Student Subscriptions

THE *WALL STREET JOURNAL* PRINT AND INTERACTIVE EDITIONS SUBSCRIPTION

Prentice Hall has formed a strategic alliance with the Wall Street Journal, *the most respected and trusted daily source for information on business and economics. For a small additional charge, Prentice Hall offers students a fifteen-week subscription to the* Wall Street Journal *Interactive Edition (www.wsj.com) and a fifteen-week complimentary print edition subscription. Upon receipt of ten student registrations from an adopting institution, we will provide the course instructor with a one-year subscription to the print and interactive versions as well as weekly, subject-specific* Wall Street Journal *educators' lesson plans.*

THE *FINANCIAL TIMES*

Covering far more than just finance, The Financial Times *is universally acknowledged as the world's leading business newspaper of global affairs. It is the only worldwide daily concentrating on international business, and its team of 600 journalists presents economic and business news from a truly global perspective. For a small additional charge, Prentice Hall offers students a fifteen-week subscription to* The Financial Times. *Upon receipt of ten student registrations from an adopting institution, we will provide the course instructor with a one-year subscription to* The Financial Times.

THE *ECONOMIST.COM*

Economist.com is the premier online source for the analysis of world business and current affairs, providing authoritative insight and opinion on international news, world politics, business, finance, science and technology, as well as overviews of cultural trends and regular industry, business, and country surveys. For a small additional charge, Prentice Hall offers students a twelve-week subscription to Economist.com. *Upon receipt of ten student registrations from an adopting institution, we will provide the course instructor with a six-month subscription to* Economist.com.

To offer these and many other valuable packages for your students, contact your Prentice Hall sales representative for ISBNs and current pricing!

THIRD EDITION

INTERNATIONAL ECONOMICS

W. Charles Sawyer

Texas Christian University

Richard L. Sprinkle

University of Texas at El Paso

PEARSON
Prentice Hall

Pearson Education International

AVP/Executive Editor: Chris Rogers
AVP/Editor-in-Chief: Eric Svendsen
Product Development Manager: Ashley Santora
Project Manager: Susan Abraham
Editorial Assistant: Vanessa Bain
Media Project Manager: Denise Vaughn
Marketing Manager: Andrew Watts
Marketing Assistant: Ian Gold
Senior Managing Editor, Production: Judy Leale
Production Manager: Kerri Tomasso
Permissions Coordinator: Charles Morris
Senior Operations Supervisor: Arnold Vila
Operations Specialist: Nick Sklitsis
Cover Design: Studio Indigo
Cover Photo: Getty Images, Inc.
Composition/Full-Service Project Management: TexTech Inc.
Printer/Binder: RRD Harrisonburg
Typeface: 10/12 New Baskerville

Credits and acknowledgments borrowed from other sources and reproduced, with permission, in this textbook appear on appropriate page within text.

Pearson Education LTD., London
Pearson Education Singapore, Pte. Ltd
Pearson Education Canada, Inc.
Pearson Education–Japan
Pearson Education Australia PTY, Limited
Pearson Education North Asia, Ltd., Hong Kong
Pearson Educación de Mexico, S.A. de C.V.
Pearson Education Malaysia, Pte. Ltd.
Pearson Education Upper Saddle River, New Jersey

PEARSON
Prentice Hall

10 9 8 7 6 5 4 3 2 1
ISBN-13: 978-0-13-208997-5
ISBN-10: 0-13-208997-1

About the Authors

W. Charles Sawyer is a Professor of Economics at Texas Christian University. He earned both a B.A. and an M.A. from St. Mary's University and a Ph.D. from the University of Arkansas. He has taught at the University of Arkansas, the University of Southern Mississippi, Louisiana State University, and the Helsinki School of Economics and Business. In addition to his academic teaching, he has taught in a number of executive development programs for both the public and private sectors. He has served as a consultant for the United Nations Industrial Development Organization and the United Nations Conference on Trade and Development. Professor Sawyer is also the Hal Wright Professor of Latin American Economics at TCU.

Professor Sawyer's primary research interests have been in the areas of international trade and economic development. He has authored or coauthored a number of research articles that have appeared in journals such as the *Review of Economics and Statistics,* the *Journal of Regional Science, Economic Development and Cultural Change,* and *Weltwirtschaftliches Archiv.* His current research focuses on the effects of international trade on U.S. states and regions. He is a member of the American Economic Association and the International Economics and Finance Society.

Richard L. Sprinkle is a Professor of Economics at the University of Texas at El Paso. Professor Sprinkle holds a Ph.D. in Economics from the University of Arkansas with specializations in international economics, international finance, and applied econometrics. He currently teaches macroeconomics, econometrics, and international economics. Over the last thirty years he has been affiliated with the College of the Ozarks, Louisiana State University, the Helsinki School of Economics and Business, the University of Arkansas, and the University of Texas at El Paso.

Professor Sprinkle's research has focused on U.S. international trade relations and the effects of trade agreements on trade and employment. He has published numerous journal articles, book chapters, and technical documents. Professor Sprinkle is a coauthor of two books, *The Demand for Imports and Exports in the World Economy* and *Regional Case Studies in International Business and Strategic Policy.* Both his teaching and research have been recognized by a number of professional awards. Professor Sprinkle is the former Director of the Center for the Study of Western Hemispheric Trade at UTEP and currently holds the Western Hemispheric Trade Research Professorship.

Brief Contents

Contents

Preface

It is difficult to get through a day without the world economy touching our lives in some way. Every day, we spend much of our time either consuming goods and services from or producing goods and services for other countries. Our exposure to the language of international economics is pervasive, with terms like *exchange rate* and *trade balance* and the names of organizations (e.g., WTO) and trade agreements (e.g., NAFTA) frequently appearing in newspapers, magazines, news programs, and the Internet. In addition, the profitability of many businesses depends on their ability to effectively manage an increasingly global business environment. Governments also must deal with the world economy's influence on public policy. In most countries, international trade in goods and services is becoming an increasingly large percentage of total economic activity. As a result, national governments need to consider the international implications of their policies. Despite the growing importance of international economics, general knowledge about the subject is often superficial at best. This lack of understanding has resulted in an increasing number of students who are enrolling in international economics courses.

AUDIENCE: A DIVERSE MIX OF STUDENTS

Until recently, international economics was a course that only economics majors who had completed courses in intermediate microeconomic and macroeconomic theory took. As international economics has become a more important subject in business, government, and our daily lives, the enrollment in international economics courses has been increasing. This increase is not due to a sudden boom in the number of economics majors. Rather, it is related to the growing number of students taking the course who are *not* majoring in economics. Many business majors now take International Economics as part of their core degree requirements, and the course has become a common elective for MBA students attempting to get a more global perspective on business problems. An international economics course is a natural part of the curriculum for liberal arts students majoring in international or regional studies. Finally, an increasing number of political science or public administration students take the course, as global economic conditions may have important effects on the public sector. The diversity of students enrolled in international economics courses today is the main reason why we wrote *International Economics.*

APPROACH: PREPARING STUDENTS FOR SUCCESSFUL CAREERS

Most international textbooks are written with two unstated assumptions. The first is that the students enrolled in the course are economics majors. The second is that most students need to learn international economics in a way that prepares them to take the *next* course in international economics. Increasingly, neither of these assumptions is correct, as an ever-larger percentage of the students taking this course are not economics majors. Further, the vast majority of economics majors are not planning to attend graduate school in economics. The typical economics major is headed for law school, an MBA program, or a career. Even a book designed to prepare students for graduate work in economics is not likely to serve the interests of economics majors—much less nonmajors.

The reality is that most students studying international economics need to prepare for success in their chosen careers. To us, this means two things. First, students need to learn the parts of international economic theory that they will most likely need to know for a career in the public or private sector. Second, learning some theory will not do these students much good if they cannot apply it. This book's approach is to apply basic economic theory to international economic issues. In one sense, the approach in *International Economics* is simpler because it is less purely theoretical. However, learning some economic theory—what the theory *means* and how to use it—is not so easy.

Our approach is driven by what we are trying to accomplish. Most students entering this course have only a vague understanding of the terminology associated with international economics. The main goal of *International Economics* is to guide students to the point at which they can easily understand any information on international economics that they may encounter in their careers. If students can understand and apply international economics, they have a good chance of having a more successful career. Both of us have spent some time teaching in executive MBA programs and have found that the average midcareer manager knows little more about international economics than the typical junior in college. This lack of knowledge makes managers uncomfortable and, in many cases, may be costing them higher salaries and/or promotions. These students have been invaluable in teaching us what our younger students need to know before they start their careers, namely, basic theory and how to apply it.

PEDAGOGY: TEACHING AND APPLYING THEORY

Most international economics textbooks are trying, in varying degrees, to do three things. First, they are teaching some new theoretical tools. Second, they are teaching students how to apply these tools in a "real world" context. Finally, they are preparing students for further study in international economics. But teaching international economics to a diverse group of majors using a book designed for economics majors is like trying to juggle too many balls. It can lead to a lot of frustration. To make the course easier to teach and more useful to the new students taking this course, we have adopted a different pedagogical approach to the subject. Because most students taking this course have had either a one-semester survey course or the traditional two-semester Principles of Microeconomics and Macroeconomics, the theory that we use throughout this book to analyze economics is the same theory that students have already learned in their "principles" course(s). This approach accomplishes two things. First, instructors have to teach little if any "new" theory. This allows them to move at a much faster pace and cover much more of the subject than would be the case if they had to spend a substantial amount of class time teaching theory that many of the students have not been prepared to easily learn. Second, it becomes much easier to focus on applying the theory. Since the students are seeing the theory for the "second" time, they can spend more time on learning how to apply it and use it in their careers.

The book employs a number of pedagogical features to reinforce this basic approach.

- The book is written in a user-friendly style that emphasizes how to use international economic theory and where to apply it.
- Students cannot possibly comprehend international economics unless they know the specialized terms of the discipline. That is why we define important terms in the margins. The marginal definitions provide a quick way for students to recognize the terms that are important to know. In addition, students may not always have time to read the entire chapter before class and studying the marginal terms beforehand should improve their understanding of it.
- We cannot assume that students will remember everything that they learned in their Principles of Economics course. That is why we provide a quick review of economic principles at key points in the text. This gives instructors the flexibility to review the material in class or to let students review the material on their own. To accommodate those students who have had only the one-semester survey course (which is usually less oriented toward macroeconomics), these reviews are more extensive in the second half of the book.
- Although applications of international economics are liberally distributed throughout the text, each chapter includes a number of boxes that provide more extensive examples or applications of the previously described theory.
- The end-of-chapter questions accomplish two things. First, many of the questions are designed to encourage students to describe what they know in their own words. This allows them to discover what they *don't* know before it really matters (i.e., an exam). Second, the remaining questions are designed to motivate students to either apply the theory or to think about issues that the theory implies.
- Each chapter ends with a "Suggested Readings and Web Sites" section. These sections provide students with options for exploring both traditional and Internet-based sources of information on the concepts they have learned in the chapter. For instructors who want to assign out-of-class coursework, these sections enable them to easily direct students to the information needed for these assignments. Unlike most books, the readings in these sections are easily accessible for undergraduate students, as the primary sources are publications such as *The Economist, The Wall Street Journal, The New York Times, The Financial Times, Newsweek, Business Week, Fortune,* and *Forbes.*

FEATURES: CONTENT THAT MAKES A DIFFERENCE

Beyond the book's basic approach and pedagogy, *International Economics* contains some content-oriented features that represent a somewhat different approach to teaching the course.

- Data—The world of international economics is full of numerical data. However, this is not always reflected in the way that international economics textbooks teach the subject. In this book, there is a more extensive presentation of international economic data than is usually the case. For example, it is quite possible for an international economics text to neglect to mention the size of the world economy. In *International Economics*, that number is just the starting point for discussing other types of international economic data. However, in the discipline of international economics, the numbers can seem, at first glance, to be implausibly large. To remedy these perceptual problems, we put the data into perspective with regard to national economies and the world economy so that students can see how international economic data compares with national economies and the world economy. For example, learning that U.S. exports are over $1 trillion is a useful thing to know. If you also learn that the size of the U.S. economy is $13 trillion and the size of the world economy is $45 trillion, then the information on U.S. exports has more meaning. Students learn not only how large exports are but how they fit into the economy overall.

- Intraindustry Trade—Intraindustry trade has become an extremely important part of total international trade. The explanations for this type of trade are different than those used to explain interindustry trade. To adequately cover both the phenomenon and its explanations, intraindustry trade is covered in a separate chapter (Chapter 5).
- Factor Movements—The international movements of labor and capital play a critical role in the world economy. Immigrants are now a large part of the population in many developed countries, and firms building plants and investors buying stocks and bonds in other countries are just a normal part of the global business environment. The importance of these labor and capital movements is one of the reasons why we cover factor movements in a separate chapter early in the book (Chapter 6). Since the factors that drive these movements can be related to the traditional explanations of international trade, the early placement of this chapter makes the material easier to teach and learn.
- Public Choice—Tariff and nontariff barriers to trade are policies made in a political market. Students need to know not only what effects these barriers have on trade but also why they exist in the first place. The chapter on public choice (Chapter 9) is designed to explain the process that leads to trade barriers. This chapter also enables students to better understand both today's trade policy debates and those they will no doubt encounter during their careers.
- The Relationship between the Current Account and Capital and Financial Accounts—In addition to the traditional emphasis on the current account, *International* Economics highlights the role of the capital and financial accounts. The discussion focuses on the relationship among the current account, the capital and financial accounts, GDP, and the components of GDP. These relationships are identified first in Chapter 12 and are an integral part of the discussion of open economy macroeconomics in Chapters 17 through 20.
- Asset-Market Approach to Exchange-Rate Determination—The approach that we use to explain the determination of exchange rates is the modern asset-market approach. The focus is on how interest rates and other factors cause short-run changes in exchange rates. Chapter 16 on purchasing power parity emphasizes the modern asset-market approach as a useful reference point in analyzing commonly used terms such as *overvalued* or *undervalued* exchange rates.
- Open Economy Macroeconomics—The focus of *International Economics* is on how changes in the exchange rate affect output and the price level. In much of our discussion, we assume that the exchange rate and the current account are usually allowed to adjust to macroeconomic policies aimed at inflation and unemployment. This allows the discussion to be more representative of macroeconomic policy in most countries.

- Fixed versus Flexible Exchange Rate Systems—Despite the wide use of flexible exchange rate systems, fixed exchange rates are still an important part of the international monetary system. However, there are newer forms of fixed exchange rate systems such as currency boards and monetary unions that countries are now using to replace more traditional ways of fixing the exchange rate. In order to cover both exchange rate systems adequately, *International Economics* covers flexible and fixed exchange rate systems separately in Chapters 18 and 19, respectively. Chapter 20 summarizes the discussion as a choice entailing different mixes of costs and benefits.

Changes in the Third Edition

Most of the changes in the third edition are related to the primary purpose of the book. Our intention has always been to teach international economics in a way that will enhance the ability of students to use what they learn during their careers. In the third edition, this led to one significant change and the addition of new material in a number of chapters.

- The material on absolute and comparative advantage has been expanded and is now contained in two chapters. Chapter 2 now contains the most basic approach to teaching this material. The same chapter also now contains a discussion of trade and the world market price as well as the addition of the new research on the dynamic gains from trade.
- A new Chapter 3 is designed to allow instructors to cover comparative advantage in more detail. The new organization of the material should allow instructors more flexiblility in how they choose to present the concept of comparative advantage.
- Chapter 8 now contains a section on the Gravity Model. This material provides an interesting extension and empirical examples to the material on transportation costs and trade.
- A completely new section on Economic Sanctions has been added to Chapter 8. Students frequently ask about this issue in our classes, as economic sanctions of some sort are frequently in the news. In response to this, we felt that this material would be useful in most international economics classes.
- Chapter 8 now contains a section on Corruption and International Trade. The issue of corruption frequently arises in our classes. Fortunately, it is also an active topic of academic research. This new section blends the basics of corruption and trade with the research on this topic.
- A new section on Dark Matter in the U.S. Balance of Payments has been added to Chapter 12. The disconnect between the U.S. as a debtor nation and investment income is one of the more interesting puzzles in international finance.
- A completely new section on the Incompatible Trinity has been added to the end of Chapter 19 on fixed exchange rate systems. The inability of a country to simultaneously fix its exchange rate, manage the money supply, and have free flows of capital is both a good way to end the discussion of fixed exchange rates and set the stage for Chapter 20 on International Monetary Systems.
- The Problems and Questions for Review section for each chapter has been expanded and revised to reflect changes in the book. Also, the Suggested Readings and Web Sites for each chapter has been updated to reflect ongoing changes in the world economy.

Alternative Course Designs

International Economics was designed to be used in two commonly used course formats. The first half of the book on international trade, factor movements, and trade and economic development are frequently covered in most international economics courses. The final ten chapters on international finance can be divided into at least three parts: national income accounting and exchange rate determination; purchasing power parity and the real exchange rate; and open-economy macroeconomics. The result is that instructors have the flexibility to design a course appropriate for both the content of the course and the background of the students.

The traditional international economics course is a one-semester course covering both international trade and finance. Students in this course normally are either majoring in economics or in a related discipline such as finance or international business. *International Economics* was written concisely to allow instructors to finish all of the chapters and/or omit chapters in order to cover readings or other material. In this type of course, Chapter 6 (International Factor Movements), Chapter 11 (International Trade and Economic Growth), Chapter 13 (International Transactions and Financial Markets), or Chapter 21 (Capital Flows and the Developing Countries) could be omitted without loss of continuity.

It is increasingly common for International Economics to be taught as a one-semester survey course to classes where the majority of students are not majoring in economics. *International Economics* also was designed to accommodate this type of course. Throughout the book, the basic material is presented using only the tools the students learned in Principles of Economics. The more technical points are always covered in separate sections to allow instructors to move at a faster pace by omitting this material. Most courses of this type are more heavily weighted toward international trade and add some international finance at the end of the course. The present book is organized to allow instructors to cover all of the essential parts of international trade. The second half of the text was written to allow for flexibility of coverage in international finance. The ten chapters on international finance can be considered in a number of different ways. Chapters 12, 14, and 17 cover the "core" topics of the balance of payments, exchange rate determination, and open-economy macroeconomics. These chapters can be combined with groups of other chapters to produce a course with a focus on exchange rates, open-economy macroeconomics, or a combination of the two. Adding Chapters 13, 15, 16, and 20 produces a course with a focus on exchange rates. A course with a focus on open-economy macroeconomics can be obtained by covering Chapters 18 through 21. A blend of the two topics can be covering Chapters 15, 16, 18, and 20. These alternatives are shown at the end of the Preface.

SUPPLEMENTARY MATERIALS

Instructor's Manual with Testbank. The Instructor's Manual with Testbank contains a chapter outline and summary for each chapter, answers to end-of-chapter questions, lecture suggestions, and a complete bank of questions for quizzes and tests. The **TestGen-EQ test generating software** allows instructors to custom design, save, and generate classroom tests. The test program allows instructors to edit, add, or delete questions from the test banks; edit existing graphics and create new graphics; analyze test results, and organize a database of tests and student results. This software allows for greater flexibility and ease of use. It provides many options for organizing and displaying tests, along with a search and sort feature. The software, as well as the Testbank, is available for download from the link for the **Instructor Resource Center** on the book's Companion Web site.

The **Companion Web site (www.prenhall.com/sawyer)** is a Web site with resources related specifically to *International Economics*. **For Students**, the **Online Study Guide** offers another opportunity for them to sharpen their problem-solving skills and to assess their understanding of the text material. The Online Study Guide grades each question submitted by the student, provides immediate and detailed feedback for correct and incorrect answers, and allows students to e-mail results to up to four e-mail addresses. **For instructors**, the Companion Web site contains the **Syllabus Manager** which allows instructors to create a syllabus that they may publish for their students to access. Instructors may add exams or assignments of their own, edit any of the student resources available on the Companion Web site, post discussion topics, and more. Instructors may find **downloadable resources** (including the **Instructor's Manual, Testbank, TestGen EQ software**, and **PowerPoint Presentations**) from the link on the site for the **Instructor Resource Center**.

PowerPoint Lecture Presentation: This lecture presentation tool offers outlines and summaries of important text material, tables and graphs that build, and additional exercises. The package will allow for instructors to make full-color, professional-looking presentations while providing the ability for custom handouts to be provided to the students. Instructors may download the **PowerPoint Presentations** from the link for the **Instructor Resource Center at www.prenhall.com/sawyer**.

ACKNOWLEDGMENTS

During the writing and revising of this book, we received a number of both small and large comments from reviewers that have improved both the economic content and the method of presentation. The following list of reviewers for the third edition is presented not just as a formality but also as a way of saying thanks for all the help.

Ugur Aker,
Hiram College

Richard Ault,
Auburn University

Jeff Bruns,
Bacone College

Jen-Chi Cheng,
Wichita State University

Michael Cook,
William Jewell College

Arthur Cyr,
Carthage College

Anusua Datta,
Philadelphia University

Yamanishi David,
Michigan State University

Juan J. DelaCruz,
FIT-SUNY and Lehman College-CUNY

Steve Ford,
University of the South

Joseph Foudy,
Stern School of Business

Sucharita Ghosh,
University of Akron

John Gilbert,
Utah State University

Michael Goode,
University of North Carolina, Charlotte

Jack Julian,
Indiana University of Pennsylvania

Kishore G. Kulkarni,
Metropolitan State College of Denver

Mary Lesser,
Iona College

Isobel Lobo,
Benedictine University

Mary Lovely,
Syracuse University

Bernard Malamud,
University of Nevada Las Vegas

Richard McIntyre,
University of Rhode Island

R. J. Mody,
University at Albany

Joe Nowakowski,
Muskingum College

Ilan Noy,
University of Hawaii

Ebere Oriaku,
Elizabeth City State University

Eun Soo Park,
University of Missouri, Rolla

E. Wesley Peterson,
University of Nebraska-Lincoln

Susan Pozo,
Western Michigan University

Michael Quinn,
Bentley College

Reza Ramazani,
Saint Michael's College

Artatrana Ratha,
St. Cloud State University

Monica Robayo,
University of North Florida

Michael Ryan,
Western Michigan University

Luis San Vicente Portes,
Montclair State University

Sunil Sapra,
California State University

Aaron Schavey,
Bethel College

Patricia Schneider,
Mount Holyoke College

Deep Shikha,
College of St. Catherine

Millicent Sites,
Carson-Newman College

Niloufer Sohrabji,
Simmons College

Richard Stahl,
Louisiana State University

Robert M. Stern,
University of Michigan

Sue Stockly,
Eastern New Mexico University

Edward Stuart,
Northeastern Illinois University

Grigor Sukiassyan,
California State University, Fullerton

Evert Van der Sluis,
South Dakota State University

Jonathan Warner,
Dordt College

Claudia Williamson,
West Virginia University

Janice Yee,
Worcester State College

Ben Zissimos,
Vanderbilt University

In addition, we would like to thank the following list of reviewers for their thoughtful comments that helped the development of previous editions of the text.

Richard V. Adkisson, *New Mexico State University*

Richard T. Bailie, *Michigan State University*

Peter Brust, *University of Tampa*

William W. David, *Western Kentucky University*

Elynor Davis, *Georgia Southern University*

Harmut Fisher, *University of San Francisco*

Ira Gang, *Rutgers University*

Thomas Grennes, *North Carolina State University*

Darrin Gulla *University of Georgia*

Andrew T. Hill, *Federal Reserve Bank of Philadelphia*

S. Hussain Ali Jafri, *Tarleton State University*

William Laird, *Florida State University*

Anil Lal, *Pittsburgh State University*

David Lehr, *Longwood College*

Bozena Leven, *The College of New Jersey*

Jacquelynne W. McLellan, *Frostburg State University*

Shannon Mitchell, *Virginia Commonwealth University*

Franklin G. Mixon, Jr. *University of Southern Mississippi*

Masoud Moghaddam, *St. Cloud State University*

Anthony Negbenebor, *Gardner-Webb University*

Dorothy Petersen, *Washington University*

Reza Ramazani, *St. Michael's College*

Michael Ryan, *Western Michigan State University*

Jeff Sarabaum, *UNC at Greensboro*

Gerald P. W. Simons, *Grand Valley State University*

Carol Ogden Stivender, *UNC at Charlotte*

Leonie Stone, *SUNY-Geneseo*

James Swofford, *University of South Alabama*

Charlie Turner, *Old Dominion University*

Laura Wolff, *Southern Illinois University-Edwardsville*

George K. Zestos, *Christopher Newport University*

Writing a book involves the accumulation of a number of debts.This includes the following colleagues and friends. We would like to thank Don Clark of the University of Tennessee for discussions on a number of points in international trade that show up in the first part of the book. Several former colleagues at the University of Southern Mississippi have contributed to the book. Tyrone Black is the author of the diagram on intraindustry trade in Chapter 5; James McQuiston taught us much of what is contained in Chapter 9. Several users of the first edition have provided useful comments on various points. These include James Dunlevy of Miami University of Ohio; Isobel Lobo of Benedictine University; and Sunny Wong of the University of San Francisco.

We are deeply indebted to a number of people at Prentice Hall that have worked to make this a better book. Rod Banister (Executive Editor) and Rebecca Johnson (Development Editor) were instrumental in making the first edition possible. We are very grateful to David Alexander (Executive Editor) for his support during the second edition. In finishing the third edition, we owe a particular debt to both Chris Rogers (Executive Editor) and Mary Kate Murray (Editorial Project Manager). Their understanding of the book and their ability to get things done led to substantial improvements in this edition. Finally, Kerri Tomasso (Production Project Manager) again worked through the maze of details involved in getting a rough draft into the form you're now reading. Our debt to all of these people is immense.

Finally, there are a couple of acknowledgments that go beyond the narrow confines of a textbook. We would like to thank Tracy Murray for both his instruction and support for more years than any of us would like to recall. In a different vein, we owe debts to our families who have put up with not only this book, but a lot of other "projects" over the years. Without their support, none of this work would have been possible.

ALTERNATIVE COURSE DESIGNS

International Trade	Core	Focus on Trade and Factor Movements	Focus on Trade and Development
1 Introduction: An Overview of the World Economy	X		
2 Why Countries Trade	X		
3 Comparative Advantage and the Production Possibilities Frontier		X	
4 Factor Endowments and the Commodity Composition of Trade	X		
5 Intraindustry Trade	X		
6 International Factor Movements		X	
7 Tariffs	X		
8 Nontariff Distortions to Trade	X		
9 International Trade Policy	X		
10 Regional Economic Arrangements	X		
11 International Trade and Economic Growth			X

ALTERNATIVE COURSE DESIGNS (SEQUENTIAL)—International Trade

Complete International Trade Coverage

1 Introduction: An Overview of the World Economy
2 Why Countries Trade
3 Comparative Advantage and the Production Possibilities Frontier
4 Factor Endowments and the Commodity Composition of Trade
5 Intraindustry Trade
6 International Factor Movements
7 Tariffs
8 Nontariff Distortions to Trade
9 International Trade Policy
10 Regional Economic Arrangements
11 International Trade and Economic Growth

Focus on Trade and Factor Movements

1 Introduction: An Overview of the World Economy
2 Why Countries Trade
4 Factor Endowments and the Commodity Composition of Trade
5 Intraindustry Trade
6 International Factor Movements
7 Tariffs
8 Nontariff Distortions to Trade
9 International Trade Policy
10 Regional Economic Arrangements

Focus on Trade and Development

1 Introduction: An Overview of the World Economy
2 Why Countries Trade
4 Factor Endowments and the Commodity Composition of Trade
5 Intraindustry Trade
7 Tariffs
8 Nontariff Distortions to Trade
9 International Trade Policy
10 Regional Economic Arrangements
11 International Trade and Economic Growth

ALTERNATIVE COURSE DESIGNS

International Finance	Core	Focus on Exchange Rates	Focus on Open Economy Macroeconomics	Basics of Exchange Rates and Open Economy Macroeconomics
12 National Income Accounting and the Balance of Payments	X			
13 International Transactions and Financial Markets		X		
14 Exchange Rates and Their Determination: A Basic Model	X			
15 Money, Interest Rates, and the Exchange Rate		X		X
16 Price Levels and Exchange Rates in the Long Run		X		X
17 Output and the Exchange Rate in the Short Run	X			

(continued)

ALTERNATIVE COURSE DESIGNS (*Continued*)

International Finance	Core	Focus on Exchange Rates	Focus on Open Economy Macroeconomics	Basics of Exchange Rates and Open Economy Macroeconomics
18 Macroeconomic Policy and Floating Exchange Rates			X	X
19 Fixed Exchange Rates and Currency Unions			X	X
20 International Monetary Arrangements		X	X	
21 Capital Flows and the Developing Countries			X	

ALTERNATIVE COURSE DESIGNS (SEQUENTIAL)—International Finance

Focus on Exchange Rates	Focus on Open Economy Macroeconomics	Basic Exchange Rates and Open Economy Macroeconomics
12 National Income Accounting and the Balance of Payments	12 National Income Accounting and the Balance of Payments	12 National Income Accounting and the Balance of Payments
13 International Transactions and Financial Markets	14 Exchange Rates and Their Determination: A Basic Model	14 Exchange Rates and Their Determination: A Basic Model
14 Exchange Rates and Their Determination: A Basic Model	17 Output and the Exchange Rate in the Short Run	15 Money, Interest Rates, and the Exchange Rate
15 Money, Interest Rates, and the Exchange Rate	18 Macroeconomic Policy and Floating Exchange Rates	16 Price Levels and Exchange Rates in the Long Run
16 Price Levels and Exchange Rates in the Long Run	19 Fixed Exchange Rates and Currency Unions	17 Output and the Exchange Rate in the Short Run
17 Output and the Exchange Rate in the Short Run	20 International Monetary Arrangements	18 Macroeconomic Policy and Floating Exchange Rates
20 International Monetary Arrangements	21 Capital Flows and the Developing Countries	19 Fixed Exchange Rates and Currency Unions

Chapter 1

Introduction: An Overview of the World Economy

"Merchants have no country. The mere spot they stand on does not constitute so strong an attachment as that from which they draw their gains."
—THOMAS JEFFERSON

INTRODUCTION

Today, no country inhabits an economic island. Its firms and industries, its commercial activities in goods and services, its technology and available capital, its standard of living, and all other features of its economy are related to the economies of other countries. These relationships form a complex flow of goods, services, capital, labor, and technology between countries. As the world economy becomes increasingly integrated, every country must come to terms with this increased interdependence.

Until the early 1970s, this interdependence was perceived to be a one-way street. To most consumers and businesses located within the United States, the economy appeared to be and acted like a self-sufficient and closed economy. At the time, the U.S. economy's absolute and relative size led consumers, businesses, and policy makers to conclude that the economy was immune to economic events that occurred abroad, such as oil prices in the Middle East, automobile production in Japan and Germany, textile and apparel production in Latin America, and the currency crisis of countries located in the Far East. In contrast, foreign countries were greatly influenced by events that took place in the U.S. A recession would mean that the rest of the world's economy would suffer greatly. In addition, the U.S. could raise import tariffs on steel, automobiles, or lumber without effective retaliation from other countries. Further, the U.S. could ignore the international value of the dollar because exchange rates were fixed.

However, over the last several decades, this interdependence truly has become a two-way street. In the United States and the rest of the world, goods, services, capital, technology, and people flow across borders with greater frequency and in increasingly greater volumes. Between 1975 and 2005 global trade in goods has increased by 350 percent. For some individuals and businesses, international transactions and international relationships have become more important than interactions within their own country. Every country benefits tremendously from its interactions with other countries. National policies that affect trade, investment, the value of the country's

microeconomics the study of the production and consumption of various goods and services and how particular industries and markets work

currency, and the level of national output can be used to enhance these benefits and lessen the costs of interdependence. To reap these additional benefits, each country needs to base its national policies on an objective analysis of international economics.

The purpose of international economics is to explain these patterns of international trade, investment, and other cross-border transactions that we currently observe in the real world. Much of our examination of international economics is based on analyzing the economic data of individual countries and the world economy. In this chapter, we describe several different aspects of a country's interdependence within the world economy. Throughout the rest of the text, we will refer to economic data as it pertains to selected international economic issues. We begin by describing how international economics relates to the concepts you have learned in previous economics courses. From there we will examine the overall landscape of the world economy. We will do this by first looking at the output of the world economy. With this information we can then consider how international transactions such as international trade and capital movements fit into the picture. At that point, some of the more important issues that are discussed later in the book can be introduced.

THE SCOPE OF INTERNATIONAL ECONOMICS

macroeconomics the study of an entire economy's operation by examining the factors that determine the economy's total output

The discipline of economics can be divided into two major parts: microeconomics and macroeconomics. **Microeconomics** deals with the production and consumption of various goods and services and how particular industries and markets work. Using microeconomic theory, you can analyze the activities of individuals and the behavior of individual businesses in choosing what to produce and how much to charge. **Macroeconomics** deals with the operation of the entire economy and examines the factors that determine the economy's total output and the overall price level. In a sense, economics is like medicine. Many physicians are general practitioners who can deal with practically any minor ailment. On the other hand, a large number of physicians are specialists who primarily work on one particular disease or system of the body. Economics has evolved in much the same way. The study of economics is now subdivided into a number of different areas such as labor economics, natural resource economics, economic development, and international economics.[1]

international economics the study of the production, distribution, and consumption of goods, services, and capital on a worldwide basis

International economics is the study of the production, distribution, and consumption of goods and services on a worldwide basis. As such, international economics is a blend of microeconomics and macroeconomics. In Chapters 1 through 11, we extend our study of microeconomics by examining international trade. In many respects, international trade is similar to domestic trade. However, each country has different codes or rules that make one national economy different from another. These national or political boundaries determine not only the legal, linguistic, social, and currency barriers to trade, but also the nature of economic policies. These national laws tend to partially isolate each country and cause significant differences in the way trade is conducted domestically versus how it is carried out internationally.

Chapters 12 through 21 are an extension of macroeconomics. In your Principles of Economics course, the text you read may have assumed that the U.S. economy was

[1]A description of the major fields of economics can be found in any recent volume of *The Journal of Economic Literature.*

something like an economic island. To simplify the analysis, the effects of changes in other countries' economic conditions on the U.S. economy may have been downplayed or ignored. This simplification was based on the idea that the economy can be more easily understood by considering only domestic consumption, investment, government spending, and various government policies. Adding factors, such as changes in the exchange rate or trade flows, creates a model that is more realistic. However, this added degree of realism may get in the way of teaching the basic principles of macroeconomics.

The purpose of the second half of this book is to expand the model you learned in your principles courses in two important ways. First, changes in foreign economic conditions at times may noticeably affect the domestic economy. Further, changes in any domestic economy can have noticeable impacts on foreign economies. Second, changes in government policies have significant impacts not only on the domestic economy but also on the sectors of the economy related to international trade. These extensions to microeconomics and macroeconomics have now become so important and so extensive that they easily constitute an extra semester of study.

Although international economics is important, it is essential to keep it in perspective. For the U.S. and many other countries, international trade is an important adjunct to domestic economic activity. Most economic activity in the world is domestic in nature. However, the international exchange of goods, services, and assets is now large and growing at a rapid rate. While no one can predict how long this process of "internationalization" or "globalization" will continue, it currently shows no signs of abating. This chapter provides basic information about the world economy; the importance and trends in international trade; the significance of trade in services; the size and importance of international capital flows; and the position of the U.S. in the world economy.

This material is important for several reasons. First, everyone needs a sense of the size of the world economy in order to keep the size of trade and flows of assets in perspective. Second, there are startling differences between countries and regions of the world in terms of physical size, population, and their economic importance in the world economy. For instance, while many know that Canada is a large country in terms of its physical size and is small in terms of population, the absolute size of the Canadian economy is probably less well known. Third, there are substantial differences in the absolute size of the world's economies and standards of living. Fourth, imports and exports of goods and services are an important part of both the world economy and the U.S. economy. While most individuals are aware of this importance, they are unsure about the specifics. Fifth, international trade in services and the movements of real and financial capital between countries are becoming increasingly important. Until recently, both of these subjects have been given relatively brief attention in the study of international economics. However, the rapid growth of trade in services and the volume of trade in real and financial assets have made these critical issues in international economics. In the last part of the chapter we examine several trends in the world economy over the last two decades and consider what these trends imply.

THE OUTPUT OF THE WORLD ECONOMY

Describing the world's economic output is important for two reasons. First, we have all heard the terms *world economy, internationalization, globalization,* or any number of

Table 1.1 Distribution of World Population and Economic Output, 2005[a]

	GDP per capita	Population (millions)	% of World Population	Total GDP (millions of $)	% of World GDP
Low-Income Economies	$602	2,352	36.5%	$1,416,212	3.2%
Middle-Income Economies	$2,782	3,075	47.8%	$8,553,721	19.2%
High-Income Economies	$34,316	1,011	15.7%	$34,687,058	77.7%

[a] *The countries included in the table are shown in the endpaper table and each country is classified as high-, middle-, or low-income.*
Source: World Bank, *World Development Indicators,* Washington, D.C.: World Bank, 2007.

Gross Domestic Product (GDP) measures the market value of all final goods and services that a country produces during a given period of time

World Bank a multilateral institution that makes loans to developing countries to enhance economic development

variations on this basic idea. What is missing is some sense of the world economy's size and the magnitude of internationalization. It is important to know these facts before we begin our analysis. Second, while absolute size is important, relative size matters as well. That is why our analysis throughout this text considers the relative size of various countries and regions of the world.

The size of the world economy is measured as the sum of **Gross Domestic Product (GDP)** for each country.[2] GDP measures the market value of all final goods and services that a country produces during a given period of time. In 2005, world output was estimated to be $44,656,991 million or approximately *$44.7 trillion.*[3] This estimate of total world output is likely a conservative one because the calculation of GDP has two major omissions. First, all economic activity that is not sold in a market is excluded. For example, the production of services that a homemaker provides is excluded from GDP. For developing countries, the production of a farmer's own food may be excluded from GDP. Second, some economic activities are not reported because participants are attempting to escape taxation and/or government regulation or are engaging in illegal activities. This underground economy can cause an underestimate of world production.

Table 1.1 provides a summary of the distribution of the world's economic output. For comparison purposes, the **World Bank** classifies each country of the world into low-income, middle-income, and high-income economies. This classification is based on GDP per capita, which is calculated by dividing the GDP of a country by its population. In 2005, the average GDP per capita for low-, middle-, and high-income economies was $602, $2,782, and $34,316, respectively.[4] Notice that the high-, middle-, and low-income economies are producing 77.7 percent, 19.2 percent, and 3.2 percent of the world's economic output, respectively.

[2]GDP can be calculated using the income approach or the expenditures approach. Given the focus of this text on production and consumption in the world economy, when we refer to GDP it may be useful to think of it in the sense of expenditures. For a quick review of this distinction, see Karl E. Case and Ray C. Fair, *Economics,* 8th ed., Upper Saddle River, NJ: Prentice Hall, 2007, pp. 520–25.
[3]The data is from World Bank, *World Development Indicators,* Washington, D.C.: World Bank, 2007. All data in this chapter is shown in nominal or current dollars unless otherwise noted.
[4]See the appendix at the end of the book for a complete list of countries and GDP per capita.

This distribution of world output affects how we look at international economics. With minor adjustments, GDP measures both the total production and the total income of a country. As a result, there is an obvious relationship between the distribution of world production and the distribution of world income. This distribution of world income affects the study of international trade because the production of goods and income is unevenly distributed among the world's economies. As we will see, the pattern of international trade is likewise skewed.

IMPORTS AND EXPORTS OF GOODS IN THE WORLD ECONOMY

exports **the part of domestic production that is sold to residents of other countries**

imports **the part of domestic consumption and/or investment that a country purchases from foreign producers**

Imports and exports of goods dominate the interdependence of countries in the world economy. **Exports** are the part of a country's domestic production that is sold to residents of other countries. **Imports** are the part of a country's domestic consumption and/or investment that is purchased from foreign producers.[5]

From Table 1.1, the total value of GDP for the world economy is approximately \$44.7 trillion. To gain some perspective on the relative importance of international trade, we need the information on the value of exports and imports contained in Table 1.2. In 2005, exports and imports of goods were \$10,434,024 and \$10,684,945 million, respectively.[6] In terms of percentages, exports and imports are approximately 23.4 percent and 23.9 percent of world output, respectively. These percentages reflect trade in goods and do not include international trade in services. We can now define one aspect of the term *globalization,* which is the amount of domestic consumption produced in other countries (imports) and, conversely, the amount of domestic production shipped to other countries (exports).

In the preceding section, we saw that world economic output was not evenly distributed among the world's economies. The high-income economies account for approximately 78 percent of the world's output. A similar distribution is observed when examining total imports and exports. As Table 1.2 shows, the low-income economies account for approximately 2.7 percent of international trade. Notice in Table 1.1 that

Table 1.2 Distribution of Imports and Exports of Merchandise in the World Economy 2005

	Imports (millions of \$)	% of World Total	Exports (millions of \$)	% of World Total
Low-Income Economies	\$316,559	3.0%	\$261,853	2.5%
Middle-Income Economies	\$2,552,089	23.9%	\$2,795,181	26.8%
High-Income Economies	\$7,816,297	73.2%	\$7,376,990	70.7%
World Total	\$10,684,945	–	\$10,434,024	–

Source: World Bank, *World Development Indicators,* Washington, DC: World Bank, 2007.

[5]A more detailed description of a country's international trade statistics is given in Chapter 12.
[6]The reader may wonder about the discrepancy between world exports and world imports. This discrepancy is not unusual and will be discussed in more detail in Chapter 12.

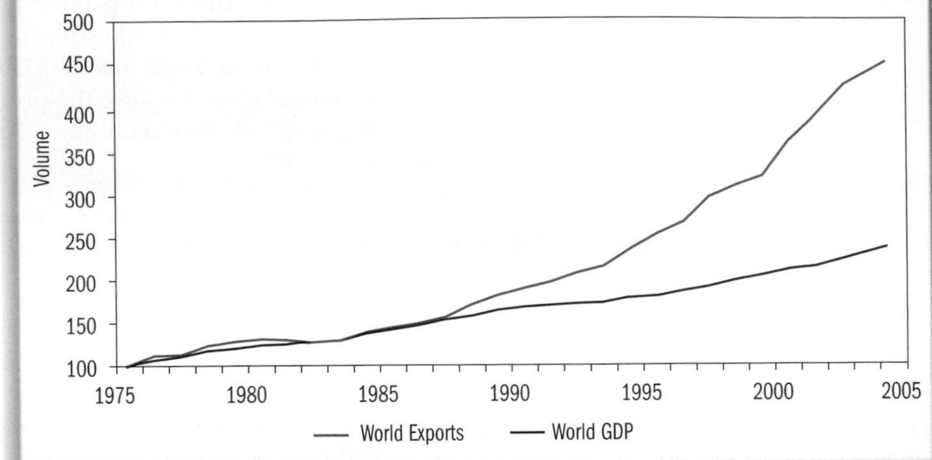

Figure 1.1 Real World Exports of Good and Real GDP, 1975–2005

Source: Adapted from World Trade Organization, *International Trade Statistics, 2006,* Geneva: WTO, 2007, Table A1.

these countries have only 3.2 percent of the world's economic output. A similar situation exists for the middle- and high-income economies. The middle-income economies account for 25.3 percent of world trade and 19.2 percent of world production. Not surprisingly, the high-income economies account for 72.0 percent of world trade and 77.7 percent of world production.[7]

This similarity in world production and trade is not difficult to explain. For a country to export a product, it first must produce the product. Because the high-income economies have the overwhelming part of world production, a corresponding share of world exports originates within these economies. Similarly, imports are a form of consumption or investment spending that is produced in another country. For a country to import a product, the buyer has to have the income to purchase the good (i.e., effective demand). High-income economies are not a misnomer. Countries with high levels of income consume not only more domestically-produced goods but also more foreign-produced goods. As a result, the high-income economies also have a high share of world imports.

In addition, the economic interdependence among countries has increased over time. Figure 1.1 shows real GDP growth and real export growth in goods from 1975 through 2005. Notice that over the period, export growth has been faster than GDP growth. To make both series comparable we have converted each series into an index number that equals 100 in 1975. As the figure shows, real GDP and real exports grew at approximately the same rate between 1975 and 1985. Beginning in the mid-1980s world exports began to rise faster than world GDP. By 2005, world exports were 350 percent larger than in 1975 and world GDP was only 138 percent larger.

[7]There is approximately 6 percent difference in the distribution of world output and trade among the middle-income and high-income countries. In part, this difference stems from classifying many of the oil-exporting countries as middle-income countries.

U.S. States and Regions in the World Economy

An emerging topic of discussion in economics is the potential link between international economics and regional economics.[8] Regional economics analyzes why there are substantial economic differences between regions within countries, the United States being one example. Recently, economists have been exploring how U.S. states and regions would fit into the global economy if these entities were independent countries. If you examine the appendix at the end of the text, you will notice that the different countries of the world are ranked by total GDP. The table also contains data on population, GDP per capita, exports, and exports per capita. Similar data for the different census regions of the U.S. is listed in CAPITALS, and the various states within the U.S. are listed in *italics.*

What if any of the listed regions or states in the table were a country? The results are quite interesting. Four U.S. census regions would be among the world's top ten economies. If California were a country, it would, in economic terms, be slightly smaller than Italy and slightly larger than Spain. The smallest U.S. state (Vermont) would still have an economy smaller than Sri Lanka or slightly larger than Costa Rica. Look at the data for your home state, region, or country. It may help to bring the idea of the global economy and international trade a bit closer to home.

[8]One can pick up almost any volume of the *Journal of Regional Science* and find an article on the relationship between regional economics and international economics. One of the seminal works in this area is Paul Krugman, *Geography and Trade,* Cambridge: MIT Press, 1991.

INTERNATIONAL TRADE IN SERVICES

When describing international trade, many commentators describe trade in goods, such as cars, bananas, diamonds, and so forth, while ignoring trade in services. There are several reasons for this bias. First, you can more readily see the trade in goods, which is sometimes called visible trade. The export goods are shipped to a port on a visible truck or railroad car. The goods are then loaded into a ship or, with increasing frequency, a cargo plane. The merchandise is then shipped to a foreign country and the process reverses. When most of us think about international trade, this is what comes to mind. However, this characterization of international trade ignores the less visible trade in services. Service trade consists of business services, such as transportation and insurance. Individuals also consume international services, with tourism being a prominent example. Trade in services is less "visible" than trade in merchandise and is sometimes called invisible trade. For example, the consumption of car insurance is considerably less visible than the consumption of a car.

Second, international trade in services is more difficult to measure than merchandise trade. Goods must pass through a country's border where they are assessed some value. This is not necessarily the case for international trade in services. For example, when a British citizen vacations in Disney World, these expenditures are considered a U.S. export just like a U.S. product that is sold to a British company. In the latter case, U.S. officials would record this transaction as it left a U.S. port and British customs officials would record it as the good entered the United Kingdom. However, how do the U.S. and the U.K. count the spending of the British tourist in the U.S.? Although the dollars that tourists spend are a U.S. export, these transactions may not be recorded because they are difficult to monitor. This same monitoring problem plagues much of international trade in services. What is difficult to see and measure becomes something that is not thought about and/or studied.

Third, the study of international trade in services is in its infancy. As we will see in the next two chapters, we can explain the determinants of international trade in goods. The same cannot be said for international trade in services. At this point, there is not a general theory of what causes international trade in services, and this leads to a tendency to downplay its importance. Finally, international trade in services comprised, until recently, a relatively small portion of total trade. This relatively small size coupled with the factors mentioned earlier has led to little or no emphasis on this type of trade.

The inattention to international trade in services is difficult to reconcile with the reality of the absolute size of the trade flows. As Table 1.3 indicates, the absolute volume of international trade in services is now quite large. Imports and exports of services in the world economy are approximately *$2.4 trillion.* While this number is large, its size in relation to trade in goods is perhaps even more revealing. International trade in services is approximately 23 percent of the size of international trade in goods. Since the 1970s, international trade in services has been growing faster than trade in goods with the exception of the period 2000 through 2005. Since the terrorist attack on the World Trade Center in the U.S., international trade in services has grown at the same rate as international trade in goods.

Table 1.3 also provides information on the distribution among countries of international trade in services. As they do with trade in goods, the high-income economies dominate international trade in services. These countries account for 76.6 percent of the imports of services and 79.8 percent of the exports. This dominance occurs for two reasons. First, these countries' dominance in both production and income also means that they should account for the majority of international trade, in both goods and services. Second, as a country's GDP increases, the percentage of GDP allocated to the service industry increases. For example, in the low- and middle-income economies, the service sector accounts for approximately 50 percent and 53 percent of economic activity, respectively. In the high-income economies, the service sector accounts for

Table 1.3 Distribution of International Trade in Services in the World Economy 2005

	Imports (millions of $)	% of World Total	Exports (millions of $)	% of World Total
Low-Income Economies	$101,435	4.3%	$84,840	3.4%
Middle-Income Economies	$449,275	19.1%	$412,960	16.8%
High-Income Economies	$1,800,743	76.6%	$1,962,711	79.8%
World Total	$2,351,453	–	$2,460,511	–

Source: World Bank, *World Development Indicators,* Washington, D.C.: World Bank, 2007.

The U.S. Position in the World Economy

The United States has a truly unique position in the world economy for a number of reasons. First, the sheer size of the U.S. economy makes it important. The GDP of the U.S. is approximately $12.4 trillion. The second largest economy is Japan's, with a GDP of approximately $4.5 trillion. The U.S. economy accounts for nearly a quarter of the world's economic output. Second, the U.S. is also the world's largest exporter. In 2005, the U.S. exported and imported approximately $1,256 billion and $2,014 billion in goods and services, respectively. In both an absolute and a relative sense, the U.S. is the world's largest trading nation. In the concern over U.S. trade deficits, these facts are frequently overlooked. Third, the U.S. has the world's largest financial market. Consequently, a substantial amount of the capital flows and currency trading directly or indirectly involves these financial markets. Finally, the dollar is the dominant vehicle currency for transactions in the world economy.[9]

Despite these statistics, the discussion of international trade and the U.S. economy has been a focus of controversy for some time. If the U.S. is simultaneously the world's largest economy and the world's largest trading nation, why should international trade issues remain so controversial? Figure 1.2 is useful in resolving this seeming paradox. The chart tracks two conflicting trends for the

Figure 1.2 (A) U.S. Exports as a Percentage of U.S. Output.
(B) U.S. Output as a Percentage of World Output

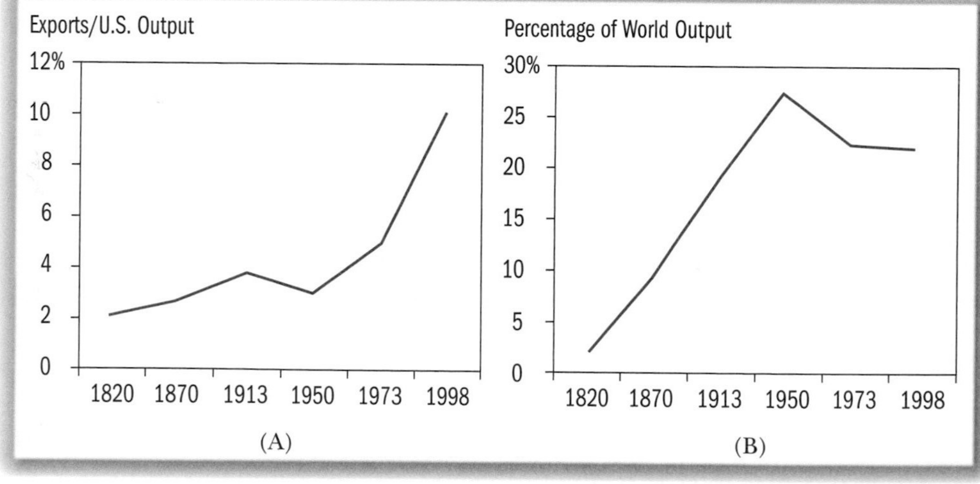

Source: Angus Maddison, *The World Economy: A Millennial Perspective,* Paris: Organization for Economic Co-Operation and Development, 2001, Tables B-18 and F-2.
(A) Based on Table B-18 from Angus Maddison, "The World Economy: A Millennial Perspective", © OECD 2001.
(B) Based on F-2 from Angus Maddison, "The World Economy: A Millennial Perspective", © OECD 2001.

[9]An excellent summary of the dollar's role is contained in Craig S. Hakkio, "The Dollar's International Role," *Contemporary Policy Issues* 11(2), April 1993, pp. 62–75.

(*continued*)

U.S. economy. First, over the last fifty years the percentage of the U.S. economy that produces exports has risen from approximately 2 percent to nearly 10 percent. For industries that emphasize exports, this increasing "openness" of the U.S. economy has created opportunities for increased sales and profits. However, for the part of the economy that produces domestic goods that compete with imports, clothing, steel, and lumber, for example, the adjustment to this new level of competition has been difficult, as sales and profits have fallen. While trade is beneficial to the economy as a whole, the same cannot be said for all segments of the economy. Perhaps the chronic trade deficits the U.S. has run over the last twenty years have focused too much attention on import competition and not enough attention on the U.S. as a successful exporter of goods and services.

The second part of the chart tracks U.S. GDP as a percentage of the economic output of the world economy. In the middle of the twentieth century, the U.S. economy was approximately 27 percent of the economy of the world. The U.S. during that period was not just a relatively large economy—it was the dominant economy. In the ensuing fifty years, the U.S. economy has become "smaller" relative to the rest of the world economy. This means that for some time the economy of the rest of the world has grown faster than that of the U.S. Whether or not this relative decline is of any importance or not has been a subject of some debate.[10] However, being the world's largest economy, the world's largest trading nation, and having one of the highest standards of living in the world is not a particularly terrible position for a country to be in.

A closer examination of the chart reveals that the time frame covers more than one hundred years. This historical perspective is intentional. If one examines the position of the U.S. economy in the late nineteenth century, the parallels with the late twentieth century are interesting. In terms of both trade as a percentage of GDP and U.S. GDP relative to the rest of the world, the U.S. position today is not so different from what it was a hundred years ago. At that time, the U.S. was the world's largest economy. Also, exports were approximately 40 percent as important a component in GDP as they are now. Looking at a longer stretch of history, the position of the U.S. economy as a relatively "closed" economy seems abnormal. The same may be true for the dominant position that the U.S. economy had in the mid-twentieth century. Despite the U.S. economy's large absolute size, its dominance in the mid-twentieth century may have been something of an aberration created by the lingering effects of the Great Depression and World War II. While the position of the U.S. in the world economy is now somewhat different from what it was twenty or thirty years ago, this position may, in a longer historical view, be more typical.[11]

[0]For example, see Paul M. Kennedy, *The Rise and Fall of the Great Powers,* New York: Random House, 1987.
[1]For a more extensive treatment of these subjects see "America: A Survey," *The Economist,* October 26, 1991; or Douglas A. Irwin, "The United States in A Global Economy? A Century's Perspective," *American Economic Review* 86(2), May 1996, pp. 41–45.

approximately 72 percent of economic activity. With more of their total economic activity engaged in the production and consumption of services, the high-income economies tend to trade more services. Given the increasing importance of international trade in services, we have made an effort to include this type of trade in our study of international economics.

CAPITAL FLOWS IN THE WORLD ECONOMY

International trade in goods and services is just one part of international economics. During every business day, a substantial amount of capital flows around the world that

multinational corporations (MNCs) companies that own, control, or manage production and distribution facilities in several countries

portfolio capital the purchase of financial assets, such as stock and bonds, in a foreign country

foreign direct investment (FDI) a corporation's purchase of real assets, such as production facilities and equipment, in a foreign country

is not directly related to the buying or selling of goods and services.[12] These flows take several forms. First, capital flows between countries when domestic residents purchase equities or bonds in a foreign financial market.[13] While the flow of capital to buy or sell foreign financial assets is important, many financial flows between countries are much more mundane. For example, **multinational corporations (MNCs)** own, control, or manage production and distribution facilities in several countries. Quite naturally, a MNC would maintain a number of bank accounts denominated in different currencies. For these firms, simply maintaining the desired level of cash in these accounts may involve substantial movements of financial capital. This type of capital movement is frequently referred to as the movement of **portfolio capital**. In addition, there are movements of capital between countries to effectuate **foreign direct investment (FDI)**. Foreign direct investment is the purchase of real assets (such as production facilities and equipment) by a domestic firm in a foreign country. For example, if a German corporation builds a production facility in Alabama, this entails a movement of capital from Germany to the U.S. Lastly, governments and central banks frequently move capital between countries or buy and sell foreign currencies.[14]

In the cases just mentioned, capital flows are not an import or an export of a good or a service. Consequently, these flows are not included in the figures on international trade of goods and services reported in Tables 1.2 or 1.3. As Table 1.4 indicates, portfolio capital flows to low- and middle-income countries for 2005 were $10.3 billion and $108.5 billion, respectively. Although net private capital flows are not reported for the high-income countries, the U.S. imported $785.4 in net portfolio capital in 2005. In the case of foreign direct investment, a total of $974.3 billion flowed between countries worldwide in 2005. Of the total foreign direct investment flows for 2005, 71.2 percent of these flows occurred among the high-income countries. The low- and middle-income economies received 2.1 percent and 26.7 percent of the world's foreign direct investment flows, respectively.

To facilitate international trade in goods, services, and capital, individuals, businesses and governments need to buy or sell foreign currencies. The exchange of one country's currency for another country's currency occurs in the **foreign**

Table 1.4 Distribution of International Capital Flows in the World Economy 2005

	Net Private Capital Flows (millions of $)	Foreign Direct Investment (millions of $)	% of World Total
Low-Income Economies	$10,327	$20,522	2.1%
Middle-Income Economies	$111,463	$260,273	26.7%
High-Income Economies	–	$693,488	71.2%
World Total	–	$974,283	–

Source: World Bank, *World Development Indicators*, Washington, D.C.: World Bank, 2007.

[12]A formal discussion of the differences in these flows will be covered in Chapter 12.

[3]However, any dividends or interest earned on these types of investments would be recorded elsewhere.

[4]The reasons for this activity by central banks are discussed in the second part of the book.

foreign exchange market the market where currencies are bought and sold

exchange rate the price of one currency in terms of another currency

exchange market. In most cases, this currency exchange occurs as banks respond to their customers' needs. An international firm may need a large amount of Euros this week and Thai baht the next. If you totaled these currency exchanges during a year, you would see that the volume of trading in the foreign exchange market is staggering. In 2004, trading in foreign exchange reached almost $2 trillion per day. This daily trading activity in foreign exchange has increased from only $600 billion since the late 1980s.[15] While the volume of international trade in goods and services is large, the volume of trading in foreign exchange dwarfs it. Comparing the numbers in Tables 1.1, 1.2, 1.3, and 1.4, the volume of traditional international exports or imports for a year is less than a week's worth of foreign exchange trading. The volume of foreign exchange trading for one month is greater than the total output of the world economy. With trading of foreign currencies at these levels, it is small wonder that the **exchange rate**, the value of currencies in terms of other currencies, is so widely reported.

TRENDS IN INTERNATIONAL PRODUCTION AND TRADE

The data presented in Tables 1.1 through 1.4 is a snapshot of production and trade in the world economy. Among the low-, middle-, and high-income economies, production, international trade, and population are growing at different rates. As time passes, these differentials in the rates of growth will alter the economic landscape of the world economy. The differing growth rates of the three groups of countries are presented in Table 1.5.

The first three columns of the table present data on the growth rate of output in the world economy during the 1980s and 1990s and first five years of the 2000s. During the 1980s, world economic output grew at 3.3 percent per year. Notice that the low-income economies were growing faster than the other country groups. During the 1990s, world economic growth slowed to 2.7 percent per year. Only the middle-income economies increased their rate of growth over the two decades. The growth rates of both the low-income and high-income economies slowed. During the first five years of the 2000s, world economic output increased at 2.8 percent per year. However, growth in the low- and middle-income economies increased to 6.1 percent and 5.2 percent, respectively. The trends, with respect to the growth rate of exports for the same time periods for the various economies, are shown in columns 4 and 6.[16] During the 1980s, world exports grew at 5.2 percent per year and increased to 6.9 percent during the 1990s. During the first five years of the 2000s, world exports grew at 5.7 percent per year. Over the two decades, exports in the low-income economies were growing at a slower rate than world exports. However, during the 2000s, exports of the low-income economies grew quicker than world exports, 11.1 percent per year. For the middle-income economies, export growth has been faster than world export growth over all three periods. The last three columns of the table show the population growth rates for the same groups of countries. World population growth decreased

[15]Bank for International Settlements, *Triennial Central Bank Survey: Foreign Exchange and Derivatives Market Activity in 2004,* Basel: Bank for International Settlements, March 2005.

[16]The growth rates refer to the growth of real exports, and real GDP. Real values are calculated by taking nominal values and adjusting them for changes in prices over the period.

Table 1.5 Rates of Growth of GDP, Exports, and Population

	GDP Growth		
	1980–1990	1990–2000	2000–2005
Low-Income Economies	4.50%	3.20%	6.10%
Middle-Income Economies	3.30%	3.60%	5.20%
High-Income Economies	3.30%	2.50%	2.20%
World	3.30%	2.70%	2.80%
	Export of Goods & Services Growth		
	1980–1990	1990–2000	2000–2005
Low-Income Economies	3.30%	5.30%	11.10%
Middle-Income Economies	7.30%	8.80%	10.40%
High-Income Economies	5.00%	6.50%	4.10%
World	5.20%	6.90%	5.70%
	Population Growth		
	1980–1990	1990–2000	2000–2005
Low-Income Economies	2.30%	2.00%	1.90%
Middle-Income Economies	1.70%	1.20%	0.90%
High-Income Economies	0.60%	0.70%	0.70%
World	1.70%	1.40%	1.20%

Source: World Bank, *World Development Indicators*, Washington, D.C.: World Bank, 2004 and 2007, World Bank, *World Development Report*, New York: Oxford University Press, 2003.

from 1.7 percent in the 1980s to 1.4 percent in the 1990s to 1.2 percent in the 2000s. The low-income countries during the period had population growth rates that were equal to or greater than that of the world. Both middle-income and high-income countries had populations growing at a slower rate than that of the rest of the world during the 1990s.

These differences in the growth rates of production, exports, and population imply several things. First, the faster production growth rates in the middle-income

The Growth of the World Economy: Historical Perspectives and Future Trends

When the term *economic growth* is used, almost invariably what is being discussed is a country's GDP growth rate. In the United States, data on past and current GDP growth and forecasts of future growth are commonplace. Announcements concerning the growth of countries like Japan, Germany, and Mexico are becoming increasingly common. If you think about it, something important is missing. GDP growth is usually put in the context of a domestic economy. Occasionally you will hear announcements concerning the growth of a region such as Europe, Asia, or Latin America. However, no country or region is an economic island. Since all countries are to a greater or lesser extent integrated into the world economy, it is reasonable to think about world economic growth. If the world economy is growing at a faster or slower rate, then it will be, accordingly, easier or harder for a national economy to grow.

To get some idea of the rate of growth of the world economy, economic historians have been constructing estimates of past GDP growth in various countries and aggregating these estimates over the past several decades. In general terms, they have identified distinct periods of growth in the world economy over the last 150 years. From 1850 to 1914, the world economy experienced a prolonged period of rapid economic growth. Rapid advances in transportation and communication helped fuel the growth of trade both domestically and internationally in many countries.[17] A period of slow growth began with the start of World War I and ended in 1945 with the end of World War II. This period included two world wars and a global depression.

A prolonged period of rapid world economic growth began in 1945. The period 1945 to 1973 was a golden age for the world economy characterized by rapid increases in output and especially international trade. Growth in trade was partially a function of the dismantling of many of the trade barriers erected during the 1930s. Unfortunately, this "golden age" ended abruptly in 1973 with the rapid increase in oil prices. Since 1973, the world economy has been growing at an abnormally low rate compared to the two earlier booms.[18]

Since 1993, the world economy has been growing at a rate of between 3 and 4 percent per year. These few years of fast growth have led some to believe that the slow growth era that began in 1973 is ending and a new higher growth path for the world economy has begun. The reasoning is that the widespread use of information technology and the expansion of "economic freedom" in both developing countries and former Communist countries will usher in a new "golden age" for the world economy.[19] It is a bit early to call a few years of faster growth a trend, but, if true, the implications are important. For our purposes, this would mean an even larger increase in economic growth and international trade. The trade growth rate is very sensitive to the growth rate in world output. Since world growth has been somewhat slow for the last 20 years, it is safe to say that this has been a drag on the growth rate of international trade. The growth rates of output and trade given in the chapter are possibly somewhat conservative. Extrapolating to the future, it would be unlikely that the growth rates of output and trade would be slower than that given in the chapter. Further, there is a possibility that those growth rates could turn out to be low. More rapid growth in the world economy would make it easier for the U.S. economy, or any other economy, to grow at a faster rate.

---

[17]For an excellent study of this period, see Kevin O'Rourke and Jeffrey G. Williamson, *Globalization and History: The Evolution of a Nineteenth-Century Atlantic Economy,* Cambridge: MIT Press, 1999.

[18]For a more complete discussion of world economic growth and it's implications for developing countries, see Lloyd G. Reynolds, "The Spread of Economic Growth to the Third World: 1850 to 1980," *Journal of Economic Literature* 21(3), September 1983, pp. 941–80.

[19]For an excellent discussion of these issues, see "The Right Mix: Global Growth Attains a New, Higher Level That Could Be Lasting," *Wall Street Journal,* March 13, 1997, pp. A1 and A8.

economies imply that over time, these economies will account for an increasingly important part of world output. Because income growth is tied to production growth, this means that income in these economies is also rising. Over time, the higher production growth is leading to a higher growth rate of exports of goods and services for these economies. Further, the rapid growth of GDP for these economies leads to a faster growth rate for imports. Keep these trends in mind as you read this book. Of necessity, our discussion will focus on production and trade in high-income economies because they constitute the largest portion of the world economy. However, we need to remember that the focus of international economics and business will shift to production and trade in developing countries as these countries' absolute and relative size in the world economy increases.

GLOBALIZATION

A commonly heard word in discussions of international trade is *globalization.* In one sense, everyone knows what this word means but usually only in a vague manner. For the most part, globalization is usually taken to mean that international transactions of one sort or another are becoming increasingly important. In our case, we would like to be more precise about this term. In the first part of this section we clarify the term globalization. Following this, we discuss various aspects of globalization and how they relate to what we will cover as we move through the book. In the last part of the section we will cover how to think about the controversy surrounding globalization.

First, globalization can be thought of in two ways. One way is to discuss globalization at the country level. Table 1.6 shows exports plus imports of goods as a percent of GDP for a sample of forty countries. Countries with a high ratio are generally more open to the world economy than are countries with a low ratio. Notice that the ratios are not uniform. Some countries are noticeably more open than others. Further, these ratios change over time. In most cases, the ratio tends to rise at a faster or slower rate for each country. For countries where the ratio is rising rapidly, the structure of the economy is likely to be changing rapidly because industries linked to exports will be expanding. As we will see, countries with rapidly growing exports will likely have rapidly growing imports as well. In this case, some industries will be experiencing more competition from imports. These latter changes can be difficult for a country to manage. Globalization, or the increasing openness of an economy, means changes that are not universally positive.

If the globalization of countries is now common, this implies that the same is true of the world economy. The concept of globalization can be extended to the world economy as well. The sample of countries shown above is not unique; the same thing is happening on a global basis. This is illustrated in Figure 1.3. In this figure, world exports of goods are shown as a percentage of world output from 1950 to 2005. During this time period, world exports have increased from approximately 12 percent to 23 percent of world output. International trade is becoming an increasingly important component of total economic activity for both individual countries and the world economy. In part, this is a function of the reduction of the barriers to trade that will be the focus of Chapters 7 through 10.

The concept of globalization is complex and involves more than international trade alone. It has other aspects that are not purely linked to international trade. Not

Table 1.6 Exports Plus Imports as a Percentage of GDP for Selected Countries

Country	Real Export plus Imports as a Percent of GDP
Singapore	462.9%
Hong Kong	343.4
Luxembourg	282.0
Hungary	180.0
Ireland	176.7
Belgium	174.0
Netherlands	146.9
Taiwan	118.1
Honduras	109.7
Philippines	107.7
Austria	103.0
Costa Rica	96.4
Korea	95.5
Denmark	94.5
Switzerland	90.7
Sweden	88.9
Canada	81.8
Indonesia	81.7
Portugal	79.9
Nicaragua	79.3
Iceland	78.9
Israel	78.3
Finland	77.9
Ecuador	76.9
Germany	76.6
Norway	76.4
Turkey	71.2
Chile	71.1
Poland	69.5
Mexico	66.8
Spain	65.1
U.K.	59.9
France	57.5
Italy	54.5
China	54.4
South Africa	54.4
Greece	54.3
Australia	48.9
U.S.	26.6
Japan	23.4

Source: Alan Heston, Robert Summers and Bettina Aten, *Penn World Table Version 6.2,* Center for International Comparisons of Production, Income and Prices at the University of Pennsylvania, September 2006.

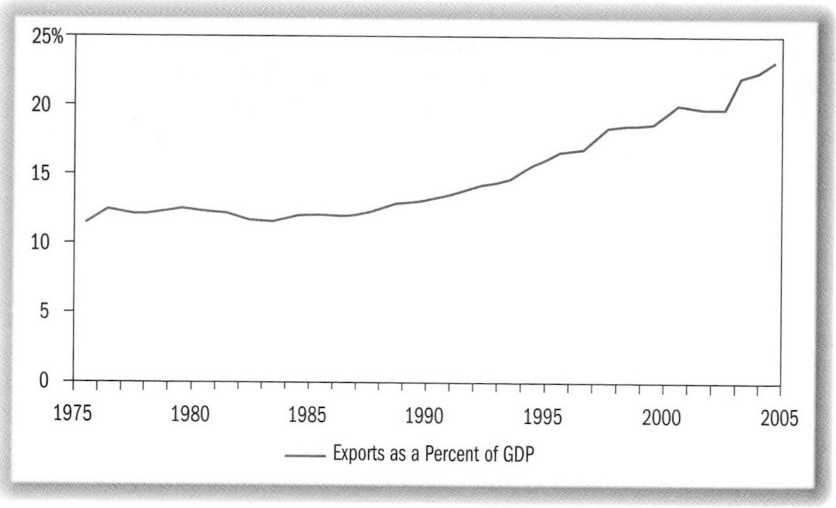

Figure 1.3 Real World Exports of Goods as a Percentage of Real World GDP

Source: Adapted from World Trade Organization, *International Trade Statistics, 2006,* Geneva: WTO, 2007, Table A1.

only goods and services move in the world economy; resources do as well. In Chapter 6, we will consider the movement of people, of money for foreign direct investment, and the role of multinational corporations in the world economy. In a related vein, there are large movements in the world economy of portfolio capital. These movements will be highlighted in Chapters 13 through 15. Globalization also affects the way the economies of countries function in terms of the growth rate of GDP and changes in a country's overall price level. In Chapters 17 through 20, the way changes in the world economy affect the macroeconomic performance of individual countries is presented. Finally, globalization is especially important for the developing countries. For countries that are developed, globalization is an important issue. However, for the developing countries, integration into the world economy is critical for their economic development. Because most of the world's population resides in the developing countries, we will focus on the relationship between certain aspects of globalization and economic development in Chapters 11 and 21.

From the above it is obvious that globalization is a complex issue. In order to examine it in a coherent manner, it is useful to think in the economic terms of benefits and costs. This is a natural way of thinking about most things to an economist. Economic phenomena always have both benefits and costs. The trick is to consider *both* and to analyze concepts like globalization in this way. As we will see as we move through the book, most international transactions improve welfare as long as they are voluntary. By definition, an international transaction is one that involves market participants in more than one country. Market participants such as individuals or businesses do not normally engage in transactions where the costs outweigh the benefits. International transactions occur because both parties expect the transaction to improve their welfare.

If globalization is such a positive thing, then one may well ask why it is so controversial. As we have pointed out, globalization has both benefits and costs. A consistent theme of the book will be to point out both. However, as we will see in many cases it is much easier to see the costs than to identify the benefits. For example the closing of a manufacturing plant is highly visible. On the other hand, the hiring of new workers or the expansion of an existing plant to increase exports would go practically unnoticed. One of the purposes of this book is to teach you to see both the benefits and the costs more clearly. With this information, you will be able to more clearly assess and judge the positive and negative sides of globalization. As we will see, on balance globalization is a positive thing. However, to be honest it is necessary to be clear about the costs. We will see that globalization, in all its forms, provides one more example of the economist's saying that there is no such thing as a free lunch.

SUMMARY

1. International economics is the study of the production, distribution, and consumption of goods, services and capital on a worldwide basis.
2. For most countries, international trade is an important adjunct to domestic economic activity. However, the international exchange of goods, services, and real and financial assets is now large and is growing at a rapid rate.
3. The distribution of world economic output is not evenly distributed among the world's economies. High-income economies account for almost 80 percent of the world's output, and a similar percentage of imports and exports. The low-income economies account for only 3 percent of the world's economic output and international trade.
4. International trade in services is now nearly one-quarter the size of international trade in goods. This type of trade is large and has been growing faster than trade in goods.
5. During every business day financial capital (money) that is not related to the buying and selling of goods and/or services moves around the world. These financial flows are so large that they equal the total output of the world economy in less than a month. Consequently, the exchange rate, or the value of one currency in terms of another, has become very important.
6. Among the different groups of countries in the world, production and trade are growing at different rates. As time passes, the focus of international economics will shift more toward production and trade in developing countries as their absolute and relative size increases.
7. Globalization is the term used to convey the idea that international factors are becoming a more important part of the world economy. This concept can be used for either a country or the world economy as a whole. The simplest measure of globalization is the ratio of foreign trade to total economic activity.

KEY CONCEPTS AND TERMS

- microeconomics p. 2
- macroeconomics p. 2
- international economics p. 2
- Gross Domestic Product (GDP) p. 4
- World Bank p. 4
- exports p. 5
- imports p. 5
- multinational corporations (MNCs) p. 11
- portfolio capital p. 11
- foreign direct investment (FDI) p. 11
- foreign exchange market p. 12
- exchange rate p. 12

PROBLEMS AND QUESTIONS FOR REVIEW

1. Why is it important to study international economics?
2. Conduct an Internet search for the term *international economics*. How many items related to international economics show up?
3. How is international economics related to your earlier study of microeconomics and/or macroeconomics?
4. How is the economic output of the world distributed among low-, medium-, and high-income economies?
5. The world's biggest economic problem is GDP per capita in the low-income countries. Is this statement true?
6. What can be said about the distribution of merchandise trade among low-, medium-, and high-income economies? How does this compare with the distribution of output?
7. If your state were a country, how would it fit into the world economy?
8. What is international trade in services composed of?
9. How does the distribution of trade in services compare with the distribution of output and merchandise trade?
10. How important is international trade in goods and services relative to the economic output of the world?
11. Compare the position of the U.S. economy to other large economies such as Japan or Germany.
12. How has the position of the U.S. in the world economy changed since 1820?
13. What is the difference between foreign direct investment and movements of portfolio capital?
14. Describe the distribution of FDI in the world economy.
15. Describe the size of trading in foreign exchange. Why is this type of activity so large?
16. Explain the trends in production and trade in the world economy over the last twenty-five years. What do these trends imply for the low- and middle-income economies?
17. Describe the three different periods of world economic growth that have occurred since 1850. Is the world economy now emerging from a period of slow growth?
18. Some now argue that the world economy is now entering a new phase of fast growth. What could cause this to happen?
19. Describe what the term globalization means. What is the easiest way to define it in numerical terms?
20. Recently, the consulting firm A. T. Kearney has been publishing a globalization index for countries of the world. Go to www.atkearney.com and look at the most recent ranking of countries. Next look at the sixteen factors used to create the globalization index.

SUGGESTED READINGS AND WEB SITES

As you begin your study of international economics, it would be a good idea to start keeping up with international economic news. The most common sources of information and their associated Web sites are as follows:

The Financial Times (www.ft.com)
The Economist (www.economist.com)
The Wall Street Journal (www.wsj.com)
Other resources that may be useful for this chapter are:
Nancy Birdsall, "Life is Unfair: Inequality in the World," *Foreign Policy* 111 (Summer 1998), pp. 76–93.
A readable examination of the extent and causes of income inequality in the world economy.
"Globalization and Its Critics: A Survey of Globalization," *The Economist,* September 29, 2001, pp. S3–S30.
An excellent survey article on some of the issues in the globalization debate.
Kevin O'Rourke and Jeffrey Williamson, *Globalization and History: The Evolution of a Nineteenth-Century Atlantic Economy,* Cambridge: MIT Press, 2000.
The integration of the world economy is not something that is entirely new. This book shows that it has all happened before and could even be reversed.

Howard Lewis, III and J. David Richardson, *Why Global Commitment Really Matters!,* Washington, D.C.: Institute for International Economics, 2001.

A careful study of the costs and benefits of globalization for the U.S. economy. The unusual feature is the discussion of the benefits of imports, U.S. investment overseas, and the transfer of U.S. technology.

Penn World Tables (www.datacentre.2chass.utoronto.ca/pwt/)

The best general data source for information on the world's economies.

Kenneth Pomeranz and Steven Topik, *The World That Trade Created: Society, Culture, and The World Economy,* New York: M.E. Sharpe, 1999.

A fascinating collection of anecdotes on international trade over the last five centuries.

Resources for Economists on the Internet (www.rfe.org)

A good place to start looking for the data on international economics.

Kenneth F. Scheve and Matthew Slaughter, *Globalization and the Perception of American Workers,* Washington, D.C.: Institute for International Economics, 2001.

A careful survey of the attitudes of American workers toward the increasing globalization of the U.S. economy.

Chapter 2

Why Countries Trade

"It is the maxim of every prudent master of a family, never to attempt to make at home what it will cost him more to make than to buy. The taylor does not attempt to make his own shoes, but buys them from the shoemaker. The shoemaker does not attempt to make his own clothes, but employs a taylor. The farmer attempts to make neither the one or the other, but employs those different artificers. . . . What is prudence in the conduct of every private family, can scarce be folly in that of a great kingdom. If a foreign country can supply us with a commodity cheaper than we can make it, better buy it of them with some part of the produce of our own industry, employed in a way we have some advantage."
—ADAM SMITH

INTRODUCTION

International trade theory as we know it today had its beginning with Adam Smith's presentation over two hundred years ago on the causes of international trade. Since the publication of *The Wealth of Nations,* economists have sought answers to a number of questions concerning international trade theory such as: Why do countries trade with one another? What specific benefits can a country obtain through international trade? Which country produces which good(s)? Why do countries export and import certain goods? At what prices do countries exchange exports and imports? How does international trade differ from interregional trade?

In this chapter, we begin our analysis of international trade theory and we answer these questions by comparing international trade to interregional trade. To appreciate Adam Smith's contribution to the development of international trade theory, we begin by discussing international trade for a single product. We then discuss international trade based on Adam Smith's theory of absolute advantage. Next, we explain the pattern of trade and the gains from trade based on David Ricardo's theory of comparative advantage. We continue the development of international trade theory by explaining the theory of comparative advantage in terms of opportunity cost. Finally, we describe the gains from trade that are difficult to quantify and occur over time.

INTERNATIONAL TRADE VERSUS INTERREGIONAL TRADE

Why do countries trade with one another? For that matter, why does one region of a country trade with another region of the same country? Among the various regions of the United States, there is a tremendous flow of goods and services on a daily basis.

The Southeast sells cotton to regions where cotton cannot grow. Northern California sells wine to the rest of the U.S. where conditions are less favorable for producing wine. New York City sells financial services to other regions where the cost of these services is higher.

Interregional trade and international trade are similar. For example, Massachusetts buys cotton from Mississippi for the same reason the United States buys coffee from Brazil. It makes little economic sense for a country to produce a good that can be purchased from another country at a lower price. The difference lies in the perception that trade between two regions of the same country, such as the U.S., is *us buying from and selling to ourselves,* whereas trade between one country and another country, is *us buying from and selling to them—another country.* For example, many Americans have trouble endorsing purchases of foreign steel, clothing, cars, meat, sugar, and other foreign goods because they may lead to a loss of U.S. jobs in those industries. Also, there are varying degrees of opposition to U.S. sales of Alaskan oil to Japan, U.S. weapons to foreign governments, and technological expertise to Russia. This difference in perception is illustrated as follows:[1]

A domestic entrepreneur announces that he has discovered a method of transforming agricultural products into electronic products. The agricultural products are fed into one side of a big black box and transformed electronic products of all kinds come out of the other side of the box. (You need to suspend disbelief to appreciate the idea that we are developing.) This method of transforming goods is a great innovation for society. Although this means a loss of jobs for the domestic electronics industry, the public nevertheless accepts it as a reasonable price for economic progress. However, eventually it is discovered that the agricultural goods are not transformed within the black box. What actually occurs is that the entrepreneur takes the agricultural products going into the black box, and without anyone noticing, he sells them abroad. The entrepreneur then uses the income from those sales to buy foreign electronic goods at a much lower cost and those electronic goods come out of the black box. When the public finds out what the entrepreneur is doing, he is denounced as a fraud and a destroyer of domestic jobs.

For more than 200 years, economists have tried to convince the public and policy makers that countries trade for the same reason that individuals do. Countries, like individuals, are not equally capable of producing every good or service that they want or need. All countries, like individuals, can benefit if each country specializes in producing those goods that it can produce best and satisfy their other wants and needs by trading for them. Specialization and trade makes total world output of goods and services larger than it would be without trade. One goal of this chapter is to show how international trade is not like a poker game where one person's gain is another person's loss.[2] Rather, in international trade all countries gain and are better off than they would be if they pursued the alternative: buying and selling goods restricted to their own domestic markets.

---

[1]This anecdote is adapted from James C. Ingram, *International Economics,* New York: Wiley, 1983.

[2]Poker and games like it are called zero-sum games. An n-sum game is one where all parties potentially gain. Mutually beneficial international trade is an n-sum game.

TRADE IN AN INDIVIDUAL PRODUCT

In this section, we begin to put the ideas expressed in the previous section into a more formal format. First, consider who makes interregional or international trade happen. For the most part, trade occurs because a businessperson feels that he or she can make a larger profit by moving goods from where they are currently produced to someplace else where they can be sold at a higher price, resulting in higher profits. Goods tend to move from where they can be produced relatively cheaply to where they can be sold at a relatively higher price. This is true for both interregional and international trade. Since our focus is on international trade, we begin our analysis with a simple example of one good moving between two countries. For purely illustrative purposes, we will assume that the good being traded is cloth and that only two countries are involved in international trade—the U.S. and India. To do this, we use the familiar supply and demand model that you learned in your Principles of Economics courses. This model is a form of partial equilibrium analysis. This means that you must assume that the impact of trade in one individual product does not influence the overall state of the domestic economy. As we move through the book, we will continue to use cloth and the U.S. and India to maintain the continuity of the discussion. However, keep in mind that the principles are general and the goods and countries used are not important. The U.S. and India are just examples that are convenient, in part, because the countries have different economic characteristics.

As we begin our analysis, consider the domestic cloth market in the U.S. This is shown in the left-hand panel of Figure 2.1. As you may recall from your Principles of Economics course, the demand for cloth in the U.S. (D_{US}) slopes downward to the right. The demand curve slopes downward because, other things being equal, the quantity of cloth demanded by U.S. consumers increases as the price of cloth falls. The U.S. supply of cloth (S_{US}) should also look familiar. The supply curve slopes upward because, other things being equal, the quantity of cloth supplied by U.S. producers increases as the price of cloth rises. Before international trade opens between the U.S. and India, equilibrium in the U.S. cloth market occurs at point E, where the quantity demanded in the U.S. equals the quantity supplied in the U.S. The U.S. price is P_{US} and the quantity of cloth produced and consumed is Q_{US}. This equilibrium shows what would happen in **autarky**. Autarky is the word used by economists to express market outcomes in a situation where there is no trade with other countries.

autarky a situation where a country does not conduct international trade

The analogous situation for India is shown in the right-hand panel of Figure 2.1. As before, the demand for cloth in the Indian market (D_{INDIA}) slopes downward to the right, and the supply curve (S_{INDIA}) slopes upward to the right. In autarky, the equilibrium in the Indian market occurs at point F, where quantity demanded in India equals quantity supplied in India. In the Indian market, the equilibrium quantity is Q_{INDIA} and the equilibrium price is P_{INDIA}.

Normally, the U.S. supply and demand for cloth will depend on the price of cloth in terms of U.S. dollars, and India's supply and demand for cloth will depend on the price of cloth in terms of India's currency, rupees. Assuming that the exchange rate between the U.S. dollar and the Indian rupee is not affected by whatever trade policy is undertaken in both countries with respect to the cloth market, we can state prices of cloth in both the U.S. and India in terms of one currency, dollars.

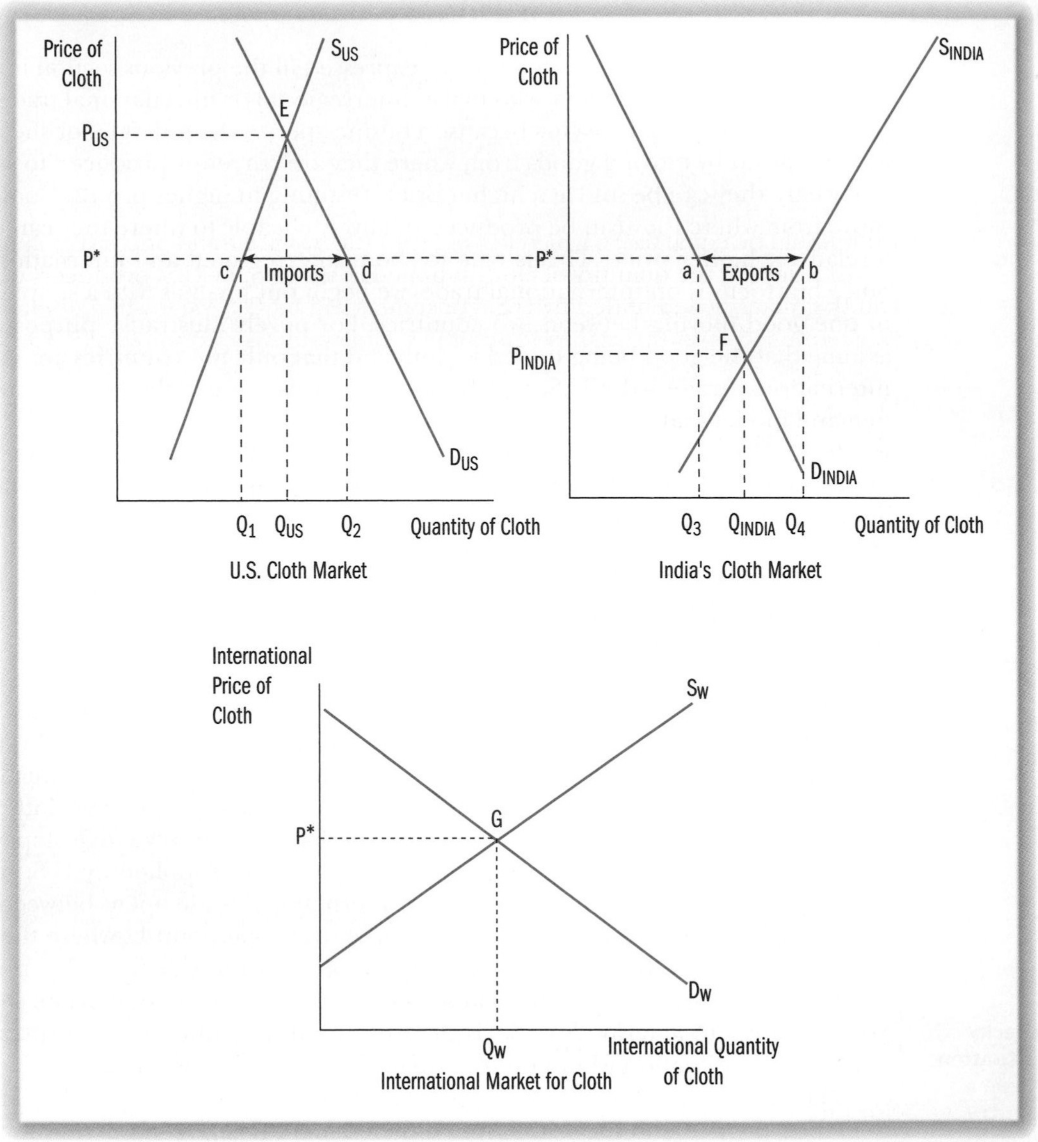

Figure 2.1 **The Effects of Trade on Production, Consumption and Price of Cloth**

For an individual product, like cloth, international trade equalizes the international price at P. As the figure illustrates the U.S. imports and India exports cloth at the international price.*

Comparing the two countries in a state of autarky, one can notice an immediate difference. Given different supply and demand conditions, the equilibrium price in India is lower than the equilibrium price in the U.S. At this point, what causes of the price differences between the U.S. and India is immaterial. However, the existence of this price differential is very important.

Since the price of cloth is lower in India than it is in the U.S., it is easy to imagine that U.S. consumers may purchase Indian cloth at price P_{INDIA} which is lower than the price of cloth in the U.S. (P_{US}).[3] The process of international trade involves moving cloth from India to the U.S. More precisely, cloth is exported from India and imported into the U.S. As this occurs, the price of cloth in the U.S. will decline, while the price of cloth in India will rise. This movement in the price of cloth in both countries will continue until the two prices converge at a single "international price." In Figure 2.1, the international price of cloth would be equal to P*, which lies between the two pre-trade prices (P_{US} and P_{INDIA}).

At price P*, the quantity of cloth supplied in the U.S. by U.S. producers will be Q_1, and the quantity demanded by U.S. consumers will be Q_2. Meanwhile, the quantity of cloth supplied in India will be Q_4 and the quantity demanded will be Q_3. For the international market to clear, the excess demand in the U.S., Q_1 to Q_2, must equal the excess supply in India, Q_3 to Q_4. That is the quantity of cloth available for export from India (ab) must be equal to the quantity of cloth imports demanded by the U.S. (cd).

Let us first examine the more commonly noticed effects in the importing country, the U.S. The effects of imports in the U.S. market are conceptually similar to adding suppliers. However, in this case the new suppliers are from India. The new equilibrium occurs at a higher equilibrium quantity (Q_2) and a lower equilibrium price (P*). American consumers buy more cloth at a lower price. As most of us intuitively understand, imports are good for domestic consumers.[4] For domestic producers, imports are not a positive change in the market. Imports cause the domestic price to drop from P_{US} to P*. You can trace the effects of this drop in the price on U.S. producers of cloth by moving down the supply curve (S_{US}). The lower price causes a decrease in the quantity supplied by U.S. cloth producers. At the new equilibrium price, U.S. production of cloth is Q_1. The U.S. cloth industry has reduced its output by an amount equivalent to Q_{US} minus Q_1. Since the quantity demanded is Q_2, imports are equal to Q_2 minus Q_1. The overall effects of trade in the U.S. market are now clear. U.S. consumers get to purchase a larger amount of cloth *and* pay a lower price. The U.S. cloth industry produces a lower amount of cloth and receives a lower price.

As one could anticipate, the effects on the cloth market in India are the reverse. These effects are shown in the right-hand panel of Figure 2.1. In India, exports of cloth to the U.S. are conceptually similar to adding consumers. However, in this case the new consumers are from the U.S. The new equilibrium for India occurs at a higher equilibrium quantity (Q_4) and a higher equilibrium price (P*). In India the price of cloth has risen and the quantity produced by the Indian cloth industry rises. This is clearly a positive development for the Indian cloth industry. The industry is both producing more cloth and receiving a higher price. However, there is another effect in India that is not so positive. As the price rises, the quantity demanded by Indian consumers of cloth falls. As the price rises from P_{INDIA} to P*, domestic consumption of cloth

---

[3]At this point we will assume zero transportation costs and no government imposed barriers to trade. The effects of transportations costs on trade will be discussed in Chapter 8. Similarly, the effects of any barriers to trade will be covered in Chapters 7 and 8.

[4]To make an overall judgment regarding the gains from trade for a country as a whole within this model, we would need to discuss the concepts of producers' surplus and consumers' surplus. Both consumers' and producers' surplus and the welfare gains from trade are discussed in Chapter 7, where we demonstrate that free trade will provide overall benefits to both countries.

falls from Q_{INDIA} to Q_3. In this case, total exports of cloth in India are Q_4 minus Q_3. The overall effects of trade in the Indian market are now clear. Indian consumers get to purchase a smaller amount of cloth *and* pay a higher price. The Indian cloth industry produces a larger amount of cloth and receives a higher price.

International trade in cloth between the U.S. and India has created an "international" market for cloth. The international supply of cloth consists of the excess supply of cloth from India (the difference between cloth produced in India and Indian consumption of cloth). International demand for cloth consists of the excess demand for cloth from the U.S. (the difference between U.S. consumption of cloth and cloth produced in the U.S.). This situation is shown in the bottom panel of Figure 2.1. The international demand for cloth is shown as Dw. Likewise, the international supply of cloth is shown as Sw. The intersection of the two curves at point G shows the equilibrium price in the world market for cloth at P* and the equilibrium quantity at Qw. Notice from the start that P* is not the same as the autarky price of cloth in either the U.S. or India.

The above example illustrates the simple dynamics of international trade between two countries for a single product. The analysis is in general the same whether the product is cloth or semiconductors. Trade occurs because of prices for products are different between countries. However, what has been left out of the analysis is what *causes* of the differences in prices between countries. Why is the price of cloth low in India and high in the U.S.? In the material that follows we will examine what economists have learned about this over the last 200 years. The answer to that question is important in two respects. First, both domestic and international trade occur for the same reasons—price differences. Understanding what causes these price differences also means understanding what causes trade. Second, as we pointed out in the previous chapter, international trade is becoming an ever larger part of the economic activity of the world. Without a clear understanding of the causes of international trade,

Football Games, Rats, and Economic Theory

For many students, the terms "economic theory" and "rationality" are often associated with unrealistic assumptions. However, economic theory is not nearly as "unrealistic" or removed from reality as it is frequently perceived to be. The purpose of any theory, economic or otherwise, is to explain and to predict events.

The first step in the process of developing a theory is abstraction. Most economic events, such as international trade, are influenced by a myriad of factors. In most cases there are too many factors to consider simultaneously. International trade is a good example. Virtually millions of factors influence the international trade of a country. That's why it is important to first limit the number of factors to be considered to some manageable number. Once this has been done, the second task is to formulate a theory of how these factors interact, which explains past economic events such as exports and imports of a country. Finally, it is desirable to test the theory against real-world data to see if it does explain past exports and imports of a country. With a little luck the theory then *might* be useful in predicting future exports and imports of a country.

Abstracting and formulating a theory is not exclusive to economics. It is something all of us do frequently. The "unrealism" of economic theory is usually perceived to be a result of the first part of the process (abstraction). However, abstraction is necessary. Many events are influenced by too many factors to be considered simultaneously. Football games are a good example. How many factors can influence the outcome of a football game? Literally thousands of greater or lesser factors could influence the outcome. The next time you hear people discussing who will win a football game, or any other type of athletic contest, you will probably be hearing theory at work. A person with an opinion on the outcome cannot consider all possible factors. Listen carefully and you'll hear abstraction. He or she has picked out a few important factors from all possible factors and used this limited number of factors to arrive at a prediction. Arguments over the outcomes of athletic contests are usually over differences in the factors that the abstraction process produced. Notice also that people focus on important factors and "unrealistically" ignore many things that can influence the game's outcome.

The principle is general. When you buy a car, do you consider *all* possible features of every car on the market? Most likely not, as this would be "unrealistic." Similarly, we cannot consider every factor that would influence international trade. We have to limit ourselves to a few main factors in much the same way that we do in analyzing the outcomes of football games. The only real difference is that economists are simply more precise about exactly what the assumptions are.

A second problem that students frequently have with economics is the concept of rationality. In this text, we consider the participants in the world economy to be rational. When hearing the term *rational,* one often thinks of a world where everyone runs around with HP financial calculators and computes utility before buying an ice cream cone. In fact, rationality as used in economics is not that formal.

By economists' standards, even rats are rational. Researchers have found that rats enjoy both root beer and cherry cola. In an experiment, the rats were "charged" for their consumption of these two soft drinks by pressing on a bar to obtain a drink of one or the other. The researchers were able to change the "price" of the two drinks by changing the number of times the rat had to press each bar to obtain one soda or the other. Not surprisingly (at least to economists), as the price of one drink went up the rat would switch its consumption to the other drink. The rats would consume more of the "cheaper" drink and less of the "expensive" one.[5] Rats are just as rational in their consumption as students are in their consumption of Taco Bell versus McDonald's. The bottom line is that the assumption of rationality is not very "unrealistic."

[5]The experiments are described in Gordon Tullock and Richard B. McKenzie, *The New World of Economics,* 4th edition, Homewood, Ill.: Irwin, 1985.

it is virtually impossible to understand the world economy. In the following section, the most basic explanation of what causes price differences between countries and, by implication, in international trade are presented.

TRADE BASED ON ABSOLUTE ADVANTAGE

In the late 18th century, Adam Smith formulated the concept of mutually beneficial trade between countries. His original purpose was to refute the mercantilist view of international trade (see the box on mercantilism) and to provide a case for free trade between countries. According to Adam Smith, in order for two individuals, two regions,

absolute advantage **the ability of a country to produce a good using fewer resources than another country**

or two countries to trade with one another, both must gain from the exchange. Smith wanted to show that international trade was not a zero-sum game like poker, but an n-sum game where all countries can benefit. To do this he created the concept of **absolute advantage** which is the ability of a country to use fewer resources to produce a good than other countries. In this section, we will demonstrate exactly how this is possible.

Absolute Advantage

To illustrate Adam Smith's idea of the mutual gains from trade, we will assume that there are only two countries, the U.S. and India, and that both countries produce just two goods, machines (M) and cloth (C). Suppose, further, that labor within a country is homogeneous and is the only factor of production used to produce both machines and cloth. In addition, suppose that the U.S. and India have a fixed amount of labor to produce the goods and that within the U.S. and India labor is fully employed. Also, the level of technology used to produce the goods is constant and production costs are constant. With free trade, goods can move freely between the U.S. and India, but labor

Mercantilism

"The ideas of economists and political philosophers, both when they are right and when they are wrong, are more powerful than is commonly understood. Indeed the world is ruled by little else. Practical men, who believe themselves to be quite exempt from any intellectual influence, are usually the slaves of some defunct economist."

JOHN MAYNARD KEYNES

Why do individuals in many countries consider interregional trade to be more acceptable than international trade? To answer this question, we need to look back to the 17th and 18th centuries when the doctrine of mercantilism dominated political and economic thought throughout the world. The doctrine of mercantilism is based on the premise that a country can promote its self-interest by discouraging imports and encouraging exports in order to increase its wealth. Underlying the mercantilists' view of international trade was the belief that a person's wealth or a country's wealth was based on their holdings of precious metals, which were gold and silver. Because gold and silver circulated as money, a country could increase its wealth by exporting more goods than it imported. This would occur as:

- Exports created inflows of gold and silver—foreigners' payments for domestic goods.
- Imports created outflows of gold and silver—domestic resident's payments to foreigners for their goods.

When a country's exports exceeded its imports, its stock of gold and silver rose, and the country's wealth increased. This situation implied that international trade was a zero-sum game, in the sense that exports were "good" and imports were "not good at all." To encourage a net inflow of gold and silver, the mercantilists advocated regulating international trade in a way that would promote large exports and small imports, meaning a favorable trade balance. To accomplish this, tariffs and quotas would be combined to restrict imports and cheap raw materials, and low wages would be used to encourage low-cost exports. Today, there are still traces of the old mercantilist doctrine in evidence around the world.[6] For example, public officials who argue that exports are "good" because they create jobs in a country, and imports are "not good" as they take jobs from the same country, still view international trade as a zero-sum game. Adam Smith challenged this view of international trade in the late 18th century when he formulated the concept of mutually beneficial trade between countries based on absolute advantage. His original purpose was to refute the mercantilist view of international trade and to demonstrate that trade between countries was beneficial to both.

[6]For a modern discussion of mercantilism see Robert B. Ekelund and Robert D. Tollison, *Mercantilism as a Rent Seeking Society: Economic Regulation in Historical Perspective,* College Station, TX: Texas A&M Press, 1981.

is mobile only within a country and remains immobile between countries.[7] Transportation costs between countries are zero and the two countries engage in barter trade, where goods are exchanged for other goods without the use of money.

Given these assumptions, Table 2.1 demonstrates the mutually beneficial gains from trade. The first row shows that one worker in the U.S. can produce either 5 machines or 10 yards of cloth in one day. The second row shows that one worker in India can produce either 2 machines or 15 yards of cloth in one day. Comparing the two countries, U.S. workers are more productive in machine production and Indian workers are more productive in cloth. In this situation, the U.S. has an absolute advantage in machine production because the U.S. can produce more machines than India can with a given amount of labor. As a result, the U.S. can produce lower-cost machines. Likewise, India has an absolute advantage in cloth production and it can produce lower-cost cloth because India can produce more cloth than the U.S. with a given amount of labor.

The Gains from Specialization and Trade with Absolute Advantage

Assuming that trade opens up between the two countries, the U.S. could benefit from importing cloth from India and exporting machines to India. India could benefit from

Table 2.1 Absolute Advantage: Production Conditions When Each Country Is More Efficient in the Production of One Commodity

	One Person Per Day of Labor Produces	
Country	**Machines**	**Cloth**
U.S.	5 machines	10 yards of cloth
India	2 machines	15 yards of cloth

[7]In Chapter 6 we will relax this assumption and consider what happens if labor and/or capital can move between countries.

Table 2.2 Change in World Output Resulting from Specialization According to Absolute Advantage

	Change in the Production of	
Country	**Machines**	**Cloth**
U.S.	+5 machines	−10 yards of cloth
India	−2 machines	+15 yards of cloth
Change in World Output	+3 machines	+5 yards of cloth

importing machines from the U.S. and exporting cloth to the U.S. Each country would, in its own self-interest, import the cheaper product in an attempt to profit from trade. This is an important point in our analysis. In our example, for each worker that the U.S. transfers from cloth production to machine production, U.S. output of machines increases by 5 units and U.S. output of cloth falls by 10 yards. For each worker that India transfers from machine production to cloth production, Indian cloth production increases by 15 yards and Indian machine production falls by 2 units. These results are shown in Table 2.2. As the table indicates, world output increases by 3 machines and 5 yards of cloth. This increase in output occurs as each country transfers one worker into the production of the good in which it has an absolute advantage. The gains from trade are the increase in world output that results from each country having specialized its production according to its absolute advantage. This increase in output would be allocated between the two countries through the process of international trade. The U.S. would export machines and import cloth, and India would export cloth and import machines.

labor theory of value the theory that the cost of a good is determined solely by the amount of labor used to produce it

In our example, what causes the difference in labor productivity and the difference in costs between each country is not crucial. Adam Smith's concept of cost, and the one that we use in our example, is based on the labor theory of value. The **labor theory of value** assumes that labor is the only relevant factor of production. This implies that the cost of a product depends solely on the amount of labor needed to produce it. Workers who produce more output per day produce less costly goods. Specialization and trade by countries based on absolute advantage results in the world using its resources more efficiently and causes an increase in world output that is distributed to the two countries through international trade. However, absolute advantage can explain only a small part of international trade. For example, absolute advantage can explain international trade based on a country's climate or natural resources, such as Brazil's capacity to export coffee or South Africa's capacity to export diamonds. In the next section we present a more generalized case of the gains from international trade.

TRADE BASED ON COMPARATIVE ADVANTAGE

Smith's explanation of mutually beneficial trade is an effective case for free trade. However, Smith's analysis leaves an unanswered question. Why would trade occur between two countries if one country had an absolute advantage in the production of

comparative advantage the ability of a country to produce a good at a lower (opportunity) cost than another country

both goods? In the late 18th and early 19th centuries, the United Kingdom was the most advanced country in the world with an absolute advantage in the production of most goods. Given this situation, why would the U.K. trade with a less productive area such as the American colonies? David Ricardo, a British economist, developed the answer. Expanding upon Adam Smith's work based on absolute advantage, Ricardo formulated the theory of **comparative advantage**.[8]

Comparative Advantage

To see how comparative advantage works, refer to Table 2.3 where the data shows that one U.S. worker can produce either 5 machines or 15 yards of cloth per day (first row), and that one Indian worker can produce 1 machine or 5 yards of cloth per day (second row). Comparing the two countries in Table 2.3, notice that the U.S. has an absolute advantage in the production of both machines and cloth. If you were using the concept of absolute advantage alone as the basis for trade, no trade would occur between the U.S. and India. However, Ricardo's theory of comparative advantage shows that mutually beneficial trade can still occur between these countries.

As the table indicates, U.S. labor has a 5 to 1 absolute advantage in the production of machines. In other words, U.S. workers can produce 5 machines for every 1 machine produced by Indian workers. U.S. labor also has a 15 to 5 or 3 to 1 absolute advantage in the production of cloth. This means that U.S. workers can produce 3 yards of cloth for every 1 yard of cloth produced by Indian workers. India has an absolute disadvantage in the production of machines and cloth. That is, U.S. workers can produce more machines and more yards of cloth than workers in India.

In this example, the U.S. has a greater absolute advantage in producing machines than it does in producing cloth. However, India's absolute disadvantage is smaller in producing cloth than in producing machines. Notice we are comparing the degree of absolute advantage or disadvantage in the production of both goods between these countries. Using Ricardo's logic, the U.S. has a comparative advantage in machines because its degree of absolute advantage is higher, and a comparative disadvantage in cloth because its degree of absolute advantage is lower. Similarly, India has a comparative advantage in cloth because its degree of absolute disadvantage is lower, and it has a comparative

Table 2.3 Comparative Advantage: Production Conditions When the U.S. Is More Efficient in the Production of Both Commodities

	One Person Per Day of Labor Produces		
Country	**Machines**	**Cloth**	**Relative Cost**
U.S.	5 machines	15 yards of cloth	1M = 3C
India	1 machine	5 yards of cloth	1M = 5C

[8]David Ricardo, *The Principles of Political Economy and Taxation,* London: Cambridge University Press, 1966. This work was first published in 1817.

disadvantage in machines because its degree of absolute disadvantage is higher. Comparative advantage, as opposed to absolute advantage, is a relative relationship.

Ricardo illustrated the principle of comparative advantage with the following example:

> "Two men can make shoes and hats, and one is superior to the other in both employments; but in making hats he can only exceed his competitor by one-fifth, or 20 percent, and in making shoes he can excel him by one-third or $33\frac{1}{3}$ percent. Will it not be for the interest of both that the superior man should employ himself exclusively in making shoes, and the inferior man in making hats?"

If Babe Ruth had played baseball 100 years earlier, Ricardo might have used him to illustrate comparative advantage. Babe Ruth began his baseball career as a pitcher for the Boston Red Sox. As a pitcher he won 89 games in 6 seasons but he was also an outstanding hitter. The New York Yankees traded for the Babe and turned him into an outfielder so he could specialize in his greater advantage, hitting. As a result he once hit 60 home runs in one season and 714 home runs in his career. In the same way, the U.S. has a comparative advantage in the production of machines and should specialize in producing machines. India has a comparative advantage in the production of cloth and should specialize in producing cloth.

The Gains from Specialization and Trade with Comparative Advantage

Now, assuming that trade opens up between the U.S. and India, the U.S. could benefit from importing cloth from and exporting machines to India. India could benefit from importing machines from and exporting cloth to the U.S. For each worker that the U.S. transfers from cloth production to machine production, U.S. output of machines increases by 5 units and U.S. cloth production falls by 15 yards. As India transfers 3 workers from machine production to cloth production, Indian cloth production increases by 15 yards and Indian machine production falls by 3 units. In this case, there is a net increase in world output, since cloth production remains constant and machine production increases by 2 units. These results are shown in Table 2.4.

Table 2.4 Change in World Output Resulting from Specialization According to Comparative Advantage

	Change in the Production of	
Country	**Machines**	**Cloth**
U.S.	+5 machines	−15 yards of cloth
India	−3 machines	+15 yards of cloth
Change in World Output	+2 machines	0 yards of cloth

Again, the gain from specialization and trade is the increase in world output that results from each country specializing its production according to its comparative advantage. This increase in output would be allocated between the two countries through the process of international trade. Exactly how this increase in output is distributed between the two countries is a question we will answer later.

TRADE BASED ON OPPORTUNITY COSTS

Our explanation of comparative advantage between the U.S. and India in the previous section was possible because we assumed that labor was homogeneous and was the only factor of production used to produce cloth and machines. Without this assumption,

Labor Costs as a Source of Comparative Advantage

Despite its limitations, the simple Ricardian model of international trade describes trade based on comparative advantage quite well. Since the 1950s, economists have conducted several empirical tests of the Ricardian model. The easiest way to test the theory is to examine the relative productivity of labor within two countries. In our chapter example, this examination would consist of the ratio of labor productivity in the U.S. to labor productivity in India. As noted, the productivity of labor and real wages are highly correlated. The more productive that U.S. labor is relative to Indian labor, the more that U.S. exports to India tend to be larger than U.S. imports.

MacDougall (1951) did the original study that tested the Ricardian model, and the results were essentially replicated by Stern (1962) and Bhagwati (1963).[9] A more recent study by Golub (1995) indicates that the theory seems to hold up quite well.[10] Golub studied U.S. trade with Asian countries and found that relative productivity differences and trade flows were in general correlated.

This study also shows why low-wage countries do not dominate international trade. For example, the wage rate in Malaysia is about 15 percent of the wage rate in the U.S. Not surprisingly, labor productivity in Malaysia is about 15 percent of U.S. labor productivity. In this case, is Malaysia really a "low-wage" country? The alleged unfair advantage of low-wage countries in most cases is nothing of the sort because low wages usually go hand in hand with low labor productivity. The U.S. and other industrialized countries import goods from low-wage countries to the extent that these countries have a comparative advantage in a particular product and not because the country pays low wages. Table 2.5 provides unit labor costs relative to the U.S. in 24 developing countries and 5 selected sectors for each country. As the table indicates, adjusted for productivity differentials, low wages are of themselves no guarantee of success in international markets.

[9]For details see G.D.A. MacDougall, "British and American Exports: A Study Suggested by the Theory of Comparative Costs, Part 1," *Economic Journal* 61(244), December 1951, pp. 697–724; Robert M. Stern, "British and American Productivity and Comparative Costs in International Trade," *Oxford Economic Papers* 14(3), October 1962, pp. 275–96; and Bela Balassa, "An Empirical Demonstration of Classical Comparative Cost Theory," *Review of Economics and Statistics* 45(3), August 1963, pp. 231–38.

[10]For details see Stephen Golub, "Comparative and Absolute Advantage in the Asia Pacific Region," *Federal Reserve Bank of San Francisco*, Pacific Basin Working Paper Series, No. 95-09, October 1995.

(*continued*)

Table 2.5 Unit Labor Costs in 24 Developing Economies for Selected Sectors, 2000 (Ratios relative to the U.S.)

Country	Food Products	Textiles	Clothing	Electrical Machinery	Transport Equipment
Argentina[a]	1.95	1.28	0.64	2.11	1.78
Bolivia	0.61	0.76	0.65	1.00	1.34
Brazil[a]	0.74	0.65	0.47	0.81	0.53
Chile	0.80	0.89	0.51	0.90	0.74
Colombia	0.62	0.66	0.47	1.01	0.97
Cote d'Ivoire[b]	1.50	1.06	1.02	1.34	1.69
Ecuador[c]	0.88	0.30	0.34	1.20	0.55
Egypt	1.45[d]	1.21[d]	0.38[e]	1.10[e]	0.71[e]
Ghana[a]	0.82	0.96	0.60	0.39	1.63
India	1.29	1.57	0.47	0.98	1.43
Indonesia	0.71	0.42	0.45	0.62	0.26
Kenya[c]	1.31	2.20	0.96	0.74	3.34
Malaysia	1.08	0.59	0.84	1.01	0.69
Mexico	0.90	0.88	0.64	1.06	0.43
Morocco[c]	1.61	1.38	1.05	1.49	0.92
Nigeria[a]	0.29	0.80	0.11	0.56	0.04
Peru[a]	1.02	0.62	0.46	0.95	0.50
Philippines[b]	0.65	0.67	0.59	0.80	0.40
Korea	0.73	0.63	0.62	0.56	0.71
Taiwan[a]	1.93	1.45	0.80	1.81	1.17
Thailand[f]	0.92	0.87	1.07	0.65	0.41
Turkey	1.09	0.96	0.43	0.97	0.65
Uruguay[c]	1.64	0.74	0.69	1.52	1.22
Venezuela[b]	0.93	0.72	0.49	0.68	0.17

Note: Unit labor costs calculated as wages (in current dollars) divided by value added (in current dollars).
[a]1995; [b]1997; [c]1999; [d]1996; [e]1998; [f]1994.
Source: Adapted from United Nations Conference on Trade and Development, *Trade and Development Report, 2003,* Geneva: UNCTAD, 2004, p. 108.

comparing the productivity of U.S. workers to India's workers would not be possible. Since labor is *not* homogeneous between countries and is just one of several factors of production, we must develop a more general theory of comparative advantage that is not based on the labor theory of value.

Opportunity Costs

The concept of **opportunity cost** enables us to develop a general theory of comparative advantage that takes into account all factors of production. In this context, opportunity cost is the amount of a good—machines—that must be given up to release enough

opportunity costs the cost of a good is the amount of another good that must be given up to release enough resources to produce the first good

marginal rate of transformation (MRT) the amount of one good that a country must forego to produce each additional unit of another good. This is another name for opportunity cost

resources to produce another good—cloth. Return to Table 2.3 and consider what would happen if the U.S. transferred one worker (and other resources) from machine production to cloth production. In this case, the U.S. would gain 15 yards of cloth but would have to forego the production of 5 machines. The opportunity cost of gaining the 15 yards of cloth is the loss of 5 machines. Economist's term the amount of one good that a country must forego to produce each additional unit of another good the **marginal rate of transformation (MRT)**, which in this example is 1 machine for 3 yards of cloth or 1 yard of cloth for 1/3 of a machine.

For India, the opportunity cost of 1 machine is 5 yards of cloth, or 1 yard of cloth costs 1/5 of a machine. This means that in India the marginal rate of transformation for the two goods is 1 machine for 5 yards of cloth. Notice that the marginal rate of transformation for the U.S. and India is different—the U.S. can exchange 1 machine for 3 yards of cloth, and India can exchange 1 machine for 5 yards of cloth.

Comparing the different marginal rates of transformation for both countries, the U.S. opportunity cost is lower for machines. The U.S. gives up 3 yards of cloth to produce 1 machine, whereas India must give up 5 yards of cloth to produce 1 machine. India's opportunity cost is lower for cloth. India must give up only 1/5 of a machine to produce 1 yard of cloth, whereas the U.S. must give up 1/3 of a machine to produce 1 yard of cloth.

Although the U.S. has an absolute advantage in the production of both machines and cloth, it has a comparative advantage in the production of machines. While India has an absolute disadvantage in the production of both machines and cloth, it has a comparative advantage in the production of cloth. Because the opportunity costs of the same goods differ within each country, both countries could benefit from trade. Traders can buy cloth in India and ship it to the U.S. to sell at a profit. In the same way, traders can buy machines in the U.S. and ship them to India to sell for a profit there.

The Gains from Specialization and Trade with Opportunity Costs

In Table 2.3, notice that there are limits to mutually beneficial exchange. No one in the U.S. would pay more than 1/3 of a machine for a yard of cloth. Why would anyone pay more for an imported good if the domestic price was lower? Similarly, no one in India would pay more than 5 yards of cloth to obtain a machine no matter where it was produced. For profitable exchange to take place, the price of machines relative to the price of cloth would have to be between 1 machine at a price of 3 yards of cloth, or 1M = 3C and 1 machine at a price of 5 yards of cloth, or 1M = 5C.[11]

Given the 1M = 3C and 1M = 5C limits to trade, let us assume that the exchange ratio for trade between the two countries is 1 machine costs 4 yards of cloth, or 1M = 4C. With this exchange ratio, we can examine Table 2.6 to determine the gains from trade. The first row of the table shows each country's maximum production of the two goods when all a country's resources are used to produce the good in which it has

[11]If you have been thinking that transportation costs affect comparative advantage, you're right. We have ignored transportation costs and will continue to ignore them throughout most of the analysis for simplicity. If the degree of comparative advantage is not sufficient to overcome transportation costs, then the good is not traded. In our example, the introduction of transportation costs would narrow the limits of mutually beneficial exchange. The effects of transportation costs on trade will be discussed in Chapter 8.

Table 2.6 Production and Consumption With and Without Trade: Based on an Exchange Ratio of 1 Machine = 4 yds. of Cloth

	Country	
	U.S.	**India**
Production at Full Employment	100 machines 0 yds. of cloth	0 machines 300 yds. of cloth
Consumption with Trade	50 machines 200 yds. of cloth	50 machines 100 yds. of cloth
Domestic Production and Consumption Without Trade (autarky)	50 machines 150 yds. of cloth	40 machines 100 yds. of cloth
Gains from Specialization and Trade	50 yds. of cloth	10 machines

a comparative advantage. For example, the U.S. is capable of producing 100 machines per day if all of its resources are devoted to the production of machines. Similarly, India could produce 300 yards of cloth per day if all of its resources are devoted to the production of cloth.

Let us assume that the U.S. consumes 50 machines and trades (exports) 50 machines to India. At the exchange ratio 1M = 4C, the U.S. would obtain (import) 200 yards of cloth from India. Looking at this exchange from the other perspective, India would be exporting the 200 yards of cloth and obtaining (importing) 50 machines. These exchanges are identified as "consumption with trade" in the second row of Table 2.6.

The gains from specialization and trade are what each country can consume with trade beyond what it can consume under conditions of autarky or without trade. If these two countries decided not to trade with each other, how much of each good could they consume? The U.S. could produce and consume 50 machines, and use its remaining resources to produce and consume cloth. Given the U.S. opportunity cost (MRT), 1M = 3C, it could have produced and consumed only 150 yards of cloth. This means that without trade, the U.S. has 50 yards less of cloth (200 with trade versus 150 without trade) to consume. By trading at the international exchange ratio of 1M = 4C, the U.S. is able to consume more cloth through trade.

The situation is the same for India. India could produce and consume 100 yards of cloth and devote its remaining resources to the domestic production of machines. Given its opportunity costs (MRT) of 1M = 5C, India could have produced and consumed only 40 machines. Without trade, India has 10 fewer machines (50 with trade vs. 40 without trade) to consume. As the example shows, both countries are better off when they specialize and trade than they would be if they produced and consumed without trade.

DYNAMIC GAINS FROM TRADE

We have seen that under both constant and increasing cost conditions international trade is mutually beneficial to the U.S. and India. In our example, both countries consume more goods with trade than they could without trade. However, these gains from

static gains from trade the increase in world production and consumption resulting from specialization and trade

dynamic gains from trade gains from trade over time that occur because trade causes an increase in a country's economic growth or induces greater efficiency in the use of existing resources

trade are a one-time event. Gains in world output that result from specialization and trade are the **static gains from trade**. Empirical estimates of the static gains from international trade tend to show that, in total, these gains are small. For example, empirical studies indicate that if the U.S. decided not to trade with all countries, the loss in U.S. GDP would be less than 1 percent.[12]

In addition to the static gains from trade, there may be additional **dynamic gains from trade**. These dynamic gains from trade are the gains from trade that occur over time because trade induces greater efficiency in the country's use of existing resources. Everything else being equal, this greater efficiency causes an increase in the rate of economic growth. These additional gains from trade may be difficult to measure, but they can be felt within the economy. To see what we mean, consider the following.

First, a country engaging in international trade uses its resources more efficiently. Businesses in search of a profit will naturally move resources, such as labor and capital, from industries with a comparative disadvantage to industries with a comparative advantage. The resources employed in the industry with a comparative advantage can produce more output, which leads to a higher real GDP. A higher real GDP tends to lead to more savings and, therefore, more investment. This additional investment in plant and equipment usually leads to a higher rate of economic growth. With faster economic growth, a country can produce even more goods and services over time. In a roundabout way, the gains from international trade grow larger over time. What is happening is that economies that are more open to trade grow faster than more closed economies, all else being equal.[13]

Second, there may be even greater benefits from trade for small countries, as large potential gains from trade are available in some industries that are subject to increasing returns to scale. Increasing returns to scale means that as the output of an industry increases, the unit costs of production decline. For industries subject to increasing returns to scale, free trade may allow an industry in a small country the opportunity to expand its production and lower its unit costs. This reduction in costs makes the industry more efficient and allows it to compete in world markets. Imagine the loss of opportunities for producers in small countries such as Belgium, the Netherlands, and Denmark if they did not have free access to all European markets. The same is true for the Canadian economy, which is about one-tenth the size of the U.S. economy.

Third, international trade increases not only the quantity of the goods we consume but, in many instances, their quality. For firms competing with imports, the issue may be more than the price of the product. It may also be the quality of the product. Increased competition usually leads to lower prices, as well as higher quality and greater diversity of the goods we can consume.

Fourth, international trade can be a very effective way to enhance competition in a country's domestic market. In the 1950s and 1960s, the lack of competition in the U.S. automobile and steel industries was considered a major public policy problem. In particular, firms like General Motors and U.S. Steel were considered to have had sufficient monopoly power to affect market prices. As the auto and steel industries encountered

---

[12]See Robert E. Feenstra, "How Costly is Protectionism," *Journal of Economic Perspectives* 6(3), Summer 1992, pp. 159–78.

[13]For an extensive survey of this subject see Sebastian Edwards, "Openness, Trade Liberalization, and Growth in Developing Countries," *Journal of Economic Literature* 31(3), September 1993, pp. 1358–93.

increased foreign competition, imports rose and the market share of General Motors and U.S. Steel declined. Foreign competition can be an effective remedy for insufficient competition in the domestic market.

SUMMARY

1. Modern international trade theory is concerned with the reasons for trade, the direction of trade, and the gains from trade.
2. Prior to Adam Smith, the dominant theory of international trade was mercantilism. This doctrine emphasized the accumulation of gold and silver as the source of a country's wealth. The implication of this theory was that trade was not mutually beneficial. Exports were considered to contribute to a county's welfare while imports subtracted from it.
3. In the late 18th century, Adam Smith formulated the concept of mutually beneficial trade based on absolute advantage. Specialization and trade based on absolute advantage results in the world using its resources more efficiently and causes an increase in world output.
4. David Ricardo expanded on the concept of absolute advantage by introducing the concept of comparative advantage. Even when one country has an absolute advantage in the production of all goods, mutually beneficial trade between the two countries is possible based on comparative advantage.
5. Modern trade theory employs comparative advantage based on opportunity cost. For example, when the relative prices of two commodities differ within each of the two countries, both countries can benefit from trade by specialization.
6. In addition to the static gains from trade there are also dynamic gains from trade. The dynamic gains include: (a) faster economic growth; (b) increasing returns to scale; (c) an increase in the quality of the goods we consume; and (d) an increase in competition within the domestic market.

KEY CONCEPTS AND TERMS

- autarky p. 23
- absolute advantage p. 28
- labor theory of value p. 30
- comparative advantage p. 31
- opportunity costs p. 35
- marginal rate of transformation (MRT) p. 35
- static gains from trade p. 37
- dynamic gains from trade p. 37

PROBLEMS AND QUESTIONS FOR REVIEW

1. How is international trade similar to trade among the regions of a country?
2. Show how differences in the price of a good among countries could lead to trade.
3. Trade can lead to price differences between one country and another becoming smaller. Show why this is true.
4. Exports may not be a positive thing for consumers in the exporting country. Is this statement true?
5. Describe the economic doctrine of mercantilism. What are the policy implications of this doctrine?
6. Is international trade a zero-sum game or an n-sum game? Why does this matter?
7. The theory of comparative advantage is useless because it is so unrealistic. Explain why this statement is true or false.
8. According to Adam Smith, what is the basis for trade? How are the gains from trade generated?
9. Explain how a country can have an absolute disadvantage in the production of all goods but still have a comparative advantage in the production of some goods.

10. What is the basis for trade according to David Ricardo? How are the gains from trade generated?
11. With a constant level of world resources, international trade brings about an increase in total world output. Explain why this statement is true.
12. If the wages in a country are low, then it obviously has cheap labor. Explain why this statement is false.

Table 2.7

	Case I		*Case II*		*Case III*		*Case IV*	
	Japan	**Korea**	**Japan**	**Korea**	**Japan**	**Korea**	**Japan**	**Korea**
Corn (bushels)	4	1	4	1	4	1	4	2
Wine (bottles)	1	2	3	2	2	2	2	1

13. Table 2.7 shows the bushels of corn and the bottles of wine that Japan and Korea can produce from one day of labor under four different hypothetical situations. For each case identify the commodity in which Japan and Korea have an absolute advantage or disadvantage.
14. From the Table 2.7, indicate for each case the commodity in which each country has a comparative advantage or disadvantage.
15. From the Table 2.7, indicate for each case whether or not trade is possible and the basis for trade.
16. Suppose that in Case II, in Table 2.7, Japan exchanges 4 bushels of corn for 4 bottles of wine with Korea.
    a. How much does Japan gain?
    b. How much does Korea gain?
    c. What is the range for the terms of trade for mutually beneficial trade?
    d. How much would each country gain if they exchanged 4 bushels of corn for 6 bottles of wine?
17. Assume that there are two countries, Mexico and Brazil, and one product—beer that is produced and consumed in both countries. Before international trade opens between Brazil and Mexico, given the Mexican peso-Brazilian real exchange rate, Mexico's equilibrium price for beer is higher than Brazil's equilibrium price for beer. Explain and show the effects on consumers, producers, and the countries as a whole if we allow them to internationally trade beer (and trading beer has no effect on the exchange rate).
18. Assume that there are two countries, the U.S. and Mexico, and one product—tequila that is produced only in Mexico but after trade will be consumed in both countries. Using supply and demand curves for the individual domestic markets and for the international market, show and explain the effects on consumers, producers, and the countries as a whole if we allow them to internationally trade tequila (and trading tequila has no effect on the exchange rate).
19. List and explain the dynamic gains from trade.

SUGGESTED READINGS AND WEB SITES

Douglas A. Irwin, *Against the Tide: An Intellectual History of Free Trade,* Princeton, NJ: Princeton University Press, 1996.

An extensive but readable history of the idea that free trade maximizes national and world welfare.

Lori G. Kletzer, *Job Losses from Imports: Measuring the Costs,* Washington, D.C.: Institute for International Economics, 2001.

A carefully done study of the losses to U.S. workers from import competition. It documents that the losses are not widely spread but very concentrated for specific types of workers.

Paul Krugman, "What Do Undergrads Need to Know About Trade?," *American Economic Review* 83(2), May 1993, pp. 23–26.

A quick synopsis on what an educated person should know about international trade.

R. A. Radford, "The Economic Organization of a P.O.W. Camp," *Economica* 12, November 1945, pp. 189–201.

The classic story of how simple trade improves economic welfare.

Chapter 3

Comparative Advantage and the Production Possibilities Frontier

"Comparative advantage is one of the few things in economics that is true, but not obvious."
—Paul Samuelson

INTRODUCTION

In the previous chapter, we considered a number of things about international trade. We first showed that international trade occurs for the same reason that domestic trade occurs. Next we considered trade as a way for businesses to make a profit and for consumers to obtain lower-priced goods. This initial look at international trade showed that trade is driven by the existence of different prices for goods in different countries. The analysis to this point left one important question unanswered: why are the prices different? To answer this question, we first considered the theory of trade based on absolute advantage. Some countries can produce goods at a lower price because labor in that country is more productive in producing that particular good. As we saw, trade based on absolute advantage is deficient in some respects as a complete explanation of trade. To remedy these problems, we then considered the theory of comparative advantage. Countries have a comparative advantage in the production of goods where the opportunity cost of producing those goods is low.

While the theory of comparative advantage is quite general, our discussion of the reasons for international trade is not complete. Specifically, we made an assumption in Chapter 2 that is not always realistic. In our previous analysis, we assumed constant costs. This is not an unreasonable assumption in many cases. However, you may recall from Principles of Economics that there are other cost conditions. We start this chapter by analyzing international trade under constant costs in a more rigorous way. Using the same framework, we will be able to consider how differences in the demand for goods in different countries influences the outcome of trade. From that point, we can then show how the existence of increasing costs influences international trade. While the models developed in this chapter cannot cover every conceivable aspect of international trade, they can be used to consider situations that could not be analyzed using the more limited tools in Chapter 2.

THE PRODUCTION POSSIBILITIES FRONTIER AND CONSTANT COSTS

production possibilities frontier (PPF) **a curve showing the various combinations of two goods that a country can produce when all of a country's resources are fully employed and used in their most efficient manner**

To start our analysis, let us go back to some information we covered in the last chapter. The theory of comparative advantage explains how specialization and trade lead to gains from trade for both countries. Table 3.1 contains the same information that we used in Chapter 2. However, now we will use this information to construct a graphical analysis that will allow us to get a more visual understanding of the theory of comparative advantage.

The Production Possibilities Frontier

The focus of our graphical analysis is the **production possibilities frontier (PPF)**. A production possibilities frontier shows the different combinations of two goods that can be produced when all of a country's factors of production are fully employed in their most efficient manner. By *efficiency,* we mean that the economy is producing a given mix of goods (machines and cloth) at the least cost given the current state of technology.

Table 3.2 shows hypothetical production possibilities frontiers (based on the information contained in Table 3.1) for the U.S. and India, assuming that each country produces both cloth and machines under **constant costs**. By fully using all of its resources, the U.S. could produce either 100 machines and 0 yards of cloth or 0 machines and 300 yards of cloth. Because resources are mobile within a country, any combination between these two extremes could be produced. As Table 3.2 indicates, for each group

Table 3.1 Production and Consumption With and Without Trade: Based on an Exchange Ratio of 1 Machine = 4 yds. of Cloth

	Country	
	U.S.	India
Production at Full Employment	100 machines	0 machines
	0 yds. of cloth	300 yds. of cloth
Consumption with Trade	50 machines	50 machines
	200 yds. of cloth	100 yds. of cloth
Domestic Production and Consumption	50 machines	40 machines
Without Trade (autarky)	150 yds. of cloth	100 yds. of cloth
Gains from Specialization and trade	50 yds. of cloth	10 machines

Table 3.2 Production Possibilities Schedules for the U.S. and India at Full Employment

U.S.		*India*	
Number of Machines	Yds. of Cloth	Number of Machines	Yds. of Cloth
100	0	60	0
90	30	50	50
80	60	40	100
70	90	30	150
60	120	20	200
50	150	10	250
40	180	0	300
30	210		
20	240		
10	270		
0	300		

constant costs the amount of a good (assumed to be unchanging) that a country must forego to produce each additional unit of another good

of 10 machines the U.S. does not produce, just enough resources are released to produce an additional 30 yards of cloth. This means the opportunity cost (MRT) of 10 machines is 30 yards of cloth, or 1 machine for 3 yards of cloth.

India can produce either 60 machines and 0 yards of cloth, 0 machines and 300 yards of cloth, or any combination between these two extremes. This means that India can increase its output by 50 yards of cloth for each group of 10 machines it does not produce. India's opportunity cost (MRT) is 1 machine for 5 yards of cloth. The production possibilities frontiers in Table 3.1 are graphed in Figure 3.1 where each point on a country's production possibilities frontier represents one combination of cloth and machines that the country can produce. These frontiers are straight lines because the opportunity cost of each good is constant.

Production and Consumption Without Specialization and Trade

Without specialization and trade, the U.S. and India can produce and consume at any point along their respective production possibilities frontiers as shown in Figure 3.1. Points inside or below the production possibilities frontier, like points B or B', represent possible production combinations that can be produced but are inefficient because there would be some unemployed and/or underemployed resources. Points outside or above the production possibilities frontier, like points C or C', represent production combinations that are not possible for a country to produce with available resources and technology. The downward or negative slope of the production possibilities frontier shows that both countries must give up machine production to increase the production of cloth, and vice versa. Although the opportunity costs are constant in both countries, these costs differ between the two countries.

The opportunity cost, or marginal rate of transformation, for each country is graphically equal to the slope of the production possibilities frontier. Figure 3.1 shows

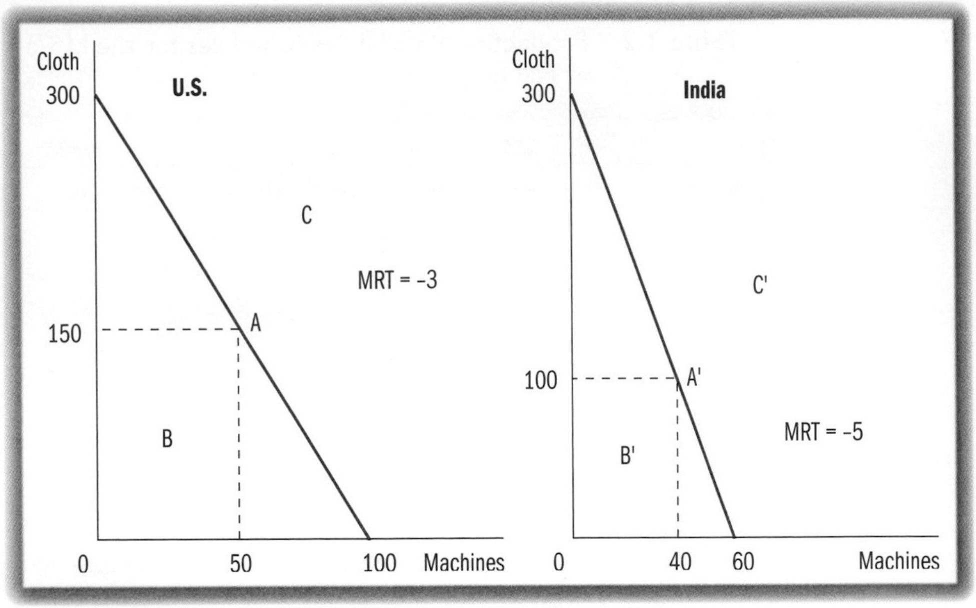

Figure 3.1 Production Possibilities Frontiers Under Constant Costs for the U.S. and India

The two production possibilities frontiers show the amounts of machines and cloth that the U.S. and India can produce domestically. These production possibilities frontiers are straight lines because we are assuming constant costs. The different cost ratios, MRT = −3 for the U.S. and MRT = −5 for India, are reflected in the different slopes of the two curves.

that the slope of the U.S. curve is –3 yards of cloth per machine. This means that the U.S. must give up 3 yards of cloth to get 1 machine. The slope of India's production possibilities frontier is –5 yards of cloth per machine, so India must give up 5 yards of cloth to get 1 machine.

When product markets are perfectly competitive, the price of a product will equal its average cost. Under this condition, the price of 1 machine in the U.S. will be 3 times the price of a yard of cloth $[(P_M/P_C) = 3]$ or 1 yard of cloth will be 1/3 the price of a machine $[(P_C/P_M) = 1/3]$. For India the price of 1 machine will be 5 times the price of a yard of cloth $[(P_M/P_C) = 5]$ or 1 yard of cloth will be 1/5 the price of a machine $[(P_C/P_M) = 1/5]$. Notice that the relative price ratios in the two countries reflect the opportunity costs of producing each good.

Let us suppose the U.S. decides to produce and consume at point A on its frontier—50 machines and 150 yards of cloth; and India decides to produce and consume at point A′ on its frontier—40 machines and 100 yards of cloth. Total world production and consumption of machines and cloth is the sum of the output of the two countries—90 machines and 250 yards of cloth. Because the opportunity costs are different in the two countries, mutually beneficial trade is possible.

Production and Consumption with Specialization and Trade

Now, assume that trade opens up between the U.S. and India. The U.S. could benefit from importing cloth from India and exporting machines to India. India could benefit

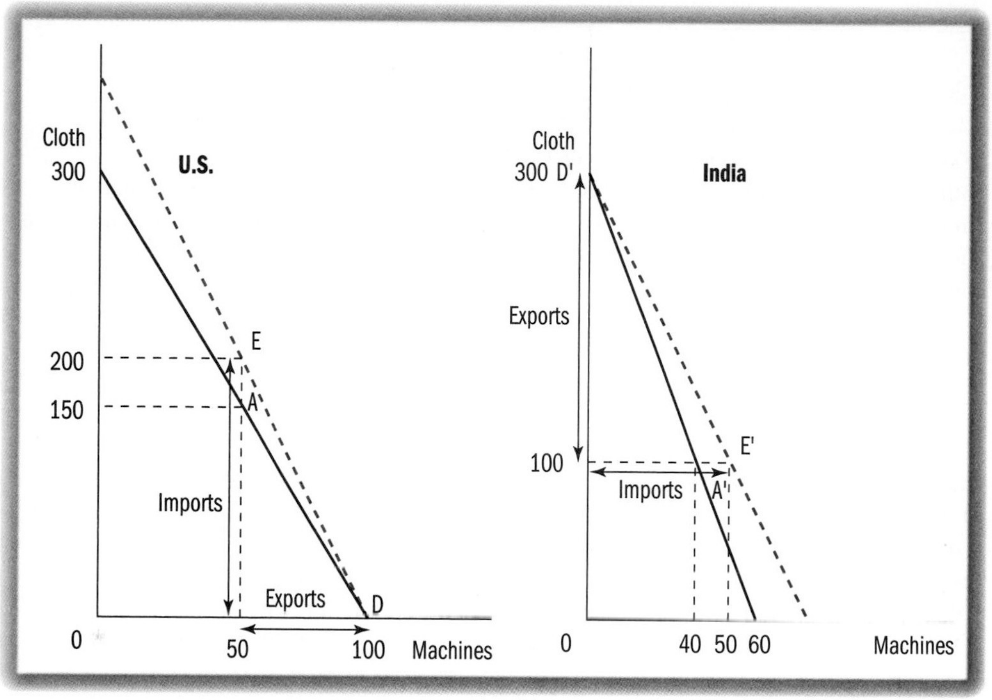

Figure 3.2 Specialization and Trade Under Constant Costs

As a result of international specialization and trade, both the U.S. and India can both have levels of consumption that are superior to those attainable on their production possibilities frontiers. The U.S. can move from point A on its production possibilities frontiers to point E on its trading possibilities line. India, too, can move from point A' to point E'.

from importing machines from the U.S. and exporting cloth to the U.S. In Figure 3.2 the production possibilities frontiers of the U.S. and India show the U.S. and India before specialization and trade producing and consuming at points A and A′, respectively. Given different opportunity costs in the two countries, the U.S. would specialize in the production of machines, transferring its production from point A to point D (100 machines and 0 cloth) on its production possibility frontier. India specializes in the production of cloth, moving from point A′ to point D′ (0 machines and 300 yards of cloth). With each country specializing in the production of the good in which it has a comparative advantage, world output increases to 100 machines and 300 yards of cloth (Table 3.1, line1). In other words, 10 more machines and 50 more yards of cloth are produced in the two countries.

Before trade, the U.S. and India's consumption possibilities were limited to points along their respective production possibilities frontiers. With specialization and trade, both countries can achieve consumption points beyond or above their respective frontiers. With trade, the set of consumption points that a country can achieve is determined by the terms of trade—the relative price of trading machines for cloth, and vice versa. For there to be mutually beneficial trade, the price of machines and cloth would have to be between 1M = 3C and 1M = 5C.

Patterns in U.S. Trade

Each month the U.S. Department of Commerce publishes data on the value of U.S. exports and imports in a number of broad categories. In addition, these government statistics record the distribution of U.S. trade among trading partners, and the U.S. trade balance with each partner. Here we summarize the trade of the U.S. in 2005 in terms of types and goods and destinations and sources of exports and imports.

Figure 3.3 depicts U.S. export and import shares by destination for 2005. In addition, the top data in Table 3.3 shows U.S. exports by destination and commodity group. In 2005, the majority of U.S. exports went to Western Europe, Canada, Asia (excluding Japan), Latin America, and Mexico. Overall, this data suggests that the U.S. exports mainly to other developed countries. In addition, U.S. exports are concentrated in capital goods, such as office and telecommunications equipment (excluding automotive). Other major export categories include industrial supplies and materials, automotive vehicles, parts and engines, and consumer goods.

The bottom data in Table 3.3 depicts U.S. imports by source and commodity group. The major trading partners as defined by imports are the same as for exports. Partners are mainly developed economies and include the two NAFTA partners, Canada and Mexico. U.S. imports are divided fairly equally among capital goods, industrial supplies and materials, consumer goods, and automotive vehicles, parts, and engines.

Figure 3.3 U.S. Export and Import Shares

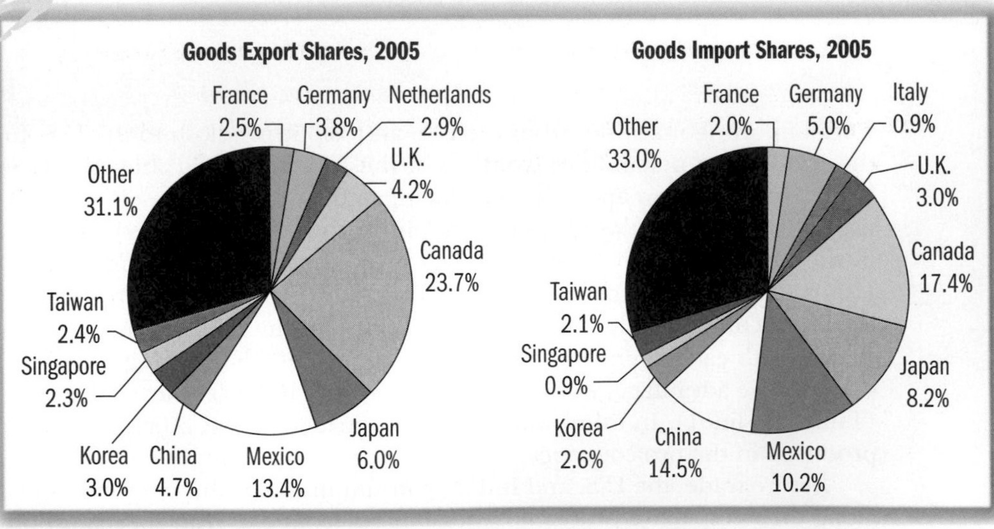

Table 3.3 U.S. Trade in Goods by Major End-Use Category for Selected Areas and Countries, 2005

	Canada	Europe	United Kingdom	Germany	Japan	Latin America	Mexico	Asia, excluding Japan	Hong Kong, Korea, Singapore, Taiwan	China
EXPORTS	**$211,528**	**$207,814**	**$37,610**	**$33,555**	**$53,234**	**$137,446**	**$119,946**	**$197,683**	**$85,023**	**$41,743**
Foods, feeds, and beverages	12,198	8,339	1,117	1,044	8,677	9,804	8,526	12,944	4,980	3,479
Industrial supplies & materials	54,981	48,218	8,064	5,939	11,950	42,144	39,705	47,995	19,715	16,155
Capital goods (except automotive)	59,920	90,988	16,954	16,240	22,251	51,330	42,012	104,741	49,278	18,842
Automotive vehicles, parts & engines	52,769	12,839	1,739	5,079	2,022	15,192	16,089	8,332	1,313	1,100
Consumer goods (non-food)	25,593	41,268	8,435	4,309	7.228	14,065	9,569	18,550	7,476	1,889
Other Exports	6,067	6,162	1,301	944	1,106	4,911	4,045	5,121	2,261	278
IMPORTS	**290,797**	**354,364**	**50,719**	**84,531**	**138,064**	**206,049**	**171,478**	**523,977**	**102,629**	**243,484**
Foods, feeds, and beverages	13,965	16,773	1,547	963	511	15,458	9,132	12,586	727	2,892
Industrial supplies & materials	134,023	95,850	15,147	14,261	14,002	60,317	40,334	95,119	16,291	21,714
Capital goods (except automotive)	35,027	92,193	13,670	28,097	48,574	37,874	38,276	156,775	38,799	74,000
Automotive vehicles, parts & engines	71,184	45,447	7,123	27,148	52,706	43,880	44,433	21,975	13,766	5,755
Consumer goods (non-food)	19,161	88,036	9,936	10,755	13,301	40,072	31,929	227,260	29,138	136,294
Other Imports	17,437	16,065	3,296	3,307	3,970	8,448	7,374	10,262	3,908	2,829

Source: U.S. Department of Commerce, *Survey of Current Business,* April 2006, p. 33.

trading possibilities curve a curve showing the various combinations of two goods that a country can consume through international trade

Given these limits to trade, let us assume that the terms of trade are 1M = 4C. With this exchange ratio, the possibility of trading on these more favorable terms permits each country to enhance its no-trade production possibilities frontier with a trading possibilities curve shown as the dashed lines in Figure 3.2.[1] A **trading possibilities curve** shows the options a country has when it specializes in the production of one good and trades, or exports, its specialty to obtain the other good.

Suppose that the U.S. decides to specialize and export 50 machines to India in exchange for 200 yards of cloth. Starting at point D in Figure 3.2, the U.S. will move along the trading possibilities curve to point E, which represents U.S. consumption. Compared to no trade, point E represents a gain in consumption for the U.S. At point A, the U.S. produces and consumes 50 machines and 150 yards of cloth. At point E, the U.S. consumes 50 machines and 200 yards of cloth. The gain from trade for the U.S. is 50 yards of cloth.

India, specializing in cloth, exports 200 yards of cloth for 50 machines. As a result, India moves along its trading possibilities curve to point E′. Compared to its consumption with no trade at point A′, there also is a gain in consumption for India at point E′. At point A′, India produces and consumes 40 machines and 100 yards of cloth. At point E′, India consumes 50 machines and 100 yards of cloth. The consumption gain for India is 10 machines. As the example shows, both countries are better off by specializing and trading than they would be without trade.

THE TERMS OF TRADE

terms of trade the relative price at which two counties trade goods

In our example, both countries gain from trade at the international exchange ratio, 1M = 4C. This ratio represents the relative price at which two countries trade goods. The commonly used phrase for the ratio is the **terms of trade**. A change in this ratio toward 1M = 3C or toward 1M = 5C would change the distribution of the gains from trade. The closer the ratio moves toward 1M = 3C, the more favorable the exchange is for India because it obtains more machines for each yard of cloth. Obviously, changes in this direction are less favorable for the U.S. because it will obtain fewer yards of cloth for each machine. However, the closer the ratio moves toward 1M = 5C the more favorable the exchange is for the U.S. and less favorable for India. Outside these two limits, one of the two countries will not trade, for it could do better without trade.

Changes in the Gains from Specialization and Trade

How each country fares trading at 1M = 3.5C is illustrated in Table 3.4. Let us see what the gains are at this new international exchange ratio. In the second row in Table 3.4, we see the U.S. has traded 50 machines with India. At this exchange ratio, the U.S. receives 175 yards of cloth, as compared to 200 yards when the exchange ratio was 1M = 4C. India obtains (imports) 50 machines, but gives up fewer yards of cloth to gain those 50 machines. India is better off at the 1M = 3.5C ratio. The U.S. is worse off relative to the international exchange ratio of 1M = 4C, but the U.S. is still considerably

[1]Sometimes, this line is referred to as the terms of trade line.

Table 3.4 Production and Consumption With and Without Trade: Based on an Exchange Ratio of 1 Machine = 3.5 yds. of Cloth

	Country	
	U.S.	**India**
Production at Full Employment	100 machines	0 machines
	0 yds. of cloth	300 yds. of cloth
Consumption with Trade	50 machines	50 machines
	175 yds. of cloth	125 yds. of cloth
Domestic Production and Consumption Without Trade (autarky)	50 machines	40 machines
	150 yds. of cloth	100 yds. of cloth
Gains from Specialization and Trade	25 yds. of cloth	10 machines
		25 yds. of cloth

better off trading than attempting to transform machines into cloth domestically (the third row of the table).

The results shown in Table 3.4 are illustrated using production possibilities frontiers in Figure 3.4. As the international exchange ratio (terms of trade) changes from 1M = 4C to 1M = 3.5C, the trading possibilities curve moves (rotates) for each country.

Figure 3.4 Changes in the Terms of Trade for the U.S. and India

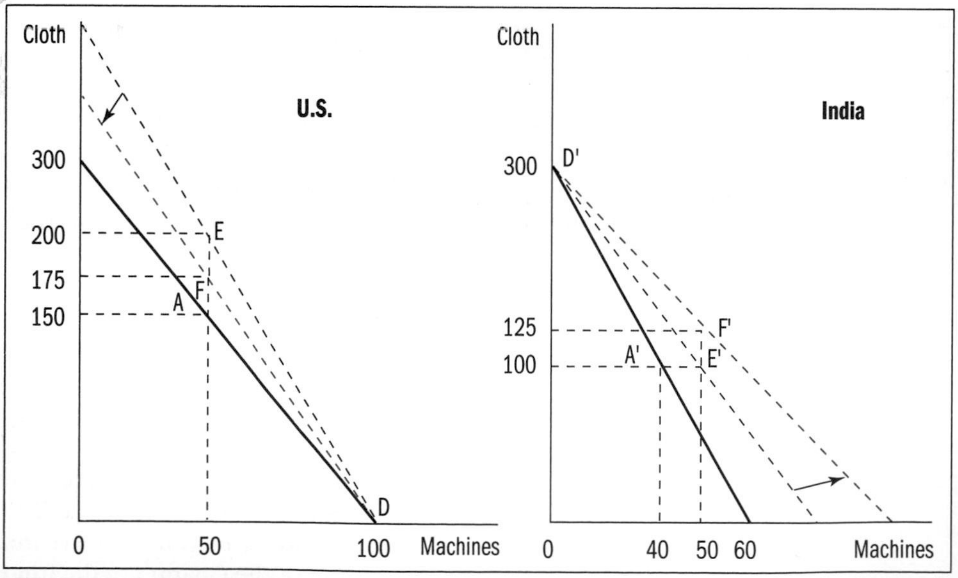

As the terms of trade change, the trading possibilities frontier rotates for both countries. India's consumption point moves from E' to F', and the U.S. consumption point moves from E to F.

For the U.S. the trading possibilities curve rotates inward, indicating a less favorable trading condition. For India, its trading possibilities curve rotates outward, indicating a more favorable trading condition. As the figure shows, without specialization and trade the U.S. produces and consumes at point A and India produces and consumes at point A′. With specialization trade at an international exchange ratio of 1M = 4C, the U.S. produces at point D and consumes at point E. For India, they produce at point D′ and consume at point E′. With the new international exchange ratio of 1M = 3.5C, the U.S. produces at point D but now consumes at point F. The U.S. is worse off relative to the previous trading position but is still better off than not trading with India. For India, the new international exchange ratio allows it to produce at point D′ and consume at point F′. In India's case, it is better off relative to the previous trading as more of the gains are distributed to their country.

Demand Conditions and the Terms of Trade

Of particular interest is the determination of the actual or final international exchange ratio. In our previous examples, we simply picked a ratio within the limits to mutually beneficial trade. Recall that the opportunity cost of producing the two goods in each country determines the limits to mutually beneficial trade. The actual international exchange ratio will fall between these limits and will depend on the relative strength of each country's demand for the two goods. This theory of **reciprocal demand** suggests that the actual international exchange ratio at which trade takes place depends on each trading partner's interacting demands. Suppose that the U.S. has an immense demand for cloth and is willing to pay high prices for cloth. In this case, the U.S. would be willing to give up more machines to obtain cloth, and a ratio such as 1M = 3.5C might result. However, if India has an immense demand for machines, the price that India is willing to pay for machines would rise. In this case, India would be willing to give up more cloth to obtain machines, and a ratio such as 1M = 4.5C is more likely.

reciprocal demand **the interaction of the demand by two countries for the other country's export good in determining the international exchange ratio**

The reciprocal demand theory indicates that the final international exchange ratio depends on the relative strength of each country's demand for the other country's product. The country with the greater demand for the other country's product will be willing to sacrifice more of its goods in exchange for that product. The resulting exchange ratio will distribute more of the gains from trade to the country whose good has greater demand relative to the demand of the other country.

In addition, if the two countries are of unequal size (population or income), it is possible that the larger country's demand would be greater than the smaller country's demand. As a result, the smaller country gains more from trade than the larger country. For example, in 2005 the gross national income per capita of India and the U.S. were $730 and $43,560, respectively. Because of the relationship between the demand for most goods and income, the U.S. demand for Indian goods would be greater than the Indian demand for U.S. goods. This differential demand affects the international exchange ratio in India's favor. The prices of the traded goods will be closer to the marginal rate of transformation of the U.S., and India would receive more of the gains from trade. As we illustrated in the beginning of the Chapter 2, the international price of the traded goods will continue to adjust until U.S. imports of cloth equal India's exports of cloth, and U.S. exports of machines equal India's imports of machines.

Distribution of the Gains from Trade

The distribution of the gains from international trade can be a source of friction among countries. Given that the gains from trade rarely are perfectly balanced between countries, there is often the perception that trade makes the country receiving the smaller share of the total gains somehow "worse off." However, it is not true that a country with the larger demand is not gaining anything from trade, because international trade within the mutually beneficial limits to trade is always preferable to no international trade. As our example illustrates, suppose that the U.S. trades at a low international exchange ratio such as 1M = 3.1C. It is still better off than it would be if it did not trade at all. At this very low international exchange ratio, the U.S. receives more cloth in imports than it can produce itself.

The difference between the opportunity cost of producing the product domestically and the cost of purchasing the product from another country determines the gains that a country receives from trade. The terms of trade measures the relationship between the price that a country receives for its exports and the price that the country pays for its imports. In our example, the terms of trade for the U.S. would be the price of machines divided by the price of cloth. The higher this price ratio, the more favorable are the terms of trade for the U.S. If the terms of trade changed from 1M = 4C to 1M = 4.5C, then the U.S. would be better off because a smaller quantity of U.S. export goods is required to obtain a given quantity of imports. In this case, the U.S. is paying less for each unit of cloth. For India, the situation is the reverse. India's terms of trade would be the price of cloth divided by the price of machines. Over time, changes in a country's terms of trade indicate whether a country can obtain more or fewer imports per unit of exports. However, an improvement in a country's terms of trade does not necessarily reflect an improvement in that country's overall welfare. Likewise, deterioration in a country's terms of trade does not necessarily reflect an analogous deterioration in that country's overall welfare.

A change in a country's terms of trade may reflect a change in international economic conditions or it may reflect a change in domestic economic conditions. Let us assume that a country's terms of trade change as a result of a change in international conditions. For example, suppose that there is an increase in the demand for U.S. exports. As a result, the price of U.S. exports increases and the U.S. terms of trade improve. We can conclude that an improvement in the terms of trade resulting from a change in international conditions enhances U.S. welfare, and that a deterioration in the terms of trade is equivalent to a reduction in U.S. welfare.

When the terms of trade change as a result of a change in domestic economic conditions, the effect on a country's welfare is uncertain. Suppose for example, that the U.S. has a tremendous increase in technology and now can produce a large number of machines inexpensively. The increase in the supply of machines will cause the world price of machines to decline, which in turn will cause a deterioration in the U.S. terms of trade. Is the U.S. worse off because of this change in its terms of trade? The reduction in the U.S. terms of trade decreases U.S. welfare, but the additional machines that the U.S. produces increases U.S. welfare. The net effect on total welfare depends on which is larger—the decrease due to the change in the terms of trade or the increase due to increased production. Although changes in the terms of trade do not accurately measure the changes in a country's welfare, business and government officials often use it as a rough indication of how a country is doing in the world economy.

The Commodity Terms of Trade

The most frequently used measure of changes in the gains from trade is the commodity terms of trade. The commodity terms of trade measures the relationship between the average prices a country receives for its exports and the average prices a country pays for its imports. This measure is calculated by dividing the price index of a country's exports by the price index of its imports:

$$\text{Terms of Trade} = \frac{\text{Export Price Index}}{\text{Import Price Index}} \times (100)$$

Table 3.5 shows the commodity terms of trade for 7 large industrial countries for the years 1995 through 2005. The terms of trade are measured with 2000 as the base year (equal to 100). The table shows that each country's terms of trade have changed over the decade. Japan's terms of trade worsen from 105.5 in 1995 to 97.6 in 2005. The U.S. terms of trade improved over the period 1995–1998 and then deteriorated to 97.2 in 2005. Canada's terms of trade improved from 97.2 to 111.3 over the period 1995–2005.

Table 3.5 Commodity Terms of Trade for 7 Industrial Countries, 1995–2005 (2000 = 100)

	Terms of Trade Index										
Country	**1995**	**1996**	**1997**	**1998**	**1999**	**2000**	**2001**	**2002**	**2003**	**2004**	**2005**
Canada	97.2	98.2	97.1	103.2	110.5	100.0	98.9	94.9	101.9	106.5	111.3
France	106.5	105.2	103.3	104.4	104.9	100.0	108.3	110.1	110.1	110.8	110.6
Germany	107.5	107.2	104.8	106.7	107.1	100.0	101.9	104.4	107.2	107.2	105.2
Italy	95.9	100.0	101.5	106.6	107.7	100.0	100.9	102.7	103.9	103.3	101.0
Japan	105.5	98.2	94.4	100.6	105.4	100.0	107.5	103.7	105.4	103.1	97.6
U.K.	100.1	100.9	102.5	102.8	102.2	100.0	99.2	101.7	104.3	105.2	104.9
U.S.	103.3	102.9	104.0	107.1	104.8	100.0	102.8	104.4	103.0	101.2	97.2

Source: International Monetary Fund, *International Financial Statistics,* Washington, D.C.: International Monetary Fund, July 2007.

TRADE UNDER INCREASING OPPORTUNITY COSTS

In our examples demonstrating the gains from trade based on comparative advantage, each country produces both cloth and machines and does not trade. When we allow for international trade, each country then specializes completely in the production of the good in which it has a comparative advantage and imports the other good. The opening of trade ends up "wiping out" the industry in each country that has a comparative disadvantage. The cloth industry ceases to exist in the U.S. and the machine industry disappears in India.

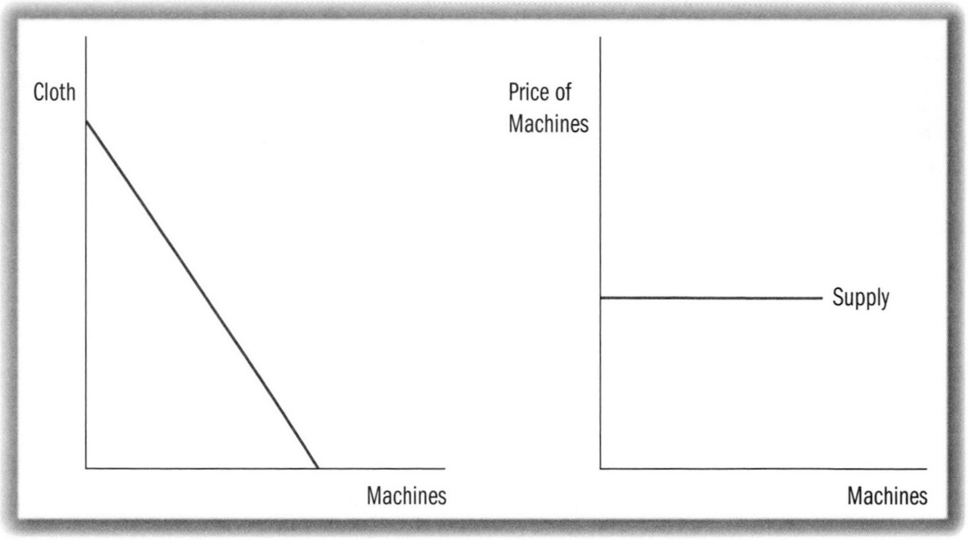

Figure 3.5 Supply Curves of a Good and the Production Possibilities Frontier Under Constant Cost Conditions

Constant opportunity costs lead to straight-line production possibilities frontiers and supply curves for goods that are horizontal.

complete specialization the use of all of a country's resources to produce only one good

Complete specialization occurs because as production expands in the industry with a comparative advantage, the domestic cost of producing the product does not rise. *Constant costs* are assumed to prevail over the entire range of production. In this case, the firm's cost curves and the product's supply curves are horizontal. Constant costs are illustrated in Figure 3.5. Constant costs imply that the resources used to produce both machines and cloth are completely adaptable or flexible in the production of both goods. When constant costs prevail, a country does not lose its comparative advantage as it produces more of the good. As a result, the country completely specializes its production in the good in which it has a comparative advantage.

increasing costs the increasing amount of a good that a country must forego to release enough resources to produce each additional unit of another good

Increasing Costs and the Production Possibilities Frontier

In the real world, the constant cost assumption may not be realistic. Rather, a country may be subject to **increasing costs** as more of a good is produced. With increasing opportunity costs, as the production of one good, such as machines, increases, the economy must give up ever increasing quantities of the other good, cloth. Increasing costs are illustrated in Figure 3.6, which shows a positively sloped product supply curve. This implies that the production possibilities frontier of a country that is concave to (bowed out from) the origin.

Referring to Figure 3.6, suppose that a country is currently producing at point A, 300 yards of cloth and 0 machines. As the economy moves from point A toward point F, it produces more and more machines. As a result, the output of cloth falls by increasing amounts. To produce the first 20 machines, only 20 yards of cloth are not produced. To produce the second 20 machines, an additional 40 yards of cloth are not

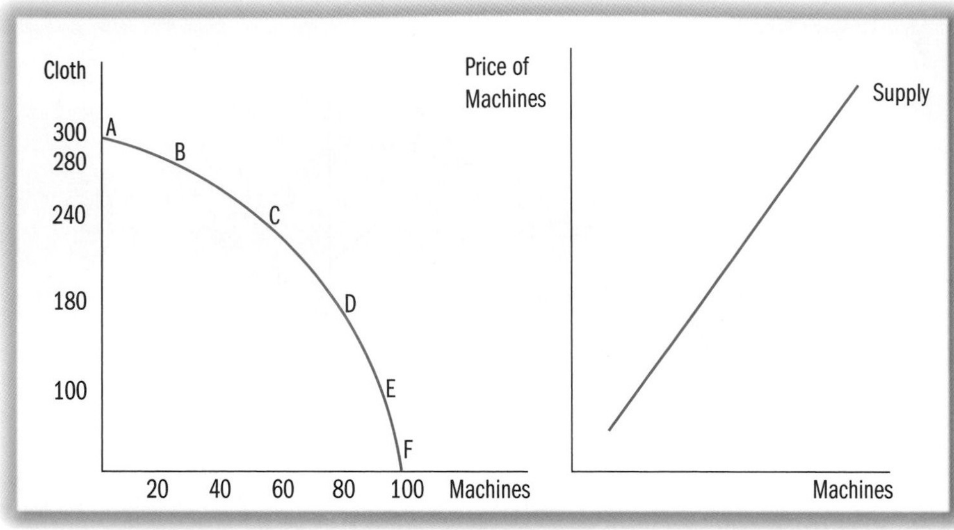

Figure 3.6 **Supply Curves of a Good and the Production Possibilities Frontier Under Increasing-Cost Conditions**

Increasing opportunity costs lead to production possibilities frontiers that are concave to the origin and supply curves for goods that are upward sloping.

produced. To produce the third 20 machines, an additional 60 yards of cloth are not produced. Notice that each successive machine produced requires an ever larger amount of foregone output of cloth. The same increasing-cost phenomenon occurs for the production of each additional yard of cloth. Moving along the production possibilities frontier in the other direction, from point F toward point A, the production of cloth also has increasing opportunity costs.

Just as in the constant-cost case, the marginal rate of transformation is equal to the slope of the production possibilities frontier. However, with increasing costs the slope of the production possibilities frontier changes at every point along the curve. The slope of the production possibilities frontier at any point is represented graphically by the slope of a line tangent to that point. For example, in Figure 3.7 the slope of the production possibilities frontier at point B is equal to the slope of the tangent line DE. Similarly, the slope of the tangent line FG represents the slope of the production possibilities frontier at point C. Notice, the tangent line DE is flatter than the tangent line FG, implying increasing costs.

There are two reasons why a country may have increasing opportunity costs. One reason is that the factors of production (i.e., labor and capital) used to produce the products are specialized in the production of a particular product, such as machines. An example of product-specific resources would include highly skilled labor for the production of machines that is *not* skilled in the production of cloth.[2] Therefore, as the country moves from point A toward point F in Figure 3.7, the first resources used to produce machines

[2]See Chapter 4 for a more extensive discussion of the concept of specific factors of production.

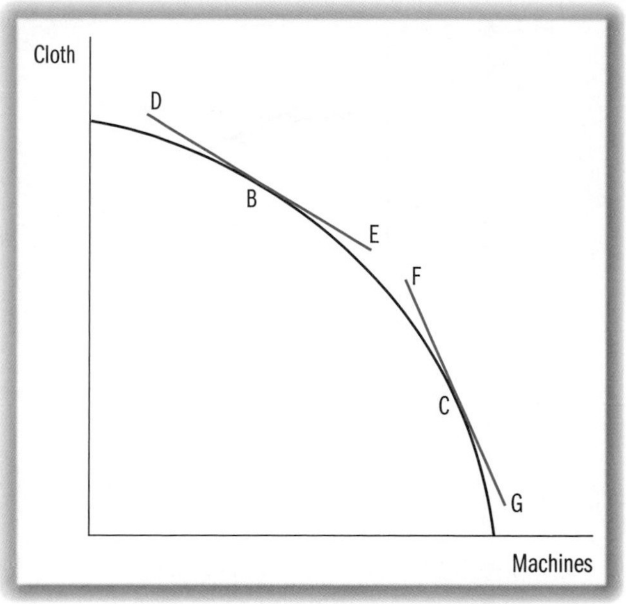

Figure 3.7 Production Possibilities Curve with Increasing Costs and the Marginal Rate of Transformation

Under increasing costs, the slope of the production possibilities frontier at point B is equal to the to slope of the tangent line DE. Similarly, the slope of the tangent line FG represents the slope of the production possibilities frontier at point C. The tangent line DE is flatter than the tangent line FG, implying increasing costs.

are better equipped to manufacture machines than cloth and the cost of a machine is relatively low. As the country continues to move toward point F, additional resources are used to produce machines, although some of these resources are better suited to produce cloth than machines. The opportunity cost of machines increases because each additional machine produced requires larger reductions in cloth production.

The other reason for increasing opportunity costs is the premise that all resources are identical in the sense that all workers and capital have the same productivity in the production of both machines and cloth. However, if the machine and cloth industries use resources in different relative proportions, increasing opportunity costs will occur. For instance, the cloth industry may require large amounts of labor, while the machine industry may require large amounts of capital. As resources move between the two industries, the different production mixes cause costs to rise. If unit costs rise with an increase in production, then as the U.S. expands its production of machines and contracts its production of cloth, the price of machines rises and the price of cloth falls. As India contracts its production of machines and expands its production of cloth, the price of machines falls and the price of cloth rises.

Production and Consumption Without Specialization and Trade

Without specialization and trade, the U.S. and India can produce and consume at any point on their production possibilities frontier. The only difference is that these two

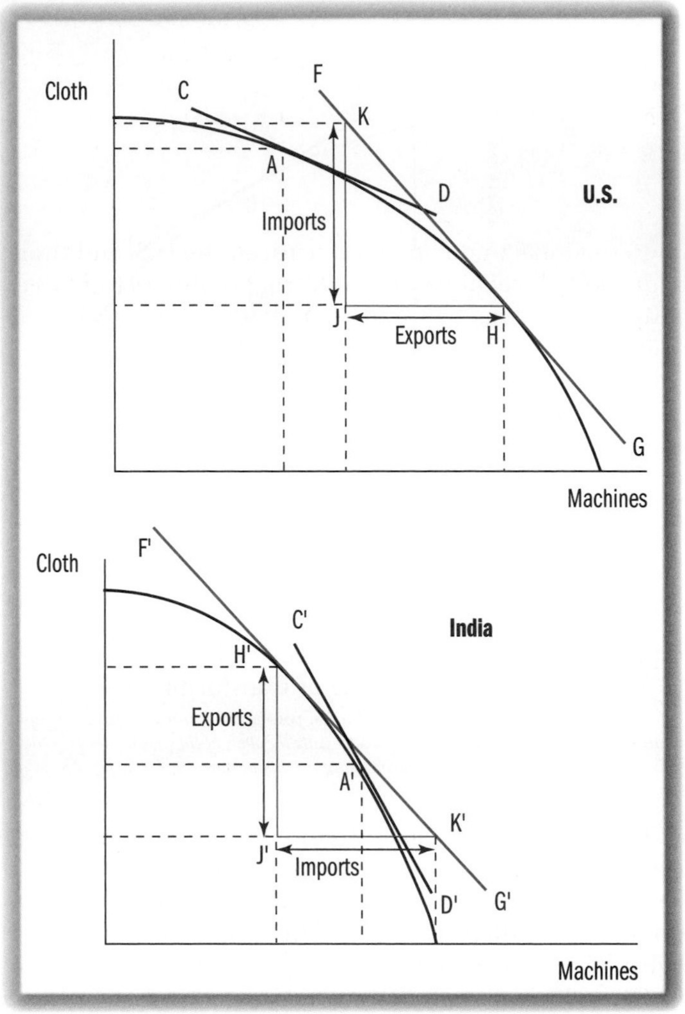

Figure 3.8 Specialization and Trade Under Increasing Costs

As a result of international specialization and trade, the U.S. and India can each have levels of consumption that are superior to those attainable on their production possibilities frontiers. The U.S. can move from point A on its production possibilities frontiers to point K on its trading possibilities line. India, too, can move from point A′ to point K′.

countries now have increasing opportunity costs. In Figure 3.8 let us assume that, given tastes and preferences of the consumers in both countries, the U.S. decides to produce at point A on its frontier and India decides to produce at point A′ on its frontier.

With no trade, the line CD represents the U.S. marginal rate of transformation, or opportunity cost, and is equal to the slope of the production possibilities frontier. Let us say that this slope is –3—the opportunity cost of machines in the U.S. is one machine for 3 yards of cloth. Similarly, without trade, the line C′D′ represents India's marginal rate of transformation. Also, we will assume that the slope of line C′D′ is –5—India's opportunity cost of machines without trade is 1 machine for 5 yards of cloth. Comparing the U.S. and India's marginal rates of transformation, one can see that machines are less costly in the U.S. than in India (–3 > –5). In a world of constant opportunity costs, a country should specialize in the production of the product that it produces at a lower cost relative to the cost that another country incurs in producing that product. The same is true in the world of increasing opportunity costs. As before, the U.S. should specialize in the production of machines and India in cloth.

Production and Consumption with Specialization and Trade

As international trade opens up between the U.S. and India, the U.S. specializes in the production of machines by transferring resources from its cloth industry to its machine industry. This means that the U.S. would move downward along its production possibilities frontier from point A toward point H, as illustrated in Figure 3.8. As its specialization increases, the U.S. opportunity cost of machines in terms of cloth increases. The opposite movement occurs in India as it transfers resources from its machine industry to its cloth industry. This means that India would move up along its production possibilities frontier from point A′ toward H′ and its opportunity cost of machines in terms of cloth decreases. International specialization continues until the opportunity cost of machines and cloth are the same in both countries. This is just another way of expressing the concept that trade tends to move differences in prices closer to equality.

Figure 3.8 also illustrates the final outcome of international specialization according to comparative advantage based on an assumed terms of trade of 1 machine for 4 yards of cloth. This terms of trade, or relative price, coincides with the absolute slopes of the U.S.'s and India's trading possibilities curves, FG and F′G′, respectively. The U.S. shifts its production from A to H and India shifts its production from A′ to H′. The U.S. consumes at point K on its trading possibilities curve, FG, and achieves this consumption point when it exports JH machines to India in exchange for JK yards of Indian cloth. India consumes at point K′ on its trading possibilities curve, F′G′, by exporting J′H′ yards of cloth to the U.S. in exchange for J′K′ machines.

Specialization and trade under increasing cost conditions does not significantly change the conclusions that we reached concerning the benefits of trade. Specializing and exporting the good in which the country has a comparative advantage, and trading for other goods, enables both countries to become better off by consuming beyond their respective production possibilities frontiers. However, production under increasing-cost conditions constitutes a mechanism that forces prices to converge and results in neither country specializing completely in the production of the good in which it has a comparative advantage. In the case of increasing costs, both countries continue to produce both goods after trade.

INTERNATIONAL TRADE UNDER INCREASING COSTS: AN ADVANCED ANALYSIS

Up to this point, we have assumed the consumption positions of each country by stating that "given tastes and preferences of the consumers in both countries, the U.S. decides to produce at point A on its frontier, and India decides to produce at point A' on its frontier." In this section, we explicitly introduce each country's demand conditions by employing indifference curves to show the role of consumers' tastes and preferences in determining how the gains from trade are distributed. An **indifference curve**

Principal Exports and Export Concentration of Selected Countries

Under constant costs, a country should specialize completely in the production of the good in which it has a comparative advantage. In the increasing-cost case, a country should increase production of the good in which it has a comparative advantage even though complete specialization is not likely. In both cases, specialization and trade should result in a country's exports being concentrated in goods in which it has a comparative advantage.

Table 3.6 The Principal Exports and Export Concentration of Selected Countries

Country	Principal Export	Principal Export as a Percentage of the Country's Total Exports
Algeria	Crude Oil & Natural Gas	38.1%
Argentina	Agricultural Products	33.8
Australia	Minerals & Metals	44.4
Bangladesh	Clothing	67.9
Brazil	Transport Equipment	15.3
Canada	Machinery & Industrial Equipment	23.4
Chile	Copper	34.9
China	Office & Telecom Equipment	24.6
Denmark	Manufactured Goods	76.1
France	Intermediate Goods	30.1
Germany	Machinery & Road Vehicles	33.1
India	Engineering Goods	21.4
Iran	Oil & Gas	81.6
Ireland	Chemicals	53.1
Israel	Diamonds	28.6
Italy	Engineering Products	29.0
Japan	Transport Equipment	24.3
Malaysia	Electronic & Electrical Machinery	52.1
Mexico	Manufactured Products	97.0
Norway	Oil & Gas Products	79.1
Philippines	Electrical & Electronic Equipment	63.9
Russia	Mineral Products	51.6
Saudi Arabia	Crude Oil & Refined Petroleum	80.6
Singapore	Machinery & Equipment	62.7
South Korea	Electronic Products	35.2
Sweden	Machinery & Transport Equipment	51.1
Switzerland	Chemicals	34.6
United Kingdom	Finished Manufactured Products	54.7
United States	Capital Goods	40.4

Source: The Economist, *World in Figures,* 2003, London: Profile Books Ltd., 2006.

Table 3.6 presents each country's principal export as a percentage of total exports. Many countries in the sample (Algeria, Iran, and Mexico) have very concentrated exports. The degree of export concentration in this sample indicates that many countries specialize their production in favor of goods in which they have a comparative advantage. For the most part, developing countries specialize in food, clothing, textiles, and raw materials, and developed countries specialize in the production of machinery, transport equipment, and capital goods.

represents the various combinations of two goods—machines and cloth—that enable the consumer to attain a given level of satisfaction or utility.

Figure 3.9 illustrates an indifference map, which consists of a set of indifference curves. Indifference curves have the following characteristics:

- an indifference curve will pass through every point in Figure 3.9;
- indifference curves slope downward;
- indifference curves never intersect;
- indifference curves represent different levels of satisfaction or utility. For example, a movement from a lower to a higher indifference curve (such as from curve 1 to curve 2) represents an increase in the consumer's utility; and
- indifference curves are convex to the origin.

As a consumer moves along an indifference curve from A to B, he or she is substituting the consumption of machines for the consumption of cloth. The consumer is equally

Figure 3.9 Indifference Curves and Map

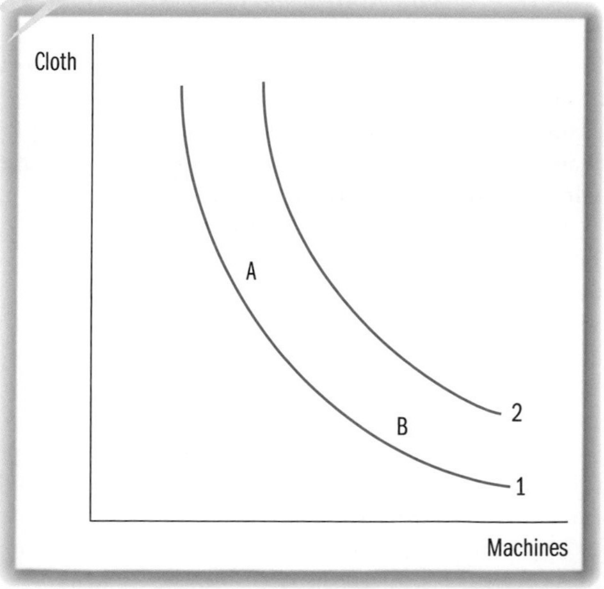

satisfied with any of the combinations of the two goods represented along the curve. Because the consumer is equally satisfied with the combination of goods represented at any point, he or she is indifferent to the combinations.

The rate at which consumers are willing to substitute machines for cloth is called the **marginal rate of substitution (MRS)** of machines for cloth. Graphically, the marginal rate of substitution is the slope of the indifference curve at a point on the curve. As a consumer moves from A toward B, the slope of the indifference curve becomes more negative, so the marginal rate of substitution diminishes. A diminishing marginal rate of substitution reflects diminishing marginal utility, and it is this characteristic that makes indifference curves convex to the origin.

To use indifference curves to represent an entire country's demand conditions we need to make two assumptions.

- The tastes and preferences of an entire country (as opposed to the tastes and preferences of individual consumers) can be represented graphically by a social indifference curve. Social indifference curves have the same characteristics as the indifference curves of an individual consumer.
- A country will behave as if it is trying to attain the highest possible social indifference curve.

As a result, a social indifference curve is not the sum of all the individual indifference curves. Rather, a social indifference curve is designed to represent the tastes and preferences of all consumers within a country as a group. To represent a country's welfare using a social indifference curve, we need to know the distribution of income within that country. Different income distributions within the country would result in a different set of indifference curves. This is important in international economics in that trade may benefit exporters while domestic producers competing with imports may be harmed. Trade may very well change a country's income distribution and cause a new set of social indifference curves. Suppose that one individual in a country becomes better off because of trade and, at the same time, another becomes worse off. We cannot say what happens to social welfare unless we find a way to compare the first individual's gain with the second individual's loss. Such a comparison cannot be made objectively. Different observers would pass different judgments. In this case, whether or not social welfare has increased is unclear. To resolve this issue, we employ the compensation principle. We will assume that social welfare may potentially improve when the gainers can use part of their gains to compensate the losers so that everyone potentially becomes better off.

In the absence of trade, a country acts like a huge consumer, as shown in Figure 3.10. The production possibilities frontier, line AB, shows all possible combinations of the two goods that a country can produce given its level of resources and technology. The social indifference curves, lines 1 and 2, represent that country's tastes and preferences for the two goods. Equilibrium occurs at the point where the production possibilities frontier is tangent to the highest possible social indifference curve at point E. In equilibrium this country would produce and consume OG yards of cloth and OF machines. At point E, the slope of the production possibilities frontier and the slope of the social indifference curve are equal. This also determines the equilibrium price of machines in terms of cloth. In equilibrium the price ratio, line CD, is equal to both the opportunity cost of machines in terms of cloth and is also equal to the marginal rate of substitution in consumption.

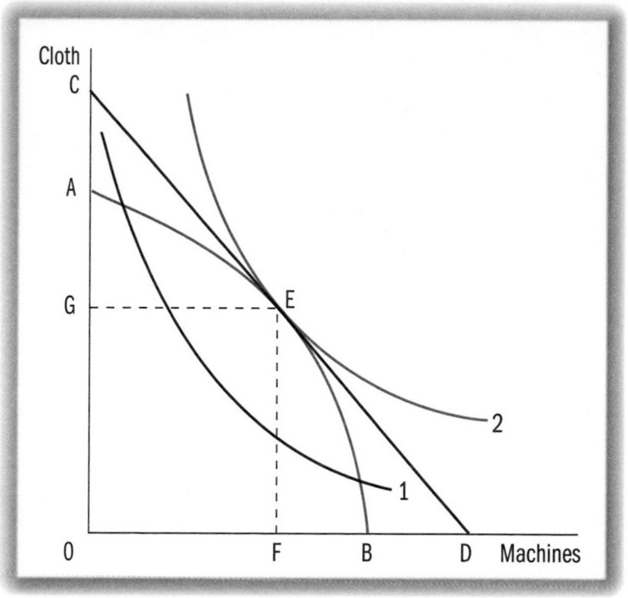

Figure 3.10 Equilibrium for a Country in Autarky

Let's see how a country's production possibilities frontier and social indifference curves can show the effects of international trade. In Figure 3.11, the U.S. produces and consumes at E, where its production possibilities frontier, line AB, is tangent to its social indifference curve 1. With no trade, the line CD gives the U.S. price of machines in terms of cloth. This is equal to the slope of the production possibilities frontier and the slope of indifference curve 1. Now suppose that this slope is –3—the opportunity cost in the U.S. is one machine for 3 yards of cloth. Similarly, without trade, India is in equilibrium at E′ where its production possibilities frontier, line A′B′, is tangent to its social indifference curve 1′, and its price of machines in terms of cloth is given by the line C′D′. In this case we will assume that this slope is –5—India's opportunity cost without trade is 1 machine for 5 yards of cloth. Machines are less costly in the U.S. than in India (–3 > –5).

In a world of constant or increasing costs, a country should specialize in producing the good that it produces at a lower cost relative to the other country's cost of producing it. As before, the U.S. should specialize in the production of machines and India in cloth. As the U.S. specializes in the production of machines by transferring resources from the cloth industry to the machine industry, it moves downward along its production possibilities frontier, line AB, from the no-trade point, point E, toward point H. As its trade increases, the U.S. opportunity cost of machines in terms of cloth increases. The same happens in India as it shifts from no trade. India transfers resources from its machine industry to its cloth industry. As India moves up along its production possibilities frontier from point E′ toward H′, India's opportunity cost of machines in terms of cloth decreases. International specialization continues until the

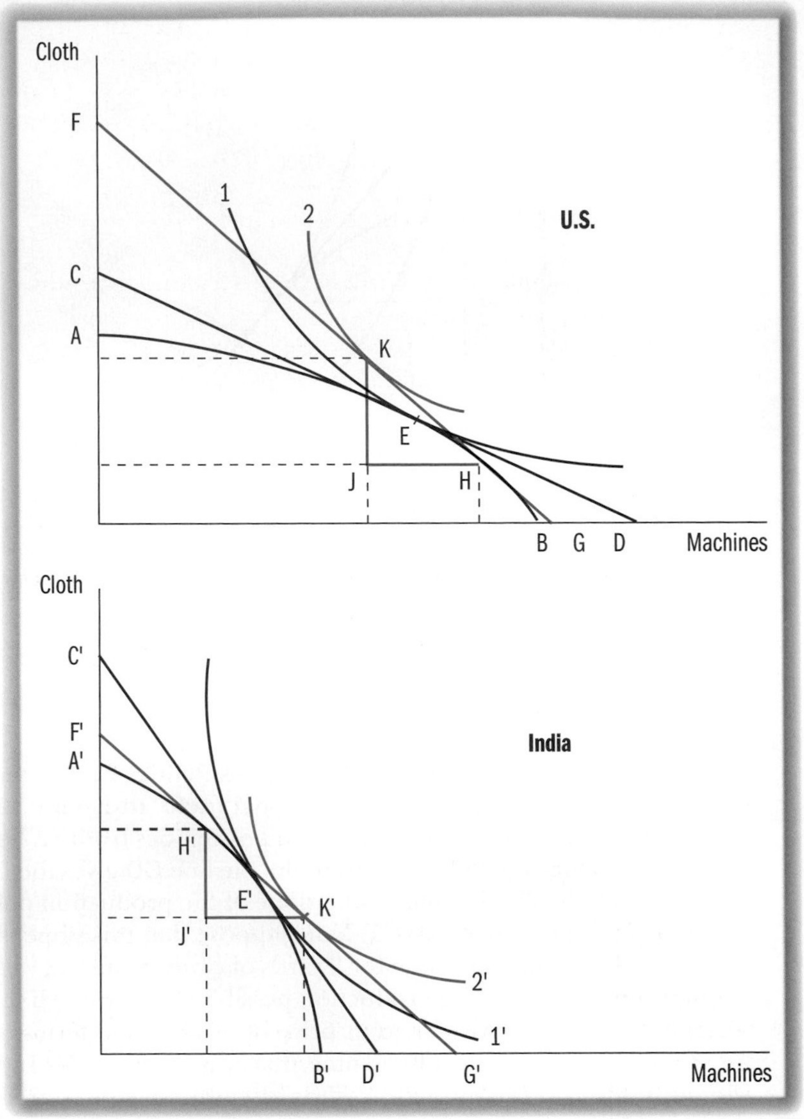

Figure 3.11 Specialization and Trade Based on Comparative Advantage and the Gains from Trade

opportunity cost of machines is the same in both countries, and what one country exports, the other country imports.

Figure 3.11 illustrates the final outcome of international specialization according to comparative advantage. The equilibrium relative price of machines—terms of trade—is assumed to be 1 machine can be traded for 4 yards of cloth. This relative price coincides with the absolute slopes of the U.S.'s and India's trading possibilities lines, FG and F′G′, respectively. The U.S. shifts its production from E to H and India shifts its production from E′ to H′. The U.S. consumes at K, where its trading possibilities line, FG, is tangent to indifference curve 2. The U.S. achieves this new equilibrium by exporting JH machines to India in exchange for JK yards of Indian cloth. India consumes at point K′, where its trading possibilities line, F′G′, is tangent to indifference curve 2′. India achieves this consumption point by exporting J′H′ yards of cloth to the U.S. in exchange for J′K′ machines.

Note the following points in this example:

- The equilibrium terms of trade lies between the no-trade price ratios of the two countries.
- Specialization and free trade enable both countries to become better off, consuming beyond their respective production possibilities frontiers.
- Neither country specializes completely and each continues to produce both goods.

Now, what happens if both countries produce the two goods at the same cost but each country has different tastes for each good? This is shown in Figure 3.12. Because both countries have equal capacity to produce both goods at the same costs, their production possibilities curves are identical. Let's assume that the U.S. prefers cloth and India prefers machines. In the absence of trade, a good would cost more in the country that has the stronger preference for it. This means that machines cost more in India and cloth costs more in the U.S., as illustrated in Figure 3.12. In the absence of trade, the U.S. produces and consumes at point E. This is where the production possibility curve, line AB, is tangent to the U.S. social indifference curve 1. India produces and consumes at point E′ where the production possibility curve of India, line A′B′, is tangent to India's social indifference curve 1′. Under these circumstances, the no-trade relative price of machines in the U.S., line CD, is less than the no-trade relative price of machines in India, C′D′. The comparative advantage for the U.S. is in machines and for India it's in cloth.

Trade between the two countries equalizes the relative commodity prices at line FG for the U.S. and at line F′G′ for India. In the last example, international trade between the two countries causes production within the two countries to become more dissimilar. In this example, international trade causes production within the two countries to become similar. That is because trade equalizes the relative prices and both countries produce at the same point—H for the U.S. and H′ for India. The U.S. satisfies its preference for cloth by exporting JH machines in exchange for GK yards of cloth. As a result, the U.S. reaches the higher indifference curve 2 at point K. India satisfies its preference for machines by exporting H′J′ yards of cloth and importing J′K′ machines, consuming at point K′, which lies on higher indifference curve 2′. The two countries become more specialized in their consumption patterns while reducing the amount of their specialization in the production of each good.

In the above two examples, either the production possibilities curves are different or the indifference curves are different. Generally, both will likely be different. As long as the no-trade relative prices are different between the two countries, specialization and trade are beneficial to both countries. Each country's no-trade relative prices determine the pattern of comparative advantage and the direction of trade. There are no potential gains from trade except under the unusual case where the no-trade relative prices are identical in both countries.

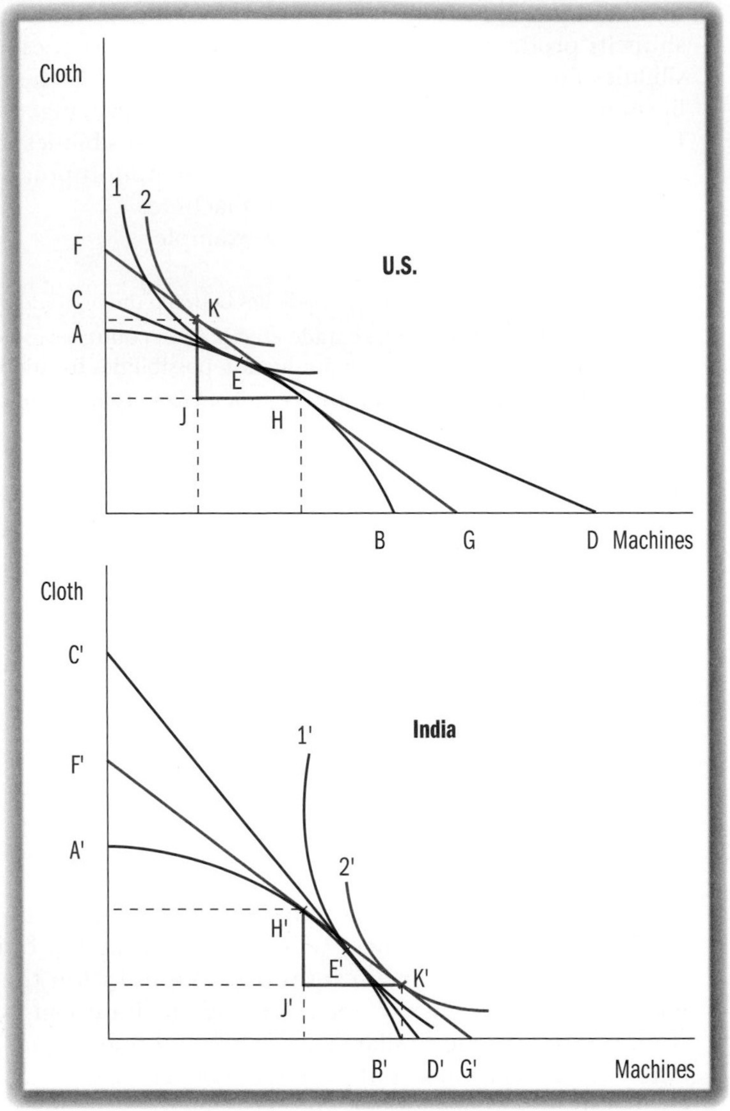

Figure 3.12 Specialization and Trade Based on Different Tastes and the Gains from Trade

The analysis that we have presented in Chapters 2 and 3 is useful for showing why international trade occurs and how countries can benefit from trade. However, the analysis has left an important question unanswered. Most of the analysis hinges on the existence of differences in prices of the two goods between countries. Up to this point, we have explained those differences in prices by asserting that there are differences between countries in the opportunity cost of producing various goods. Trade occurs because one country has a lower opportunity cost of producing a good than another country. Up to this point, we have ignored a deeper question. What *causes* the opportunity cost to be lower in one country relative to the other country? In the next chapter, we take up this somewhat more basic question. The answer to this question will not only help us to understand why international trade occurs but also to appreciate global patterns of production in industries.

SUMMARY

1. A production possibilities frontier (PPF) is a way of showing how an economy allocates its production between goods. If costs are constant, the PPF is linear.
2. The PPF can be used to show that trade is mutually beneficial. Specifically, we can demonstrate that a country can consume combinations of goods by trading that are not obtainable in autarky.
3. The assumption of constant costs leads to the result that countries that trade will completely specialize in the production of one good.
4. The terms of trade is the price of exports divided by the price of imports. It is always between the relative prices of two goods in the two countries that trade.
5. The terms of trade determines the distribution of the gains from trade. For any country it is more advantageous if the ratio is closer to that which prevails in the other country.
6. Production costs set the limits to mutually beneficial trade. However, differences in the demand for the goods in the two countries will determine the final price.
7. Trade can still occur even if the costs of production in the two countries are the same. Differences in the demand for goods in the two counties could cause a sufficient difference in price that could make trade mutually beneficial.

KEY CONCEPTS AND TERMS

- production possibilities frontier (PPF) p. 42
- constant costs p. 43
- trading possibilities curve p. 48
- terms of trade p. 48
- reciprocal demand p. 50
- complete specialization p. 53
- increasing costs p. 53

PROBLEMS AND QUESTIONS FOR REVIEW

1. Analyze the quote at the start of the chapter. What exactly isn't obvious about comparative advantage?
2. Demonstrate how a PPF can be used to illustrate the choices available in autarky to an economy in the production of two goods.
3. Graphically demonstrate how trade allows a country to consume at a point beyond its production possibilities frontier.
4. What is the meaning of the term *reciprocal demand?* How does it provide a meaningful explanation of the terms of trade?
5. Describe what the phrase *terms of trade* means.
6. Describe how changes in the terms of trade can lead to changes in the distribution of the gains from trade.
7. If a country cannot trade at a terms of trade such that it obtains most of the gains from trade, then it should not trade. Is this statement true or false?

8. Explain why the existence of constant costs leads countries that trade to completely specialize in the production of the good in which the country has a comparative advantage.
9. If the U.S. and Mexico trade, which country is more likely to obtain more favorable terms of trade?
10. How do increasing cost conditions affect the extent of international specialization and trade?
11. Compare and contrast international trade under conditions of constant costs and increasing costs.
12. Without trade suppose that Country A has constant costs, and currently produces 12 tons of wheat and 8 tons of corn. In addition, suppose that Country A has a marginal rate of transformation of 1 ton of wheat for 2 tons of corn
    a. Construct Country A's production possibilities frontier, and label the diagram.
    b. Suppose that Country A has the opportunity to trade with Country B at an international exchange ratio of 1 ton of wheat for 1 ton of corn. Assume after trade that Country A consumes 10 tons of corn.
    c. What will Country A produce after trade?
    d. What will Country A consume after trade? Show this consumption point on your diagram.
    e. What are the gains from trade for Country A?

Table 3.7

	U.S.	Mexico
Beer	30,000	12,000
Chips	5,000	3,000

13. Table 3.7 shows the maximum output of beer or chips that the U.S. and Mexico can produce under constant cost conditions.
    a. Graph the production possibilities frontiers for Mexico and the U.S. In the absence of trade, assume that the U.S. produces and consumes 18,000 beers and 2,000 chips and that Mexico produces and consumes 8,000 beers and 1,000 chips. Denote these points on each country's production possibilities frontiers.
    b. Determine the marginal rate of transformation for each country. According to the theory of comparative advantage, should the two countries specialize and trade with one another? If so, which country should specialize in the production of which product? Once specialization has occurred, what is the increase in output?
    c. Suppose that the terms of trade between the U.S. and Mexico is 1 chip for 5 beers. Illustrate the trading possibilities curve for both countries. Assume that 2,000 chips are traded for 10,000 beers. Are the consumers in the U.S. and Mexico better off? If so, by how much?
14. Assume that there are two countries, America and Europe, both producing food and clothing from land and labor. America is relatively abundantly endowed with land, compared to Europe, and land is used more intensively in the production of food than in the production of clothing. On the axes below, draw production possibility frontiers, and indifference curves for America and Europe, and then use them to illustrate and explain the movement to the free-trade equilibrium pattern of production, consumption, trade and the gains from trade for the two countries.

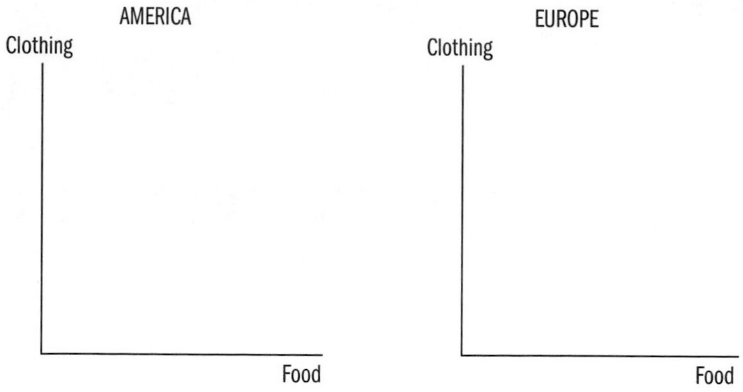

SUGGESTED READINGS AND WEB SITES

International Monetary Fund, *International Financial Statistics,* Washington, D.C.: International Monetary Fund, selected issues.

This monthly publication contains the import and export price indexes usually used to calculate the terms of trade.

Michael Cox and Richard Alm, *The Fruits of Free Trade, 2002 Annual Report,* Dallas: Federal Reserve Bank of Dallas, 2003.

A good synopsis of how trade improves the welfare of a country.

Penn World Tables (www.datacentre.2chass.utoronto.ca/pwt/)

An excellent data source for the importance of international trade for most of the world's countries.

U.S. Bureau of the Census, *U.S. Commodity Imports and Exports Related to Output,* Washington, D.C.: U.S. Government Printing Office, selected issues.

A very detailed classification of U.S. foreign trade as well as the relationship of foreign trade to domestic production.

Chapter 4

Factor Endowments and the Commodity Composition of Trade

"Generally, abundant factors are relatively cheap, scanty factors are relatively dear, in each region. Commodities requiring for their production much of the former and little of the latter are exported in exchange for goods that call for factors in the opposite proportions. Thus indirectly, factors in abundant supply are exported and factors in scanty supply are imported."
—Bertil Ohlin

INTRODUCTION

So far, we have shown that two countries can benefit from trade if each country specializes in the production of a good that it can produce at a lower comparative cost than the other country can, and imports a good that would require it to bear a higher comparative cost to produce. In a world with free trade, the activities of businesses and individuals will produce these benefits for the country as a byproduct of their desire to make a profit. International trade will increase until the point where all profitable opportunities for trade are exhausted. The model developed in the previous chapter was able to produce these results.

However, the model left us with some important but unanswered questions. The model developed in this chapter addresses the following questions: What determines a country's comparative advantage? How does international trade affect the size of an economy's various industries? How does international trade affect the payments or returns to the factors of production such as labor and capital? How does international trade affect the distribution of income within a country? In answering these questions, you will learn why international trade is a major public policy issue within a country.[1]

Further, determining the best location to produce a particular product is one of the more challenging problems in international business. Investment in plant and equipment requires a firm to commit substantial resources over a long period of time. A production facility that is profitable in a country means the managers, who had to decide where to locate it, had an understanding of the determinants of comparative advantage for the good that is produced there. The opposite of comparative advantage is comparative *disadvantage.* A successful exporter has figured out which goods can be produced domestically and determined which countries have a comparative disadvantage in the production of that good. Knowledge of the basis for international trade can help a businessperson spot opportunities that others might miss. Also, without a solid understanding of what determines comparative advantage, any type of long-term corporate strategy is likely to be flawed. It is necessary to understand not only what causes comparative advantage but also how the factors influencing comparative advantage can change over time.

In the next section, the basic theory that explains the causes of comparative advantage is presented. This basic theory is then extended to explain how international trade affects the returns to factors of production and the distribution of income within a country. Once we understand the causes of comparative advantage, we then consider the situation where a factor of production cannot move from one industry to another. The final section of the chapter discusses various empirical tests of the theory. These tests are useful in expanding our understanding of the basic theory of what causes comparative advantage.

THE FACTOR-PROPORTIONS THEORY

factor-proportions theory **the theory that states that a country's comparative advantage is based on its endowment of the factors of production**

For nearly one hundred years economists could explain trade based on comparative advantage, but they could not explain what *caused* comparative advantage. In the early part of the 20th century two Swedish economists, Eli Heckscher and Bertil Ohlin, explained the causes of comparative advantage. Paul Samuelson later refined their basic idea, which is referred to as the **factor-proportions theory**. The factor-proportions theory states that a country's comparative advantage is determined by its initial resource endowments.[2]

We begin our analysis with the simplest version of the factor-proportions theory. From the research on the basic theory, we can extend it to cover many more goods and/or countries without affecting the validity of its results.[3] The next section covers the assumptions of the basic theory. These assumptions are important for two reasons. First, it is necessary to look at the theory in its most basic form in order for it to be

[1]For a more extensive discussion see Paul Krugman, "What Do Undergrads Need to Know About Trade?" *American Economic Review* 83(2), May 1993, pp. 23–26.

[2]The factor-proportions theory is variously referred to as the factor-endowment model, the Heckscher-Ohlin theory (HO), or the Heckscher-Ohlin-Samuelson model.

[3]Some types of international trade are difficult to explain using the factor-proportions theory. These types of trade are covered in Chapter 4.

perfect competition a market structure in which firms produce a homogeneous good and each firm has no control over its own price

factors of production resource inputs—e.g., labor and capital—used to produce goods

constant returns to scale a production condition in which proportionate changes in factors of production lead to proportionate changes in output

capital intensive requiring a high capital-to-labor ratio to produce (said of a good) as compared with that of another good

easily understood. Second, much of what we do in the next several chapters involves changing one or more of these assumptions. As we will see the theory is much more "realistic" than the basic version outlined below.

Assumptions of the Factor-Proportions Theory

We begin our explanation of the factor-proportions theory by picking up where we left off in Chapter 2. To illustrate the factor-proportions theory of trade, we will assume that:

- As before, the U.S. and India each produce two goods, machines (M) and cloth (C), respectively.
- The production and consumption of the goods occur under **perfect competition** both in the product and factor markets. This means that:
  - firms are price takers and their individual actions cannot influence conditions in their respective markets;
  - the prices of the two goods and the prices paid to the factors of production are determined by supply and demand in each market;
  - and in the long run, the prices of the goods are equal to their respective costs of production.
- There are no transportation costs, taxes on trade, or other obstructions to the free flow of goods between the two countries.
- The introduction of international trade does not cause complete specialization in the production of one of the goods in either country. Both countries will continue to produce both goods.
- Consumers in the two countries have equal tastes and preferences. This means that when the price of machines in terms of cloth is the same in the two countries, both countries will consume the same proportion of the two goods.
- Both countries are endowed with two homogeneous **factors of production**, capital (K) and labor (L); and both resources are employed in the production of the two goods.[4]
- The technology available to produce the two goods is the same in both countries, and each good is produced under constant returns to scale. **Constant returns to scale** is a production condition in which proportionate changes in the factors of production lead to proportionate changes in output. In this case, if the amount of labor and capital used to produce cloth doubles, then the output of cloth doubles.
- Labor and capital are mobile domestically. This means that within each country, labor and capital can flow freely from one industry to the other. As a result, both industries within a country will pay the same wage rate and the same return to capital.
- Labor and capital cannot move between the two countries. This allows for differences in wage rates and the return to capital between the two countries. It also rules out the possibility of eliminating wage differences between countries through migration.[5]
- The production techniques available to produce machines and cloth in both countries are such that the production of machines is everywhere **capital intensive** and the

[4]This is sometimes called the 2 by 2 by 2 model, where each 2 refers to the number of countries, goods, and factors of production. Most conclusions generalize to higher dimensional models such as 3 by 3 by 3.
[5]Exceptions to this are sufficiently important that the implications of having mobile factors internationally will be considered in Chapter 6.

Table 4.1 Production Conditions in the U.S. and India

	Input Requirements to Produce	
Country	**1 Machine**	**10 yards of Cloth**
U.S.	10 units of capital +4 days of labor	4 units of capital +8 days of labor
India	10 units of capital +4 days of labor	4 units of capital +8 days of labor

labor intensive requiring a low capital-to-labor ratio to produce (said of a good) as compared with that of another good

capital-to-labor ratio (K/L) the amount of capital per unit of labor used to produce a good

production of cloth is everywhere **labor intensive**. This means that the production of machines tends to use a lot of capital relative to labor—in other words, it has a high **capital-to-labor ratio (K/L)**. On the other hand, the production of cloth requires a substantial amount of labor relative to capital—in other words, the K/L ratio for cloth is low relative to that for the production of machines.

Referring to Table 4.1, you can see that the production of machines and cloth occurs using a fixed ratio of the factors of production. Notice that the production of machines in both countries requires more units of capital than units of labor. Further, the capital-to-labor, or K/L, ratio for the machine industry is 2.5 (= 10/4). In both countries, the production of cloth requires more inputs of labor than capital and the cloth industry's K/L ratio is 0.5 (= 4/8). Comparing the K/L ratios, one observes that the cloth industry's K/L ratio (= 0.5) is low relative to the K/L ratio of the machine industry (= 2.5). This indicates that the production of machines in both the U.S. and India is relatively capital intensive.

➤ The U.S. is a relatively **capital-abundant** country, and India is a relatively **labor-abundant** country. This means that the capital-to-labor ratio in the U.S. is greater than the capital-to-labor ratio in India. The important point here is not whether the U.S. has more units of capital than India, but whether the U.S. has a larger capital-to-labor ratio than India. To illustrate, the capital-to-labor ratio in the U.S. is approximately $35,993 and the capital-to-labor ratio in India is approximately $1,997.[6] In this case, the U.S. is capital abundant relative to India and India is labor abundant relative to the U.S.

capital abundant having a high capital-to-labor ratio (said of a country) relative to that of another country

In the factor-proportions theory of international trade, the K/L ratio of a country plays an important role in determining the relative abundance of capital and labor in that country. One of the reasons that the theory we describe below can explain international trade is that the various countries of the world have widely differing capital-to-labor ratios. These ratios are presented in Table 4.2. The countries shown on the left side of the Table are all high-income countries, while those on the right are middle- and low-income countries. The lowest K/L ratio for the group of high-income countries is over $22,000 for the United Kingdom. On the other hand, the highest K/L ratio for a middle- to low-income country is a little over $16,000. The K/L ratios for Kenya and Nigeria are less than $1,000. Our point is that some countries are

[6]Both capital-to-labor ratios are measured as nonresidential capital stock per worker for 1992 and were obtained from Penn World Tables on the Internet at http://datacentre.epas.utoronto.ca:5680/pwt/pwt.html.

Table 4.2 Capital Stock per Worker of Selected Countries in 1992 (in 1985 international dollar prices)

High-Income Country	Capital-to-Labor Ratio	Middle & Low Income Country	Capital-to-Labor Ratio
Switzerland	$76,733	Mexico	$13,697
Canada	44,970	Poland	11,811
Japan	41,286	Chile	11,306
Australia	38,729	Turkey	7,626
France	37,460	Thailand	5,853
United States	35,993	Philippines	3,598
Netherlands	34,084	India	1,997
Italy	33,775	Kenya	822
Spain	30,888	Nigeria	735
United Kingdom	22,509		

Source: Penn World Tables, 5.6: //dc1.chass.utoronto.ca/pwt56/docs/topic.html

labor abundant having a low capital-to-labor ratio (said of a country) relative to that of another country

relatively capital abundant or relatively labor abundant. These substantial differences among countries serve to make the theory of comparative advantage described below much more realistic.

The Factor-Proportions Theorem

Given our assumptions, we can explain what determines a country's comparative advantage. We assumed that consumers in the U.S. and India have equal demand conditions for machines and cloth. Because of this assumption, the supply of resources, as reflected by each country's resource endowments, will be the sole determinant of factor prices. This means that before the U.S. and India trade with one another, capital would be relatively less expensive in the capital-abundant country and labor would be relatively less expensive in the labor-abundant country. In the U.S., capital would be relatively cheap and labor would be expensive. The reverse would be true for India, capital would be relatively expensive and labor would be cheap. This would be reflected in the ratio of the payment made to labor—wages—and the payment made to capital—which economists call rent. In this case, the ratio is higher in the U.S. than in India. This can be seen in the following relationship:

$$\left[\frac{\text{Wages in U.S.}}{\text{Rent in U.S.}}\right] > \left[\frac{\text{Wages in India}}{\text{Rent in India}}\right]$$

Because the wage-rent ratios are different, a country will have a lower opportunity cost of production in goods where the production technique requires greater quantities of the abundant factor and smaller quantities of the scarce factor. In our example, the U.S. will have a lower opportunity cost in goods produced using more capital and less labor. India's opportunity cost will be lower in goods produced using more labor and less capital. This leads to the following two important conclusions concerning the U.S. and India.

factor-proportions theory **the theory that states that a country's comparative advantage is based on its endowment of the factors of production**

- The U.S. has a comparative advantage in the production of machines because the production of machines is capital intensive and the U.S. has an abundance of capital.
- India has a comparative advantage in the production of cloth because the production of cloth is labor intensive and India has an abundance of labor.

The abundance of a particular factor of production in a country tends to make that factor less expensive relative to the cost of that same factor in other countries. Given this, a country will tend to produce and export goods that intensively use their less expensive factor of production. The **factor-proportions theorem**[7] can be expressed in the following way.

> A country will have a comparative advantage in goods whose production intensively uses its relatively abundant factor of production. A country will have a comparative disadvantage in goods whose production intensively uses its relatively scarce factor of production.

This is one of the most powerful statements in international economics. If you examine the U.S. pattern of trade, much of what the U.S. imports are goods from countries where labor is abundant relative to capital. The reverse also is true. Much of what the U.S. exports are capital-intensive goods. We have reached this conclusion using a simplified model with only two countries, two goods, and two factors of production, but the results can be generalized to many factors and many goods.

This theory provides an explanation of what determines a country's comparative advantage—but keep in mind the other side of the coin, comparative disadvantage. A country will have a comparative disadvantage in the production of goods that

U.S.–China Trade

If we compare the resource endowments of the U.S. to China, we find that the U.S. possesses abundant skilled labor (human capital) and scarce unskilled labor. China possesses abundant unskilled labor and scarce skilled labor. Thus, the factor-proportions theory would predict that the U.S. has a comparative advantage and should export goods that intensively use skilled labor in its production, and that China has a comparative advantage and should export goods that intensively use unskilled labor in its production.

Table 4.3 shows the results of a recent study that tested this prediction based on U.S.–China trade in 1990. In this study, the authors divided a sample of 131 industries into 10 groups based on their skill intensity. Group 1 industries embodied the most skill-intensive, and Group 10 industries the least skill-intensive. This table provides sample industries for each group and shows each group's share of both U.S. exports to China and China's exports to the U.S.

Notice that the pattern of U.S.–China trade shown in Table 4.3 fits the prediction of the factor-proportions theory well. U.S. exports to China are concentrated in the high-skilled industries, as industry groups 1 through 3 account for 78 percent of

[7] Often the factor-proportions theorem is referred to as the Heckscher-Ohlin theorem or the H-O theorem.

Table 4.3 The Factor-Proportions Theory and U.S.–China Trade

Skill Group	Industry Examples	Percent of Chinese Exports to the U.S	Percent of U.S. Exports to China
Most Skilled			
1	Periodical, office & computing machines	4.8%	7.7%
2	Aircraft & parts, industrial inorganic chemicals	2.6	48.8
3	Engines & turbines, fats & oils	3.9	21.3
4	Concrete, nonelectric plumbing & heating	11.5	4.3
5	Watches, clocks, toys, sporting goods	18.9	6.3
6	Wood buildings, blast furnaces, basic steel	8.2	1.3
7	Ship building & repair, furniture & fixtures	4.1	2.8
8	Cigarettes, motor vehicles, iron & steel foundries	5.2	1.8
9	Weaving, wool, leather tanning & finishing	17.2	0.4
10	Children's outerwear, nonrubber footwear	23.5	5.2
Least Skilled			

Source: Jeffery Sachs and Howard Shatz, "Trade and Jobs in U.S. Manufacturing," *Brookings Papers on Economic Activity* 1, 1994, pp. 18–53.

U.S. exports to China. Also, China's exports to the U.S. are concentrated in the least skilled industries. Industry groups 9 and 10 account for more than 40 percent of China's exports to the U.S.

intensively uses its scarce factor of production. We usually focus on a country's comparative advantage. However, comparative disadvantage is just as important in generating the gains from trade. Remember: the gains from trade are realized when a country exports goods based on its comparative advantage and imports goods based on its comparative disadvantage.[8]

[8]For a more thorough explanation of the factor-proportions theory and factor-price equalization, see Appendix 4.1.

FACTOR-PRICE EQUALIZATION AND THE DISTRIBUTION OF INCOME

The premise of the factor-proportions theory is that comparative advantage and international trade occur because countries are endowed with different factor proportions. Employing the results of the theory, we also can illustrate several other phenomena associated with international trade. For example, what happens to the relative size of industries as an economy moves from autarky to free trade? What happens to the payments or returns to factors of production such as labor and capital within an economy? What is the relationship between international trade and the distribution of income within a country?

Factor-Price Equalization

factor-price equalization theorem **the premise that international trade will reduce or equalize factor prices between countries**

In Chapters 2 and 3 we described how free trade equalizes the price of cloth and machines in both countries at the same terms of trade. Within the factor-proportions theory this adjustment to free trade produces a very interesting result known as the **factor-price equalization theorem**. This theorem states that when international trade occurs between two countries based on different factor proportions, not only will free trade equalize the price of the traded goods but also the relative factor prices in the two countries will tend to converge. The changes in the relative factor prices will occur over a period of years or decades. Such changes have long-run implications for businesses that want to exploit short-run differences in the costs of production between countries.

To illustrate the factor-price equalization theorem, let's return to our previous example. The U.S. has a comparative advantage in capital-intensive machine production because it is a capital-abundant country, and India has a comparative advantage in labor-intensive cloth production because it is a labor-abundant country. As trade opens up between the U.S. and India, the price of cloth and machines in the U.S. and India equalize as both countries trade at the same terms of trade. Because each country will specialize its production in its comparative-advantage good, the size of the machine and cloth industries in each country will change as each country moves along its production possibilities frontier.

industrial structure **the percentage of output that is accounted for by each industry within a country**

For the U.S., machine production expands and cloth production contracts as international trade allows the U.S. to specialize in the production of machines. For India, machine production contracts and cloth production expands as international trade allows India to specialize in the production of cloth. This change in machine and cloth production within each country changes each country's **industrial structure**. Industrial structure refers to the percentage of output accounted for by each industry within a country. Without any trade, both the U.S. and India would have a certain percentage of their total industrial capacity devoted to producing machines and cloth. By allowing international trade, each country specializes its production and changes the percentage of its production that is allocated to produce machines and cloth.

With international trade, the U.S. machine industry experiences an increase in demand for its output, as the industry will have to supply not only the U.S. market but also—in the form of exports—India's. As a result, the price of machines rises relative to the price of cloth. The U.S. machine industry expands its production to meet this increase in demand. To expand production, the machine industry requires more resources, meaning more capital and more labor. This expansion requires a greater increase in capital relative to the increase in labor because machine production is capital intensive. Assuming the economy is at full employment, the additional resources that the machine industry needs will come from the cloth industry.

As trade opens up, the U.S. cloth industry experiences a decrease in demand for its output, and the price of cloth declines relative to the price of machines. The cloth industry produces less cloth as imports from India replace domestic production. As the cloth industry contracts, it uses less capital and less labor. This contraction releases more labor relative to the release of capital because cloth production is labor intensive. However, this shift of capital and labor from one industry to another is not a perfect fit. The expanding machine industry is capital intensive. To expand, this industry needs a lot of capital and only a little more labor. On the other hand, the contracting cloth industry is releasing a lot of labor and only a little more capital.

Refer to the production conditions shown in Table 4.1. As the cloth industry contracts, it releases 4 units of capital and 8 days of labor. The expanding machine industry requires 10 units of capital and 4 days of labor. In this case, the 4 units of capital supplied is less than the 10 units of capital demanded. The result is a shortage of capital, and the price paid to capital (rent) rises. The opposite occurs in the labor market, where the 8 days of labor supplied is greater than the 4 days of labor demanded. The result is a surplus of labor, and the price paid to labor (wages) falls. Given these conditions, the relative price of the factors of production (the ratio of wages to rent) decreases. The introduction of international trade sets in motion market forces that cause a change in the relative price of machines in terms of cloth. The changes in the prices of the two goods cause changes in the industrial structure of the U.S. In turn, this change in the industrial structure causes changes in the prices paid to the factors of production.

A similar situation occurs in India, where the introduction of trade leads to an increase in the price of cloth relative to machines. The change in the price of cloth relative to machines causes changes in India's industrial structure. In India, the production of cloth expands and the production of machines contracts. This change in India's industrial structure causes the price paid to the abundant factor in India (labor) to increase and the price paid to the scarce factor (capital) to decrease. As a result, the relative price of the factors of production (wages/rent) in India increases.

In the U.S., labor becomes less costly, and in India it becomes more expensive. The difference in the price of labor between the two countries narrows. The same thing is happening with respect to capital. In the U.S., the price paid to capital increases, and in India it decreases. The difference in the price of capital in the two countries also narrows with trade. Would the price of each factor of production in the U.S. ever reach perfect equality with the price of the corresponding factor in India? Under the very strict assumptions of the factor-proportions theorem, the answer is yes. However, under practical conditions, the answer is no. Absolute factor-price equalization may not occur for a variety of reasons. Among these are less than perfect competitive conditions in the product and/or factor markets, differences in technology, and the existence of transportation costs and/or trade barriers. Nevertheless, we can view the factor-price equalization theorem as a consistent tendency. This is true because international trade puts market forces in motion that tend to move relative factor prices in the two countries closer together in the long run. They may never reach perfect equality, but the direction of change in relative factor prices is clear.

The factor-price equalization theorem also has important implications for multinational corporations. Companies located in countries where labor is relatively expensive could profit by importing products from companies located in countries where labor is relatively less expensive. As we will see in Chapter 6, a multinational corporation might also consider building a plant in a relatively low-wage country if profits are potentially higher from products produced there. However, establishing a plant and purchasing equipment normally is an investment for ten to thirty years. If the managers of the multinational corporation assume that the labor-cost differential between countries that exists today will persist for decades, they could be partially wrong. At a minimum, the relatively labor-cost differential would tend to narrow over time and affect the potential profitability of the investment. Factor-price equalization is another factor that multinational corporations need to consider when making long-run investment decisions in the global marketplace.

Trade and the Distribution of Income

We have just explained how international trade changes the prices paid to the factors of production in the two trading countries. We showed that the price paid to the abundant factor of production would rise and the price paid to the scarce factor of production would fall within a country. These factor-price results have significant implications regarding the effects of international trade on a country's distribution of income.

In our example, as trade opens up the price paid to capital (the abundant factor) in the U.S. would rise, and the price paid to labor (the scarce factor) in the U.S. would fall. In India, the price paid to labor (the abundant factor) would rise, and the price paid to capital (the scarce factor) would fall. Carrying this analysis one step further produces an interesting result. Because we assume that labor and capital remain fully employed both before and after trade, the real income of both labor and capital will move in the same direction as the factor-price movements.

In our example, the percentage of national income that capital receives would increase in the U.S. and the percentage of national income that labor receives would decrease. For India, the percentage of national income that capital receives would fall and the percentage of income that labor receives would increase. The result is that international trade has discernible effects on the distribution of income within a trading country. Specifically, the abundant factor tends to receive a larger share of the income pie and the scarce factor tends to receive a smaller share of the income pie. This effect is called the **Stolper-Samuelson theorem**.

Stolper-Samuelson theorem **the premise that international trade will reduce the income of the scarce factor of production and increase the income of the abundant factor of production within a country**

International trade enhances a country's total welfare, but the gains from trade are not necessarily equally distributed among the factors of production. In many cases, the changes in the distribution of income may be very subtle, in the sense that the incomes of the abundant factor may be growing faster over time than are the incomes of the scarce factor. The main point is that international trade has the potential to change the distribution of income among the various factors of production in a predictable way. The same type of change would occur in India. As trade opens up, the abundant factor's income would tend to rise and the scarce factor's income would tend to fall. Labor in India would receive a larger percentage of national income and capital would receive a smaller percentage.

These effects of international trade on factor prices have implications for the world economy. In developed countries, the relatively abundant factor of production

Changes in the K/L Ratio Over Time: South Korea and India

A country's K/L ratio can change over time as its factor endowments change. For example, a country that is labor-abundant today may not be a labor-abundant country in 30 thirty years. South Korea is a good example of a country changing its factor endowments. Some basic data on the South Korean economy is given in Table 4.4. In the mid 1960s, the capital stock per worker in South Korea was a bit more than \$2,000. By the early 1990s it was nearly \$18,000. Given that Korean-produced goods can be found in almost every U.S. store; this should not be too surprising. Less than 40 years ago, South Korea was a very poor developing country. GDP per capita at the end of the Korean War was less than \$800. In less than 40 years, GDP per capita had increased to \$7,235. Some of this progress can be attributed to the relative openness of the Korean economy. In the early 1950s exports plus imports as a percentage of GDP were a little more than 10 percent. By 1990 they were more than 60 percent.

India is a good study in contrast. In the 1950s, India's GDP per capita was only slightly lower than South Korea's. India, like South Korea, was a labor-abundant country with a low capital stock per worker as evidenced in Table 4.4. The level of openness in the two economies was also similar in the early 1950s. Today India is still a poor, labor-abundant economy for many reasons. But at least part of the story can be found by contrasting the rates at which the two economies opened themselves up to trade over the last 40 years.

Table 4.4 Economic Data for South Korea and India

Economic Variable	South Korea		India	
	Year	Value	Year	Value
GDP per Capita	1953	\$796	1953	\$641
	1962	\$928	1962	\$760
	1972	\$1,45	1972	\$786
	1982	\$3,395	1982	\$936
	1991	\$7,251	1991	\$1,251
Capital/Worker	1965	\$2,093	1965	\$786
	1975	\$6,533	1975	\$1,259
	1985	\$12,036	1985	\$1,712
	1992	\$17,995	1992	\$1,997
Degree of Openness [(Exports + Imports)/ GDP]	1953	11.8%	1953	10.4%
	1962	22.1%	1962	11.2%
	1972	44.5%	1972	8.8%
	1982	71.5%	1982	14.5%
	1990	62.5%	1992	21.4%

Source: Penn World Tables, 5.6: //dc1.chass.utoronto.ca/pwt56/docs/topic.html

is capital and the scarce factor is unskilled labor. As a result, the potential gainers from free trade are the owners of capital with above average incomes and the losers are unskilled labor with the lowest incomes. For the developing countries, international trade tends to increase the incomes of the relatively abundant factor, labor. In this case, trade has the prospect of reducing the poverty prevalent in many of these countries by increasing wages. We will return to these issues in later chapters. For now, keep in mind that while international trade improves the welfare of the trading countries, the benefits are not necessarily distributed evenly and may lead to absolute or relative losses for some segments of society.

These results are based on the assumption that the factors of production are mobile between industries within a country. While a factor may be mobile in the long

Trade Adjustment Assistance

If the U.S. has a comparative disadvantage in the production of products that intensively use (unskilled or semiskilled) labor, then imports of labor-intensive products will cause labor in the U.S. to suffer losses of income even though the economy as a whole gains from trade. The abundant factor gains and the scarce factor loses. Paul Samuelson developed one possible solution to this income redistribution effect in the 1960s. He concluded that the U.S. gains from trade were large enough that society could "bribe" the losers into accepting their losses and still have money left over.[9]

In the U.S. such a system, known as Trade Adjustment Assistance (TAA), is actually in place. TAA was created under the Trade Act of 1962. Under this legislation, workers who lost jobs caused by trade liberalization were entitled to compensation. The Trade Act of 1974 greatly liberalized the program. Under this Act's new rules, displaced workers could qualify for compensation if import competition caused the job loss. Under the liberalized rules, it was easier to be certified as a worker who was displaced by import competition. Certified displaced workers were then entitled to receive extended unemployment compensation and special training benefits. During 2006, the U.S. government provided nearly $1.0 billion in funding for this program. Given the benefits of imports and the modest cost, the program seemed a bargain.

However, recent research casts some doubt on the program's economic necessity.[10] TAA is by nature discriminatory—workers who lose their jobs due to import competition become eligible for benefits in excess of what is available to other workers who lose their jobs due to other economic conditions. For example, if your firm closes due to competition from a more efficient domestic competitor, you are out of luck! Similarly, if the industry you work in is in long-run decline, then TAA becomes available only if increased imports also are associated with this decline. Indeed, Robert Lawrence has found that is often the case.[11] It is not surprising that Clark, et al. found that there are no significant differences in employment outcomes between workers in manufacturing industries who lost their jobs due to import competition and workers who lost their jobs for other reasons. TAA may be a political necessity, but it does not appear to be an economic necessity.

[9]See Paul Samuelson, "The Gains from International Trade Once Again," *Economic Journal* 72, 1962, pp. 820–29.
[10]See Don P. Clark, Henry W. Herzog, Jr. and Alan M. Schlottmann, "Import Competition, Employment Risk, and the Job-Search Outcomes of Trade-Displaced Manufacturing Workers," *Industrial Relations* 37(2), April 1998, pp.182–205.
[11]See Robert Z. Lawrence, *Can America Compete?*, Washington, D.C.: The Brookings Institution, 1984.

run, in the short-run, factors may not be able to move from one industry to another within a country. If factors of production are not mobile within a country, then our analysis needs to be modified. Since this situation is not uncommon, the next section of the chapter considers how the immobility of factors of production affects our results above.

THE SPECIFIC-FACTORS MODEL

The factor-proportions theory assumes that labor and capital can move from one industry to another industry in the same economy. In our example, if the machine industry expanded in the U.S., the capital and labor needed for this expansion would come from the cloth industry. This movement of resources is a realistic assumption in the long run, as labor and capital used in the cloth industry could move to the machine industry.

However, in the short run, moving labor between industries may require some length of time, as workers might need to acquire new or different skills. In a large country such as the U.S., this movement of labor may also require workers to relocate to another part of the country. Although not impossible, these work force adjustments take time. Moving capital from one industry in the economy to another industry also may be even more difficult. For example, capital equipment designed to produce machines may not be easily adapted to produce cloth. In the long run, reallocating capital from the cloth industry to the machine industry may mean expanding capital in the machine industry only as existing capital in the cloth industry wears out. In this way, new capital investment over time would eventually reallocate the capital between the two industries. Factor mobility between industries is realistic in the long run, but in the short run, factors of production may be somewhat immobile.

With imperfect factor mobility between industries, the gains and losses resulting from trade to the factors of production need to be modified. To examine why the payments received by the factors of production depend on the mobility of the factors of production, let's return to our example. Assume that there are three factors of production: capital used to produce machines, capital used to produce cloth, and labor that can be used to produce either machines or cloth. Capital in this case is called a **specific factor** because its use is specific to either the production of machines or the production of cloth and cannot move between industries. Labor is called a variable or **mobile factor** because over time it can move between machine production and cloth production.

specific factor a factor of production is specific to an industry or is immobile between industries

mobile factor a factor of production that can move between industries or is mobile between industries

Remember, when trade opens up between the U.S. and India, the machine industry expands and the cloth industry contracts in the U.S. Initially, if all factors of production are immobile, as the cloth industry contracts, both capital and labor in this industry suffer losses as employment contracts and factories are shut down. In the expanding machine industry, both labor and capital benefit as employment and profits increase. In fact, these initial industry-specific effects often dominate the political debate over trade policy within a country.

Now, suppose that labor can move between industries and capital is immobile between industries. Point E in Figure 4.1 illustrates the before-trade equilibrium for the U.S. In the figure, the total supply of labor in the U.S. is shown along the horizontal axis. The amount of labor employed in the machine industry is measured from O

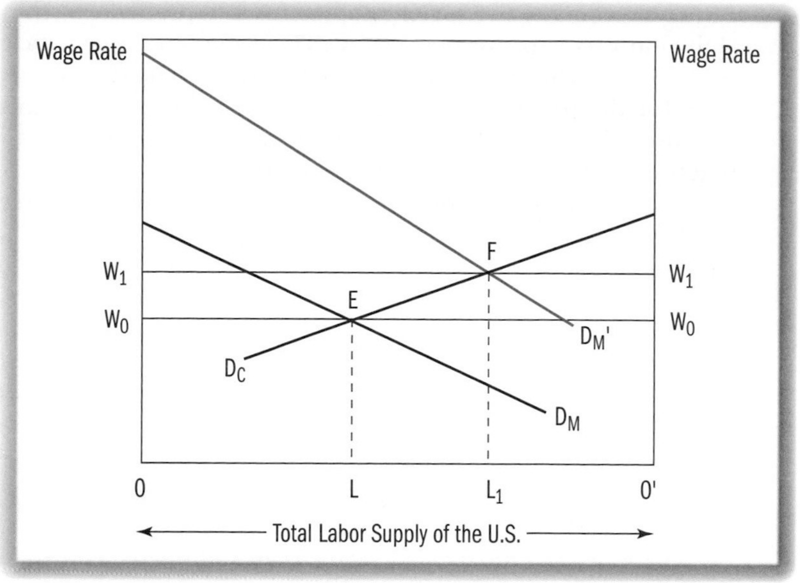

Figure 4.1 Specific Factors Model

With the specific factors model, as the demand for labor in the machine industry increases the wage rate rises and workers move from the cloth industry to the machine industry.

rightward along the axis, and the amount of labor employed in the cloth industry is measured from O' leftward along the axis. In each industry, labor is combined with a fixed amount of specific capital to produce either cloth or machines. Under these conditions, labor is subject to diminishing returns in each industry. This means that the demand for labor in each industry is downward sloping and is equal to the value of the marginal product of labor.[12] The machine industry's demand for labor is represented by D_M, and the cloth industry's demand for labor is represented by D_C. (The cloth industry's demand for labor is measured leftward from O'.) By assuming that labor is mobile between industries, both the machine industry and the cloth industry will pay the same wage rate, W_0. This equilibrium occurs at the intersection of the two demand curves at point E. At this point, OL workers are employed in the machine industry and O'L workers are employed in the cloth industry.

When trade opens up between the U.S. and India, machine prices increase in the U.S., causing the demand for labor in the machine industry to increase to D'_M.[13] As a result, the new equilibrium is at point F. Employment in the machine industry increases to OL_1 as machine production expands and employment decreases in the cloth industry to $O'L_1$ as cloth production declines. In addition, the wage rate paid in both industries increases from W_0 to W_1.

[12]The value of the marginal product of labor is equal to the price of the product times the marginal product of labor.

[13]We illustrate the impact of trade on the labor market within the U.S. by allowing the price of machines to increase while the price of cloth has remained constant.

The owners of the specific capital used to produce machines continue to benefit as the industry expands production. The owners of the specific capital used to produce cloth lose as production contracts. The effect on the mobile factor, labor, is indeterminate, for the price of machines has increased by more than the increase in wages. Because of trade, U.S. labor faces rising machine prices and lower cloth prices. Whether workers are better or worse off depends on their consumption pattern. If labor consumes more machines than cloth, labor will be worse off as their real wage has decreased. If the reverse is true, labor will be better off. The mobile factor, in this case labor, may gain or lose depending on its consumption pattern.

The results arising from the existence of specific factors are short-run effects. These short-run effects will diminish over time as factors of production move into the industry that has a comparative advantage. In the long run, the abundant factor of production (capital in the U.S.) gains, and the scarce factor of production (labor in the U.S.) loses. The difference is that some owners of sector-specific factors experience gains (owners of capital used to produce machines) or losses (owners of capital used to produce cloth) in the short run. Even with the existence of specific factors, the country as a whole still gains from trade.

The existence of specific factors can help explain why some groups resist free trade. In general, owners of the abundant factor of production in a country will likely be in favor of freer international trade, while owners of the scarce factor of production will likely favor trade restrictions. With specific factors of production, both capital and labor in an industry having a comparative disadvantage will suffer losses and may well resist free trade.

EMPIRICAL EVIDENCE CONCERNING THE FACTOR-PROPORTIONS THEORY

The factor-proportions theory provides a logical and obvious explanation of international trade. Unfortunately, economists have learned from experience that a "logical and obvious" explanation of an economic phenomenon can be misleading or wrong. It is not enough for a theory to make sense. It also needs to pass enough empirical tests to give us a sense of confidence about it. We need to be assured that what we think is true is actually true. The empirical testing of the factor-proportions theory of international trade provides an excellent example. Empirical testing of theory is designed to check the validity of a theory. In some cases, the empirical testing leads to a better understanding and/or extensions of the basic theory. As we will show, this has been the case with the factor-proportions theory.

When the factor-proportions theory of international trade was developed in the early 20th century, lack of economic data made empirical testing of economic theory nearly impossible. Economic data that is routinely reported from media outlets such as radio, TV, newspapers, magazines, and the Internet did not become available until after 1945. Similarly the statistical tools used to test economic theory and the means to process the data (computers) were not available until the 1950s and 1960s. Because the factor-proportions theory seemed so logical, most economists accepted it as true before it had been empirically tested.

The Leontief Paradox

Wassily Leontief conducted the first and most famous empirical test of the factor-proportions theory in 1954.[14] What Leontief found was surprising. He reasoned that compared to its trading partners, the U.S. was a capital-abundant country. Given the factor-proportions theory, the U.S. should export goods that are capital intensive and import goods that are labor intensive. To test this hypothesis, Leontief calculated how much capital and labor—the K/L ratio—various U.S. industries used in their production. He then compared the K/L ratios of the industries that had a net trade surplus—the net exporters—with the K/L ratios of the industries that had a net trade deficit—the net importers. He expected that U.S. industries with a trade surplus would have a high K/L ratio (capital intensive) relative to U.S. industries with a trade deficit (labor intensive).

Leontief paradox **the empirical finding (in the 1940s) that U.S. industries with trade surpluses were more labor intensive than were U.S. industries with trade deficits. This is contrary to the factor-proportions theory**

Leontief's empirical estimation of the capital-to-labor ratio in U.S. industries with a trade surplus was $14,010, and his estimate for industries with a trade deficit was $18,180. This meant that his empirical result was the reverse of what he had expected. Net export industries in the U.S. were more labor intensive than were U.S. net import industries. This result has been called the **Leontief Paradox**. This paradox is not some peculiarity of 1947, the year that Leontief did his research. Subsequent empirical studies on the factor-proportions theory, some very recent, have obtained this same perverse result. Leontief's findings caused considerable dismay among economists, who concluded that something was wrong with either the empirical test or the basic theory. The problem turned out to involve both, as we will show in the next section. In identifying the nature of the problem, economists have been able to gain a better understanding of how factor abundance influences international trade.

Explanations of the Leontief Paradox

There are a number of possible explanations for Leontief's results. One is that some imports are not based on an abundance of labor or capital but depend, instead, on the foreign country's possession of natural resources such as oil, diamonds, bauxite, or copper. Many of these natural-resource industries use highly capital-intensive production techniques to extract the product.[15] Because Leontief used only a two-factor model (labor and capital), his results may have been biased. Since the U.S. imports many natural resources, this would help to explain why U.S. imports are capital intensive.

Another explanation of the paradox is that U.S. trade policy may have biased the results. Many of the most heavily protected industries in the U.S. are labor-intensive (e.g., textiles and apparel). In our earlier discussion of trade and the distribution of income, we showed that the scarce factor of production (labor, for the U.S.) generally favors trade restrictions. The effect of imposing trade restrictions on certain

[14]See Wassily Leontief, "Domestic Production and Foreign Trade: The American Capital Position Reexamined," *Economia Internazionale* 7(1), February 1954, pp. 3–32.

[15]James Hartigan has found that the paradox disappears if natural resources are excluded from consideration. See James C. Hartigan, "The U.S. Tariff and Comparative Advantage: A Survey of Method," *Weltwirtschaftliches Archiv* 117(1), 1981, pp. 61–109. More specifically, Niroomand has found that the source of this effect may be Canada. See Farhang Niroomand, "Factor Inputs and U.S. Manufacturing Trade Structure: 1963–1980," *Weltwirtschaftliches Archiv* 127(4), 1991, pp. 744–63.

labor-intensive goods would be to diminish U.S. imports of labor-intensive products and reduce the overall labor intensity of U.S. imports.[16]

human capital **the education, training, and job skills embodied in labor, serving to increase labor's productivity and make it more valuable in the market**

The most important explanations of the Leontief paradox, however, have to do with the skill level of the U.S. workforce and the presence of high technology. Leontief's test found that U.S. exports were labor intensive. This conclusion was based on the simple two-factor version of the factor-proportions model. This simple model assumes that labor is homogeneous, or that one unit of labor is like any other unit of labor. In many cases, assumptions like this do not alter the predictions of economic models. However, in this case it did affect the model's results. Much of the U.S. labor force is highly skilled, or, to state it differently, represents valuable **human capital** (knowledge and skills). A simple way of examining the human capital that is embodied in labor is to consider a worker's wage in relation to the minimum wage. Most U.S. workers earn wages above the minimum wage. To the extent that any employer pays more than the absolute minimum wage, workers must possess something, such as skills, education, or training, which reflects their value in the labor market. Any payment to labor above the minimum wage can be viewed as a return to some form of human capital. In attempting to explain U.S. exports, it is necessary to take account of the human capital embodied in exports. When human capital is taken into account, U.S. exports appear to be not labor intensive but rather human-capital intensive.[17] In addition, U.S. exports appear to be intensive in technology, which represents another factor, different from capital, labor, or human capital. That is, U.S. exports have been shown to be intensive in research and development (R&D), and the level of R&D in an industry is a somewhat coarse but frequently used measure of that industry's level of technology.[18]

As a result of this research, we can use the factor-proportions theory with some confidence. Most empirical evidence indicates that the basic reasoning embodied in the theory is correct.[19] Countries tend to have a comparative advantage in and export goods whose production intensively uses its abundant factor of production. What needs to be considered is what constitutes a factor of production? Physical capital can be used as a factor, essentially as it was described in the simple version of the theory. The same cannot be said for labor. The knowledge and skills (human capital) that a labor force possesses need to be treated as a separate factor of production. The same

---

[16]Empirical evidence supporting this proposition can be found in Robert E. Baldwin, "Determinants of the Commodity Structure of U.S. Trade," *American Economic Review* 61(1), March 1971, pp. 126–46.

[17]On this point see Donald B. Keesing, "Labor Skills and Comparative Advantage," *American Economic Review* 56(2), May 1966, pp. 249–58. In addition, Trefler argues that the U.S. was relatively abundant in land and relatively scarce in both labor and capital. By adjusting for productivity differences across countries, the U.S. would have been classified as a labor-abundant country and expected to export labor-abundant goods. For more information, see Daniel Trefler, "International Factor Price Differences: Leontief Was Right!," *Journal of Political Economy* 101(6), December 1993, pp. 961–87.

[18]See William Gruber, Dileep Mehta, and Raymond Vernon, "The R&D Factor in International Trade and International Investment of United States Industries," *Journal of Political Economy* 75(1), February 1967, pp. 20–37.

[19]The evidence in general seems to support the factor-proportions theory. For examples of very extensive tests of the theory, see Edward E. Leamer, *Sources of Comparative Advantage: Theories and Evidence,* Cambridge: MIT Press, 1984; Harry P. Bowen, Edward E. Leamer, and Leo Sveikaukas, "Multicountry, Multifactor Tests of the Factor Abundance Theory," *American Economic Review* 77(5), December 1987, pp. 791–809; or James Harrigan, "Technology, Factor Supplies, and International Specialization: Estimating the Neoclassical Model," *American Economic Review* 87(4), September 1997, pp. 475–94.

Relative Factor Endowments for Selected Countries

One of the primary assumptions of the factor-proportions theory is that countries are endowed with different factor endowments. Table 4.5 provides some information for the abundance of capital and two different types of labor on a global basis. The table decomposes labor into two broad classes: skilled and unskilled. Notice that the OECD countries possess more than half of the world's capital and nearly half the world's skilled labor. The developing countries have a relatively small proportion of the world's capital and skilled labor but a large majority of unskilled labor. Notice how the different factor endowments illustrated in the table support the premise that underlying factor supplies vary from country to country, as the factor-proportions theory predicts.

Table 4.5 Factor Endowments of Countries and Regions, 1993 (as a Percentage of World Total)

Country/Region	Capital	Skilled Labor	Unskilled Labor	All Resources
U.S.	20.8%	19.4%	2.6%	5.6%
EU	20.7	13.3	5.3	6.9
Japan	10.5	8.2	1.6	2.9
Canada	2.0	1.7	0.4	0.6
Rest of OCED	5.0	2.6	2.0	2.2
Mexico	2.3	1.2	1.4	1.4
Rest of Latin America	6.4	3.7	5.3	5.1
China	8.3	21.7	30.4	28.4
India	3.0	7.1	15.3	13.7
Hong Kong, Korea, Taiwan, Singapore	2.8	3.7	0.9	1.4
Rest of Asia	3.4	5.3	9.5	8.7
Eastern Europe (including Russia)	6.2	3.8	8.4	7.6
Organization of Petroleum Exporting Countries (OPEC)	6.2	4.4	7.1	6.7
Rest of World	2.5	4.0	10.0	8.9
Total	100.0	100.0	100.0	100.0

Source: Adapted from William Cline, *Trade and Income Distribution,* Washington D.C.: Institute for International Economics, 1997, pp. 183–85.

is true for technology. The basic logic embodied in the factor-proportions theory is correct. We just need to broaden the concept of factors of production to include factors other than capital and labor.

International Trade Not Explained by the Factor-Proportions Theory

The factor-proportions theory is a useful explanation of international trade, but it does not explain all international trade.[20] In particular, it does not explain two types of international trade. First, international trade in products based on natural resources is not explained using the factor-proportions theory. Examples of these types of goods are diamonds, copper, coal, coffee, and oil. A country either has diamonds or it does not. A country either has a climate conducive to the growing of coffee beans or it does not. Second, there is a substantial amount of international trade that involves countries simultaneously importing and exporting very similar goods. An example of this type of trade is the U.S. export and import of automobiles. An explanation of why this type of trade occurs is the subject of the next chapter.

SUMMARY

1. The basis for trade between countries comes from differences in the price of goods between countries.
2. The factor-proportions theory is a way to explain why countries have different opportunity costs associated with producing different goods.
3. The factor-proportions theory is based on the following assumptions: (1) two countries, two goods, with two factors of production; (2) both countries have the same technology, and each good is produced under constant returns to scale; (3) both countries have perfectly competitive product and factor markets, and prices of the two goods and factors of production are determined by supply and demand; (4) there are no transportation costs, tariffs, or other obstructions to free trade between countries, and after the introduction of international trade neither country completely specializes in producing a particular good; (5) consumers in the two countries have equal tastes and preferences for each of the two goods; (6) labor and capital are assumed to be mobile domestically but not internationally; (7) the production techniques available to produce the two goods are such that one good is everywhere capital intensive, and the production of the other good is everywhere labor intensive; and (8) the resources of both countries are fully employed both before and after trade.
4. The factor-proportions theory suggests that differences in relative factor endowments between countries determine the basis for trade. The theory states that a country has a comparative advantage in, and exports, the good that intensively uses the country's abundant factor of production. Conversely, a country has a comparative disadvantage in, and imports, the good that intensively uses the country's relatively scarce factor of production.
5. The factor-price equalization theorem states that international trade would equalize factor prices between countries. As such, in the long-run there is a tendency toward factor-price equalization.

---

[20]For additional information see Donald R. Davis and David E. Weinstein, "An Account of Global Factor Trade," *American Economic Review* 91(5), December 2001, pp. 1423–53.

6. The Stolper-Samuelson theorem states that an increase in the relative price of a commodity raises the real price of the factor used intensively in the commodity's production and reduces the real price of the other factor. These changes in factor prices tend to increase the percentage of national income the abundant factor receives. The reverse is true for the scarce factor.
7. The specific-factors model shows that owners of capital specific to export- or import-competing industries tend to experience gains or losses from international trade. Workers find that their welfare may rise, fall, or remain the same depending on their consumption of the various goods.
8. Leontief, using 1947 data, conducted the first empirical test of the factor-proportions model. He found that the production of U.S. goods, which were substitutes for imports, were more capital intensive than were U.S. exports. His findings became known as the Leontief paradox. A number of possible explanations for the perverse result have been given over the years. The paradox tends to be resolved by considering human capital and technology as separate factors of production.

KEY CONCEPTS AND TERMS

- factor-proportions theory p. 69
- perfect competition p. 70
- factors of production p. 70
- constant returns to scale p. 70
- capital intensive p. 70
- labor intensive p. 71
- capital-to-labor ratio (K/L) p. 71
- capital abundant p. 71
- labor abundant p. 72
- factor-proportions theorem p. 73
- factor-price equalization theorem p. 75
- industrial structure p. 75
- Stolper-Samuelson theorem p. 77
- specific factor p. 80
- mobile factor p. 80
- Leontief paradox p. 83
- human capital p. 84

PROBLEMS AND QUESTIONS FOR REVIEW

1. In what ways does the factor-proportions theory represent an extension of the trade model presented in Chapter 2?
2. State the assumptions of the factor-proportions theory. What is the meaning and importance of each assumption?
3. What is a labor-intensive good? What is a labor-abundant country?
4. What are the basic determinants of comparative advantage and trade in the factor-proportions model?
5. Go to the Penn World Tables Web site listed in the Suggested Readings and Web Sites section of this chapter. At the home page, click on the "Variable List." Click on the choice, "Non-Res Capital Stock/Worker." You will see a list of 53 countries ranked by capital per worker. How does this information relate to the concepts of capital abundant and labor abundant used in the chapter?
6. Consider the following information on the factor endowments of two countries:

Factor Endowments	Country B	Country C
Labor Force	30 million workers	15 million workers
Capital Stock	200,000 machines	400,000 machines

   a. Which country is relatively capital abundant?
   b. Which country is relatively labor abundant?

   c. Assuming that steel is capital intensive relative to textiles, which country will have a comparative advantage in the production of steel? Explain why.
7. Explain how the international movement of goods tends to promote an equalization in factor prices.
8. The factor-proportions theory demonstrates how international trade affects the distribution of income within a country. Explain why this statement is true.
9. Labor unions in developed countries are usually opposed to free trade. Explain why this is true.
10. When trade begins, Country A imports textiles, a labor-intensive good. What does this imply about Country A's factor endowments? What is likely to be the effect of trade on wages in Country A? What group in Country A would you expect to support free trade? Who would you expect to oppose free trade in Country A?
11. How could trade help to reduce poverty in developing countries?
12. Find the Web site for Trade Adjustment Assistance listed in the Suggested Readings and Web Sites section of this chapter. Identify the two criteria that the government uses to determine if a firm and workers have been adversely impacted by imports.
13. What is the Leontief paradox? Describe the factors that have been found to resolve the Leontief paradox?
14. Describe the role of human capital in international trade.
15. Explain how R&D has become a source of comparative advantage.
16. Explain the different effects of trade on the distribution of income when the country has specific factors of production.
17. Describe the economic changes that have occurred in South Korea over the last 50 years. How has trade contributed to these changes?
18. Using the specific-factors model, explain why you might expect capital owners and labor groups arguing against expanding trade in a capital-abundant country.
19. Assume that there are two countries, Argentina and Brazil, each producing wheat and wine from capital and labor. Suppose that Argentina has abundant capital and scarce labor when compared to Brazil; that wheat is capital intensive relative to wine; and that the other factor-proportion assumptions apply.
   a. Using production possibility frontiers, and indifference curves for Argentina and Brazil, illustrate and explain the movement of both countries to the free-trade equilibrium pattern of production, consumption, trade and the gains from trade for the two countries. That is, explain the sequence of the argument as to how mutually beneficial trade between the two countries is possible.
   b. Given the above trade between the two countries, explain the trade effects on product prices, factor prices, and factor incomes. Why do these effects occur?
20. Consider a small economy, initially in autarky, in a world where there are two goods that can be produced, food and cloth. The relative price of food in the country in autarky is lower that the relative price of food on the world market. Suppose that the country now opens to free international trade. Then, for each of the models listed below, answer the following questions, graphically showing and explaining the reasoning behind your answers.
   - How will trade change the fraction of the labor force that is employed in the food and cloth sectors?
   - How will trade change the real wage of labor that was initially employed in the food and cloth sectors?
     a. A Specific Factors Model where all factors are immobile
     b. A Specific Factors Model where capital is immobile between sectors and labor is mobile between sectors
     c. The Factors-Proportions Model (assume here that food is relatively labor intensive when compared to cloth)

SELECTED READINGS AND WEB SITES

Kaitherine Baicker and M. Marit Rehavi, "Policy Watch: Trade Adjustment Assistance," *Journal of Economic Perspectives* 18(2), Spring 2004, pp. 239–56.

The latest update on trade adjustment assistance.

Keith Bradsher, "Wages Are on the Rise in China As Businesses Court the Young," *New York Times,* August 29, 2007, p. A1.

As the Chinese economy becomes more open, there is anecdotal evidence that wages in export-oriented industries are rising rapidly.

Cletus C. Coughlin, "Technology, Globalization, and Economic Policy," *Federal Reserve Bank of Atalanta International Economic Trends,* May 2004, p. 1.

An interesting comparison of the labor market effects of trade and technology.

Caroline L. Freund and Diana Weinhold, "The Effect of the Internet on International Trade," *Journal of International Economics* 62(1), January 2004, pp. 171–89.

A very readable article on how the internet stimulates international trade.

"India's Shining Hopes," *The Economist,* February 31, 2004, pp. S1–S26.

An excellent article on what went wrong with the Indian economy and the potential for future growth.

International Monetary Fund, *Directions of Trade Statistics,* Washington, D.C.: International Monetary Fund, 2003.

An annual publication with trade data on all of the world's countries.

Lori G. Kletzer, *Job Loss from Imports: Measuring the Costs,* Washington, D.C.: Institute for International Economics, 2001.

An excellent source for information on the job losses associated with import competition.

OECD, *OECD Statistics on International Trade in Services, 2000 Edition,* Washington, D.C.: OECD, 2000.

An excellent source of information on international trade in services for all OECD countries.

Penn World Tables (www.pwt.econ.upenn.edu)

The Penn World Tables web site provides information on the openness of economies (X+M/GDP) and contains data on the K/L ratio for many countries.

Eswar Prasad and Thomas Rumbaugh, "Beyond the Great Wall," *Finance and Development,* December 2003, pp. 46–49.

An excellent short article on China's integration into the world economy.

J. David Richardson, "Income Inequality and Trade: How to Think, What to Conclude," *Journal of Economic Perspectives* 9(3), Summer 1995, pp. 33–55.

A detailed summary of the theory and evidence on the issue of trade and income inequality.

"Trade and Wages," *The Economist,* December 7, 1996, p. 74.

An outstanding one page article to give further details on the effects of trade and other factors on wages.

U.S. Department of Commerce (www.doc.gov)

The web site for current data on U.S. imports and exports

U.S. Department of Labor (www.doleta.gov)

The web site for further information on Trade Adjustment Assistance.

World Bank, *World Development Report, 2004,* Washington, D.C.: World Bank 2004.

An annual publication of the World Bank containing very good summaries of international trade in goods and services.

APPENDIX 4.1

Factor-Proportions Theory: An Advanced Analysis

"Nothing adds such weight and dignity to a book as an Appendix."
—Mark Twain

An intermediate analysis of the factor-proportions theory is illustrated here for students who are familiar with advanced microeconomic theory. Assuming that the amounts of capital and labor of a country are fixed, one can determine a country's production possibilities frontier.[21] Figure 4.2 shows the production possibilities frontiers for India and the U.S., assuming that machine production is capital intensive and cloth production is labor intensive, and that

Figure 4.2 Comparative Advantage in the Factor-Proportions Model

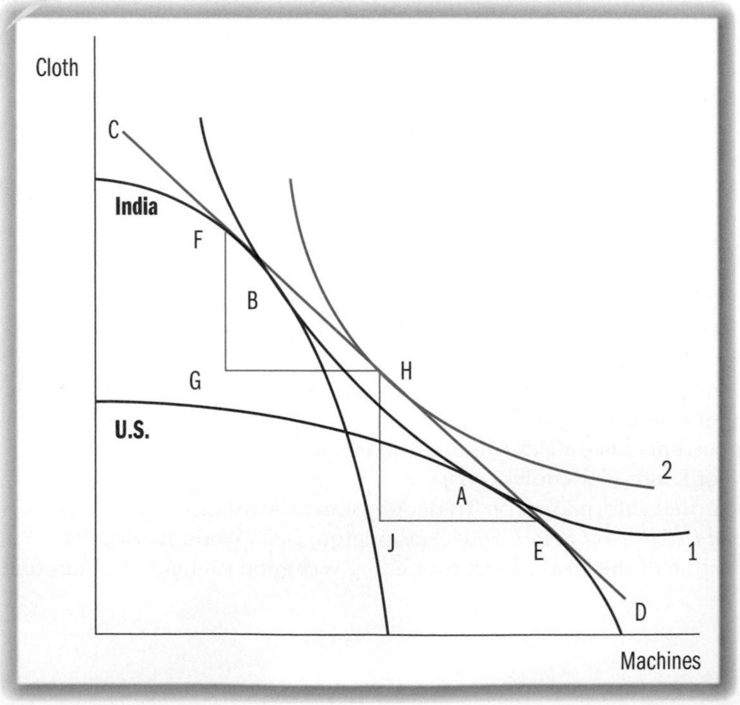

[21]Under the assumption that the amounts of capital and labor of a country are fixed, the Edgeworth-Bowley box diagram can be employed to show a country's contract curve. This curve shows the locus of points of efficient allocation of the two factors of production between the two industries. From the contract curve one can then derive a country's production possibilities frontier. It is left to more advanced international economic texts to illustrate this technical point.

capital is abundant in the U.S. while labor is relatively abundant in India. Since machine production is capital intensive and the U.S. is a capital-abundant country, the U.S. production possibilities frontier will be skewed (biased) toward machine production. This implies that the U.S. will be able to produce a lot of machines relative to cloth. India's production possibilities frontier is skewed (biased) toward cloth production because India is the labor-abundant country and cloth production is labor intensive. As such, India will be able to produce a lot of cloth relative to machines.

In addition, assume that tastes and preferences are identical in both the U.S. and India. This means that the social indifference curves for India and the U.S. are the same and are represented by curve 1 and curve 2 in Figure 4.2. The points where the social indifference curve 1 is tangent to the transformation curves of the U.S. and India indicate the no-trade (autarky) equilibriums for both countries. Without trade, the U.S. would produce and consume at point A on its production possibilities frontier and India would produce and consume at point B on its frontier. The relative price of machines in terms of cloth at these equilibrium points indicates that the U.S. has a comparative advantage in the production of machines and India has a comparative advantage in the production of cloth.

These equilibriums graphically show the factor-proportions theory, given identical tastes and preferences and homogeneous factors of production. Differences in the abundance of a country's resources determine the relative prices of a country's goods and the pattern of trade. Capital is relatively cheap in the capital-abundant country (the U.S.) and labor is relatively cheap in the labor-abundant country (India). The capital-abundant country (the U.S.) exports the capital-intensive good (machines), and the labor-abundant country (India) exports the labor-intensive good (cloth).

As the two countries trade with one another, each country specializes in the production of the good in which it has a comparative advantage. This specialization in production continues until the relative prices of machines in terms of cloth are equalized between countries. This occurs at the common terms of trade line CD. The U.S. moves its production from point A to point E (where the terms of trade line is tangent to the U.S. production possibilities frontier), and India moves its production from point B to point F (where the terms of trade line is tangent to India's production possibilities frontier). With trade, India exports FG amount of cloth for GH amount of machines. India achieves post-trade consumption on indifference curve 2 at point H. On the other hand, the U.S. exports EJ amount of machines for JH amount of cloth. With identical tastes and preferences the U.S. also achieves post-trade consumption on indifference curve 2 at point H. Both countries become better off after specialization and trade.

In Figure 4.3, the upward-sloping curve MN summarizes the basic relationship between relative factor prices and relative good prices, assuming that technology is the same in both countries. This relationship indicates that as labor becomes cheaper relative to capital or as the wage/rent ratio falls, the labor-intensive good (cloth) becomes cheaper relative to the capital-intensive good (machines) or the price ratio of cloth to machines, PC/PM, declines.

Remember that before trade, the U.S. and India produce at production points A and B, respectively, in Figure 4.2. Before trade, different factor endowments force the U.S. and India to operate at different points on the curve MN in Figure 4.3. The U.S. before trade operates at point A′, where the relative price of cloth in terms of machines is greater than in India and the relative price of labor is greater than in India. India before trade operates at point B′, where the relative price of machines is greater than in the U.S. and the relative price of capital is greater than in the U.S. Before trade, cloth is relatively expensive in the U.S. and so is labor, and machines are relatively expensive in India and so is capital.

When trade occurs between the two countries, the U.S. exports machines to India in exchange for cloth. The relative price of cloth in terms of machines falls in the U.S. and rises

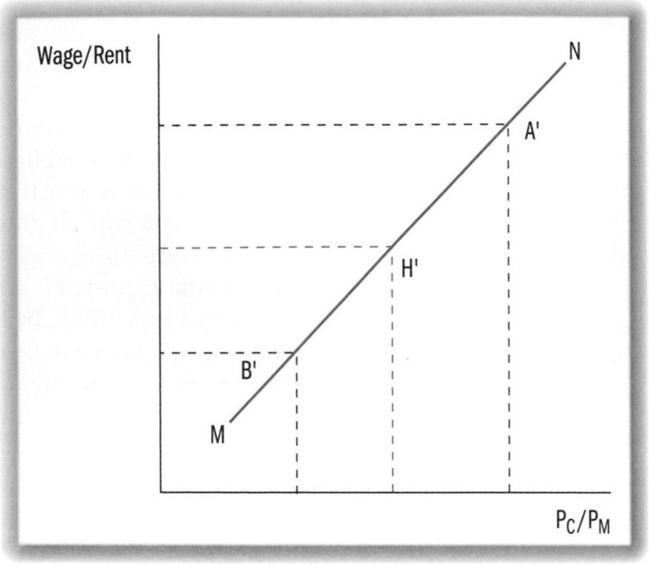

Figure 4.3 Factor-Price Equalization Between the U.S. and India

in India until they are equalized. Both countries consume at point H in Figure 4.2. What does this good-price equalization imply for the factor prices in the U.S. and India? Equalization of the good prices between countries moves the U.S. and India to the same point, H′, on curve MN in Figure 4.3. Accordingly, the same relative price for the factors of production will occur in both countries. As a result, the relative price of labor declines in the U.S. and the relative price of labor increases in India until they are equalized. Under these very strict assumptions, relative factor-price equalization would occur, and the owners of the abundant factor of production would find their incomes rising and the owners of the scarce factor of production would find their incomes falling.

Chapter 5

Intraindustry Trade

"Most students of international trade have long had at least a sneaking suspicion that conventional models of comparative advantage do not give an adequate account of world trade . . . [I]t is hard to reconcile what we see in the manufactures trade with the assumptions of standard trade theory."
—Paul Krugman

INTRODUCTION

In our analysis of international trade you have learned why countries have a comparative advantage in producing different types of goods. The U.S. has a comparative advantage in machines and India in cloth because the two countries are endowed with different factor proportions. Comparative advantage based on the factor-proportions theory is the foundation of our understanding of the gains from specialization and trade. With this foundation we can determine the impact that trade has on factor prices and a country's distribution of income.

intraindustry trade international trade that occurs when a country exports and imports goods within the same industry or product group

However, a large share of international trade is not based on comparative advantage that results from different factor endowments. Countries also trade essentially the same goods with one another. This is known as **intraindustry trade**. For example, Canada and the U.S. have a large trading relationship based on exporting and importing automobiles and automobile parts to one another. In this chapter, we will explain what intraindustry trade is and how it differs from the **interindustry trade** that we have considered in the previous three chapters. As we will see, intraindustry trade is determined by factors that differ from those involved in interindustry trade. As a result, a large part of this chapter is dedicated to explaining why intraindustry trade occurs. Finally, we will examine the welfare effects of intraindustry trade and show that it is as beneficial as interindustry trade.

INTRAINDUSTRY VERSUS INTERINDUSTRY TRADE

In Chapter 4, you learned that comparative advantage is based on different factor endowments among countries. The empirical tests of the factor-proportions theory raised some questions regarding the empirical validity of the theory but also stimulated the development of new trade theories. More specifically, the factor-proportions theory leaves unexplained a large portion of today's international trade. Up to this point, we have assumed that all international trade is interindustry trade, meaning countries trading different goods with one another. The U.S. imports cloth and exports

interindustry trade international trade that occurs when a country either exports or imports goods in different industries

machines, and India imports machines and exports cloth. Because each country has different resource endowments, countries trade very different goods. However, a large portion of international trade consists of countries exporting and importing the same goods—this is intraindustry trade. For example, the U.S. both imports and exports automobiles, beer, and steel. Intraindustry trade is not an isolated event but rather a pervasive part of international trade for many countries.

Unfortunately, intraindustry trade between countries coupled with the factor-proportions theory as the basis of trade poses a logical problem. The premise of the factor-proportions theory is that each country exports goods in which it has a comparative advantage. This comparative advantage reflects a country's ability to produce the good at a lower opportunity cost. Countries have different opportunity costs because they have different resource endowments. As a result, the factor-proportions theory provides a basis for interindustry trade but not for intraindustry trade.

With intraindustry trade, a country simultaneously imports and exports the same good. This implies that a country simultaneously has a comparative advantage *and* a comparative disadvantage in the same good. Using the factor-proportions theory as the sole basis for explaining trade, this does not make any sense. Something else must be determining the basis for intraindustry trade. However, explaining intraindustry trade is more complicated than was the case for interindustry trade. We will discuss several theories, each less general than the factor-proportions theory, and each designed to explain intraindustry trade for narrower groups of goods. In order to meaningfully discuss intraindustry trade, we must first define it more carefully.

DEFINING INTRAINDUSTRY TRADE

intraindustry trade index indicates the amount of intraindustry trade embodied in a country's international trade. The index is expressed as 1 minus the ratio of the absolute value of exports minus imports divided by exports plus imports.

Assessments of the importance of intraindustry trade vary because measuring this form of trade is not nearly as straightforward as measuring interindustry trade. For the latter, we can easily determine what goods are imported and exported. We measure such trade by calculating the value of trade in various goods. For example, the U.S. imports \$100,000 of cloth from India and exports \$100,000 of machines to India.

On the other hand, the problem in measuring intraindustry trade is that it is two-way trade in the same good—a country imports and exports the same good. For example, suppose that the U.S. imports \$50,000 in food from India and exports \$50,000 in food to India. In this case, a numerical measure of the amount of intraindustry trade in the food industry is necessary. The easiest way to measure intraindustry trade is by means of the following formula, called the **intraindustry trade index**.

$$\text{Intraindustry Trade Index} = 1 - \frac{|X - M|}{X + M}$$

For a particular industry or product group, X represents the value of exports and M represents the value of imports. The vertical bars in the numerator of the index denote the absolute value of the difference between the amount exported and the amount imported.[1]

[1]Indexes of intraindustry trade can be traced back to Bela Balassa, "Tariff Reductions and Trade in Manufactures Among the Industrial Countries," *American Economic Review* 56(2), June 1966, pp. 466–73.

In order to evaluate intraindustry trade, we first consider the situation covered in the previous three chapters. For the most part, a country either imported a particular product or exported it. As a starting point, consider the situation that we examined in Chapter 4. Suppose that the U.S. only imports $100,000 of cloth from India, without exporting anything. In this case the second term in the expression reduces to 1 by dividing ($100,000/$100,000), and the whole expressions equals 0. This indicates no intraindustry trade in the cloth industry. If the U.S. only exports $100,000 of machines to India, without importing anything, the second term in the expression reduces to 1 by dividing ($100,000/$100,000), and the whole expression equals 0. This indicates no intraindustry trade in machines. In both cases, all trade is interindustry trade.

However, if the U.S. exports $50,000 in food to India *and* imports $50,000 in food from India, the result is different. The second term in the expression reduces to 0 by dividing (0/$100,000). The whole expression now equals 1. This indicates that 100 percent of the trade in the food industry is intraindustry trade. Using these two extreme cases, the intraindustry trade index ranges from 0 (no intraindustry trade) to 1 (100 percent of the trade is intraindustry trade). The closer the index is to 1, the more intraindustry trade there is relative to interindustry trade. The closer it is to 0, the less intraindustry trade there is relative to interindustry trade in the same good or service.

The major shortcoming of using this index to measure the amount of intraindustry trade is that we get very different values for intraindustry trade depending on how we define the industry or product group. The more broadly we define the industry, the more likely we are to find that a country engages in intraindustry trade. For example,

Intraindustry Trade in U.S. Foreign Trade

The major shortcoming of using the intraindustry trade index to measure the amount of intraindustry trade is that we get very different values for intraindustry trade depending on how we define the industry or product group. The more broadly we define the industry or product group, the more likely we are to find that a country engages in intraindustry trade. In Tables 5.1 and 5.2, we examine how intraindustry trade varies across industries. U.S. merchandise trade can be subdivided by a number of different product categories. Table 5.1 shows the amount of U.S. imports and exports for 16 of these broad product categories. The intraindustry trade index varies from 0.996 in machine tools and 0.988 in medical equipment apparatus to 0.005 in crude oil. These indexes indicate that intraindustry trade for the U.S. is substantial.

Again, however, the level of intraindustry trade is sensitive to how broadly or narrowly an industry is defined. As we move to more narrowly defined product categories, the measured amount of intraindustry trade frequently falls. Intraindustry trade indexes for more narrowly defined product categories are shown in Table 5.2. Even with these more narrowly defined categories, the level of intraindustry trade is quite large in some cases. For other product categories the level is relatively low.

Can you determine what causes the difference? The more closely that trade approximates the factor-proportions theory described in Chapter 4, the less intraindustry trade there is. Products such as clothing and apparel typically now are imported from developing countries. Products such as electrical machinery are more likely to be traded *among* developed countries, where the factor-proportions model works less well.

(*continued*)

Table 5.1 Intraindustry Trade Examples: Selected U.S. Exports and Imports, 2006 ($ Million)

Category	Exports	Imports	Calculated Index of IIT
Telecommunications Equipment	$28,322	$40,250	0.826
Plastic Material	25,125	13,453	0.697
Cookware	872	6,352	0.241
Pulpwood	5,908	3,189	0.701
Finished Metal Shapes	13,941	16,373	0.920
Crude Oil	567	216,627	0.005
Electronic Apparatus	29,804	33,556	0.941
Semiconductors	52,430	27,375	0.686
Machine Tools	9,498	9,572	0.996
Furniture	3,220	24,626	0.231
Excavating Machinery	9,871	10,358	0.976
Farm Machinery	5,312	6,794	0.878
Business Machines & Equipment	2,702	8,717	0.473
Medical Equipment	22,708	23,241	0.988
Computers	11,470	33,771	0.507
Civilian Aircraft	40,832	10,607	0.412

Source: U.S. Bureau of the Census, *International Trade in Goods and Services, FT 900,* Washington, D.C.: U.S. Government Printing Office, 2007.

Table 5.2 Indexes of Intraindustry Trade for the U.S., 2006

Industry	Index of IIT
Inorganic Chemicals	0.925
Generators	0.735
Industrial Machinery	0.941
Organic Chemicals	0.820
Apparel and Textiles	0.181
Toileties & Cosmetics	0.926
TV, VCR, etc.	0.201
Vehicles	0.589
Iron & Steel	0.375
Household Appliances	0.529
Stereo Equipment	0.383

Source: U.S. Bureau of the Census, *International Trade in Goods and Services, FT 900,* Washington, D.C.: U.S. Government Printing Office, 2007.

suppose that the U.S. imports $100,000 worth of men's pants and exports $100,000 worth of women's pants. What is the amount of intraindustry trade? If we define the industry to be the pants industry, the second term in the expression reduces to 0 by dividing (0/$200,000), and the whole expression equals 1. This indicates that 100 percent of the trade in this industry is intraindustry trade. But if we define the men's pants industry and the women's pants industry separately, the intraindustry trade indexes for each industry would equal 0, indicating no intraindustry trade. As a result, measurements of the importance of intraindustry trade can vary depending on how you define the industry or product group. The general principle is that the more broadly one defines the industry, the higher the intraindustry trade index will be. Conversely, the more narrowly the industry is defined, the lower the index will be. Beyond this definitional issue, there is little doubt that intraindustry trade is an important part of international trade overall. In the next section, we consider just how important it is and how fast it is growing.

THE INCREASING IMPORTANCE OF INTRAINDUSTRY TRADE

Now that you know how intraindustry trade is measured, let's examine the data in Table 5.3. The table shows the average share of intraindustry trade in manufactured goods for various countries and groups of countries from 1970 to 2000. Manufactured goods in this case do not include trade in agricultural products, raw materials, and other primary products that can be explained by the factor-proportions theory. The combined intraindustry trade for the 22 developed economies was approximately 62 percent of their total trade in manufactured goods in 2000. Among the six largest economies, the lowest was Japan's 41 percent intraindustry trade as a percentage of its total trade in manufactured goods. France was the highest with intraindustry trade of 76.7 percent of its total trade in manufactured goods. For the U.S., intraindustry trade accounts for 59.6 percent of total manufactured goods trade. Even for the developing countries, the percentage of intraindustry trade ranged from 28.5 percent to nearly 52 percent of total trade.

The third column of Table 5.3 presents the change in the average levels of intraindustry trade in manufactured goods from 1970 to 2000. As the table indicates, intraindustry trade has grown over the period. For most countries or country groups, the average level of intraindustry trade grew by 13.8 to 38.4 percent over the 30 years from 1970 to 2000. For the developed economies, the average levels of intraindustry increased by 26.9 percent over the same time period. For the U.S., intraindustry trade increased by 23.6 percent. This data indicates that intraindustry trade has become a larger component of total manufactured trade among countries.[2] In the next section, we consider the reasons that intraindustry trade occurs.

homogeneous goods one product is identical to every other product produced within an industry

INTRAINDUSTRY TRADE IN HOMOGENEOUS PRODUCTS

So far we have assumed that the goods being traded were **homogeneous goods** (identical goods). For example, cloth and machines produced in India are identical to cloth

[2]The same results seem to hold for broader measures of trade among industrialized countries. Also, intraindustry trade is not a new phenomenon. Even in the 1960s intraindustry trade was already a large percentage of total trade. For more details see H. P. Grubel and P. J. Lloyd, *Intra Industry Trade*, London: MacMillan, 1975.

Table 5.3 Average Shares of Intraindustry Trade in Manufactured Goods by Country Group, 1970 and 2000 (Percentages), and Change in Intraindustry Trade

Economic Group/Country (Number of Countries)	Average Intraindustry Trade Index		Change in Average Intraindustry Trade Index from 1970 to 2000
	1970	2000	
Developed Economies (22)	0.351	0.620	0.269
Six Major Exporters	0.411	0.617	0.206
France	0.519	0.767	0.248
Germany	0.510	0.692	0.182
Italy	0.443	0.581	0.138
Japan	0.177	0.410	0.233
United Kingdom	0.453	0.736	0.283
United States	0.360	0.596	0.236
Other Developed Economies (16)	0.328	0.628	0.300
Developing Countries (25)	0.081	0.465	0.384
Newly Industrialized Economies (6)	0.139	0.512	0.373
Second Generation Newly Industrialized Economies (9)	0.034	0.408	0.374
Other Developing Countries (10)	0.089	0.285	0.196

Developed Economies include France, Germany, Italy, Japan, the United Kingdom, the United States, Australia, Austria, Belgium, Canada, Denmark, Finland, Greece, Ireland, Israel, the Netherlands, New Zealand, Norway, Portugal, Spain, Sweden, and Switzerland. Developing Countries include the Newly Industrialized Economies, the Second Generation Newly Industrialized Economies, and the Other Developing Countries. The Newly Industrialized Economies include Argentina, Brazil, Hong Kong, Mexico, Korea, and Singapore; Second-Generation Newly Industrialized Economies include Colombia, Indonesia, Malaysia, Peru, Philippines, Sri Lanka, Thailand, Tunisia, and Uruguay; and Other Developing Countries, Chile, Dominican Republic, Egypt, Guatemala, India, Pakistan, Panama, Turkey, Venezuela, and Yugoslavia.

Source: Adapted from Helmut Forstner and Robert Ballance, *Competing in A Global Economy: An Empirical Study on Specialization and Trade in Manufactures,* London: Unwin Hyman, 1990 and authors' calculations.

and machines produced in the U.S. The factor-proportions theory explained why there is interindustry trade in homogeneous goods. We now want to explain why there also is intraindustry trade in these goods. Intraindustry trade in homogeneous goods between countries can occur as a result of one (or more) of four possible circumstances.

entrepot trade **goods are imported into a country and sometime later the same goods are exported to another country**

First, consider a bulky material such as cement, for which the cost of transportation is high relative to its value. For example, there are several cement plants located on each side of the U.S. and Canadian border. Cement users in both Canada and the U.S. might find it cheaper to buy from a supplier on the other side of the border—that is, a foreign supplier—if that supplier is closer than the nearest domestic supplier. In such cases, exports and imports would show up as intraindustry trade for both Canada and the U.S.

Second, homogeneous services can be the basis of intraindustry trade due to the joint production of the service or peculiar technical conditions. For example, a country both exports and imports banking services, shipping services, and insurance services because these services are produced jointly with another traded product. Exports of automobiles from Germany to the U.S. must be transported and insured. Frequently a bank is involved in financing goods as they move from the German exporter to the U.S. importer. Similarly, a shipment of computers from the U.S. to Germany must be transported, insured, and financed. The export and import of these goods represent interindustry trade, but the export and import of transportation, insurance, and financing services to move these goods would show up as intraindustry trade in services for both Germany and the U.S.

re-export trade goods are imported into a country and sometime later the same goods are subjected to a small transformation and exported to another country

Third, some countries engage in substantial *entrepot* and *re-export* trade. With **entrepot trade**, goods are imported into a country and later the same good is exported to another country. The country engaging in entrepot trade is providing storage and distribution facilities for an international firm. For example, IBM may ship computers from the U.S. to a warehouse facility in Singapore. With computers stored in a warehouse in Singapore, IBM can supply other countries in the Far East. Imports and exports of computers by Singapore are classified as entrepot trade. With **re-export trade**, goods are imported into a country and then subjected to some small transformation that leaves them essentially unchanged prior to exportation to another country. For example, Singapore, Hong Kong–China, and the Netherlands collect imports and then sort, re-pack, and label these goods for use in the countries to which they will ultimately be shipped. In turn, the receiving countries may re-export the goods to countries within the region. In the case of entrepot and re-export trade, the trading country does not actually produce the good but rather transships it using its own facilities. However, this type of trade is included in a country's imports and exports and increases the reported level of intraindustry trade.

differentiated goods goods competing in the same market or industry that appear different from one another on the basis of their features

Fourth, seasonal or other periodic fluctuations in output or demand can lead to intraindustry trade in homogeneous goods. Examples would include international trade in seasonal fruits and vegetables, electricity, and tourist services.[3]

horizontally differentiated goods similarly priced goods that are perceived to be different in some slight way

INTRAINDUSTRY TRADE IN DIFFERENTIATED PRODUCTS

Most intraindustry trade is trade in differentiated goods between countries. **Differentiated goods** have features that make them appear different from competing goods in the same market or industry. Goods can be differentiated in one of two ways. **Horizontally differentiated goods** are goods that differ among themselves in some slight way, although their prices are similar. For example, candy bars may have the same price but contain very different flavors or ingredients. **Vertically differentiated goods** are those that have very different physical characteristics and different prices.[4] For example, the prices and physical characteristics of new automobiles vary enormously.

vertically differentiated goods features that make one good appear different from competing goods in the same market based on very different product characteristics and very different prices

In addition, most international trade in differentiated goods occurs under conditions of imperfect competition. A critical distinction between perfect and imperfect

[3]Most of our discussion of intraindustry trade will be limited to international trade in goods. However, from this section there is obviously a nontrivial amount of international trade in services. Unfortunately, the study of this type of trade is even less developed than our study of international trade in services in general.

[4]An explanation of intraindustry trade in terms of horizontal product differentiation is contained in Paul R. Krugman, "Scale Economies, Product Differentiation and the Pattern of Trade," *American Economic Review* 70(5), December 1980, pp. 950–59. Vertical product differentiation and intraindustry trade is covered in Kelvin J. Lancaster, "Intra-Industry Trade under Perfect Monopolistic Competition," *Journal of International Economics* 10(2), June 1980, pp. 151–75. An analysis of intraindustry trade between the U.S. and Canada is provided in Keith Head and John Ries, "Increasing Returns Versus National Product Differentiation as an Explanation for the Pattern of U.S.–Canada Trade," *American Economic Review* 91(4), September 2001, pp. 858–76.

perfect competition the market condition where there are many buyers and sellers of a good or factor of production, each buyer and seller having no control over the price of the good or factor

imperfect competition a market structure in which firms have some degree of monopoly power, including monopolistic competition, oligopoly, and monopoly markets

competition has to do with the number of firms in the marketplace. Under **perfect competition**, a firm cannot affect the market price because it is only one of many firms that produce virtually identical goods. Under **imperfect competition**, a firm is able to influence the price of the product by changing the quantity of goods offered for sale. When a firm in an imperfectly competitive market can influence the price of the product, this means that the firm has some degree of market power. Imperfect competition can occur under three different market structures—monopolistic competition, oligopoly, and monopoly.

In an industry characterized by **monopolistic competition**, there are many firms and each one has some market power derived from product differentiation. For example, there may be thirty women's clothing stores in a city. Each store may be able to differentiate itself by offering different locations, atmosphere, style, quality of the material, or quality of the service. However, each firm must compete with other firms offering close substitutes. Coffee bars, banks, radio stations, apparel stores, convenience stores, law firms, and dentists are all examples of monopolistic competition. In an **oligopoly** there are few firms and each firm has some market power that is derived from the small number of firms in the industry and high barriers to entry. Automobiles, tires, detergents, and TVs are all differentiated products sold in oligopoly markets in which one firm's actions may cause a reaction on the part of the other firms. In a **monopoly,** a firm's market power is derived from being the only firm in the industry that produces a unique product with no close substitutes. Electrical power service, water service, sewer service, natural gas service, cable TV service, and drugs under patent are all examples of virtual monopolies.

What follows are three theories that serve to explain intraindustry trade. Economies of scale, the product cycle, and overlapping demands all are used to explain intraindustry trade in differentiated products. However, these theories are not mutually exclusive. This means that you may be able to apply more than one of these explanations of intraindustry trade to a particular product or industry.[5]

Equilibrium with Monopolistic Competition

Firms face a high degree of competition when they produce differentiated products that can be distinguished from one another by the consuming public. If competition is great enough in the marketplace, the free entry of firms into the market will drive profits for all firms to zero. In this case, the demand for the product produced by any one firm is characterized by a downward sloping demand curve. As such, the firm is a price searcher in that if the firm raises or lowers its price while the prices of competing products are constant, its sales would dramatically decrease or increase, respectively.

Figure 5.1 illustrates the equilibrium level output for a single firm in this monopolistically competitive market. The demand curve, D, facing the firm is downward sloping, implying that the marginal revenue curve,

[5]For an extensive discussion of this problem, see H. Peter Gray, "Intra-Industry Trade: An 'Untidy' Phenomenon," *Weltwirtschaftliches Archiv* 124(2), 1988, pp. 212–29.

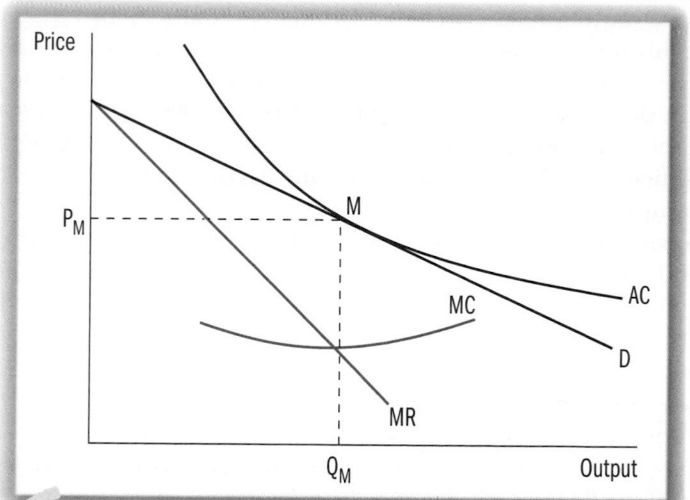

Figure 5.1 Equilibrium with Monopolistic Competition

A firm in a monopolistically competitive market achieves equilibrium by producing output level, Q_M, where marginal revenue equals marginal cost. Free entry into the market by other firms creates a situation where profits for the firm are zero at price, P_M, which is equal to average costs.

MR—meaning the change in total revenue as the firm sells one more unit—lies below the demand curve. With the firm producing in the range of decreasing costs, the average cost curve, AC, is declining. With average costs declining, the marginal cost curve—that is, the change in total costs as the firm produces one more unit—lies below the average cost curve.

The firm in this market seeks to produce an output level at which profits are maximized. This means that the firm will select the output level for which marginal revenue equals marginal cost, Q_M. If new firms are free to enter this market, the resulting maximum profits for any one firm are zero. This is shown in Figure 5.1 by the tangency of the average cost and the demand curves at point M. Output Q_M and price P_M represent the best that the firm can achieve, as any other output level results in losses for the firm.

Notice that in this market, the price of the product is greater than the marginal cost of producing the last unit of output. When consumers pay a price above the marginal cost of producing a product, then society as a whole values additional units of that product more than they value alternative products that can be produced with the resources. In addition, imperfectly competitive firms are characterized by excess capacity, which means that they produce somewhat short of the least unit cost level of output. As a result, an imperfectly competitive market tends to have underutilized plants, and consumers are penalized through having to pay higher than perfectly competitive prices to buy the product.

Economies of Scale

A common explanation of international trade in differentiated products is that this form of trade is a result of economies of scale—EOS—in the product's production. **Economies of scale** means that as the production of a good increases, the cost per unit falls. This phenomenon also is known as **decreasing costs** or increasing returns to scale.

monopolistic competition a market structure in which many firms produce slightly differentiated goods but each firm maintains some control over its own price

oligopoly a market structure in which a few firms produce all of the output for an industry, and each firm has some control over its own price

Figure 5.2 shows the effects of economies of scale on international trade. Assume that a U.S. automobile firm and a German automobile firm have identical cost conditions. This means that the firms have the same long-run average cost curve (AC) for this type of car. As the figure indicates, the economies of scale that both firms face result in decreasing unit costs over the first 250,000 cars produced in a year. Past this point, the unit cost of a car remains constant. Point C in the figure is called the minimum efficient scale of plant size. This means that 250,000 units of output are required to minimize per unit cost.

Now, suppose that the U.S. automobile firm produces and sells 50,000 cars in the U.S. and the German automobile firm produces and sells 50,000 cars in Germany, as indicated by point A. Because cost and price structures are the same, the average cost for both firms are equal at AC_0. At this point, there is no basis for international trade. Now suppose that rising incomes in the U.S. result in a demand for 200,000 cars while German demand remains constant. The larger demand allows the U.S. firm to produce more output and take advantage of the economies of scale. As output increases from 50,000 cars to 200,000 cars, unit costs for the firm change from AC_0 at point A to AC_1 at point B. Because the U.S. firm is subject to economies of scale, its unit costs have declined. Compared to the German firm, the U.S. firm now can produce cars at a lower cost. With free trade, the U.S. would now export cars to Germany. As a result, we can use economies of scale to explain interindustry trade when initial comparative costs between countries are equal. However, this example of economies of scale and international trade does not explain the existence of intraindustry trade in automobiles between Germany and the U.S.

Figure 5.2 Economies of Scale as a Basis for Trade

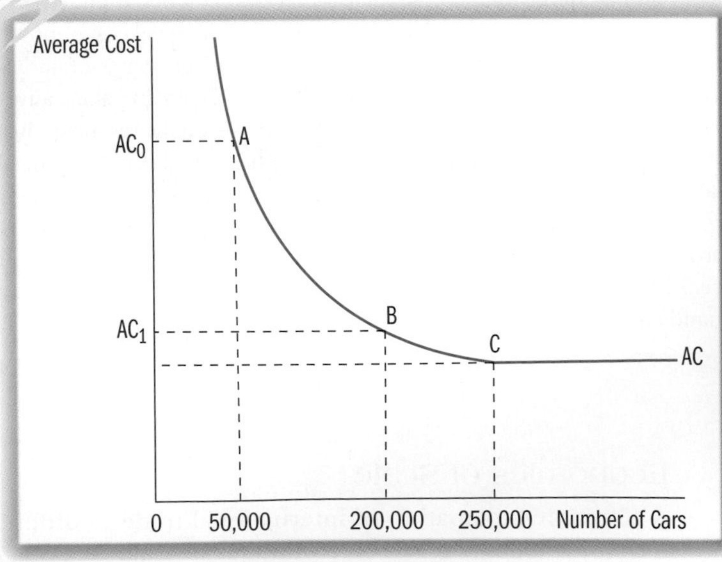

By adding to the size of the domestic market, international trade allows a firm to increase its production. This increase in production can lead to greater efficiency and reductions in unit costs.

monopoly a market structure in which one firm supplies the entire industry for a particular good and maintains considerable control over its own price

To explain intraindustry trade using economies of scale, consider a situation where both a U.S. automobile firm and a German automobile firm each produce full-size cars and subcompact cars. In addition, assume that both firms have identical cost conditions in the production of both types of cars so that they have the same long-run average cost curves (AC). As Figure 5.3 indicates, the economies of scale that both firms face result in decreasing unit costs for both full-size and subcompact cars. Assume that the U.S. automobile firm produces and sells 75,000 full-size cars in the U.S. and the German automobile firm produces and sells 75,000 full-size cars in Germany, as indicated by point A. In addition, assume that the U.S. automobile firm produces and sells 75,000 subcompact cars in the U.S. and the German automobile firm produces and sells 75,000 subcompact cars in Germany, as indicated by point A′. Because cost and price structures are the same, there is no basis for trade.

economies of scale the reduction in average costs that result from increases in the size (scale) of a firm's plant and equipment

Now, assume that both Germany and the U.S. allow free trade in the automobile market. The total demand for full-size and subcompact cars in the combined German and U.S. markets is 150,000 full-size and 150,000 subcompact cars (75,000 cars in Germany and 75,000 cars in the U.S.). This combined larger demand for full-size cars would allow the U.S. firm to produce more full-size cars and thus take advantage of economies of scale. As the U.S. firm increases output from 75,000 to 150,000 full-size cars, unit costs for the firm change from point A to point B. Because the U.S. firm is subject to economies of scale, its unit costs decline from AC_0 to AC_1. Compared to the German firm, the U.S. firm now can produce full-size cars at a lower cost. In addition, the combined larger demand for subcompact cars would allow the German firm to produce more subcompact cars and likewise take advantage of economies of scale. As the German firm increases output from 75,000 to 150,000 subcompact cars, unit costs for the firm fall from AC_0 to AC_1 (point A′ to point B′). Because the German firm is subject to economies of scale, its unit costs decline. Compared to the U.S. firm, the German firm now can produce subcompact cars at a lower cost. With free trade, the U.S. would now export full-size cars to Germany, and Germany would export subcompact cars to the U.S. As a result, economies of scale can be used to explain intraindustry trade when initial comparative costs between countries are equal.

decreasing costs the reduction in average costs that results from increases in a firm's output

While our example shows that intraindustry trade can occur between countries because of economies of scale, the actual specialization pattern is indeterminate. In the example, the U.S. produces full-size cars and Germany produces subcompact cars. As a practical matter, it does not make any difference which firm or which country produces the full-size or subcompact car. In either case, units costs decline and intraindustry trade will occur between the two countries. Very often, the determination of which country produces which type of good is a result of historical accident or is based on initial consumer tastes and preferences within the domestic economy. In our example, we assumed that the initial comparative costs and demand conditions between the two countries were identical. With differentiated products, identical costs and demand conditions are not necessary for mutually beneficial trade to occur from economies of scale.

There are two sources of economies of scale. One source is *internal* economies of scale for the firm. Scale economies are internal when the firm's increase in output causes a decline in its average cost. A firm that has high fixed costs as a percentage of its total costs will have falling average unit costs as output increases. This cost structure generally occurs when firms use a lot of capital to produce a good relative to labor or

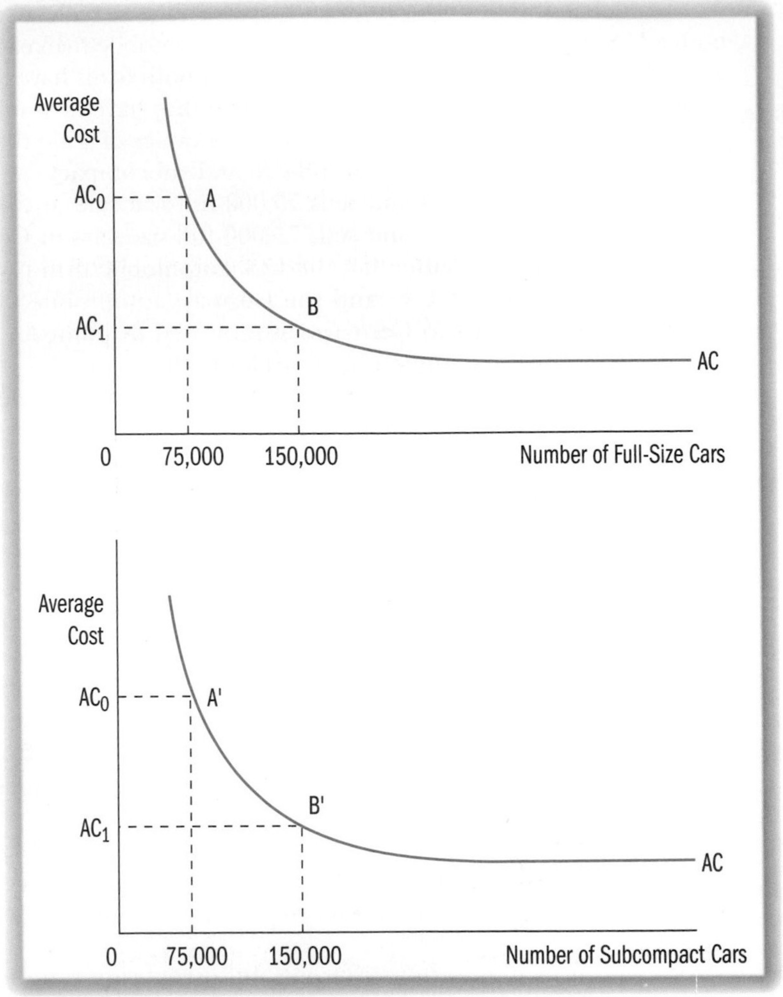

Figure 5.3 **Economies of Scale as the Basis for Intraindustry Trade**

By combining German and U.S. automobile markets, economies of scale allow the German and U.S. automobile firms to increase production. This increase can lead to greater efficiency and reductions in unit costs. As a result, intraindustry trade can occur between the U.S. and Germany in the automobile industry.

other variable factors. For example, most firms in the automobile industry are subject to internal economies of scale. Firms such as General Motors or Toyota produce a large number of automobiles at relatively low prices. Smaller firms such as Porsche or Ferrari have much higher production costs per unit. Similar economies of scale occur in industries that produce intermediate products such as steel and chemicals.

Another source of internal economies of scale occurs in high-technology products where there are high fixed costs associated with research and development (R&D). For example, nearly all of the total costs of computer software are development costs. The variable unit cost of producing and distributing the software may be small relative to the total production costs. In the pharmaceutical industry, the development costs of a new drug are quite high and the variable costs of producing and distributing it are low. In many cases, the first producer to successfully develop the product gains almost all of the market as unit costs decline.[6] The result is that internal economies of scale contribute to the existence of intraindustry trade.

On the other hand, when there are *external* economies of scale a firm's average unit cost falls as the output of the entire industry rises. As the industry expands output, several factors may influence costs for all firms. Because the industry may depend upon the existence of suppliers or a large pool of labor with the skills necessary in that industry, external economies of scale may explain why firms within an industry tend to cluster geographically.[7] Examples include the watch industry in Switzerland, the movie industry in southern California, and the financial services industry in New York City or London. Economies of scale provide a basis for intraindustry trade.[8] In markets characterized by internal or external economies of scale, international trade makes it possible for consumers to enjoy a greater variety of goods while paying a lower price to producers, whose costs are lower because of large-scale production.

product cycle **the process where goods are produced and introduced in a developed country requiring heavy R&D expenses and refinement in production, followed by product stabilization in design and production, and finally complete standardization and production in a developing country**

The Product Cycle

Another explanation for the occurrence of intraindustry trade between countries is the **product cycle**. In this case, changes in technology or a new product design can change the pattern of imports and exports.[9] The basic idea behind the product cycle is that developed countries tend to specialize in producing new goods based on technological innovations, while the developing countries tend to specialize in the production of already well-established goods. The theory of the product cycle is that as each good moves through its product cycle, there will be changes in the geographical location of where and how the good is produced. The product cycle for a typical good is shown in Figure 5.4.

In the first stage of the product cycle, manufacturers of a "new" product need to be near a high-income market in order to receive consumer feedback. Generally, a firm targets its initial small-scale production at a consumer base with substantial income in the firm's domestic market, such as the U.S. At this point, both the product's design and the production process are still evolving. The product may need to be improved and/or the production process may need to be adjusted to determine the most efficient method of production. These design and production enhancements usually require specialized scientific and engineering inputs that are available only in developed countries. During this stage of the product cycle, both consumption and production of a "new" product are likely to occur in a relatively high-income and high-cost-of-production country. Over

[6]For a firm like Boeing Aircraft, unit cost declines as output expands due to large physical capital costs and large R&D costs. This firm has a very high market share worldwide in the production of wide-bodied jet aircraft.

[7]An excellent description of these types of effects is contained in Michael Porter, *The Competitive Advantage of Nations,* New York: Free Press, 1990.

[8]An extensive empirical test of economies of scale and intraindustry trade is contained in James Harrigan, "Scale Economies and the Volume of Trade," *Review of Economics and Statistics* 76(2), May 1994, pp. 321–28.

[9]The original work on the product cycle was published in Raymond Vernon, "International Investment and International Trade in the Product Cycle," *Quarterly Journal of Economics* 50, May 1966, pp. 190–207.

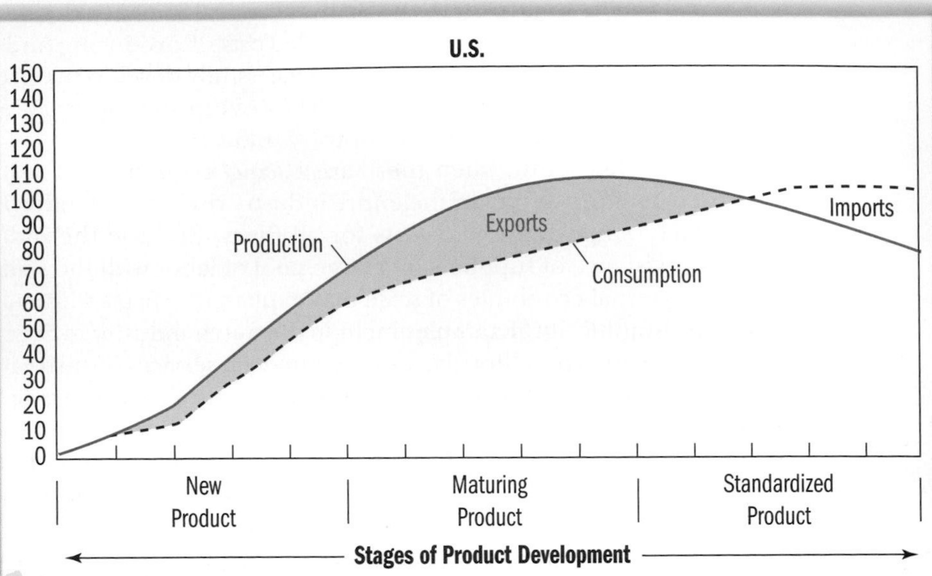

Figure 5.4 The Product Cycle

The Learning Curve

Fixed costs and R&D expenses are not the only reason unit costs decline as output expands. For some industries, another reason why costs decline as output expands is the learning curve. Learning curve analysis relates a firm's average cost of production to the total quantity of the product that is produced over time. Early work on learning curves stressed the gains in labor experience over time. Workers were organized more efficiently over time and both teams and individuals learned the production ropes. Later work extended the application of the learning curve to other costs of the firm. For example, machines could be fine-tuned or the distribution network could be improved.

For a typical learning curve, it is assumed that costs decline by a fixed percentage each time output doubles. For example, unit costs decline by 15 percent with each doubling of output. As a result of learning, unit costs decline and a firm's cost curve would look like the average cost curve in Figure 5.2. In a study by Lieberman on the chemical industry, it was estimated that on average each doubling of plant scale over time was accompanied by an 11 percent reduction of unit costs.[10] In a study of the semiconductor industry, Irwin and Klenow found an average learning rate of 20 percent for successive generations of dynamic random-access memory chips (DRAMs).[11] These types of results have been

[10]See M. B. Lieberman, "The Learning Curve and Pricing in the Chemical Processing Industry," *Rand Journal of Economics*, Summer 1984, pp. 213–28.
[11]See D. Irwin and P. Klenow, "Learning-by-Doing Spillovers in the Semiconductor Industry," *Journal of Political Economy* 102(6), 1994, pp. 1200–27.

found in other industries, such as petrochemicals and electric utilities, as well.

Learning curves have some important implications for international trade. The country that produces the greatest quantity of the products has the lowest costs, not because of different resource endowments, but because it has learned to use its labor and/or capital more efficiently. In this case, comparative advantage is something that is created. As such, it is not low costs that cause a country to specialize and trade; rather, it is specialization that causes the low unit costs.

time, the firm will perfect the product and the production process. At this point the product's consumption and production increases. In addition to serving the domestic market, the firm will begin to export the new product to other countries where there is similar demand from high-income consumers.

In the second stage of the product cycle, the product matures as it becomes more standardized in terms of size, features, and the production process. If foreign demand is sufficiently large, the firm may find it more profitable to produce the product in those foreign markets instead of exporting it. In some circumstances, the country where the product was originally developed may begin importing the product from other high-income countries where production costs are less.

In the third stage of the product cycle, the product and the production process have become so standardized that profit maximization leads firms to produce in the lowest-cost production site. At this point, the standardized production processes can be moved to developing countries where using semi-skilled labor in assembly-type operations keeps production costs low. The innovating country now becomes an importer of the product.[12] In the innovating country, attention moves on to a new product at the early stage of its product cycle. Examples of products that have experienced a typical product cycle include radios, TVs, VCRs, and semiconductor chips. The product may have started as a "new" and somewhat unique product in the first phase. In the last stage, the product has become sufficiently standardized so that factor abundance and low-production costs determine its pattern of production and trade.

The concept of the product cycle can be used to explain some of the intraindustry trade both among developed countries and between developing and developed countries. For example, a country may be exporting a new product and at the same time importing a similar product from another country. The U.S. may be exporting a new sports car to Japan and simultaneously importing another variety of sports car from Japan. With the constant flood of "new" products being developed in developed countries, intraindustry trade occurs among high-income countries as they exchange these new products with one another. The model also implies that high-income countries will be exporting "newer" versions of the product to developing countries and importing "older" versions of the product from these countries.

---

[12]The original article by Vernon cited above is quite readable for those with a greater interest in the subject. Some writers use a five-stage process to cover this in more detail. For an excellent discussion of this latter scheme, see Beth V. Yarbrough and Robert M. Yarbrough, *The World Economy,* 3rd edition, New York: Dryden Press, 1994.

Overlapping Demands

The final explanation of intraindustry trade focuses on the importance of demand characteristics in various countries. In the early 1960s, the economist Staffan Linder used the concept of overlapping demands to suggest that similarities between countries could be the basis of trade, even though factor prices were the same in both countries.[13]

overlapping demands **trade in manufactured goods is likely to be greatest among countries with similar tastes and income levels**

According to the **overlapping demands** hypothesis, trade in manufactured goods is likely to be greatest among countries with similar tastes and income levels. Linder argues that firms within a country are primarily oriented toward producing a specific variety of a good for which there is a large home market. As such, a country's tastes and preferences determine the specific variety of product that its firms will produce and that they could then export to foreign consumers. The most promising foreign markets for these exports will be found in countries with tastes and income levels similar to those of the country in which the products are produced. Each country will produce products that primarily serve its home market, but part of the output will be exported to other countries where there is a receptive market.

For example, a U.S. automobile firm will produce an automobile that satisfies the tastes and preferences of most U.S. consumers. However, there will be a small number of U.S. consumers who prefer something other than the domestic version. In Sweden and Germany, automobile producers will produce an automobile that satisfies the tastes and preferences of most Swedish and German consumers, respectively. However, it is likely that in both countries there will be a small number of consumers who prefer something other than the Swedish or German versions. In all three countries, there are some consumers who are not able to purchase the variety of automobile that they prefer. The hypothesis of overlapping demands indicates that in such a case, U.S. producers could produce for their domestic market and export automobiles to Swedish and German consumers who prefer the U.S. automobile. At the same time, Swedish and German producers could export automobiles to U.S. consumers who prefer German and Swedish automobiles. These sorts of overlapping demands can lead to intraindustry trade.

Linder states that within a country, consumers' average income level will determine their general tastes and preferences. Countries with low average incomes will demand lower-quality goods, and countries with high average incomes will demand higher-quality goods. As such, high-income countries are more likely to trade with other high-income countries because there is a greater probability of overlapping demands. For the same reason, low-income countries are more likely to trade with other low-income countries.

Overlapping demands implies that intraindustry trade would be more intense among countries with similar incomes.[14] In general, the theory of overlapping demands can explain the large and growing amount of trade in similar but differentiated goods. These conclusions concerning trade patterns between countries are interesting

[13]Staffan B. Linder, *An Essay on Trade and Transformation,* New York: Wiley, 1961. An empirical test of the hypothesis is contained in Joseph F. Francois and Seth Kaplan, "Aggregate Demand Shifts, Income Distribution, and the Linder Hypothesis," *Review of Economics and Statistics* 78(2), May 1996, pp. 244–50.

[14]See Rudolf Loertscher and Frank Wolter, "Determinants of Intra-Industry Trade: Among Countries and Across Industries," *Weltwirtschaftliches Archiv* 116(2), 1980, pp. 280–93.

The U.S. Automobile Market

According to the overlapping demand hypothesis, trade in manufactured goods as opposed to agricultural, raw material, and primary products is likely to be greatest among countries with similar tastes and income levels. Linder argues that firms within a country are primarily oriented toward producing a specific variety of a good for which there is a large home market.

In this chapter we used the U.S. automobile market as an example of overlapping demands. Table 5.4

Table 5.4 Automobile Manufactures and Products Sold in the U.S.

Automobile Manufacture	Number of Products Sold in the U.S.
ACURA	5
ASTON MARTIN	3
AUDI	9
BENTLEY	5
BMW	11
BUICK	5
CADILLAC	11
CHEVROLET	25
CHRYSLER	7
DODGE	13
FERRARI	1
FORD	21
GMC	14
HONDA	9
HUMMER	3
HYUNDAI	9
INFINITI	6
ISUZU	2
JAGUAR	4
JEEP	6
KIA	8
LAMBORGHINI	2
LAND ROVER	3
LEXUS	12
LINCOLN	6
MASERATI	1
MAYBACH	2
MAZDA	10
MERCEDES-BENZ	13
MERCURY	7

(continued)

Table 5.4 (Continued)

Automobile Manufacture	Number of Products Sold in the U.S.
MINI	1
MITSUBISHI	6
NISSAN	13
PANOZ	1
PONTIAC	6
PORSCHE	3
ROLLS-ROYCE	1
SAAB	3
SATURN	6
SCION	1
SUBARU	5
SUZUKI	6
TOYOTA	18
VOLKSWAGEN	7
VOLVO	8

illustrates the number of different automobile firms and the number of different types of automobiles for sale in the U.S. automobile market.[15] The list includes 46 manufacturers with 365 different car, van, sport utility vehicles, and trucks available within the U.S.

Notice that overlapping demands have resulted in intraindustry trade in the U.S. automobile market.

[15]The data on automobile firms and models for Table 5.4 was obtained from the internet site www.edmunds.com.

because they are not based on or predicted by the factor-proportions theory. Everything else being equal, the theory suggests that trade will be more intense between countries that have similar tastes, preferences, and incomes.

The discussion of intraindustry trade and overlapping demands indicates that countries with similar incomes would tend to have a higher percentage of their trade as intraindustry trade. Going back to Table 5.2, it would appear that in general this is the case. However, it was noted in the first part of the chapter that developing countries also engage in a substantial amount of intraindustry trade. Some of this trade can be explained as intraindustry trade with other developing countries at a similar level of income. On the other hand, it has been observed that there is a growing amount of intraindustry trade between developed and developing countries. At first glance, this would seem to be a bit odd. The explanation lies in linking vertical product differentiation with overlapping demands. In a developing country, there may be a substantial number of consumers with incomes similar to those that prevail in developed countries. These consumers may be poorly served by the domestic producers, who are producing for the majority taste and preference within the country. Satisfying the needs of these high-income consumers may be most profitably accomplished by importing higher-quality versions of products from developed countries. The reverse is true for the developed countries. In these countries there may be less affluent consumers who desire cheaper varieties of a product. These consumers may not be well served by the domestic producers if the market is too small. The solution may be to import lower-priced versions of the product designed for consumers in low-income countries. The existence of vertical product differentiation and overlapping demands between different groups of consumers in different types of countries helps to explain the growing amount of intraindustry trade between developed and developing countries.[16]

THE WELFARE IMPLICATIONS OF INTRAINDUSTRY TRADE

Recall that interindustry trade, as covered in earlier chapters, was shown to increase world economic output and welfare. Although intraindustry trade results from different associated processes, welfare gains also occur with it. Figure 5.5 shows the different types of intraindustry trade and their respective associated processes, as we discussed earlier. As the figure indicates, intraindustry trade occurs in homogeneous products and in horizontally or vertically differentiated products.

For intraindustry trade in homogeneous products, the welfare gains for a country are similar to those under interindustry trade. These gains occur as the traded goods are provided based on lower opportunity costs in the form of lower transportation, insurance, or financing costs or on the provision of low-cost seasonal products.

In the case of horizontally or vertically differentiated products, welfare gains occur but there are additional factors to consider. For one, product differentiation enhances consumers' choices, but the products are produced in a market structure of imperfect competition. In imperfectly competitive markets, the market price of the product is greater than the marginal cost of producing the last unit of output. In this case, consumers value additional units of the product more than they value alternative products that could be produced with the resources. Further, imperfectly competitive firms are characterized by excess capacity. This means that production falls somewhat short of the most efficient or least unit cost level of output because of economies of scale. As a result, an imperfectly competitive market tends to have underutilized plants, and consumers are penalized through having to pay higher than perfectly competitive prices. The introduction of imports into these markets would tend to lower prices. This, in turn, helps to reduce the social costs associated with markets that are imperfectly competitive.

Secondly, intraindustry trade in differentiated products improves the general welfare of a country to the extent that domestic consumers have more types of the product available from which to choose. Additional types of the same differentiated product increases competition and generally should result in an improvement in the average quality of the products. For example, without imports of automobiles from Japan and other countries U.S.-made automobiles would probably be of lower quality. Third, intraindustry trade is effective at reducing the monopoly power of domestic firms. More

[16]For a discussion of this type of intra-industry trade and an empirical example, see Robert H. Ballance, Helmut Forstner, and W. Charles Sawyer, "An Empirical Examination of the Role of Vertical Product Differentiation in North-South Trade," *Weltwirtschaftliches Archiv* 128(2), 1992, pp. 330–38.

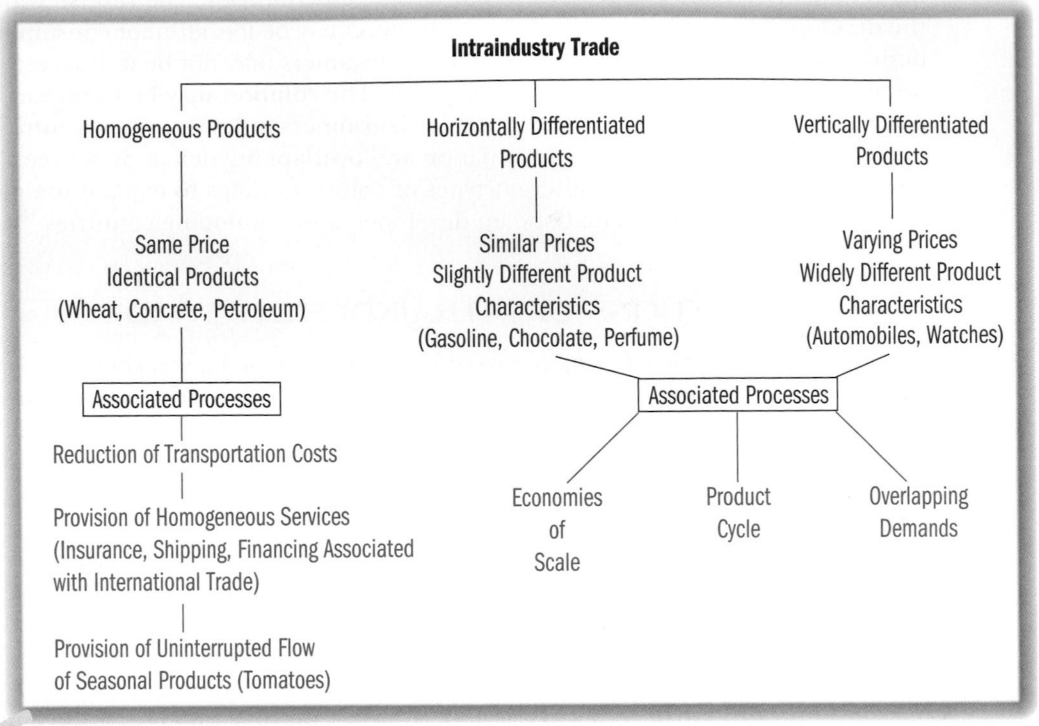

Figure 5.5 Types of Intraindustry Trade and Associated Processes

open trade among countries has reduced potential antitrust problems—the problems associated with monopoly power—and even eliminated them in a number of industries, such as the U.S. automobile and steel industries. Fourth, intraindustry trade makes it possible for companies to produce at higher levels of output. This increased output means that firms can reduce costs due to economies of scale. As a result, prices decline not only in the export market but also in the domestic market.

Fifth, when discussing interindustry trade, we described the adjustment costs of an economy moving toward free trade. For example, when factors of production used to produce cloth are being shifted to and adapted to the production of machines, the shift may be difficult or impossible in the short run. In the case of intraindustry trade, this does not necessarily happen. Recall that intraindustry trade is more intense among countries with similar incomes and factor endowments. Therefore, it is easier for resources to reallocate among industries participating in intraindustry trade because those industries have similar factor intensities. Both the contracting industry and the expanding industry are either capital intensive or skilled labor intensive.[17] In summary, the gains from intraindustry trade may be larger and the adjustment costs lower than in the case of interindustry trade.

[17]See H. Peter Gray, *Free Trade or Protection: A Pragmatic Analysis,* London: Palgrave, 1985.

Trade and Product Variety

In this chapter, we have demonstrated that international trade improves the welfare of countries that trade. In our examples, the U.S. and India improve their welfare by gaining the ability to obtain goods at a lower price than they could have if the goods had been produced domestically. In the chapter, we referred to this as the static gains from trade. In the final section of the chapter, we discussed the dynamic gains from trade. These gains are other gains from trade that are more difficult to capture in standard economic models. Everyone recognizes the importance of these sorts of gains from trade. The problem is that in many cases they are difficult to quantify. Economists being economists, this is an annoying situation. However, in some cases some progress is being made in putting numerical values on these gains.

An example of this is international trade and the variety of goods available to domestic consumers. As we will see in later chapters, international trade is

Table 5.5 The Impact of Variety

	Average Number of Suppliers per Imported Good		
Country	**1972**	**1997**	**Percent Change**
U.S.	31.4	42.7	36.1
Germany	29.1	38.2	31.2
Japan	20.6	28.8	39.9
U.K.	30.4	38.4	26.5
France	26.3	35.2	34.2
Italy	23.9	33.5	40.0
Canada	17.8	25.2	41.3
Netherlands	23.6	31.5	33.1
China	4.9	20.7	326.1
Belgium	20.8	27.6	32.8
Hong Kong	15.0	23.7	57.9
Spain	16.6	21.8	31.6
Mexico	9.1	17.3	89.3
Singapore	14.7	23.2	57.6
Former Soviet Union	8.7	27.3	213.7
South Korea	5.9	16.8	185.3
Switzerland	18.7	24.2	28.9
Taiwan	7.7	17.4	126.9
Sweden	18.8	22.8	21.5
Brazil	11.5	19.7	70.7

Source: Adapted from Christian Broda and David E. Weinstein, "Variety Growth and World Welfare," *American Economic Review* 94(2), May 2004, pp. 139–44.

(*continued*)

riddled with various barriers to trade. However, over the last 50 years there has been a substantial amount of progress in the world economy in reducing these trade barriers. As trade barriers have fallen, there has been a substantial expansion in the number of countries that individual countries trade with. A recent paper by Broda and Weinstein (2004) illustrates this trend. Table 5.5 reproduces the main result of their study. The 20 countries in the table are the world's largest importers of goods. The data shows that for each country, the average number of countries that it imports from since 1972 has increased substantially. The average increase in the number of supplying countries is 49 percent. In these researchers' study, the number of countries from which an individual country imports is taken to be a measure of the variety of imports in a particular product category. This would yield a rather conservative measure of this phenomenon.

These results imply two things: one obvious and one less so. Having choices in one's consumption has value to most consumers. As you learned in Principles of Economics, this is almost entirely the reason why many markets are characterized by monopolistic competition. For most of us, our welfare would be diminished considerably if the wide variety of goods from which we can choose were to be curtailed. For many of us, considering life without imported goods is not a pleasant thought. However, there is another benefit of variety that is less obvious but that can, to some extent, be quantified. A larger variety of imported goods tends to put downward pressure on the price of other imports. In other words, the more varieties there are of a product that are imported, the lower will be the price—all else being equal. This makes sense because the presence of a larger number of suppliers will usually cause lower prices in any market. These effects are subtle but noticeable. Broda and Weinstein calculate that the increase in the variety of imports has been lowering the price of imports by about 1.2 percent per year faster than would otherwise be the case. Given that imports in the U.S. are a rising percentage of GDP, these lower prices are having a noticeable effect on overall welfare. Overall, Broda and Weinstein estimate that the rising number of varieties available has increased consumer welfare in the U.S. by about 3 percent. In terms of nominal GDP, this is about $420 billion.

SUMMARY

1. Besides interindustry trade, the exchange of goods between countries includes intraindustry trade. Intraindustry trade is two-way trade in similar products. The common measure of intraindustry trade is the intraindustry trade index.
2. Intraindustry trade is a large and growing portion of international trade. For the U.S., approximately 60 percent of manufacturing trade is intraindustry trade.
3. Intraindustry trade can occur in homogeneous products. This type of trade can occur in the case of low value/weight ratio products; certain types of services; entrepot and reexport trade; or trade in seasonal products.
4. Differentiated goods are usually described using the market structures of imperfect competition. The market structures of imperfect competition are monopolistic competition, oligopoly, and monopoly.
5. Products may be horizontally differentiated—meaning that the prices of various types of goods are similar but the goods differ in their physical characteristics. Products also may be vertically differentiated—meaning that the good's physical characteristics and prices are different.
6. Intraindustry trade widens the size of the domestic market, permitting firms to take advantage of economies of scale. Economies of scale translate into lower production costs and, therefore, lower product prices—which improves a firm's or country's comparative advantage.

7. There are internal and external economies of scale. Economies of scale create an incentive for firms to specialize in production, which stimulates intraindustry trade.
8. There are three product stages in the product cycle theory: new product, maturing product, and standardized product. The product cycle theory explains the speed of dissemination of innovation on the basis of changing input requirements over a new product's life cycle and countries' factor endowments.
9. Linder asserted that trade in manufactured goods is best explained by overlapping demand structures between countries. A country will tend to export those manufactured goods to countries with similar per capita incomes for which there is a broad domestic market.
10. Intraindustry trade in differentiated products has two important implications for the gains from trade: (1) consumers gain from having a greater variety of goods to choose from, and (2) unit costs and prices decline because the commodities are produced under increasing returns.

KEY CONCEPTS AND TERMS

- intraindustry trade p. 93
- interindustry trade p. 94
- intraindustry trade index p. 94
- homogeneous goods p. 97
- entrepot trade p. 98
- re-export trade p. 99
- differentiated goods p. 99
- horizontally differentiated goods p. 99
- vertically differentiated goods p. 99
- perfect competition p. 100
- imperfect competition p. 100
- monopolistic competition p. 102
- oligopoly p. 102
- monopoly p. 103
- economies of scale p. 103
- decreasing costs p. 103
- product cycle p. 105
- overlapping demands p. 108

PROBLEMS AND QUESTIONS FOR REVIEW

1. Distinguish between interindustry and intraindustry trade.
2. How is intraindustry trade measured?
3. Using the formula for the intraindustry trade index, explain why the index can take on a value of 0 for industries with no intraindustry trade and a value of 1 for industries with all of their trade being intraindustry trade.
4. If a country exports $15 million in computers per year and imports $25 million in computers per year, what is the country's intraindustry trade index for computers?
5. What is the extent of intraindustry trade in the U.S. and the world economy?
6. Describe the growth of intraindustry trade in the world economy from 1970 to 2000.
7. What are the major determinants of intraindustry trade in homogeneous products?
8. What is the difference between entrepot and re-export trade?
9. What is the difference between horizontal and vertical product differentiation? Give examples of each.
10. Describe the various types of imperfect competition.
11. What is meant by economies of scale? Explain the difference between internal and external economies of scale.
12. How can economies of scale be a basis for trade?
13. State the product cycle theory of trade and identify the various stages of production.
14. What goods might be examples of products that are currently going through or have gone through the various stages of the product cycle?
15. How can the product cycle generate intraindustry trade?
16. Explain how overlapping demands between countries could lead to trade.

17. What would Linder's theory suggest about the future prospects of developing countries in exporting goods to developed countries?
18. Why is an increase in the number of varieties of a good regarded as a gain from trade?
19. Why would the adjustments to intraindustry trade perhaps be easier than the adjustments to interindustry trade?

SUGGESTED READINGS AND WEB SITES

Don P. Clark and Denise L. Stanley, "Determinants of Intraindustry Trade between the United States and Industrial Nations," *International Trade Journal* 17(3), Autumn 2003, pp. 1–17.

A recent empirical look at U.S. intraindustry trade with other OECD countries.

H. Peter Gray, "Intraindustry Trade: An 'Untidy' Phenomenon," *Weltwirtschaftliches Archiv* 124(2), 1988, pp. 212–29.

A good discussion of the problems associated with analyzing IIT.

David Greenaway and Johan Torstensson, "Back to the Future: Taking Stock on Intraindustry Trade," *Weltwirtschaftliches Archiv* 133(2), 1997, pp. 249–69.

An overall survey of the state of knowledge on intraindustry trade.

Keith Head and John Ries, "Increasing Returns Versus National Product Differentiation as an Explanation for the Pattern of U.S.-Canada Trade," *American Economic Review* 91(4), September 2001, pp. 858–76.

An excellent empirical article showing the effects of both increasing returns to scale and product differentiation on intraindustry trade between Canada and the U.S.

Farhang Niroomand, "Inter- versus Intraindustry Trade: A Note on U.S. Trends, 1963–1980," *Weltwirtschaftliches Archiv* 124(2), 1988, pp. 337–40.

An overall empirical examination of intraindustry trade for the U.S.

Michael Porter, *The Competitive Advantage of Nations,* New York: Free Press, 1990.

A classic work on a number of often neglected aspects of international trade.

Roy J. Ruffin, "The Nature and Significance of Intra-Industry Trade," *Federal Reserve Bank of Dallas Economic Review,* 4th Quarter 1999, pp. 2–9.

A good general reference on intraindustry trade that also contains recent data on intraindustry trade for the U.S.

Joe A. Stone and Hyun-Hoon Lee, "Determinants of Intraindustry Trade: A Longitudinal, Cross-country Analysis," *Weltwirtschaftliches Archiv* 131(1), 1995, pp. 67–85.

An extensive test of the determinants of intraindustry trade for a large sample of countries.

Chapter 6

International Factor Movements

"Commodity movements are at least to some extent a substitute for factor movements. The absence of trade impediments implies commodity price equalization and, even when factors are immobile, a tendency toward factor-price equalization. It is equally true that perfect mobility of factors results in factor-price equalization and, even when commodity movements cannot take place, in a tendency toward commodity-price equalization."
—ROBERT MUNDELL

INTRODUCTION

So far, we have assumed that factors of production like labor and capital are mobile within a country. This means that labor and capital could move freely among a country's industries as the industries expanded or contracted. This movement of labor and capital occurs automatically in a country, as the resources seek their best rate of return. We also assumed that the factors of production are immobile between countries. This assumption practically defines international trade theory. If both labor and capital could easily migrate across national borders, the study of international economics would be indistinguishable from the study of the economics of a country's regions.

capital flows the flow of foreign assets into a country or the flow of a country's assets abroad

However, international economics differs from regional economics. A country's laws and regulations concerning the buying and selling of foreign currency may restrict the movement of portfolio capital. National laws restricting foreign ownership may restrict the ability of foreign firms to invest in plant and equipment in a particular country. Such restrictions can be important because they may impede **capital flows** that would naturally seek out the highest rate of return. The movement of labor from one country to another, or **immigration**, is a much debated political issue. In this chapter, you will learn that there are valid economic reasons why the immigration of labor is so contentious.

immigration the movement of labor from one country to another

We begin this chapter by discussing international trade and the mobility of factors of production. Then we examine the international mobility of capital and labor. Since multinational corporations (MNCs) are responsible for some of the movements of labor and capital, the final part of this chapter discusses the nature of MNCs and how they are regulated.

INTERNATIONAL TRADE VERSUS INTERNATIONAL FACTOR MOVEMENTS

Interindustry trade as viewed from the perspective of factor-proportions theory occurs between countries because the factors of production are not mobile from one country to another. Let us see what would occur if the factors of production were mobile between the U.S. and India. Assume that the U.S. is the capital-abundant country and India is the labor-abundant country. As a result, labor earns a higher wage in the U.S. than it does in India. If labor is mobile between the two countries, some of India's labor would start migrating to the U.S. in search of this higher rate of return. How would this migration affect the labor markets in both countries? Wages would start to fall in the U.S. as the arrival of immigrant labor from India augments the supply of labor in the U.S. Likewise as the supply of labor falls in India, wages would start to rise in India. The international movement of labor would continue until the return to labor in the two countries equalized. A similar process would occur with respect to capital. Capital would migrate from the U.S. to India in search of a higher rate of return. The migration of capital to India would continue until the rates of return to capital are the same in both countries.

Consider how the international movement of factors of production compares with the movements of the factors of production from one region to another within a large country such as the U.S. Given a national capital market, capital is very mobile within the U.S. economy. Small differentials in the rate of return to capital among the different regions of the U.S. will quickly induce a substantial capital flow to the region where it can earn the highest return. As a result, the return to capital is equalized within the U.S. Although labor's mobility is not as fast or fluid, high real wages in a region within the U.S. will typically bring about an influx of workers from other regions of the country where real wages are lower. Although real wage differences exist between the various regions, the movements of labor within the country will tend to reduce these differences over time.

The movements of the factors of production from one region of a country to another are similar to the factor-price equalization that we discussed in Chapter 4. As our example illustrates, factor prices tend toward equality either through trade or through the movement of the factors of production. To a large extent, this means that international trade is a substitute for the movement of the factors of production between countries.[1] In many cases where the mobility of the factors of production is blocked, international trade is the next best option. However, international trade is considered a second-best alternative because, as we will see, moving the factors of production between countries maximizes world output. For example, if capital and labor could both earn a higher rate of return by moving to another country, blocking their movement would mean that those resources will be used in a less productive way. This implies that there is an opportunity cost associated with making resources immobile between countries. The result is that making resources immobile reduces the potential output of the world economy.

[1]The initial statement of this principle can be found in Robert A. Mundell, "International Trade and Factor Mobility," *American Economic Review* 47(3), 1957, pp. 321–35.

Here is a simple way to examine the effects of resource immobility. What if the U.S. did not exist as a whole but rather consisted of fifty independent countries occupying the areas of today's states? Assume that there are no trade barriers among these 50 fifty countries but, at the same time, labor and capital cannot move across their borders. In other words, labor cannot move from Kansas to California or from Arkansas to Texas, and capital cannot move from New York City to Dallas or from San Francisco to Seattle. If this situation held for the past 230 years, from 1776 to 2006, do you think that the collective output of the 50 countries today would equal the output of the current country? The answer is no; over time, the immobility of resources between the 50 countries would have created less output than would have been the case had factor mobility been permitted. In the sections that follow, we cover the international movement of capital and labor, beginning with the former.

INTERNATIONAL MOVEMENTS OF CAPITAL

The foreign exchange market exchanges approximately $2 trillion per day in foreign currencies. While the volume of world trade in goods and services is large, the volume of world trade for a year is less than one week's worth of foreign exchange trading. Thus, there must be some other trading activities comprising the difference. In many cases, the buying and selling of foreign exchange occurs because of the international movements of financial capital. International movements of financial capital—portfolio capital—can occur for a variety of reasons, and these reasons are described in Chapter 13.

The movements of capital that we describe in this chapter are called foreign direct investment. Foreign direct investment (FDI) represents real investments in land, nonresidential investment (buildings and other structures), and equipment and software. The investor is not furnishing financial capital but rather is directly investing in the firm's plant and equipment and actively managing the investment. This investment usually is in the form of a domestic corporation opening a foreign subsidiary or buying control of an existing foreign firm. We can measure the impact of flows of foreign direct investment in a number of ways. Table 6.1 shows various values associated with FDI for 1982, 1990, 2002, and 2005. The last four columns of the table show the growth rates of each of the variables for each of the last four years. FDI in 2005 was approximately $916 billion. As the last two columns indicate, the growth of FDI in

Table 6.1 Selected Indicators of FDI and International Production, 1982–2005

	Value at Current Prices (Billion dollars)				*Annual Growth Rate (per cent)*			
Item	1982	1990	2002	2005	2002	2003	2004	2005
FDI Inflows	$59	$202	$651	$916	–25.8%	–9.7%	27.4%	28.9%
FDI Inward Stock	647	1,789	7,123	10,130	9.7	20.6	16.1	6.1

Source: Adapted from United Nations Conference on Trade and Development, *World Investment Report, 2003 and 2006,* New York: United Nations, 2003 and 2006.

Table 6.2 Regional Distribution of FDI Flows 2003–2005

Region/Country	FDI Inflows	FDI Outflows
Developed Countries	**59.4%**	**85.8%**
European Union	40.7	54.6
Japan	0.8	4.9
United States	12.6	15.7
Other Developed Countries	5.3	10.6
Developing Countries	**35.9**	**12.3**
Africa	3.0	0.2
Latin America & the Caribbean	11.5	3.5
Asia & Oceania	21.4	8.6
Central & Eastern Europe	**4.7**	**1.8**
World	100.0	100.0

Source: Adapted from United Nations Conference on Trade and Development, *World Investment Report, 2003,* New York: United Nations, 2006.

the world economy declined in 2002 and 2003 before increasing at rates over 25 percent per year for 2004 and 2005. Over the 23-year period shown in the table, the cumulative stock of FDI grew from $647 billion to over $10 trillion. Obviously, FDI has become an important factor in the world economy.

Table 6.2 shows the percentage of total foreign direct investment originating in and received by selected regions and countries for the period 2003–2005. The table indicates that factor abundance explains some of the flows. More than 85 percent of foreign direct investment originated in developed countries, and developing countries received approximately 35.9 percent of the world's foreign direct investment. The factor abundance of countries explains where the foreign direct investment comes from. However, using factor abundance does not explain where it goes. The world's developed countries received nearly 60 percent of the world's foreign direct investment. Our discussion of world production and income in Chapter 1 indicated that approximately 80 percent of the world's total production and income occurs in developed countries. FDI mostly flows into these developed countries to more efficiently serve high-income markets. As the table indicates, the distribution of FDI among the developing countries is not equal. The developing countries of Asia receive about 21 percent of world FDI. Latin America and the Caribbean receive about 12 percent of world FDI. The countries of Central and Eastern Europe receive FDI inflows of approximately 5 percent of the total and Africa is receiving only 3 percent of world FDI. Now that we have described the overall picture of FDI, we need to consider the reasons for these movements.

Reasons for the International Movement of Capital

Firms pursue foreign direct investment to earn a higher expected rate of return. There are many additional obstacles that a firm has to deal with in building a plant in a foreign country as opposed to building the same plant at home. A firm would not go through those additional problems unless the expected rate of return on that foreign investment was higher than the rate obtainable from building the plant in its home country.

By employing the factor-proportions theory of international trade, we can explain why foreign direct investment flows from the capital-abundant countries to the labor-abundant/capital scarce countries. The return on capital in the countries where capital is scarce, as in developing countries, will be higher than will the return on capital where capital is abundant, as in developed countries. That is one rationale for the flow of foreign direct investment. There are other general reasons for firms in particular industries to engage in foreign direct investment.

For example, the extraction of natural resources may entail foreign direct investment. A multinational corporation in the petroleum industry may have no choice but to invest abroad to obtain crude oil. A similar situation occurs with respect to the aluminum industry to obtain bauxite. In some agricultural goods, firms invest abroad in countries that have climates that are conducive to growing coffee, bananas, and other food products.

Another motive for foreign direct investment has to do with when a foreign market is closed or highly restricted. In some cases, the foreign country's trade restrictions may be so severe that a good cannot be exported to that country and still earn a reasonable profit. It may be more profitable for the multinational corporation to set up a plant to manufacture its product within the closed or restricted foreign market. Also, if a country places a highly restrictive limit on the quantity of the good that can be imported, the multinational corporation may find it profitable to set up domestic production facilities in the foreign market. High transportation costs likewise can induce foreign direct investment. Consider the cement industry. If the Mexican firm Cementos Mexicanos is going to sell cement in other countries, it must establish local production facilities. Cement has such a low value-to-weight ratio that it is economically impractical to export cement from Mexico even if the production process within Mexico is very efficient.

Even where there are no restrictions on the movement of goods between countries, undertaking foreign direct investment and producing a good in a foreign country may be preferable to exporting that good to the foreign country. As we described in Chapter 5, many goods sold to domestic consumers and businesses are differentiated, and product differentiation is very important in an international context. Goods sold in one country may have to be modified in some way to be acceptable in another country. For example, as we discuss in Chapter 8, many countries have national standards for health, safety, and product labeling. In most cases, when a firm exports, it will at a minimum have to change the label to translate the product information and otherwise conform to foreign labeling standards. In many cases, the good will have to be modified to one degree or another to make it saleable in a foreign market. For a U.S. firm to sell cars in Japan or a number of other countries, for example, the steering wheel and other components have to be moved from the left side of the vehicle to the right side. In addition, the firm may need to have an extensive presence in a foreign market to fully understand consumer tastes and preferences. This results in foreign direct investment. In this situation, a multinational firm would horizontally differentiate its production processes by producing and selling slightly different versions of the same good at similar prices in different countries.

Finally, multinational corporations whose production operations are separated into several distinct stages may find it profitable to set up production facilities in foreign markets in order to take advantage of lower operating costs. In such a situation, a multinational firm would vertically integrate its production processes. An example of vertical integration is the automobile industry. Raw materials are transformed into parts in one country; the parts are assembled into components such as engines and transmissions in another country; and these components are then moved to a third country where the final assembly occurs. In this case, a vertically integrated firm separates its production process and locates each process in a country where production costs are lower.

Welfare Effects of International Capital Movements

source country **the country that sends the factor of production to another country**

Now that we understand the reasons for foreign direct investment, let us examine the welfare effects of capital flows with respect to the source and host countries. First, consider the effect of foreign direct investment in the **source country**—the country where the capital originates. As capital moves out of the source country to the foreign country, the supply of capital decreases in the source country. This reduction in the supply of capital causes an increase in the rate of return to capital in the source country and the owners of capital in the source country benefit. The owners of the capital that is moved from the source country to the foreign country also benefit, as the capital invested in the foreign country earns a higher rate of return than it would have earned if it had remained in the source country. As a result, the overall return to capital in the source country rises.

The effect of this capital movement on labor in the source country can be negative. As capital is moved from the source country to foreign countries, there will be less capital in the source country for labor to work with. With less capital, the capital-to-labor ratio declines in the source country, and the productivity of labor also declines. If the capital movement is small, its effect will be a slower rate of growth of labor productivity in the source country. Because of these results, organized labor in the U.S. has opposed investing U.S. capital in plant and equipment in foreign countries. Notice, that these effects are similar to those of international trade. Remember our discussion in Chapter 4 concerning the effect of international trade on a country's factor prices and its distribution of income. If a country has abundant capital and scarce labor, the opening of trade results in an increase in the return to capital and a decrease in wages within the country. As such, the scarce factor, labor, loses relative to the abundant factor, capital.

host country **the country that receives the factor of production from another country**

The effects in the **host country**—the country receiving the capital—are the reverse. The return to capital in the host country will decrease as the domestic supply of capital is increased with foreign direct investment flows. As capital migrates to the host country, labor within the country benefits from the increased amount of capital per worker, which increases labor's productivity. The return to labor (wages) increases in the host country and the welfare of the labor force increases. These effects are similar to those that international trade has with regard to a country's factor prices and its distribution of income. If a country has abundant labor and scarce capital, the opening of trade results in an increase in wages and a decrease in the return to capital within the country. As such, the scarce factor, capital, loses relative to the abundant

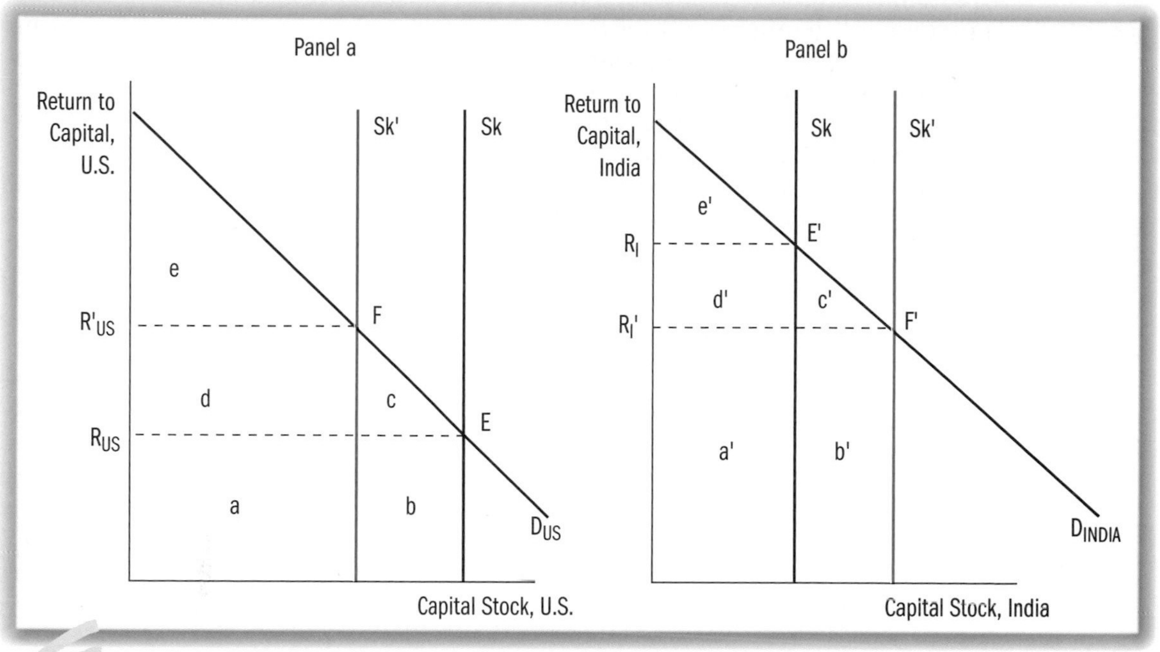

Figure 6.1 Output and Welfare Effects of International Capital Mobility
Allowing capital to flow between countries will equalize the return to capital in both countries and increase world output.

factor, labor. These welfare effects on the factors of production reinforce the notion that international trade and the international movements of factors of production are substitutes.

We can use the familiar tools of supply and demand analysis to determine how the international movements of capital affect welfare. More specifically, we can determine the effects of the movement of capital on the factors of production and on world economic output. To do this, consider the two graphs in Figure 6.1. Panel a represents the demand and supply of capital in the U.S., and Panel b represents the same for India. The return to capital (rent) in the U.S. is shown as R_{US}, and the return to capital in India is shown as R_I. As is usually the case, the demand for capital slopes downward and to the right. However, now we are discussing the demand for a factor of production. As a result, the demand curve represents the value of the marginal product of capital (VMP). VMP is the marginal product of capital multiplied by the price that producers receive for the last unit sold. In other words, it is the amount of money received by producers for the last unit produced with an extra unit of capital. Producers will use capital up to the point where the price of capital equals the VMP of capital. Thus, equilibrium in the U.S. and India are shown at points E and E′, respectively.

As before, we will assume that the U.S. is a capital-abundant country and India is a labor-abundant country. This implies that capital is more abundant in the U.S. than it is in India. The figure shows this graphically. The supply of capital (Sk) is higher (larger) in the U.S. than it is in India. In equilibrium, the return to capital (R) is lower in the U.S. than it is in India. Given this difference, capital will begin to migrating from the U.S. to India to obtain a higher rate of return. This is shown by a leftward movement of the supply of capital in the U.S. from Sk to Sk′. As capital moves into India, the supply of capital increases from Sk to Sk′. Thus, the return to capital in the U.S. increases and the return to capital in India decreases. The movement of capital from the U.S. to India will stop when R is the same in both countries. Equilibrium in both countries changes to point F for the U.S. and F′ for India.

To analyze the effects more clearly, the area under the demand curve in both countries has been divided into 5 areas labeled a, b, c, d, and e. These 5 areas represent the total output of the economy that is divided between capital and labor. Before the movement of capital, owners of capital in the U.S. received areas (a + b). The rest of the output (c + d + e) goes to the other factor, labor. As the supply of capital falls in the U.S. several effects occur. First, the owners of capital gain as the return to capital increases from R_{US} to R_{US}'. The return to capital in the U.S. is equal to areas (a + d) plus the (b′), which is earned by U.S. capital located in India and is larger than before. Notice that part of the return to U.S. capital is now capital that is located in India. U.S. labor now receives only area e and has lost area (c + d). Finally, the total output of the U.S. economy is lower because there are fewer resources. Prior to the movement of capital, the total output of the economy was area (a + b + c + d + e). After the movement of capital to India, output has fallen to area (a + d + e). In summary, the owners of capital in the U.S. have gained, labor has lost, and economic output has fallen.

As one would expect, the situation in India is the reverse. As the supply of capital shifts from Sk to Sk′, the return to capital falls from R_I to R_I'. Again, the area under the demand curve has been split into the areas a′ + b′ + c′ + d′ + e′. Prior to the inflow of capital the total output of the Indian economy was area (e′ + d′ + a′). The owners of capital in India received areas (a′ + d′) and labor received area e′. The inflow of capital causes Indian output to expand by area (c′ + b′). The owners of Indian capital now receive only area a′; area b′ is earned by U.S. capital located in India, and Indian labor now receives areas (e′ + d′ + c′). Clearly the owners of capital have lost; labor has gained; and the output of the Indian economy has increased.

For the world, economic output has increased. Intuitively, this should make sense, for the value of an extra unit of output in India is larger than the value of such a unit in the U.S. As capital is reallocated from the U.S. to India, it is moving from where its value is lower to where it is higher. The situation is analogous to moving capital from a comparative-disadvantage industry to a comparative-advantage industry within a country. The total output of the country rises. Global output, too, rises as the world's stock of capital is being used more efficiently.

Capital Movements and Public Policy

Restrictions on foreign trade, such as tariffs, are common in most countries. Less well known are the restrictions on the flow of foreign direct investment. Firms can sell their products to foreigners either by exporting the goods or services or by establishing factories or subsidiaries in foreign countries. As we will show in Chapters 7 and 8, trade barriers, such as tariffs and quotas, distort international trade. Restrictions placed on foreign direct investment also distort international investment. The issue is far from trivial, as can be seen by the fact that flows of foreign direct investment in 2005 were $974 billion.

Governments restrict the free flow of foreign direct investment in several ways. First, they frequently require foreign firms to seek approval before investing within a country. This process may be simply a check on whether or not the proposed investment is in accord with existing business regulations. However, the process may include negotiations between the MNC and the proposed host country concerning what is required for the investment to be approved. Second, many countries make it more difficult for foreign firms to invest in their country by placing restrictions on FDI in some industries, such as telecommunications or national defense industries. In addition, it also is common for restrictions on FDI to be put in place as a form of protectionism for domestic firms. Restrictions on FDI in many service industries can be particularly restrictive. For example, if General Motors or Ford has difficulty in producing cars in a country because of restrictions on foreign direct investment, at least they have the option of exporting cars to that country. To provide services, firms frequently have little choice but to establish a local subsidiary. However, if a country restricts FDI in the service industry, a foreign firm does not have the option of exporting the service to the country. Third, even if there is no overt discrimination against foreign firms, a country's **industrial policy** tends to favor local firms at the expense of foreign firms. A coutry's industrial policy refers to the many ways in which government tax policy, direct subsidies, or trade policies affect the development of business within a country. Fourth, we saw above that FDI usually increases the welfare of the host country. To obtain these benefits, some countries may offer incentives to attract FDI. These incentives often distort FDI flows by placing more investment in a particular location than would otherwise be the case. The result is that global flows of FDI are being distorted by the substantial variance in the way governments encourage or discourage it. Public policy on FDI is far less uniform than it is for international trade. Since trade and FDI are substitutes, distortions in the latter cause distortions in the former. In the next section, we consider the international movements of labor and the highly visible public policies toward immigration.

industrial policy a government policy designed to stimulate the development and growth of an industry

INTERNATIONAL MOVEMENTS OF LABOR

The migration of labor from one country to another is an important issue in international economics and public policy. To understand why, let us first consider what encourages an immigrant to migrate, and then examine some data from both the world economy and the U.S. Immigrants are people who permanently change their country of residence. Using this definition, international immigrants do not include tourists, business travelers, religious pilgrims, or persons seeking medical treatment—who collectively make millions of visits to foreign countries every year. Only 75 million people throughout the world resided outside their country of birth in 1965. By 2000, the number of immigrants residing in a new country had grown to more than 150 million. From 1965 to 1975, immigration increased at an annual rate of 1.2 percent. More recently, the annual rate of growth of immigration has increased to approximately 2.6 percent. Currently, immigrants constitute approximately 3 percent of the world's population.

The traditional destination for immigrants in the world economy has been the developed countries. Table 6.3 shows immigrants as a percentage of the population and of the labor force for a number of these developed countries. In the U.S., over 10 percent of the population is made up of immigrants, and an even higher percentage

Table 6.3 Immigrants as a Percentage of the Population and the Labor Force, 2005

Country	Percentage of Population	Percentage of Labor Force
Europe		
Austria	9.7%	12.0%
Belgium	8.6	9.1
Denmark	5.0	4.0
France	5.6	5.3
Germany	8.8	9.3
Italy	4.6	6.0
Luxembourg	39.6	62.6
Netherlands	4.2	3.4
Sweden	5.3	4.8
Switzerland	20.3	20.9
United Kingdom	5.2	5.4
Japan	1.6	0.3
Traditional Immigrant Countries		
Australia	23.8	24.9
Canada	19.1	19.9
United States	12.9	15.2

Source: OECD, *International Migration Outlook,* Paris: OECD, May, 2007.

of the labor force is comprised of immigrants. However, the U.S. is hardly an unusual developed country. Austria, Belgium, and Germany all have similar percentages of immigrants. The percentage of immigrants is far higher in Switzerland, Luxembourg, Canada, and Australia. Canada and Australia have percentages of immigrants that represent approximately one-fifth and one-quarter of their labor forces, respectively. It should not be surprising that the immigration policy of many countries is controversial, and we seek to explain some of the reasons why next.[2]

Reasons for the International Movement of Labor

Our discussion of immigration is concerned with the motives and effects of immigrants who voluntarily leave one country to enter another.[3] This voluntary migration generally occurs for economic reasons. As a result, this labor movement between countries is much like the movement of capital that we discussed in the last section.

[2]The information in this section was obtained from United Nations, International Organization for Migration, *World Migration Report* 2005, New York: United Nations, 2005.

[3]Every year, people move from one country to another for reasons that are not exclusively related to economics. Some individuals are forced to move from their home countries as a result of war, revolutions, natural disasters, or ethnic or religious persecution. These forced emigrants are not included in our discussion.

Immigration to America Before the Revolutionary War

The immigration of labor to America before the Revolutionary War (1776) illustrates the importance of both "push" and "pull" factors in inducing labor to move from one country to another. By 1760 the population of the British Colonies in North America was approximately 700,000. In the prior 140 years, approximately 4,500 people per year immigrated to the British Colonies. There was a substantial increase in the number of immigrants between 1760 and 1775. During these 15 years, approximately 15,000 people immigrated to the British Colonies each year. By 1775, this wave of immigration accounted for 10 percent of the population of the British Colonies. These numbers are startling. For example, 3 percent of Scotland's total population and 2.3 percent of Ireland's total population left for the British Colonies during these 15 years.

Many emigrants were farmers and laborers whose livelihoods were being severely diminished by large rent increases on the land that they worked. For farmers, the prospect of cheap land in the British Colonies was a powerful incentive to migration. In Britain, labor was abundant relative to land. The rents on land were rising and the return to labor to work the land was falling. When asked why they were leaving Britain for the Colonies, farmers said that they were searching for an improved economic environment. For the common farm laborer the answer was frequently "the lack of bread." In the British Colonies the situation was reverse. For the immigrants who were artisans, craftsman, and skilled construction workers, there were serious labor shortages for all types of workers—and that meant the possibility of a higher standard of living.

What is interesting in this case was the British government's reaction. By 1770, British landlords had become alarmed at the flight of their tenant farmers. British industrialists were concerned that emigration might diminish the supply of cheap labor. There were proposals in Britain to put an end to the emigration or to regulate the conditions of passage to the Colonies. This proposal was an attempt to make emigration prohibitively expensive for the poor. In any event, the owners of land and/or capital in Britain realized that emigration was not in their economic interest and lobbied the government for measures to eliminate or reduce it. In the end the government settled for collecting information on emigrants from Britain from 1773 to 1775. Although the events described here occurred more than 225 years ago, the information has left us with an unusually detailed record of the movement of people from one area to another for the usual economic reasons.[4]

[4]For a through and fascinating account of this, see Bernard Bailyn, *Voyagers to the West: A Passage in the Peopling of America on the Eve of the Revolution,* New York: Knopf, 1986.

The source countries that labor tends to leave are predominantly developing countries. As we saw in Chapter 1, GDP per capita in these countries is low relative to that of developed countries. Immigrants want to leave their home countries where the standard of living may be so low that they are living in poverty or close to it. With respect to the immigration of skilled labor, some developing countries are producing more highly-trained people than their economies currently need. In these cases, workers with advanced degrees in developing countries may experience high rates of unemployment and decide to seek employment in developed countries.

Both poverty and unemployment are considered "push" factors that lead to emigration. These push factors would not be very important if the distribution of income among the world's economies were evenly distributed. However, approximately 78 percent of the world's output and income originates in 45 countries possessing, collectively, less than 16 percent of the world's population. The high incomes in these countries create a "pull" factor. Workers from developing countries can improve their standard of living by moving to a developed country, where the standard of living is higher. Likewise, workers from low-income countries may seek to migrate to a middle-income country. For a worker in a low-income country, the standard of living in a middle-income country may seem affluent.

The combination of the "push" factors of poverty and unemployment in developing countries and the "pull" factor of higher wages and a higher standard of living in developed countries creates an environment conducive to the migration of labor. Neither "push" nor "pull" factors by themselves are sufficient to induce labor to move from the home country to a foreign country. Both groups of factors need to be present for migration to occur.

Welfare Effects of the International Movement of Labor

Again, consider the situation in which India is relatively labor abundant and the U.S. is relatively capital abundant. Under these conditions, U.S. wages would be higher than wages in India, and Indian labor would migrate to the U.S. This migration affects India's economy and factors of production. First, workers in India who do not migrate to the U.S. benefit. As labor leaves India, India's capital-to-labor ratio rises, resulting in an increase in labor's productivity. With this productivity increase, Indian wages rise. However, with less labor, India's total output falls. The returns to the owners of capital in India also fall, as such owners pay higher wages and produce less output.

The U.S. economy gains in this process. As immigrant labor enters the U.S, the existing labor force loses, as each worker has less capital to work with. The capital-to-labor ratio in the U.S. falls, resulting in a decrease in the productivity of the existing labor force. This decrease in labor productivity causes wages to fall. However, with more total labor (existing labor plus immigrants), total U.S. output rises. The returns to the owners of capital in the U.S. also increase, as they pay lower wages and produce more output.

Because wages paid to existing U.S. workers decline as a result of immigration, labor will oppose open immigration. However, owners of capital will favor open immigration, as their returns increase due to additional output and lower labor costs. A country's immigration policy is usually an attempt to balance lower wages with higher total output. Immigration may lower wages, but it augments the country's total output. The output effects on the world economy are positive. The workers who have emigrated from India to the U.S. are more productive. As a result, the output of the world economy rises because workers can move to countries where they are more productive.

You can analyze the welfare effects of international labor migration on the countries involved using the same graphical technique that was used to describe the effects of foreign direct investment. To do this, consider the two graphs in Figure 6.2. Panel a represents the demand and supply of labor in the U.S., and Panel b represents the same for India. The price of labor in the U.S. is shown as the wage rate, W_{US}, and the rate in India

Does Immigration Lower Wages?

Because immigration has a potentially depressing effect on domestic wages, it is a major public policy issue. Economists have conducted a number of studies looking at the effect of immigration on wages, and the general conclusion is that the effects are relatively small. The size of the U.S. labor force is approximately 150 million. In an average year, about 1 million immigrants enter and stay in the U.S. and not all enter the work force immediately. Further, the U.S. labor force grows by approximately 1.5 million a year owing to changes in the domestic population. In most years, the demand for U.S. labor increases. The predicted effects of immigration would be to slightly reduce the *rate of increase* of wages, not a catastrophic drop in the average wage.[5]

Immigration turns out to be more of a regional economic issue than a national one. Recent immigrants tend to settle where earlier immigrants from the same country or region have settled. In these cases, immigrants can noticeably change the local supply of labor. For instance, during the 1970s new immigrants in the metropolitan Los Angeles area increased the labor supply by more than 30 percent. The "Mariel boatlift" of 1980 increased the labor supply of Miami by 7 percent in a single year. Even in these extreme cases, there is little evidence of the lowering of wages. In fact, most of the effects appear to occur from immigrants who arrived earlier. Even in this case, the effects on wages appear to be small.[6] Given the current level of immigration, immigration's critics may be gravely overstating their case.

[5]We are speaking here of legal immigration, which is augmented to some extent by illegal immigration. For a discussion of the latter see Barry R. Chiswick, "Illegal Immigration and Immigration Control," *Journal of Economic Perspectives* 2(3), Summer 1988, pp. 101–15.

[6]For an excellent summary of this literature, see Robert H. Topel, "Factor Proportions and Relative Wages: The Supply-Side Determinants of Wage Inequality," *Journal of Economic Perspectives* 11(2), Spring 1997, pp. 55–74.

is shown as W_I. As before, the demand curve represents the value of the marginal product of labor (VMP), and it slopes downward to the right in both countries. VMP is the marginal product of labor multiplied by the price that producers receive for the last unit sold. In other words, it is the amount of money received by producers for the last unit produced with an extra unit of labor. Producers will hire labor up to the point where the price of labor equals the VMP of labor. The equilibrium points for the U.S. and India are shown as E and E′, respectively.

As before we will assume that the U.S. is a capital-abundant country and India is a labor-abundant country. With respect to labor, this implies that it is more abundant in India than it is in the U.S. This is shown graphically in the figures as the supply of labor (Sl) is lower in the U.S. than in India. As a result, the wage rate is higher in the U.S. (W_{US}) than it is in India (W_I). Given the difference in wages, labor will begin to migrate from India to the U.S. to obtain a higher wage. This is shown by a leftward movement of the supply of labor in India from Sl to Sl′. As labor moves into the U.S., the supply of labor increases from Sl to Sl′. Thus, wages in the U.S. decrease and wages in India increase. The movement of labor from India to the U.S. will stop when wages

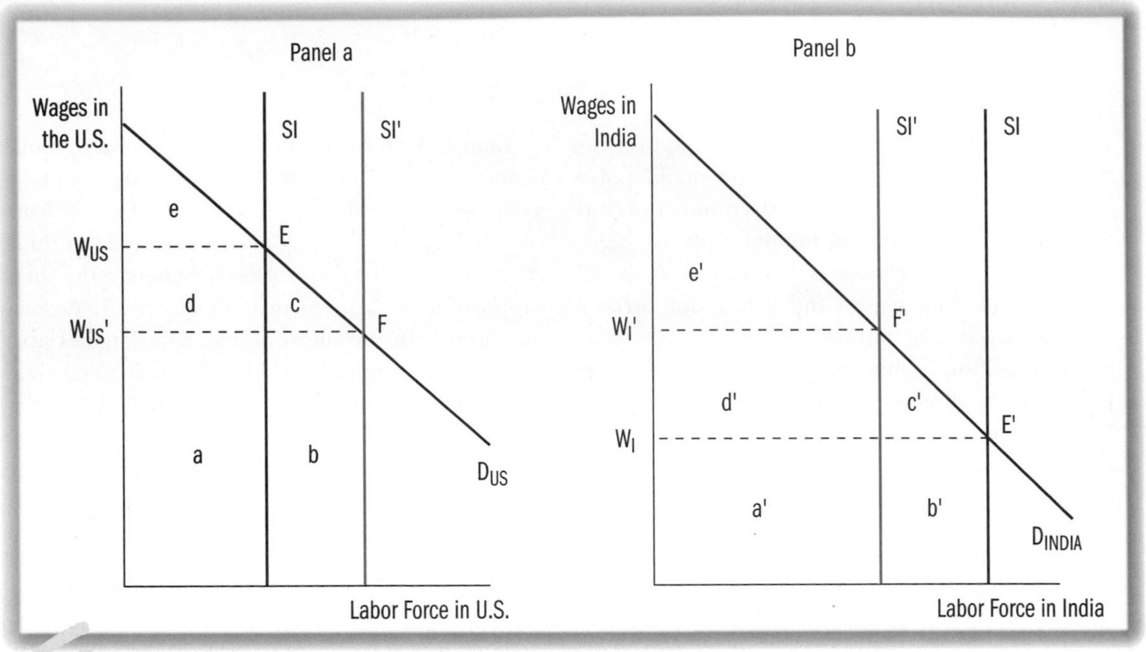

Figure 6.2 **Output and Welfare Effects of International Labor Migration**

Allowing labor to migrate completely between countries will equalize wages in both countries and increase world output.

are the same in both countries. The equilibrium in both countries changes to point F for the U.S. and point F′ for India.

To analyze the effects more clearly, the area under the demand curve in both countries has been cut into 5 areas labeled a, b, c, d, and e. These 5 areas represent the total output of the economy that is divided between capital and labor. Before the movement of labor, labor in India received area (a′ + b′). The rest of India's output (c′ + d′ + e′) goes to the other factor, capital in the form of rent. The reduction in the supply of labor has several effects. First, labor that remains in India gains as wages increase and the new return to labor is (a′ + d′), which is larger than area a′. Capital in India now receives only area e′ and has lost area (c′ + d′). Finally, the total output of the Indian economy is lower because there are fewer resources. Prior to the movement of labor, the total output of the economy was (a′ + b′ + c′ + d′ + e′). After the migration of labor, output has fallen to area (a′ + d′ + e′). In summary, labor in India has gained, capital has lost, and economic output has fallen.

As one would expect, the situation in the U.S. is the reverse. The supply of labor shifts from from Sl to Sl′ and the wage falls. Again the area under the demand curve has been split into the areas a + b + c + d + e. Prior to the inflow of labor, the total output of the U.S. economy was area (e + d + a). U.S. labor received areas (a + d) and capital received area e. The inflow of labor causes U.S. output to expand by area (c + b). U.S. residents now receive only area a in the form of wages, immigrants receive area b, and U.S. capital now receives areas (e + d + c). Clearly, the owners of capital have gained and U.S. labor has lost and the output of the U.S. economy has increased.

For the world, economic output has increased. Output has fallen in India but risen in the U.S. The loss of output will be lower in India than the gain in output in the U.S. This is because as labor is reallocated from the U.S. to India, it is moving from where its value is lower to where it is higher. The situation is analogous to moving resources from a comparative-disadvantage industry to a comparative-advantage industry within a country. As such, the total output of the country rises.

Immigration and Public Policy

Immigration policy is a persistent political problem within many developed countries as they try to balance the impact that immigration has on wages within their countries with the total output that their countries produce. An immigration policy designed to maximize a country's total output would be a policy of completely open immigration. In this case a country's output would be maximized, but labor's economic interest—wages—could be harmed. This is why few countries have a totally open immigration policy. On the other hand, few countries have a complete ban on immigration. Restricting immigration to zero would result in a high opportunity cost in that the absence of immigrant workers would result in lost output.

While neither open immigration nor zero immigration are likely, some sort of political process must shape a government's immigration policy. The government must balance the welfare of society against the welfare of particular groups that immigration affects. However, both economic and political factors change over time. As a result, immigration policies, especially in developed countries, are prone to changes over time.

The political difficulties associated with open immigration have lead countries to design immigration policies that allow companies to use less expensive foreign labor. Countries have been able to design immigration policies that allow market forces to allocate labor efficiently on a global basis and remain compatible with public preferences on immigration. For example, the guest worker programs of Europe allow workers from developing countries to work there temporarily rather than immigrate permanently. This policy allows firms to hire lower-skilled workers who are in short supply without the government committing to granting these workers permanent residency. However, these programs have been troublesome whenever the host country experiences increased social costs through larger expenditures for safety net programs like unemployment insurance, education, housing, and health care.

offshore assembly provisions **the section of the tariff schedule that allows U.S. firms to export materials and parts of a good to foreign countries for final assembly; when the assembled goods are returned to the U.S., duties are assessed only on the value added in the foreign country**

For the U.S., **offshore assembly provisions** provide the most common method of using foreign labor without allowing immigration. These provisions are contained in Section 9802 of the *Harmonized Tariff Schedule of the United States.* This section of the tariff schedule allows U.S. firms to export materials and parts of a good to foreign countries for final assembly. When the final assembled goods are imported back into the U.S., duties are assessed only on the value added in the foreign country. This allows U.S. firms to take advantage of lower foreign labor costs without actually importing the labor to assemble the parts domestically. Use of this provision of the tariff schedule has been especially popular among U.S. firms in setting up assembly plants in northern Mexico. The term for these assembly plants, *maquiladoras,* has become synonymous with offshore assembly.

Recently, the decline in the price of international transportation and communications has allowed some industries to use foreign labor without directly importing it. Firms in the service sector, insurance for one, have been able to use less-costly foreign

The Brain Drain

The "brain drain" alludes to highly-skilled and/or trained professionals migrating from developing countries to developed countries. In recent years, there has been migration of skilled workers from the former Soviet Union and the Eastern European countries to Western Europe and other OECD countries. This type of migration creates a complicated mix of economic gains and losses.

Let's examine the winners and losers in this brain drain. The migrants and the developed countries gain because better wages and working conditions in the richer industrialized nations foster migration. In some areas, such as the hard sciences or medicine, the working conditions in developed countries are also a lure, as some of what these scientists wish to accomplish is simply impossible in their home country owing to a lack of money and/or equipment. The world economy as a whole gains from this migration, as the productivity of these migrants is higher in the industrialized countries and potentially new products and processes may be discovered that would not have occurred without the migration.[7] In the recent debates over immigration in the U.S., many high-technology companies have feared the potential loss of this talent source. This will become more important as the rate of growth of the U.S. labor force slows to approximately 1 percent.[8]

The losers are the developing countries. These countries have invested in the initial training of these workers. If these workers migrate, the country faces the "loss" of the investment because educational resources are scarce in developing countries. A common proposal to mitigate this loss is a tax on emigrants—a tax that developing countries cannot collect and the developed countries do not want to impose. In many cases, though, the migration is not a total loss for the developing country. High-income workers who have moved to developed countries may remit money home to support relatives. In this case, the developing country has recouped some of the loss, and if the wage differential is high enough, it may be such that a fraction of the migrant's earnings remitted may cover the entire initial "investment."[9]

More recently, the brain drain has been reversing. As time passes, the country from which the migrant left may have grown economically from a developing country into a developed country. As this occurs, the migrants are returning to their home countries.[10] For example, many foreigners receive advanced degrees in the U.S. and return to their home countries and become successful business leaders.

[7]An example is the "low fat" potato chip. A Nigerian scientist who had immigrated to the U.S discovered this exceptionally important process. For the fascinating details of this story, see *Texas Monthly,* January 1996, pp. 104–8, 112–14.
[8]See Alex Markels, "Institute Urges More Immigration of Skilled Workers," *The Wall Street Journal,* April 16, 1997, p. B4.
[9]For an analysis of this topic, see Nicholas P. Glytsos, "Measuring the Income Effects of Migrant Remittances: A Methodological Approach Applied to Greece," *Economic Development and Cultural Change* 42(1), October 1993, pp. 131–68 or Nicholas P. Glytsos, "Remitting Behavior of 'Temporary' and 'Permanent' Migrants: The Case of Greeks in Germany and Australia," *Labour* 11(3), Autumn 1997, pp. 409–35.
[10]See Andrew Tanzer, "Brain Drain in Reverse," *Forbes,* April, 17, 1989, pp. 114–15.

labor to process paperwork, shipping documents by air freight to and from foreign countries. In addition, it is now feasible to subcontract design and engineering work to foreign countries and have these workers tied to the home firm through computer technology. While most developed countries limit immigration, both market forces and technology can produce labor market conditions that are similar to actual immigration.

The Outsourcing Debate

Over the last several years, there has been an intense debate over the issue of outsourcing. Outsourcing refers to the movement of certain service-sector jobs from a developed country to some developing countries. Although the term is relatively new, the movement of jobs from developed to developing countries is not. As mentioned in the text, some manufacturing assembly jobs have moved from the U.S. to Mexico. In the 1970s there was alarm that virtually all U.S. manufacturing jobs would move to Mexico. In fact only a small minority of jobs migrated to Mexico, mostly for the final assembly of products. What seems new now is the migration of service-sector jobs. In some sense this is disconcerting for service workers, as such jobs until recently have been immune from foreign competition. Or have they? For a number of years U.S. insurance companies have been using Irish labor to process insurance claims. The newest outsourcing story is the migration of low-end service-sector jobs such as call centers to Asian countries. Another part of this story has been the movement of some IT jobs to India. All of these stories represent the concept of comparative advantage at work. MNCs will tend to move jobs to locations where unit costs are lowest. The new twist is that because of modern transportation and communications, some service-sector jobs now can be moved. There are estimates that several million service-sector jobs might move outside the U.S. over the next 10 years. Superficially, this seems like a lot of lost jobs. However, one needs to keep in mind that the U.S. labor force is now over 150 million. Second, these job losses are spread out over a decade, or roughly 200,000 jobs per year. If one looks at new claims for unemployment compensation data, it is not at all unusual for that many American workers to lose their jobs in a *week*. When the data is looked at in a different light, the numbers aren't quite so alarming.

As is usually the case with free trade, the costs are easy to see and the benefits less so. First, IT trade has been shown to increase U.S. GDP. This isn't surprising, as trade usually leads to higher output. Second, the fear of the massive outsourcing of services is at variance with the data. As shown in Chapter 1, the U.S. exports more services than it imports, and this positive imbalance is growing over time. Finally, we should point to the term *insourcing*. Although the U.S. definitely now outsources jobs, there are also millions of jobs moving into the U.S. It has become more difficult for observers to complain about some jobs leaving the U.S. when other jobs are migrating to the country. By this point in the text, you should appreciate the benefits of specialization and trade for a country based on comparative advantage.

THE MULTINATIONAL CORPORATION

Up to now, we have been considering the international movements of the factors of production between countries. Much of the movement of capital and labor in the global economy occurs as a result of the activities of multinational corporations (MNCs). Labor shortages in one country may induce firms to recruit labor from another country, or the firm may decide to move workers from one country to another to address the shortage. In addition, the activities of multinational corporations are the primary determinant of international movements of capital or foreign direct investment. The most fundamental question concerning multinational corporations is why they exist. The answer is that they are efficient. Large multinational firms derive these efficiencies from *internalizing* certain activities as opposed to contracting them out to a second party.[11] Among other things, managing a firm involves deciding which activities the firm will carry out itself and which activities will be contracted out to firms or individuals external to the firm. Beyond this fundamental issue, a firm may decide to operate business units outside the home country for reasons related to its business specialization. In this section, we first consider the importance of MNCs in the world economy followed by a discussion of some of the reasons MNCs exist. Since MNCs are sometimes controversial, we conclude this section with a discussion of the various public policy issues countries face with respect to MNCs.

The Importance of MNCs

MNCs are sometimes the subject of controversy in the world economy. As we will see, there are reasons for this controversy. First, consider the relative importance of MNCs in the world economy by examining the data presented in Table 6.4. As MNCs spread out from their home country, they set up affiliate operations in foreign countries. The various forms that these affiliates can take are considered in the next section. We can describe the relative importance of MNCs and their affiliates by examining three related variables: sales, assets, and employment. Table 6.4 shows data for these three variables for 1982, 1990, and 2005. In addition the table shows the growth rates of these variables from 2002 to 2005. For comparison purposes, analogous data on world GDP and world exports of goods and services are given in the last two rows.

Over the last 23 years, the sales of affiliates of MNCs have grown from less than $3 trillion to approximately $22 trillion. Such sales now are large in comparison to world output, but these sales are especially striking compared to world exports

Table 6.4 Selected Indicators of FDI and International Production, 1982–2005

	Value at Current Prices (Billion dollars)			*Annual Growth Rate (percent)*			
Item	**1982**	**1990**	**2005**	**2002**	**2003**	**2004**	**2005**
Sales of Foreign Affiliates	$2,620	$6,045	$22,171	11.2%	30.4%	11.4%	5.6%
Gross Product of Foreign Affiliates	646	1,481	4,517	1.9	20.3	22.8	5.4
Total Assets of Foreign Affiliates	2,108	5,956	45,564	36.7	27.9	3.5	6.4
Exports of Foreign Affiliates	647	1,366	4,214	4.9	16.5	21.0	12.9
Employment of Foreign Affiliates (thousands)	19,537	24,551	62,059	10.0	−0.5	20.1	4.4
GDP (in current prices)	10,899	21,898	44,674	3.9	12.1	12.1	9.1
Exports of Goods and Services	2,247	4,261	12,641	4.9	16.5	21.0	12.9

Source: Adapted from United Nations Conference on Trade and Development, *World Investment Report, 2006,* New York: United Nations, 2006.

[1]See Ronald Coase, "The Nature of the Firm," *Economica,* November 1937, pp. 368–405.

of goods and services. In 1980, there was a rough equality of sales and exports. By 2005, sales of foreign affiliates were approximately twice as large as exports of goods and services. Clearly, if one considers globalization only in terms of international trade, one misses the large impact of MNCs in the world economy. Given the growth of sales, it is not surprising that the total assets of these foreign affiliates have grown significantly. These assets were slightly over $2 trillion in 1980 but had grown to over $45 trillion in 2005. The employment of these affiliates has grown along with sales and assets. Total employment has grown from 19 million to over 62 million from 1980 to 2005.

The growth rates of these variables for the last 4 years for which data is available are given in the last four columns of the table. Virtually all of the variables tend to grow faster than either world output or world exports of goods and services. Even as growth in the world economy slowed in the early part of this decade, sales, assets, and employment continued to grow. If growth in the world economy accelerates in the next several years, it is likely that all three of these variables will resume their previous, higher growth paths. Given these trends, there must be some underlying reasons why MNCs are growing so quickly. In the next section, we consider the reasons for the existence of MNCs.

Reasons for the Existence of MNCs

Many large firms find it necessary to be horizontally or vertically integrated. With both horizontal and vertical integration, firms may find it profitable to set up business units in other countries to service their customers more efficiently or to reduce costs. Firms that sell goods and services in foreign countries, or firms that produce goods in foreign countries for sale domestically, must decide how they want to control their assets in the foreign country. There are several alternative modes of foreign investment. The main choices include:

wholly owned subsidiary a foreign operation incorporated in the host country and owned by a parent corporation in the source country

- The firm can export its product to a foreign firm and let the foreign firm handle all aspects of selling it in the foreign market.
- The multinational corporation may set up a **wholly owned subsidiary** to serve the foreign market. In this type of subsidiary, the firm has complete control from the production of the product or service to the end sale and service to the ultimate consumer.
- They can establish joint ventures with a firm in the foreign market.[12] The firm may need to operate in a foreign country to obtain raw materials not available in the home market. Increasingly, multinational corporations are choosing to manufacture sub-components in foreign markets to reduce overall production costs.

The motivations for foreign direct investment, and the reasons for the existence of multinational corporations, are similar but not identical. A firm may "go multinational"

[2]The potential types of joint ventures are too numerous to mention here. For an excellent summary of joint ventures and some of the problems common to this type of organization, see Robert Miller, et al., "International Joint Ventures in Developing Countries," *Finance and Development,* March 1997, pp. 26–29.

for reasons beyond the motivations for foreign direct investment. The most popular method of analyzing this phenomenon is John Dunning's OLI approach.[13]

OLI approach **a framework that explains why multinational corporations use foreign direct investment**

The **OLI approach** is a framework that explains why multinational corporations engage in foreign direct investment. The O in OLI stands for *ownership*—commonly, ownership of an intangible asset. An intangible asset is a good or process that a firm has developed and that competing firms find difficult to replicate. Usually it is valuable because it is a source of considerable competitive advantage.[14] The firm may believe that maintaining control over this asset makes it necessary to set up subsidiaries in foreign markets rather than relinquish control over the production and/or distribution of the product. For example, Coca-Cola feels that the formula used to make its product is so valuable that the company must maintain extremely tight control over production and distribution in foreign markets.

licensing agreement **a domestic firm licenses the right to produce and market a good or to use a technology to a foreign firm in a foreign country**

The ownership of intangible assets relates to the issue of technology transfer. When a firm owns a technology that can be profitably employed or sold in a foreign market, the simplest and, in the short run, most profitable option is to license the technology to a foreign firm. This **licensing agreement** immediately increases the domestic firm's profits because the marginal cost of obtaining this extra revenue is usually quite low. However, such an agreement may allow a foreign firm to gain access to the technology and potentially become a competitor at a later date. To prevent this from happening, the domestic firm may feel that it is necessary to serve the foreign market in some other fashion.

L in the OLI framework represents *locational* advantages. In some cases, it may be in a firm's global interests to locate outside its home country. This may occur for a number of reasons. The location of natural resources is an obvious example. Less obvious is the firm's motive to take advantage of cheaper foreign inputs in a vertically integrated production process. Usually this involves multinational corporations moving part of the production process to developing countries to take advantage of cheaper labor or raw materials in the production of components for more sophisticated products. Likewise, horizontal integration in an industry may induce firms to set up subsidiaries to more profitably serve foreign markets. In addition, various natural and legal barriers to trade may induce firms to locate in foreign markets that might not otherwise exist.

Finally, I in the OLI framework represents *internalization*. Internalization refers to firms' propensity to perform functions internally that outside firms could do. In this case the firm derives some benefit from internalizing production as opposed to allowing other firms to participate to one extent or another in producing the product. The OLI model provides a useful way of thinking about the activities of multinational corporations. Most of the time, one or more of these three factors can explain the activities of a firm in foreign markets.[15]

---

[3]For an extensive treatment of this approach, see John H. Dunning, *Explaining International Production*, London: Unwin Hyman, 1988.

[4]It should be noted that it is entirely legitimate for one to speak of a *firm* having a competitive advantage over other firms.

[5]For further details on the theory of MNCs, see James R. Markusen, "The Boundaries of Multinational Enterprises and the Theory of International Trade," *Journal of Economic Perspectives* 9(2), Spring 1995, pp. 169–89.

The World's Largest Multinational Corporations

Table 6.5 provides information on the world's largest 20 nonfinancial corporations. Included in the table is the name of the corporation, the parent firm's home country, the major industry, the level of foreign and total assets, the level of foreign and total sales, and the level of foreign and total employment. From the table, we see that 5 of the largest multinational firms have headquarters in France and Germany, 4 in the U.S., and 3 in the U.K. Four are motor vehicle firms, 4 are petroleum firms, 4 are electricity, gas and water firms, 3 are telecommunications firms, and 2 are electrical and electronic and/or computer firms.

Table 6.5 The World's Largest 20 Nonfinancial Multinational Corporations Ranked by Foreign Assets, 2005 (Billions of Dollars and Number of Employees)

				Assets (in Billions of $)		*Sales (in Billions of $)*		*Employment (in Thousands)*	
Ranking	**Corporation**	**Home Country**	**Industry**	**Foreign**	**Total**	**Foreign**	**Total**	**Foreign**	**Total**
1	General Electric	USA	Electrical & Electronic Equipment	$447.9	$750.5	$56.9	$152.99	142.0	307.0
2	Vodafone	UK	Telecommunications	247.9	258.6	53.3	62.5	46.0	57.4
3	Ford Motor Company	USA	Motor Vehicles	179.9	305.3	71.40	171.6	102.7	225.6
4	General Motors	USA	Motor Vehicles	173.7	479.6	59.1	193.5	114.6	324.0
5	BP	UK	Petroleum	154.5	193.2	232.4	285.1	85.5	102.9
6	Exxonmobil Corporation	USA	Petroleum	134.9	195.3	202.9	291.3	53.0	105.2
7	Royal Dutch/Shell Group	UK/ Netherlands	Petroleum	129.9	192.8	170.3	265.2	96.0	114.0
8	Toyota Motor Corporation	Japan	Motor Vehicles	123.0	233.7	103.0	171.5	94.7	285.8
9	Total	France	Petroleum	98.7	114.6	24.3	58.6	81.7	206.5
10	France Telecom	France	Telecommunications	85.7	131.2	24.3	58.6	81.2	206.5
11	Volkswagen Group	Germany	Motor Vehicles	84.0	172.9	80.0	110.5	165.2	342.5
12	Sanofi-Aventis	France	Pharmaceuticals	82.6	104.5	15.4	18.7	68.8	96.4
13	Deutsche Telekom AG	Germany	Telecommunications	79.7	146.8	47.1	71.9	73.8	244.6
14	RWE Group	Germany	Electricity, Gas & Water	78.7	127.2	23.6	52.3	42.4	97.8

(*continued*)

Table 6.5 *(Continued)*

Ranking	Corporation	Home Country	Industry	Assets (in Billions of $) Foreign	Assets Total	Sales (in Billions of $) Foreign	Sales Total	Employment (in Thousands) Foreign	Employment Total
15	Suez	France	Electricity, Gas & Water	74.1	85.8	38.8	50.6	100.5	160.7
16	E. On	Germany	Electricity, Gas & Water	72.7	155.4	22.0	61.0	32.8	72.5
17	Hutchison Whampoa Ltd	Hong Kong, China	Diversified	67.6	84.2	17.0	23.0	150.7	180.0
18	Siemens AG	Germany	Electrical & Electronic Equipment	65.8	108.3	59.2	93.3	266.0	430.0
19	Nestle SA	Switzerland	Food & Beverages	65.4	77.0	68.6	69.8	240.4	247.0
20	Electricite De France	France	Electricity, Gas & Water	65.4	200.1	17.9	55.8	50.5	156.2

Source: Adapted from United Nations Conference on Trade and Development, *World Investment Report, 2006,* New York: United Nations, 2006.

Public Policy toward Multinational Corporations

A final issue concerning multinationals is how they are regulated. Every national government regulates business within its borders. Multinational firms potentially pose a unique situation in that they operate in foreign countries (the host country) but, to a greater or lesser extent, are managed from the home (source) country. In general, there are two public policy issues. The first is how are multinational corporations regulated in the host country. The second is how both the home and the host country tax multinational corporations.

national treatment treating a multinational corporation as if it were a domestic firm, thus eliminating legal and/or regulatory restrictions that otherwise might apply to it as a foreign firm

A host country's treatment of multinational corporations can vary considerably. At one extreme, the host country could ban the activities of multinational corporations. On the other extreme, the host country could treat the multinational corporations as though they were a domestic firm without making legal and/or regulatory distinctions between domestic firms and foreign-owned firms. This situation is called **national treatment**. Alternatively, a host country could treat multinational corporations somewhere in between these two extremes. National treatment is the most desirable situation for a multinational corporation, as market forces would determine foreign direct investment flows without being either hindered or induced in one way or another. There are many possibilities between these two extremes. In most countries, including the U.S., there are restrictions on the activities of foreign-owned firms in at least a few industries. National defense, transportation, and telecommunications are three industries that commonly include restrictions on the activities of foreign companies. In addition, countries may choose to put any number of restrictions on multinational corporations' ability to operate in the host country. Such restrictions may include the percentage of the industry that foreign firms can own; the percentage of the firm's output that must be exported; and the firm's ability to repatriate profits. The point here is that for a number of reasons most countries choose to treat foreign-owned firms differently than they treat domestic firms.

transfer pricing the over-pricing or under-pricing of goods in intrafirm trade of multinational corporations that is designed to shift income and profits from high-tax to low-tax countries

The same is true of tax issues. Generally, multinational firms must pay taxes on the profits of their local subsidiary in the foreign country. In the home country, the firm is generally given a tax credit against its local tax liability for any taxes paid abroad. However, what if the domestic and foreign taxes differ? Suppose taxes in the home country are far less than the taxes in the host country. The firm would then have an incentive to try to transfer income (profits) from the host to the home country. Just how would the firm accomplish this? Usually, the firm in the host country is shipping some inputs or at least providing headquarter services such as accounting and the like to the subsidiary in the host country. These transactions are occurring intrafirm. Of course, what the parent firm is charging the subsidiary for inputs and/or services is quite flexible. In this case, it becomes possible for the parent firm to raise the price of these inputs and effectively lower the foreign subsidiary's profits. The profit would have been transferred back to the home country and taxed at a lower rate. This **transfer pricing**, the over- or under-pricing of goods in intrafirm trade of multinational corporations, allows firms to use intrafirm pricing to maximize the after-tax profits allocated to the home country or its subsidiary. Initially transfer pricing was used to transfer profits out of countries with exchange controls.[16] Unless countries adopt similar income tax rates, at least some transfer pricing by multinational corporations to lower their total tax liability will continue to occur.

SUMMARY

1. In many ways, the movement of the factors of production between countries is a substitute for international trade in goods.
2. Nearly 90 percent of foreign direct investment (FDI) originates in developed countries. Thirty-six percent of the world's foreign direct investment goes to developing countries, and approximately 60 percent of the world's foreign direct investment flows to developed countries.
3. The international movement of capital can occur for a variety of reasons. Foreign direct investment represents the capital flow between countries to purchase land, structures, and equipment and software. This investment usually is in the form of a domestic corporation opening a foreign subsidiary or buying control of an existing foreign firm.
4. The owners of capital in the source country benefit from capital flows while the effect on labor in the source country is negative. Organized labor in the U.S. has almost always opposed the investment of U.S. capital in plants and equipment in other countries. The effects on the country receiving the capital are the reverse.
5. One of the most controversial areas in international economics and public policy is immigration. The international migration of labor usually is an economic phenomenon that pushes workers out of low-wage countries and pulls them into high-wage countries.
6. For the country losing emigrants, immigration benefits the workers left behind. For the country gaining the immigrants, immigration may lower the return to existing labor within the

[6]See Chapter 18 for a further discussion of exchange controls.

country but it augments the country's total output.

7. Countries have been able to design policies that allow market forces to allocate labor efficiently on a global basis in a way that seems compatible with public preferences on immigration. Examples of this are the guest worker programs of Europe and the offshore assembly provisions of the U.S. More recently, improved communications have made it possible to move certain services to foreign countries.
8. A multinational corporation is a firm that conducts part of its business across national boundaries. A firm may decide to form subsidiary business units outside the home country for reasons related to the firm's business specialty.
9. Firms become multinationals in order to maintain ownership of an intangible asset; to obtain locational advantages; and/or to internalize certain aspects of the business.
10. There are two major public policy issues concerning multinationals: How are the multinational corporations regulated in the host country and how do both the home and the host country tax multinational corporations.

KEY CONCEPTS AND TERMS

- capital flows p. 117
- immigration p. 117
- source country p. 122
- host country p. 122
- industrial policy p. 125
- offshore assembly provisions p. 131
- wholly owned subsidiary p. 135
- OLI approach p. 136
- licensing agreement p. 136
- national treatment p. 138
- transfer pricing p. 139

PROBLEMS AND QUESTIONS FOR REVIEW

1. In what sense are international movements of the factors of production a substitute for international trade in goods?
2. What is the meaning of foreign direct investment? List some of the factors that induce companies to invest abroad.
3. Describe the distribution of FDI in the world economy. To what extent does this distribution reflect differences in the relative abundance of capital?
4. Explain the effects of foreign direct investment on the welfare of the source country, the host country, and the world as a whole.
5. Explain why organized labor in the U.S. opposes FDI by U.S. corporations.
6. What are the motives for the international migration of labor? Explain the effects of labor migration on the host country, the source country, and the world as a whole.
7. Discuss the balance a country tries to achieve with its immigration policy.
8. Why would a country employ the use of a guest worker program? Why would a country include offshore assembly provisions in its tariff code?
9. Why are multinational corporations important? What are the reasons for their existence?
10. Explain how the OLI approach accounts for the existence of multinationals.
11. What does the term *national treatment* mean to a multinational corporation?
12. What are some of the more common restrictions on the activities of multinational corporations in host countries?
13. Suppose that a German firm is producing automobiles in the U.S. Assume that 40 percent of the value of one of its vehicles is produced in Germany and exported to the U.S. plant. If the U.S. corporate income tax is 35 percent and the German tax is 50 percent, what would the German firm be tempted to charge the American subsidiary for the German components?

SUGGESTED READINGS AND WEB SITES

Daniel W. Drezner, "The Outsourcing Bogeyman," *Foreign Affairs,* May/June 2004, pp. 22–34.
An exceptionally clear discussion of the costs and benefits of outsourcing.

Robert C. Feenstra, "Integration of Trade and Disintegration of Production in the Global Economy," *Journal of Economic Perspectives* 12(4), Fall 1998, pp. 31–50.
An interesting look at how vertical specialization in trade may be leading to an increased volume of trade.

"Footloose Firms," *The Economist,* March 27, 2004, p. 77.
An excellent article on the propensity of MNCs to move their operations around the world.

"Free Trade, Fettered Investment," *The Economist,* September 14, 1996, p. 80.
A short article on the often overlooked issue of how distortions of FDI also end up distorting trade.

Edward Graham, *Fighting the Wrong Enemy: Antiglobal Activists and Multinational Enterprises,* Washington, D.C.: Institute for International Economics, 2000.
A detailed look at the activities of MNCs in the world economy.

Catherine Mann, et al., *Global Electronic Commerce: A Primer,* Washington, D.C.: Institute for International Economics, 2000.
A quick analysis of the newer forms of trade in IT.

"The New Jobs Migration," *The Economist,* February 21, 2004, p. 11.
A good short discussion on the topic of outsourcing.

"Open Up: A Special Report on Migration," *The Economist,* January 5, 2008, pp. 1–16.
An excellent survey of the current state of migration in the world economy.

"Relocating the Back Office," *The Economist,* December 13, 2003, pp. 67–69.
A detailed article on the movement of service work in the world economy.

United Nations Conference on Trade and Development, *World Investment Report, 2006,* Geneva: United Nations, 2006.
The annual report on global FDI contains a large amount of information on global capital flows.

United Nations International Organization for Migration, *World Migration Report, 2005,* New York: United Nations, 2005.
An excellent summary of trends in migration in the world economy.

U.S. Department of Commerce, *Survey of Current Business,* Washington, D.C.: U.S. Government Printing Office.
The August issue of this monthly publication includes detailed statistics on U.S. FDI.

Chapter 7

Tariffs

"We up in Massachusetts do not want that duty upon molasses, we trade our fish for molasses, and if you shut out molasses you shut in fish."
—U.S. CONGRESSIONAL DEBATES, 1790

"A protective tariff is immoral and dishonest, because its sole purpose is to increase prices artificially, thereby enabling one citizen to levy unjust tribute from another."
—CORDELL HULL

INTRODUCTION

So far we have assumed that international trade is similar to trade among the various regions of a country in that it is not impeded by government action. As such, we have shown that free trade leads to the most efficient allocation of world resources and maximizes world output. However, governments do restrict or influence the international flow of goods and services through the use of trade barriers. In this chapter we begin our study of the effects of trade barriers. Our analysis begins by examining the most basic barrier to trade—the tariff. To describe the effects of a tariff, we employ a basic supply and demand model by returning to our discussion of international trade for a single product. This model allows us to focus on the effects that tariffs have with respect to imports, domestic consumption, and domestic production. In the final section of the chapter, we cover some of the common arguments in favor of tariffs and show that, usually, there is a better public policy option available than imposing tariffs.

TARIFFS: SOME PRELIMINARY DETAILS

tariff
a tax on imports imposed by a government

A **tariff** is simply a tax on an imported good.[1] Like all taxes, a tariff does the following:

- It affects the domestic consumption of an imported good.
- It affects the domestic production of goods that compete with the imported good.
- It affects the foreign production of the imported good.
- It changes the structure of the domestic economy.

In many respects, the effects of a tariff are no different than those of any other tax imposed by a government.[2] While tariffs are no longer a major form of tax revenue for

[1]Taxes on exports are theoretically possible and occasionally observed. Further, their effects are symmetrical to those for imports. However, the U.S. Constitution specifically prohibits taxes on exports, so we will limit our discussion to import tariffs.

[2]However, a tariff is a sneaky government tax. Have you ever seen the amount of tariffs paid by the importer on *any* imported item that you have purchased? It is safe to say that there would be fewer tariffs if this information were provided to consumers.

revenue tariff a tariff imposed by government on a good that is not domestically produced

protective tariff a tariff that is imposed by a government on a good to protect a domestic industry from foreign competition

the U.S. government, they still have important economic effects. For example, the tax—tariff—imposed on an imported good determines or influences what you consume and how much of the good you consume. Although the average tariff in the U.S. is approximately 4 percent, the tariff on many imported products remains quite high.

Some tariffs imposed by governments are designed as revenue tariffs. A **revenue tariff** is an import tax levied on a good that is not domestically produced. There are some revenue tariffs in the U.S., although they are rare.[3] As we will see below, revenue tariffs are most common in the developing countries. Tariffs in developed countries are designed primarily to be **protective tariffs**. The purpose of a protective tariff is to protect a domestic industry from foreign competition. Although not its principal purpose, any protective tariff also generates revenue. In fiscal year 2006, U.S. tariffs generated tax revenues of $26.7 billion. In this chapter, we will be concerned with the effects of tariffs that are imposed to protect domestic industries, rather than tariffs that are imposed to raise revenue for the domestic government.

Types of Tariffs

specific tariff a tariff that is measured as a fixed amount of money per unit imported –$1 per ton

One of the simplest forms of a tariff is a specific tariff. A **specific tariff** is expressed as a per-unit tax on imported goods, such as 6 cents per imported liter or $4 per imported ton. A specific tariff is relatively easy for a government to administer—it is a certain amount of money per unit of whatever is imported. However, if there are large differences in the imported price per unit, the effects of a specific tariff are not uniform across lower-priced and higher-priced items. For example, a specific tariff of $1,000 imposed on automobiles would yield a high percentage tariff relative to the import price of inexpensive Hyundais and a low percentage tariff relative to the import price of expensive Porsches. In this case, a specific tariff is regressive as Hyundais and Porsches are likely to be purchased by lower-income and higher-income consumers, respectively. In this case, the lower-income consumers would be paying a higher percentage tariff than would the higher-income consumers. As a result, the less well off pay a larger percentage of their income in tariffs than do those who are more affluent. In addition, the degree of protection given domestic producers varies with the price of the imported good. In this case, a specific tariff provides domestic producers of low-priced cars a high percentage tariff and a low percentage tariff on high-priced cars. The result of a specific tariff would be to encourage domestic producers to produce lower-priced or less expensive goods.

ad valorem tariff a tariff that is measured as a percentage of the value of the imported good

To avoid the regressive nature of specific tariffs, many governments impose ad valorem tariffs. An **ad valorem tariff** is expressed as a percentage of the value of the imported good, such as 5 percent. This constant percentage tariff avoids the regressive nature of a specific tariff. However, with an ad valorem tariff the valuation, or the price, of the imported good becomes critical in determining the dollar amount of the tariff. The higher the price of the imported good, the higher the dollar amount of the tariff. In this case, importers facing an ad valorem tariff have an incentive to *under-invoice* the price of the imported good. Under-invoicing means that importers may place a lower

[3]A major goal of the developing countries in trade negotiations is the elimination of revenue tariffs in the developed countries. These are particularly noticeable with respect to some natural resources and tropical food products.

value on the imported good than the true market price in order to reduce the dollar amount of the tariff.[4]

Under-invoicing also may occur when a multinational corporation ships intermediate products from one of its plants located in one country to one of its plants in another country. This type of under-invoicing is related to the firm's transfer-pricing policy that we discussed in the previous chapter. In part, these transfer-pricing practices determine in which country the profits of the multinational corporation are reported and taxed. In the case of under-invoicing, customs officials must be extremely knowledgeable about the market prices for all imported goods. As a result, ad valorem tariffs are more difficult for a country to administer than are specific tariffs.

compound tariff a tariff that includes a specific tariff and an ad valorem tariff

A tariff that is comprised of both a specific tariff and an ad valorem tariff is a **compound tariff**. An example would be $4 per imported ton plus 3 percent of the value of the imported good. Such compound tariffs are common on agricultural products whose prices tend to fluctuate. Table 7.1 lists various U.S. tariffs on selected imported items. Notice that some tariff rates are specific tariffs, some are ad valorem tariffs, and some are compound tariffs.

Methods of Valuing Imports

One of the issues that a country faces in administering and collecting tariffs is that its customs valuation can be based on one of three different methods of valuing imports.

Table 7.1 Selected U.S. Tariffs

Product	Duty Rate
Live, Chickens	0.9 cents each
Hams	1.4 cents/kg
Butter	12.3 cents/kg
Rice wine or Sake	3 cents/liter
Cheddar Cheese	16%
Caviar	15%
High Quality Beef Cuts	4%
Photographic Film in Rolls, 35mm	3.7%
Tire of Rubber for Motor Vehicles Radial	4%
Bicycles	11%
Mushrooms	8.8 cents/kg + 20%
Cigars each valued at less than 15 cents	$1.89/kg + 4.7%
Cigarettes, paper-wrapped	41.7 cents/kg + 0.9%
Women's or Girl's Overcoats made of wool	55.9 cents/kg + 16.4%

Source: U.S. International Trade Commission, *Tariff Schedules of the United States*, Washington, D.C.: U.S. Government Printing Office, 2007, (www.usitc.gov).

[4]An extreme form of under-invoicing is smuggling. If the tariff were high enough, importers would have an incentive to try to avoid the tariff altogether. In some developing countries this is not a trivial problem. For an excellent discussion of smuggling in the world economy, see Kate Gillespie and J. Brad McBride, "Smuggling in Emerging Markets: Global Implications," *Columbia Journal of World Business* 31(4), Winter 1996, pp. 40–54.

free alongside a measurement of the value of imports that includes the price of the good shipped to the side of the ship but without loading costs

One such method is the **free alongside (F.A.S.)** price. This valuation method defines the price of the imported good as the foreign country's market price before the good is loaded into the ship, train, truck, or airplane for shipment to the importing country.

Another method of valuing imports defines the imported price of the good as the **free on board (FOB)** price. The FOB price defines the price of the imported good as the foreign country's market price plus the cost of loading the good into the means of conveyance.

The third method of valuing imports is the **cost, insurance, and freight (C.I.F.)** price. This method defines the price of the imported good as the foreign country's market price plus the cost of loading the good into the means of conveyance plus all inter-country transportation costs up to the importing country's port of entry. Most countries use the C.I.F. price for calculating ad valorem tariffs. However, the U.S. currently uses the free on board price for calculating ad valorem tariffs.

WELFARE EFFECTS OF TRADE IN AN INDIVIDUAL PRODUCT

free on board a measurement of the value of imports that includes the price of the good loaded onto the ship but without the cost of international shipping or insurance

To analyze a tariff's economic impact, we need to separate the effects that a tariff has on consumers from the effects it has on producers. To separate these effects, we use a supply and demand model for an individual product, incorporating a separate measure for consumer and producer welfare.

Consumer and Producer Surplus: A Review

We begin by examining the benefits that consumers and producers receive from buying and selling a good in a market. Once we have a measure of consumer and producer welfare, the benefits of exports and imports for a country as a whole can be examined. These welfare measures are known as consumer and producer surplus. In the left panel of Figure 7.1, we illustrate the domestic demand for cloth for consumers in the U.S.[5] The vertical axis represents the maximum price that consumers are willing and able to pay for a given quantity of cloth, which is represented on the horizontal axis. The demand for cloth slopes downward to the right. All else being equal, this indicates that as the price of cloth falls; consumers are willing and able to buy more cloth.

cost, insurance, and freight a measurement of the value of imports that includes the cost of the good plus insurance and freight

Suppose that the market price of cloth in the U.S. is P, as illustrated in Figure 7.1. The quantity that consumers purchase at that price would be Q yards of cloth. Total expenditures on cloth by consumers—meaning price times quantity—is represented by the area of rectangle OPEQ. In this market, all consumers pay the same price, P. However, the demand curve for cloth indicates that there are some consumers who are willing to pay a higher price. For example, let us examine the highest price at which no consumers are willing to buy cloth. At price P_1 where the demand curve intersects the vertical axis, the quantity demanded is zero. Below P_1, there is some quantity demanded by consumers. These consumers are paying a lower price, P, than the maximum price they would be willing to pay.

[5]Although we could use any product, we chose cloth to be consistent with the earlier trade theory chapters.

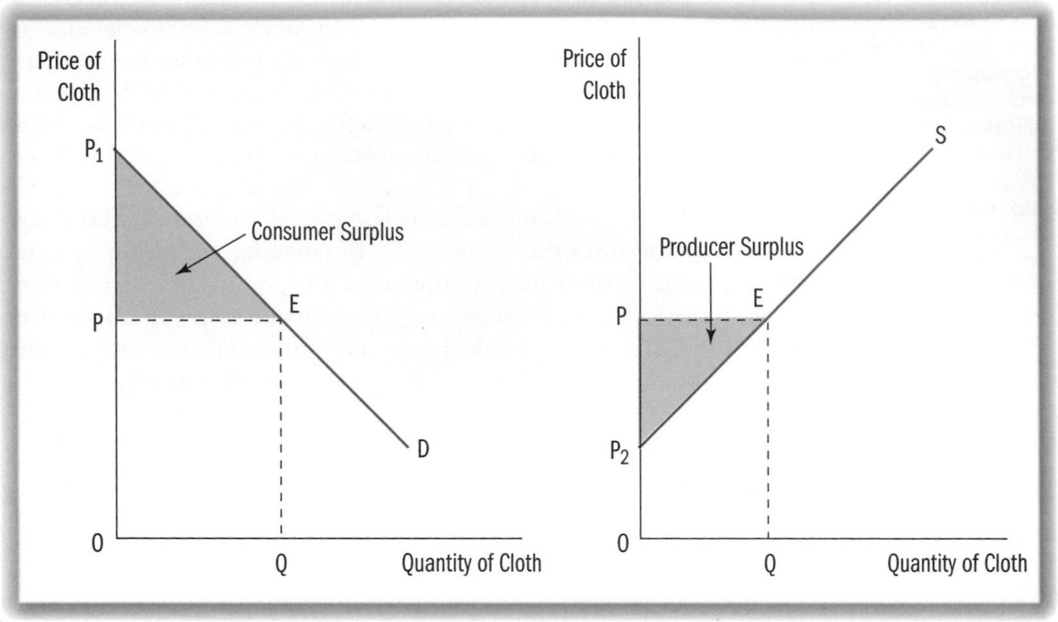

Figure 7.1 Domestic Demand and Supply of Cloth with Consumer and Producer Surplus

Consumer surplus is the difference between the price a consumer would be willing to pay for the good and the market price. Graphically, consumer surplus is represented by the area under the demand curve and above the market price, P_1EP. Producer surplus is the difference between the price at which a good is sold and the minimum price that the seller would be willing to accept. Graphically, producer surplus is represented by the area above the supply curve and below the market price, P_2EP.

consumer surplus the difference between the price that a consumer would be willing to pay for a good and the actual market price

This difference between the price that consumers are willing to pay and the price that they actually pay is known as **consumer surplus**. Consumer surplus is represented graphically by the triangular area P_1EP. This area represents the difference between the total amount of money that consumers were willing to spend on cloth and what consumers actually spent on purchasing cloth. Notice that the size of consumer surplus varies inversely with the price of cloth. A decrease in the market price would increase consumer surplus, while a higher market price would decrease consumer surplus.

To complete the analysis, we need to consider U.S. producers of cloth. In the right panel of Figure 7.1 the market supply of cloth is illustrated. The vertical axis represents the minimum price that producers would be willing to accept for a given quantity of cloth, which is represented on the horizontal axis. This supply curve slopes upward to the right. Everything else being equal, as the price of cloth rises, producers are willing and able to produce more cloth.[6]

Suppose that the market price of cloth in the U.S. is P, as illustrated in Figure 7.1. The quantity supplied by all producers would be Q yards of cloth. The total revenue that all producers receive—meaning price times quantity—is represented by the area of

[6]The supply curve includes all costs of production including a normal profit for the producer. A normal profit is defined by the producer's opportunity cost.

producer surplus the difference between the price at which a good is sold and the minimum price that the seller would be willing to accept for it

rectangle OPEQ. In this market for cloth, all producers receive the same price, P. The supply curve indicates that there are some producers willing to sell at a lower price. For example, let us examine the lowest price, at which no producers are willing to sell cloth. At price P_2 where the supply curve intersects the vertical axis, the quantity supplied is zero. Above P_2, there is some quantity supplied by producers. These producers are receiving a higher price, P, than the minimum price they would be willing to accept.

This difference between the price that producers are willing to accept and the price that they receive is known as **producer surplus**. Producer surplus is represented graphically by the triangular area P_2EP. This area represents the difference between the total amount of money that producers were willing to accept for cloth and what producers actually receive for selling cloth. Again, notice that the size of producer surplus varies directly with the price of cloth. A decrease in the market price of cloth would decrease producer surplus, while a higher market price of cloth would increase producer surplus.

Now, consider the domestic market for cloth without international trade. In this case, the equilibrium price and quantity of cloth in the U.S. is determined by domestic supply and demand. As Figure 7.2 illustrates, equilibrium occurs at point E, where the price of

Figure 7.2 Domestic Supply and Demand for Cloth with Consumer and Producer Surplus

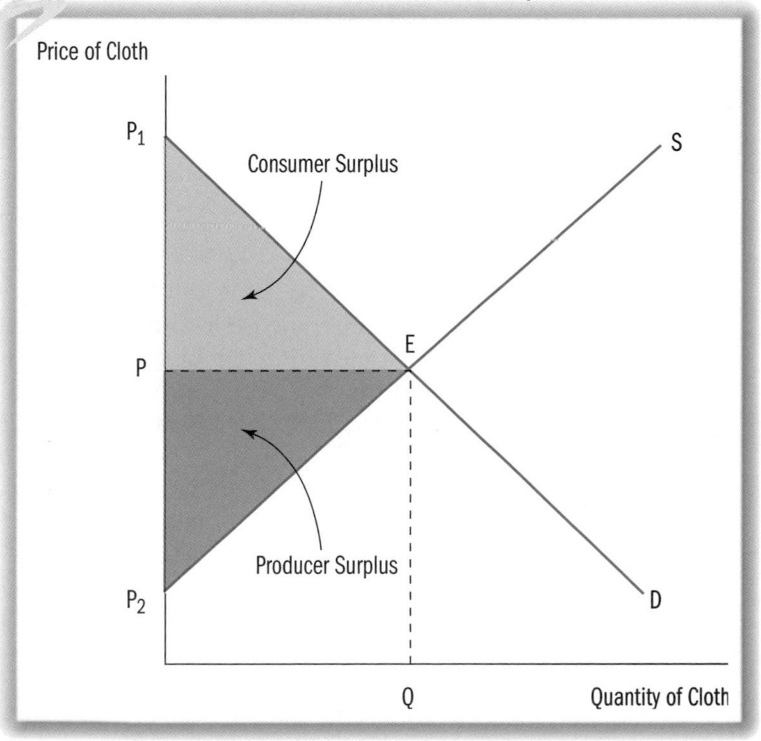

Equilibrium in the cloth market is represented at point E, where the equilibrium price and quantity are P and Q, respectively. Consumer surplus is represented by the area under the demand curve and above the equilibrium price—the triangle PEP_1. Producer surplus is represented by the area above the supply curve and below the equilibrium price—the triangle PEP_2.

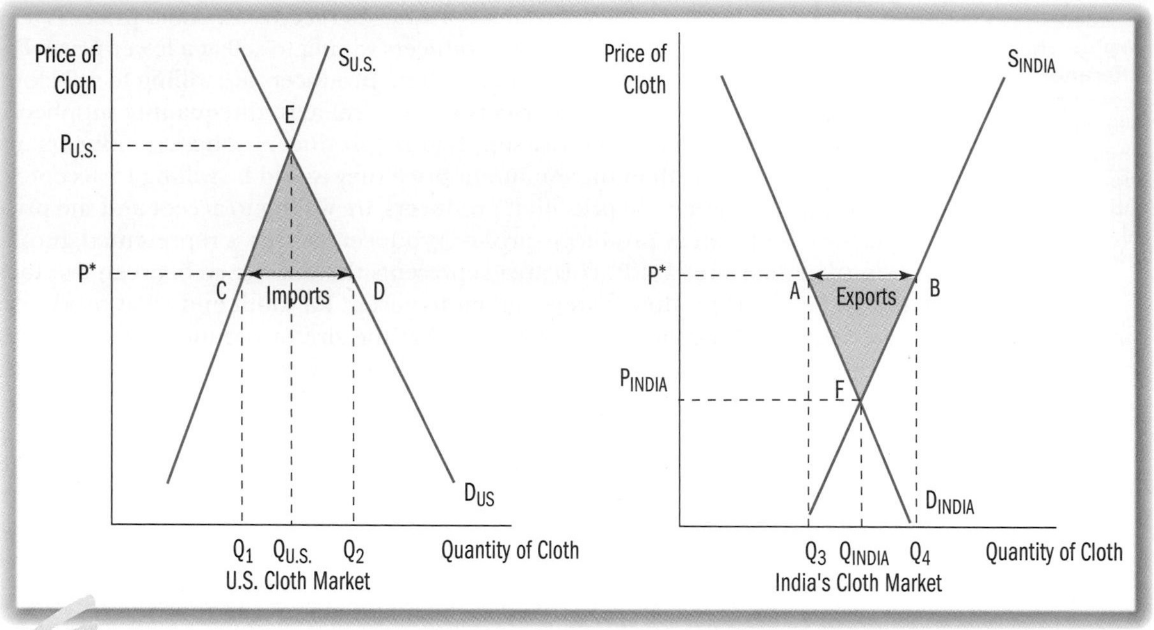

Figure 7.3 **Supply and Demand For Cloth Under Conditions of Free Trade**
Free trade in cloth between the U.S. and India causes the U.S. to gain by the area CED and India to gain by the area ABF.

cloth is P (the domestic price) and the equilibrium quantity of cloth is Q. The equilibrium market price of cloth represents the amount that consumers pay and producers receive for each unit of cloth sold in the market. Graphically, consumer surplus is represented by the triangular area P_1EP and producer surplus is represented by the triangular area P_2EP.

The Effects of Free Trade

To measure the effects of free trade on a country's welfare, consider the market for cloth as shown in Figure 7.3. As we begin our analysis, consider a world consisting of two countries—India and the U.S.—and one product—cloth—that is produced and consumed in both countries. Figure 7.3 shows the domestic supply and demand conditions for cloth within the U.S. and India. The supply and demand curves for cloth in the U.S. are shown in the left-hand panel by S_{US} and D_{US}, respectively. The analogous supply and demand curves for cloth in India are given in the right-hand panel as S_{INDIA} and D_{INDIA}, respectively.[7]

Before international trade opens between the two countries, equilibrium in the U.S. cloth market occurs at point E, where the equilibrium price and quantity of cloth

[7]Normally, the U.S. supply and demand for cloth will depend on the price of cloth in terms of U.S. dollars, and India's supply and demand for cloth will depend on the price of cloth in terms of India's currency, rupees. By assuming that the exchange rate between the U.S. dollar and the Indian rupee is not affected by whatever trade policy is undertaken in both countries with respect to the cloth market, we can state prices of cloth in both the U.S. and India in terms of one currency, dollars.

is P_{US} and Q_{US}, respectively. Equilibrium in the Indian cloth market occurs at point F, where the equilibrium price and quantity of cloth is P_{INDIA} and Q_{INDIA}, respectively. Because of the lower price of cloth in India, U.S. residents will begin purchasing Indian cloth and reduce their purchases of U.S. cloth once trade opens up. As residents in the U.S. reduce their demand for U.S. cloth, the price of cloth in the U.S. will decline. On the other hand, the price of cloth in India will rise. This occurs as the new U.S. demand for Indian cloth is added to domestic demand. This movement in the price of cloth in both countries will continue until the two prices converge at a single "international price." In Figure 7.3 the international price of cloth would be equal to P*, which lies between the two pre-trade prices (P_{US} and P_{INDIA}).

At price P*, the quantity of cloth supplied by U.S. producers will be Q_1, and the quantity demanded by U.S. consumers will be Q_2. Meanwhile, the quantity of cloth supplied in India will be Q_4 and the quantity demanded will be Q_3. For the international market to clear, the excess demand in the U.S., Q_1 to Q_2, must equal the excess supply in India, Q_3 to Q_4. That is, the quantity of cloth available for export from India (AB) must be equal to the quantity of cloth imports demanded by the U.S. (CD).

The opening of trade between the two countries has several important effects. First, the price of the traded good (cloth) will rise in the exporting country (India) and fall in the importing country (the U.S.), establishing a common international price. This means that consumers in the exporting country will have to pay a higher price for the good (cloth) than before trade, while consumers in the importing country will pay less. Second, because of these price changes, consumers in the exporting country (India) will consume less of the traded good (Q_3 is less than Q_{INDIA}), while consumers in the importing country (the U.S.) will consume more (Q_2 is greater than Q_{US}). Third, the quantity of the traded good (cloth) produced in the exporting country (India) will increase as trade opens (Q_4 is greater than Q_{INDIA}), and fall in the importing country (the U.S., Q_1 is smaller than Q_{US}).

Within the supply and demand model, a discussion of the effects of trade on the economic well-being of consumers and producers in the trading countries can also be conducted using consumer and producer surplus. For example, consumers of cloth in the U.S. have benefited from the opening of trade because the quantity of cloth consumed has increased and they pay a lower price. Obviously the welfare of U.S. consumers has increased. This increase in consumer welfare is represented by the increase in U.S. consumer surplus. The increase in consumer surplus is shown as area $P^*P_{US}ED$. However, producers of cloth in the U.S. have lost since they produce a smaller quantity of cloth and receive a lower price. This results in lower welfare for U.S. producers. Graphically, the decrease in producer welfare is represented by a decline in producers surplus of $P^*P_{US}EC$. Imports of cloth have clearly benefited U.S. society as a whole. Producer surplus has been reduced by the area $P^*P_{US}EC$ while consumer surplus has increased by the area $P^*P_{US}ED$. Since the gain in consumer surplus is larger than the loss in producer surplus, the U.S. as a whole gains. The area bounded by the points CED represents this gain.

For producers and consumers in India the opposite occurs. Consumers of cloth in India have lost due to the opening of trade. Their quantity of cloth consumed has decreased and they pay a higher price. The decrease in consumer welfare in India is shown as the area $P_{INDIA}P^*AF$. The producers of cloth in India have benefited since they produce a larger quantity of cloth and receive a higher price. The increase in producer welfare in India is shown as the area $P_{INDIA}P^*BF$. Exports of cloth by India have clearly benefited Indian society as a whole. Consumer surplus has been reduced by the area $P^*P_{INDIA}AF$ while producer surplus has increased by the area $P^*P_{INDIA}BF$. Since the gain in producer surplus is larger than the loss in consumer surplus, India as a whole gains. The area bounded by the points ABF represents their gain.

What we have described is why free trade increases a country's welfare. Recall that in Chapter 3 we illustrated that free trade was beneficial to a country overall using production possibilities frontiers. We also showed that the import competing industry suffered losses; the export industry reaped gains; and the country as a whole gained from international trade. Using the supply and demand model, we have illustrated the same results.

Figure 7.3 illustrates one of the most difficult policy issues in international trade. The gains to society as a whole are greater than the losses that occur within a particular industry. On the export side of the market, the losses are diffused among thousands or even millions of consumers as they pay a higher price for the exported good. Although the losses are diffused among consumers, the gains to producers and workers are concentrated. For example, firms in the export sector experience higher profits. Further, workers in such an industry frequently see wage increases and/or more job opportunities because of the opportunity to export the product.

On the import side of the market, the gains are diffused among thousands or even millions of consumers. The fact that greater imports are saving consumers (through lower prices) money on their purchases of cloth often goes unrecognized. The large gains to consumers in total come from relatively small gains over a very large number of purchases. The gains from trade are large in total, but the gains for any particular item frequently are small. Although the gains are diffused among consumers, the losses to producers and workers are concentrated. For example, firms in an industry that competes with imports face lower or even negative profits or in the extreme case, bankruptcy. Workers in such an industry may see wage increases that are lower because of competition from imports. If the import competition is large enough, the workers may experience reduced hours or even loss of employment. Given these losses, it is asking a lot for the industry to calmly accept this as the price paid for the greater economic good.[8]

THE ECONOMIC EFFECTS OF TARIFFS

To analyze a tariff's economic impact, we need to separate the effects that a tariff has on consumers from the effects it has on domestic producers. To separate these effects, we can use the concepts of producer and consumer surplus developed above. The central point of the analysis is that there is a net loss to a country's welfare that results from putting a tariff on imported goods.

The Effects of a Tariff for a Small Country

Now, let us use the concepts of consumer and producer surplus that we just developed to analyze the impact of a tariff. We begin our analysis by considering the case of

[8]Industry losses are routinely accepted if another, more efficient domestic industry hurts a domestic firm.

a country whose imports constitute a very small portion of total world imports. The importing country is referred to as a price taker because it is so small that it cannot influence world market conditions. In Figure 7.4, the domestic demand and supply of cloth is illustrated. Before international trade, equilibrium in the domestic cloth market occurs at point E. The equilibrium price and quantity of cloth associated with this point are P and Q, respectively.

Now, assume that the small country has a comparative disadvantage in the production of cloth and decides to engage in international trade. In this case, the small country will be able to import at a world price (P_w), which is below its domestic price, P. Point F is the new free-trade equilibrium. As we indicated earlier, this new equilibrium is clearly beneficial for cloth consumers. It is as though a marketwide sale of cloth were occurring as the price of cloth declines from P without imports to P_w with imports. In addition, the quantity of cloth that consumers are willing and able to buy increases from Q to Q_2. However, with free trade the amount supplied by the domestic cloth industry contracts from Q to Q_1 as the price of cloth declines and imports increase.

Let's assume that the domestic government imposes a tariff on cloth of the amount T to restrict imports. Because we have assumed that the importing country is a small country, it cannot influence world market conditions. In this case, the world

Figure 7.4 Domestic Effects of a Tariff

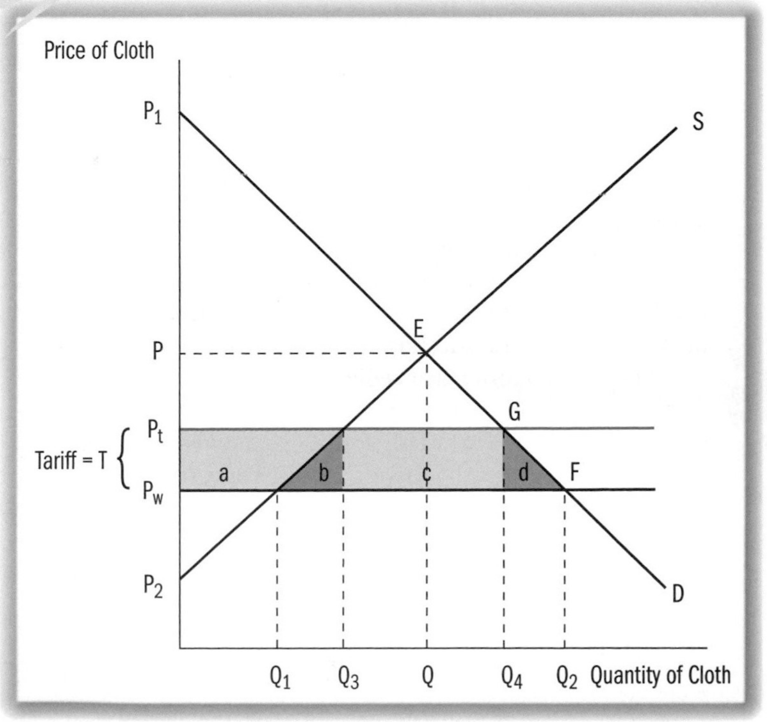

The tariff placed on imported cloth raises the price of cloth from Pw to Pt. As a result of the price increase, consumer surplus declines and producer surplus expands. The country's welfare falls by the amount equal to the production effect—triangle b—and the consumption effect—triangle d.

price of cloth will remain constant at P_w. The imposition of a tariff raises the price of cloth in the importing country by the full amount of the tariff, T. The result of this is the price of cloth in the importing country rises from P_w to P_t. The imposition of the tariff results in a new equilibrium at point G.[9]

The higher price of imported cloth has two effects. First, the quantity imported falls from the horizontal difference Q_1 to Q_2 to the smaller amount Q_3 to Q_4. The decline in imports is a result of lower domestic consumption of cloth—Q_2 to Q_4—and greater domestic production—Q_1 to Q_3. Second, consumers of cloth are clearly worse off. The price of cloth has increased and the quantity of cloth consumers buy has declined. As a result, consumer surplus within the country has declined. Specifically, the loss in consumer surplus is represented by the area $(a + b + c + d)$. As a result of the government imposing a tariff, consumers within the country lose. The remaining question is: Who gains? The gainers in the case of a tariff are the domestic government and domestic producers.

The rectangular area c represents the tariff revenue that the domestic government collects. The quantity imported after the tariff is imposed is the horizontal difference between Q_3 and Q_4. The tariff (T) is the difference between the world price, P_w, and price paid by domestic consumers, P_t. Multiplying the quantity imported by the amount of the tariff gives us the total tariff revenue collected by the government, area c. As a result, the government gains this area and the consumers lose it. If one assumes that the utility derived from government spending is the same as that derived from private consumption, there is no net loss to society as a whole from the consumer losing area c and the government gaining it.[10]

The area a represents a transfer of consumer surplus to producer surplus. This transfer of welfare from consumers to domestic producers represents the domestic producers' gains from a tariff. From the standpoint of the domestic cloth producer, a tariff is not as good as autarky but it is preferable to free trade.

The small triangle (b) represents the cost of resources transferred from their best use to the production of more cloth—Q_1 to Q_3. This represents a loss to society, because in a free market these resources would have been used to produce a product in which the importing country has a comparative advantage. Transferring resources to the tariff-ridden industry necessarily entails a loss of resources to some other, more productive industry.[11] Finally, the area d represents a consumption effect caused by a tariff as consumers purchase less cloth—Q_3 to Q_4.

dead-weight loss **the loss of welfare by a country from the imposition of a tariff**

The areas a and c are redistributed from consumers to the producers and government, respectively. The net loss to society and the loss of consumer welfare is composed of area (b + d). This loss to society is referred to as the **dead-weight loss** of a tariff. The dead-weight loss of a tariff represents a real loss to the country. Since it is not transferred to another sector of the economy and at represents a waste of resources in economic terms.

---

[9]For simplicity, the tariff in this case is assumed to be a specific tariff. The effects of an ad valorem tariff are the same when the importing country is small.

[10]However, it should be pointed out that some resources would be expended by an industry to obtain protection. The technical term for this waste of resources is *rent seeking*. For more details, see Chapter 9.

[11]This point is sometimes difficult to see. However, read the last quote (box) by Henry George and the point could not be clearer. Transferring resources to the tariff-ridden industry necessarily entails a loss of resources to some other, more productive industry.

Henry George on Free Trade

The U.S. economist Henry George (1839–1897) is best known for his proposed single tax on land. However, he was also an eloquent critic of protectionism in an age when it was rampant. The following are some of his better quotes concerning the folly of protectionism.[12]

"It might be to the interests of [lighting] companies to restrict the number and size of windows, but hardly to the interests of a community. Broken limbs bring fees to surgeons, but would it profit a municipality to prohibit the removal of ice from sidewalks in order to encourage surgery? Economically, what difference is there between restricting the importation of iron to benefit iron-producers and restricting sanitary improvements to benefit undertakers?"

"If to prevent trade were to stimulate industry and promote prosperity, then the localities where he was most isolated would show the first advances of man. The natural protection to home industry afforded by rugged mountain-chains, by burning deserts, or by seas too wide and tempestuous for the frail bark of the early mariner would have given us the first glimmerings of civilization and shown its most rapid growth. But, in fact, it is where trade could best be carried on that we find wealth first accumulating and civilization beginning. It is on accessible harbors, by navigable rivers and much traveled highways that we find cities arising and the arts and sciences developing."

"To have all the ships that left each country sunk before they could reach any other country would, upon protectionist principles, be the quickest means of enriching the whole world, since all countries could then enjoy the maximum of exports with the minimum of imports."

"What protection teaches us, is to do to ourselves in time of peace what enemies seek to do to us in time of war."

"However protection may affect special forms of industry it must necessarily diminish the total return to industry-first by the waste inseparable from encouragement by tariff, and second by the loss due to transfer of capital and labor from occupations which they would choose for themselves to less profitable occupations which they must be bribed to engage in. If we do not see this without reflection, it is because our attention is engaged with but a part of the effects of protection. We see the large smelting-works and the massive mill without realizing that the same taxes which we are told have built them up have made more costly every nail driven and every needle full of thread used throughout the whole country."

[12]This collection of quotes is taken from C. Lowell Harriss, "Guidance from an Economics Classic: The Centennial of Henry George's 'Protection or Free Trade," *American Journal of Economics and Sociology* 48(3), July 1989, pp. 351–56.

The Effects of a Tariff for a Large Country

Now, consider a country like the U.S. that is large enough to influence the world price of cloth if there is a change in its consumption. The difference between the large-country and small-country assumption is that, in the case of a large country, changes in the quantity imported influence the world price of the product. Figure 7.5 illustrates the economic effects of a tariff imposed by a large country. As we begin our analysis, once again consider a world consisting of two countries—India and the U.S. One product—cloth—is produced and consumed in both countries. Figure 7.5 shows the domestic supply and demand conditions for cloth in the U.S. and India. In the left-hand panel, the supply and demand curves for cloth in the U.S. are shown as S_{US} and D_{US}, respectively. Similar

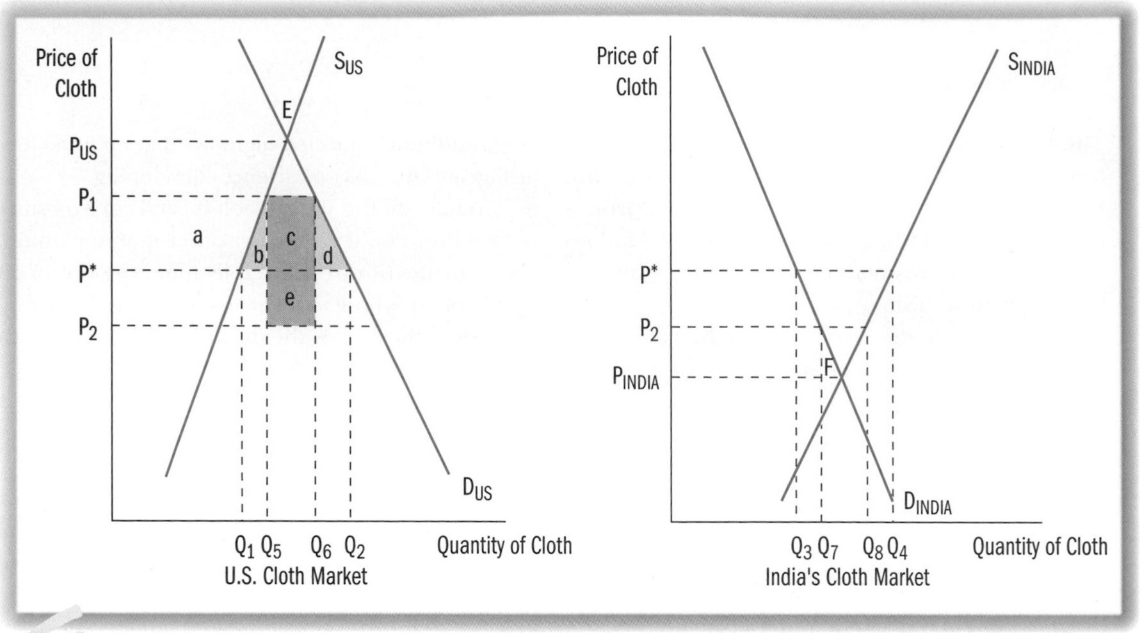

Figure 7.5 Domestic Effects of a Tariff in a Large Country

In a large country, a tariff on imports may be partially shifted to the domestic consumers through a higher price, P_1 to P, and partially shifted to foreign producers through a lower export price, P_2 to P*. The country's welfare effects are: 1) the loss of consumer surplus, area (b + d), and 2) the gain of welfare through the terms of trade effect, area e.*

supply and demand curves for cloth in India are shown in the right-hand panel by S_{INDIA} and D_{INDIA}, respectively. As we have previously illustrated, the world price of cloth under free trade would be equal to P*. At price P*, the quantity of cloth supplied by U.S. producers will be Q_1, and the quantity demanded by U.S. consumers will be Q_2. Meanwhile, the quantity of cloth supplied in India will be Q_4 and the quantity demanded will be Q_3. For the international market to clear, the excess demand in the U.S., Q_1 to Q_2, must equal the excess supply in India, Q_3 to Q_4. Put another way, the quantity of cloth exported from India must be equal to the quantity of cloth imported by the U.S.

Now assume that the U.S. imposes a tariff—T—on imported cloth, causing the price of cloth to rise from P* to P_1. As the price of imported cloth rises, the quantity of imported cloth falls from the horizontal difference Q_1 to Q_2 to the smaller amount Q_5 to Q_6. Because we have assumed that the U.S. is a large country, the U.S. tariff affects India's price of cloth. When a large country (U.S.) imposes a tariff to decrease its consumption of imports, this causes the price in the exporting country (India) to fall. As illustrated in Figure 7.5, the price of cloth in India falls from P* to P_2. India's price of cloth will fall until U.S. imports of cloth (Q_5 to Q_6) equals India's exports of cloth (Q_7 to Q_8.).

The higher price of imported cloth in the U.S. causes a decline in U.S. consumer surplus. Specifically, the loss in consumer surplus is represented by the area (a + b + c + d). Consumers within the country lose as a result of the government imposing a tariff. Remember, the area represented by (a), is a transfer of consumer surplus to producer surplus. The small triangle (b) represents the cost of resources transferred from their best use to U.S. production of more cloth. This represents a loss to society, because in a free market these resources would have been used to produce a product in which the U.S. has a comparative advantage. The small triangle (d) is the consumption effect caused by a tariff as U.S. consumers purchase less cloth.

The difference between a tariff imposed by a large country and a tariff imposed by a small country is that part of the tariff burden falls on consumers of cloth in the U.S., and part of the tariff burden falls on producers of cloth in India. The total government revenue collected from the tariff is equal to the amount imported (Q_5 to Q_6)

The Economic Effects of Selected U.S. Import Tariffs

Table 7.2 shows both tariff rates and the economic effects of the tariff on selected U.S. imported products. These estimated effects are based on 1990 data. The consumer cost refers to the loss in consumer surplus as a result of the tariff. The tariff revenue is the amount of revenue that the U.S. government collects. The producer gain refers to the increase in producer surplus as a result of the tariff. The dead-weight loss is the protection cost of the tariff. Also indicated in the table is cost per domestic job saved by the tariff. This cost is calculated by dividing the consumer cost by the number of domestic jobs saved as a result of the tariff. Note the very high cost of protection to the U.S. consumer for saving each job in the U.S. We wonder how many luggage workers in the U.S. really earn $934,000 per year.

Table 7.2 The Economic Effects of Selected U.S. Import Tariffs in 1990 (in millions of $)

Product	Tariff (%)	Consumer Cost	Tariff Revenue	Producer Gain	Dead-Weight Loss	Consumer Cost per Job in Thousands
Ceramic Tiles	19.0%	$139	$94	$45	$2	$401
Costume Jewelry	9.0	103	51	46	5	97
Frozen Concentrated orange juice	30.0	281	145	101	35	57
Glassware	11.0	266	95	162	9	180
Luggage	16.5	211	169	16	26	934
Rubber Footwear	20.0	208	141	55	12	122
Women's Footwear	10.0	276	295	70	11	102
Women's Handbags	9.0	103	51	46	5	97

Source: G. C. Hufbauer and K. A. Elliott, *Measuring the Cost of Protection in the United States,* Washington D.C.: Institute for International Economics, 1994, pp. 9–13.

multiplied by the import tariff (T) and is illustrated by area (c + e). The revenue of the import tariff includes two components. The first component is the amount of the tariff revenue shifted from domestic consumers to the U.S. government. This amount is illustrated by area c and is determined by the increase in the price of cloth from P* to P_1 multiplied by the amount of cloth imported, Q_5 to Q_6. The second component is the amount of the tariff revenue shifted from foreign producers in India to the U.S. government. This amount is illustrated by area e and is determined by the decrease in the price received by the foreign firm after the tariff is paid, P* to P_2, multiplied by the amount of cloth imported, Q_5 to Q_6. This second component is called the *terms of trade effect* and represents a redistribution of income from the foreign country to the U.S. This terms of trade effect improves the welfare of the U.S. at the expense of the foreign country.

In the case of a large country, the welfare effects of a tariff are: (1) the loss of consumer surplus, area (b + d), and (2) the gain of welfare through the terms of trade affect, area e. As a result, one of three possible cases can occur with respect to the overall impact of a tariff on the welfare of the large country. First, the U.S. could find that its total welfare has decreased if area (b + d) is greater than area e. Second, the U.S. could find that its total welfare has remained constant if area (b + d) is equal to area e. Finally, the U.S. could find that its total welfare has increased if area (b + d) is less than area e. The last case is interesting in that a country could theoretically increase its welfare by imposing a tariff. In this situation, the optimum tariff for a country to impose is that tariff that would maximize its own welfare at the expense of the foreign country's welfare.

THE EFFECTIVE RATE OF PROTECTION

effective rate of protection **a measurement of the amount of protection provided to an industry by a country's tariff schedule**

It is tempting to assume that domestic producers with high import tariffs receive a high degree of protection, and domestic producers with low import tariffs receive a low degree of protection. However, such a simple relationship between tariff rates and the degree of protection does not necessarily hold. To determine the actual degree of protection an industry receives, one must consider not only the tariff on the final good but also any tariffs on the intermediate inputs that the industry uses to produce the final good. This means that we need to consider the impact of tariffs on the value of the product produced domestically. A measure that accounts for the importance of these items is called the **effective rate of protection**.

For example, consider two DVD players. One is produced in the U.S. and the other is produced in a foreign country. For simplicity we will assume that both DVD players sell for $100 in the U.S. under conditions of free trade. Further, let us assume that half of the value of the foreign and domestically produced DVD players—$50—is imported components from a third country, and domestic and foreign production—value-added—accounts for the other half of the cost of the DVD players—$50. Now, suppose that a 20 percent tariff is imposed on the imported DVD player, and this tariff raises the imported price of the DVD player to $120—$100 for the DVD player and $20 for the tariff. The tariff rate is 20 percent, but what is the effective rate of protection for U.S. producers of DVD players? The effective rate of protection is equal to the percentage increase in domestic value-added made possible by the tariff.

Domestic value-added before the tariff was \$50, and domestic value-added after the tariff is \$70.

The domestic value-added after the tariff can be determined in one of two ways. First, it can be calculated as the difference between the tariff inclusive price—\$120—and the price of the imported components—\$50. Second, it can be calculated as the sum of the tariff—\$20—plus the domestic value-added before the tariff—\$50. The percentage change in the domestic value-added is determined as \$20/\$50, or 40 percent. In this case, a 20 percent tariff rate allows domestic value-added to rise by 40 percent, and this measures the effective rate of protection for domestic producers. Table 7.3 shows the impact of the tariff on U.S. valued-added in detail. A 20 percent tariff rate does not always imply an effective rate of protection of 40 percent. The relationship between the tariff rate and the effective rate of protection depends on the percentage of imported components used in the production process and the presence or absence of tariffs on the imported components and the final good.

The general formula for determining the effective rate of protection is:

$$ERP = (T_f - aT_c)/(1 - a)$$

In our example, T_f is the tariff rate on the imported final product—the DVD player; a is the percentage of imported components used in producing the final product [(\$50/\$100) = .5]; and T_c is the tariff rate on the imported components used to produce a DVD player. For example, if the imported components were taxed (tariff) at 10 percent, and DVD players faced a 20 percent tariff, the effective rate of protection would be 30 percent. $[.20 - .5(.1)]/(1 - .5)$

Since the effective rate of protection is determined by the interaction of three variables, the potential outcomes are infinite, and the effective rate of protection can even be negative. This occurs when the tariff on imported components multiplied by the percentage of imported inputs into the production process is larger than the tariff on the final good.

The tariffs on final goods in the U.S. tariff schedule are frequently small. However, a seemingly small nominal tariff coupled with a large percentage of the product

Table 7.3 The Effective Rate of Protection

	Under Free Trade		*With a 20% Tariff*	
	Foreign DVD Player	**Domestic DVD Player**	**Foreign DVD Player**	**Domestic DVD Player**
Component Parts	\$50	\$50	\$50	\$50
Assembly Cost (Value Added)	\$50	\$50	\$50	\$70
Tariff			\$20	
Price	\$100	\$100	\$120	\$120

coming from imported inputs can yield a large effective rate of protection. This phenomenon is so common that it is referred to as tariff escalation. The tariff schedules of many developed countries are structured in such a way as to have low tariffs on imported inputs coupled with higher tariffs on the final goods. In effect, the effective rate of protection on final products in developed countries is frequently higher than the nominal tariff posted in the tariff schedule. This tariff escalation encourages the final processing of imported inputs to occur in developed countries. This **structure of protection** discourages the processing of intermediate products into final goods in the foreign country where the intermediate products are produced. A consistent complaint of developing countries is that this structure of protection hinders their ability to transform raw materials into intermediate or final goods. While the magnitude of this effect may be debatable, the existence of this effect is not. Any time the tariff escalates with the stage of processing, foreign producers who wish to produce the final product with local inputs are being discriminated against. Since these producers are frequently in developing countries, the escalation of tariffs in developed countries makes the world distribution of income more unequal than if there were no tariffs at all.

structure of protection an analysis of the variation in tariffs by product for a country

ARGUMENTS FOR TARIFFS

In Chapter 2, we showed that free trade increases a country's welfare as resources are better utilized by countries that specialize and engage in trade. Our analysis showed that the total output of each individual country would rise. Further, this implies that the economic output of the world would rise. In Chapter 4, we showed the causes of comparative advantage. Comparative advantage occurs because countries are endowed with relatively different amounts of capital, labor, human capital, and/or technology. The result in terms of the economic output of the countries engaging in trade was the same. The total output of the two countries both increased as a result of trade. Again, the economic output of the world increased as well. Under these circumstances, one may well wonder why there is any public policy toward trade in the world economy that represents a departure from free trade. With a few notable exceptions, such as Hong Kong, virtually all countries choose to impose restrictions on free trade. In this section, we will consider some of the more widely used arguments for the protection of domestic industry. Very few of these arguments have much, if any, economic merit. The purpose here is to illustrate the fallacies embodied in the arguments for imposing tariffs. In the final part of this section, we will consider a policy that is normally preferable to tariffs if there is some reason society wishes to produce more output in a particular industry than would be dictated in the free market.

Infant Government

The most reasonable case that can be made for a country to impose tariffs is the infant government argument. In a developed country, the tax revenue that the government needs to finance its operations is relatively easy to collect. Income taxes are automatically deducted from your paycheck. Sales taxes are automatically collected by the merchant and electronically passed on to the government. In a developing country, this rather automatic form of tax collection does not exist. Many if not most transactions occur in cash. Collecting income and/or sales taxes may be beyond the technical capabilities of the government. Like all governments, the governments of developing countries need money to finance their operations, but collecting taxes is much more difficult. In these cases, the tariff is an attractive method of raising government revenue. For example, Cameroon, the Congo, the Dominican Republic, Guinea, Nepal, and Sierre Leone collect more than 30 percent of government revenues from tariffs. As we will see in Chapter 9, today's developed countries once collected most of the government's revenues from tariffs. In such a circumstance, it is somewhat understandable that a developing country would be willing to sacrifice some overall economic efficiency in the interests of collecting an adequate amount of money to finance the government. In the process of collecting this revenue, developing countries frequently design a system of tariffs that accomplishes other purposes.

For a developing country, tariffs can be an attractive form of taxation for several reasons. First, imports legally must pass through customs. In effect, this is a choke point where the government can easily collect revenue. The goods cannot pass into the country until the tariff is paid. The administrative costs of such a tax are also small relative to income or sales taxes. Second, in a developing country GDP per capita frequently is low. Many of the country's citizens would have difficulty paying even a modest income tax. However, not all of the country's citizens are poor. The challenge is to design a tax that is based on the ability to pay. A country's tariff structure can be structured to accomplish this. Tariffs may be levied on intermediate goods or on capital equipment that is only going to be purchased by producers of final goods. These firms can recoup at least part of the tariff in the form of higher prices. However, most firms will not be able to pass along the entire amount of the tariff to consumers. In this case, the tariff acts something like a corporate income tax. Also, tariffs can be used as a highly progressive income tax. A high tariff on "luxury" consumer goods such as automobiles or air conditioners can amount to a very progressive income tax. The point is that by putting different tariffs on different imports, the government can collect revenue in a way that is something like a progressive tax on corporate or individual income. Finally, such a system has the potential to alter the distribution of income within the country.

National Defense

A common argument for tariffs is the national defense argument. A country has a legitimate need to take steps to ensure that its military forces can operate effectively if necessary. Soldiers do not fight in a vacuum. Frequently, enormous supplies of goods and services are needed at short notice in the case of potential or actual military conflict. The argument in this case is that certain industries need to be protected from foreign competition to ensure an adequate output of the industry in the case of a conflict. There are two problems with this argument. The first problem is defining which industries are essential for national defense. Since this may not be entirely clear in all cases, industries with only a tenuous connection to national defense may obtain protection. The national defense argument ultimately entails a large amount of protection in the forms of tariffs or other nontariff barriers to trade.[13]

[13]See the next chapter for another form of protectionism for the defense industry in the U.S.

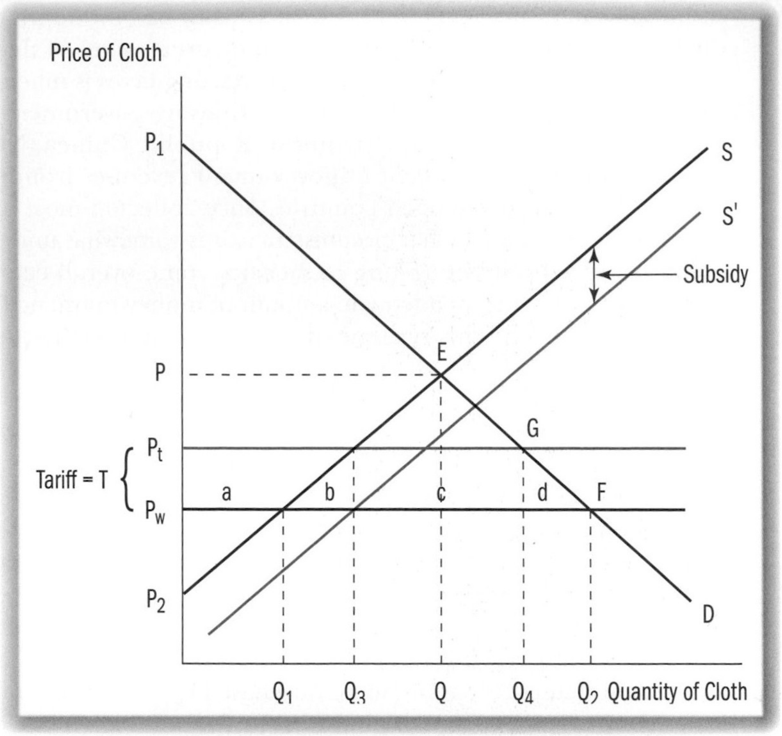

Figure 7.6 The Effects of a Domestic Production Subsidy

A government subsidy leads to an increase in domestic output, with less dead-weight loss than under an equivalent tariff.

The second problem is that a tariff is a costly means of accomplishing this end. Almost invariably, the optimal policy in this case and others is a domestic production subsidy. To illustrate the effects of a subsidy, we reproduce the figure that illustrates the effects of a tariff for a small country in Figure 7.6. If a country was to impose a tariff, T, on this product there would be a loss of consumer surplus equivalent to the area (a + b + c + d). As before, areas a and c are transferred to the producers and the government, respectively. The dead-weight loss from the tariff is equal to area (b + d). In the case of the tariff, domestic output increases from Q_1 to Q_3. However, the same increase in domestic production can be accomplished at a lower cost to the country by providing a production subsidy. Let us assume that the government simply furnishes the industry with a production subsidy of S, which is equal to the price they would obtain with a tariff in place. In this case, the effect of the subsidy is to shift the domestic supply downward by the amount of the subsidy. This effect is illustrated with the supply curve S', and the industry would be willing to produce the larger output associated with a tariff, Q_1 to Q_3. However, in this case the consumer is still paying the world price, P_w, for the good. The consumer would still be purchasing the same amount of the good at the same price. The dead-weight loss is now only area b and not area (b + d). Our example of protection in this case was firms located in the defense industry, but the principle can be generalized. The least expensive way to encourage domestic output of a good is through a production subsidy, not a tariff.

Infant Industries

The infant industry argument has been a staple of the economic development literature for a long time. Most developing countries go through a stage where resources are moving out of a declining agricultural sector into a growing manufacturing sector. However, in the initial stages of the development of a manufacturing sector, many of the industries within the sector look weak compared to world competition. The premise is that "new" industries in developing countries initially may need protection to allow them to grow in the face of more established foreign competition. The temporary protection also may allow the industry to become large enough to establish sufficient economies of scale to effectively compete in world markets. Once the industry has become internationally competitive, the protectionism is withdrawn to allow the industry to become even more efficient.

Superficially, this argument is plausible, but in practice it has been fraught with problems. The first problem is that an eligible infant industry is one that will eventually become internationally competitive. The problem for the government is picking the industries that will in fact become internationally competitive. It is an old joke among economists that any government bureaucrat who could really do this should quit being a bureaucrat and become an investor. This is just a way of pointing out that what seems easy, really is not. Secondly, the infant industry may never grow up. Protectionism is very attractive for the producers and possibly for the workers. Industries that have been protected are frequently unwilling to give up this protection. If the government is not careful, the "temporary" protection may go on for so long that the industry never really becomes efficient. If this policy is pursued on a large scale in a country, the risk is that large parts of the manufacturing sector may become permanently uncompetitive in world markets. Once this has happened, the eventual adjustments necessary to restructure the country's manufacturing sector may be difficult. As we will see in Chapter 11, the optimal policy may be a more market-oriented approach to industrial development that emphasizes the development of a manufacturing sector based on factor abundance and comparative advantage.

Senile Industry Protection

For many developed countries, there are forms of protection that have been designed for industries that are not new. These old or "senile" industries may have once had a comparative advantage in world markets. However, as was indicated in Chapter 4, factor abundance can change over time. An industry in a developed country that once had a comparative advantage based on relatively inexpensive labor, may be hard pressed by imports from developing countries where labor is now cheaper. The apparel industry in most developed countries is a common example. The problem in this case is how to transfer the resources from the comparative-disadvantage industry to other activities where the resources can produce more output. The problem is exacerbated by the existence of the sector-specific resources also discussed in Chapter 4. Some resources used in these industries cannot be easily transferred to other uses.

The argument for protecting these industries is to provide a method of moving resources out of them in such a way as to ensure that the overall output of the economy does not fall. If firms in the industry fail and the resources cannot be easily put to use elsewhere, the overall output of the economy could fall in the short run. The argument here is that temporary protection of older industries may actually increase output if the protection is gradually withdrawn as the resources reach the end of their useful life. The argument is plausible and has one advantage that the infant industry argument does not. Picking future comparative advantage industries is difficult. However, anyone can determine the comparative disadvantage industries: imports are rising, profits are falling, firms are failing, and employment in the industry is falling. Picking the senile industries is not hard to do. Again, the difficulty lies in the execution. The protection must be temporary and should be withdrawn as the assets in the industry depreciate to the end of their economically useful lives. This process will not be easy. Unless the protectionism is withdrawn at an appropriate rate, it will be all too easy for a country to be permanently saddled with an old, inefficient industry. The protectionism in the agricultural sector of many developed countries is a case in point.

A more efficient strategy in this case is to aid firms and workers in making the adjustment to another part of the economy. The owners of capital can be encouraged and/or subsidized to find new ways to use the capital that will earn a higher rate of return in the long run than leaving the capital in a comparative-disadvantage industry. Governments can also pursue policies to assist workers in finding new employment. This may involve subsidies for education, training, and the payment of relocation expenses. As was shown earlier in the chapter, the costs of saving jobs in declining industries is very high. Compared to these costs, subsidies to firms and workers rather than protectionism may be a relative bargain for society.

Tariffs, Trade, and Jobs

The final and most common argument for tariffs is the creation of jobs in the economy. Like most arguments for tariffs, it seems plausible at first. Returning to Figure 7.4, a tariff increases the output of the domestic industry. Presumably as output expands, the amount of employment in the industry likewise will expand. Rather simplistically, the tariff has produced more "jobs." As we will see, the tariff has not really produced any jobs and if there are enough tariffs on imports the total number of jobs may well be less than without tariffs.

The key to seeing this is considering employment in the industry as opposed to the overall level of employment in the economy. The tariff has created jobs in this particular industry but there are fewer jobs in other industries. This is because consumers spend more on goods from the protected industry but less on other goods. The tariff has not increased the total number of jobs, it has just rearranged them. Protected industries have more jobs, and other industries have fewer jobs. The overall level of employment has not changed. The total number of jobs in the economy is determined by macroeconomic forces such as the rate of economic growth in the long run and the state of fiscal and monetary policy in the long run. Tariffs don't change the total number of jobs, they just put jobs in places that the market would not.

Unfortunately, in the long run tariffs may reduce the overall level of employment. As we saw in Chapter 2, there is a gain from moving resources such as labor from comparative-disadvantage industries to comparative-advantage industries. The reverse is true. Tariffs move jobs into comparative-disadvantage industries. This entails a loss in the overall output of the economy (GDP). Since the total level of employment is tied to the total output of the economy, tariffs may easily produce fewer jobs overall. Finally, an economy with a lot of tariffs will usually grow more slowly than a more open economy. The number of new jobs in the future is dependent on the rate of economic growth. The faster the growth rate, the more jobs will become available. This also works to reduce the number of jobs. The bottom line is that the number of jobs in both the short run and the long run is reduced by the presence of tariffs.

Petition of the French Candlemakers

French economist Fredric Bastiat's "The Petition of the French Candlemakers" (1873) is often used to illustrate what protection of a domestic industry from foreign competition implies. In this amusing anecdote, he illustrates the flaws in the argument for protectionism.

"We are subjected to the intolerable competition of a foreign rival whose superior facilities for producing light enable him to flood the French market at so low a price as to take away all our customers the moment he appears, suddenly reducing an important branch of French industry to stagnation. This rival is the sun.

We request a law to shut up all windows, dormers, skylights, openings, holes, chinks, and fissures through which sunlight penetrates. Our industry provides such valuable manufactures that our country cannot, without ingratitude, leave us now to struggle unprotected through so unequal a contest. . . . In short, granting our petition will greatly develop every branch of agriculture. Navigation will equally profit. Thousands of vessels will soon be employed in whaling, and thence will arise a navy capable of upholding the honor of France. . . .

Do you object that the consumer must pay the price of protecting us? You have yourselves already answered the objection. When told that the consumer is interested in free importation of iron, coal, corn, wheat, cloth, etc., you have answered that the producer is interested in their exclusion. You have always acted to encourage labor, to increase the demand for labor.

Will you say that sunlight is a free gift, and that to repulse free gifts is to repulse riches under pretense of encouraging the means of obtaining them? Take care you deal a death blow to your own policy. Remember: hitherto you have always repulsed foreign produce because it was an approach to a free gift; and the closer this approach, the more you have repulsed the good. . . .

When we buy a Portuguese orange at half the price of a French orange, we in effect get it half as a gift. If you protect national labor against the competition of a half-gift, what principle justifies allowing the importation of something just because it is entirely a gift? . . . The difference in price between an imported article and the corresponding French article is a free gift to us. The bigger the difference, the bigger the gift. . . . The question is whether you wish for France the benefit of free consumption or the supposed advantages of laborious production. Choose, but be consistent."

SUMMARY

1. A tariff is a tax on imports and like all taxes it can have important effects on consumption, production, and the structure of a domestic economy.
2. Tariffs have two basic functions. A revenue tariff is an import tax levied on a good that is not produced domestically. A protective tariff is designed to protect a domestic industry from foreign competition.
3. There are several types of tariffs. A specific tariff is a per-unit tax and is expressed as a certain amount per unit imported. An ad valorem tariff is expressed as a percentage of the value of the import. A compound tariff is a tariff comprised of both a specific tariff and an ad valorem tariff.
4. The administration of tariffs is complicated because a country's customs valuation can be based on one of three different methods of valuing imports. The free alongside (F.A.S.) price defines the price of the imported good as the foreign market price before it is loaded into the ship, train, truck, or airplane for shipment to the foreign country. The free on board (F.O.B.) price defines the price of the imported good as the foreign price plus the cost of loading the product into the means of conveyance. The cost, insurance, and freight (C.I.F.) price defines the imported price as the product's value as it arrives at the port of entry.
5. The difference between the price that consumers are willing to pay and the price that they actually pay is known as consumer surplus. The difference between the price at which a good is sold and the minimum price that the seller would be willing to accept for it is known as producer surplus.
6. A tariff's welfare effects can be measured by the gains and losses of consumer and producer surplus. The imposition of a tariff raises the price of the imported good and results in the following: (1) fewer imports, (2) a decrease in consumer surplus, (3) an increase in producer surplus, and (4) an increase in government revenue. The net effect of the tariff is lost consumer welfare.
7. In the case of a large country, a tariff's welfare effects are the loss of consumer welfare and the gain of welfare through a change in the terms of trade.
8. There are several arguments for the imposition of a tariff. They include the infant government, infant industry, national defense, senile industry, and domestic jobs.

KEY CONCEPTS AND TERMS

- tariff p. 142
- revenue tariff p. 143
- protective tariff p. 143
- specific tariff p. 143
- ad valorem tariff p. 143
- compound tariff p. 144
- free alongside p. 145
- free on board p. 145
- cost, insurance, and freight p. 145
- consumer surplus p. 146
- producer surplus p. 147
- dead-weight loss p. 152
- effective rate of protection p. 156
- structure of protection p. 158

PROBLEMS AND QUESTIONS FOR REVIEW

1. What is the difference between a revenue tariff and a protective tariff?
2. In general, are there differences in countries that primarily use tariffs for revenue versus protection of domestic industries?
3. Describe the differences among specific tariffs, ad valorem tariffs, and compound tariffs.
4. What are some of the problems associated with using specific tariffs for differentiated products.
5. Describe the differences in the valuation of imports between FAS, FOB, and CIF.
6. Describe consumer and producer surplus.
7. Show what happens to both producer surplus and consumer surplus when the price increases or decreases.

8. Describe the economic effects that occur when a small country imposes a tariff.
9. Show how a tariff reduces the welfare of consumers by a larger amount than it increases the welfare of producers.
10. What is the dead-weight loss from a tariff?
11. Explain the economic effects of a tariff that is imposed by a large country.
12. Suppose that the free-trade price of a domestic product is $10,000 and contains 25 percent imported components. Assume that the tariff on the final product is 10 percent and a 5 percent tariff is imposed on the imported components.
    a. What is the product's price after the imposition of the tariff?
    b. What is the domestic value added before and after the imposition of the tariff?
    c. What is the effective rate of protection?
13. Explain what is meant by the effective rate of protection.
14. Under what conditions does a tariff applied to an imported product overstate or understate the effective rate of protection?
15. Describe how the structure of protection in developed countries could impede the development of manufacturing industries in developing countries.
16. Why are tariffs still used for revenue by developing countries?
17. Demonstrate why a production subsidy is less costly than a tariff if the goal is to expand the output of a particular industry.
18. Describe the national defense argument for a tariff. In many cases, is this the most efficient solution?
19. Is protecting new industries from foreign competition an efficient way to develop these industries?
20. Do tariffs increase the overall level of employment in an economy?

SUGGESTED READINGS AND WEB SITES

Jagdish N. Bhagwati, *Free Trade Today,* Princeton, NJ: Princeton University Press, 2002.

A collection of three essays on the history of free trade, labor and environmental issues, and approaches to free trade. Accessible for good undergraduate students.

Cletus C. Coughlin, "The Controversy Over Free Trade: The Gap Between Economists and the General Public," *Federal Reserve Bank of St. Louis Review* 84(1), January/February 2002, pp. 1–21.

A short summary of the debate over free trade coupled with some interesting polling data both from economists and the general public.

Douglas A. Irwin, *Free Trade Under Fire,* Princeton, N.J.: Princeton University Press, 2002.

A careful collation of the ways that free trade is subverted in the world economy.

Johannes Overbeek, *Free Trade versus Protectionism,* Northampton, MA: Edward Elgar, 1999.

The subtitle of this book is "A Sourcebook of Essays and Readings." It is a wonderful collection of many of the classic essays on free trade.

Russell Roberts, *The Choice, A Novel of Free Trade and Protectionism,* 3rd ed, Upper Saddle River, N.J.: Prentice Hall, 2007.

A fascinating way to learn about most of the issues involved in the debate over free trade.

Nelson D. Schwartz, "Bent but Unbowed," *Fortune,* July 22, 2002, pp. 118–26.

A close-up look at the problems of the American steel industry and why tariffs won't solve the industry's problems.

U.S. International Trade Commission, *Tariff Schedules of the United States,* Washington, D.C.: U.S. Government Printing Office, 2004. (www.usitc.gov)

This is the source for information on tariffs in the U.S.

Chapter 8

Nontariff Distortions to Trade

"In itself the abolition of protection is like the driving off of a robber. But it will not help a man to drive off one robber, if another, still stronger and more rapacious, be left to plunder him."
—HENRY GEORGE

"The American automobile industry had a very good year in 1983: New-car sales jumped up by nearly one million units, and, as has been well-publicized, after tax profits soared to a record $6.2 billion. But the industry is not quite as robust as these statistics suggest. U.S. automobile companies have been playing with a home-field advantage: quotas on Japanese imports, . . . Given the scant evidence that these quotas are advancing the competitiveness of the U.S. automobile industry, their desirability turns on whether Americans wish to pay large premiums on their cars in order to increase the employment of auto workers at wages far above the manufacturing average."
—ROBERT W. CRANDALL

INTRODUCTION

In the last chapter, we described how tariffs protect domestic industries from foreign competition. However, from the standpoint of governments and domestic producers, tariffs have a couple of disadvantages. First, they do not necessarily completely protect a domestic industry over time. Unless the tariff is prohibitively high, domestic producers still have to worry about competition from imports. In the first part of this chapter, you will learn about quotas, which provide domestic firms with a more certain form of protection. Second, tariffs imposed by a government are a visible form of protectionism. For example, a 10-percent tariff on an imported good provides a domestic producer a 10-percent price advantage over foreign producers. Governments and both foreign and domestic producers know the size of this price advantage. If possible, governments would prefer to protect a domestic industry using a means that is not quite so visible. In the second part of this chapter, we discuss ways in which governments attempt to protect domestic industries without being so obvious about it. As you will learn, these forms of protectionism are becoming common in the world economy. Up until this point, we have made the assumption that the costs involved in moving goods from one country to another are zero. The existence of transportation costs constitutes an implicit form of protection for domestic producers, and in the last section of the chapter we consider transportation costs and how they affect international trade.

NONTARIFF BARRIERS TO TRADE

Tariffs have been and remain a serious impediment to international trade, but they are less of a barrier than they used to be. In developed countries, tariffs have declined to less than 10 percent on average. In developing countries, tariffs are generally higher than they are in developed countries. Successive rounds of international trade negotiations have been successful in significantly reducing the average level of tariffs within this group of countries. If the decline in tariff rates had occurred in isolation for both developed and developing countries, the world would have made significant progress toward freer international trade. Unfortunately, everything else has not stayed the same. As tariffs declined in most countries, domestic firms and industries have sought protection from imports in other areas. Part of the protectionist pressure has been shifted to bureaucratic regulations that allow tariffs to be increased in the presence of "unfair" foreign trade practices.[1] Beyond this administrative (bureaucratic) track, governments can engineer regulations that do not look like protectionism but amount to the same thing. For industries with sufficient political influence, there is the possibility of obtaining more overt forms of protection.

nontariff trade barriers (NTBs) government policies other than tariffs that distort trade

Nontariff barriers to trade (NTBs) are government policies other than tariffs that tend to distort trade. Figure 8.1 illustrates that NTBs affect between 10 and 20 percent of the tariff lines of the EU, Japan, and the U.S. These forms of protection are less visible but they have a significant impact on international trade in many industries. In some cases, an NTB may prevent international trade between countries. Even in less extreme cases, NTBs reduce international trade because they implicitly make imported goods more expensive than comparable domestic goods. As the level of tariff protection diminishes over time, NTBs are becoming a relatively more important deterrent to trade.

QUOTAS

quota a government policy that limits imports of a product to a certain number of units

One of the more restrictive forms of protectionism is the quota. **Quotas** restrict imports of a good to a certain quantitative level. In practice, this means that a country imposing a quota imports only a certain number of units of the good on an annual basis. Quotas are considered such an extreme form of protectionism that they are banned under international trade rules. Nevertheless, quotas still exist in various forms for five reasons.

First, not all countries are members of the World Trade Organization (WTO). These countries are still free to impose quotas. Countries that are not members of the WTO include Afghanistan, Algeria, Azerbaijan, Belarus, Ethiopia, Iran, Iraq,

[1]These laws are covered in the next chapter.

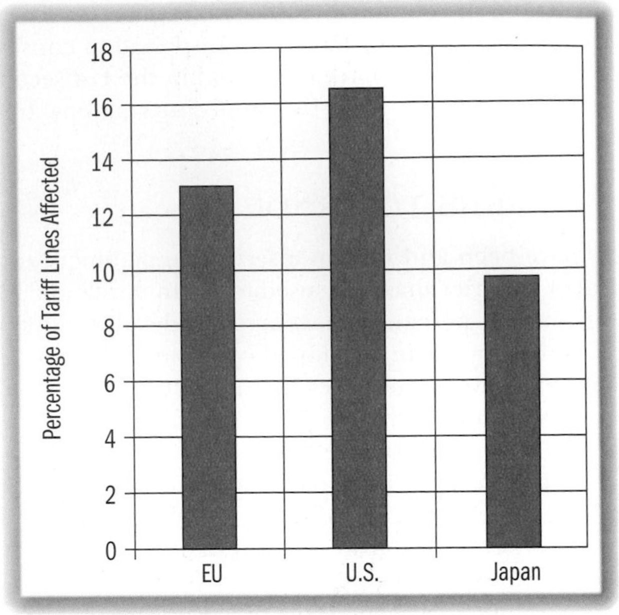

Figure 8.1 Frequency of Nontariff Barriers, 1996

Source: *Market Access: Unfinished Business—Post Uruguay Round, Inventory and Issues,* (Special Study No. 6), Geneva: World Trade Organization, 2001, p. 21.

Lebanon, Libya, Russian Federation, Sudan, Yemen, Ukraine, Kazakhstan, Tajikistan, and Uzbekistan. Quotas provide protection for domestic industries, but they also can accomplish another objective. For example, some countries may experience difficulties obtaining adequate amounts of foreign exchange to finance or buy all of their imports. In these circumstances, a country may choose to restrict imports through the use of a quota as a means of conserving foreign exchange. In the past, many developing countries were reluctant to join the GATT/WTO because the elimination of quotas was a condition of membership.

Second, new members of the WTO are allowed to maintain their previously existing quotas for a specified period of time. For example, when a country joins the WTO, its trade regulations do not have to be in immediate compliance with WTO rules. Usually, an agreement is negotiated between the WTO and the country concerning a transition period. This transition period is designed to allow the country time to implement new trade regulations that are in compliance with WTO standards. To make this transition easier for countries joining the WTO, a lengthy transition period is normally granted. For example, when Mexico joined GATT (General Agreement on Tariffs and Trade) in 1986, the transition period was 15 years. Such a situation is not untypical. From 1990 until the creation of the WTO in 1995, 31 countries joined the international trade organization, and since the WTO's creation an additional 37 countries have joined. For example, between 2000 and 2006, Albania, Armenia, Cambodia, China, Croatia, Georgia, Jordan, Lithuania, Macedonia, Moldova, Nepal, Oman,

Table 8.1 Number of Import Quotas in the Major Industrialized Countries

Country	Total Number of Import Quotas	Quotas on Agricultural Products	Quotas on Industrial Products
United States	7	1	6
Canada	5	4	1
United Kingdom	3	1	2
France	46	19	27
Germany	4	3	1
Italy	8	3	5
Benelux	5	2	3
Japan	27	22	5

Source: William R. Cline, "The Micro- and Macroeconomics of Foreign Sales to Japan," in *Trade Policy in the 1980s,* William R. Cline, ed., Washington, D.C.: Institute for International Economics 1983, p. 261.

Saudi Arabia, Chinese Taipei (Taiwan customs area), Tonga, and Viet Nam joined the WTO. As such, all of the newly joined members of the WTO are in the process of eliminating their quotas.

Multifibre Arrangement (MFA) **a system of bilateral quotas for imports and exports of textiles and apparel in which each country is allowed to send or receive a specific quantity of textiles and/or apparel items**

Third, some countries implement quotas on some goods in defiance of WTO rules. The U.S. quota on sugar is an example.[2] A listing of import quotas for major industrial countries is given in Table 8.1. As the table indicates, the French government seems to impose more import quotas than the other countries in the table.

Fourth, international trade in textiles and apparel was profoundly distorted by the **Multifibre Arrangement (MFA)**. As a result of trade negotiations in the Uruguay Round, the MFA was phased out by 2005. For each developed country, the MFA managed trade in these two industries by enforcing a quota *by product and by country* for imports of textiles and apparel. The size of each quota was a major issue for both producers and consumers in each industry and in each country. The previous quota protection has been replaced by tariffs. Since the system was in operation in various forms for decades, the adverse effects of the MFA on world consumption and production of these products will linger for a long time.

Fifth, until recently world trade in agricultural products was not covered by WTO standards. For agricultural products, the use of quotas to protect domestic producers has been a prominent feature of world trade in this sector. Quotas are extensively used by the developed countries to protect farmers from low-cost imports. As we will see in the next chapter, the conversion of these quotas into tariffs is a major issue in the current round of WTO negotiations.

[2]For more details on U.S. quotas, see C. Fred Bergsten, *Auction Quotas and U.S. Trade Policy,* Washington, D.C.: Institute for International Economics, 1987. To be fair, the U.S. is a fairly average industrial country in this regard.

U.S. Sugar Quotas

"I do not make jokes. I just watch the government and report the facts."
—WILL ROGERS

Since 1816, the U.S. has provided protection for domestic sugar producers. As such, international trade in sugar is not a new issue for the U.S. and its trading partners. However, the issue has become more contentious. First, the U.S. government virtually guarantees domestic sugar producers a price that is generally higher than the world market price. Second, the subsidy to domestic sugar producers is provided through loan guarantees. As a result, the U.S. government lends the sugar farmers money and agrees to take the sugar as repayment of the loans. Thus, the government has a financial stake in maintaining the domestic price. Otherwise, the government would take a loss on this sugar transaction if prices are lower than the amount to pay off the loans. To maintain the high prices, the government has imposed a quota on imports of sugar since the early 1980s. This quota is changed annually to reflect market conditions. The list below is a partial enumeration of the effects of this policy.

1. In total, U.S. consumers lose $1.646 billion annually.[3]
2. The average sugar producer gets $170,000 annually. The average American family loses $25 per year.
3. Since this is a quota and not a tariff, nearly 25 percent of the loss accrues to foreigners.
4. There are currently about 12,000 people employed in the sugar industry, and the implicit subsidy per job is $90,000.
5. Estimates of the jobs lost in the industry under free trade are from 2,000 to 3,000 jobs. The cost of each job saved is approximately $500,000.
6. This does not count the loss of jobs in "upstream" industries. The industries that use sugar are somewhat smaller than they would be if their input (sugar) were cheaper. This would make it more difficult for U.S. firms attempting to compete in world markets with firms that have access to much cheaper sugar.
7. The program imposes losses on poor countries trying to export a product where they have a comparative advantage. The U.S. tries to aid nations in the Caribbean Basin through a program that provides for duty-free entry of some products from these countries.[4] However, the restrictions on sugar for these countries remain in place.
8. The program has created the crime of the illegal importation of sugar. Sentences can go up to 2 years in prison and a $250,000 fine.
9. Other countries have complained to the WTO that the system is illegal. The U.S. system was found to be illegal under international trade rules, but the U.S. has virtually ignored these findings. This severely undermines U.S. credibility when it complains about other countries' violations of WTO rules.

If you have ever wondered why so many food products contain high-fructose corn syrup instead of sugar, now you know. At this trade-restricted price for sugar, it is profitable for food companies to extract sugar from corn rather than to use sugar.

[3]See Gary Clyde Hufbauer and Kimberly Ann Elliot, *Measuring the Costs of Protection in the United States*, Washington, D.C.: Institute for International Economics, 1994.

[4]For more information on the Caribbean Basin trade policy, see W. Charles Sawyer and Richard L. Sprinkle, "Caribbean Basin Economic Recovery Act: Export Expansion Effects," *Journal of World Trade Law* 18(5), September 1984, pp. 429–36.

voluntary export restraint (VER) an agreement by a country to limit its exports to another country to a certain number of units

Finally, until 1999 a number of countries introduced a form of protection known as a **voluntary export restraint (VER)**. A voluntary export restraint is an agreement in which the exporting country agrees to limit its exports to another country to a certain number of units. The primary difference between a quota and a VER is the name. For example, an importing country, such as the U.S., that wanted to limit its imports of a particular product negotiates with the exporting country, such as Japan, for it to "voluntarily" limit its exports to the U.S.[5] In this case, the exporting country, not the importing one, administers the restraint—a quota. In this form, the quota (VER) on imported goods technically was legal under WTO regulations. While such an agreement may not violate the letter of international trade law, it clearly violates its spirit. Although this form of protection has been phased out, one often hears the term VER when discussing nontariff barriers to trade. Like the MFA, the effects of past VERs can still be observed in some markets such as automobiles.

THE ECONOMIC EFFECTS OF A QUOTA

In the previous chapter, we analyzed the effects of a tariff. In that case it was useful to separate the effects it had on consumers from its impact on producers. In our analysis of the quota we also want to separate these effects. To illustrate these effects, we once again employ a supply and demand model to show that the economic effects of a quota are very similar to the effects of a tariff.[6] Figure 8.2 illustrates the effects of quota on the domestic market for cloth of a small importing country. The domestic demand and supply curves of cloth are shown as D and S, respectively. In the absence of international trade, equilibrium would occur at point E with the domestic price of cloth equaling P.

Now, assume that this country has a comparative disadvantage in the production of cloth, and decides to open its borders to trade. In this case, the country will import cloth at price P_w, and the free-trade equilibrium is located at point F. Under conditions of free trade, the domestic price of cloth would fall to the world price, P_w, with Q_1 amount of cloth being produced domestically and the amount Q_1 to Q_2 being imported. Remember, if a tariff were imposed in this market, the domestic price of cloth would rise. As a result, domestic production of cloth would expand and imports would decline. Identical effects on the domestic price, domestic production, and the amount imported can occur if the government imposed an import quota.

Let's assume the government imposes an import quota that restricts the supply of imported cloth to X units. The imposition of the quota changes the amount of cloth supplied to the importing country. For all prices above the world price, P_w, the total supply of cloth in the importing country would equal the domestic supply, S, plus the quota amount, X. This total supply of cloth in the importing country is illustrated by the supply curve S + Q. Because the supply of imported cloth is reduced at the world price of P_w, the price of cloth will begin to rise until a new equilibrium is reached at G.

---

[5]However, this is about as "voluntary" as handing your purse or wallet to a mugger.

[6]For the non-economist, the discussion that follows will almost always be adequate. For professional economists, the circumstances in which a tariff and a quota are not *exactly* equivalent has been a source of seemingly endless fascination.

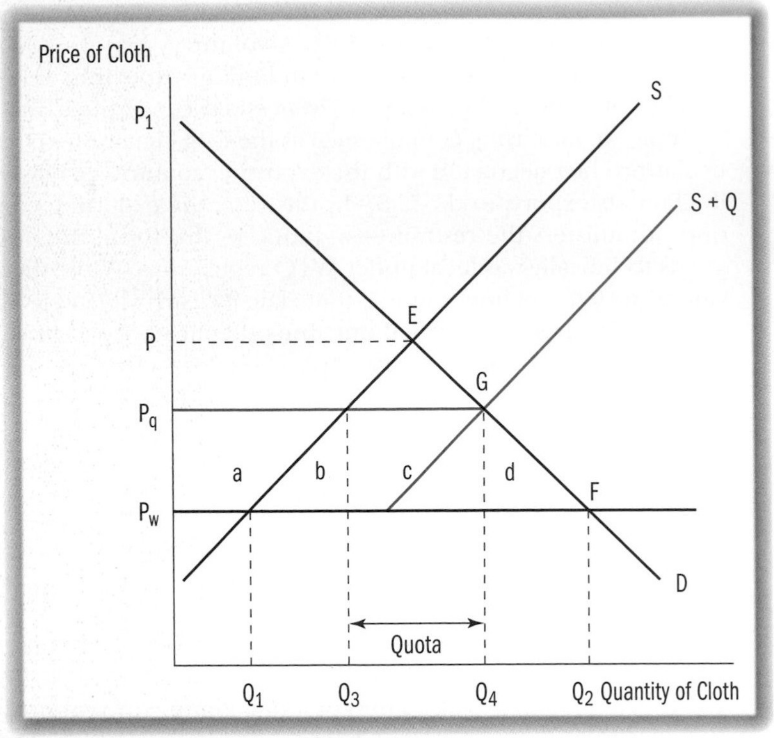

Figure 8.2 **Domestic Effects of a Quota**

A quota placed on imported cloth raises the price of cloth from P_w to P_q. This higher price of cloth results in a decrease in consumer surplus. The welfare loss to the importing country consists of the production effect—triangle b—the consumption effect—triangle d—and the revenue effect—box c—that is captured by the foreign exporters.

In this case, domestic consumers are harmed as consumer surplus declines by areas (a + b + c + d). Like our analysis of a tariff, domestic producers benefit as they produce more of the product and sell it at a higher price. The increase in producer welfare (surplus) by imposing a quota is represented by area a. In addition, there are efficiency losses of areas b and d. Remember, the small triangle b represents the cost of resources transferred from their best use to the production of more cloth. In a free market, this represents a loss to society, as these resources would have been used to produce a product in which the importing country has a comparative advantage. Transferring resources to the quota-restricted industry necessarily entails a loss of resources to some other, more productive industry. Finally, the area d is a consumption effect caused by a quota as consumers purchase less cloth.

The matter of who receives area c is the only difference between a tariff and a quota. In the case of a tariff, area c is the amount of tariff revenue the domestic government collects. In the case of a quota, area c accrues to the foreign producers and makes them more profitable. The net welfare loss to the quota-imposing country is larger under a quota. The country loses areas (b + c + d) under a quota but only areas (b + d) under a tariff. With a tariff, the domestic government gains revenue, area c, which can be spent on the provision of public goods. With a quota, area c is lost

auction quota the government auctions quotas in a free market in order to receive the quota rents

to the foreign producers. Estimates of the revenue lost to the U.S. government that quotas cause are approximately $10 billion.[7]

There are two methods available for a government or society to capture area c from foreign producers under a quota. First, the domestic government could auction quotas to foreign producers in a free market. The advantage to this **auction quota** method is that the domestic government would gain area c, which now accrues to foreigners. The limited quota supply would go to those importers most in need of the product who would pay the highest prices.[8]

tariff equivalent the replacement of a quota with a tariff which restricts imports to the same level

Another method available to a government to capture area c is to convert the quota into an equivalent tariff. The conversion of a quota into a tariff has several advantages. First, tariffs are legal under the WTO and quotas are not. If foreign firms find the quota sufficiently restrictive, they can perhaps petition their government to complain to the WTO for relief or an alternative remedy.[9] Second, calculating a **tariff equivalent** for an existing quota is relatively easy to do. To calculate a tariff equivalent, one would take the difference between the good's world market price and the its quota-constrained domestic price, and divide that difference by the good's world market price. Calculating these tariff equivalents has become an important process in world trade. In phasing out the MFA, the developed countries are not forgoing protection in these industries. Rather, they are simply converting their quotas into tariff equivalents. This process also is occurring in the developing countries as they phase out their quotas to bring their countries into compliance with WTO standards. Also, the trade negotiations in agricultural products allow countries to replace their quotas with equivalent tariffs.

Finally, and most importantly, a tariff is much less restrictive in the domestic market when the domestic demand for the product increases. This is illustrated in Figure 8.3, where we have assumed that the demand for cloth increases from D to D′ after a quota has been imposed. As a result of the quota, the quantity imported, Q_3 to Q_4, cannot increase when there is an increase in demand and the price of cloth rises from P_q to P_q'. In the case of a tariff, the price would remain constant at P_t and the additional demand for cloth would cause additional imports of cloth.[10] However, in the presence of a quota, the domestic producers supply the increase in demand. In this case, the foreign producers of cloth also gain as the price they receive for their product increases. The important point is that the losses for consumers and society are much larger in the case of a quota than in the case of a tariff when demand increases. These losses are shown by the areas (b + c + d) (the shaded area). As the figure indicates, losses to society increase as the demand for the product increases.

---

[7]See C. Fred Bergsten, et al., *Auction Quotas and United States Trade Policy*, Washington, D.C.: Institute for International Economics, 1987.

[8]One could argue that if the "winner's curse" applied, the government might end up with even more money. The winner's curse is the idea that the winners of auctions tend to be the most optimistic bidders who frequently end up overpaying.

[9]This raises an interesting point. Currently, only governments can file a complaint with the WTO. It might be highly useful to allow *companies* to file complaints. See Edward Graham, *Global Corporations and National Governments,* Washington, D.C.: Institute for International Economics, 1996.

[10]This occurs because the supply of imports is horizontal. If the supply of imports were upward sloping, the price of cloth would rise somewhat and both domestic and foreign producers would supply the additional demand for cloth. The exact split in sales would depend on the elasticity of the supply of imports and domestic production. It would be an unusual case if none of the increase in demand were satisfied by imports.

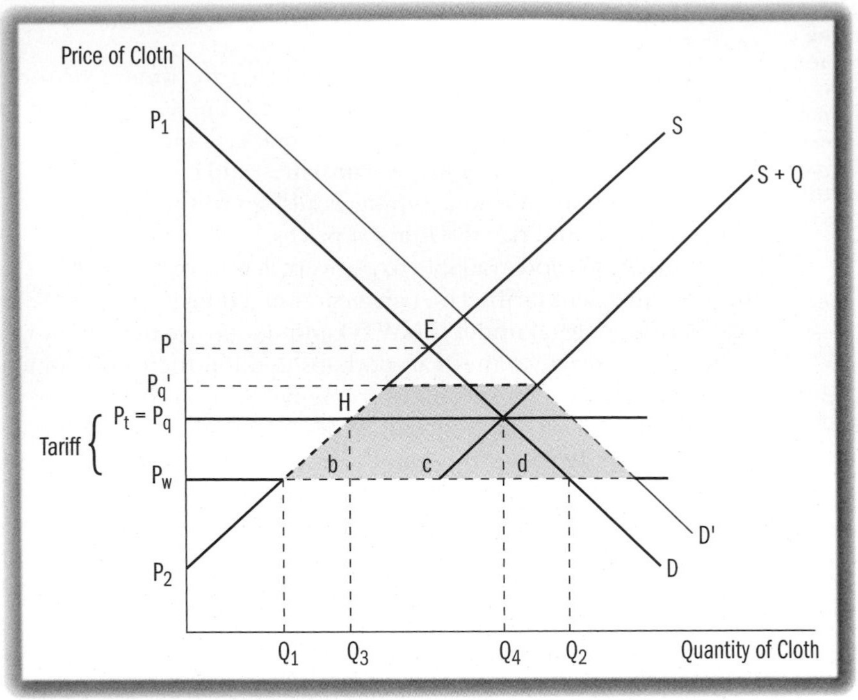

Figure 8.3 Domestic Effects of a Quota When Demand Increases

An increase in demand induces an increase in the price of cloth from P_t to P_t'. This price increase leads to an increase in domestic production, and a fall in domestic consumption. As a result, the welfare loss to the importing country increases.

While quotas reduce foreign competition in the short run, the long-run anticompetitive effects may be greatly diminished for several reasons. First, quotas may entice foreign firms that are exporting to the domestic market to engage in foreign direct investment in the quota-constrained market. If the domestic market in the importing country is large enough, and the barriers to exporting are sufficiently high, foreign firms may find it profitable to build production facilities in the importing country. This effect is analogous to firms building plants to jump over high tariffs.

Second, when an importing country enforces a quota, the quota is stated as a specific number of units without regard to their price. In this case, the exporters have a clear incentive to export the highest quality and the most expensive versions of the product. For example, the U.S. imposed a quota on imports of apparel from Italy in the 1930s. At that time, Italian apparel exports were not the high-quality items we see today. To maximize their revenue from a limited number of exports, Italian firms had a clear incentive to produce higher-quality items for export. Exports of automobiles from Japan are a perfect example of both effects. With the passing of the VER on exports of Japanese cars in the early 1980s, Japanese firms had an even greater incentive to build plants in the U.S. This also gave the Japanese companies a clear incentive to export higher-priced vehicles from Japan. In retrospect, the pressure that U.S. companies placed on government officials to obtain a VER may have been a relatively short-sighted strategy. As a result, a quota or VER can be a two-edged sword. In most cases, a quota will benefit the domestic industry by raising profits in the short run. Whether this will also hold for the long run is another matter.

OTHER NONTARIFF DISTORTIONS

Quotas are usually considered the most important nontariff barrier to trade. Like tariffs, quotas have effects on international trade that are relatively easy to analyze. However, quotas over time will become less of a barrier to trade, as many quotas are or will be phased out and replaced with tariffs. If tariffs and quotas were the only trade restrictions that businesses engaged in international trade had to deal with, conducting international trade would be relatively simple. Businesses would merely need to consider whether a profit could be made given the constraint of a quota and/or a tariff. Unfortunately, governments pursue many other policies that either directly or indirectly affect international trade. These policies may not necessarily prohibit trade, but frequently they distort the amount of trade relative to domestic production. In some cases, the distortion is just a byproduct of a government attempting to accomplish some other objective unrelated to international trade. In other cases, the clear goal is to favor domestic production at the expense of imports. These distortions are becoming increasingly important in the world economy. As explicit trade barriers are reduced worldwide, these other nontariff distortions of trade are becoming relatively more important.

Industrial Policy

Every country in the world conducts what is known as industrial policy. An industrial policy is the effect of government regulation on the industrial structure of the country. In some cases this policy is very specific, as the government may want to clearly favor one industry over another. In other countries, the industrial policy is simply a residual effect. All governments pass regulations that impact business even if the purpose of the regulation is not specifically aimed at favoring one industry over another. Since we cannot consider every possible governmental policy that influences international trade, we will consider taxes and labor regulations as examples of industrial policies that can distort trade. Later in this section, we consider the effects of government subsidies and environmental regulation.

First, consider how differences in taxation could affect trade. For example, suppose that in the U.S. companies are taxed on the basis of gross income, both domestic and export income. Further suppose that U.S. firms compete with European firms that are also taxed on the basis of gross income. However, let us assume that European firms do not have to pay taxes on income earned from exports. Given this situation, U.S. firms have to pay taxes on any income earned from exports to Europe, but European firms do not have to pay any taxes on exports to the U.S. Obviously, this differential tax treatment will distort trade flows between the two countries. European exports to the U.S. will be higher and U.S. exports to Europe will be lower because of the difference in taxation. The example is an extreme case, but the principle can be generalized. National differences in the level of business taxes have the potential to distort trade.

Second, consider how differences in labor regulations can distort trade. Assume that in the U.S., workers are able to work a standard 40-hour week and can also work overtime. Overtime in the U.S. is paid at a higher wage rate, but the employer has the ability to determine the number of hours worked so as to maximize the profitability of the firm. Suppose that in Europe the work week is 35 hours with no legal overtime. Thus, to produce more output, the European firm must hire more workers. Further, we will assume that laying off workers in Europe is prohibitively expensive due to mandated government labor regulations. In this case, U.S. firms have an advantage over European firms because they can more easily adjust their operations to accommodate changes in demand. For European firms, this is much harder to do. Expanding output is more costly, as additional workers must be employed and trained. In addition, since laying off workers in the face of declining demand is difficult, European firms are reluctant to expand output and their workforce in the first place. In this case, U.S. firms will have an advantage in world markets relative to European firms because changes in exports can be more easily accommodated by U.S. firms relative to European firms.

Such differences in industrial policy have created some interesting issues in international economics. As tariffs have declined, national differences in industrial policy have a greater chance of altering the pattern of world production and trade. This is especially true given the increasing number of free-trade agreements between countries. Once countries have entered into a free-trade agreement that abolishes tariffs and quotas, the differences in business regulations among the countries become more important. For example, as Canada and the U.S. have abolished trade restrictions, resulting differences in each country's regulation of an industry can have noticeable effects on the trade flows between the two countries. If Canada decides to heavily regulate an industry that the U.S. does not, the industry will likely shrink in Canada and expand in the U.S. The result is that, as traditional trade barriers fall, industrial policy takes on increasing importance.

Technical Barriers to Trade

technical barriers **laws that apply technical standards to goods or services that may distort trade**

An even larger and more difficult protectionist problem to address is technical barriers to trade. **Technical barriers** refer to a country's national standards for health, safety, and product labeling. Even when these regulations are designed solely for the protection of the domestic population, they can distort international trade. For example, most firms produce products primarily for domestic consumption and the exportation of the product provides a secondary source of demand. However, when a firm decides to export its product, it will have to change the product label. In most cases, the new label will have to conform to the importing country's product labeling standards and be printed in the country's official language.

In addition to labeling changes, many domestic products that are exported are also modified to meet government technical standards. A classic example is automobiles. For a U.S. firm to sell cars in Japan or in the U.K., the steering wheel and other driving-related components have to be moved from the left side of the car to the right side. These product modifications are not free for domestic firms, and the additional cost amounts to a tariff on exported cars to countries with right-side-oriented cars. The numerous changes that domestic firms must make to comply with foreign governments' technical standards distort international trade.

These technical standards affect not only trade in goods but also trade in services. The negotiations over international trade in airline services offer a clear example. When the deregulated U.S. airline industry attempts to compete in a foreign market where the airline industry is heavily regulated with regard to gates, routes, landing times, fares, and safety regulations, the possibility of a trade dispute is rather high. The difficulty in resolving the dispute lies in the intent of the regulations. If the intent of the regulation is an

Strategic Trade Policy

For the last 10 ten years, a lively topic of economic debate has been the role and effects of strategic trade policy. In general, strategic trade policy refers to industrial policies that exporting countries pursue. Such policies are aimed at maximizing a country's exports. A country's strategic trade policy requires that the trade ministry of a country identify an industry in which the country has a comparative advantage. The country then nurtures this industry by subsidizing its development and protecting it from imports. Once the industry has developed, the industry can export the product to the world market, devastating similar industries in the target countries. With foreign competition disposed of, the industry now has the monopoly power to raise prices and earn excess profits. The effective use of strategic trade policy is often applied to Japan and its Ministry of International Trade and Industry (MITI) during the 1980s, when Japanese imports of automobiles, steel, and semiconductors were flooding the U.S. market.

Within the U.S., there was gloomy talk of the deindustrialization of the U.S. economy and the dominance of Japanese industries. From the start, various policy makers in the U.S questioned the validity of strategic trade policy. First, the argument for strategic trade policy presupposes that employees in a ministry can spot profitable opportunities that the market cannot. Second, if economies of scale are necessary to make the policy successful, it is difficult to determine which industries will have significant economies of scale in their future development.[11] Finally, no empirical studies were completed to determine if Japanese industrial policy was really any better than any other country's. For example, France has had an active industrial policy for much longer than Japan, and no one ever discussed the success of French industrial policy. New research on Japanese industrial policy has demonstrated what economists have long suspected.[12] Japanese industrial policy does not work much better in Japan than it does anywhere else. The empirical test to determine this was that there should be a positive correlation between how fast Japanese industries grow and the government's support of the industry. In fact, the authors found a negative correlation. Japanese trade bureaucrats do what most governments do, which is support industries that are having a hard time competing with imports.

This result is not surprising. In 1776, Adam Smith wrote in *The Wealth of Nations* on the "folly and presumption" of government attempts to intervene in free markets.

"The statesman, who should attempt to direct private people in what manner they ought to employ their capitals, would only load himself with a most unnecessary attention, but assume an authority which could safely be trusted, not only to no single person, but to no council or senate whatever, and which would no-where be so dangerous as in the hands of a man who had folly and presumption enough to fancy himself fit to exercise it."

Of course the same logic would apply to strategic trade policy.

[11]See Farhang Niroomand and W. Charles Sawyer, "The Extent of Scale Economies in U.S. Foreign Trade," *Journal of World Trade* 23(6), December 1989, pp. 137–46.
[12]See "Picking Losers in Japan," *The Economist,* February 24, 1994, p. 69.

expression of national preference, and the adverse effects on foreign competitors are just a byproduct of that preference, then it is difficult for U.S. firms or the government to complain to the WTO concerning this discrimination. However, if the regulation's intent is to protect the domestic industry from competition, countries can complain to the WTO or threaten retaliation. Efforts by the WTO to control these types of government

The Scope of Trade Negotiations

When it comes to trade negotiations, there is usually an implicit notion that everyone knows what to negotiate. For a number of years this was true. Tariffs were high and the goal was lower tariffs. Similarly, discriminatory government procurement is considered "bad" and should be an object of negotiation. Once you move to the areas of product-specific standards or more general areas such as labor law, however, things get murkier. Clearly, standards, which are mainly designed to reduce imports, need to be the subject of negotiation. But as negotiators have found, intent is a difficult thing to discern. A seemingly elegant way out of this problem is to harmonize international standards. However, governments jealously guard their sovereignty, and international harmonization of standards necessarily means the surrender of some small part of that sovereignty.

As one would expect, the path that many economists advocate is to leave each country to its own devices. This is not an elegant answer but it may be the most workable. Countries with higher standards may pay a price in terms of their comparative advantage. As long as the country can accept that price (cost), the results may not be suboptimal. In most countries, domestic economic activity is more important than international trade. To the extent that standards apply to international trade, their detrimental impact on domestic economic activity may be less important. For poorer countries, the economist's argument seems incredibly crass to non-economists because these countries can ill afford high labor and environmental standards. Basic human necessities usually take precedence over "luxuries" such as labor regulation and a cleaner environment.[13]

[13]For an exceptionally clear statement of these problems, see Paul Krugman, "What Should Trade Negotiators Negotiate About?" *Journal of Economic Literature* 35(1), March 1997, pp. 113–20.

restriction have not been successful, and disputes of this kind are some of the most difficult areas for businesses and governments to negotiate in international trade.

Subsidies

There are few if any governments in the world that do not subsidize some form of business activity. Subsidies may take the form of actual money being given to a firm or industry. In many cases, the subsidy is more indirect or subtle in the form of reduced taxes for certain activities, lower utility rates, or a lower level of business regulation. In a world where trade barriers are on average falling, government subsidies are becoming more important. A significant subsidy to domestic business has the potential to increase the level of domestic production relative to imports. This effect was illustrated in Figure 7.6 in the last chapter. Also, a domestic subsidy could increase the level of exports to other countries. The main point is that significant government subsidies have the potential to change the pattern of trade among countries from what it would be without the influence of government.

When one thinks of subsidies and international trade, attention is usually focused on an explicit export subsidy. An export subsidy is a certain amount of money paid by a government and tied to the level of exports, such as $1 per ton. These types of subsidies clearly distort trade. They give exporters in world markets an advantage over other competitors that do not receive the subsidies. However, such subsidies are less troublesome than one might think. These subsidies are clearly illegal under WTO rules and can be legally offset by domestic tariffs. As a result, they are less common than one might think.

The other type of government subsidy is more troublesome. Consider a domestic subsidy that is given to a firm or industry that is not explicitly tied to international trade. Generally, these subsidies are being given to the firm or industry to accomplish some domestic policy objective. Most countries have some form of domestic subsidies as part of an overall industrial policy. The problem is that these subsidies can also distort trade. Trying to eliminate the effects on trade of domestic subsidies is an extremely difficult problem in world trade. As we will discuss in the next chapter, the problem is particularly acute with respect to world trade in agricultural products.

Government Procurement

government procurement laws that direct a government to buy domestic-made products unless comparable foreign products are substantially cheaper

One of the most obvious cases of government rules and regulations that distort trade is in the area of government procurement. **Government procurement laws** are laws that direct a government to buy domestically made products unless comparable foreign-made products are substantially cheaper. In a free market, consumers purchase products that are of the highest quality for any given price. However, government agencies differ somewhat from consumers in that the agencies spend public funds rather than their own money. Government purchases of goods and services are subject to constraints, and frequently governments have regulations that give preferences to domestic firms. The rationale for these regulations is that buying domestic is more beneficial to the country than buying an imported product. In this case, it seems that the mercantilists' views on international trade remain active. The issue of government procurement has become important because in most countries government purchases account for 10 to 15 percent of GDP.

Like most governments, the U.S. government has a "buy domestic" requirement when purchasing goods and services. Under the Buy American Act of 1933, domestic producers are given a 6 to 12-percent margin of preference over foreign suppliers—meaning that a foreign producer must sell the good at a price that is at least 6 percent below an American producer's in order to win the contract. This buy domestic requirement means that foreign producers implicitly face at least a 6-percent tariff on all federal government purchases. For military or defense-related goods, the preference margin expands to 50 percent.[14]

However, the U.S. differs from many other countries in that its government does not own private industries. In some countries, the government may own part of a particular firm or industry. For example, in many developing countries the government owns or is part owner of the domestic telecommunication industry and/or public utility companies. This governmental ownership can be a serious barrier to trade when the government both owns a domestic industry and has "buy domestic" requirements.[15] In these cases, the discrimination against foreign firms is much larger. The WTO has attempted to deal with this issue but has had only limited success. A government procurement code was adopted

[14]In the incessant wrangling over reducing government spending, these preferences would be a good place to start. There might be fewer problems with overpriced military goods if American firms had less protection.

[15]However, in the U.S. a number of states give preferences to firms within the state when bidding on government contracts. This also distorts international trade. The distortion is no small matter as a number of large states have economies bigger than some large industrial economies.

during the Tokyo Round of trade negotiations. It was expanded in scope as a result of negotiations during the Uruguay Round. However, countries that are WTO members are not obligated to be a party to the government procurement code. At this point, approximately 50 out of 151 total WTO members are parties to this code. Rather obviously, governments seem to be very reluctant to part with this particular form of protectionism.

CORRUPTION AND INTERNATIONAL TRADE

A recurring issue that comes up when discussing international trade is "corruption." Unfortunately the term *corruption* is too general for our discussion, so we need to narrow our focus to corruption in government. Specifically, corruption refers to the use of public office for private gain. In the private sector, the profit motive tends to motivate workers in firms to perform their jobs in an appropriate way. As a result, when we talk about corruption, it is almost universally understood to be corruption in government. Since we are discussing international trade, we want to further narrow our discussion to corruption in government as it relates to international trade.[16]

What this leads us to is the passing of money from a company in the private sector into the hands of some government employee. There is a tendency to assume that any money changing hands in this manner is corruption—but legally the situation is not that clear cut. Suppose that it is routine practice in Country X to pay a customs official a carton of cigarettes to process goods through customs in the next 24 hours instead of sometime during the next week. All that has been done is to encourage the official to do his or her job at the "normal" speed. Frequently this is called a "grease payment" or a "facilitation payment." You have not paid the official to do anything illegal; you have simply paid to get the regular work of government done. Facilitation payments are common practice in many countries and constitute a small NTB. They may be troublesome, but they are not the heart of the problem of corruption in international trade.

A bribe is a whole different matter. In this case, a business has paid a government employee to do something illegal. It might be the reclassification of a shipment of goods to allow for a lower tariff or a payment to evade quota restrictions. Notice that both high tariffs and quotas on international trade tend to induce bribes to government officials. Government procurement is a large part of the problem of corruption in international trade. In a smaller country, government officials may routinely buy foreign goods because there is no domestic production of the product. Unfortunately there is also no profit motive in government agencies. Officials may buy more expensive and/or lower quality products with no immediately obvious effects. In such cases, it may be tempting to bribe government officials to purchase goods or services that they would not otherwise have purchased.

Bribes are usually illegal in the country where the payment is being made. However, the governments of developed countries have also moved to make it illegal for businesses in these countries to bribe foreign officials. The U.S. was the first country to enact such a law. Passed in 1977, the Foreign Corrupt Practices Act (FCPA) prohibits U.S.

[16]For an outstanding discussion of corruption in general, see Chapter 6 of *World Development Report: The State in A Changing World Economy,* Washington, D.C.: World Bank, 1997. For an excellent summary of the problem of corruption in international trade, see "The Short Arm of the Law, *The Economist,* March 2, 2002, pp. 63–65.

Ranking Countries by Degree of Corruption

In the previous section, we covered the relationship between government procurement and the potential for corruption. While the logical connection is clear, it would be extremely interesting to know something about the degree of overall corruption in government among the world's countries. Fortunately, there is a well-known source for just this sort of information. The German organization, Transparency International, publishes an annual ranking of countries by the degree of overall corruption in government. The rankings are based on an index (CPI) that measures the extent to which public officials and politicians are perceived as being corrupt. One of the best features of the index is that it is a composite one that uses data from 12 different polls and surveys from 9 independent institutions. The respondents to the polls and surveys are either businesspeople or country analysts. Only 163 of the world's 193 countries are included in the rankings due to a lack of reliable data for some countries. A corruption-free political-economic environment is equal to 10 in the rankings, while a completely corrupt environment would be equal to zero. A number near 5 indicates a borderline condition. Table 8.2 shows the 10 countries that in the 2006 survey were the least corrupt and the 10 that were most corrupt. he entire survey can be easily accessed at www.transparency.org.

Table 8.2 Corruption Perceptions Index for Selected Countries, 2006

Country Rank	Country	CPI Score	Country Rank	Country	CPI Score
1	Finland	9.6	151	Belarus	2.1
1	Iceland	9.6	151	Cambodia	2.1
1	New Zealand	9.6	151	Côte d'Ivoire	2.1
4	Denmark	9.5	151	Equatorial Guinea	2.1
5	Singapore	9.4	151	Uzbekistan	2.1
6	Sweden	9.2	156	Bangladesh	2
7	Switzerland	9.1	156	Chad	2
8	Norway	8.8	156	Congo, Dem. Rep.	2
9	Australia	8.7	156	Sudan	2
9	Netherlands	8.7	160	Guinea	1.9
11	Austria	8.6	160	Iraq	1.9
11	Luxembourg	8.6	160	Myanmar	1.9
11	United Kingdom	8.6	163	Haiti	1.8

firms from engaging in the bribery of foreign officials, political parties, party officials, and candidates. Corruption in international trade became a more important issue in 1997 when the OECD countries committed themselves to passing laws similar to the FCPA. At this point 35 countries both in and outside of the OECD have committed themselves to the principles of the original convention. While this convention and subsequent legislation in many countries will not eliminate corruption in international trade, at least the process of significantly reducing the problem has begun.

ECONOMIC SANCTIONS

One frequently hears from the popular press that the U.S. or some other government has imposed economic sanctions on another country or group of countries. The purpose of this section is to explain in a brief way what economic sanctions are; a bit of the history of sanctions; what they are meant to accomplish; and why they usually fail to accomplish the goals that caused them in the first place. The section is a logical extension of our discussion of NTBs. While sanctions could involve just increasing tariffs over the usual MFN level, they normally involve some other prohibition on trade or investment. In a sense, the topic does not fit neatly into either international trade or finance. However, since sanctions frequently involve interference with international trade or FDI, it is convenient to cover them in this part of the book even though at times the interference may be in the area of international finance.

economic sanctions **government interference with normal trade and capital flows to accomplish foreign policy goals**

At the start, we need to define what economic sanctions are. **Economic sanctions** are the deliberate withdrawal caused by the government of normal trade or financial relationships in order to achieve foreign policy goals. No one in the private sector would in most cases voluntarily withdraw from a profitable economic relationship. It takes the coercive power of government to cause such an interruption. In the literature, the government imposing the sanctions is referred to as the sender country, while the country that is the object of the sanctions is the target country. In effect what is happening is that the sender country is attempting to impose significant costs on the target country. The hope is that these costs will induce the target country to change its policies in order to avoid these costs. In a sense, this is just another application of cost/benefit analysis. Is the target country willing in incur the costs of maintaining its current policies? One also needs to distinguish actual sanctions from the *threat* of sanctions. In some cases, the sender government will attempt to accomplish its ends by threatening to impose sanctions before actually doing so.

Sanctions can take on a number of forms. The imposition of economic sanctions usually is less than the total severance of economic ties between two countries. It is not uncommon for the sanctions to be imposed on only part of the trade that is important to the target country. The sanctions may involve a suspension of imports. In this case, domestic consumers are "financing" the conduct of foreign policy. Sanctions may also involve the suspension of exports. Note that in this case there are costs of conducting foreign policy that are being borne by domestic firms. The sanctions may be imposed on FDI. Domestic companies may be barred from investing in the target country. Finally, the sanctions may include or be limited to movements of portfolio capital. The aim may be to prevent the target country from acquiring capital or "trap" its capital in foreign financial markets. The above discussion presumes that the sanctions are bilateral in nature. However, in some cases the sanctions are legitimized by a multilateral organization such as the U.N. and may be imposed on the target country by a large number of countries. Finally, the WTO has the authority to allow economic sanctions against members that violate the rules of international trade.

Economic sanctions are hardly a new thing in the world economy. A documented case of economic sanctions occurred as long ago as 432 BC. This was not an isolated incident. Prior to the twentieth century, economic sanctions were commonly used. However, in the past economic sanctions usually were adjuncts to outright warfare. Sanctions were just another way to damage an enemy's ability to engage in war. The use of sanctions as a tool of foreign policy separate from military conflict emerged after World War II. Instead of being complementary to military action, sanctions became a substitute for such actions. This makes sense as the motives for economic sanctions became much broader than just national defense. A partial list of reasons for economic sanctions includes: the destabilization of obnoxious regimes; the protection of human rights in foreign countries; the prevention of nuclear proliferation; the settling of expropriation claims; combating terrorism; and the support of democracy. The attempt by a sender government to achieve these "softer" foreign policy goals calls for policy measures that are decidedly less extreme than military action.

Economic sanctions are usually imposed by large countries in the world economy with active foreign policy agendas. They are attractive because they occupy a middle ground in foreign policy between simple complaints about the target government's behavior and outright warfare. They demonstrate resolve in the issue, as the government is imposing costs on domestic consumers, domestic firms, or both groups. They may also have a deterrence effect of sending a message to the target country about how seriously the sender country perceives the issue to be.

This leads to an important question: Do economic sanctions work? It depends on how one defines success. If success is defined as the frequency with which sanctions demonstrably change the target country's behavior, then the answer is that they usually fail. There are many reasons for this. First, sanctions may be too weak a response to a serious foreign policy dispute. Second, in an era of rapid globalization, sanctions may not be effective. A country facing restrictions on its exports or imports may be able to find another buyer or seller, respectively. Third, the imposition of sanctions may invoke more support for the target country's government from both the domestic population and allies. Finally, the imposition of sanctions is imposing costs on parts of the sender country's population. The losses to these groups may weaken support for the sanctions. However, sanctions may be effective in another sense. In some cases, the point of the sanctions is the accomplishment of domestic political goals. If the imposition of sanctions is politically popular in the sender country, then the effects of the target country may be less important. In any case, the use of economic sanctions has become a common part of the landscape of the world economy. As in the case of the WTO, they are now an official part of the machinery of policing world trade. Because they are so commonly used, economic sanctions must be perceived to be effective in some sense. This being the case, it seems safe to assume that we will all continue to hear or read about the use of economic sanctions as a tool of foreign policy.[17]

LABOR AND ENVIRONMENTAL STANDARDS

Two of the more controversial aspects of the debate over globalization are the issues of labor and environmental standards and international trade. The argument of the

[17] The basic reasoning in this section is a brief summary of the classic work on sanctions, Kimberly Ann Elliot, Gary Clyde Hufbauer and Jeffrey J. Schott, *Economic Sanctions Reconsidered, 3rd ed, Washington, DC: Peterson Institute, 2008.*

opponents of globalization usually proceeds along these lines. It is asserted that the more intense competition fostered by globalization drives companies engaged in international trade to aggressively cut costs. This forces companies to try to reduce their labor costs in any way possible. With respect to environmental issues, it is asserted that companies will tend to locate production processes in countries where environmental regulations are low. In both cases, this creates "a race to the bottom" as companies will endlessly attempt to cut both labor and environmental costs. Over time, this would tend to produce ever poorer working conditions and an increasingly polluted global environment. If this argument is correct, then the solution would be some form of global standard with respect to labor and environmental regulations. In effect, the standards that prevail in the developed countries would be imposed on the developing countries as a condition of international trade. If such rules became embodied within the international trade rules, this would constitute an important nontariff barrier to trade. In this section, we will discuss both the labor standards and the environmental standards arguments.

labor standards laws that apply labor standards to manufactured products, resulting in some cases in import restrictions

All countries regulate their domestic labor markets with respect to wages, conditions of work, and occupational safety. These **labor standards** and their enforcement vary from country to country. It has been empirically shown that wages and working conditions are positively correlated with GDP per capita. As GDP per capita increases, wages and working conditions also improve. In developed countries, there is a concern over the ability to compete with countries that have lower labor standards for wages, working conditions, and occupational safety. The fear is that countries with "low" standards will enjoy an "unfair" advantage over countries with higher standards. To a large extent the argument is over comparative advantage. As we illustrated in Chapter 4, developing countries tend to have a comparative advantage in labor-intensive products. Companies will tend to produce such products in countries where unit labor costs are low relative to the developed countries. This is not so much a "race to the bottom" as it is a firm's trying to take advantage of a country's comparative advantage. The placement of labor-intensive production in developing countries increases these countries' specialization in products in which they have a comparative advantage and, over time, will increase relative wages through factor-price equalization within the country. For these reasons, the developing countries view the drive to impose developed country's labor standards on them as a condition of exports as nothing more than thinly veiled protectionism. They point out that when the now-developed countries were at the same level of economic development, labor standards were low. As these developing economies become wealthier, labor standards will become more like those now observed in developed countries. The proponents of the "race to the bottom" argument on labor standards no doubt are well intentioned. However, such standards would tend to rob the developing countries of one of the best avenues available to reduce the level of poverty.

environmental standards laws that apply environmental standards to manufactured products, resulting in some cases in import restrictions

The same type of argument applies to national differences in **environmental standards**. Environmental standards are laws that apply environmental standards to the manufacture of products. Again, the "race to the bottom" argument is that companies will move pollution-intensive plants to countries having low environmental standards. Many countries with high environmental standards fear that countries with low standards and/or enforcement may enjoy an "unfair" advantage in industries that are relatively pollution intensive. Superficially, this argument has some merit. Countries do have different environmental standards. This opens up the possibility that globalization

Sweatshops?

The U.S. has recently become concerned about imports of products from developing countries that are produced in "sweatshops." But just what is a sweatshop? Generally, one imagines a "sweatshop" to be a plant where low-wage workers work long hours under poor working conditions. Unfortunately, all of the adjectives (*low-wage, long,* and *poor*) are relative terms. A hard reality is that Bangladesh is not Kansas. What seems to be impossibly long hours in the U.S. may be the average work week in many poor countries. For example, many of our grandparents worked what we would consider to be very long days or weeks. Even college students once went to class on Saturday mornings. By a developed country's standards, working conditions in poor countries are, in some cases, appalling. However, these standards were once common in what are now developed countries. In 1870, the average American worked approximately 3,000 hours per year as opposed to nearly half that time now. GDP per capita in the U.S. in 1890 was approximately $2,500, or equivalent to what a worker in Guatemala, Jamaica, or the Russian Federation now earns.[18]

The same is true with respect to a discussion of wages. While many workers in developing countries may be poorly educated, they are not irrational. They are willing to work in factories because their next best opportunity is *worse.* Attempts to impose wages and working conditions equivalent to those in developed countries would reduce these countries' comparative advantage in the production of products intensively employing unskilled or semiskilled labor. Such an imposition might make some in the developed countries feel better, but it would not make developing countries or their citizens better off. When asked if he were concerned about sweatshops in Africa, the economist Jeffrey Sachs offered the following: "My concern is not that there are too many sweatshops but that there are too few. Those are precisely the jobs that were the stepping stone for Singapore and Hong Kong and those are the jobs that have to come to Africa to get them out of their backbreaking rural poverty."[19] For many of these workers, the alternative employment is even poorer paid and harder agricultural labor.

[18]The data is from Angus Maddison, *Monitoring the World Economy: 1820–1992,* Paris: OECD, 1995.
[19]Quoted in "In Principle, A Case for More Sweatshops," *The New York Times,* June 22, 1997, p. 5E.

could lead to a concentration of pollution-intensive industries in part of the world where environmental standards are low. However, there is not a substantial amount of evidence that this actually occurs. To illustrate why this in general is not occurring, we need to look at two important aspects of pollution within the world economy.

First, consider the issue of the location of a new plant in the world economy. As we discussed in Chapter 6, there are a large number of factors that go into deciding where to locate a plant. Among these are the proximity to natural resources coupled with the proximity to the final market. Firms will frequently locate plants so as to minimize transportation costs. Comparative advantage matters, and plants will tend to be located with respect to minimizing capital or labor costs. Trade barriers are part of the location decision as well as local taxes and business regulations. Among this multitude of factors, environmental costs would no doubt be considered. However, it is not the only factor involved. If it were, firms would clearly locate the majority of pollution-intensive plants in areas of the world known for their low environmental regulations. Researchers in this area have attempted to empirically verify that firms tend to locate pollution-intensive plants in low regulation countries. So far, the evidence indicates that this effect does have a small effect on plant location and trade flows. This result should not be too surprising. Lowering pollution costs is just one among many factors involved in plant location.

Secondly, pollution levels seem to be related to GDP per capita. In a famous paper, the economists Gene Grossman and Alan Krueger showed that for low-income economies, pollution and GDP per capita were positively related. This means that as economies grew richer, pollution levels increased. However, once a certain level of GDP per capita had been reached, the relationship became the reverse. Pollution levels decline with increases in GDP per capita for low- and middle-income countries. The overall relationship looks like an inverted U and is known as the environmental Kuznets curve.[20] If this relationship is correct, it has interesting implications for the debate over globalization and pollution. For very poor countries, it seems that the faster economic growth that may accompany a more open economy may initially worsen the level of pollution. However, once a certain GDP per capita is reached, pollution levels begin to fall even as economic growth continues. If the empirical results are correct, the problem of pollution levels in developing countries is somewhat self-liquidating beyond a certain level of GDP per capita. This produces the interesting result that the antidote for pollution is more economic growth.[21]

The central question concerning environmental standards is whether the environmental policies of the developed countries should be applied to the developing countries as a precondition for trade. This type of nontariff barrier would not have the same devastating effects on developing-country exports that labor standards would. However, it would reduce the comparative advantage of some developing countries in some pollution-intensive goods. This would tend to slow the economic growth of these countries. In turn, this might actually increase pollution levels if it slowed the transition of countries from the left side of the environmental Kuznets curve to the right side. Second, it appears that plant location decisions are not very sensitive to environmental standards, as other locational factors seem to dominate these decisions. However, any such regulation would tend to put more plants in the developed countries and fewer in the developing countries. Again, this would tend to slow down the rate of economic growth in the developing countries. The response of the developing countries is that this sort of regulation should be left to the domestic government to determine, so that a level of environmental standards appropriate to the country's level of economic development can be set.

Given the strength of the developing countries in the WTO, global standards on labor and environmental issues are unlikely. However, the debate has had a positive effect by stimulating research on economic development, wages, working conditions, and environmental standards that probably would not have occurred in its absence. As a result, our understanding of how labor standards and environmental standards affect

[20]For more details, see Gene M. Grossman and Alan B. Krueger, "Economic Growth and the Environment," *Quarterly Journal of Economics* 110(2), May 1995, pp. 353–77.
[21]For an excellent summary of the literature on trade and the environment, see Brian R. Copeland and M. Scott Taylor, "Trade Growth and the Environment," *Journal of Economic Literature* 42(1), March 2004, pp. 7–71.

The Gravity Model and International Trade

Up to this point in the text, we have been considering international trade in a certain way. Specifically, we have considered trade between countries for individual industries. In our examples, the U.S. exports machines and imports cloth. India imports machines and exports cloth. We were interested in which countries had a comparative advantage or disadvantage in which industries. The point was to explain the *composition* of trade. The same approach has been taken in the last two chapters. We were examining the degree of protection of a particular industry in a particular country. What we did not consider was the absolute *volume* of trade among countries. In other words, rather than ask what countries trade with one another, one can ask how much trade is occurring irrespective of what is being traded. Traditionally, this has been a topic that has been considered important in international finance. As we will see in the second half of the book, the total volume of imports and exports has important implications for issues such as the exchange rate and the balance of trade.

Recently, economists have been investigating the determinants of the volume of trade in a way that relates more to international trade. Specifically, a model known as the gravity model of international trade has been widely used to explain the total volume of trade between countries. In order to illustrate this, we will again use the example of trade between U.S. and India. A simple form of the equation is given below.

$$VOT_{UI} = A \times Y_U \times Y_I / D_{UI}$$

Where VOT_{UI} is the volume of trade between the U.S. and India; A is the constant term; Y_U is GDP in the U.S.; Y_I is GDP in India; and D_{UI} is the distance between two countries. The total amount of trade between the U.S. and India, or any two countries, becomes a function of the product of the countries GDPs and the distance between the two countries. The model makes good sense. Notice that as the GDPs increase, trade increases. As we will see in the second part of the text, the amount of trade is positively correlated with income. As countries become richer, consumers buy both more domestic goods and more foreign goods. The gravity model simply puts this logic into a more formal model. The model would predict that trade between the U.S. and India would not be immense. The GDP of India is relatively small and the two countries are not exactly in the same zip code.

At this point, our primary interest is on the effect of distance on trade. In a sense, one doesn't even have to estimate a model. If one looks at the trade of almost any country, there tends to be more trade among "neighbors" than among countries that are more geographically distant. However, the empirical estimation of the gravity model can shed some light on the degree to which distance acts as a barrier to trade. In these empirical estimates of the effect of distance on trade, the effect is as expected negative. No one study gives a precise result. However, the general results of these models suggest a rough proportionality. If the distance between countries increases by 10 percent, then trade tends to decrease by about 10 percent. This is exactly what the model we developed in the previous section indicates. What the simple model was unable to convey was the *magnitude* of the effect. However, one should be cautious in using this result. This is the effect of distance between countries on overall trade. The effects on any particular industry could be greater or less depending on the particular transportation costs associated with that industry. To summarize, the results of the gravity model show that distance effects trade flows in the same way that government imposed trade barriers do. Distance adversely affects trade in much the same way that tariffs and quotas deter trade.

international trade is much better than it was a decade ago. A possible compromise to this policy issue may lie in the trade negotiations that the U.S. has conducted with Mexico and is now conducting with other developing countries. In these agreements, all parties commit themselves to rigorously enforcing their own domestic labor and environmental standards. Many developing countries have fairly rigorous labor and environmental standards, but these standards may not be strictly enforced. For a developing country to have lower labor and environmental standards than the U.S. is not unusual. GDP per capita in such countries may be substantially below the U.S. level. However, the standards written into law presumably reflect appropriate standards for the country's level of development. If the trade agreement requires the local level of standards to be enforced, the agreement may both improve labor and environmental standards and not significantly hinder the rate of economic growth necessary to improve the standard of living in the country.

TRANSPORTATION COSTS AND TRADE

The supply and demand model that we used to analyze the effects of trade barriers also can be used to show the effects of transportation costs on international trade, prices, and domestic production and consumption. Up to this point, we have assumed that transportation costs between countries are zero. With zero transportation costs and perfect competition, a single world price would result for a good after free trade opens up between countries.

The effects of transportation costs can be seen by comparing trade in a single good under conditions of zero transportation costs between countries to a condition in which transportation costs are positive. In Figure 8.4, we illustrate the economic effects of transportation costs for both the importing and exporting countries. As we begin our analysis, once again consider a world consisting of two countries—India and the U.S.—and one product—cloth, which is produced and consumed in both countries. Figure 8.4 shows the domestic supply and demand conditions for cloth in the U.S. and India. The U.S. supply and demand curves for cloth are given in the left-hand panel by S_{US} and D_{US}, respectively. The same curves for India are shown in the right-hand panel by S_{INDIA} and D_{INDIA}, respectively. As we have previously illustrated, under free trade with zero transportation costs between the U.S. and India, the world price of cloth would be equal to P*. At price P*, the quantity of cloth supplied in the U.S. by domestic producers will be Q_1, and the quantity demanded by U.S. consumers will be Q_2. Meanwhile, the quantity of cloth supplied in India will be Q_4 and the quantity demanded will be Q_3. For the international market to clear, the excess demand in the U.S., Q_1 to Q_2, must equal the excess supply in India, Q_3 to Q_4. That is, the quantity of cloth available for export from India must be equal to the quantity of cloth imports demanded by the U.S.

Now, assume that positive transportation costs are included in the analysis. The effect of these costs will be to place a wedge between the price of cloth in the U.S. and the price of cloth in India. As such, a single world price of cloth will no longer exist. The difference between the price of cloth in India and the U.S. exists because in order for Indian exporters to be willing to sell to consumers in the U.S., they must receive a price that covers the additional costs of transporting cloth to the U.S. In equilibrium,

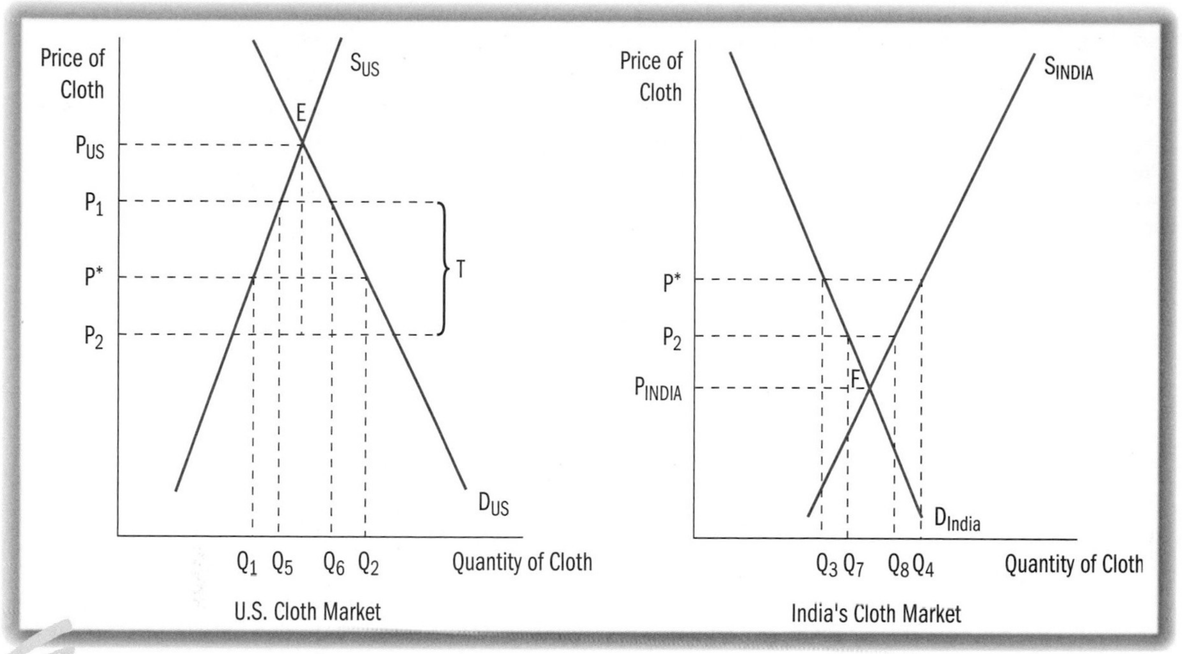

Figure 8.4 **Effects of Transportation Costs on International Trade**

With positive transportation costs the U.S. produces more cloth, consumes less cloth, and imports less cloth. The exporting country, India, produces less cloth, consumes more cloth, and exports less cloth.

the difference in cloth prices between the two countries will be equal to the per-unit transportation costs.

Suppose that transportation costs per unit of cloth are equal to T, as illustrated in Figure 8.4. This means that the price of imported cloth by the U.S. will rise from P* to P_1. As the price of imported cloth rises, the quantity of imported cloth falls from the horizontal difference Q_1 to Q_2 to the smaller amount Q_5 to Q_6. In addition, the net price (the price of imported cloth in the U.S. minus transportation costs) of exported cloth from India falls. As illustrated in Figure 8.4, the price of cloth in India falls from P* to P_2. India's price of cloth will fall until U.S. imports of cloth (Q_5 to Q_6) equals India's exports of cloth (Q_7 to Q_8.). The difference between the U.S. price, P_1, and India's price, P_2, is equal to the transportation costs, T.

With positive transportation costs, the quantity of cloth traded is lower; imports by the U.S. and exports by India both have decreased. In addition, the consumption of cloth in the U.S. has declined while the production of cloth in the U.S. has increased. For India, the consumption of cloth has increased while the production of cloth has decreased. Thus, the effect of transportation costs is to move the price of cloth and the quantities traded partially back toward the no-trade situation. As such, transportation costs act as a barrier to trade much as tariffs and other nontariff barriers do. Indeed, if transportation costs were equal to or greater than the no-trade price differences

nontradable goods goods whose transportation charges are so large that they become unprofitable to trade

between the U.S. and India, there would be no trade between the two countries. You may be able to think of numerous goods that are not typically traded between countries for just this reason.

Often, the analysis of trade between countries distinguishes between tradable and nontradable goods. This distinction is determined by transportation costs between countries. **Nontradable goods** are those goods whose transportation costs are so large that it makes trade unprofitable—whereas tradable goods are those whose transportation costs are low enough to make it potentially profitable to trade the goods between countries.

SUMMARY

1. The decline in tariffs in the past several decades has made nontariff trade barriers more important as a measure of protection. Between 10 and 15 percent of imports in the EU, Japan, and the U.S. are affected to one extent or another by nontariff barriers to trade.
2. An import quota is a government-imposed limit on the amount of a good that can be imported. Quotas have many of the same effects as tariffs but are generally more restrictive.
3. Quotas exist because some countries are either not members or new members of the WTO or simply ignore WTO rules. Also, quotas are common for agricultural products.
4. The major difference between a quota and a tariff is that the government does not collect any revenue in the case of a quota, and this revenue generally accrues to the importer. If the government wants to capture this revenue, it could auction the import quota or impose an equivalent tariff.
5. Different industrial policies such as taxes, labor standards, and business regulations can distort international trade.
6. Governments discriminate against foreign suppliers in purchasing goods and services. This is important, as this buying constitutes 10 to 15 percent of world output.
7. There are a variety of different technical barriers to trade.
8. Government subsidies distort trade flows. Such subsidies can be directly tied to exports, but more commonly they are domestic subsidies that indirectly influence trade.
9. The imposition of labor and/or environmental standards on developing countries would inhibit the growth of these countries. Labor standards would reduce the developing countries comparative advantage and make workers worse off. The effects of environmental standards on growth would be less.
10. Countries sometimes impose economic sanctions on other countries in an attempt to induce the other country to make some change in their policy. While sanctions rarely succeed in changing the behavior of governments, they may be a useful way for governments to indicate their degree of concern about another country's actions.
11. Transportation costs tend to reduce the quantity of trade between countries by raising the price of imported goods. A good will be traded internationally if transportation costs are low enough to make it potentially profitable to trade the goods between countries. Otherwise, the good will not be traded.

KEY CONCEPTS AND TERMS

- nontariff barriers to trade (NTBs) p. 167
- quotas p. 167
- Multifibre Arrangement (MFA) p. 169
- voluntary export restraint (VER) p. 171
- auction quota p. 173
- tariff equivalent p. 173
- technical barriers p. 176
- government procurement p. 179
- economic sanctions p. 182
- labor standards p. 184
- environmental standards p. 184
- nontradable goods p. 190

PROBLEMS AND QUESTIONS FOR REVIEW

1. How common are NTBs in the EU, the U.S., and Japan?
2. What does an import quota mean? How does an import quota differ from an import tariff?
3. List the reasons that quotas still exist.
4. Describe the U.S. quota on sugar.
5. Which is more restrictive, an import tariff or a quota? Why?
6. Graphically illustrate and explain the economic effects of a quota that is placed on imported steel.
7. Describe why a quota is far worse than a tariff if the demand for the quota-constrained product increases over time.
8. How can the domestic government capture the additional revenue that accrues to foreign producers under a quota?
9. Describe what a tariff equivalent is.
10. Explain how a foreign firm could mitigate the effects of a quota.
11. How do differences in industrial policy affect trade?
12. Why is government procurement important in international trade?
13. Describe how national standards for health and safety be used as trade barriers.
14. What are the two types of government subsidies that affect international trade? Which one is more difficult to deal with?
15. Describe the argument that globalization will lead to a decline in the welfare of workers in developing countries. Given what you learned in Chapter 4, is this argument likely to be the case?
16. How does corruption influence international trade?
17. Would imposing developed-country labor standards on developing countries as a condition of trade improve the welfare of workers in developing countries?
18. Describe the relationship between pollution levels and GDP per capita.
19. What are economic sanctions? How do countries use them to accomplish foreign policy objectives?
20. Explain the effects of positive transportation costs on international trade, prices, production, and consumption.

SUGGESTED READINGS AND WEB SITES

Werner Antweiler, Brian R. Copeland, and M. Scott Taylor, "Is Free Trade Good for the Environment?" *American Economic Review* 91(4), September 2001, pp. 877–908.

An outstanding article on the effects of international trade on the environment. The introduction to the article is a great synopsis of what is known about the issue.

Aaron Bernstein, "Do-It-Yourself Labor Standards," *Business Week,* November 19, 2001, pp. 74–75.

There are no internationally agreed upon standards for trade, labor, and the environment. In this vacuum, private firms are making up their own. A good look at how businesses react to controversial policy issues.

Drusilla K. Brown, "Labor Standards: Where Do They Belong on the International Trade Agenda?" *Journal of Economic Perspectives* 15(3), Summer 2001, pp. 89–112.

An extensive and readable paper on labor standards and international trade.

Gary Burtless, "Workers Rights: Labor Standards and Global Trade," *Brookings Review* 19(4), Fall 2001, pp. 10–13.

A short article on the debate on labor standards and international trade.

Judith M. Dean, "Measuring the Impact of Freer Trade on the Environment," *International Economic Review,* August/September 2000, pp. 3–6.

A very useful summary of the state of knowledge on the issue of trade and the environment.

Alan V. Deardorff and Robert M. Stern, *Measurement of Nontariff Barriers,* Ann Arbor: University of Michigan Press, 1998.

A good reference on the measurement of NTBs. A byproduct of this book is that one learns a lot about NTBs themselves.

Robert C. Feenstra, "How Costly is Protectionism?" *Journal of Economic Perspectives* 6(3), Summer 1992, pp. 159–78.

Still a good piece on the costs of protectionism.

Robert L. Heilbroner, *The Economic Transformation of America,* New York: Harcourt Brace, 1977.

Chapter 7 (Workers and Work) gives a vivid picture of wages and working conditions in the U.S. when GDP per capita was similar to that in many developing countries today.

Kala Krishna and Ling Hui Tan, *Rags and Riches: Implementing Apparel Quotas under the Multi-Fibre Arrangement,* Ann Arbor: University of Michigan Press, 1999.

The unfortunate details of an unfortunate NTB.

Robyn Meredith, "China's Cheating," *Forbes,* October 14, 2002, pp. 108–10.

A perfect example of how a country can use NTBs to accomplish the same thing as tariffs. The article shows how China is using questionable regulations on imports of food to offset the tariff reductions agreed to when the country joined the WTO.

Carolyn Tuttle, *Hard at Work in Factories and Mines: The Economics of Child Labor During the British Industrial Revolution,* Boulder: Westview Press, 1999.

One of the more heartbreaking parts of international trade is the debate over child labor in the world economy. This book provides a fascinating and dispassionate look back at where the developed countries once were.

Fareed Zakaria, "Sleepwalking to Sanctions, Again" *Newsweek,* October 15, 2007, p. 34.

This article argues that economic sanctions have become almost a default form of foreign policy imposed because governments can't think of any other response.

Chapter 9

International Trade Policy

"If there were an Economist's Creed, it would surely contain the affirmations "I understand the Principle of Comparative Advantage" and "I advocate Free Trade." For one hundred seventy years, the appreciation that international trade benefits a country whether it is "fair" or not has been one of the touchstones of professionalism in economics. Comparative advantage is not just an idea both simple and profound; it is an idea that conflicts directly with both stubborn popular prejudices and powerful interests. This combination makes the defense of free trade as close to a sacred tenet as any idea in economics."
—Paul Krugman

"A government that robs Peter to pay Paul can always depend upon the support of Paul."
—George Bernard Shaw

INTRODUCTION

In Chapters 7 and 8, we examined the effects of tariff and nontariff barriers to trade and discussed how protectionism tends to make a country as a whole worse off. However, these effects are not uniform. The gains to consumers tend to be widely dispersed and in many cases hardly noticeable. However, the losses to domestic producers and workers are very concentrated. As a result, some firms and workers might seek protection from the government. In this chapter, we will explain why most countries provide protection to some domestic industries. We begin by analyzing the political economy of protection. Protection from imports may not be in the country's best interest, but it is in the interest of selected special interest groups. We also explain a country's structure of protection by describing why the tariff is high for some goods and low for others. Next, we explain what is known as administered protection as it has become difficult for governments to explicitly raise tariffs. These bureaucratic mechanisms have been developed to allow tariffs to be increased in the presence of allegedly unfair foreign competition.

The second part of the chapter presents the evolution of U.S. trade policy from 1792 to today. As we will see, U.S. trade policy is the product of over 225 years of legislation. The nature and fundamental principles of U.S. trade law are much easier to understand if you know something about their historical roots. The last section of the chapter describes the evolution of the global trading system since World War II. The WTO is the product of nearly 50 years of international trade negotiations. This section discusses the history of those negotiations. Finally, we discuss the troubled state of world trade negotiations and the issues left to be negotiated.

THE POLITICAL ECONOMY OF PROTECTIONISM

Given that a country as a whole gains from trade, one would expect free trade to dominate most countries' international trade policy. Trade barriers cost the economy more in lost consumer surplus than is gained by producers and the government. However, as we saw in the last two chapters, firms and workers in import competing industries gain from trade barriers. As we will see in what follows, the interaction between the gains from trade for the country and the gains from trade barriers for producers explains the existence of trade barriers. The result is that free trade is not most countries' international trade policy.

In economics, *policy* refers to an action or actions that a government implements. For example, governments regulate industries and firms in a number of areas. These regulations are designed to strengthen, facilitate, supplement, or modify economic activity. In the presence of market failures, government regulation can improve the welfare of society. Such regulations are commonly observed for pollution or in the food and pharmaceutical industries. Not all government regulation of industries and firms works to the benefit of society as a whole; some regulations favor one segment of society. Industries and firms that benefit from regulation favor it.[1] For example, it is illegal for firms to conspire to fix or raise prices. However, firms can legally raise prices if the government regulates and enforces minimum prices for an industry's product. In this case, firms in this industry may find it in their own interest to accept regulation if it can enhance their profitability.[2]

special interest groups groups within a country that lobby for changes in laws and regulations that will benefit them

The existence of a demand for regulation means that there is a potential market for government regulation.[3] One area where a market for government regulation exists is international trade. Imports of goods and services have conflicting effects. Consumers want the benefits that come from free trade, but firms and workers in the industries that compete with imports want to restrict trade. In the U.S., **special interest groups** lobby for changes in laws and regulations that will benefit them, although not society as a whole. Lobbying to restrict international trade has a long history in the U.S. and in most other countries. For example, the U.S. steel industry petitioned for increased trade barriers in 2002 and the president authorized additional trade restrictions on imported steel to protect the domestic industry. The question to be answered is why the activities of special interest groups may succeed even if the regulation they favor lowers the welfare of the society as a whole.

public choice an economic analysis of the government decision making political process to develop economic policy

Protectionism and Public Choice

Over the last 30 years, economists have developed the theory of **public choice** to describe political behavior.[4] The premise underlying the theory of public choice is that

[1]See Sam Pelzman, "Toward A More General Theory of Regulation," *Journal of Law and Economics,* August 1976, 19(2), pp. 211–240.
[2]Before 1980 the U.S. government was doing precisely this in the trucking and airline industries.
[3]The government in this case is something like a monopsonist (i.e., the only buyer of a goods or service).
[4]A similar literature has arisen in political science and is referred to as *positive political science.*

politicians, like all individuals, attempt to maximize their utility. Utility maximization for a politician in most cases means maximizing the number of votes he or she will receive in the next election. This implies that politicians tend to favor programs having immediate and clear-cut benefits combined with vague, difficult to measure, or deferred costs. Likewise, politicians generally do not support programs having future benefits that are vague and difficult to measure coupled with immediate and easily identifiable costs.

For example, consider a country contemplating freer trade. At first, it might seem that a politician's optimal strategy for securing votes would be to favor the reduction of trade barriers. As we have shown using trade theory, the abundant factor of production gains from free trade, and the scarce factor of production loses from free trade. Furthermore, there are more consumers that would benefit from lower trade barriers than there are firms producing goods that ineffectively compete with imports. For both political and economic reasons, it would seem that free trade would be the optimal vote maximizing strategy for a politician.

Unfortunately, it is not that simple. In a democracy, individuals have an incentive to form groups designed to influence the government to pass laws that serve their collective interest. This behavior is called collective action.[5] In the case of international trade policy, while a country benefits from free trade, the gains to individual consumers are relatively small per good consumed. Usually an individual consumer cannot quantitatively feel the gains from trade. The result is that in general individuals do not form groups to lobby the government for freer trade. In addition, tariff rates and the price increases associated with nontariff barriers to trade are not explicitly known by consumers. As a result, the effects of restricted trade may go unnoticed by the consuming public. The other group that gains from free trade are industries that have a comparative advantage. However, what these export-oriented firms are interested in is the international trade policy of other countries. As a group, these firms want free trade or at least fewer restrictions on their exports to foreign countries. They have an interest in domestic trade policy only to the extent that they use imported inputs. The result is that these industries do not have a strong incentive to lobby for lower domestic trade barriers.

rent-seeking occurs when the government approves a program that benefits only a small group within society but the society as a whole pays the cost

The group with a clear economic interest to lobby the domestic government concerning trade policy is the group that ineffectively competes with imports. They have a strong incentive to form special interest groups and engage in collective action to obtain protection from imports. Although protectionism is not in the country's interest, it is in the interest of this special interest group. For example, the debate over the increased protection of the U.S. steel industry focused on the gains to the steel industry and its workers versus the increased cost of steel to the U.S. economy as a whole.

Activities that are designed to benefit a special interest group are called rent-seeking activities.[6] **Rent-seeking** is the act of obtaining special treatment by the government at the expense of society as a whole. For example, requesting that the government raise or not lower a tariff on a particular good is a form of rent-seeking behavior. Such behavior also may help maximize the votes a politician receives in the next election.

---

[5]See Mancur Olsen, *The Logic of Collective Action,* Cambridge: Harvard University Press, 1965.

[6]See Anne O. Krueger, "The Political Economy of the Rent-Seeking Society," *American Economic Review* 64(3), June 1974, pp. 291–303.

Voting for protection may gain a politician a few additional votes from the industry, firm, and workers that receive the protection.

In this case, the politician attempts to gain the extra votes that are contingent on voting for protection and simultaneously minimize the harmful effects of protection on society as a whole. In the U.S. and virtually all other countries, the tariff imposed on goods varies considerably from one good to another. In fact, the U.S. tariff schedule is an extremely complicated document[7] because tariffs are levied on very specific goods or very specific product categories. Complexity in a country's tariff schedule provides two advantages. First, a producer of a good that competes with imports can focus their lobbying efforts for protection on a particular good. For example, it is easier to gain protection for a product like imported bacon than for all imported food products. After all, consumers are not likely to notice a small increase in the price of bacon because prices on all products constantly change to reflect market conditions. However, if a tariff is imposed on all imported food products, the price increases might not go unnoticed by consumers (voters). Second, a detailed tariff schedule makes it possible for a politician to pick up votes by protecting one specific good without inducing protests from the average consumer (voter). For these reasons, most countries have developed very complicated tariff schedules and the tariffs on very similar goods may be dramatically different. In the following section, we present a more precise explanation what causes the differences in tariffs for different products.

The Structure of Protection

structure of protection **an analysis of the variation in tariffs by product for a country**

In most countries, the tariff schedule is as complicated as the example indicated in the box below. Tariffs can vary considerably even for reasonably similar goods. This analysis of variation in tariffs by product for a country is called the **structure of protection**.[8] Researchers have been studying why the tariff on one specific good is low and on another specific good is high. In general, this research indicates that the interaction between politicians and special groups described above is useful in describing the structure of protection. More specifically, the research provides a list of factors that influence the probability that an industry will receive or maintain protection.

First, large industries that are important to a country are more likely to receive protection than are small, unimportant industries. This implies that it may be easier for automobile producers to obtain protection than it would be for motor-scooter producers. Second, the fewer number of firms (more concentrated) in the industry, the more likely it is protected from imports. This is because it is easier for the firms to organize and lobby the domestic government for protection when there are fewer firms in the industry.[9] Third, it is easier for firms to obtain protection if they produce an intermediate product, such as steel, in which the voters are unlikely to notice price increases. Fourth, the potential voting strength of the industry's employees impacts the degree of protection. Industries that have a larger number of employees are more

[7]The official tariff code of the U.S. is called the Harmonized Tariff Schedule of the United States. A copy of one page of it is provided in the box on the Complexity of Fruit Juice.

[8]For a review of this literature, see Robert E. Baldwin, "The Political Economy of Trade Policy," *Journal of Economic Perspectives* 3(4), Fall 1989, pp. 119–36.

[9]Empirically, this would mean a high CR4 index that is the percentage of sales accounted for by the four largest firms in the industry.

The Complexity of Fruit Juice

Table 9.1 is a copy of several pages of the tariff schedule for the U.S.[10] It includes the most-favored-nation (MFN) tariff for fruit and fruit juices that are applied to WTO member countries.

Note that frozen orange juice importers pay a tariff of 7.85 cents per liter to the U.S. government. Orange juice has a tariff of only 4.5 cents per liter, and the tariff is even lower for grapefruit juice. Yet foreign-produced apple juice is imported into the U.S. duty free. Apparently, the grapefruit growers and apple growers associations are not as efficient in lobbying for their interests as is the orange growers association. Examine the different juices listed and notice the mixture of tariffs in place on each product. If you were to examine any page of the U.S. tariff schedule, you would find the same dramatic differences in tariffs by product.

Table 9.1 Chapter 20: Preparations of Vegetables, Fruit, Nuts or Other Parts of Plants

Heading/ Subheading	Statistical Suffix	Article Description	Rates of Duty
2009		Fruit juices (including grape must) and vegetable juices, not fortified with vitamins or minerals, unfermented and not containing added spirit, whether or not containing added sugar or other sweetening matter:	
		Orange juice:	
2009.11.00		Frozen	7.85¢/liter
	20	In containers each holding less than 0.946 liter	
	40	In containers each holding 0.946 liter or more but not more than 3.785 liters	
	60	In containers of more than 3.785 liters	
2009.12		Not frozen, of a Brix value not exceeding 20:	
2009.12.25	00	Not concentrated and not made from a juice having a degree of concentration of 1.5 or more (as determined before correction to the nearest 0.5 degree)	4.5¢/liter
2009.12.45	00	Other	7.85¢/liter
		Grapefruit juice:	
2009.21		Of a Brix value not exceeding 20:	
2009.21.20	00	Not concentrated and not made from a juice having a degree of concentration of 1.5 or more (as determined before correction to the nearest 0.5 degree)	4.5¢/ liter
2009.21.40		Other	7.9¢/liter
	20	Frozen	
	40	Other	

(continued)

Table 9.1 *(Continued)*

Heading/ Subheading	Statistical Suffix	Article Description	Rates of Duty
2009.29.00		Other	7.9¢/liter
	20	Frozen	
	40	Other	
		Juice of any other single citrus fruit:	
2009.31		Of a Brix value not exceeding 20:	
		Lime:	
2009.31.10		Unfit for beverage purposes	1.8¢/kg
	20	Not concentrated	
	40	Concentrated	
2009.31.20		Other	1.7¢/liter
	20	Not concentrated	
	40	Concentrated	
		Other:	
2009.31.40		Not concentrated	3.4¢/liter
	20	Lemon juice	
	40	Other	
2009.31.60		Concentrated	7.9¢/liter
		Lemon juice:	
	20	Frozen	
	40	Other	
	60	Other	
2009.39		Other:	
		Lime:	
2009.39.10	00	Unfit for beverage purposes	1.8¢/kg
2009.39.20	00	Other	1.7¢/liter
2009.39.60		Other	7.9¢/liter
		Lemon juice:	
	20	Frozen	
	40	Other	
	60	Other	
		Pineapple juice:	
2009.41		Of a Brix value not exceeding 20:	
2009.41.20	00	Not concentrated, or having a degree of concentration of not more than 3.5 (as determined before correction to the nearest 0.5 degree)	4.2¢/liter
2009.41.40		Other	1¢/liter
	20	Frozen	
	40	Other	
2009.49		Other:	

Table 9.1 *(Continued)*

Heading/ Subheading	Statistical Suffix	Article Description	Rates of Duty
2009.49.20	00	Not concentrated, or having a degree of concentration of not more than 3.5 (as determined before correction to the nearest 0.5 degree)	4.2¢/liter
2009.49.40		Other	1¢/liter
	20	Frozen	
	40	Other	
2009.50.00		Tomato juice	0.14¢/liter
	10	In airtight containers	
	90	Other	
		Grape juice (including grape must):	
2009.61.00		Of a Brix value not exceeding 30	4.4¢/liter
	20	Not concentrated	
		Concentrated	
	40	Frozen	
	60	Other	
2009.69.00		Other	4.4¢/liter
	40	Frozen	
	60	Other	
		Apple juice:	
2009.71.00	00	Of a Brix value not exceeding 20	Free
2009.79.00		Other	Free
	10	Frozen	
	20	Other	
2009.80		Juice of any other single fruit or vegetable:	
		Fruit juice:	
2009.80.20	00	Pear juice	Free
2009.80.40	00	Prune juice	0.64¢/liter
2009.80.60		Other 1/	0.5¢/liter
	10	Cherry juice	
	20	Berry juice	
	90	Other	
2009.80.80		Vegetable juice	0.2¢/liter
	31	In airtight containers	
	39	Other	
2009.90		Mixtures of juices:	
2009.90.20	00	Vegetable	0.2¢/liter
2009.90.40	00	Other	7.4¢/liter

[10]Actually the tariff schedule below is less complicated than it used to be. The previous *Tariff Schedule of the United States* was in use until 1988. This tariff schedule was considerably more complicated than the new Harmonized Tariff Schedule (HTS). The advantage of the new HTS is that it makes tariff schedules more similar across countries. This is an obvious advantage in trade negotiations and for companies exporting to more than one country. The HTS was authorized in Section 1207 of the Omnibus Trade and Competitiveness Act of 1988. It is currently in its ninth edition.

likely to be protected than those that have fewer employees. In addition, if the industry is regionally concentrated and/or unionized, the workers are able to lobby more effectively for protection. Finally, industries that have a comparative disadvantage are more likely to be protected. Firms and workers in these industries have more to lose from freer trade than those industries that have a comparative advantage. This is particularly true for U.S. industries that intensively use unskilled labor.

This research indicates that an industry characterized by one or more of these factors does not guarantee it will be protected. However, if an industry has one or more of

Uniform Tariffs in Chile

"Although there are no efficiency reasons for *uniform* import tariffs, there are practical political economy considerations for advocating a flat import structure."

—SEBASTIAN EDWARDS[11]

Economists have long advocated a uniform tariff that would solve a number of problems associated with a complicated tariff schedule. One, the tariff becomes easy to administer because customs officials would not have to worry about classifying a product into whatever category it might best fit. For example, is a sport utility vehicle a car or a truck? (The U.S. tariff on a car is 2.5 percent while the tariff on a truck is 25 percent.) Two, a uniform tariff makes lobbying for protectionism *much* harder. If an import-competing industry wants an increase in the tariff, the tariff would have to increase on all imports. This is likely to create some resistance for several reasons.

- A general increase in the tariff is unlikely to pass by consumers completely unnoticed.
- Other industries capable of lobbying the government would likely do so.
- Firms purchasing imported intermediate products would see the increase in the tariff as a direct increase in their costs and would complain to the government. Under most supply and demand conditions, the firms could not pass all of this cost increase on to consumers and, therefore, profits would fall.
- The same would be true of firms that are purchasing imports for final sale to the consumer. Firms that export may find tariff increases especially harmful as it may dilute their ability to compete in international markets. The net result is that more firms may lose from the higher tariff than the number of firms that might gain from it.
- Add consumer preferences to the mix and the optimal public-choice strategy for a politician may well be *lower* tariffs.

What we have just described is much like what happened in Chile during the last twenty years. In the early 1970s, Chile had tariffs that were high and very complex. These tariffs were replaced by a 10 percent uniform tariff in 1979. In response to an economic crisis in the 1980s, the uniform tariff was raised to 35 percent. Since the mid 1980s, the uniform tariff has fallen to 7 percent.

Economists have long advocated a uniform tariff as the best alternative to free trade. In Chile where it has been tried for 20 years, it appears to work fairly well.[12]

[11]From Sebastian Edwards, "Trade Liberalization Reforms and the World Bank," *American Economic Review* 87(2), May 1997, pp. 43–48.

[12]For a discussion of this process, see Vittorio Corbo, "Trade Reform and Uniform Import Tariffs: The Chilean Experience," *American Economic Review* 87(2), May 1997, pp. 73–77.

these characteristics, there is a higher *probability* that it will have a higher tariff.[13] For example, the U.S. steel industry has consistently obtained high levels of protection. The steel industry is large in terms of output and employment; the workers are unionized; the industry is highly concentrated and is somewhat regionally concentrated; and it is an intermediate product. Given these conditions, the steel industry has been able to obtain a higher tariff than the national average for manufacturers.[14] In addition, recent research on this issue has focused on developing more formal theoretical models to describe the process of obtaining protection. However, this newer research does not alter the conclusions given earlier.[15]

THE EVOLUTION OF U.S. TRADE POLICY

The U.S. tariff structure has been evolving throughout the last 225 years. Figure 9.1 provides a convenient way to view the history of U.S. trade policy. The figure shows the average tariff imposed on U.S. imports from 1792 to 2005. Over that period of time, one can see that the U.S. has gone through several periods of protectionism followed by periods of freer trade. Currently, U.S. tariffs have fallen to an average of approximately 2.5 percent.

For the U.S. and many other countries in the late eighteenth century, tariffs were a convenient and important way for countries to raise revenue. For example, Table 9.2 shows that U.S. tariffs were an important source of revenue for the federal government until the early 1900s.[16] There are two things to keep in mind about U.S. trade policy up to the beginning of the 20th century. First, Congress and the president could impose *any* tariff on *any* narrowly defined good imported from *any* country. Second, the tax revenue use to support federal government expenditures came mainly from the imposition of tariffs.

In the years before the federal government instituted an income tax, the "tariff bill" was a potential source of gain for industries as well as the major source of government revenue. According to the economist Henry George, the process of passing the tariff bill was described as follows:

> "To introduce a tariff bill into congress or parliament is like throwing a banana into a cage of monkeys. No sooner is it proposed to protect one industry than all industries that are capable of protection begin to screech and scramble for it."[17]

---

[13]The same logic applies to the existence or lack thereof of a nontariff barrier to trade.

[14]For details, see Mordechai E. Kreinin, "Wage Competitiveness in the U.S. Auto and Steel Industries," *Economic Inquiry*, January 1984, pp. 39–50.

[15]See, for example, Gene M. Grossman and Elhanan Helpman, "Protection for Sale," *American Economic Review* 84(4), September 1994, pp. 833–850.

[16]Tariffs are now a minor source of revenue (less than 2 percent of government revenue). Interestingly, one of the weaknesses of the Articles of Confederation was the inability to pass a national tariff because of the unanimous vote requirement. Article 2 of the U.S. Constitution gives Congress the power to regulate and tax trade. The initial U.S. tariff was a modest 5 percent. Until the start of the 20th century, tariffs were still the major source of revenue for the U.S. government. Tariffs are still an important source of revenue for some developing countries.

[17]From Henry George, *Protection or Free Trade: An Examination of the Tariff Question with Especial Regard to the Interests of Labor* (1886), New York: Robert Schalkenbach Foundation 1980.

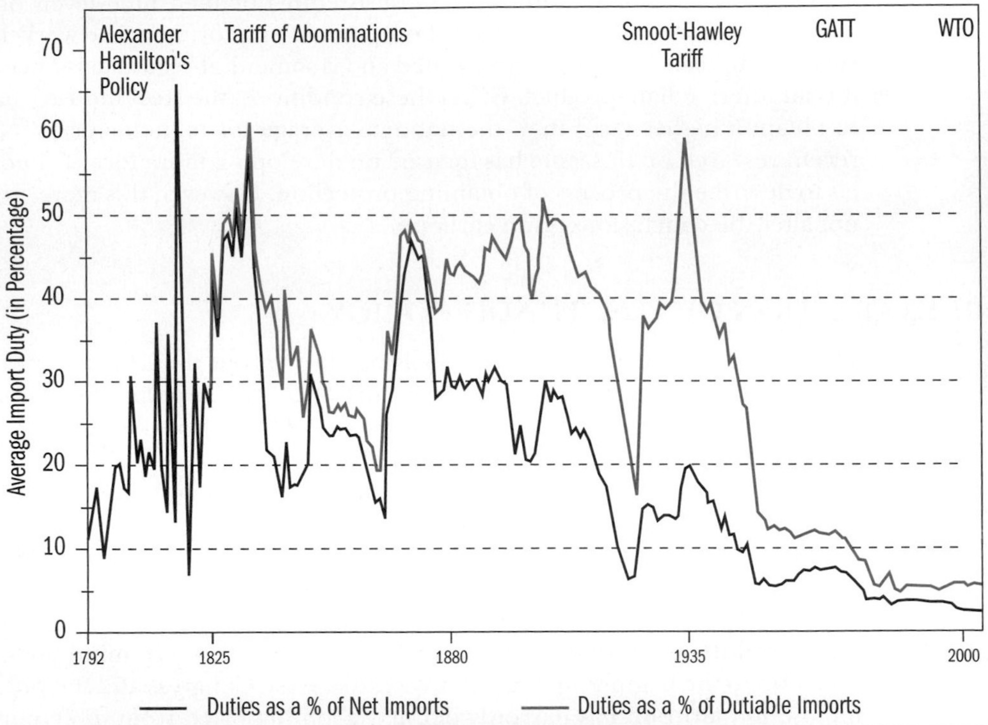

Figure 9.1 United States Average Import Duties 1792–2005

Average tariff rates on dutiable imports reached a high of approximately 60 percent in 1828 and in 1932. Currently, average tariff rates on dutiable imports are approximately 4 percent.

Table 9.2 Percentage of Federal Revenue from Tariffs (Customs Duties)

Date	% of Federal Revenue
1789–91	99.6%
1850	91.0
1910	49.4
1920	4.9
1970	1.3

Source: U.S. Department of Commerce, *Historical Statistics of the United States: Colonial Times to 1970,* Washington D.C.: U.S. Government Printing Office, 1975, pp. 1105–6.

infant-industry protection the argument that an industry's costs of production will be high when it is beginning, and as a result it will need protection from imports

By the late eighteenth century, governments recognized tariffs for their potential to protect domestic industries. In England, there was political anguish over the effects of the "corn laws" and whether or not British tariffs protected agricultural interests to the detriment of manufacturing industry.[18] In the U.S., Alexander Hamilton's "Report on Manufactures" recommended high tariffs on manufactured goods as a means of developing U.S. industry capable of competing with the British. This policy of **infant-industry protection** was gradually adopted and tariffs were raised from 5 percent in 1792 to 12.5 percent by 1812.

Tariff of Abominations a very high level of tariffs adopted by the U.S. in 1828

Tariffs leveled off for a few years following the War of 1812 but increased dramatically reaching a peak of over 60 percent with the **Tariff of Abominations** of 1828. This high average rate of tariff protection by the U.S. government provoked a strong reaction from the Southern states.[19] Northern states and Northern manufacturers favored high tariffs as a way of protecting new industries. This policy also led to an increase in the profits of the protected industries. The Southern states favored low tariffs to reduce the cost of the manufactured goods they imported. This difference of opinion concerning tariffs hampered the degree of solidarity within the country. The Southern states felt so strongly about the tariff issue that the Confederate Constitution prohibited the protection of any *specific* industry.[20]

Because tariff revenue was a major source of revenue for the U.S. government, tariffs increased dramatically to finance the Civil War and remained high until 1913. In addition, protectionism was brewing on the other side of the Atlantic during the last decades of the nineteenth century. Germany was raising tariffs to protect its industries against low-priced imports from the U.K., and World War I resulted in the U.K. increasing its tariffs to finance its war effort.

Smoot-Hawley Tariff a high level of tariffs adopted by the U.S. in 1930 and that caused a large decline in world trade

In 1913, the U.S. reduced tariffs significantly to their lowest level since the Civil War. However, in the early 1920s the Republican Party returned to power in Congress and the White House and quickly raised tariffs to protect domestic industry.[21] The last tariff bill Congress passed was the famous **Smoot-Hawley Tariff** of 1930. This tariff law resulted in the highest general tariff structure in U.S. history, with average tariffs of approximately 60 percent on dutiable imports. Other nations retaliated by raising their tariffs against goods imported from the U.S. While this tariff escalation did not *cause* the Great Depression, it did not help. As a result of the Great Depression and the tariff increases, the volume of world trade declined from nearly $3 billion in 1929 to less than $500 million in 1933.[22]

Considering that trade policy is in part a political process, in 1933 the Roosevelt Administration persuaded Congress to transfer the authority to negotiate tariffs and

[18]Corn was at that time a common euphemism for food grains in general.

[19]As an example of this reaction, South Carolina threatened to secede from the Union over the issue.

[20]Article I, Section 8 of the Constitution of the Confederate States of America contains the following phrase: "nor shall any duties or taxes on importations from foreign nations be laid to promote or foster any branch of industry."

[21]For much of it's early history, the Republican Party tended to be protectionist and the Democratic Party tended to be more liberal on trade issues. In the post World War II era, the parties more or less reversed their roles.

[22]See Charles P. Kindleberger, *The World in Depression*, 1929–1939, Berkeley: University of California Press, 1973.

Reciprocal Trade Agreements Act passed in 1934, the general principles of this law remain the basis for all subsequent trade legislations in the U.S.

tariff reductions to the President. In 1934 Congress passed the **Reciprocal Trade Agreements Act**. This Act is the basis for current U.S. trade policy. The three provisions of this Act that are still important include the following:

1. Tariff reciprocity. This means that the U.S. will negotiate tariff reductions on its imports only in return for tariff reductions on its exports by its trading partners. This reciprocity principle is based on the idea of fairness, as mutual tariff reductions benefit U.S. consumers and foreign producers through an increase in U.S. imports while the increase in exports benefit U.S. producers and foreign consumers. Reciprocity is still deeply embedded in current trade negotiations.

2. The Act transferred U.S. trade policy from Congress to the president by giving the president authorization to negotiate trade agreements with foreign countries. This provision allows foreign countries to negotiate with the executive branch of the U.S. government without having to negotiate every detail of the agreement with individual members of Congress. Once an agreement has been negotiated, Congress votes to approve or reject the agreement in total, without amendments.[23]

most favored nation (MFN) when one country promises to offer another country having most-favored nation status the lowest tariff which it offers to any other country

3. The Act, and all future trade legislation passed by Congress, is based on the **Most Favored Nation** (MFN) principle.[24] This nondiscrimination principle means that any tariff cuts the U.S. agrees to with one country would apply to the products of all other trade partners that have most-favored-nation status. Most Favored Nation is a very old trading principle, and the first trade treaty that the U.S. signed with France in 1778 contained this principle. In the early 1900s, the U.S. administered separate tariffs by product *and* by country. The administrative details involved with having separate tariffs proved unworkable and was abandoned in the 1920s. MFN makes administering tariffs much easier as approximately 145 countries have MFN status. In addition, trade legislation based on MFN makes international trade far less risky for businesses when compared to a world where tariffs could be changed on a political whim.

From a political standpoint, the fact that tariffs cannot be raised easily has both benefits and costs. The benefits outlined above come at the cost of inflexibility. As we saw in Chapter 4, comparative advantage can change over time. Industries that once had a comfortable comparative advantage in world markets may find increasing competition from imports lowers profits and may lower employment in the industry. This situation has led to mechanisms that change in response to this situation. In effect, governments have had to create mechanisms to protect comparative disadvantage industries by raising tariffs on particular imports from particular countries. In the next section, we cover what these mechanisms are and how they work.

ANTIDUMPING, COUNTERVAILING DUTIES, AND THE ESCAPE CLAUSE

One of the effects of a country imposing a tariff is that domestic firms and industries gain additional producer surplus through additional sales and higher prices. Current WTO rules have made it difficult for a country to unilaterally increase tariffs on selected products. Effectively, the tariff on any particular product by a country is

[23]Formerly, this provision was known as "fast track" trade legislation. The current term used to describe this provision is "trade promotion authority."

[24] The current term used to describe most favored nation status is "normal trade relations."

administered protection increasing the tariff on a particular good by a country through the use of antidumping, countervailing duties, or escape clause regulations

"bound." What this means is that any member country of the WTO cannot simply raise the tariff because of pressure from an industry or a special interest group. As a result, countries have developed several forms of what is known as **administered protection**.[25]

Although there are several different forms of administered protection, they all involve increasing the tariff on a particular imported good. These forms of administered protection are sanctioned by the WTO. What this means is that it is possible for an industry in the U.S. or another country to obtain an increase in a tariff in a manner that is consistent with WTO rules. To obtain the protection, the industry must proceed through a complex set of rules. The goal of these rules is to protect domestic industries from "unfair" foreign competition.[26] Administered protection by the U.S. is not trivial in size. The U.S. International Trade Commission (USITC) has estimated that antidumping statutes alone cost the U.S. economy $1.16 billion per year.[27]

Antidumping

antidumping law a law that does not allow an international firm to sell its product in an export market for less than what it is sold for in its home market

The first type of administered protection that a country can impose is called the antidumping law.[28] An **antidumping law** is a law that does not allow a firm to sell its product in an export market for less than it is sold for in its home market. Dumping by a firm or industry can be defined in two ways. Cost-based dumping occurs when a firm sells a product at a price below its cost of production in a foreign market. Price-based dumping is when a firm sells a product in a foreign market at a price lower than the price charged in its home market. The U.S. antidumping laws are based on either form of dumping.

Types of Dumping

sporadic dumping the occasional sale of a product by a firm in a foreign market at a price below that sold in the home market

Dumping by a foreign firm can occur for three reasons. First, a foreign firm may find it in their best interest to sell their product at a lower price in a foreign market for a relatively short period of time. This is called **sporadic dumping**. For example, if the foreign firm finds itself with excess inventory, the quickest way to reduce the inventory may be to "dump" the unwanted inventory in foreign markets. This is the international equivalent of a "sale." This form of dumping can occur due to the international asymmetry of the business cycle. For example, suppose that the Japanese economy is in the middle of a recession and the U.S. economy is in the middle of an economic expansion. In this case, it is easy to see why Japanese producers would attempt to sell excess inventory in the U.S. market. With slack domestic demand in Japan, a firm may not be able to make a profit but may be concerned with minimizing losses in the short run. So long as the firm sells the product at anything above marginal cost, losses for the firm would be minimized. Such behavior by firms is routine and would pass unnoticed in a large domestic market such as the U.S. Such sporadic

[25]The term originally appeared in J. M. Finger, H. Keith Hall, and Douglas R. Nelson, "The Political Economy of Administered Protection," *American Economic Review* 72(3), June 1982, pp. 452–66.

[26]It has been suggested that things have gotten to the point where the possession of comparative advantage has become an unfair trade practice.

[27]Protected firms and workers gain $685 million and the rest of society loses $1.85 billion. This is a good example of Figure 7.4 at work. See U.S. International Trade Commission, "The Economic Effects of Antidumping and Countervailing Duty Orders and Suspension Agreements," Investigation No. 332–344, Publication 2900, June 1995.

[28]Technically, this is Section 703 of the Tariff Act of 1930.

persistent dumping the sale of a product by a firm in a foreign market at a price below that sold in its domestic market over an extended period of time

predatory dumping the sale of a product by a firm in a foreign market at a price below that sold in its domestic market in order to drive competing firms out of business

dumping is often seen as a part of doing business, but in an international context it can draw legal action from the industry in the importing country.[29]

The second type of dumping, **persistent dumping**, is the sale of a product in a foreign market at a price below that sold in the domestic market over an extended period of time. If different markets have different elasticities of demand, then it is often in the firm's best interest—maximization of profits—to charge different prices in each market.[30] If the differences in these elasticities of demand between the two markets persists, then the "dumping" may likewise persist. Unlike sporadic dumping, persistent dumping may cause lasting damage to the domestic industry.

A final type of dumping is **predatory dumping**. The intent of a firm engaged in predatory dumping is to price its product in such a way so as to drive domestic firms out of business. Once the domestic competitors exit the market, the foreign firm then is in a position to raise prices and maximize profits in the long run. Such predatory pricing is illegal in the U.S., even if no foreign firms are involved. In addition, no foreign firm has ever been found guilty of predatory dumping.

History of Antidumping Law in the United States

The original U.S. antidumping law passed in 1916 prohibited only predatory dumping.[31] This law simply extended the Sherman Antitrust Act to the activities of foreign firms. The intent of the law was to create a legal level playing field for domestic and foreign firms. The legislative changes that have followed the original antidumping law have created a bias in favor of domestic firms. With the Antidumping Act of 1921, Congress loosened the requirements on antidumping to permit federal government action to further restrict imports. Under this Act, foreign companies now could be charged with dumping even if there was no proof of predatory pricing. It is this Act that forms the basis for current U.S. antidumping law. The Antidumping Act was incorporated into the 1930 Tariff Act and subsequently amended in 1979, 1984, and 1988.[32] The result of these amendments has been to make it easier to restrict foreign imports sold at lower prices than similar U.S. goods.

From its inception in 1948, the General Agreement on Tariffs and Trade (GATT) sanctioned the concept of antidumping laws. The Kennedy Round of the GATT led to the adoption of the GATT Antidumping Code. This code provides guidelines under which countries may act against foreign firms that engage in predatory pricing that result in material injury to an industry based in the importing country. The antidumping code simply creates the guidelines and countries can adopt their own antidumping laws to prevent dumping. This code was amended during the Tokyo Round of the GATT, but only 25 countries have signed this amended code. According to the amended code, each signatory country can legislate and administer its antidumping law as long as it conforms to WTO standards. As recently as 1992, the WTO ruled that

[29]What was described has been called cyclical dumping which is really just a special case of sporadic dumping.

[30]This concept may be familiar from principles of economics. If not, see Appendix 8.1 for a quick review.

[31]This law is still on the books. It requires showing an intent to injure. It has rarely been used and has never been successfully invoked.

[32]The Trade Agreements Act of 1979 was a watershed piece in the history of antidumping law. It transferred the determination of the dumping margin from the Treasury Department to the Department of Commerce.

the U.S. was violating the intent of international guidelines to which the laws of signatory countries must conform. Specifically, the WTO alleged that the U.S. antidumping law made it too easy for U.S. firms to obtain punitive tariffs against imports. To date, the U.S. has ignored these warnings concerning its antidumping law.

The original intent of U.S. antidumping law was to prevent predatory pricing of foreign firms. The law over time was amended to prevent foreign firms from engaging in price-based dumping and cost-based dumping. The immediate and obvious problem for foreign firms selling goods in the U.S. is that they can be legally prevented from pursuing pricing strategies that are perfectly legal for U.S. firms. In essence, the antidumping regulations have been "captured" by U.S. firms for their own advantage. While the announced aim of the antidumping law is to protect U.S. industry from predatory dumping, the real aim is protectionism in the form of allowing U.S. firms the option to under-price foreign competition without foreign producers being able to retaliate. While this misdirection seems to be the reason for the continued existence of antidumping laws in their current form, obfuscation is what keeps them going. The administration of antidumping laws in the U.S. has now become a complex process that only a few business people, economists, and lawyers understand.

dumping margin the difference between the domestic market price of a product and the foreign market value of the product

Between 1980 and 2005, U.S. firms filed 1,102 antidumping cases. Once a case is filed, a regulatory process is set in motion that can take from 20 days to over a year to complete. Simply put, there are two investigations that the U.S. government conducts. First, the International Trade Administration (ITA)[33] conducts an investigation to determine if the imports in question are being "dumped" and if so, by how much. Second, the U.S. International Trade Commission (USITC) conducts an investigation to determine if the alleged dumping is harming the domestic industry or firm. If an affirmative preliminary decision is reached by both investigations, then a tariff equivalent to the difference between the U.S. market price and the foreign market value (called the **dumping margin**) is ordered. Both agencies continue their investigations in order to make a final determination on the question of injury and the exact dumping margin. Many antidumping cases are "terminated" at one point or another in the process. What occurs, in many cases, is that the foreign firms have simply agreed to raise prices in order to avoid explicit tariffs.[34] Alas, the shoe is increasingly on the other foot. U.S. exporters are now finding that foreign governments are adopting similar antidumping laws, and U.S. firms are increasingly having antidumping cases filed against them overseas.

countervailing duty a tariff imposed by a country that is designed to increase the price of the imported good by an amount equal to any export subsidies

Countervailing Duties

The second form of administered protection is a **countervailing duty**. This is a tariff designed to offset the effects of foreign government subsidies for exports. Between 1980 and 2005, 459 countervailing duty cases were filed in the U.S. Like many economic issues, there are two views on this subject. If the increase in U.S. imports does not harm a domestic industry, one possible response by the government to such subsidies

[33]The ITA is a division of the Department of Commerce.

[34]This "harassment" effect has been demonstrated in Mark G. Herander and J. Brad Schwartz, "An Empirical Test of the Impact of the Threat of U.S. Trade Policy: The Case of Antidumping Duties," *Southern Economic Journal* 51(1), July 1984, pp. 59–79. The same effects have been more recently estimated in Robert W. Staiger and Frank A. Wolak, "Measuring Industry Specific Protection: Antidumping in the United States," *Brookings Papers on Economic Activity, Microeconomics,* 1994, pp. 51–103.

would be to send a "thank you" note to the foreign government. In this case, if a foreign government wishes to subsidize the consumption of U.S. citizens, then so much the better. The U.S. would have a higher standard of living at the expense of some other country's taxpayers. On the other hand, while it may be perfectly legitimate to ask our firms to compete with foreign firms, it may be asking a bit much for them to compete with foreign governments. In order to prevent this, U.S. trade law allows domestic firms to petition the U.S. government for a "countervailing duty" to offset foreign government subsidies on exports. The process of obtaining a countervailing duty is very similar to that of an antidumping petition.

While this countervailing duty is conceptually clear, determining the size of government subsidies is quite difficult in practice. There are two problems that arise in countervailing duty cases. First, there is the difficult issue of which government subsidies can be countervailed. Optimally, one would like to countervail direct subsidies on exports. A clear example would be a government subsidy of a certain monetary amount for each unit exported. However, government subsidies to firms and industries are rarely that clear. For example, assume that a foreign government subsidizes the R&D expenses of an industry that subsequently exports the product. In this case, can that subsidy be countervailed? In some cases, the answer is yes and in other cases no. What about industry specific tax breaks? The list of indirect subsidies to firms and industries can go on endlessly. Indeed, it is difficult to find any firm in any country that has not received some form of a government subsidy.

This leads to the second problem with countervailing duty cases. The problem is disentangling a country's trade policy from its industrial policy. For a variety of reasons, governments subsidize one industry or another. This encouragement or industrial policy may take the form of direct subsidies, partial or total government ownership, and tax relief. However, there is a potential conflict between a government's ability to pursue an active industrial policy and a level playing field in international markets. This conflict is not yet severe but it is unlikely to go away. Other countries have similar laws. As a result, U.S. firms that export are not immune from these effects. Any firm receiving substantial government assistance is at risk of having its exports "countervailed" in foreign markets.

The Escape Clause

Occasionally, a country's comparative advantage can shift more quickly than the domestic industry can adjust. This situation leads to the final type of administered protection, the escape clause. The **escape clause** allows a domestic industry to petition the government for temporary protection to allow the industry a chance to adjust their operations to compete with the more intense import competition. The purpose of the escape clause is to protect domestic firms, which might be profitable in the long run, from being driven out of business due to an increase in imports that has occurred in a short period of time.

escape clause a provision in U.S. law that allows temporary protection for U.S. industries that are under pressure from imports

In this case, the USITC investigates the industry and makes a determination on whether or not the industry is being harmed by imports. The final decision on whether or not to protect the industry is made by the president. Surprisingly, the filing of escape clause petitions is fairly rare. Since 1975, approximately 75 cases have been filed. Virtually all countries have this type of administered protection, which is perfectly legal under the WTO. The escape clause may be particularly important in a

Harley-Davidson and the Escape Clause

In the early 1980s, the classic American motorcycle firm, Harley-Davidson, was on the brink of bankruptcy. The firm was in dire straights owing to a combination of adverse factors. First, by its own admission, Harley-Davidson had been poorly managed in the 1970s. Second, the firm was facing a flood of cheaper, higher-quality imports from Japan. Japanese firms were obviously intent on penetrating the U.S. market, but a Japanese recession was giving them even more incentive to export than usual. Third, the U.S. was just emerging from a recession in the early 1980s, so domestic sales were below average even without imports. Finally, the dollar was becoming increasingly overvalued, making it even easier for Japanese firms to sell in the U.S. market at very competitive prices.

Faced with this situation, Harley-Davidson filed a petition for escape-clause relief arguing that the firm could survive and compete with the Japanese given some time to adjust. In 1983, the USITC recommended to President Ronald Reagan that the firm be granted relief. Tariffs were increased to 45 percent from 4 percent the first year and were to decline progressively to 10 percent in 1987. A year ahead of schedule, Harley-Davidson notified the government that it was now competitive and did not need the final year of protection. The rest, of course, is history.

period of floating exchange rates. A loss of comparative advantage coupled with an overvalued exchange rate may produce a situation where the firms might be able to deal with efficient foreign competitors or an overvalued exchange rate, but not both. When protection is granted, the tariff is usually raised on the particular good and then gradually lowered over a period of time such as five years.

An example of relief under the escape clause occurred in 2002, when President George Bush imposed tariffs ranging from 8 percent to 30 percent on a variety of imported steel products. Under this relief, the new tariffs were to be phased out over a three-year period. The design of the import relief is to give the U.S. steel producers time so that they can bring the costs under control and upgrade equipment. Critics of the import relief argue that protecting the U.S. steel industry raises the cost to steel-using industries and causes a decrease in employment in the steel-using sectors of the economy.

THE GENERAL AGREEMENT ON TARIFFS AND TRADE (GATT)

During World War II, there was no opportunity to reform the world's trading system. However, as the war was ending, the major trading nations moved quickly to reform the international trading system. After the war ended, there was a fear that the depressed economic conditions of the 1930s would return. In the past, most major wars had been followed by recessions that national governments caused in part by their attempt to return to balanced budgets. In 1944, the allied powers met in Bretton Woods, New Hampshire, to determine some guidelines for the operation of the world

International Trade Organization (ITO) an organization conceived by the Bretton Woods conference to develop the international trading system. The actual implementation of the ITO did not occur because the U.S. Congress did not ratify the agreement.

General Agreement on Tariffs and Trade (GATT) an agreement reached in 1947 that established principles to govern international trade. Until 1995 this organization administered multilateral trade agreements and settled trade disputes.

economy after the war. The International Monetary Fund (IMF) and the World Bank were conceived at this conference.[35] In addition, a framework for conducting international trade was developed to repair the damage that the escalation of tariffs in the 1930s caused and to prevent this type of tariff escalation from recurring. The conference proposed the **International Trade Organization (ITO)** to develop the international trading system and to complement the activities of the IMF and the World Bank. The charter to implement the ITO was signed in Havana, Cuba, in 1948. However, the actual implementation of the ITO did not occur because the U.S. Congress did not ratify the agreement.[36]

Fortunately, at the Bretton Woods Conference an interim committee or organization had been created to launch the ITO. This interim committee was authorized by an administrative agreement between the countries and was called the **General Agreement on Tariffs and Trade (GATT)**. This administrative agreement did not require U.S. Congressional ratification. Its purpose was to operate as an interim committee until the ITO was established. In this case the interim was 50 years. Because GATT was not an official international organization, countries that joined GATT were called contracting parties. One scholar of international trade relations described GATT in the following way:

> "In one of the happiest examples of ingenuity in the history of international organization, the GATT has risen above the legalistic confines of the text of the General Agreement and has improvised numerous procedures."[37]

From its inauspicious beginning, GATT changed world trade. One measure of GATT's success was its growth. The GATT began in 1947 with 23 contracting parties and grew until it comprised more than 100 contracting parties.[38] In total, the contracting parties (countries) covered more than 90 percent of world trade. To become a contracting party of GATT, a country had to give most-favored-nation status to all other contracting parties and had to eliminate any quotas (quantitative restrictions on imports) that restricted international trade.

GATT and Multilateral Trade Negotiations

The first goal of GATT was to reduce the high levels of tariffs remaining since the 1930s. Over the next fifty years, a number of **Multilateral Trade Negotiations (MTNs)** successfully reduced tariffs. A multilateral trade negotiation proceeds in the following manner.

First, there would be a GATT ministerial meeting of the trade ministers from the contracting parties to set up a proposed agenda for what was to be negotiated. Next, the trade ministers of each country would then request authorization from their respective governments to participate in the multilateral trade negotiations. The U.S.

[35]The IMF will be discussed in greater detail in Chapter 20.
[36]Although Congress made several attempts to ratify this agreement, none passed.
[37]Kenneth W. Dam, *The GATT: Law and the International Economic Organization,* Chicago: University of Chicago Press, 1970.
[38]The WTO now has 145 member countries. For further details see "Fifty Years On," *The Economist,* May 16, 1998, pp. 21–23.

multilateral trade negotiations a process of reducing tariff and nontariff barriers to trade among member countries of GATT or the WTO

government's position concerning the multilateral trade negotiations was critical. Given the size of the U.S. economy, the negotiations could not proceed without the U.S. Also, the other contracting parties did not want to enter into negotiations with the U.S. government without assurances that it would honor the negotiated agreement. In part, the other contracting parties felt this way because the U.S. had not ratified the International Trade Organization. Normally, the other contracting parties waited until the U.S. Congress passed legislation that authorized the executive branch to participate in the multilateral trade negotiations. Embodied within the U.S. legislation was a statement that the U.S. Congress would vote to ratify the negotiated trade agreement without modifying or amending the trade agreement. This statement is called Congressional fast-track approval. The multilateral trade negotiations between the contracting parties began and continued over a period of years. Several multinational trade negotiations have occurred since World War II.[39] Table 9.3 illustrates the success that the MTNs had on reducing tariffs and the number of countries involved in the process. Once a trade agreement was reached, the U.S. Congress would then decide whether to accept or reject the agreement without modification. (Every MTN trade agreement has passed Congress.) The tariff cuts mandated by a multilateral trade negotiation would then be phased in over a number of years.

To keep the process of tariff reductions moving forward, a subsequent multilateral trade negotiation would be planned and started as soon as possible. The process of reducing tariffs was like the movement of a bicycle: it needed to keep going forward or

Table 9.3 GATT and WTO Multilateral Trade Negotiations

Multilateral Trade Round	Dates	Tariff Cuts	# of Countries	Major Negotiation
Pre-GATT	1934–1947	33.2%	23	Tariffs
First Round	1947	21.1	23	Tariffs
Second Round	1949	1.9	13	Tariffs
Third Round	1950–1951	3.0	38	Tariffs
Fourth Round	1955–1956	3.5	26	Tariffs
Dillon Round	1961–1962	2.4	26	Tariffs
Kennedy Round	1964–1967	36.0	62	Tariffs, Agriculture, Dumping
Tokyo Round	1974–1979	29.6	99	Tariffs, NTBs
Uruguay Round	1987–1994	38.0	125	Tariffs, Services, Agriculture
Millennium Round	1999	Aborted		
Doha Round	2001–		142	See Text for Details

Source: Data adapted from R. P. Lavergne, "The Political Economy of U.S. Tariffs" (Ph.D. Thesis, University of Toronto, 1981); reproduced in R. E. Baldwin, "U.S. Trade Policy Since World War II," in *The Structure and Evolution of Recent U.S. Trade Policy,* edited by R. E. Baldwin and A. O. Kruger (Chicago: University of Chicago Press, 1984). Updated to include the Uruguay and later rounds.

[39]Several smaller negotiations had occurred in the 1940s and 1950s. For details see Wilson B. Brown and Jan S. Hogendorn, *International Economics: Theory and Context,* New York: Addison-Wesley, 1994.

Who Makes U.S. Trade Policy?

Most countries have a ministry or department that is exclusively charged with setting international trade policy for the country. For example, Japan has the Ministry for International Trade and Industry (MITI), which deals with both domestic business and international trade issues. In Japan, international trade policy decisions move much faster than we are accustomed to in the U.S. Ministers serve at the prime minister's pleasure and can be appointed or replaced very quickly. Thus, when the "government" (the ruling party or coalition of parties) makes a decision regarding international trade, things happen fairly fast.

In the U.S., things work differently because there is no Department of International Trade and Industry. The closest equivalent in the U.S. is the Office of the United States Trade Representative (USTR). This office was created by the Trade Expansion Act of 1962 and as part of the Trade Act of 1974, the office was established as a cabinet-level agency within the Executive Office of the President. This office has responsibility for *coordinating* and *administering* U.S. trade policy. The trade representative is a cabinet-level official with the rank of Ambassador. The agency provides trade policy leadership and negotiating expertise in its major areas of responsibility.

More than 17 federal agencies and offices are involved in international trade issues, not including input from Congress and the input from representatives of various interests in the private sector. The combination of this form of government and the diffusion of responsibility on international trade issues around the government is what makes trade policy a "mess" or at least complicated for the U.S.

it would fall down.[40] For example, the tariffs reductions negotiated in the Kennedy Round were completely phased in by January 1, 1972. The Tokyo Round was initiated at a meeting of trade ministers in Tokyo in 1973. The Tokyo Round agreement was negotiated among the contracting parties between 1975 and 1979. The tariff reductions that were agreed to in the Tokyo Round were phased in through January 1, 1987. Before the Tokyo Round reductions were completed, the Uruguay Round was initiated at a meeting of trade ministers in 1986 and the Uruguay Round negotiations began in 1987.[41]

Each of the multilateral trade negotiations was successful in reducing trade barriers. Tariffs under the Kennedy, Tokyo, and Uruguay Rounds were cut by approximately one-third in each round of trade negotiations. Although average tariffs have been reduced, tariffs continue to be a problem for two reasons. One, tariffs on some products are still high, even in developed countries—as shown in the box on the complexity of fruit juice. Two, the developing countries and, lately, the transition

[40]See William R. Cline, "Introduction and Summary," in *Trade Policy in the 1980s,* William R. Cline, ed., Washington, D.C.: Institute for International Economics, 1983, pp. 1–54.

[41]One may have noticed that the negotiations are rather lengthy. The old joke is that GATT stood for the General Agreement to Talk and Talk. Another problem may be that the negotiations are held in Geneva and the pleasant environment there may be inducing the negotiators to linger. For more details on this problem see "For GATT Officials, Talking Only Stops If Mouth Are Full," *The Wall Street Journal,* November 8, 1993, p. A1.

economies of Eastern Europe have been latecomers in joining the WTO and reducing their tariffs. As such, average tariff levels in many of these countries remain high.

THE WORLD TRADE ORGANIZATION

The Uruguay Round's most important achievement was the creation of the **World Trade Organization (WTO)**. On January 1, 1995 the ITO's Interim Committee, GATT, became an international organization headquartered in Geneva, Switzerland. This distinction between a treaty and an organization is important. The old GATT was an international treaty that had gone beyond being just a treaty. It essentially was an organization. However, over time this arrangement had become difficult to administer. The arrangement was workable with only a few dozen members negotiating tariff cuts. With the increasing number of countries in GATT and the increasing complexity of the issues, the organizational arrangement was becoming increasingly unworkable.

Under the original GATT, treaty there were a relatively simple set of rules governing world trade in goods. However, as tariffs fell, other issues not included in the original agreement became the subject of negotiation. Among these issues were international trade in services, government procurement, and antidumping regulations. Since many countries were unwilling to negotiate trade agreements on these issues, GATT had developed a number of "side" agreements in these areas. Countries were and still are free to pick and choose which parts of international trade rules they wished to conform to in which areas of trade. Nonetheless, all countries that are members of the WTO must adhere to a core set of rules governing trade that have been negotiated over the years.

However, the most important difference between GATT and the WTO is the dispute settlement mechanism. Under GATT, a country could file a trade complaint against another country and a GATT Council would investigate the complaint. However, the investigation was slow and the GATT panels' findings were routinely ignored because GATT could not enforce their rulings. Under the WTO, a country can file a trade complaint against another country and a WTO dispute panel will investigate the complaint. The WTO dispute panel will issue its findings within six months and the offended country will legally be able to retaliate against the other country.[42] Thus, the WTO has an effective enforcement mechanism that was lacking in GATT. The new mechanism has been successful in the sense that it is being actively used. The U.S. has filed 24 complaints with the WTO and has prevailed in 22 of these.

THE FUTURE OF INTERNATIONAL TRADE NEGOTIATIONS

How future WTO negotiations will proceed remains to be seen. A WTO ministerial meeting was held in Singapore in 1996, and another WTO ministerial meeting was held in Seattle in 1999, where riots disrupted the meetings. In November 2001, ministers from the 142 countries attending the WTO meeting in Doha, Qatar, agreed to launch a new round of global trade negotiations. In August of 2002, the U.S. Congress

[42]There is a complicated appeals process that can delay the retaliation. Details are available on the process at www.wto.org/wto/webds_wpf.html.

passed trade promotion authority legislation authorizing the executive branch of the U.S. government to participate in this multilateral trade negotiation. The ministers at Doha gave themselves three years to complete this round of trade negotiations. This means the negotiations on all areas should have been completed by January 1, 2005.

The agenda for the Doha Round is complex. However, the agenda effectively provides a roadmap of what remains to be completed in terms of modernizing WTO rules to fit the more modern aspects of international trade. The following is a list of the major issues facing the negotiators.

International Trade in Agricultural Products—Previous GATT negotiations, have for the most part, avoided the contentious issue of countries protecting their agriculture industry. The issue is so sensitive that it this issues alone almost derailed the whole Uruguay Round. However, the agreement reached under the Uruguay Round was that agriculture should be a topic of negotiation in the Doha Round. World trade in agriculture is largely distorted in two ways. First, there are a substantial amount of trade barriers (tariffs and nontariff barriers) in agricultural products. Second, even if there were no trade barriers, agricultural production in many countries is heavily subsidized. The primary goal of the Doha Round is the reduction of agricultural subsidies primarily in the developed countries. This is an important issue as the size of the subsidies are quite large. The WTO has estimated that the total amount of farm subsidies for its members is $221 billion.

General Agreement on Trade in Services (GATS) commits WTO members to a set of agreed upon rules for trade in services

Market Access—The WTO describes tariff reductions as market access. In this case, the issue for negotiators is developed countries' tariffs on agricultural and primary products and developing countries' high tariffs on manufactured products. Many developed countries still impose what are essentially revenue tariffs on products that they do not produce. Many of the developing countries only recently have joined the WTO and still have high tariffs on average. There is potentially room for the two groups to bargain reciprocal tariff reductions on these two issues.

International Trade in Services—One of the major accomplishments of the Uruguay Round was the creation of the **General Agreement on Trade in Services (GATS)**. GATS commits WTO members to a set of agreed-upon rules for trade in services. Unfortunately, the only concrete commitment by all members is that the principle of MFN should be applied to services. At this point, world trade in services is hindered by applying by-service-by-country barriers similar to the by-product-by-country barriers that plagued world trade in goods before GATT. Needless to say, these negotiations are extremely complex. However, the gains for countries and the world economy are potentially large as the service industries have become a major part of the world's domestic production.

Trade Related Intellectual Property (TRIPs) trade in intellectual property, such as music, software, writing, and pharmaceuticals, all of which are protected in the form of patents or copyrights

Trade-Related Intellectual Property (TRIPS)—World trade in intellectual property such as music, writings, software, and pharmaceuticals is an increasingly important part of the world economy. However, this trade can be efficiently conducted only if intellectual property in the form of patents and copyrights is respected. The development of intellectual property is encouraged when the producers are free to charge market prices for the property and are protected from the theft of this property. However, in a world with large disparities in income, a completely free market may make it difficult for low-income countries to purchase adequate amounts of some essential products such as pharmaceuticals. The function of the WTO in this case is to mediate between these conflicting interests. The result is that the Doha Round negotiations involve the developing countries offering to more rigorously enforce intellectual property rights in exchange for access to some products at prices appropriate to their level of economic development.

Trade Related Investment Measures (TRIMs) government policies in which foreign direct investment in a country are allowed only if the investing firm meets certain trade performance goals

Trade-Related Investment Measures (TRIMS)—As we saw in Chapter 6, international trade and the movement of factors of production are substitutes. If goods can flow freely but factors of production cannot, then international trade has been distorted. The WTO cannot negotiate the movements of labor, but restrictions on FDI are being negotiated. Specifically, some rules on FDI have an obvious effect on international trade. For example, if a new plant in a country must export a specified amount of total output this has an obvious effect on trade flows. The goal in the Doha Round are the reduction in regulations on FDI that also distort trade flows.

The Future of MTNs

The brief list of major issues being negotiated in the Doha Round shows the challenges and opportunities of the current and any future MTNs. With so many issues and so many countries involved, MTNs are becoming difficult to negotiate. The Uruguay Round was almost ruined by the negotiations over agriculture. As one can see from the above discussion, the Doha Round was difficult, even, to begin. Likewise, the actual negotiations have proved to be very difficult. Once again, negotiations over agriculture have threatened to ruin the entire negotiations. The Doha Round is further complicated by the timetable for negotiations. Previous MTNs were becoming ever longer as both the negotiating agenda and the number of countries involved became ever larger. To combat this problem, the Doha Round was to be concluded by December of 2006. No agreement had been reached by that point. One cannot conclusively say that the Doha Round has failed, but the current state of negotiations is uncertain. Since no major trade negotiation has failed since the 1930s, all parties seem uncertain as to how to proceed.

The opportunities for further expansion of world trade are enormous if MTNs are successful. Trade barriers, however, terribly distort world trade in agriculture. The developed countries spend enormous sums of money on agricultural subsidies. The liberalization of world trade in this sector holds the promise of both rationalizing the production of food and feeding the world's hungry. The gains to consumers of lower prices with free trade could hardly be more important than in trade in agricultural products. On a different level, international trade in services are hindered by the lack of trade rules that take us back in time before the development of GATT. Practically speaking, countries are now free to restrict trade in services in any way they wish. In this sense, the fact that world trade in services is currently growing faster than world trade in goods is remarkable. With rules for services that are anything like the rules for goods, the growth of world trade in services in the 21st century could be one of the more important factors in world economic growth.

Despite these opportunities, progress in liberalizing trade within the framework of MTNs has been slow. Further, there is still opposition to the WTO itself and the idea of global trade liberalization. The WTO is essential as a referee of world trade and as a forum for negotiating new rules in areas where few or none exist. Unfortunately, for many countries the pace of negotiations within the WTO is too slow. Increasingly, many countries are searching for a means of liberalizing trade at a faster rate than that which is likely to come out of an MTN. However, these countries also want to do so in a way that is consistent with existing WTO rules. In the next chapter, we consider the means for countries to accomplish this.

SUMMARY

1. A country's international trade policies are measures that the country's government designs to affect its trade relations with the rest of the world.
2. An industry or firm will seek government regulation that enhances the profits of nearly all firms in the industry.
3. International trade can create losses for firms and workers in the industries that compete with imports. As a result, firms and workers will have an incentive to seek protection from imports. Both firms and workers will use special interest groups to lobby for changes in laws and regulations that will benefit them, although these changes may not benefit the larger public.
4. The study of politics by economists is called public choice. The theory of public choice states that politicians attempt to maximize their utility, in the same way that consumers try to maximize their utility, or firms try to maximize profits. The group that will lobby for or against freer trade is most likely the group that has a comparative disadvantage. Economists refer to these activities by special interest groups as rent-seeking.
5. In general, industries and/or products receive high tariffs when: (1) the industry is large and important to the country; (2) the industry is concentrated regionally or has few firms; (3) the industry produces an intermediate product; (4) the industry's employees have significant voting strength; and (5) the industry has a comparative disadvantage in the world marketplace. Firms and workers in these industries have more to lose from freer trade than firms and workers in industries that have a comparative advantage.
6. During the late 18th and the 19th century, the U.S. government used tariffs as a way to raise revenue. Tariffs were also used as a way of developing American industry through infant-industry protection. Also, Northern manufacturers sought high tariffs as a way of avoiding foreign competition. High tariffs were opposed by Southern states and the disagreement culminated with the passing of the Tariff of Abominations in 1828.
7. In response to the onset of the Great Depression, the U.S. passed the Smoot-Hawley Tariff. This raised tariffs to the highest level in U.S. history.
8. The U.S. government passed the Reciprocal Trade Agreements Act in 1934, which is the basis of all subsequent U.S. trade policy. The Act mandated reciprocity in trade negotiations; transferred much of Congressional authority in trade policy to the president; and required the use of MFN.
9. There are three forms of administered protection: antidumping, countervailing duties, and the escape clause. Antidumping law prohibits the sale of foreign goods in the U.S. if they are being sold at less than the cost of production or at a price lower than that charged in the foreign market. Countervailing duties are used to offset foreign export subsidies. The escape clause is a means by which U.S. imports suffering from import competition can obtain temporary protection in order to restructure and become more competitive.
10. In 1944, the allied countries met at Bretton Woods, New Hampshire, to set guidelines for the operation of the world economy after the war. The International Trade Organization (ITO) was developed to complement the activities of the IMF and World Bank but was never ratified by the U.S. Congress and did not go into effect. Through an administrative agreement, an interim committee called General Agreement on Tariffs and Trade (GATT) had been created to launch the ITO. GATT remained in existence for nearly 50 years.
11. Upon entering GATT, countries must adopt most-favored-nation tariffs with respect to all other contracting parties. GATT's first order of business was to reduce the high tariffs left over from the 1930s and over the next 50 years, tariffs were reduced in a number of multilateral trade negotiations.
12. The agenda for the Uruguay Round covered the following issues: (1) tariffs would be reduced by the contracting parties by approximately 33 percent; (2) quotas and voluntary export restraints would be phased out; (3) trade-related investment measures were discussed; (4) the General Agreement on Trade in Services was created; (5) the rules governing government procurement were discussed; (6) the contracting parties tried

once again to reduce the trade distortions caused by government subsidies to farmers; and (7) the World Trade Organization (WTO) was created to replace GATT.

13. The agenda for the Doha Round included a reduction in farm subsidies in developed countries; a lo`wering of tariffs in both developed and developing countries; and agreements on trade in services, intellectual property, and FDI. The lack of progress in the Doha Round leaves the whole future of MTNs uncertain.

KEY CONCEPTS AND TERMS

- special interest groups p. 194
- public choice p. 194
- rent seeking p. 195
- structure of protection p. 196
- infant-industry protection p. 203
- Tariff of Abominations p. 203
- Smoot-Hawley Tariff p. 203
- Reciprocal Trade Agreements Act p. 204
- Most Favored Nation (MFN) p. 204
- administered protection p. 205
- antidumping law p. 205
- sporadic dumping p. 205
- persistent dumping p. 206
- predatory dumping p. 206
- dumping margin p. 207
- countervailing duty p. 207
- escape clause p. 208
- International Trade Organization (ITO) p. 210
- General Agreement on Tariffs and Trade (GATT) p. 210
- multilateral trade negotiations (MTNs) p. 211
- General Agreement on Trade in Services (GATS) p. 214
- Trade-Related Intellectual Property (TRIPs) p. 214
- Trade-Related Investment Measures (TRIMs) p. 215

PROBLEMS AND QUESTIONS FOR REVIEW

1. Describe what the theory of public choice means.
2. Explain what the term *rent-seeking* means.
3. How does public choice relate to the existence of protectionism?
4. Why is the U.S. tariff schedule so complicated?
5. List the factors that would increase the probability that an industry would receive a higher level of protection.
6. What are the advantages of a uniform tariff?
7. Why do some industries have greater protection than others?
8. Describe the evolution of U.S. trade policy from 1792 to the 20th century.
9. At what stages in U.S. trade history did protectionism reach its peak?
10. Identify the main provisions of the Reciprocal Trade Agreements Act.
11. Why is MFN so important?
12. What does the term *fast track* mean in the context of U.S. trade policy? Why is it important?
13. What are the various forms of dumping?
14. Describe the evolution of antidumping law in the U.S.
15. How do governments protect domestic industries from export subsidies?
16. Describe how the escape clause is different from the other forms of administered protection.
17. Why was the creation of GATT an important event in world trade?
18. List the MTNs, when they occurred and the major issues negotiated.
19. How is the WTO different from GATT?
20. What are the major issues being negotiated in the Doha Round?

SUGGESTED READINGS AND WEB SITES

Robert J. Barro, "Big Steel Doesn't Need Any More Propping Up," *Business Week,* April 1, 2002, p.24.
A short article outlining why the steel industry is a poor candidate for escape clause protection.
Jagdish Bhagwati, *In Defense of Globalization,* New York: Oxford University Press, 2004.
An outstanding collection of essays on most aspects of international trade and trade policy.
Kenneth W. Dam, *The Rules of the Global Game: A New Look at U.S. International Policymaking,* Chicago: University of Chicago Press, 2001.
A good look at how the lobbying industry in the U.S. affects U.S. international economic policy from one of those rare academics that has made the successful transition to government service.
"Domestic Demands Limit U.S., EU Bargaining at Trade Talks," *Wall Street Journal,* November 12, 2001, p. A24.
An unusually frank look at how domestic political pressures influence U.S. and EU trade negotiators.
Nina Easton, "Ahoy! Can This Woman Save Free Trade?" *Fortune,* October 1, 2007, pp. 172–178.
A fascinating look at the work of the current U.S. Trade Representative.
Peter Engardio, "Dumping: China Strikes Back," *Business Week,* July 5, 2004, p. 58.
Other countries also have antidumping laws and U.S. exporters are now feeling the effects.
Michael J. Ferrantino, "Import Restraints: Special Focus on Labor Transitions," *International Economic Review,* July/August 2002, pp. 1–7.
This excellent study shows the anticipated effects of the removal of all significant barriers to trade on both a national and a state basis.
"Fifty Years On," *The Economist,* May 16, 1998, pp. 21–23.
Perhaps the best short reference piece available on the history of the GATT/WTO.
Robert Z. Lawrence, *Crimes and Punishments? Retaliation under the WTO,* Washington, D.C.: Institute for International Economics, 2003.
An excellent book on the new enforcement mechanism of the WTO.
Brink Lindsey and Daniel J. Ikenson, *AntiDumping Exposed: The Devilish Details of Unfair Trade Laws,* Washington, D.C.: Cato Institute, 2003.
An excellent book on U.S. antidumping law.
Jakob B. Madsen, "Trade Barriers and the Collapse of World Trade During the Great Depression," *Southern Economic Journal,* April 2001, 67(4), pp. 848–68.
An excellent article that gives quantitative estimates of the effects of the trade war of the 1930s on world trade.
Keith Maskus, *Intellectual Property Rights in the Global Economy,* Washington, D.C.: Institute for International Economics, 2000.
A good reference on the issues involved in trade related intellectual property.
Arvind Panagairya, "Cost of Protection: Where Do We Stand?" *American Economic Review* 92(2), May 2002, pp. 175–79.
A readable short synopsis of what we know about the cost of protection as a percentage of GDP. The article also includes a short piece on the costs of rent-seeking activities and a discussion of the costs of X-efficiency.
"Patches of Light," *The Economist,* June 9, 2001, pp. 69–71.
A short article on world trade in agriculture. The graph on page 70 showing the difference in the growth of world trade in agriculture versus manufactures neatly shows the damage being done by trade barriers and subsidies.
"The Right to Good Ideas," *The Economist,* June 23, 2001, pp. 21–23.
An excellent short article on the issues involved in world trade in intellectual property.
U.S. International Trade Commission (www.ustic.gov).
The USITC is the best source for the details of administered protection.
U.S. Trade Representative (www.ustr.gov)
The official web site of the U.S. Trade Representative. The best place to keep up with U.S. international trade negotiations.
World Trade Organization (www.wto.org)
The official web of the WTO. It is both easy to use and contains an incredible amount of information.

APPENDIX 9.1

Price Discrimination

A major cause of persistent dumping is international price discrimination. A firm's practice of price discrimination can occur when the firm is able to separate its total market into two or more markets with different elasticities of demand for its product. Under these conditions, the firm can increase its profits by charging different prices in each market. In the case of international price discrimination, the firm in question is serving both a domestic market and an export market. In many cases, a domestic firm has more competitors in its export markets than in its domestic market. This implies that the demand for the domestic firm's product in the export market is more elastic than the demand for the firm's product in its home market. This situation creates an incentive for international price discrimination.

Figure 9.2 illustrates the relationship between international price discrimination and persistent dumping. A firm producing cloth faces both a home market demand and an export market demand for its product. These demand curves indicate that the firm faces a more elastic demand

Figure 9.2 Persistent Dumping as International Price Discrimination

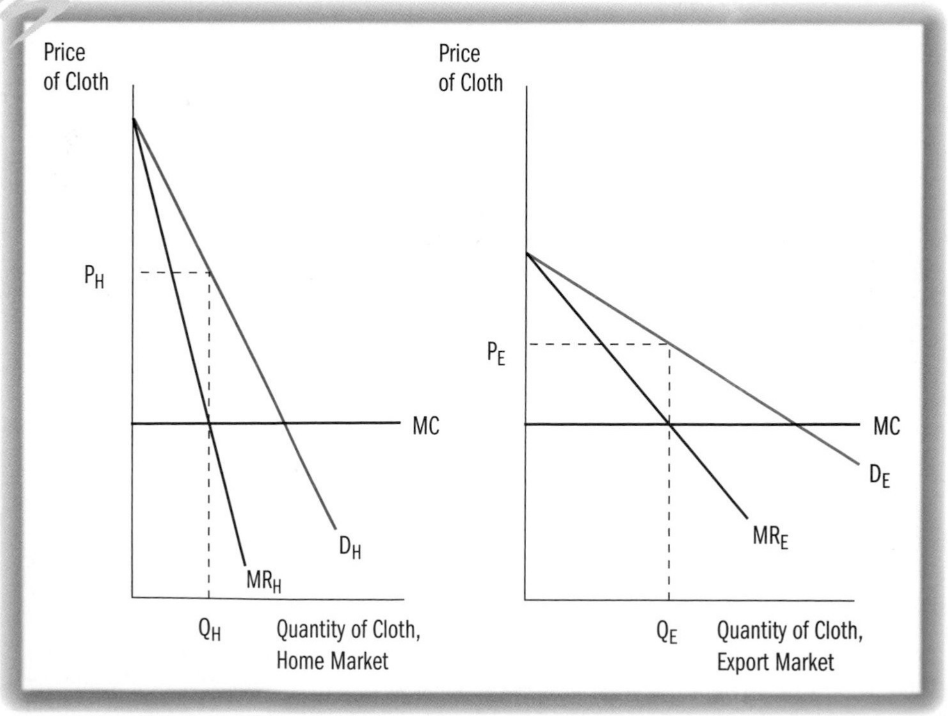

for its product in its export market. This implies that the firm has more market power in the home market than in the export market.

Under these conditions, the firm will maximize its profit in each market by producing and selling that level of output at which marginal cost equals marginal revenue. The price charged in the home market for cloth is P_H, and the price charged in the export market for cloth is P_E. In addition, the price charged in the export market is less than the price charged in the home market for the same unit of cloth. The important point is that under this situation, the firm is persistently dumping cloth in the export market and could be subjected to the antidumping laws of the importing country.

Chapter 10

Regional Economic Arrangements

"The multilateral system and the Uruguay round are important and should not be abandoned or jeopardized. But multilateralism moves at the pace of the slowest. Regional Integration can open economies further and faster. It should be given free rein"
—RUDIGER DORNBUSCH

INTRODUCTION

regional trade agreements **a trade agreement between two or more countries that provides tariff reductions for only those countries that are members of the agreement**

One of the most important trends in the world economy is the increasing number of **regional trade agreements** between countries. Regional trade agreements are trade agreements between two or more countries that reduce trade barriers for only those countries that are members of the agreement. These reductions in trade barriers differ from the reduction of trade barriers on a multilateral basis. Under multilateral trade negotiations, tariffs and other barriers to trade are reduced for all countries that are members of the WTO. As such, multilateral reductions in trade barriers are nondiscriminatory.

Since tariffs and other trade barriers are reduced for some countries but not for all, regional trade agreements and the associated reduction of trade barriers embodied in them are discriminatory. As a result, the negotiating countries which are a part of these agreements obtain a margin of preference over other countries that are not a part of the agreement.[1] The GATT/WTO has been notified on some 367 regional trade agreements, of which more than 180 notifications have occurred since the creation of the WTO in 1995. Currently 214 regional trade agreements are in force between countries. Out of the total 158 cover trade in goods, 43 cover trade in services, and 13 are accessions to existing RTAs. The WTO currently estimates that by the end of 2005, approximately 300 regional trade agreements will be in effect. Figure 10.1 illustrates the number of RTAs in force and RTAs that have notified the WTO by type of notification. As the figure illustrates, the global trading system has seen a dramatic increase in the

[1]Actually, the term *regional trade agreement* is misleading. Countries do not have to be geographically close to one another to reduce trade barriers. In addition, such trade agreements are inherently preferential. However, the term *preferential trade agreement* usually describes an agreement between developed and developing countries where the former cuts trade barriers while the latter does not.

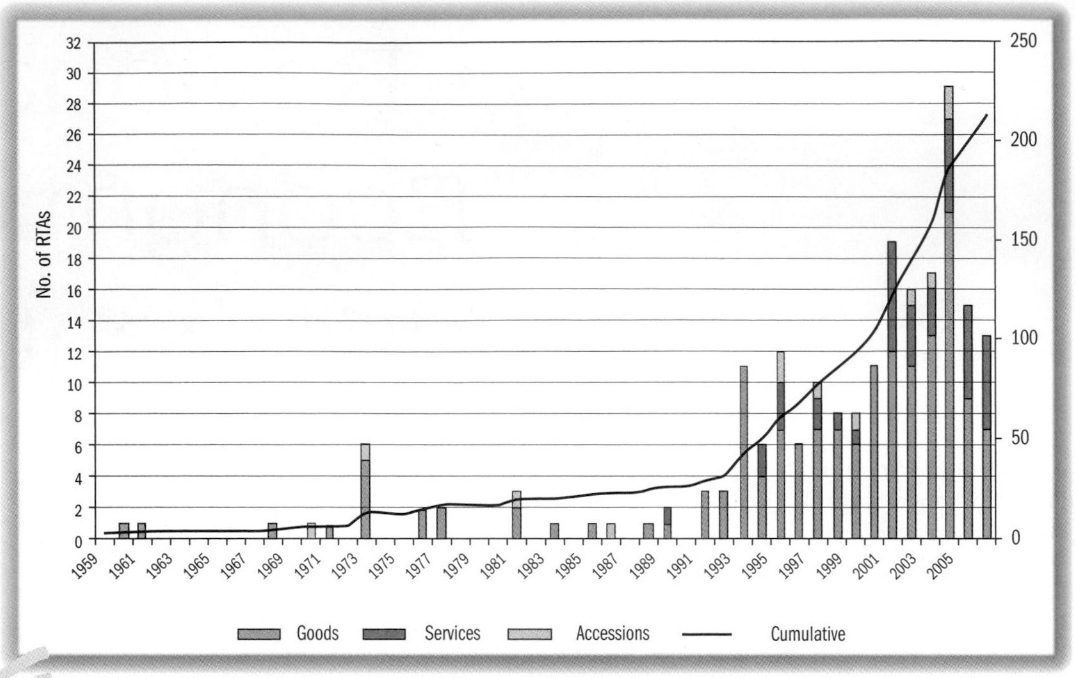

Figure 10.1 Number of Regional Trade Agreements

Source: Roberto Fiorentino, Luis Verdeja and Christelle Toqueboeuf, "The Changing Landscape of Regional Trade Agreements: 2006 Update," World Trade Organization, Discussion Paper No. 12, 2007.

number of regional trade agreements over the past 15 years. While the recent growth of regional trade agreements began in the 1990s, the seeds of this development were sown in the 1980s. Part of the trend toward regionalism occurred because of the difficult and sometimes slow progress in the multilateral trade negotiations during the Uruguay Round. In addition, during this period the U.S. began to implement the regional trade agreement approach to trade by signing a free trade agreement with Israel, followed by Canada, and the North American Free Trade Agreement (NAFTA).

Although regional trade agreements between countries strike at the very heart of the most favored nation principle, the WTO has accepted them. The reasoning behind this exemption is relatively straightforward. The implementation of a regional trade agreement entails both benefits and costs. Simplistically, the reduction of trade barriers increases the amount of trade between the countries involved and the countries that are not a part of the agreement lose some trade. If the gains in new trade are greater for member countries than the losses to nonmember countries, the volume of world trade expands and the world economy is better off. However, this total benefit is not free as there are some losers.

This chapter on international trade addresses these regional economic issues, beginning with a discussion concerning the different types of regional economic integration and the importance of the rules of origin. We then analyze the economic impact of regional integration on the countries involved and the rest of the world. The European Union (EU) and the various U.S. trade agreements then are used as the major examples of how regional trade agreements operate. The concluding section considers the relationship between future multilateral trade negotiations and regional trade agreements.

DEGREES OF ECONOMIC INTEGRATION

There are various degrees of international economic integration between countries, and regional trade agreements between countries tend to change over time. The different degrees of international economic integration can be placed along a continuum as illustrated in Figure 10.2. On one end of the continuum is a regional trade agreement between countries that provides a limited reduction in trade barriers between those two countries. On the other end of the continuum is an agreement among a group of countries to act as if the group is a distinct country in every economic respect. As the figure shows, there are a number of different possibilities between these two extremes.

Consider a regional trade agreement where two or more countries reduce or abolish tariffs on a limited number of products. This level of economic integration is referred to as a preferential trade agreement between the two countries. Generally, this type of agreement is illegal under the rules of the WTO. WTO regulations state that in order for a regional trade agreement to be legal under their guidelines, trade barriers must be lifted on "substantially all" of the trade between the two countries. Like many rules and regulations of the WTO, it is possible to obtain a waiver from this restriction. An example of a regional preferential trade agreement is the 1962

Figure 10.2 Levels of Economic Integration

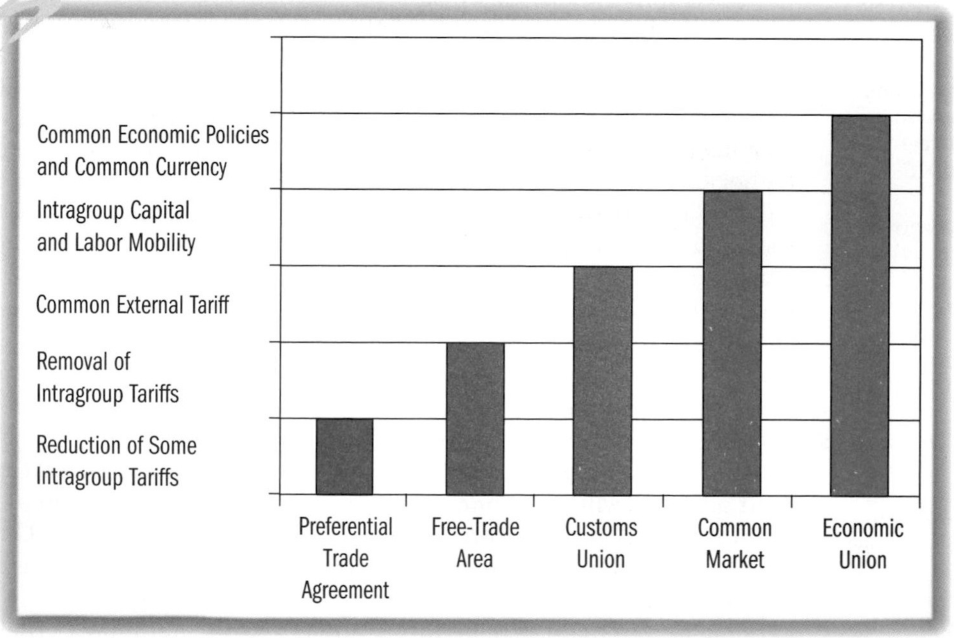

free-trade area an agreement between countries to reduce or eliminate trade barriers between countries while maintaining separate national tariff schedules

trade deflection the diversion of exports to a country within a free trade area that has lower tariffs on a good

customs union an agreement between countries to maintain a free trade area and a common external tariff

common external tariff an agreement between countries to eliminate their respective national tariff schedules and replace them with a common tariff schedule

U.S.-Canadian Agreement on Trade in Automobiles and Parts. By the early 1960s, the U.S. automobile industry had spread north of the border into Canada. As a result, U.S. manufacturers were paying tariffs on what were essentially intrafirm transactions. To reduce the cost of production, it made sense to eliminate the trade barriers in automobiles between the two countries. As a result, GATT granted a waiver for this preferential trade agreement.

The second level of economic integration is a **free-trade area (FTA)**. In a free-trade area, the countries agree to eliminate tariffs and other nontariff barriers to trade between each other. First, in order for a free-trade area to be legal under international trade law, it must cover "substantially all" trade among the members. In general, this statement means that the reduction of trade barriers must cover nonagricultural products. The European Union has free-trade agreements with countries such as Israel and Turkey that only cover such trade. Second, the agreement must be completed within a reasonable period of time. Almost all trade agreements between countries are "phased in" over time. In practice 15 years has become the limit of reasonable. Further, a free-trade agreement may cover more than just trade in goods. The free-trade agreements the U.S. has with Israel, Canada, and Mexico include trade in services, portfolio investment, and FDI. With these qualifications, a free-trade area between countries is usually *less* than the name implies. Just because two countries have signed a free-trade agreement does not mean that trade between these two countries is or will become identical to trade between, say, New Hampshire and Vermont.

Finally, with an FTA each country maintains its own separate national tariff schedule. For example, an automobile company exporting from Japan to the three NAFTA countries would face three different tariffs. Because each country uses its own tariff schedule, trade deflection may occur within a free-trade area. **Trade deflection** is the diversion of exports to a country within a free-trade area that has lower tariffs on a specific good. For example, suppose the tariff on cars is 4 percent in the U.S. and Canada and 20 percent in Mexico. A car exporter to this free-trade area has an incentive to ship cars to say San Diego, pay the 4 percent U.S. tariff, and then ship the car to Mexico to sell it to a Mexican customer. In this case, the exporter is attempting to avoid the 20 percent tariff on cars to Mexico. Thus, when the national tariffs of the free-trade area members are very different, exporters have a clear incentive to try to evade the higher tariffs. This problem can also arise if the member countries have large differences in quotas or other nontariff barriers. Differences in tariffs and/or quotas can also lead to the establishment of "screwdriver plants." These plants are designed to provide minor assembly work on a product that is essentially produced in a foreign country but assembled within the free-trade area to avoid the higher tariffs.

A third level of economic integration is a **customs union**. A customs union is an agreement between countries to maintain a free-trade area and to construct and maintain a common external tariff. As such, a customs union is similar to a free-trade area but with two differences. First, a customs union has a common external tariff for member countries. A **common external tariff** means that each country replaces its own national tariff schedule with a common tariff schedule applicable to all member countries. For example, a U.S. firm exporting to countries within the European Union faces one tariff schedule—the tariff on computers is the same for Germany as it is for Portugal. When a customs union is formed or expanded it takes some time for the different national tariff schedules to be "harmonized" to the common external tariff. Again, this phase-in may take many years. The second difference between a free-trade area and a customs union is not all free-trade areas include trade in agricultural products, services, and financial flows. However, most customs unions include a very broad range of international trade. Thus, the level of international economic integration implied by a customs union is usually "deeper" than the level of integration implied by a free-trade area.

The final two types of economic integration are somewhat more difficult to define. The fourth level of economic integration is referred to as a common market. A **common market** is a custom union with the addition of factor mobility between member countries. Thus, with a common market both restrictions on the mobility of capital and labor are eliminated and these factors are free to move within the member countries. Recall that the free mobility of capital allows for a more efficient allocation of capital within the common market and results in additional output. In addition, the mobility of labor also allows for a more efficient allocation of human capital within the member countries and also results in additional output. However, allowing the free mobility of workers between countries is not a minor issue because any substantial wage differentials among the member countries may induce a large migration between countries that would noticeably affect national wage rates.

common market an agreement between countries to maintain a free trade area, a common external tariff, and free mobility of capital and labor

Since its inception, the European Union has been moving toward a common market and doing so has proven to be difficult. In the 1980s, the EU enacted the Single European Act, which was designed to "harmonize" nearly 300 different regulations among the member countries. An example may help in understanding the problem. If the Greek government has approved a drug for use in Greece, it may not necessarily be sold everywhere in the European Union. In other words, the European Union does not yet have a European equivalent of the U.S. Food and Drug Administration. The effects in any one market may be small but the overall effects can be substantial.

The last form of economic integration is the creation of an economic union. An **economic union** is an agreement between countries to maintain a free trade area, a common external tariff, the free mobility of capital and labor, and some degree of unification in government fiscal and monetary policies. Thus, there are two additional requirements for an economic union. The first requirement is the creation of a common currency. This implies the abolition of each country's central bank and the creation of a common central bank. The advantages of a common currency are much like the advantages of lowering tariffs. Every time one national currency has to be changed into another, a fee is charged for this change. These transaction costs are similar to a tax on international transactions. Even if the tax is relatively small, the volume of transactions among closely allied economies can make the absolute size of the tax relatively large. The second requirement is that each national government has to align its national policies with those of the other member countries. The policies that need be aligned between countries cover such issues as tax rates, antitrust law, labor regulations, environmental regulations, and so forth. As such, any national policies that tend to distort trade flows would be candidates for harmonization. The world economy does not yet have an economic union that contains many countries. However, the European Union is determinedly moving in that direction.[2]

economic union an agreement between countries to maintain a free trade area, a common external tariff, free mobility of capital and labor, and some degree of unification in government policies and monetary policies

[2]However, it could be argued that the U.S. under the Articles of Confederation (the precursor to the current U.S. Constitution) had many of the features of a common market or economic union.

Foreign Trade Zones

If a country cannot join with other countries in a free-trade agreement, it has the option of making part of its country free of trade barriers. However, one must keep in mind that a Foreign Trade Zone (FTZ) is not the same thing as an FTA. There is a lot of difference between the two. Under the rules of the WTO, a country can designate certain geographical areas as zones of free trade, even when the rest of the country is subject to normal trade restrictions. These zones of free trade within a country are called Foreign Trade Zones. Currently there are approximately 400 zones in over 80 countries and these zones process approximately 10 percent of world trade.

FTZs have been allowed in the U.S. since 1934. The first U.S. FTZ was established at Staten Island, N.Y. For many years these zones were used for warehousing goods in transit, and for inspection, remarking, and repackaging. By 1970, there were still only 8 U.S. zones. Since the initial legislation authorizing FTZs, Congress has amended the law on several occasions. Currently, firms can manufacture inside a FTZ and the domestic processing costs incurred in the zones and profits earned there are free from duty. As a result, tariffs apply only to the imported inputs. The changes in the law governing FTZs have caused an increase in their growth. Currently, there are approximately 250 zones and 450 sub-zones.

RULES OF ORIGIN IN INTERNATIONAL TRADE

rules of origin laws that determine what country actually produced a good

In most countries, a certificate indicating where the imported product was produced or its country of origin must accompany the imported good. The determination of what country actually produced the good is known as the **rules of origin**. As part of its routine enforcement of U.S. trade laws, the U.S. Customs Service makes this determination on all imports at the time the good enters the country. The rules of origin are necessary for several reasons. First, the U.S. gathers information concerning the origin of imports to report statistical data on trade flows. Second, to enforce health, sanitary, and technical regulations within the U.S., the origin of imports is necessary to protect the health and safety of the public. The recent ban on imports of some food products from China or the recent discussion concerning the importation of Canadian drugs are just two examples. Third, not all countries are members of the WTO and the U.S. can enforce higher tariffs or import restrictions on goods originating in these countries. Fourth, to administer antidumping and countervailing duties on goods imported into the U.S., a determination of the country of origin is necessary. Fifth, the U.S. administration of quotas on textiles or agricultural products requires the determination of country of origin. Sixth, the U.S. administration of trade sanctions such as those against Cuba and Iraq also require knowledge of the country of origin. Finally, the recent trend toward the adoption of regional trade agreements has made the rules of origin even more critical in order to restrict the amount of trade deflection.

Traditionally, the U.S. has relied on the substantial transformation test to determine the "nationality" of a good. *Nationality* is conferred to the country where the good last went through a substantial transformation. What constitutes substantial transformation is something the U.S. legal system has been trying to precisely determine for nearly 100 years. In addition, U.S. trade agreements also contain wording concerning what percentage of the value-added in a good must be added within a country in order for the good to qualify for duty-free treatment. These rules were instituted approximately 25 years ago with the passage of the U.S. Generalized System of Preferences (GSP). The GSP specifies that in some cases, 35 percent of the value-added must occur in the preference receiving country. This 35 percent specification was continued in the Caribbean Basin Initiative of 1983 and the U.S.-Israel FTA of 1985. Under the U.S.-Canada FTA of 1990 the value-added test was increased to 50 percent for some products.

Under NAFTA, the rules of origin became even more complicated. To qualify for preferential treatment, the product must pass one of five different rules for granting North American origin. For some industries the product must also pass a minimum North American percentage of value-added test that varies from 50 percent to 60 percent of the product. Adding the NAFTA rules of origin to the various rules of origin for other preferences may yield in excess of 30 different rules of origin for the U.S. Obviously rules of origin have become an increasingly complicated feature of international trade.

trade creation (TC) an efficiency gain that results from a free trade area because more efficient member countries displace less efficient member countries

This complexity in the rules of origin can create a potential problem. Trade deflection occurs when a good that is really produced in a country that does not receive the reduced tariffs is shipped to a country that does receive the reduced tariffs for minimal processing in order to qualify for duty-free treatment. For this reason, it is common for the rules of origin to be more restrictive for preferential trade agreements than it is for imports from countries not being granted some form of preferential status. However, rules of origin are costly for firms to comply with. When the compliance costs exceed the value of the tariff reduction, rules of origin effectively become a nontariff barrier to trade.[3] This situation allows countries to legally engage in a new form of protectionism. International trade law allows each country to specify rules of origin as they see fit. It is not surprising that countries are increasingly using rules of origin as a disguised form of protectionism. The problem is now large enough that rules of origin were part of the negotiations associated with the Uruguay Round under GATT. Negotiations continue worldwide to try to "harmonize" the different rules of origin that countries employ under various trade agreements.

TRADE EFFECTS OF ECONOMIC INTEGRATION

Earlier we stated that the reduction of tariffs and nontariff barriers to trade in a regional trade agreement has both benefits and costs. For example, if two countries mutually eliminate their tariff and nontariff barriers to trade, trade between the two countries will increase. This favorable effect on world trade is known as **trade creation (TC)**. What is less obvious is that there are losses for countries that are not members of the trade agreement. For example, let us assume that the U.S. tariff on automobiles is 4 percent and the Mexican tariff on automobiles is 20 percent. If the U.S. and Mexico both eliminate their tariffs on trade between the two countries, what will happen? As the tariff falls on automobiles imported from Mexcio, the U.S. will import more cars

[3]This problem has been theoretically understood for quite some time. For an early treatment see Max Corden, *The Theory of Protection,* Oxford: Oxford University Press, 1971.

from Mexico. Further, the U.S. also may import fewer cars from other countries and more cars from Mexico. Why? Automobiles made in Mexico are now 4 percent cheaper than those made elsewhere. These export losses to the other countries are known as **trade diversion (TD)**. What happens to Mexican imports of U.S. cars? Again, there will be trade creation although much larger in relative terms because the tariff was much higher. However, the trade diversion will also be substantially larger. U.S. manufacturers now have a 20 percent margin of preference over manufacturers in other countries. Mexican imports from the U.S. will increase substantially. A part of the increase in Mexico's imports will be trade creation, but part of it will be trade diversion.

trade diversion (TD) an efficiency loss that results from a free trade area because less efficient member countries displace more efficient nonmember countries

Whether or not a trade agreement between two countries like the U.S. and Mexico increases world welfare depends on whether trade creation is larger than trade diversion.[4] Trade creation is the creation of new trade between countries that would not have occurred if the tariff had not fallen. As such, trade creation increases world welfare. On the other hand, trade diversion entails a loss of world welfare. Suppose that Mexico was importing all of its automobiles from countries other than the U.S. because they were 10 percent cheaper. With a 20 percent tariff on all countries, the lowest cost producers would dominate the Mexican automobile market. With the reduction of the 20 percent tariff to zero for only U.S. producers, what would Mexican importers do? They would begin to import all of the cars from the U.S. because these cars are now cheaper. This can be seen from Figure 10.3.

Figure 10.3 Price of Cars in Mexico

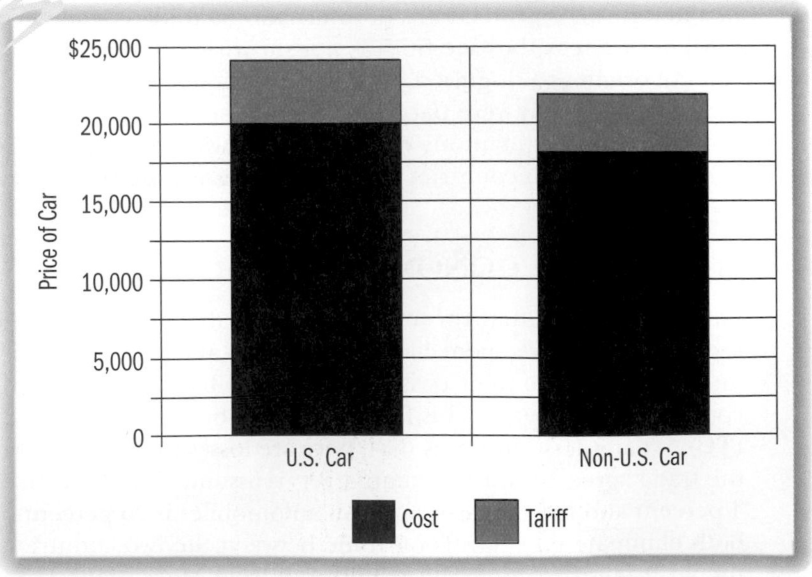

[4]This is a particularly good example of the theory of the second best. Simply stated this means that the elimination of an economic distortion such as a tariff in the presence of other distortions may or may not be welfare improving.

Suppose for example that before NAFTA, U.S.-made cars cost $20,000 and with the 20 percent tariff they would cost the Mexican importer $24,000. Also, let's assume that cars from other countries cost $18,000 and with the tariff, the cars cost $21,600. In this case, Mexican importers would buy from non-U.S. producers. After the preferential tariff reduction, cars from outside producers would still cost $21,600. However, for the Mexican importer, cars from the U.S. now cost $20,000. Mexican importers now have an incentive to buy from less efficient suppliers and trade is diverted from more efficient producers to less efficient producers. This rearranging of world production from more efficient to less efficient producers yields losses in world welfare. If trade diversion is larger than trade creation, the implementation of a regional trade agreement would result in an overall loss for the world economy.

The GATT/WTO has provided an exception to most-favored-nation status for regional trade agreements. To receive the exception, it was necessary to show that the level of protection after the implementation of the agreement would not on average be higher for the member countries than it was before the agreement.[5] Implicit in this exemption is the assumption that trade creation normally is larger than trade diversion. Fortunately, empirical estimates of trade creation and trade diversion that result from regional trade agreements indicate that this is the case under most if not all trade agreements.[6]

However, this does not mean that trade diversion is insignificant. First, while overall trade creation may well be larger than overall trade diversion, this does not mean that trade creation will be larger than trade diversion for all products. In any trade agreement, there are likely to be sectors where trade diversion is larger than trade creation. While such agreements may be beneficial for overall world welfare, they may create substantial losses for some producers in countries outside of the agreement. Second, the number of regional trade agreements between countries is rising rapidly. With each new agreement world welfare expands but the amount of trade diversion also increases. For companies operating on a global scale, the situation may begin to look suspiciously like a world without most-favored-nation tariffs. While these agreements generally free up trade, they also may create significant problems for companies trying to do business in a number of different markets.

THE STATIC EFFECTS OF A CUSTOMS UNION

Using the supply and demand model, we can illustrate the static welfare effects of lowering trade barriers among member countries of a customs union. Assume that the world is composed of three countries: Mexico, the U.S. and Japan. Now, suppose that the U.S. and Mexico decide to form a customs union and Japan is a nonmember.

[5]In the case of the formation of a customs union or the addition of a large country, this can be an interesting problem.

[6]Technically, the ex ante estimation of trade creation is fairly easy. A similar estimation of trade diversion is not so easy. However, the conditions necessary in order for trade diversion to be larger than trade creation are unusual. For a more complete discussion of the issues involved see W. Charles Sawyer and Richard L. Sprinkle, "Alternative Empirical Estimates of Trade Creation and Trade Diversion: A Comparison of the Baldwin-Murray and Verdoorn Models," *Weltwirtschaftliches Archiv* 125(1), 1989, pp. 61–73.

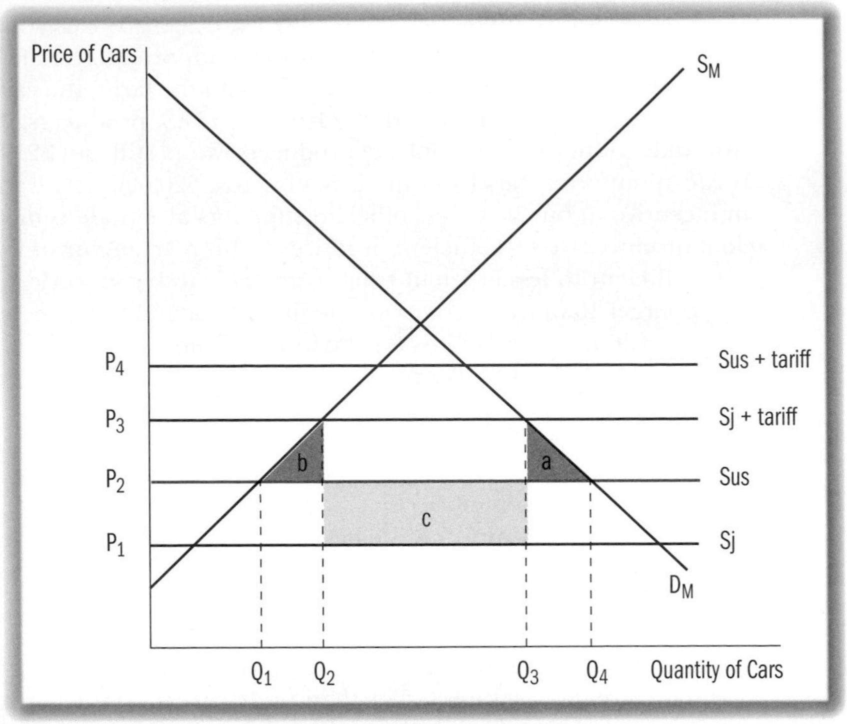

Figure 10.4 Static Welfare Effects of a Customs Union

The formation of a customs union leads to two effects. The welfare increasing trade creation effect—triangles a and b—and the welfare decreasing trade diversion effect—box c. The total effect of a customs union on world welfare depends on the size of these two effects.

Referring to Figure 10.4, assume the domestic supply and demand curves for Mexico to be S_M and D_M. In addition, assume that Mexico is a small country relative to Japan and the U.S. As such, Mexico cannot influence the price of the product so that the foreign supply curves for cars are perfectly elastic (horizontal). Also, we will assume that Japan is the most efficient supplier of cars at a free-trade price of P_1 and tariff inclusive price of P_3 (where P_3 equals P_1 plus the tariff). However, the U.S. can supply cars at a free-trade price of P_2 and a tariff inclusive price of P_4 (where P_4 equals P_2 plus the tariff). Before the formation of the customs union, Mexico buys all of its imports from Japan at a price of P_3. The U.S. does not export any cars to Mexico because its supply price, P_4, exceeds that of Japan. Thus, consumers in Mexico buy a total of Q_3 amount of cars of which Q_2 are domestically produced and Q_2 to Q_3 are imported from Japan.

After the formation of the customs union, Mexico removes the tariff on U.S.-produced cars but not on Japanese-produced cars. This means that the U.S. is now the low-price supplier of cars to Mexico. The U.S. can supply cars at price P_2, and Japan can supply cars at price P_3. Mexico now buys all of its imported cars from the U.S., and Japan does not export any cars to Mexico. The movement to freer trade under a customs union affects world welfare in two opposing ways. First, trade creation increases world welfare. In this case, consumers in Mexico buy more total cars, Q_4. Mexican production is Q_1 and Q_1 to Q_4 are imported from the U.S. The welfare gain

Estimating Trade and Employment Effects of Trade Agreements

In all of the debates concerning NAFTA, there were several estimates concerning the number of jobs gained or lost under the agreement. Both opponents and proponents of NAFTA could marshal "evidence" that thousands of jobs would be gained or lost depending on which side of the issue a person chose. Several items concerning the agreement need to be kept in mind. First, the agreement with Canada was phased in over 10 years and over 15 years for Mexico. Second, U.S. trade with both countries is small relative to the GDP of the U.S. Finally, the U.S. labor market now has approximately 150 million workers and routinely adds 200,000 jobs *per month.* So when one claims that 100,000 jobs would be lost or gained because of NAFTA, this is not a very large number. In any case, just where do these estimates come from?

Two methods are used to estimate the economic impacts of a trade agreement. The first method is tedious but relatively simple. Suppose that Mexico has a 10 percent tariff on a particular product imported from the U.S. Further suppose that the price elasticity of demand for this product is 1.0. Thus if the tariff were eliminated, exports of this product from the U.S. to Mexico would rise by 10 percent. Next, the Department of Labor produces estimates of the number of employment opportunities involved if production changes in a U.S. industry. If you know how much production changes because of the tariff reduction, you now have an estimate of the number of jobs gained. For U.S. tariff reductions, you can estimate the increase in imports from Mexico, and as U.S. output falls, the amount of lost U.S. jobs. By totaling up the effects for all industries you can estimate the total employment effect of NAFTA.[7] Only a little creativity is needed to come up with total job gains and losses. One side could argue that total "jobs" would rise while the other side could claim that they would fall. Aside from the politics, these *partial equilibrium* estimates are useful in the negotiating process. To reduce the political opposition, industries in which the effects were large had the tariff reductions conveniently phased in toward the end of the 15-year transition period.

A more recent method of calculating the effects of trade agreements is to use a computable general equilibrium model (CGE). The difference in this estimating method is that CGE models allow for the interactions among related industries. For instance, if the automobile industry is affected by a trade agreement, this will indirectly affect many other industries that provide inputs into the production process. Building such a model requires four steps. First, one needs to collect data on production, consumption, prices, and trade flows. The second step is to construct a mathematical representation of the structure of the economy. Third, various parameters, price elasticity being one, are added into the model. The model is then calibrated to ensure that it generates known results that make sense. Finally, one can use the model to answer questions concerning changes in economic policy. These models are now widely used to determine the possible effects of changes in trade policy as well as other economic policies. While these models are informative, they are not perfect. For an exercise such as NAFTA, the policy change for the U.S. was so small that the results of the exercise were also small. Partial equilibrium models are still useful for capturing the changes at the narrowly defined industry level where the changes for the economy as a whole are small. For Canada and Mexico, the relative size of the policy change was substantially larger and the effects on the structure of their economies would be larger.

[7]This is actually a loose description of estimating TC. In practice, you also have to estimate TD and add it to TC to arrive at the total effects on trade flows and jobs.

associated with this increase in consumption equals triangle a. In addition, lower-price imports from the U.S. replace some of Mexico's domestic production (Q_1 to Q_2). This represents a favorable production effect and the welfare gain associated with this production change equals triangle b. The overall trade-creation effect is the sum of the triangles (a + b).

The second effect of a customs union is trade diversion, which decreases world welfare. Trade diversion occurs when a higher-price supplier within the union (the U.S.) replaces imports from the low-price supplier outside the union (Japan). As a result of the customs union, world production is organized in a less efficient manner. In Figure 10.4, the box c indicates this welfare loss to Mexico and the world as a whole. In summary, the formation of a customs union will increase the welfare of its members, as well as the rest of the world, if the trade creation effect (a + b) is larger than the trade diversion effect (c).

THE EUROPEAN UNION

> "Guided by treaties that scarcely anybody can understand, towards a destination on which nobody can agree, the European Union has survived, and often thrived for almost half a century."
>
> —ROBERT COTTRELL

European Union an association of European countries that agrees to a free trade area and imposes a common external tariff

Treaty of Rome an agreement between six European countries to reduce tariffs and nontariff barriers to trade. It was the beginning of the European Union

The world's largest and most successful regional trade agreement is the **European Union (EU)**, Now 50 years old, the EU currently contains 27 countries with a combined population of 459 million and a combined GDP larger than the U.S. A chronological history of the EU is shown in Table 10.1. The European Union began its development in 1951 with the formation of the European Coal and Steel Community (ECSC). This agreement provided for the elimination of tariffs and quotas for the coal and steel industries between Belgium, France, Italy, Luxembourg, the Netherlands, and West Germany. The basic idea of the ECSC was to promote free trade in two important commodities (coal and steel) as a deterrent to future military conflicts in Europe. While we usually view trade arrangements as economic creatures, there is frequently also a political goal involved. In this case, the goal was to reduce the probability of another European military conflict. The basic premise behind the ECSC was that the more closely integrated countries are economically, the less likelihood of war between them.[8]

In 1957, the countries involved in the ECSC signed the **Treaty of Rome**, which provided for the elimination of tariffs and nontariff barriers to trade between member countries and the institution of a common external tariff. This treaty established the European Economic Community (EEC) as a customs union, which has been continually enlarging itself to cover more and more of Europe. In 1960, most of the countries not included in the EEC formed an alternative preferential trade arrangement called the European Free Trade Association (EFTA). This organization provided for free trade in nonagricultural products among its members. In addition, EFTA also provided

[8]For example, the close economic relationship between the U.S. and Canada would make a military conflict virtually inconceivable.

Table 10.1 Chronological Development of the European Union

European Coal and Steel Community		ECSC	1951
	Belgium, France, Lux., the Netherlands, Italy Germany		
European Atomic Energy Community		EURATOM	1957
European Economic Community		EEC	1957
	Treaty of Rome provided elimination of tariffs and nontariff barriers and the institution of a common external tariff		
	Received GATT waver under the Lome Convention		
European Free Trade Area		EFTA	1960
	Most European countries not included in the EEC provided for free trade in nonagricultural products		
Common Agriculture Policy		CAP	1962
European Community		EC	1967
	Combined EEC, ECSC, and EURATOM		
Added	The UK, Ireland, and Denmark		1973
Added	Greece		1981
Added	Spain and Portugal		1986
Added	East Germany		1990
European Union		EU	1993
Added	Finland, Austria and Sweden		1995
European Monetary Union		EMU	1999
EU			
Added	Cyprus, Estonia, Czech. Rep. Hungary, Latvia, Lithuania, Malta, Poland, Slovakia and Slovenia		2004
Added	Bulgaria and Romania		2007

for free trade in these products between itself and the EEC.[9] In 1967, the EEC and ECSC merged to form the European Communities (EC). Over time, the enlargement of the European Union has occurred mostly as countries within Europe left EFTA and joined the EU. Thus, while the EU membership grew, the EFTA membership declined. The U.K., Ireland, and Denmark joined the EC in 1973; Greece joined in 1981; Spain and Portugal joined in 1986; and Austria, Finland, and Sweden joined in 1995. In addition, 10 countries became members in 2004. These countries include Cyprus, Estonia, the Czech Republic, Hungary, Latvia, Lithuania, Malta, Poland, Slovakia and Slovenia. The newest members, Bulgaria and Romania, joined in 2007.

As the EU has "widened" to include more countries it has also "deepened." What this means is that the EU has always been something more than a customs union.

The current arrangement is formally known as the European Economic Area (EEA). In addition, it now provides for free trade in services and labor and capital mobility between it and the EU. EFTA is now composed of Iceland, Liechtenstein, Norway, and Switzerland and they have opted to stay out of the EU. In addition, Switzerland does not participate in the EEA.

common agricultural policy (CAP) an agreement between the European countries to subsidize agricultural uniformly. All EU member countries' farmers are paid subsidies by the EU rather than by each national government

Maastricht Treaty an agreement between the European countries to establish an economic union and common currency, the Euro

Euro the new currency for eleven countries of the European Union. This currency replaced the eleven national currencies in 2002

Technically, all that a custom union requires is a common external tariff and eliminating most of the trade barriers between member countries. However, from its beginning the EU has had something extra called the **Common Agricultural Policy (CAP)**. Under the CAP, all of the countries in the EU subsidize their agricultural sector in a similar manner. When countries form a regional trade agreement, free trade in agriculture is potentially a problem. This is because to one extent or another every country subsidizes its farmers. If the subsidy schemes among countries vary, free trade in agricultural products becomes problematic. To solve this problem, the EU adopted a common agricultural policy for all members. Belgian farmers are subsidized in the same way as Portuguese farmers. All member countries provide revenue to the EU, and the EU, rather than each national government, pays subsidies to farmers within the EU. Currently, approximately half the EU total budget is spent on farm subsidies. The CAP guarantees prices for all farm commodities within the EU. Further, the EU purchases whatever farmers cannot sell on the open market. In addition, farmers are protected by a variable levy (tariff) from international competition. If farm prices within the EU decline, the tariff rises and vice versa. Since the support prices are generous, there has been a problem of chronic oversupply of agricultural commodities in Europe. In addition, the surplus agricultural commodities are sometimes dumped on world markets to reduce the EU losses.

As a result, the common agricultural policy has created constant trade frictions between the U.S. and other more efficient producers of agricultural commodities such as Canada, Australia, New Zealand and many developing countries in selected products. Such countries not only lose exports to the EU but at times suffer losses in other export markets when the EU sells or dumps its agricultural surpluses. Demands by countries that the EU reform the CAP in order to produce less damage in international trade of agricultural products delayed the completion of Uruguay Round and is similarly proving to be a difficult issue in the Doha Round. In all likelihood, any future negotiations concerning world trade in agriculture will have as its central issue the common agricultural policy. The situation is politically charged because European farmers, particularly French farmers, are very active in their defense of the system. This problem is likely to be very contentious in the years ahead as many of the newest members of the EU have large agricultural sectors.

Aside from agriculture, the EU is taking a number of steps to create a full economic union. Beginning in 1985, an EU commission set about determining the steps necessary to create a genuinely barrier-free internal market in the EU. This commission listed hundreds of actions that member governments needed to take in order to create something like a unified market. Most of the governmental actions were completed by 1992, with much fanfare about the single market. The **Maastricht Treaty** of 1992 laid out plans for a new European currency (the **Euro**) that replaced 12 of the separate national currencies in January 2002.[10] This treaty also completed the evolution of the EU into a true common market. Barriers to the movement of labor and capital among the countries were removed. Capital and labor are now free to migrate in the EU in the same way they can migrate within a country.

[0]We analyze the indications of the EU adopting a single currency in Chapter 19.

The future evolution of the EU is uncertain. The EU has one of the major characteristics of an economic union, a common currency. However, a true economic union has other characteristics. To achieve a true economic union, the EU would need to have other characteristics such as a common fiscal policy, common levels of business taxation, common labor laws, and commonality in any other regulations that distort economic activity. In some areas, noticeably competition policy, this commonality is a reality. However, in other areas such as taxation and labor regulation, there are still large disparities within the EU that distort economic activity. The issue is further clouded by the uncertainty over the degree of sovereignty that member countries wish to hand over to a supranational body such as the EU. This issue is evident in the refusal of the U.K., Denmark, and Sweden to abandon their national currencies. What is clear is that the EU is moving in the direction of creating an economic union. However, the speed with which it will move on the various issues is another matter. The only certainty is that this evolution should be an interesting economic and political process to observe.

NAFTA AND OTHER U.S. TRADE AGREEMENTS

North American Free Trade Agreement (NAFTA) **an agreement to establish a free trade area consisting of the U.S., Canada, and Mexico**

From the creation of GATT until the early 1980s, U.S. trade policy was focused on reducing trade barriers through the various MTNs. Regional trade agreements were mostly centered around the expansion of the EU, and the U.S. government showed little interest in such agreements. However, beginning in the 1970s there was a slight change in U.S. policy. First, the U.S. began granting preferential trade status to developing countries under the Generalized System of Preferences. These preferences had the advantage of enhancing economic growth in developing countries without the monetary and political complications normally associated with foreign aid. This trend continued with the passage of the Caribbean Basin Initiative (CBI) in 1981 as a means of encouraging economic development in that area. The result of these agreements was that the U.S. was now deviating from a purely multilateral approach to reducing trade barriers. Also, there was rising frustration with the slow pace of trade liberalization in several areas of interest to the U.S. As we discussed in Chapter 1, international trade in services is a fast-growing part of world trade. However, liberalizing trade in services has been a very slow process. For the U.S., this is frustrating because the country has a comparative advantage in many areas of service trade, such as financial services and insurance. Secondly, the U.S. government is also interested in liberalizing trade in agricultural products. Liberalization in this sector under the auspices of the GATT/WTO has been even slower. For these and other reasons, beginning in the early 1980s the U.S. government began pursuing trade liberalization via regional trade agreements.

The first such agreement is the little known U.S.-Israel FTA. This agreement was negotiated in the early 1980s and went into effect in 1985. This initial FTA was important for the U.S. because it has served as a template for all subsequent regional trade agreements. First, this FTA covers trade in all goods, including the agricultural sector. Second, the agreement covered virtually all trade in services. Third, the agreement liberalizes all capital flows, both portfolio capital and FDI. Finally, the agreement was phased in over ten years to give both economies, especially Israel's, time to adjust to these changes. The regional trade agreements that have been signed by the U.S. are not all identical to the U.S.-Israel FTA. However, as we will see the main features of this FTA have been retained in all subsequent agreements.[11]

NAFTA

Very few economic issues over the past several years have generated as much debate as NAFTA. To many international economists, this debate has been puzzling. First, NAFTA is a very straightforward trade agreement. Second, the agreement's economic effects on the U.S. are relatively small. Simply put, NAFTA is a free-trade area between the U.S., Canada, and Mexico with a few added touches.

On January 1, 1989, the U.S. and Canada signed a free-trade agreement. The tariff reductions required under this agreement were to be phased in over a 10-year period. The U.S.-Canada agreement covered trade in goods and services, investment, and eliminated national preferences on most government contracts. In general, this trade agreement eliminated the last barriers to trade between these two developed countries. Most of the trade between the U.S. and Canada was duty-free prior to 1989. Further, the majority of Canadian trade is transacted with the U.S. and about one-fifth of U.S. trade is transacted with Canada. For the most part, this FTA simply freed a large trading relationship from its remaining restrictions.

In 1992, Canada, the U.S., and Mexico agreed to broaden the free-trade area to include Mexico. After much discussion, the U.S. Congress authorized the free-trade area in 1993 and it went into effect in 1994. The tariff reductions provided for the NAFTA agreement are to be phased in over a 15-year period. The Agreement covers all merchandise trade as well as trade in services, investment, and intellectual property rights. In addition, any trade disputes under the agreement are to be adjudicated by a member panel. Also, two additional agreements were signed in the areas concerning labor standards and environmental issues. These two agreements simply commit each country to enforce its own labor and environmental laws.[12] It is estimated that the NAFTA agreement's economic effects on the three economies are small.[13]

For the U.S. and Canada, the agreement was useful in the sense that it eliminated some of the last vestiges of protectionism in a large trading relationship. In Canada's case, the agreement would enable Canadian firms to grow larger because they would have unrestricted access to a much larger market. For both the U.S. and Canada, free trade with Mexico had its appeal in the long run for two reasons. First, while Mexico is still a developing country, its economy is growing much faster than the individual economies of the U.S. and Canada. Second, at the time the agreement was signed, Mexican tariffs were still relatively high compared to U.S. and Canadian tariffs. The prospects of entering a fast-growth market with a large margin of preference were an incentive to include Mexico in the free-trade area. For Mexico, access to two of the world's largest markets seemed to be an excellent way to advance export-led growth and

[1]For details on this agreement, see W. Charles Sawyer and Richard L. Sprinkle, "The Trade Expansion Effects of the U.S.-Israel Free-Trade Agreement," *Journal of World Trade Law* 20(5), September/October 1986, pp. 526–539.

[12]These side agreements have become politically troublesome though. Opponents of further "widening" of NAFTA are using them to block further expansion.

[13]For details see Cletus C. Coughlin, "What Do Economic Models Tell Us About the Effects of the U.S.-Canada Free-Trade Agreement?" *Federal Reserve Bank of St. Louis Review,* September/October 1990, pp. 40–58.

attract the investment capital the country needed. Further, it was a way of making Mexico's economic reform process since the 1980s permanent.

Other U.S. Trade Agreements

The past and future course of U.S. trade agreements is summarized in Table 10.2. The first coluMN1 shows the countries involved in the agreement. The second column indicates the status of the agreements. Some of the agreements such as NAFTA have been passed by Congress and either have been fully implemented or are in the process of being phased in. One agreement is in the process of being implemented. Four agreements that have been successfully negotiated are awaiting Congressional approval. Four other agreements are still in the process of negotiation. These agreements are denoted as implemented, pending implementation, pending Congressional approval, or under negotiation. The countries involved in these agreements are useful in pointing out several trends in U.S. trade policy.

Free Trade Area of the Americas (FTAA) an agreement by thirty-four countries to pursue the implementation of an FTA for the Western hemisphere

First, notice that many of the agreements are with countries in the Western Hemisphere. To a large extent, this reflects the failure of the proposed **Free Trade Area of the Americas (FTAA)**. In late 1994, 34 governments in the Western hemisphere agreed to pursue an FTA for virtually the entire hemisphere by 2005. The actual negotiations were launched in 1998. However, progress in the negotiations has been slow. This is in part due to concerns by many South American governments regarding certain types of

Table 10.2 U.S. Regional Trade Agreements

Country	Status of the Agreement	Date of Implementation
Israel	Implemented	1985
Canada	Implemented	1989, 1994
Mexico	Implemented	1994
Jordan	Implemented	2001
Chile	Implemented	2003
Singapore	Implemented	2003
Australia	Implemented	2004
Bahrain	Implemented	2004
Morocco	Implemented	2004
Central American FTA	Implemented	2005
Oman	Pending Implementation	
Peru	Pending Congressional Approval	
Panama	Pending Congressional Approval	
Korea	Pending Congressional Approval	
Colombia	Pending Congressional Approval	
Malaysia	Under Negotiation	
Thailand	Under Negotiation	
South Africa	Under Negotiation	
United Arab Emirates	Under Negotiation	

Source: United States Trade Representative (www.ustr.gov).

MERCOSUR

MERCOSUR is an acronym for a free-trade area that is on its way to becoming a customs union. This free-trade area is currently composed of Argentina, Brazil, Uruguay, and Paraguay. The first phase of the agreement, signed in 1991, is to cut intra-regional tariffs to zero by the year 2000. For the most part, tariffs are at zero for most trade within the region. Starting in 1995, the countries set about harmonizing their tariffs to a common external tariff by 2006. Beginning in 1995, the countries began negotiating the harmonization of regulations necessary for creating a "single market." As the Europeans discovered when they tried to create a common market, this project is quite difficult and will take time to complete. There is also a commitment to the free movement of labor within the countries, but no formal date has yet been made. MERCOSUR has signed a free-trade area agreement with Chile that will be implemented in phases through 2014. However, substantial tariff cuts have already been made on both sides. MERCOSUR and Chile is now a trade area containing 240 million people with a total economic output of over $1 trillion. The agreement has had an explosive effect on trade. From 1990 to 1995, intra-regional trade expanded from less than $6 billion to over $14 billion. The trade flows could grow even larger. Intra-group trade in NAFTA is 4.5 percent of GDP and in the EU, it is 14 percent. Within MERCOSUR, intra-group trade is still only 1.6 percent. MERCOSUR is also likely to expand as it is currently negotiating with Bolivia and will likely expand to the other members of the Andean Group.[14] Thus, while the U.S. contemplates the expansion of NAFTA, a substantial trade bloc is forming in South America. In this case, the usual view of hemispheric free trade as being a creature of NAFTA is not quite correct.

[4]Peru, Ecuador, Colombia, and Venezuela.

protectionism in the U.S. and U.S. government subsidies to agriculture. At this point the status of the entire venture is uncertain. The U.S. response to this apparent failure has been to include Mexico as a part of NAFTA and to continue bilateral negotiations with other countries in Central and South America. An FTA has been signed with Chile and CAFTA-DR (Costa Rica, El Salvador, Guatemala, Honduras, Nicaragua, and the Dominican Republic). Negotiations have been completed with Peru, Colombia, and Panama and are awaiting Congressional Approval. However, the overall plan of the FTAA may be difficult to complete. As a result, current U.S. government policy simply may be reflective of the fact that the completion of the FTAA may take longer than was provided for by the arbitrary date of 2005 set over a decade ago.

Second, the U.S. is using FTAs to enhance economic development in selected countries that wish to pursue a more export-oriented economic development strategy.[15] This allows the U.S. to gain the benefits of assisting developing countries while at the same time gaining access to markets that potentially grow faster than the U.S. economy. A further attraction for the U.S. is that trade barriers usually are much higher in developing countries than they are in the U.S. This means that the developing country is sacrificing

[5] See Chapter 11 for more details on this.

relatively more protection of its domestic industries than is the U.S. Finally, the pace of trade liberalization within the WTO framework has been slow and is now uncertain. For countries like the U.S. that wish to liberalize trade faster than negotiating an MTN, the use of regional trade agreements with countries that have similar preferences becomes a logical step. As we discuss in the next section, this policy may make sense, but it is also controversial.

MULTILATERALISM VERSUS REGIONAL TRADE AGREEMENTS

One of the more contentious issues in international economics is the debate over trade liberalization. Aside from the formation and expansion of the EU, until the 1980s trade liberalization occurred mostly within the framework of the various MTNs. However, since then there has been a rapid proliferation of regional trade agreements. Like most economic phenomenon, this development has both benefits and costs. The main difference is that the benefits and costs of RTAs cannot be perfectly calculated. This lack of certainty has developed into a situation where some economists have serious reservations about the rapid spread of RTAs. As one would expect, this group of economists emphasizes the costs of RTAs relative to the benefits. The other side of the debate does just the opposite. Their conclusion is that the potential benefits of RTAs outweigh the admitted costs. At this point, there is no precise answer to this debate. The purpose of this section is to provide you with an idea of what these costs and benefits are and to outline the why RTAs are controversial among economists.

Until the 1980s, trade liberalization was occurring primarily through multilateral trade negotiations under the auspices of GATT. Theoretically, this nondiscriminatory reduction in trade barriers is the optimum method to reduce trade barriers. If trade barriers are reduced only on an MFN basis, there is only trade creation and no trade diversion. Trade diversion occurs only if trade liberalization is discriminatory, meaning that one country is treated differently than another country. In a perfect world, trade liberalization would occur only on a multilateral basis, with no discrimination between countries. This is one of the strongest arguments for MTNs. RTAs inherently threaten this process. An RTA is *inherently* discriminatory. Member countries are treated differently than nonmember countries. As we illustrated, RTAs enhance world welfare if total trade creation is larger than trade diversion. However, this enhancement may come at a high cost. First, as RTAs spread, world trade becomes more complicated. For example, what is the tariff on a particular product? With RTAs, the answer depends on which country you are talking about. Let us consider a current example. What is the U.S. tariff on steel? If the steel comes from Israel or Canada, the tariff is zero. If the steel comes from Mexico or Jordan, one must go to the U.S. tariff schedule to see what the current status of the steel tariff is because the FTAs with these countries are not fully phased in. If the steel is coming from a developing country, it might qualify for duty-free entry under a number of U.S. trade agreements designed to assist developing countries. This is just one example of a product imported into the U.S. Since there are many countries now involved in many different RTAs, world trade has become more complicated. The world trading system is at risk of going back to the situation that existed prior to GATT. Each country potentially had a different tariff for each product for specific countries. In economic terms, this causes an increasing amount of trade diversion that potentially reduces world welfare.

A second cost of RTAs is more subtle. Countries only have a limited amount of time and expertise to expend on the issue of trade liberalization. As RTAs spread, governments will spend more resources on RTA negotiations. This implies that they will expend fewer resources negotiating under the WTO framework. As a result, the process of obtaining multilateral trade liberalization becomes more difficult with the spread of RTAs. The opponents of RTAs emphasize these costs. They fear that the spread of RTAs is jeopardizing the nondiscriminatory nature of world trade that had been developed under the GATT/WTO framework. Further, they fear that RTAs tend to distract government attention away from the process of liberalizing world trade in a nondiscriminatory fashion.[16] There is not a lot of argument among economists about these points. World trade is becoming more complicated, and the amount of trade diversion is rising. No doubt part of the problem with the Uruguay and Doha MTNs has been that governments no longer view them as the only way to liberalize world trade.

However, other economists are not so concerned about the development of RTAs. They freely admit that the opponents of the spread of RTAs are correct in the points made above. However, they consider other factors that make the spread of RTAs look considerably less ominous. First, it must be pointed out that RTAs are legal under the WTO. To be WTO legal, an RTA must cover substantially all trade; be completed within a reasonable period of time; and result in an average level of protection against nonmembers that was not higher than before the agreement. This has always been the case, as RTAs normally produce more trade creation than trade diversion. Slowing the spread of RTAs probably would involve an amendment of WTO rules to make it harder for countries to form RTAs. Such a development is unlikely. Subject to the current rules, the spread of RTAs is something like a free market where governments can engage in RTAs or not depending on their preferences.

Also the spread of RTAs may be saying something about the preferences of governments for RTAs. In the first place, suppose that two countries such as Germany and Austria naturally have a close economic relationship. The two countries are geographically close and share a common language. Further suppose that Germany and Austria wish to form an FTA or an even deeper RTA. In this situation, should WTO rules make this difficult for the two countries to accomplish? The point is that it would be awkward to establish WTO rules that would make an RTA easy to form for Austria and Germany but hard for the U.S. and Singapore. Secondly, there is the issue of the depth of economic integration. In the first part of the chapter, we discussed the various types of RTAs. The difference in types is related to the depth of integration. One of the current problems with multilateral liberalization is that the depth of integration being pursued is not very deep. If one compares the agenda of the Doha round to the current depth of integration in the EU or even NAFTA, the issue becomes obvious. In some cases, countries want to pursue a level of economic integration that is not possible in a multilateral framework. If a country wants to pursue deeper levels of economic integration with other countries, it has little choice but to negotiate RTAs. One final advantage of RTAs relates to the adjustment of the domestic economy to higher levels of import competition. While multilateral trade liberalization may be desirable, the adjustment costs for some domestic industries may be quite high. If trade barriers are reduced on a global

[6]For an example of these arguments, see Jagdish Bhagwati, David Greenaway, and Arvind Panagariya, "Trading Preferentially: Theory and Policy," *Economic Journal* 108(449), 1998, pp. 1128–48.

Trade Diversion in Action: The EU-Mexico Free-Trade Agreement

In this chapter, we have described the concept of trade diversion. Any type of preferential trade agreement creates the potential for trade diversion. Lowering tariffs to zero for one or more of a country's trading partners creates potential losses for other countries that are not party to the agreement. Countries that are outside any preferential trade agreement are placed into an interesting position. If they do nothing, they stand to lose exports to the countries within the preferential trade agreement. Or, they can mitigate or eliminate these losses by joining the party so to speak. A recent FTA agreement between the EU and Mexico offers a textbook (pun intended) example of the latter reaction.

On November 24, 1999, the EU and Mexico concluded a FTA. The agreement allows for the bilateral phasing out of tariffs by 2010. The agreement also liberalizes trade in services and covers other issues such as public procurement, investment, competition and intellectual property rights, and a dispute settlement procedure.[17] While this agreement is interesting, it is at least superficially a bit puzzling. EU exports to Mexico are a bit less than $10 billion and EU imports from Mexico are a bit more than $4 billion. In percentage terms, each of these numbers is less than 1 percent of EU exports and imports. On the surface, this small amount of trade hardly seems worth the trouble of an FTA. Even though EU exports to Mexico are small, the EU was concerned about a trend in its trade with Mexico. The share of the EU imports in total Mexican imports has been on a downward trend since the mid 1990s. The EU had concluded that the most likely suspect was NAFTA. As tariffs fell for the U.S. and Canada, exporters from the EU were losing business in Mexico due to trade diversion. Since Mexican MFN tariffs are still fairly high, the amount of trade diversion inflicted on outsiders such as the EU could be quite high. For example, the Mexican MFN tariff on cars is 20 percent. In order to prevent this trade diversion, the EU evidently decided that signing an FTA with Mexico was its best option. The trade numbers also suggest that the FTA made sense for the EU in a public choice sense. Some domestic producers in the EU will lose profits as a result of this FTA. However, from the information given above EU exports to Mexico are over twice the size of EU imports from Mexico. On the Mexican side, the motivation for the agreement is less clear. They may feel that the agreement is largely just replacing some imports from the U.S. and Canada with competitive imports from the EU. In technical terms, they may feel that the agreement produces little trade creation for the EU. Thus, Mexico may feel that by leveling the table for the U.S., Canada, and the EU they have little to lose in terms of domestic production. On the other side, better access to the EU market also may allow Mexico to more effectively compete with other developing countries. Some of these countries have preferential access to the EU market through the trade agreements the EU has with former colonies. For both the EU and Mexico, the agreement seems to make sense in terms of public choice. The logic above is still continuing. Mexico is currently negotiating an FTA with Japan.

---

[17]For a more complete description of this FTA, see Joanne Guth, "European Union and Mexico Conclude Free Trade Agreement," *International Economic Review,* April/May 2000, pp. 1–3.

basis, imports in a particular product category potentially could increase by a large amount. The costs for domestic industries in terms of lost profits and/or job losses likewise could be high. The costs for domestic industries by an RTA may well be lower, as trade barriers are being reduced for a smaller number of countries. Since the agreements are phased in over a period of time of up to 15 years, the short-run adjustment costs are even smaller. These adjustment costs and the opposition to liberalization probably are positively correlated. In this case, it may be easier for a country to liberalize trade using RTAs than to do so through multilateral liberalization.

A useful way of summarizing this debate is to think in terms of substitutes and complements. Those who fear the spread of RTAs really fear that they are a substitute for multilateral liberalization. Economists who are less concerned about the spread of RTAs tend to view them as complementary to MTNs. MTNs move at a slow pace on a limited number of issues. Despite the complications, there is little or no support for abandoning that process. The WTO is still a work in progress. In the Doha Round, many of the negotiations involve spreading the authority of the WTO to some types of trade such as agriculture and services that were not adequately addressed under GATT. Such negotiations are essential to further the process of the liberalization of world trade. Even if an MTN does not produce much in the way of trade liberalization, coming up with acceptable rules for certain types of trade and other issues is worth the cost of the negotiations. The world economy needs an organization to set the rules of world trade and to referee disputes among countries. While the WTO may no longer be the force for multilateral liberalization that it once was, its role in the world economy may still be increasing rather than diminishing.

SUMMARY

1. Reductions of trade barriers between countries can be nondiscriminatory through GATT/WTO or discriminatory through regional trade agreements.
2. Economic integration refers to the elimination of restrictions on international trade, flows of the factors of production, and/or capital flows between countries.
3. The different types of economic integration are: (1) a free-trade area, (2) a customs union, (3) a common market, and (4) an economic union.
4. Rules of origin reduce the amount of trade deflection that may occur with an RTA. Such rules also can be used as nontariff barriers to trade.
5. RTAs have two conflicting effects: trade creation and trade diversion. *Trade creation* refers to the increase in trade caused by the reduction of trade barriers. *Trade diversion* is the loss of exports suffered by nonmember countries that still face trade barriers.
6. The European Union (EU) was formed in 1957 with the Treaty of Rome. Today the EU consists of 27 countries with a population larger than the U.S. and GDP larger than the U.S.
7. One of the major international problems associated with the EU is its common agricultural policy (CAP). The system generates persistent surpluses of agricultural commodities that depress farm incomes outside of the EU.
8. In addition to widening, the EU is being deepened to produce an entity that is in the process of becoming more like an economic union. An example of this is the creation of the Euro.
9. The U.S. and Canada successfully negotiated a free trade agreement in 1989, with a phase-in period of 10 years. In 1994, the North American Free Trade Agreement (NAFTA) was negotiated between the U.S., Canada and Mexico. This agreement has a phase in period of 15 years.

10. The U.S. government attempted to negotiate the Free Trade Area of the Americas that would have created an FTA for most of the Western hemisphere. Despite the failure of the FTAA, the U.S. has continued to pursue FTAs both in and outside the Western hemisphere.
11. The spread of RTAs weakens the principle of nondiscrimination embodied the GATT/WTO framework. However, the spread of RTAs is likely to continue as governments may want to pursue trade liberalization at a faster rate than is possible through MTNs.

KEY CONCEPTS AND TERMS

- regional trade agreements p. 221
- free-trade area (FTA) p. 224
- trade deflection p. 224
- customs union p. 224
- common external tariff p. 224
- common market p. 225
- economic union p. 225
- rules of origin p. 226
- trade creation (TC) p. 227
- trade diversion (TD) p. 228
- European Union (EU) p. 232
- Treaty of Rome p. 232
- Common Agricultural Policy (CAP) p. 234
- Maastricht Treaty p. 234
- Euro p. 234
- North American Free Trade Agreement (NAFTA) p. 235
- Free Trade Area of the Americas (FTAA) p. 237

PROBLEMS AND QUESTIONS FOR REVIEW

1. Explain how reductions in trade barriers occur on a nondiscriminatory basis versus a discriminatory basis. Give examples of each.
2. What does the term *economic integration* mean?
3. What are the different types of economic integration? Explain the differences between them.
4. Describe the growth of RTAs in the world economy since 1948.
5. Why do countries have rules of origin? Why are they so important in the context of an RTA?
6. Explain how trade deflection can lead to a free-trade area becoming a customs union.
7. Define trade creation and trade diversion.
8. How could the existence of trade diversion lead to the formation of more regional trade agreements.
9. "The formation of a customs union is a partial movement toward free trade and therefore must improve world welfare." Do you agree? Explain why or why not.
10. Using graphical analysis, demonstrate the net welfare effects of a customs union.
11. Describe the evolution of the EU both in terms of widening and deeping.
12. What does the term *deepening* mean in the context of an RTA?
13. Why has the CAP of the EU been so disruptive in international negotiations?
14. Describe the history of the formation of NAFTA.
15. Compare the economic effects of NAFTA to the general perception of the effects of the FTA.
16. Describe the evolution of U.S. trade policy toward RTAs.
17. Describe the evolution of MERCOSUR.
18. What are the issues involved in multilateralism versus bilateralism?

SUGGESTED READINGS AND WEB SITES

"A Question of Preference," *The Economist,* August 22, 1998, p. 62.
One-page article on the trade creating effects of the EU, NAFTA, and MERCOSUR.
Soamiely Andriamananjara, "Preferential Trade Agreements and the Multilateral Trading System," *International Economic Review,* January/February 2001, pp. 1–4.

A short summary of the uneasy relationship between preferential trade agreements and the WTO.
The Economist (www.economist.com)
The leading source of information on developments in the EU.
European Union (www.europa.eu.int)
"Free Trade on Trial," *The Economist,* January 3, 2004, pp.13–16.
A short survey on the progress of NAFTA.
The EU's official web site.
Peter Hoeller, Nathalie Girouard, and Alessandra Colecchia, *The European Unions Trade Policies and Their Economic Effects,* Washington, D.C.: OECD, 2001.
An excellent short reference to the trade policies of the EU.
Anne O. Krueger, "Are Preferential Trading Arrangements Trade-Liberalizing or Protectionist?" *Journal of Economic Perspectives* 13(4), Fall 1999, pp. 105–24.
A readable guide to the current debates over RTAs.
MERCOSUR (www.mercosur.org)
The official web site of MERCOSUR.
Patrick A. Messerlin, *Measuring the Costs of Protectionism in Europe: European Commercial Policy for the 2000s,* Washington, D.C.: Institute for International Economics, 2001.
A comprehensive study of the cost of protectionism in the EU. The author finds that protectionism is costing the EU approximately the GDP of Spain.
NAFTA (www.nafta-sec-alena.org)
The official NAFTA web site.
Patricia S. Pollard, "The Creation of the Euro and the Role of the Dollar in International Markets," *Federal Reserve Bank of St. Louis Review* 83(5), September/October 2001, pp. 17–36.
An outstanding article on the evolution of the Euro and its potential place in international trade.
Geri Smith, "Farmers are Getting Plowed Under," *Business Week,* November 18, 2002, p. 53.
The article highlights the difficulties Mexican farmers will face as the tariff reductions under NAFTA are phased in. A perfect example of how trade agreements are slowly implemented. The article details the price differentials between Mexico and the U.S. on certain agricultural products. The article then goes on to show how even with free trade the differences in agricultural subsidies creates a playing field that is not level and Mexico is considering NTBs to slow the inflow of American food products.
Nicholas Stein, "Yes, we have no profits," *Fortune,* November 26, 2001, pp. 182–196.
Perhaps the best article written on the "banana wars." Contains a great description of how a change in EU trade policy virtually ruined a healthy company and how U.S. trade policy was used to "protect" the affected company. A truly rare glimpse at how trade policy can affect an individual company.
U.S. Trade Representative (www.ustr.gov)
The best source of information on current U.S. government trade policy.
Howard J. Wall, "Have Regional Trade Blocs Diverted U.S. Exports?", *International Economic Trends,* Federal Reserve Bank of St. Louis, February 2001, p. 1.
A short, readable piece on the effects of regional trade blocs in the Western hemisphere on U.S. exports.
World Trade Organization (www.wto.org)
An excellent source on the relationship between the WTO and RTAs.
Wendy Zellner, "The Highest Court You've Never Heard Of," *Business Week,* April 1, 2002, pp. 76–77.
Although it is almost never mentioned, most trade agreements have some sort of dispute-settlement mechanism. This is an accessible article about how the dispute-settlement process works with NAFTA.

Chapter 11

International Trade and Economic Growth

"The main losers in today's very unequal world are not those who are too exposed to globalization, but those who have been left out."
—Kofi Annan

INTRODUCTION

As we indicated in Chapter 1, most of the world's population is concentrated in the developing countries. In various other chapters, we have touched on some of the relationships between international trade and factor movements with respect to the developing countries. However, up to this point most of our focus and analysis has been concentrated on the developed countries. As we discussed in Chapter 1, this focus on developed countries made sense because most of the world's trade and investment occurs among the developed countries. In this chapter, we turn our attention to how international trade affects economic conditions in the developing countries. This is an important topic for two reasons. First, improving the standard of living in the developing countries is arguably one of the most important topics in all of economics. Approximately 5.3 billion people or 85 percent of the world's population live in the low- or middle-income countries (i.e., developing countries). As a result, the sheer magnitude of people living in poverty makes this an important topic. Second, the relationship between international trade and economic growth has been a controversial subject over the years. Fortunately, in the last two decades economists have learned a lot about the relationship between the two. Armed with this new knowledge, we can now explain the linkages in a straightforward manner.

economic development the development of a standard of living in the developing countries equivalent to that of the developed countries

In the first part of the chapter, we will cover the concept of **economic development** in more detail and examine some aspects of the universe of countries known as the developing economies. As we will see, the critical factor for these countries is their rate of economic growth. In the second part of the chapter, we will discuss the basic aspects of the theory of economic growth. The third part of the chapter shows how international trade can be used to enhance economic growth. This is followed by a discussion of the various strategies that have been used by developing countries to enhance their economic growth. The final section deals with the role of developed-country governments and international organizations in their efforts to increase economic growth in developing countries.

THE DEVELOPING COUNTRIES

In this section, some of the aspects of economic development and the developing countries that were omitted in Chapter 1 are discussed. First, we need to describe the concept of economic development. Second, we need to take a closer look at the economics and geography of the developing countries. From there, we will be able to begin to understand why economic growth is so important and how international trade can enhance economic development.

Economic Development

Economic development is one of those terms that everyone intuitively understands, for some countries are relatively rich and others are relatively poor. However, these concepts need to be refined somewhat. Economic development is defined as a goal that each country attempts to achieve. The goal of economic development is the attainment of a standard of living roughly equivalent to that of the average citizen in a developed country. A way to measure the average income of individuals within a country is using GDP per capita. However, this measurement is really just a proxy for a variety of factors. In most of the world's countries, low GDP per capita is associated with a host of other factors that reduce the quality of life for most of humanity. In the poorest countries there is pervasive malnutrition and chronically poor housing. The first goal of economic development is the alleviation of these dire conditions for billions of people. Beyond basic food and housing, the lack of access to basic health care is equally a threat to the lives of billions of people. In many cases, this lack of health care is more acute because of the lack of basic infrastructure to provide amenities such as clean water that can drastically reduce the standard of living. As we saw in Chapter 4, human capital is an important factor in international trade. It is even more important in the context of economic development. In low- and middle-income countries 17 and 38 percent of the male and female population is illiterate, respectively. It is difficult, at best, for people to improve their standard of living without access to basic education.

From the brief sketch above, you can see that economic development is at once an easy but also a complicated concept. This is precisely why there is an area of economics known as economic development. In a single chapter, we cannot possibly hope to summarize a different area of economics. To simplify our analysis, we are going to make an important assumption. This assumption is that the various aspects of economic development all are positively correlated with a country's GDP per capita. This means that a country with a GDP per capita of $1,000 has on average a higher standard of living than a country with a GDP per capita of $500. This is reasonable, for countries with higher GDPs per capita will normally have higher standards of living in most respects. There is another reason for making this assumption. In international economics, there has been a large amount of research on the issue of international trade and economic development. For the most part, the research has been concerned with the relationship between international trade and the rate of economic growth. In the discussion that follows, we will focus on economic growth and the associated concept of GDP per capita.

GDP of Developing Countries

As we saw in Chapter 1, there are approximately 145 developing countries in the world economy. This information is reproduced in Table 11.1. For use as a benchmark, the data for the high-income economies is shown. GDP per capita in the high-income economies is on average $34,316. These economies have a population of approximately one billion people or 15.7 percent of world population. The distinguishing characteristic of these economies is that they produce approximately 77.7 percent of world output. In general terms, the problem of economic development is to increase GDP per capita for the 84.3 percent of humanity that lives in low- to middle-income countries.

Table 11.1 also shows the data for the middle-income countries. However, one has to be careful with the term *middle*. In 2005, GDP per capita in the middle-income countries was only $2,782 per year. This is less than a tenth of GDP per capita in the high-income countries. By global standards, this is the world's middle class. However, by the standards of high-income countries, GDP per capita is extremely low even in middle-income countries. The economic development problem in these countries is substantial in the world economy. Over 3 billion people reside in these countries, or only slightly less than half of the world's population. The encouraging trend is that this group of countries has the fastest rate of growth of GDP of the three groups. These countries now produce nearly 20 percent of world economic output. Unfortunately, this output is spread over a large number of people, depressing the level of GDP per capita. Comparing the growth rate of population to the growth rate of GDP,

Table 11.1 Distribution of World Population and Economic Output, 2005[a]

	GDP per capita	Population (millions)	% of World Population	Population Growth 1990–2000	Total GDP (millions of $)	% of World GDP
Low-Income Economies	$602	2,352	36.5%	2.1%	$1,416,212	3.2%
Middle-Income Economies	$2,782	3,075	47.8%	1.3%	$8,553,721	19.2%
High-Income Economies	$34,316	1,011	15.7%	0.7%	$34,687,058	77.7%

[a]*The countries included in the table are shown in the endpaper table, and each country is classified as high- middle-, or low-income.*
Source: World Bank, *World Development Indicators,* Washington, DC: World Bank, 2007.

it is apparent that the situation is improving. Some familiar examples of middle-income countries are Mexico, Thailand, Malaysia, South Africa, and Egypt.

While the standard of living in middle-income countries is low, it pales in comparison to the economic problem of the low-income countries. GDP per capita in these countries is on average approximately $600 per year. To put this into perspective, this means a standard of living of more or less $1.60 per day. In these countries, some of the worst effects of poverty, such as malnutrition, lack of housing, and lack of medical care, are not anomalies but the norm. If these conditions were isolated to a few countries, the problem would not be quite as pressing. However, the reality is that about 2.4 billion people or over 35 percent of the world's population live in dire poverty. This group of countries produces only 3.2 percent of the world's output. With such a small percentage of output and the large size of the population, it will take an enormous increase in the collective GDPs of these countries to substantially alter the situation. Fortunately, GDP growth in these countries is outstripping the growth rate of population. Unfortunately, the gap is not large enough to quickly improve living standards in these countries. Some familiar examples of low-income countries are Haiti, India, and many countries in sub-Saharan Africa.

In an economic geography sense, levels of development are not spread evenly around the world.[1] The high-income economies are concentrated in North America and Western Europe. The former communist countries of Eastern Europe are middle-income countries that have a good chance of becoming high-income countries. In the Western hemisphere, virtually all of the countries except the U.S. and Canada are either low- or middle-income countries. The situation in Asia is similar. Japan, Singapore, Australia, and New Zealand are the only high-income countries. The rest of Asia is either in the low- or middle-income categories. The distinguishing characteristic of this region is the concentration of over 2 billion people in the low- and middle-income economies of India and China, respectively. The continent of Africa is split between low- and middle-income economies. The countries along the Mediterranean Basin are middle-income countries. Most of the countries of sub-Saharan Africa with the exception of South Africa are in the low-income category.

From the above, it is obvious that the problem of economic development is primarily a problem of raising the economic output of the low- and middle-income economies. To do this, one must first know something about the basic theory of economic growth. In the next section, we will consider both the basic theory and the factors that can help to contribute to rapid economic growth.

ECONOMIC GROWTH

In this section, we consider what determines the rate of economic growth. The first consideration is defining the factors of production that contribute to economic growth. The next step is to show how these determinants interact to produce both GDP growth and growth in GDP per capita. However, before starting on the theory of economic growth, we need to consider some preconditions that are necessary for the theory to work properly.

[1]See the Appendix at the end of the book for a complete listing of GDP, GDP per capita, population, and exports for low-, middle-, and high-income countries.

Preconditions for Growth

In many areas of economics, there is an implicit assumption concerning some preconditions that need to be in place within a single market (in the case of microeconomics) or the entire economy (in the case of macroeconomics). If these preconditions are not met, the usual theory we use in economics may not work as well. While there are a number of factors that can interfere with the workings of the market, there are two factors that are absolutely critical: property rights and the rule of law.

Property rights are essential to the workings of a market economy. For markets to work, it must be clear who owns what. If the buyer in a transaction cannot be certain that the seller actually owns the property, the transaction may not occur. Buyers need to be assured that the seller has the right to sell the property. If this is not the case, at some point another party might appear and claim that the seller had no right to sell the property in question. Further, the buyer needs to be confident that once some property is acquired, it cannot be arbitrarily taken away by another individual or the state. In a developed economy, all of us take this for granted. Unfortunately, in a number of countries this is not the case. The ownership of property may be arbitrary in the sense that property rights are not properly enforced. Such an environment takes a huge toll on the overall level of economic activity. Far fewer transactions occur, with the result that every lost transaction entails a loss of GDP.

The second precondition is the rule of law. Normal economic transactions involve legally binding contracts. Sometimes, contracts lead to disputes among the parties involved. When this occurs there needs to be a sufficiently developed legal system for the state to determine what the appropriate outcome is and which parties have what obligations under the contract. If there is no effective referee to enforce business contracts, far fewer business contracts occur. Market participants become reluctant to engage in normal economic activities because they cannot be sure that contracts will be enforced. Once again, the outcome is a lower level of economic activity.

In the sections that follow, we will assume that property rights are respected and that business contracts are enforceable. These are minimum preconditions for the growth theory we discuss to work properly. One needs to keep in mind that for some developing countries the problem is not just the theory of economic growth; in many cases, the problem is that the preconditions to normal economic growth are not being met. Sadly, this situation is so common it has a name: failed state.

Economic Growth and the Factors of Production

In order for an economy to grow, it needs resources, or what economists call the factors of production. In general terms, these resources are referred to as land, labor, capital, and technology. In the discussion that follows, we assume that land is a constant. Although, it is possible for this factor to grow, it is extremely difficult to increase it. Land can be reclaimed from the sea, as in the Netherlands, and it can be acquired by purchase from other countries or by war. For our purposes, however, it is a constant. The discussion below will focus on labor, capital, and technology.

The economic growth of a country can be enhanced by having a country's labor force grow over time. This increase can occur either through an increase in its natural population growth or through immigration. This is particularly significant for developing countries. The low-income countries typically have high birth rates, as infant

Economic Freedom Indexes

In the section above, the preconditions for economic growth were discussed. These are the minimum conditions necessary for markets to function properly. However, past these minimums governments can pursue any number of policies that can aid or hinder the rate of economic growth. To enhance economic growth, governments need to pursue policies that make it easier for both producers and consumers to maximize their respective profits and welfare. In an effort to compare countries in this regard, economists have created indexes of economic freedom to measure the extent to which government policies in a country enhance or retard growth. One of the oldest and most popular of these indexes is produced annually by the Heritage Foundation. Their index includes 10 different government policies: trade, taxation, government intervention, monetary policy, foreign investment, banking, wages and prices, property rights, regulation, and the existence of a black market in foreign exchange.[2] Such indexes are not perfect measures of government policies with respect to economic growth. However, they can be broadly indicative of whether or not government policy in a country is on balance discouraging economic growth or enhancing it. Table 11.2 shows the 10 countries that score the highest in the economic freedom index and the 10 countries that score the lowest. Notice that most of the top ten are either countries that are already developed or if not growing rapidly. The bottom ten countries are uniformly poor developing countries.

Table 11.2 Economic Freedom Index, 2007

Highest-Ranking Countries	Economic Freedom Index	Lowest-Ranking Countries	Economic Freedom Index
Hong Kong	89.29	Guinea-Bissau	45.71
Singapore	85.65	Angola	43.47
Australia	82.69	Iran	43.33
U.S.	81.98	Rep. of Congo	43.00
New Zealand	81.59	Turkmenistan	42.54
U.K.	81.55	Burma	40.14
Ireland	81.31	Zimbabwe	35.81
Luxembourg	79.31	Libya	34.48
Switzerland	79.05	Cuba	29.68
Canada	78.72	North Korea	3.00

Source: Adapted from Tim Kane, Kim Holmes, and Mary Anastasia O'Grady, eds., *2007 Index of Economic Freedom,* Washington, D.C.: The Heritage Foundation, 2007.

[2]A black market in foreign exchange occurs when individuals in a country face restrictions on their ability to buy and sell foreign currency at a mutually agreeable exchange rate. For details on these markets see Chapter 20.

mortality is quite high. Also, these countries still have a large percentage of their populations in the agricultural sector. In this sector, large families may make economic sense as a way to grow the family labor force. However, mortality rates may also be high. Population growth can be especially high in some of the wealthier low-income countries. Once a country has reached a certain stage of economic development, basic public health measures such as clean water are implemented. This can cause a large drop in mortality rates. The result of these two factors can be a period of time when the population is growing at a rapid rate. Eventually this would translate into fast growth in the labor force. This effect is temporary, for population growth rates fall with the level of economic development, as shown in Table 11.1.

This increase in the labor force will tend to increase GDP. However, there is a potential problem lurking here. Notice from Table 11.1 that population growth in the developing countries can be as high as 2 percent. To increase the level of economic development, it is necessary to have GDP per capita growing as fast as possible. In this case, it would be necessary to have GDP growth that is in excess of population growth by as much as possible. In the discussion that follows, one should keep this in mind. A fast growth rate of GDP is important in developing countries because of rapid growth in population.

Economic growth also requires an increase in the stock of capital. In economic terms, capital is the amount of money invested in business structures and equipment. The latter term refers not only to the type of equipment that goes into a manufacturing plant but also to the type of business equipment needed to process information, such as computers and software. In the models we use in the next section, economic growth can be enhanced by the ability of an economy to increase the stock of capital as fast as possible. For a developing country, the stock of capital outside of the private sector may be critically important. In order for capital and labor to produce the maximum output, the economic infrastructure of the country needs to be appropriate to the level of economic development. This sort of infrastructure includes water and sewage systems, paved roads, reliable supplies of electricity, and so on. Since much of this type of capital is developed in the public sector, we will cover this type of investment later in this chapter.

The final factor of production is technology. In economics, technology carries a somewhat different meaning than it does in common usage. Economists define a change in technology as anything that causes resources to be used in a more efficient way. Much of the time this means a change in technology as we usually understand it, such as an improvement in computer technology. For economists, however, the term is much broader. What we are interested in is the relationship between inputs and outputs. For our purposes, a change in technology means that a country can either produce more output with the same amount of resources or, alternatively, produce the same level of output with fewer resources. This might occur because of better machinery or equipment. However, in this sense a change in management practices could have the same effect. When we discuss changes in technology in the next section, keep in mind that we are talking about technology in a very broad way.

Basic Growth Theory

Given the factors of production that we described above, we can now illustrate how these factors interact to produce a higher level of GDP. This relationship is illustrated in Figure 11.1. The vertical axis measures the level of real GDP (Y), and the horizontal axis measures the size of the labor force (L). In this case, GDP is shown as a function of the size of the labor force. To graph the relationship between GDP and the labor force, we have held the stock of capital (K) and the level of technology constant. For the moment, we want to look only at the relationship between GDP and the labor force. This relationship is known as a **production function**.

production function a graph showing the relationship between GDP and the factors of production

First, notice that the relationship between GDP and the labor force is positive. Everything else being equal, as the size of the labor force increases, the amount of real GDP that an economy can produce increases. Notice that the relationship is not linear. This is because we have assumed that the capital stock and the level of technology are fixed. The changing slope of the production function reflects the phenomenon of diminishing returns. Diminishing returns occurs when an increasing amount of a variable factor of production is added to a fixed factor of production. As the amount of the variable factor increases, the resulting increase in output becomes smaller. In this case, the fixed factor of production is the capital stock and the variable factor of production is labor. When the first few units of labor begin working with a large stock of capital, initially output rises rapidly. This is shown in Figure 11.1. As the amount of labor used increases from L_1 to L_2, GDP increases sharply from Y_1 to Y_2. However, the slope of the production function is not constant because of diminishing returns. Suppose that the same amount of labor is added shown by the increase in labor used from L_3 to L_4. In this case, GDP still increases but by the smaller amount represented by the movement of GDP from Y_3 to Y_4.

The effects shown in Figure 11.1 are especially applicable to developing countries. In many cases, the initial level of GDP is low or closer to Y_1 than Y_3. In such cases, an

Figure 11.1 Production Function for a Country

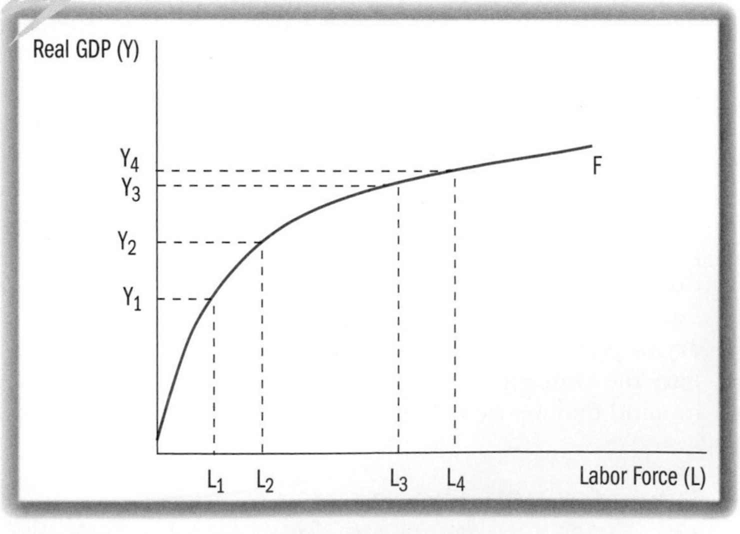

A country's production function shows the relationship between the country's labor force (L) and its total output (GDP).

increase in the labor force will yield a larger increase in output than would occur if the economy started at Y_3. Second, the labor force in a developing country may be increasing rapidly due to high rates of population growth. Everything else being equal, combining both effects indicates that a country with a low GDP has the potential to grow rather fast. However, keep in mind that since population is also growing rapidly, GDP growth must be high in order to increase GDP per capita. To do this countries need increases in both the capital stock and the level of technology.

Changes in Capital Stock and Technology

Fortunately, changing the size of the labor force is not the only way to increase GDP. In the previous section, the stock of capital and the level of technology were held constant. Here, we examine what happens if one or both of these variables change. First, let us assume that the economy accumulates more capital. In the usual course of economic activity, all current income is not immediately spent. Usually, both consumers and businesses save part of their current income. Even if a country has only a rudimentary financial system, these savings may be loaned to a business. The business then may use the proceeds of the loan to invest in a new structure and/or plant and equipment. Notice that this new investment is a flow variable that adds to the country's stock of capital. This increase in the country's capital stock changes the production function shown in the previous section. Figure 11.2 illustrates the effect of an increase in a country's capital stock on its production function. The change in the capital stock shifts the production function upward. If the labor force is at L_1, then the level of real GDP given the initial production function is Y_1. An increase in the capital stock shifts the production function from F_1 to F_2. With no change in the labor force, the level of

Figure 11.2 Shift in the Production Function for a Country

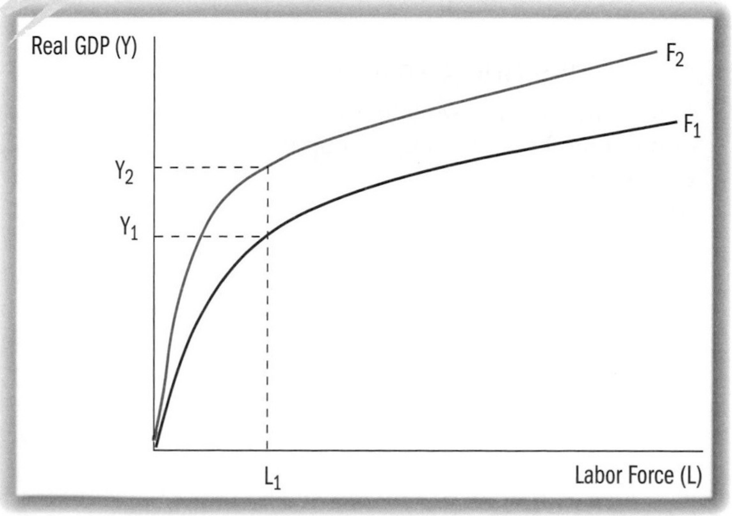

A country's production function will shift upward if the country's capital stock or technology increases.

GDP increases from Y_1 to Y_2. The economy can now produce more goods and services for any given size of the labor force. This occurs because the capital-to-labor ratio has increased. A worker with more capital can produce more goods and/or services than can one with less. As the average capital-to-labor ratio rises, real GDP rises.

A similar situation occurs when the level of technology increases. Remember that technology in this case is the relationship between inputs and output. An improvement in technology should allow the economy to produce more goods and services with the same level of labor *and* capital. In other words, something is happening in the economy that increases the ability to mix labor and capital more efficiently. Graphically, the effect is the same. An improvement in technology again shifts the production function upward from F_1 to F_2. The economy can now increase output from Y_1 to Y_2 in Figure 11.2 with the same amount of labor. However, in this case the stock of capital has not changed. The increase in real GDP occurs solely as the result of being able to utilize the same amount of capital and labor to produce more goods and services. Technology is especially important in examining the relationship between international trade and economic growth. In the next section, we consider the relationship between economic development and international trade and the international movement of factors of production.

INTERNATIONAL TRADE AND ECONOMIC GROWTH

Over the last several decades, the issue of how international trade affects economic growth has been extensively researched. The purpose of this section is to explore the potential connections between international trade and factor movements and economic growth. First, the issue of openness to trade and growth is presented. Next, the movements of capital and the transfer of technology between countries and their effect on economic growth are presented. Finally, the role of MNCs in the process of economic development is discussed.

Openness and Growth

One of the more researched topics in international economics and economic development has been the relationship between the degree of openness of an economy and the rate of economic growth. Conceptually, we have already covered this relationship. In Chapters 2 and 4, it was shown that international trade based on comparative advantage causes a reallocation of resources. From the framework developed in Chapter 2, we know that trade based on comparative advantage causes the comparative disadvantage industry to contract and the comparative advantage industry to expand. Under the factor proportions model developed in Chapter 4, we know that this implies that capital and labor would be moving from comparative-disadvantage industries to comparative-advantage industries. These resources will be able to produce more output in total because the loss of output in the comparative-disadvantage industry will be smaller than the gain in output in the comparative-advantage industry. The total output of the economy will be higher, as resources are moved to more productive uses. In terms of economic growth, the implications are clear. All else being equal, the more a country trades the faster its economy should be able to grow.

While this is logically true, economists are always searching for empirical confirmation of the predictions of economic theory. Frequently, economic phenomenon are complicated, and economists have learned not to completely trust a theoretical prediction even if it seems impossible that it is not true. The relationship between openness and growth is a perfect example of this process at work. In the late 1980s and early 1990s, economists started empirically investigating this relationship. The obvious way to start was to see if there was a good statistical correlation between the degree of openness of an economy and economic growth. These simple empirical tests usually yielded the same result: the more open an economy was to international trade, the faster it would grow.[3] While suggestive, these tests were not conclusive. What had been demonstrated was a statistical correlation. One has to be careful about the next step. Does a high correlation prove *causation*? Of course not. Just because there is high correlation, it does not necessarily mean that there is also causation.[4]

In order to more definitively demonstrate that openness is a *cause* of economic growth, it is necessary to show that openness shifts the production function upward. As indicated in the previous section, there are two possibilities. Because we know that international trade would not necessarily cause the capital stock to increase, it must have some sort of an effect on technology. Technology was defined above as a way to increase output with the same level of inputs. In this sense, openness causes an improvement in technology. By shifting resources from less productive to more productive uses, an economy can get more output from the same level of inputs, such as labor and capital. Economists refer to this as **total factor productivity**. Technically, this is the amount of economic growth that cannot be accounted for by increases in the amount of labor or capital used. If one could show that openness is highly correlated with total factor productivity growth, then one could be more certain that openness is a contributing factor to economic growth. Fortunately, this relationship has been established. Edwards (1998) has shown that more open economies tend to have higher rates of growth of total factor productivity. The implication of this is that countries that are more open would tend to grow faster, all else being equal.[5] However, "all else being equal" covers a lot of territory if one is speaking about large issues such as international trade *and* economic development. As a result, no one study is likely to be conclusive. There are many other factors that need to be controlled for in order to make stronger conclusions about the relationship between openness and economic growth. In a further study of the issue, Frankel and Romer (1999) examined the relationship between openness and GDP per capita. In this study, the researchers controlled for the effects of distance (which reduces trade) and the size of the economy (which increases income). Their study showed again that trade does seem to increase GDP per capita. The results of these studies indicate that openness is associated with higher levels of economic growth.[6] The remaining question has to do with the size of

total factor productivity an increase in GDP not accounted for by changes in the labor force or the stock of capital

[3]For an excellent survey of this literature, see Sebastian Edwards, "Openness, Trade Liberalization, and Growth in Developing Countries," *Journal of Economic Literature* 39(1), September 1993, pp. 1358–93.

[4]For example, sunrise is frequently preceded by an elevated level of vocal activity by male chickens. Does this mean that the chickens' activity causes the sun to rise?

[5]Sebastian Edwards, "Openness, Productivity, and Growth: What Do We Really Know?" *Economic Journal* 108(447), March 1998, pp. 383–98.

[6]Jeffrey A. Frankel and David Romer, "Does Trade Cause Growth?" *American Economic Review* 89(3), June 1999, pp. 379–99.

the effect. What is not in doubt is the basic proposition that more open countries tend to grow faster than less open ones. This has implications for the economic development strategies discussed below.

Openness and Growth

The section above indicates that openness and growth are positively correlated. Although the research on this subject is large, a study by Dollar and Aart (2001) is a good example of the literature. They start by identifying three groups of countries: the rich countries, globalizers, and nonglobalizers. The rich countries are the 24 OECD countries plus some of the more successful developing countries such as Chile, Hong Kong, Singapore, South Korea, and Taiwan. To differentiate the developing countries the authors studied 73 countries for which trade and tariff data were available. 24 countries were defined as globalizers. These were the top third of the developing countries in terms of increases in trade as a percentage of GDP and reductions in tariffs. The nonglobalizers are the other 49 developing countries that have experienced a smaller increase in openness or reductions in tariffs.

The differences in GDP growth for the last four decades for the three groups can be seen in Table 11.3. The rich countries have seen a declining trend in economic growth from 4.7 percent in the 1960s to 2.2 percent in the 1990s. For the group of globalizers, the results have been the reverse. Growth in these countries has increased dramatically from less than 2 percent in the 1960s to 5 percent in the 1990s. The nonglobalizers have not fared as well. Growth in these countries increased from the 1960s to the 1970s. However, growth dropped to less than 1 percent in the 1980s and has only increased to 1.4 percent in the 1990s. In many of these countries, GDP per capita has fallen.

Again remember that the results of this one study are not conclusive. However, it is illustrative of a large body of literature on the subject of openness and growth. Overwhelmingly, the conclusion of the literature is that greater economic openness enhances growth. Also note that there is more to economic growth than international trade. During these four decades, the rich countries were becoming more open and were reducing trade barriers. Despite this, rates of economic growth fell. International trade is just one factor in a complex mix of factors that influence economic growth. In the case of the rich countries, it may well be true that growth would have slowed even more if these economies had not become more open.

Table 11.3 Average Growth of Real GDP of Rich Countries, Globalizers, and Nonglobalizers, 1960s–1990s

Country Group	1960s	1970s	1980s	1990s
Rich Countries	4.7%	3.1%	2.3%	2.2%
Globalizers	1.4%	2.9%	3.5%	5.0%
Nonglobalizers	2.4%	3.3%	0.8%	1.4%

Source: Dollar, D. and A. Aart, "Trade, Growth and Poverty," *World Bank Research Paper,* March 2001, p. 28.

Capital Flows, Technology Transfers, and Economic Growth

The preceding section showed that both a larger capital stock and higher technology increase economic growth. They both cause upward shifts in the production function. However, increasing either one of these factors is difficult for a developing country. It is hard for a poor country to save enough out of current income to rapidly increase its stock of capital. Likewise in a developing country the level of technology is likely to be considerably below the world average and difficult to accumulate. Part of the solution to this problem lies in the inherent activities of MNCs and FDI.

FDI obviously helps developing countries increase their capital stock. Most MNCs are headquartered in developed countries. As indicated in Chapter 6, there is a tendency for MNCs to move capital into developing countries, where the rate of return may be higher. This movement of capital tends to increase the rate of economic growth in developing countries. As FDI flows into a country, the production function would shift upward, producing a higher level of real GDP. In this way, FDI would tend to increase the rate of economic growth.

The same type of effect would be the case for the transfer of technology from developed to developing countries. The global transfer of technology is one of the most interesting subjects in international economics. The difficulty is that technology and knowledge are extremely hard to measure. This measurement problem severely limits our ability to make statements about the effects of these technology transfers on growth in developing countries. The direction of the effect is clear. Improvements in technology imported from the developed countries will increase the rate of economic growth. FDI flows from developed to developing countries is a case in point. FDI flows bring in not only capital but also a higher level of technology. A higher level of technology would tend to shift the production function upward. This, in turn, produces a higher level of real GDP for any given level of resources. However, determining the exact extent of the transfer of technology associated with this FDI would be difficult at best.

What is less obvious is that international trade in goods and services can lead to technology transfers even in the absence of FDI. An example of this is learning by doing. International trade usually involves countries becoming more specialized in the production of certain products. Because of specialization, countries become better at producing certain goods or services. This sort of specialization causes an improvement in knowledge that increases total factor productivity. The process of exporting intensifies the learning by forcing firms to compete with other specialized firms in the world economy. The same types of effects occur when domestic firms are forced to compete with efficient foreign firms. The result is that international trade leads to an increasing accumulation of knowledge that can increase total factor productivity.[7]

ECONOMIC DEVELOPMENT STRATEGIES

Missing from the discussion of economic growth, above, is one important factor. To this point, we have not discussed the role of government except as a neutral referee of economic activity. However, governments frequently use international trade policy, as

[7]For more details on these effects, see Robert Z. Lawrence and David E. Weinstein, "Trade and Growth: Import-Led or Export-Led? Evidence from Japan and Korea," *NBER Working Paper 7264,* July 1999.

discussed in Chapters 7 through 9, as part of more general policies on economic development. In this section, three common development strategies with respect to international trade are examined. The purpose of this section is to familiarize you with some of the more common forms of development strategy and how these strategies have changed. This should make the analysis and understanding of many developing economies more comprehensible. The developing countries are not all alike, and which countries have pursued which strategies is frequently an important determinant of how certain countries have developed.

Primary Products

The endowment of natural resources is not evenly distributed around the world. Some countries have mineral resources and others do not. Some countries are able to produce certain agricultural products and others cannot. In a generic sense, these natural resources or the ability to produce agricultural products are referred to as **primary products**. Primary products can be used as the basis for a more comprehensive development strategy. If managed wisely, primary products can be used to enhance the economic development of a country.

primary products natural resources or the ability to produce certain agricultural products

First, the production and export of primary products can be quite profitable. If the product is cheap to extract or easy to cultivate, production costs may be lower than the world market price. As a result, primary products can be a major source of tax revenue. In these cases, the government may be able to use this tax revenue to enhance economic development. Countries tend to move in stages from a dependence on agricultural production to a stage where manufacturing becomes more important. However, the development of manufacturing may require a substantial investment in the country's infrastructure. Revenues from the production of primary products may allow the country to finance this more easily than a country without such resources. The result is that the country may be able to grow faster. Second, the development of infrastructure may require imports such as capital equipment from the developed countries. In turn, these imports will require foreign exchange. The export of a primary product can allow the country to more easily afford these types of imports. Third, a country with primary products may find it easier to transition into manufacturing than a country without such resources. Many primary products are the start of the process of producing a final good. For example, sugar can be refined into a product that is sold to consumers essentially as is. It can also be used to produce more sophisticated products such as candy or rum. The obvious first step in this process for a country with primary products is to add value to the primary product. As a result, countries with primary products may be able to make the transition to manufacturing more easily than countries without such products.

In practice, this process has been fraught with difficulties. Recall from Chapter 7 the concept of the effective rate of protection. If the tariff on the primary product is lower than the tariff on the intermediate or finished good, the effective rate of protection increases with the level of processing. For example, if the tariff on coffee is lower than the tariff on instant coffee, the effective rate of protection may be quite high for instant coffee. This is precisely what many developed countries have done in order to encourage the processing of primary products in their countries. The reverse of this is that it makes it more difficult for countries with primary products to fully exploit their comparative advantage. The escalation of tariffs by level of processing is a major source of tension between the developed and developing countries in international trade negotiations. It also helps to explain why so few developing countries are able to fully utilize their resources.

Primary products can be a problem with respect to economic development, as well. The prices of primary products tend to be volatile. If both the demand and supply of the product are inelastic, then most of the changes in demand and supply are reflected in the price. Figure 11.3 shows the supply and demand curves for a representative primary product such as oil. The initial supply and demand curves are labeled D and S, with an equilibrium indicated at point E. Suppose that the supply of oil diminishes by a small amount, represented by a shift of the supply curve from S to S_1. Now suppose that there also is an increase in the demand for oil. This is represented by a shift of the demand curve from D to D_1. As shown in the figure, the equilibrium would change from E to F and price of oil would rise rapidly from P to P_1. If the situation were reversed, prices could fall just as rapidly. Although the example is oil, the analysis is general. The demand and supply of primary products are frequently relatively inelastic and can make the prices of these products quite volatile. It is easy to see these price swings in world markets. Table 11.4 shows the annual changes in the prices of different classes of primary commodities from 2000 to 2005. Even for all commodities averaged together, the price changes can be large. Examining the various subcategories, shows that even in a year when the average price of commodities did not change much, the price of some classes of commodities still changed by a large amount. The point is that these types of products frequently have large price changes over relatively short periods of time.

Figure 11.3 Equilibrium Price of Primary Products

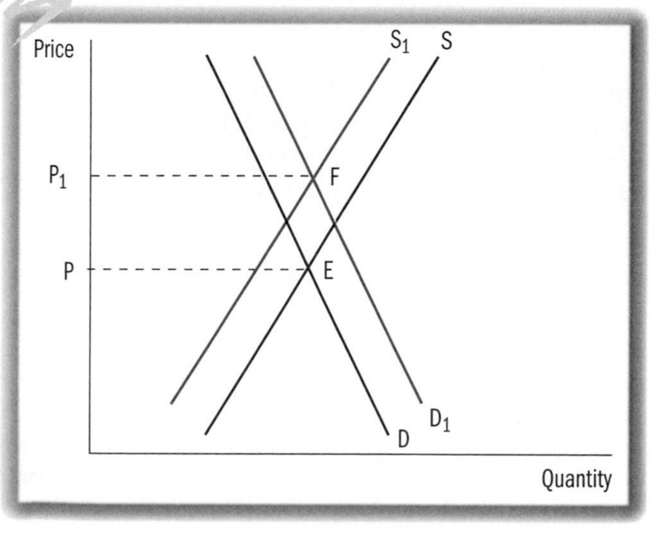

Small changes in the demand and/or supply of primary products can cause large changes in the price of the product.

Table 11.4 World Primary Commodity Prices, 2000–2005 (Percentage change over previous year)

Commodity Group	2000	2001	2002	2003	2004	2005
All Commodities	1.7%	−3.6%	0.8%	8.1%	19.4%	12.1%
Food & Tropical Beverages	−0.1	0.4	0.4	2.3	13.2	8.8
Vegetable Oilseeds & Oils	−20.3	−6.4	24.9	17.4	13.2	−9.5
Agricultural Raw Materials	3.1	−3.9	−2.4	19.8	9.9	7.1
Minerals, Ores, & Metals	12.4	−10.8	−2.7	12.4	40.7	26.2
Crude Petroleum	56.6	−13.3	2.0	15.8	30.7	41.3

Source: Adapted from United Nations Conference on Trade and Development, *Trade and Development Report,* Geneva: United Nations Conference on Trade and Development, 2006.

For many countries, primary products are a high percentage of either exports or GDP. If primary product exports are a high percentage of total exports, price instability can cause major changes in the terms of trade. In these cases, the export price index is much more volatile than the import price index. In other countries, the primary product may be a large percentage of GDP. In these cases, instability in the price of one product can mean instability for the whole economy. This would make it harder to keep the economy on a stable growth path than in the case of countries that are developing without primary products.[8] The growth record in the former type of country is mixed. On the one hand, revenues from primary products may help to more successfully transition to other types of economic activity. On the other hand, primary products may be a major source of instability in countries that are very dependent on these products as a major source of export revenue or a high percentage of GDP.

import substitution a development strategy based on developing industries that will reduce imports

Import Substitution

Import substitution is another common development strategy. The basic idea is not new. In a U.S. context, this development strategy can be found in Alexander Hamilton's *Report on Manufactures* to Congress in 1790. As mentioned in the previous section, it is common for low-income developing countries to have a large agricultural sector. Usually, middle- or high-income economies have much smaller agricultural sectors and much larger manufacturing sectors. The purpose of an import substitution development strategy is to increase the relative size of the manufacturing sector. Such an increase may have several advantages for economic development. First, it may allow the manufacturing sector initially to grow faster than would be the case under free trade. Second, it may help the country conserve on supplies of foreign exchange by importing fewer manufactured products. In turn, this may improve the trade balance. This may be especially important for countries relying on exports of primary commodities. In some years, when the prices of primary commodities are low, the supply of

[8]This situation also may create problems for the value of a country's currency. This effect is covered in Chapter 21.

OPEC

As indicated in the previous section, price fluctuations can be a serious problem if a primary product is an important part of exports and/or GDP. A theoretically attractive option is for countries producing these products to form a cartel. A cartel is an organization of producers that attempts to stabilize the price of a primary commodity by changing the supply of the product in response to changing market conditions. In a technical sense this is easy to accomplish, as the supply is adjusted by the cartel to achieve the desired price. In practice, however, this is not easily accomplished.

The most well known cartel in the world economy is the Organization of Petroleum Exporting Countries (OPEC). OPEC was formed at a meeting on September 14, 1960. The current members of OPEC are Algeria, Indonesia, Iran, Iraq, Kuwait, Libya, Nigeria, Qatar, Saudi Arabia, the United Arab Emirates, and Venezuela. OPEC currently accounts for 41 percent of the world's crude oil production and 55 percent of the oil traded in world markets. The purpose of OPEC is to provide stable prices for both producers and consumers of oil in the world market. In order to do this, it must attempt to adjust the supply of oil in response to changing market conditions. It does this by establishing a quota or a maximum amount of oil each member country can produce. This stability is more apparent than real. Figure 11.4 shows the world price of crude oil since 1990. What seems obvious from the figure is that the cartel is not particularly successful at the task of managing the price of oil.

In OPEC's defense, the task of stabilizing prices is almost impossible. First, since the supply of oil

Figure 11.4 Dollar Price of Crude Oil, 1990–2005

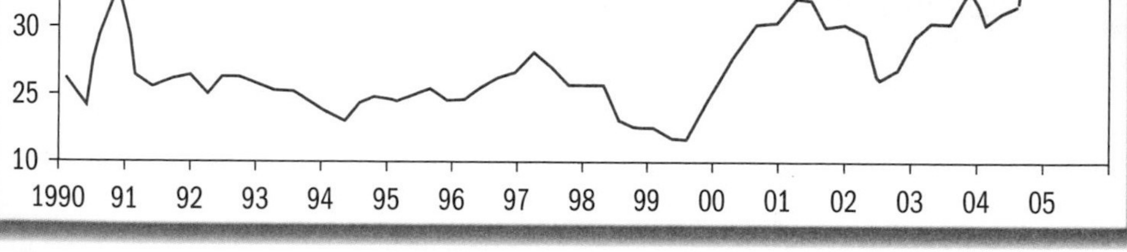

Source: International Monetary Fund, *International Financial Statistics, CD-ROM,* Washington, D.C.: International Monetary Fund, July 2007.

(*continued*)

cannot be changed quickly OPEC is inevitably in the business of forecasting world demand for oil. As in any other type of forecasting, it is easy to make mistakes. Second, notice from the information above that OPEC accounts only for slightly over half of the world oil market and an even smaller percentage of world production. Since these other producers can produce and/or export as they see fit, it is difficult for OPEC to truly "control" the supply of oil. A final problem is with its own members. OPEC cannot force countries to produce the amount of oil recommended by the cartel. In some cases countries have been known to "cheat" on the quota assigned to it. Under these circumstances, it is not surprising that OPEC has a difficult time stabilizing the world market price of oil.

foreign exchange likewise may be low. Finally, some of the protected industries might in the future have a comparative advantage. These "infant" industries initially are protected from foreign competition to allow them to develop at a faster rate. As the industry matures, the protectionism would be gradually withdrawn. However, if the economy at an early stage of economic development does not have a comparative advantage in manufactured products, is there a way to increase the size of this sector?

The answer to this question is yes, and the means of addressing it is to pursue government policies that explicitly favor the manufacturing sector. This can be accomplished through domestic policies such as low taxes on manufacturing and/or direct government subsidies. Using trade policy to favor the manufacturing sector is an attractive choice. As we saw in Chapter 7, tariffs increase the domestic production of a product. If the tariffs are high enough, it is possible to rapidly increase manufacturing output, as importing becomes a less profitable activity. If tariffs are not sufficient to increase output, then quota protection could be instituted instead of or along with tariffs.[9] While once popular as a development strategy, import substitution has created a number of problems for the countries that have pursued it. Tariffs and quotas may well produce an infant manufacturing sector; however, this sector is not internationally competitive and is producing substitutes for imports that cost more and may be of lower quality. This imposes a cost on the economy in two ways. First, all consumers and other industries in the country are paying higher prices. This reduces their welfare and/or their ability to produce other goods and services at competitive prices. Second, the protected industries are larger than they should be in a free market. This means that other industries are by definition smaller than they should be. The major loss, here, is that since the economy is not using its resources efficiently, it is not growing as fast as it could. In a poor country, an economy growing at a 4 percent rate develops much more slowly than an economy growing at a 6 percent rate. In the first case, GDP would double about every 18 years, and in the second case it would double about every 12 years. Unfortunately, countries pursuing import substitution development policies tend to grow at the slower rate. Since employment creation is highly correlated with GDP growth, the economy in these circumstances may create fewer jobs. Given that developing countries tend to have rapid growth in their labor forces, slower

[9]Another facet of import substitution development policy is the maintenance of a fixed exchange rate that is not appropriate. This situation is covered in detail in Chapter 20.

employment growth is something that these countries can ill afford. Further, this policy may reduce job creation in another way. Developing countries frequently have a comparative advantage in labor-intensive industries. An import substitution policy tends to make the domestic industry more capital-intensive than would otherwise be the case. The result can be that there are fewer manufacturing jobs than if the manufacturing sector was developing more along the lines of comparative advantage.

A second problem relates to the material on public choice covered in Chapter 9. In an economy with a lot of protectionism, there is also a lot of rent-seeking activity. Recall that the optimum situation with an import substitution policy calls for the gradual withdrawal of protectionism. In a public choice sense, this won't be easy. Firms and workers in the protected industry will lobby to keep the current level of protection from being removed. This means that high levels of protectionism in these countries may persist for decades. The industries never adjust fully to world competition and over time become relatively more inefficient. The lobbying activity increases over time as the ability of the industry to withstand foreign competition decreases. The country is now saddled with an "infant" industry that never grew up and cannot realistically adjust to even more intense foreign competition than was present at the start of the process. The combination of an import substitution development policy and rent-seeking behavior has had consequences for many developing countries that was not anticipated at the start of the process.

This implies that once an import substitution development policy has been started, it is difficult to get rid of. However, beginning in the 1970s and continuing into the 21st century, most countries pursuing this strategy are in the process of abandoning it. As indicated earlier in the chapter, developing countries need to allocate resources properly in order to have rapid growth in real GDP. In this case, many developing countries are in the process of dismantling the trade barriers associated with this process. The adjustment of these economies to more intense foreign competition is frequently painful. Whole industries may shrink rapidly or in some cases disappear altogether. Countries are willing to go through this process now due to the widespread realization that an inefficient manufacturing sector does not enhance overall economic growth. The large increase in the number of developing countries joining the WTO over the last two decades is in many cases a sign of the failure of import substitution development policies. This failure is made even more noticeable by the success of countries pursuing the type of development policy discussed below.

Export Promotion

export promotion **a development strategy based on developing industries in line with a country's comparative advantage**

As many countries are slowly abandoning import substitution policies, what is the alternative? A development strategy that has proven to be more effective at enhancing economic growth has been the promotion of exports. What this involves is allowing the country to develop along the lines dictated by comparative advantage. In this section, we will consider the role of government in enhancing exports and discuss the advantages of this development strategy.

An export promotion strategy implies an increase in the relative size of manufacturing sector. For manufacturing to thrive, there is an active role for government. First, the preconditions for growth mentioned earlier in the chapter become extremely important. The more developed an economy becomes the more important these

Economic Development in East Asia versus Latin America

A common topic in the economic development literature has been the growth of a selected group of economies in East Asia relative to countries in Latin America. The former group of countries has been extremely successful at raising GDP per capita and the latter group of economies less so. To illustrate this, consider the data in Table 11.5. On the left-hand side of the table are GDP growth rates 1990 to 2000 for Latin America as a whole and for selected economies in the area. The right-hand side of the table shows the same data for Asia as a region and selected economies.

The average growth rate for Latin America and Asia from 1990 to 2000 was 3.3 and 6.0 percent, respectively. The average growth rate for developing economies as a whole during this period was 4.8 percent. During the period, the economies of Latin America grew noticeably slower than the average rate of growth of developing economies. The reverse was true for the developing economies of Asia. These economies grew faster than the world average for the decade. This was accomplished in spite of the Asian debt crisis of the late 1990s that lowered the economic growth rate of the region to

Table 11.5 GDP Growth in Developing Countries in Latin America and Asia, 1990–2000 (Percentage Change)

Region/Country	Percent Change in GDP 1990–2000	Region/Country	Percent Change in GDP 1990–2000
Developing Countries	4.8%		
Latin America	3.3	Asia	6.0%
Argentina	4.3	China	10.3
Brazil	2.9	Hong Kong	4.0
Chile	6.7	India	5.9
Colombia	3.0	Indonesia	4.2
Ecuador	1.8	Iran	3.6
Mexico	3.1	Israel	5.1
Peru	4.7	Malaysia	7.0
Uruguay	3.4	Pakistan	3.7
Venezuela	1.6	Philippines	3.3
		Korea	5.8
		Saudi Arabia	1.5
		Singapore	7.9
		Taiwan	6.4
		Thailand	4.2
		Turkey	3.8

Source: Adapted from United Nations Conference on Trade and Development, *Trade and Development Report*, Geneva: United Nations Conference on Trade and Development, 2003.

almost zero in 1998.[10] There are many reasons for differentials in economic growth among regions. However, the most widely used explanation is economic development policy. Until recently, the economies of Latin America tended to follow import substitution development policies. On the other hand, export promotion policies were more common in Asia. The regions are not homogeneous in this regard and the exceptions to the general tendencies are instructive. Chile has had the highest grow rate in Latin America and has pursued a more export oriented development policy than most of the rest of Latin America. The reverse case is India. India has pursued one of the least open development strategies in Asia and has one of the slower growth rates in the region.

[10]See Chapter 21 for more details on the Asian crisis of the late 1990s.

basics become. For example, intellectual property rights are one of the more important factors in the development of an information technology industry. Second, manufacturing usually is more infrastructure intensive than agriculture. Normally, the development of a sufficient infrastructure to accommodate a growing manufacturing sector will involve the participation of the government. In this regard, it is also important that these services be internationally competitive in both quality and price. Third, the development of the manufacturing sector requires increases in the amount of human capital. The basic development of human capital occurs through widespread public education. Without an efficient provision of educational services by the government, it will be difficult to develop the manufacturing sector. It is important that the government spend an adequate amount on education, but spend it efficiently. It does a low-income country little good to be producing a large number of college graduates if a substantial percentage of the population is illiterate. Fourth, the taxation of industry must be competitive in relation to taxes in competitive countries. However, there is a temptation to set taxes low in order to give domestic firms a competitive advantage in world markets. The risk here is developing that an industry with an "artificial" comparative advantage based on low taxes runs the risk of encountering countervailing duty protection in export markets. Fifth, the government needs to pursue policies that are reasonable with respect to FDI. As shown earlier in the chapter, FDI is important in providing needed funds for investment and transfers of technology. Sixth, the government needs to avoid protectionism to the greatest extent possible. As was shown in Chapters 7 and 8, such policies reduce the standard of living of consumers which is something that needs to be avoided in a poor country. Further, in an environment of scarce capital, a developing country cannot afford to waste capital in comparative disadvantage industries. Finally, the exchange rate needs to be determined primarily by market forces to allow domestic firms to effectively compete in world markets.[11]

If executed properly, an export promotion development strategy has a number of advantages. More resources will flow into the comparative advantage sectors and away from comparative disadvantage sectors. Everything else equal this would tend to increase the rate of economic growth. Faster economic growth increases the rate at

[11]Again, see Chapter 20 for details on exchange rate policy in developing countries.

which new jobs are created. This is particularly important for countries in the stage of economic development where the labor force is growing at a rapid rate. Also, for many developing countries initially manufacturing will be in labor-intensive industries that provide more employment for less skilled workers moving out of the agricultural sector. Second, the policy may give the country a better chance of creating a more favorable balance between exports and imports. A larger volume of exports allows the country to more comfortably import products that it has a comparative disadvantage in. The final word on this development strategy is that it works better than import substitution. The empirical evidence on this issue is at this point virtually overwhelming. Economies developing along the lines of comparative advantage grow faster than economies utilizing policies that tend to distort the structure of the economy.

OFFICIAL DEVELOPMENT ASSISTANCE

official development assistance (ODA) **the transfer of resources from developed countries to developing countries to assist in the process of economic development**

In our previous discussion of economic development, you may have noticed a missing factor. So far we have not discussed the role of the developed countries in assisting the developing countries or what is popularly known as "foreign aid." The technically correct term for resources flowing from the developed to developing countries to assist economic development is **official development assistance (ODA)**. We have omitted official development assistance until now for two reasons. First, economic development is primarily something that is accomplished through the actions of domestic residents and governments. Without properly functioning domestic governments, rapid economic growth is difficult at best. Second, we will see that official development assistance is a small part of the picture of economic development. Resources do flow from the governments of developed countries and international institutions to the developing countries but the total amount of these flows is relatively small.

In the next section, we will consider the role of official development assistance in economic development. From there, the total amount of these transfers and how they are distributed is discussed. In the final section, the role of multilateral development institutions in the world economy is covered.

The Role of Official Development Assistance

Earlier in the chapter, we discussed the role of infrastructure in developing countries. As an economy transitions from a dominant agricultural sector to a more important manufacturing sector, some forms of basic infrastructure become more important. This is particularly true as this type of structural change frequently is accompanied by an increasing degree of urbanization. To accommodate a rising percentage of the population living in urban areas, basic infrastructure becomes more critical. Water systems need to be built to provide adequate supplies of clean water and sanitation. Urban areas need to be able to move large numbers of people around efficiently so roads and transportation systems need to be developed. Efficient supplies of electricity need to be available not only for the growing populations but to support industrial development. In a modern economy, investments must be made in basic information technology and telecommunications.

Needless to say, such investments are not cheap. In many cases the governments of poor countries are hard pressed to be able to afford these investments in the appropriate amounts at the right stage of development. Further, many of these investments require a substantial amount of foreign exchange. These investments may require purchases of expensive equipment manufactured in developed countries. This is where official development assistance can play a valuable role in the process of economic development. Usually, these investments are long run in nature. In this case it would be efficient for governments to finance these investments over long periods of time. However, developing countries typically have small and/or weak internal capital markets that do not easily accommodate this type of borrowing. Even if they exist, the government may still have the problem of obtaining the necessary quantities of foreign exchange.

This is exactly where governments and international institutions can play the most useful role in aiding economic development. The large sums of money needed for infrastructure investment in developing countries is large by the standards of those countries but is not so formidable in terms of a developed country. In the next section, we look at how official development assistance flows from developed to developing countries.

Flows of Official Development Assistance

The flows of official development assistance in the world economy are shown in Table 11.6. The first column shows the major donor countries. The second column shows the absolute amount of official development assistance. The third column shows official development assistance as a percent of the donor countries GDP. This latter number is a rough measure of the "generosity" of the donor countries. First, notice that the 22 countries listed in the table account for approximately $95 billion of official development assistance. In a world economy of $45 trillion, this is not a lot of resources. The simple fact is that official development assistance is not a major factor in economic development. The total is less than 1 percent of the collective GDPs of the developing countries. While the effects may be significant for a particular developing country at a particular point in time, the total amount of ODA is not large relative to the size of the developing countries. From the perspective of the developed countries, the flows are tiny. U.S. ODA is approximately $26 billion out of a GDP of $14 trillion or two-tenths of one percent of GDP. The average of for all developed countries is approximately 0.29 percent.

ODA flows from developed to developing countries take on two general forms. First, the money can move directly from government to government. This transfer can happen in two ways. First, the transfer may be what is known as a *grant*. The money is essentially a gift from the donor country to be used for economic development purposes. The second type of transfer is in the form of a *loan*. This money also is used for economic development purposes, but the principal plus perhaps a small amount of interest must be paid back over a period of years.[12] However, these transfers are often "tied" to the donor country. The donor may specify that the recipient country must use the money for a particular project. Further, there may be conditions that the money must be spent on goods and/or services produced in the donor country. The

[12]Some of these loans may eventually be converted to grants if the recipient country experiences difficulties in repaying the loan.

Table 11.6 Net Official Development Assistance to Developing Countries in 2005

Donor Country	Official Development Assistance ($ Millions)	% of GDP
Australia	$1,449	0.20%
Austria	$1,260	0.41%
Belgium	$1,360	0.37%
Canada	$2,816	0.25%
Denmark	$1,739	0.67%
Finland	$693	0.36%
France	$8,862	0.42%
Germany	$9,236	0.33%
Greece	$207	0.09%
Ireland	$482	0.24%
Italy	$2,686	0.15%
Japan	$17,265	0.38%
Luxembourg	$187	0.51%
Netherlands	$3,529	0.57%
New Zealand	$224	0.20%
Norway	$2,033	0.69%
Portugal	$224	0.12%
Spain	$2,362	0.21%
Sweden	$2,256	0.63%
Switzerland	$1,407	0.38%
United Kingdom	$8,509	0.39%
United States	$25,836	0.21%
Total Assistance	$94,622	0.29%

Source: World Bank, *World Development Indicators,* Washington, D.C.: World Bank, 2007.

donor country has provided ODA but the transfer of the money is not quite as generous as it appears. In some cases, the developing country may end up purchasing goods and/or services that are not completely appropriate due to restrictions on how the money must be spent. Secondly, ODA may take the form of money being transferred from the developed countries to various multilateral development organizations. These organizations then transfer the money or provide services to the developing countries. In the next section we will discuss the activities of some of these institutions.

Multilateral Development Organizations

In this section, we consider the activities of some of the well-known institutions that provide ODA. In the first part of this section, we will cover institutions that primarily loan money for infrastructure projects in developing countries. In the second part of this section, we consider some of the agencies associated with the United Nations that provide services and/or assistance to developing countries.

The World Bank and Regional Development Banks

Headquartered in Washington, D.C., the World Bank is not really one institution but a collection of five closely associated institutions. It was conceived at a conference in Bretton Woods, New Hampshire, in 1944. The heart of the institution is the *International Bank for Reconstruction and Development (IBRD)*. The original purpose of the IBRD was to provide loans for countries to reconstruct from the devastation of World War II. This mission continues today as loans are still made for reconstruction from natural disasters. The main focus of the IBRD today is loans to middle-income countries for specific infrastructure projects. These activities are financed by the World Bank borrowing funds in the world's capital markets at favorable interest rates. This allows creditworthy developing countries to borrow money at a lower rate than would be obtainable if they attempted to go to the capital markets directly. In 2006, total lending amounted to $14.2 billion for 112 new operations in 33 countries.

There are four other institutions in the World Bank Group. The *International Development Association (IDA)* provides no-interest loans to low-income countries for infrastructure. The difference is the source of capital. Money for this lending is provided by periodic infusions from developed countries that are members of the World Bank. These loans focus on very basic types of infrastructure such as water, health care, and education projects. In 2006, total IDA lending was $9.5 billion for 167 operations in 59 countries. The *International Finance Corporation (IFC)* has a fundamentally different mission. The IFC enhances economic development by investing in business opportunities in developing countries that may be underserved without IFC participation. In 2006, the IFC committed $6.7 billion for 284 investment projects in 66 countries. The final two World Bank institutions are involved in promoting FDI. The *Multilateral Investment Guarantee Agency (MIGA)* promotes FDI by providing guarantees to foreign investors for losses that cannot be covered by private sector insurance such as expropriations or civil disturbances. The *International Centre for Settlement of Investment Disputes* helps to encourage FDI by providing a facility for the conciliation and arbitration of investment disputes between companies and host countries.

On balance, the World Bank has been a successful agency for economic development but it has experienced some problems. During the 1980s, it faced difficulties with rescheduling loan repayments from some heavily indebted countries. Additionally, on occasion the Bank was found to be violating its own lending policies. These difficulties led to reforms in the 1990s of internal operations. The most common criticism the World Bank faced in the 1980s and 1990s is that in its lending policies it was not taking the environmental impacts of the projects it was funding into proper consideration. As a result, the World Bank heavily considers the environmental impacts of any proposed project as a part of decisions on which projects to fund. The most recent World Bank initiatives are concerned with funding projects for the governments of developing countries to reduce corruption.

Less well known than the World Bank are three regional development banks in Asia, Africa, and Latin America. These banks are the *Asian Development Bank,* the *African Development Bank,* and the *Interamerican Development Bank,* respectively. They were established in the 1960s to supplement the activities of the World Bank and function much like the IBRD. They use a combination of borrowing from the world capital market and money provided from developed countries to provide project loans to low- and middle-income countries. Since the World Bank is the largest multilateral lending institution, it handles lending for larger development projects. The regional banks are much smaller. However, this gives them the advantage of being able to fund projects on a smaller scale. For example, the Interamerican Development Bank has a program providing lending for microenterprises in developing countries. While not as large or high-profile as the World Bank, these institutions are important in economic development for their respective regions.

The United Nations Agencies

The United Nations (UN) has a large number of agencies that are a part of the larger organization. Many of these agencies at least partially deal with economic development issues. For example, the World Health Organization (WHO) is a leader in the global fight against HIV/AIDS. In this section we will discuss three of these agencies whose primary mission deals with economic development. These agencies are the United Nations Conference on Trade and Development (UNCTAD), the United Nations Industrial Development Organization (UNIDO), and the United Nations Development Program (UNDP). For the most part, these UN agencies do not provide ODA in the form of money. Rather, they provide valuable technical assistance in many areas of economic development.

UNCTAD was established in 1964 to assist the developing countries in the process of integrating into the world economy. This agency is the focal point within the United Nations for issues on international trade and economic development. It provides a forum for discussions among developing countries and between developing countries and developed countries on international trade issues. Headquartered in Geneva, it is well located to provide research, policy analysis, data collection, and technical assistance for developing countries on international trade issues and in international trade negotiations. At several points in this chapter, we have discussed the process of countries developing a manufacturing sector as part of the normal process of economic development. UNIDO is the United Nations agency charged with providing assistance to developing countries during this process. The agency collects data on global industry and provides technical assistance on a large range of issues involved in industrial development. Among the most important issues now addressed by the agency is managing the environmental consequences of rapid industrial development. The final agency considered is the UNDP. Unlike UNCTAD and UNIDO, this UN agency is not primarily concerned with economic issues. Rather, it is concerned with the effects of economic growth on some of the noneconomic aspects of economic development mentioned in the first part of the chapter. It acts as a coordinating agency to supervise the activities of the UN agencies that deal with various economic and noneconomic aspects of economic development.

SUMMARY

1. The economic development of a country can be defined as an increase in a country's standard of living as measured by the country's GDP per capta.
2. There are approximately 145 developing cou tries in the world economy and they contain 85 percent of the world's population. In 2005, GDP per capita in the middle-income

countries was $2,782 per year and for low-income countries GDP per capita is on average about $600 per year.

3. Economic development has many characteristics. However, most of these characteristics are positively correlated with GDP per capita.
4. There are two important preconditions for economic growth: property rights and the rule of law.
5. The economic growth of a country can be enhanced by increasing a country's labor force; increasing its stock of capital; or increasing its level of technology.
6. The theory of economic growth indicates that as the size of the labor force increases, the amount of real GDP an economy can produce increases at a decreasing rate—diminishing returns.
7. Empirical studies indicate that the more open an economy, the faster it grows. In addition, capital flows and technology transfers to developing countries increase a country's rate of economic growth.
8. There are three development strategies used by developing countries with respect to international trade: primary products, import substitution, and export promotion.
9. Developed countries assist the developing countries in their economic development through official development assistance. In 2002, approximately $95 billion in official development assistance flowed into developing countries from developed countries.
10. The World Bank Group and the regional development banks provide loans to low- and middle-income countries for specific projects.
11. The Unitied Nations has several organizations that deal with various economic and non-economic aspects of economic development.

KEY TERMS AND CONCEPTS

- economic development p. 245
- production function p. 252
- total factor productivity p. 255
- primary products p. 258
- import substitution p. 260
- export promotion p. 263
- official development assistance (ODA) p. 266

PROBLEMS AND QUESTIONS FOR REVIEW

1. Explain what the concept economic development means.
2. Describe the distribution of world economic output among low-, middle-, and high-income countries.
3. Describe the preconditions for economic growth.
4. Is an economic freedom index a good proxy for property rights and the rule of law?
5. Graphically show the relationship between GDP and the labor force.
6. What would happen to the production function and GDP if the capital stock changes.
7. Suppose that a war reduces the labor force and destroys part of the capital stock. Show what this would do to GDP.
8. How would FDI cause an increase in GDP?
9. Show how changes in technology enhance economic growth.
10. Using the production function, describe how openness increases economic growth.
11. How are FDI and technology transfers related?
12. Explain how international trade can lead to a transfer of technology.
13. Describe how primary products theoretically can increase the rate of economic growth? Why is this frequently not the case?
14. Why are the prices of primary products frequently unstable?

15. Compare and contrast economic development strategies based on import substitution versus export promotion.
16. Contrast economic development in Latin America and East Asia.
17. Describe what the term official development assistance means. Why is ODA not as important a factor in economic development as it could be?
18. Describe the amount of ODA in the world economy in relation to the collective GDPs of the high-income countries. How does ODA compare with the collective GDPs of the low- and middle-income countries?
19. How does the World Bank assist in the process of economic development?
20. What other institutions perform functions similar to that of the World Bank?
21. How is the UN involved with economic development?

SUGGESTED READINGS AND WEB SITES

Hernando De Soto and June Abbott, *The Other Path: The Economic Answer to Terrorism,* New York: Basic Books, 2002.

An update of De Soto's earlier classic book on the effects of overregulation and taxation on growth in Peru.

David Dollar and Aart Kraay, "Trade, Growth, and Poverty," *Finance & Development* 38(3), September 2001, pp. 16–19.

A very readable article on the issue of openness and growth.

Robert Klitgard, *Tropical Gangsters: One Man's Experience with Development and Decadence in Deepest Africa,* New York: Basic Books, 1991.

Spend a year in a developing country on a World Bank project. A classic story of why development assistance is not always effective.

Organization of Petroleum Exporters (OPEC) (www.opec.org)

The official website of OPEC and a good source of general information on world oil markets.

P. J. O'Rourke, *Eat the Rich,* New York: Atlantic Monthly Press, 1998.

A humorous look at economic development in a number of countries. Although the author is not an economist many of his observations are extremely perceptive.

"That Empty Nest Feeling," *The Economist,* September 8, 2007, pp. 61–62.

Successful middle income countries either no longer need funding from the World Bank or they "graduate" to high-income. As this happens, the World Bank is reevaluating its role in economic development.

World Bank (www.worldbank.org)

The World Bank is a complicated institution. Their web site is a good place to learn more about how the institution works.

Chapter 12

National Income Accounting and the Balance of Payments

"The produce of a country exchanges for the produce of other countries, at such values as are required in order that the whole of her exports may exactly pay for the whole of her imports."
—JOHN STUART MILL

INTRODUCTION

The way in which the trade balance—the difference between exports and imports—is interpreted is not necessarily an accurate assessment of an economy's health. The common opinion is that an excess of imports over exports, a trade deficit, is bad for an economy. On the other hand, an excess of exports over imports, a trade surplus, is considered good economic news. However, this "conventional wisdom" is not necessarily the case, because the trade balance is only a part of a larger economic picture.

In the first part of this chapter, we will briefly review the concept of Gross Domestic Product (GDP) so that you may understand how international trade is an important part of overall economic activity. To clarify the role of imports and exports in an economy, we will also examine the interactions among the various components of GDP. In the first part of the book, we simplified our explanation of international trade by considering only trade in goods and to a lesser degree trade in services. In the second part of this chapter, we will go beyond trade in goods and services by considering a country's balance of payments. Studying the balance of payments for a country will give you a more complete picture of a country's range of interactions with the rest of the world.

There are a number of reasons why the balance of payments is of interest to businesses and government policy makers. First, the balance of payments is an important component of GDP. Changes in the various components of the balance of payments influence the performance of all economies in the short run. For businesses trying to keep track of the performance of the economies in which they do business, information on the balance of payments and its components is important. Second, over time, analyzing the balance of payments of a country will become increasingly important as international trade in goods, services, and capital flows become a larger part of GDP in most countries. As international trade becomes a larger percentage of GDP, it will have a greater impact on the short-run performance of the economy. Also, the larger international trade becomes relative to the rest of the economy, the more business opportunities there are in foreign trade relative to domestic business. Finally, a country's interactions with the world economy can affect not only the country's production of goods and services but also its financial markets. Without an understanding of the balance of payments, the probability of making management errors could rise substantially.

NATIONAL INCOME ACCOUNTING

national income accounting **the process used by governments to keep track of GDP and its components**

National income accounting refers to the calculation of GDP for a country and the subdivision of GDP into various components. Included in the various components of GDP are exports and imports. However, exports and imports cannot be treated in isolation since they are also related to the other components of GDP. Understanding these relationships will make it easier for you to interpret how economic events affect not only international trade but also the overall economy. In the first part of this chapter, we will briefly review some of the issues to consider when calculating GDP. Next, we define the major subcomponents of GDP and then we examine the interactions among the major components of GDP in a way that highlights the role of international trade in a country's economy.

The Measurement of GDP

Recall from Chapter 1 that Gross Domestic Product (GDP) is the market value of all final goods and services that a country produces during a given period of time, usually in a year. In other words, GDP is a measure of a country's total output. This measure of total output is calculated in the country's domestic currency, with each good or service valued at its current market price. Because GDP is such an important statistic, we will spend some time considering how it is calculated. Keep in mind that, first, not every transaction in an economy has to be accounted for, and second, constant changes in prices have to be considered when comparing the output of final goods and services over time in a meaningful way. We will discuss these two factors next.

Items Excluded from GDP

Not every market transaction is included in a country's GDP. First, in our definition of GDP, *final goods and services* means that we count the value of goods and services sold only to end-users. By counting only the final value of the product, we capture the value added by all of the inputs embodied in the good or service. For example, when calculating GDP we count only the final value of cheeseburgers sold at fast-food restaurants. The price of the cheeseburger already contains the value of all of the intermediate goods such as the raw hamburger, the bun, and cheese embodied in the production of the cheeseburger. The result is that we do not have to count the value of the intermediate goods purchased for use as inputs into the production of final goods when calculating GDP.

Second, the calculation of GDP includes only reported market transactions. If a good or service is produced but not sold in the market, it is excluded from GDP. For example, the homemaker who cleans, washes, gardens, shops, and cooks, contributes to the total output of goods and services. Because the homemaker is not paid a market wage for these services, this production is excluded from the calculation of GDP. This means that GDP inherently undercounts the total production of final goods and services in any economy. Third, activities that are not reported for whatever reason (e.g., tax evasion, illegal earnings) are also not included in the calculation of GDP. As a result of these exclusions, a country's GDP is understated and provides a conservative estimate of the country's total economic activity.

GDP and Changes in Prices

real GDP a measure of GDP adjusted for changes in prices

nominal GDP the value of GDP in current dollars

Although GDP uses current prices as a measure of market value, current prices can distort our measure of real output. For example, what would happen to GDP if all prices tripled from one year to the next? This price increase would triple the value of final output. In other words, such a rise in GDP does not mean there is an increase in the quantity of goods and services that the economy produces. To distinguish increases in the quantity of goods and services a country produces from increases in GDP caused by price changes, countries construct a measure of GDP known as **real GDP** that accounts for price level changes. **Nominal GDP** is the market value of final output measured in current prices and real GDP is the value of final output measured in constant prices. When calculating real GDP the market value of goods and services produced in a year is adjusted to account for changing prices.[1] Figure 12.1 illustrates how annual real GDP has changed in the U.S. since 1959. Although real GDP generally rises over time, the rise in real GDP is not uniform and may in fact decline. For example, real GDP declined in 1974, 1975, 1980, 1982, and 1991.

The Components of GDP

Another way of examining the GDP of a country is to consider its various components. GDP can be calculated by summing the different types of expenditures that occur within a country. Thus, it can be represented using the following identity:

$$Y = C + I + G + (X - M)$$

In this relationship, Y represents GDP (total production). C represents the public's consumption of goods and services. This type of expenditure is composed of spending by individuals and families on a daily basis. I represents two types of investment spending. The first type is investment by business firms on equipment, software, structures, and changes in business inventories. The second type of investment spending is spending on housing, which is referred to as residential investment. G represents the purchase of goods and service by state, local, and federal governments. X and M represent

[1]The general formula for computing real GDP for a given base year is:

$$\text{Real GDP in year t} = \frac{\text{(Nominal GDP in year t)}}{\text{(Price Level in year t)}}$$

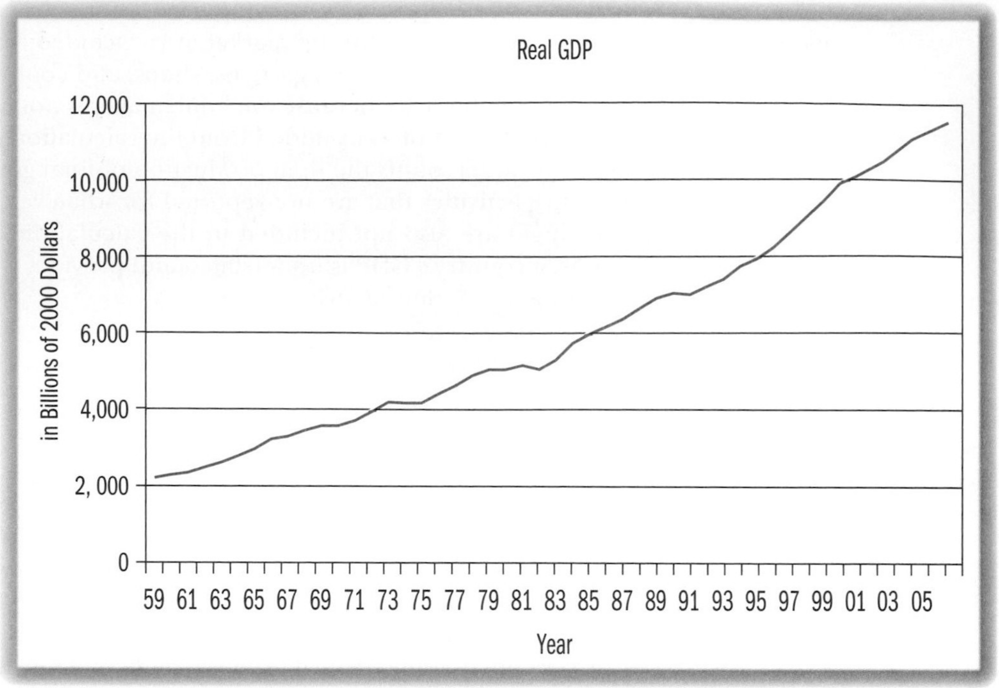

Figure 12.1 Real GDP of the U.S.

Real GDP of has increased since 1959 from approximately $2 trillion to $11 trillion. The rise in real GDP has been periodically interrupted by a decline in real GDP.

Source: Adapted from http://www.bea.gov/national/nipaweb/Index.asp and the *Economic Report of the President*, Washington, DC: U.S. Government Printing Office, 2006.

exports and imports of goods and services, respectively, and net exports is defined as [exports (X) minus imports (M)]. Figure 12.2 shows the four different components of U.S. GDP for 2006. As the figure indicates, public consumption was approximately 71 percent of GDP, and investment and government spending accounted for approximately 17 percent and 18 percent, respectively. Finally, exports minus imports accounted for a negative 6 percent of GDP indicating that the U.S. imported more goods and services than it exported. Although, we illustrate the shares of the four components of U.S. GDP for 2006 in Figure 12.2, it is important to note that the component shares are constantly changing.

Until 1970, the sum of U.S. exports and imports rarely amounted to more than one-tenth of GDP. As Figure 12.3 indicates, since 1970, the real volume of trade has grown at more than twice the rate of output. In other words, the ratios of both X and M to GDP have been rising because exports and imports have been growing faster than GDP. This growth of trade has caused an increase in the share of GDP devoted to exports and imports. By 2006 exports accounted for 11 percent of GDP, and imports were equivalent to 17 percent of GDP. In 1959, exports and imports were both less than 5 percent of GDP. When we speak of the "globalization" of the U.S. economy, we are referring to these growth trends in total imports and exports. In the next section, we examine how the components of GDP interact with one another.

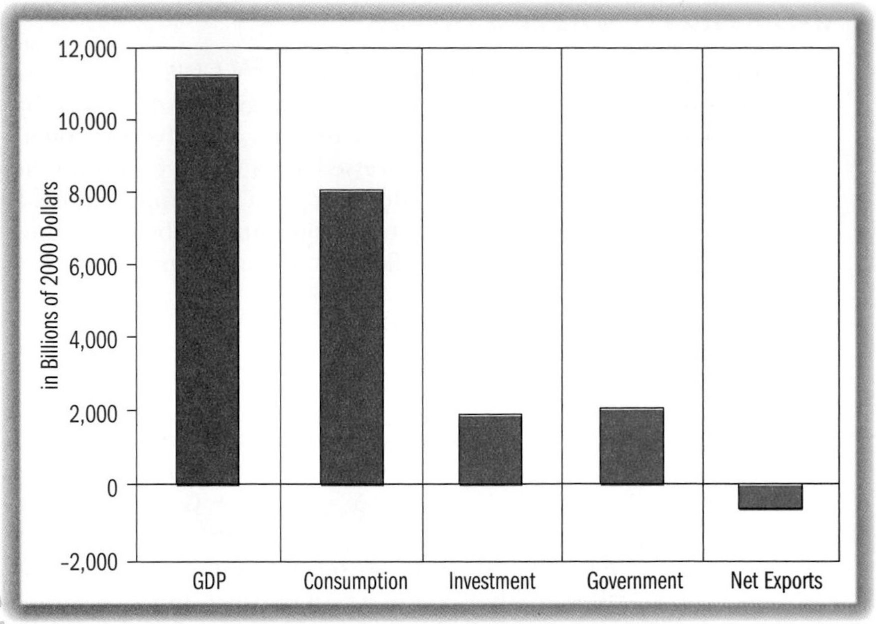

Figure 12.2 U.S. Real GDP and Its Components, 2006

GDP is composed of consumption, investment, government spending on goods and services and net exports (exports minus imports). Countries other than the U.S. may exhibit a somewhat different composition of GDP.

Source: Adapted from http://www.bea.gov/national/nipaweb/Index.asp and the *Economic Report of the President,* Washington, DC: U.S. Government Printing Office, 2006.

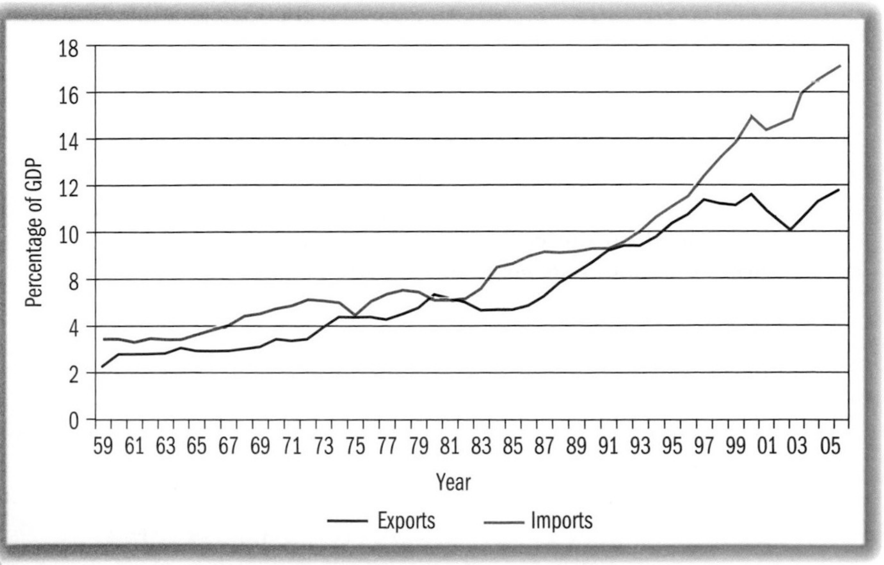

Figure 12.3 Real Exports and Imports as a Percentage of GDP

U.S. imports and exports as a percentage of GDP have increased over time. This data defines the increasing openness of the U.S. economy.

Source: Adapted from http://www.bea.gov/national/nipaweb/Index.asp and the *Economic Report of the President,* Washington, DC: U.S. Government Printing Office, 2006.

GDP AND THE TRADE BALANCE

Now that we have examined the components of GDP, we can consider how they interact with one another. In order to do this, we begin our discussion by analyzing how these components add up to GDP. Because the sum of all the components of GDP must equal GDP, the relationship can be expressed as an identity. This will help us to more clearly see the role of international trade in an open economy. Exports and imports are just a part of total economic activity (GDP) but putting them together simultaneously with the other components of GDP allows us to understand their role as a part of the total.

GDP in a Closed Economy

In a closed economy, firms must use any final good or service that individuals do not consume or the government does not purchase to produce new plant and equipment. The easiest way to express this for a closed economy (an economy that does not trade) is:

$$Y = C + I + G$$

where Y or GDP equals the sum of consumption, investment, and government spending. This equation holds in a closed economy because we have assumed that the public or government consumed and/or the business sector invested all output.

GDP in an Open Economy

To make the equation $Y = C + I + G$ work in an open economy, we have to allow for international trade. Consumers in an open economy may buy imported goods and services, so we subtract the value of imports from total domestic spending. In addition, foreign consumers may devote part of their income to the consumption of exported goods and services. So we need to add the value of exports to total domestic spending. To change the economy from a closed economy to an open economy, we add exports and subtract imports. Thus, GDP for an open economy is:

$$Y = C + I + G + (X - M)$$

This equation shows that GDP in an open economy is equal to the sum of consumption, investment, government spending and the trade balance. Since the trade balance is equal to the sum of exports and imports, there are three possibilities. It is possible, though not likely, that exports and imports would exactly match, making net exports zero. For most countries, there is a mismatch between the value of exports and imports. When a country's exports are greater than its imports, the country has a trade surplus and when imports are greater than exports, the country has a trade deficit.

Imports, Exports, and GDP

There is another way to look at how the difference between exports and imports is related to GDP in an open economy. To illustrate this, we can rearrange the open economy GDP identity to yield:

$$X - M = Y - C - I - G$$

Table 12.1 GDP for Alpha and Beta in Billions of Dollars

Country	GDP	C	I	G	X−M
Alpha	$11,319	$8,044	$1,920	$1,981	$−626
Beta	4,269	2,423	1,028	764	53

This equation highlights net exports for a country. It illustrates that exports minus imports are equal to GDP for a country minus its consumption, investment, and government spending. As such, this equation illustrates that a country's trade deficit or surplus is essentially the difference between what is produced in a country versus what is consumed. Remember, Y is the total output of final goods and services in an economy. This total output is the amount of goods and services that is available for individuals and the government to consume or for firms to invest. The sum of C, I, and G represents the domestic demand for goods and services by the various sectors in the economy. What happens if the domestic demand for goods and services is larger than the economy is capable of producing? The equation tells the story. The economy would have to import the difference from other countries. This would produce a trade deficit, as imports would exceed exports. The reverse would be true if the economy were producing more goods and services than are consumed domestically. Exports would exceed imports and result in a trade surplus. An example of these relationships is given in Table 12.1. Suppose that Y, the total output of country Alpha is $11,319 billion. Further, suppose that domestic spending C, I, and G are $8,044 billion, $1,920 billion, and $1,981 billion, respectively.[2] The sum of C, I, and G is $10,945 billion, which is larger than total domestic production of $11,319 billion. When this occurs, it must be true that (X − M) is a negative number. In this case, the trade balance of this country would be –$626 billion.

In other words, when domestic output (Y) is smaller than the sum of C, I, and G (total domestic spending), then a country is consuming more goods and services than it has produced. If this is occurring, then a country must borrow the difference from other countries. As a result, the country with a trade deficit must be increasing its indebtedness to other countries. The trade balance, X − M, is a *flow variable,* which means that it occurs over a period of time such as one year. The amount of debt a country has is a *stock variable,* which means it can be added to or subtracted from. In the case of a trade deficit the country is adding to its stock of debt to the rest of the world. There is not necessarily anything wrong with a trade deficit and the associated increased indebtedness; it is just a description of the mismatch between domestic production and domestic consumption.

Now, consider a country where total domestic output (Y) is larger than the sum of C, I, and G (domestic spending). Let's look at the equation:

$$X - M = Y - C - I - G$$

[2]With some rounding these figures are close to actual figures for the U.S. economy for 2006.

Selling the Back Forty

The phrase "selling the back forty" comes from an old story about a farmer and his family. The farmer is relatively well off and owns a fair amount of land. However, the farmer has had a bad year. The crop was poor and the farm's income will not support the family's consumption for the next year. The farmer faces an uncomfortable choice. He can either reduce his family's standard of living for the next year or sell a part of his land—the back forty acres, that have not been productive. The earnings from this sale would enable the family to maintain its standard of living in hopes of a better crop next year.

For nearly 20 years the U.S. has been living much like the farmer. It has been consuming more than it is producing—and importing the difference. These net imports have to be paid for, so U.S. residents have been selling real and financial property to foreigners. Because the stock of assets in the U.S. is so large, the country can sustain the selling. A farmer could not do this for long, but a country is not a farm. If a country's income and/or assets are rising faster than its debt, then running a trade deficit is a viable way of managing the economy. It may not feel as good as continually running surpluses, but it is sustainable.

The country must have a trade surplus—exports must be larger than imports. In this case, the extra production shows up as a trade surplus—the country "lends" the difference to foreigners. As a result, the country with a trade surplus must be reducing its indebtedness or accumulating more claims on foreign countries. Again, the main point is that a country's trade surplus is not really reflecting anything more profound than a mismatch between domestic production and domestic consumption.

We can see an example of this by considering country Beta in Table 12.1. Domestic production (Y) for this country is larger than the sum of domestic spending (C, I, and G), so country Beta will have a trade surplus.[3] Given the two countries in Table 12.1, which country is better off? There is a tendency to believe that surpluses are inherently good and deficits are inherently bad, so it is logical to assume that the country with a trade surplus is clearly better off. However, the answer to the question is not quite that simple, as we will illustrate next.

Intertemporal Trade

When a country has a trade deficit, it is consuming more than it is producing. Whether a deficit (or surplus for that matter) is good for a country depends on several factors. Generally, one of the purposes of economic activity is to provide a higher standard of living for the country's residents. In part, a higher standard of living is measured by the amount of goods and services residents consume. When a country has a trade deficit in a given year, it has consumed more than it produced during that year. Production and consumption should balance over the long run, but they do not need to balance every year. If a country has a trade deficit, it is *importing present consumption.* At some future point in time, it will have to pay for the deficit by producing more than it consumes

[3]The numbers for Beta are approximations for the GDP of Japan in 2006.

which will produce a trade surplus. When this occurs the country will be exporting future consumption. Thus, a trade deficit is the process of importing present consumption coupled with exporting future consumption. This trading of consumption and production over longer periods of time is known as **intertemporal trade**. In our example, Alpha has chosen to consume more now and less sometime in the future.

intertemporal trade countries trading production for consumption at different points in time

A country with a trade surplus is currently producing more output than it is consuming. As such, this country is *exporting present consumption* to other countries. At some point in the future the residents of the country will be able to run a trade deficit and import consumption. The result is that a country with a trade surplus is exporting current consumption and importing future consumption. Viewed in this manner, trade imbalances simply denote a country's preferences for present versus future consumption. These preferences are expressed as the result of the choices that consumers, the government, and businesses make on a daily basis.

Saving, Investment, the Government Budget, and the Trade Balance

So far we have examined total domestic spending and its relationship to total output. However, we can rearrange the relationship of GDP and its components for an open economy in a way that lets us further explore the relationship between net exports and the rest of the economy. Up to this point, we have been using GDP to measure a country's total final output. GDP also measures a country's total income. This stream of income goes to the factors of production in the form of rent, wages, interest, and profits. The public in turn spends this income on goods and services. As such, money moves in a circular flow from businesses to the public and back again.

leakages of income forms of income that are withdrawn from the circular flow of income (e.g., savings, taxes, and imports)

Although a country's total income equals GDP, not all of society's total income is immediately spent on goods and services. Some income is temporarily withdrawn from this circular flow. This income which is not spent on goods and service is referred to as **leakages** from the circular flow. There are three sources of leakages from the circular flow. First, residents of the country may choose to save a portion of their current income. This saving (S) represents a withdrawal of spending on goods and services. Second, like saving, government taxes (T) involve using part of the economy's income for purposes other than consumption by the public. Finally, imports (M) represent reduced spending on domestically produced goods and services.

injections of income additions to the circular flow of income that are not derived from current income (e.g., investment, government spending, and exports)

These outflows from the circular flow, however, do not disappear from the economy. Businesses, government, and foreigners engage in activities that inject the spending back into the circular flow. These activities can be thought of as **injections** into the circular flow. Investment (I) represents investment goods to businesses along with investment in housing. Investment represents the way in which savings is put back into the circular flow. For example, banks perform the function of accepting savings from the public that may be loaned to businesses and/or the housing sector. A second injection of spending in an economy is the amount of government spending (G) on final goods and services. Government spending does not include spending in the form of transfer payments.[4] Again, government spending is the way taxes are re-injected into

[4]Transfer payments are included in the economy in the form of consumption.

the economy. The last injection of spending into the economy is foreigners' purchases of domestically produced goods and services—exports (X). The injection of exports replaces the leakage of imports.

For any economy the sum of the leakages from the circular flow must equal the sum of the injections into the circular flow: Therefore,

$$S + T + M = G + I + X$$

In this equation the sum of saving, taxes, and imports will equal the sum of government spending, investment, and exports. However, saving (S) will not necessarily equal investment (I); government taxes (T) will not necessarily equal government spending (G); and exports (X) will not necessarily equal imports (M). This allows us to rearrange the terms to highlight the trade balance:

$$X - M = S - I + T - G$$

In this case, the trade balance becomes the mismatch between private saving (S), government saving (T − G), and investment (I). When the leakages from spending (S + T) are greater than the injections of spending (G + I), then the trade balance (X − M) will be positive. When the sum of saving and taxes is less than the sum of government spending and investment, the trade balance (X − M) will be negative. This equation illustrates that the trade balance is just the difference between the sum of leakages from spending (S + T) and injections to spending (G + I) within the economy.

Examining trade imbalances (X − M) in this manner gives us another way of looking at what causes trade imbalances. For example, consider a country with a trade deficit. A trade deficit indicates that the country's economy has an excess of domestic spending compared to domestic production. To reduce the trade imbalance, the country could produce more goods and services than it consumes. In the short run, increasing total production past some point is not very easy to do. This maximum level of production of goods and services in any economy is difficult to alter in the short run. Reducing the trade deficit in the short run requires that the country reduce domestic spending.

Adjustments to Trade Imbalances

What the leakage and injection approach indicates is that a country with a trade deficit or surplus has four potential adjustments in the leakages and injections that can be made to reduce the imbalance. Let us examine each of these adjustments listed in Table 12.2. In the table, adjustments to deficits or surpluses are given in the first and second columns, respectively. Keep in mind that these adjustments are not mutually exclusive. Most of the time, the adjustment to a trade imbalance involves movements in more than one of the leakages and/or injections at the same time.

First, everything else being equal, increasing the level of saving would tend to reduce the trade deficit. As the level of savings increases on the right hand side of the equation, there would have to be a change in X − M on the left side of the equation. For example, in the U.S., personal saving as a share of income averaged approximately 9 percent during the 1970s. The average saving rate fell to approximately 6 percent

Table 12.2 Potential Adjustments to Reduce Trade Imbalances

Country Has a Trade	
Deficit	**Surplus**
Increase Private Savings	Decrease Private Savings
Or	Or
Increase Government Taxes	Decrease Government Taxes
Or	Or
Decrease Business Investment	Increase Business Investment
Or	Or
Decrease Government Spending	Increase Government Spending

during the 1980s, fell to approximately 5 percent during the 1990s, and has fallen to approximately 2 percent in the first half of the 2000s. This decline in the national saving rate has contributed to the U.S. trade deficit. For this and other reasons, the U.S. government would like to see an increase in the private savings rate. This is a difficult change in policy for the government to implement, because it is not completely clear how to use government policy to increase the amount of saving. The other side of saving is consumption. Increasing saving and decreasing consumption are opposite sides of the same coin, and an increase in saving (a decrease in consumption) would tend to reduce the size of a trade deficit.

A second adjustment to reduce a trade deficit would be to change the level of investment. If investment spending falls with no change in savings or the government budget, the trade balance would tend to become smaller. However, there is a potential cost involved in terms of long-run economic growth. As we discussed in Chapter 11, an increase in investment tends to increase real GDP. As a result, reducing the level of investment to reduce a trade deficit is not something that economic policy makers generally advocate. The short-run solution of decreasing investment spending might cause long-run economic growth to decline, so the cure to the trade deficit may be worse than the deficit itself. Increasing the level of investment spending relative to savings may worsen the trade deficit, but it may also improve a country's economic growth.

A third adjustment to reduce the trade deficit would be to increase taxes. Increasing taxes without increasing government spending would either reduce the government budget deficit or produce a government surplus. As a result, increasing taxes would either reduce the amount government has to borrow or reduce any previously accumulated government debt. Increasing taxes without increasing government spending is similar to an increase in the level of saving. In this case, the means of increasing the level of saving is clear. This would tend to reduce a trade deficit in the same manner as increasing the level of savings.

Changing government spending is a fourth potential adjustment. Reducing the level of government spending would tend to reduce the trade deficit, and reducing government spending in conjunction with raising taxes has the potential to reduce the trade deficit to a greater extent than either policy used in isolation. Further, this combination of strategies avoids the uncertainties of increasing the private saving rate and the undesirability of reducing investment.

The second column of Table 12.2 outlines the possible adjustments for a country with a persistent trade surplus. These are the opposite of the adjustments involved in reducing a deficit. Decreasing the level of savings would tend to reduce a trade surplus. This makes sense as the alternative to saving is consumption. If the public saves less it will tend to spend more on both domestic and foreign goods and services. An increase in investment would also tend to reduce a trade surplus. Such an increase both reduces a trade imbalance and increases the economy's long-run growth potential. The public sector can also take actions to reduce a trade surplus. Increasing the level of government spending and/or reducing taxes would tend to either reduce a government budget surplus or increase the size of the deficit. Government budget decisions will not automatically reduce a trade surplus but they can influence it.

As the first part of the chapter has shown, trade deficits or surpluses are a function of macroeconomic imbalances. Persistent trade imbalances are not the result of the usual list of suspects such as unfair foreign competition and high trade barriers in foreign markets. These factors tend to have an influence on trade in particular industries but little, if any, effect on a country's overall trade balance. The purpose of the next section is to explain the details of the inflows and outflows of money in a country.

Macroeconomic Imbalances in the EU, Japan, and the U.S.

A country's total outflows of income will equal its total injections of spending. Another way of looking at this is to show that saving is equal to investment *plus* the government budget deficit or surplus *plus* the trade balance:

$$S = I + (G - T) + (X - M)$$

Table 12.3 shows the workings of this equation for the U.S., Japan, and the EU over three time periods 1978–1980, 1988–1990, and 2000–2002. The table reveals several similarities and differences among the three countries. In all three, private saving and private domestic investment declined from one period to the next. However, for the U.S. in the second two periods, an increase in foreign borrowing financed the increase in the government deficit—a trade deficit.

For Japan, each period is different. In the first period, the excess of saving over investment financed the large government deficit. In the second period the government budget was in surplus, and the excess of saving over investment was sent abroad as foreign investment. Finally, in the third period the excess of saving over investment was large enough to finance a large government deficit and to be sent abroad as foreign investment.

In the EU, the analysis is simpler. In all three periods there were large government deficits coupled with small amounts of foreign investment. A large excess of saving over investment created this situation. Notice that only the U.S. has a rough equality between saving and investment.

Table 12.3 Relationship Between Savings, Investment, the Government Balance, and Trade Balance

Country	Time Period	S	I	(G – T)	(X – M)
U.S.	1978–1980	17.6	17.1	0.4	–0.1
	1988–1990	16.6	14.8	3.2.	–1.4
	2000–2002	18.4	21.6	0.7	–4.0
Japan	1978–1980	36.5	31.7	4.9	–0.1
	1988–1990	33.6	33.1	–1.6	2.1
	2000–2002	26.7	17.4	6.9	2.5
EU	1978–1980	26.6	22.1	4.2	0.3
	1988–1990	21.7	17.6	4.2	–0.2
	2000–2002	23.6	20.9	2.2	0.5

(All Figures are Percentages of GDP).
Source: OECD, *Economic Outlook,* Paris: OECD, December 2003.

THE BALANCE OF PAYMENTS ACCOUNTS

balance of payments a summary of all the international transactions of a country's residents with the rest of the world during a year

balance on current account an accounting of international transactions that includes goods, services, investment income, and unilateral transfers

Just as a country's national income accounts keep track of GDP, savings, investment, taxes, and government spending, so does a country's **balance of payments** accounts keep track of its international transactions. The balance of payments includes a number of different accounts. The balance of payments is composed of the **balance on current account**, the **balance on financial account**, and the **balance on capital account**. The balance on current account is a record of transactions that includes payments for goods, services, and other items described below. The balance on financial account is a record of transactions that includes payments related to financial assets such as bonds. It also includes transactions involving the sale or acquisition of foreign nonfinancial assets like land. The balance on capital account is a record of other activities resulting in transfers of wealth between countries. This includes nonmarket international asset transfers including debt forgiveness and the transfer of bank accounts by foreign citizens when immigrating to the U.S.

At the most basic level, the balance of payments is a record of all economic transactions derived from the exchange of goods, services, income, and assets between residents of one country and the rest of the world. The balance of payments accounts record the total inflows and outflows of money (dollars) to and from foreign countries. The inflows and outflows are relatively large for the U.S. Indeed, tracking every dollar would be impossible. One needs to keep in mind that the balance of payments statistics for the U.S. or any country are a rough approximation of the magnitude of these flows rather than a precise number resulting from a precise accounting system. Although we are using the term *accounting* in association with the balance of payments, in this context the term means something very different from the way that accountants use the term. As a result, our first objective is to describe the terminology in the balance of payments statement. Our second objective is to ascertain what a country's

balance on financial account records the difference between the holdings of foreign assets by domestic residents and domestic assets by foreign residents

balance on capital account records that changes in the holding of nonfinancial assets including debt forgiveness and assets of immigrants

balance of payments accounts tell us about the country's domestic economy. As we will show, one can learn a lot about a country's economy from analyzing its balance of payments statement.

The Balance on Current Account

Table 12.4 shows a summary of the balance of payments statistics for the U.S. in the year 2006. The first two rows in the table are merchandise exports and merchandise imports. Notice that the former is a positive number while the latter is a negative number. This is because merchandise exports create an inflow of dollars (money) as other countries pay for U.S. goods. On the other hand merchandise imports create an outflow of dollars (money) as the U.S. pays for foreign-produced goods. The principle that inflows are recorded as a positive number and outflows as a negative number holds true for the rest of the items in the balance of payments. When the U.S. sells goods, services, or assets to foreigners, these sales create an inflow of dollars (money) and a plus sign is attached to the number. The reverse occurs, when the U.S. buys foreign goods, services, or assets, as the purchases create an outflow of dollars (money) and a negative sign is attached to the number.

Table 12.4 U.S. International Transactions, 2006 ($ billions)

Current Account transactions		
Exports of Merchandise	$1,023.1	
Imports of Merchandise	−1,861.4	
Balance of Trade (Goods)		−838.3
Exports of Services	422.6	
Imports of Services	−342.8	
Balance on Services		79.7
Balance on Goods & Service		−758.5
Income Receipts on U.S. Assets Abroad	650.5	
Income Payments of Foreign Assets in the U.S.	−613.8	
Balance on Investment Income		36.6
Balance on Goods, Services, and Income		−721.9
Unilateral Transfers, Net	−89.6	
Balance on Current Account		−811.5
Capital Account transactions, net		−3.9
Financial Account Transactions		−1,055.2
Change in U.S. Owned Assets Abroad		
U.S. Official Reserve Assets	2.4	
U.S. Government Assets, Other than Official Reserve	5.3	
U.S. Private Assets	−1,062.9	
Change in Foreign Owned Assets in the U.S.		1,859.6
Foreign Official Assets	440.3	
Foreign Private Assets	1,419.3	
Balance on Financial Account		804.4
Statistical Discrepancy		−17.8

Source: http://www.bea.gov/newsreleases/international/transactions/.

merchandise trade balance the difference between exports and imports of goods

The difference between merchandise exports ($1,023.1 billion) and imports (–$1,861.4 billion) yields the **merchandise trade balance**. As Table 12.4 indicates the U.S. had a merchandise trade deficit of–$838.3 billion. In 2006, the U.S. was a net importer of merchandise (goods), which means that merchandise imports were larger than exports. As column 2 in Table 12.5 indicates, the U.S. had a merchandise trade surplus for the three years indicated in the 1960s. In the early 1970s, the U.S. had a merchandise trade deficit. Over time this deficit has become larger as merchandise imports have grown at a faster rate than merchandise exports.

Merchandise trade does not represent all of the inflows and outflows of dollars to and from the economy. The next three rows of Table 12.4 summarize the international service flows. U.S. citizens traveling overseas take dollars out of the U.S. (outflow). When foreign citizens travel to Disney World, they bring their currency into the U.S. (inflow). We do not think of travel expenses or tourism as imports and exports, but they are because they create outflows and inflows of dollars. In addition, some companies are engaged in the provision of services across national borders. These companies

Table 12.5 Summary of U.S. International Transactions ,1964–2006 ($ billions)

Year	Merchandise Trade Balance	Service Balance	Goods and Service Balance	Investment Income Balance	Unilateral Transfers Balance	Current Account Balance
1964	6.8	–.8	6.0	5.0	–4.2	6.8
1966	3.8	–.9	2.9	5.0	–5.0	3.0
1968	.6	–.4	.3	6.0	–5.6	.6
1970	2.6	–.3	2.3	6.2	–6.2	2.3
1972	–6.4	1.0	–5.4	8.2	–8.5	–5.8
1974	–5.5	1.2	–4.3	15.5	–9.2	2.0
1976	–9.5	3.4	–6.1	16.1	–5.7	4.3
1978	–33.9	4.2	–29.8	20.4	–5.8	–15.1
1980	–25.5	6.1	–19.4	30.1	–8.3	2.3
1982	–36.5	12.3	–24.2	35.2	–16.5	–5.5
1984	–112.5	3.4	–109.1	35.1	–20.3	–94.3
1986	–145.1	6.6	–138.5	15.5	–24.1	–147.2
1988	–127.0	12.4	–114.6	18.7	–25.3	–121.2
1990	–111.0	30.1	–80.9	28.6	–26.7	–79.0
1992	–96.9	57.7	–39.2	24.2	–35.1	–50.1
1994	–165.8	667.3	–98.5	17.1	–40.3	–121.6
1996	–191.0	86.9	–104.1	22.3	–43.0	–124.8
1998	–248.2	82.1	–166.1	4.3	–53.2	–215.1
2000	–454.7	74.9	–379.8	21.1	–58.6	–417.4
2002	–485.0	61.2	–423.70	27.7	–63.6	–459.6
2004	–669.6	57.5	–612.1	56.4	–84.4	–640.1
2006	–838.3	79.7	–758.5	36.6	–89.6	–811.5

Source: U.S. Department of Commerce, *Survey of Current Business,* Washington, D.C.: U.S. Government Printing Office, selected issues.

may be compensated for these services in the form of fees. For example, an accounting firm's principal activity may be the sale of professional services. If some of these sales occur in other countries, this would create an inflow of money into the country. In other cases, individuals or companies may be receiving payments in the form of royalties or licensing fees for the sale of intellectual property. These sorts of payments must be accounted for as they create inflows and outflows of money. In 2006, service exports of $422.6 billion included travel and transportation services the U.S. provided to foreigners, and fees and royalties the U.S. received from foreigners. U.S. imports of these services from other countries amounted to –$342.8 billion. The **balance on services**, the difference between exports and imports of services was $79.7 billion in. This positive balance indicates that the U.S. had a surplus in services. As column 3 in Table 12.5 shows, the U.S. consistently has a surplus service balance, and this surplus has grown over time.

balance on services the difference between exports and imports of services

Combining the surplus of the service balance with the merchandise trade deficit yields the **balance on goods and services** of –$758.5 billion. This deficit indicates that the U.S. transferred fewer goods and services to other countries than it received from them in 2006. Column 4 in Table 12.5 lists the balance on goods and services for the U.S. from 1964–2006. The U.S. had a surplus balance on goods and services for the years indicated in the 1960s, and beginning in the early 1970s, this surplus changed into a deficit for the U.S.

balance on goods and services the difference between exports and imports of both goods and services

The U.S. Department of Commerce reports the balance on goods and services (monthly) and it is widely reported in the business media. However, monthly trade statistics should be viewed cautiously for two reasons. First, as we will see, this balance does not count all of the international inflows and outflows. Second, these monthly statistics are quite volatile. A large change in the balance on goods and services from one month to the next really does not mean much, as one month of data does not constitute a trend.

balance on investment income the difference between income earned on foreign assets and payments to foreign residents on their assets

The next section of Table 12.4 shows the inflows and outflows of money associated with U.S. investment in other countries and foreign investment in the U.S. Over the years, U.S. citizens have invested a substantial amount of money abroad in real and financial assets. As we discussed in Chapter 6, investments in real assets are called foreign direct investment (FDI). FDI by firms or individuals generates a stream of profits that eventually will be repatriated back to the U.S. Financial investments by U.S. residents overseas also yield a stream of interest payments, dividend payments, and capital gains—all of which we call "receipts." These receipts are recorded as income receipts on U.S. assets abroad. This is recorded as a positive number because it is an inflow of money to the U.S.

balance on goods, services, and income the summation of the merchandise trade balance, the balance on services, and the balance on investment income

The other side of investment income is payments to foreigners on their assets in the U.S. Again, these payments are recorded as a negative number, as the payments go to citizens or firms in foreign countries. The net of the receipts and payments can create a positive or negative number for the **balance on investment income**, the difference between income earned on foreign assets and payments to foreign residents on their assets. In 2006, the U.S. had a balance on investment income of $36.6 billion. Row 5 in Table 12.5 shows the U.S. investment income balance since 1964. This balance for the U.S. was in surplus from 1964 through 2006. The reasons for the change in this balance are outlined below. Combining the surplus of the balance on investment income with the deficit of the balance on goods and services yields a **balance on goods, services, and income** of –$721.9 billion.

unilateral transfers grants or gifts extended to or received from other countries

The next item in the balance of payments statements is **unilateral transfers**. Unilateral transfers are the inflows and outflows from the U.S. where there are no services rendered. Unilateral transfers include U.S. government pensions paid to U.S. residents living abroad and economic and military grants to foreign countries. In addition, U.S. residents create part of the outflow when they send money overseas to support family members or as part of nongovernmental charitable activities. Conversely, there are also analogous inflows of money into the U.S. Because more U.S. residents make such transfers to foreigners than do foreigners to U.S. residents, the U.S. consistently has a negative unilateral transfers balance. As Table 12.4 shows, the net of unilateral transfers to and from foreigners was –$89.6 billion in 2006. Adding unilateral transfers to the balance on goods, services, and income yields the balance on current account. As Table 12.4 shows, the U.S. had a current account deficit of –$811.5 billion. For the U.S. economy this means that outflows of money related to trade in goods and services, investment income, and unilateral transfers were smaller than the inflows of money. For all countries, this balance is the most comprehensive view of a country's total trade flows. Unfortunately, there is a tendency to confuse the current account balance with either the merchandise trade balance or the balance on goods and services. The case of the U.S. in 1980 is a prime example of this kind of potential confusion. In that year, the U.S. had a deficit in its merchandise trade balance. However, it also had a surplus in investment income that more than made up for the deficit in merchandise trade. Did the U.S. have a current account surplus or deficit in that year? It had a current account surplus: the total inflow of money on trade in goods and services plus investment income and unilateral transfers was greater than the total of outflows.

If the current account balance gives a much better picture of a country's international trade than does the balance on goods and services, why doesn't it receive more public attention? For the U.S., part of the problem is how the numbers are reported. The Department of Commerce reports the balance on goods and services monthly and the information receives some notice in the media. However, the current account balance is reported quarterly with the GDP statistics. Quite understandably the focus of the press release is on what has happened to GDP in the previous quarter and the information on the current account balance is much less widely reported.[5] While the monthly balance on goods and services statistics are of some interest to economists, the government, and the business community, the quarterly reporting of the current account balance is a better indicator of the country's trade position.

The Balance on Capital and Financial Accounts

Even though the current account balance is the most important part of the balance of payments, it is still only a part. We have not covered all possible transfers of dollars into and out of the U.S. For instance, what if a U.S. citizen buys a foreign asset? Suppose that a U.S. company purchases land and builds a manufacturing plant in Mexico. Would this transaction be recorded in the current account balance? The answer is no, because a manufacturing plant is not an import. You cannot move the plant from Mexico to the U.S. The reverse is also true. When foreigners purchase U.S. assets, these transactions

[5]The situation is somewhat analogous to the CPI and the GDP deflator. The latter is a much better price index. However, it is reported quarterly and gets less notice than the rate of growth of GDP.

change in assets abroad the change in the total amount of assets that domestic residents own

official reserve assets government holdings of gold or foreign currency used to acquire foreign assets

special drawing rights (SDRs) a form of international money created by the International Monetary Fund

International Monetary Fund (IMF) a multilateral agency created in 1946 to promote international monetary stability and cooperation

are not recorded in the current account. Such transactions include both FDI and purchases of financial assets such as bonds. These transactions are recorded in what is known as the financial account. The same is true of many governmental transactions. If the U.S. government purchases property in a foreign country, this is a capital account transaction. Something similar occurs when central banks buy or sell foreign exchange. All of these transactions are recorded in a country's capital or financial accounts.

The capital account in Table 12.4 shows the net of capital account transactions. Capital transactions are inflows and outflows of money associated with certain types of nonfinancial assets. These include debt forgiveness and the assets that immigrants bring into the country and emigrants take out of the country. In 2006, the net of these capital transactions was $3.9 billion. This represents a net outflow of money from the U.S. and enters the balance of payments with a negative sign. If we add the current account balance to the capital account balance, we find that the U.S. has an excess of outflows over inflows of –$815.4 billion. Since overall outflows and inflows of money must balance, the –$815.4 billion outflow must be matched by a $815.4 billion inflow in the bottom part of the of the balance of payments statement, the financial account.

Table 12.4 shows the transactions included in the financial account. This measures the difference between purchases of assets abroad by the U.S. and sales of U.S. assets to foreigners. Below the financial account is the **change in assets abroad**. This item totals all of the purchases of foreign assets that U.S. citizens and the U.S. government made during a year. It shows up as a negative number because these transactions create an outflow of money (dollars) as U.S. citizens receive the assets and foreign citizens receive the money. These purchases have risen dramatically, from less than $100 billion in 1980 to $1,055.2 billion in 2006. This rise consisted of an increase of $1,062.9 billion in U.S. private assets abroad and a decrease of $7.7 billion in U.S. government assets.

Changes in government assets are composed of the U.S. government's acquisition of assets abroad and changes in the amount of **U.S. official reserve assets**. These are assets that the government uses to buy and sell foreign currencies or foreign assets. Official reserve assets include gold, foreign currency holdings of the central bank, and **Special Drawing Rights (SDRs)**. SDRs are official reserve assets that are traded among the world's central banks. The **International Monetary Fund (IMF),** a multilateral agency created in 1946 to promote international monetary stability and cooperation, creates and distributes these reserves to member countries based on the countries' relative importance in international trade.

The next item in the capital account is the **change in foreign assets**. This item records all of the purchases of U.S. assets by foreigners and foreign central banks. It is a positive number, indicating that these transactions create an inflow of money (dollars) from abroad as U.S. citizens receive the money and the foreign citizens receive the assets. In 1980, foreigners purchased roughly $50.3 billion in U.S. assets. In 2006, foreigners purchased $1,859.6 billion in U.S. assets. This included an increase of $1,419.3 billion in the stock of U.S. assets that foreign residents held and an increase of $440.3 billion in the stock of U.S. assets that foreign governments and central banks held. The balance on financial account records the net of inflows and outflows for all financial account transactions. In 2006, the U.S. capital account balance was in surplus by $804.4 billion.

The final item in the balance of payments accounts, statistical discrepancy, captures any net inflows or outflows that the U.S. government failed to record. The U.S. government knows it failed to record some transactions when the total inflows and

change in foreign assets the change in the amount of assets in a country that foreign residents own

outflows of dollars (money) are not equal. In 2006 unrecorded (or misrecorded) international transactions generated a statistical discrepancy of $17.8 billion.[6] The current account balance was in deficit by $811.5 billion, the capital account was in deficit by $3.9 and the financial account was in surplus by $804.4 billion. Obviously, the U.S. government missed some of the international flows. However, the government has no way of knowing which flows it missed—goods, services, investment income, unilateral transfers, or capital. To make the balance of payments balance, we use the statistical discrepancy to force these inflows and outflows to be equal.

"Dark Matter" in the U.S. Balance of Payments

For the last 30 years the U.S. has had uninterrupted current account deficits. From the discussion above, you know what that means. A country with a current account deficit must somehow finance this deficit with a surplus in the capital/financial account. However, a surplus in the capital/financial account means that a country is borrowing from the rest of the world. The cost of this borrowing eventually shows up back in the current account. It is accounted for in Income Payments on Foreign Assets in the U.S. One would assume that if a country was a net borrower over long periods of time, the stock of the country's debt would rise. The statistics indicate that this happened. In 1980 the U.S. had a positive amount of Net Foreign Assets equal to $365 billion. In 2004, the U.S. was a net debtor with a total debt of $2.5 trillion. This is not surprising, because since 1980 the U.S. has had cumulative current account deficits of over *$5 trillion.* At some point, the Balance on Investment Income should become a large negative number.

Instead, the statistics are different from what one would expect. The Balance on Investment Income is not a negative number; it is, in fact, positive. This is a bit hard to reconcile with an external debt that is officially $2.5 trillion. There are a couple of factors that are not immediately apparent from the statistics. First, notice that the total U.S. debt is not nearly as large as the accumulated current account deficits. Part of this difference has been made up by capital gains on U.S. investments overseas. These capital gains have essentially paid for some of the previously accumulated current account deficits. That will not explain how a country can have $2.5 trillion in debt and simultaneously have a positive Balance on Investment Income. Logically, there can be only two answers. First, the U.S. may own a substantial amount of unaccounted for foreign assets. These unaccounted for assets have come to be called *dark matter* in the balance of payments. We know that they must exist because *something* is generating income that is showing up in the Balance on Investment Income. In a sense, the existence of dark matter is simply an accounting problem. Do you count a country's debt as the difference between assets and liabilities? This is the usual methodology, but over time looking solely at the accumulated stocks of assets and liabilities may give one an inaccurate view of what is happening. The Balance on Investment Income is telling a quite different story, and the numbers are much more current. If that number is positive, the country is far less likely to be a net debtor. It is possible only to the extent that, in the long run, Americans earn far higher rates of return on their foreign assets than foreigners earn on their investments in the U.S. Although you may be tempted to think that American investors are smarter than foreign investors, the existence of unaccounted for dark matter seems a more likely explanation.

[6]The numbers fail to add up exactly because of rounding error.

The Undercounting of Exports

For the U.S., the balance on goods and services was –$758.5 billion in 2006. It is quite likely that this number is too large—in other words, that the deficit is being reported as higher than it actually is. The same logic would hold for a country reporting a trade surplus. In this case, the reported surplus is probably too low. This would also affect the numbers reported in the current account. The U.S. provides a convenient example of how this happens.

The export of goods is usually undercounted by a nontrivial amount. The U.S. Department of Commerce has reported that the U.S. exports of goods may be undercounted by as much as 10 percent. For 2006, this would represent uncounted exports of approximately $145 billion. To a large extent, this occurs because U.S. exporters are not obligated to report *individual* exports with a value of less than $2,500. For example, this would mean that Amazon.com would not have to report any sales of books overseas as exports unless an individual order was in excess of $2,500. As more and more small businesses become exporters, the problem may only get worse.

The undercounting of exports is even worse with respect to services. In part this is a function of how service exports are counted. If a services exporter sells a service to a foreign buyer that is not related to the domestic company, this is recorded as an export of services. However, if a domestic company "sells" a service to a foreign subsidiary of the same company, this is not an export of services. Essentially, intracompany transactions that cross national borders are not counted as an export of services even though the foreign subsidiary may have to pay for that service. The exact size of the undercounting of exports of services is debatable, but no one is claiming that it is small. Adding the undercounting of exports and services means that the U.S. trade deficit and the current account deficit reported previously is too large by a noticeable amount.

This is not just a problem for the U.S. In one of those interesting anomalies, the world always runs a current account deficit with itself. In 2000, the world ran a current account deficit of –$127.5 billion. Between 1980 and 2000, it ran 19 current account deficits, with one exception to the rule in 1997. This means that the world economy is reporting outflows of money that are greater than the inflows.[7] Unless we are trading with another planet, exports must be undercounted in the world economy relative to imports. Given the growth of world trade, as described in Chapter 1, it is becoming increasingly important for governments to obtain a clearer picture of the amount of trade in goods and services. Exports are a large part of GDP in most countries, and an undercount of exports means an undercount of GDP. If an important part of managing an economy consists of keeping GDP at an appropriate level, it would be helpful for that data to be accurate.[8]

[7]The data is from International Monetary Fund, *Balance of Payments Statistics Yearbook,* 2001, Washington, D.C.: International Monetary Fund, 2001.

[8]For more details on these issues, see "The Trade Gap May Be Inflated," *Business Week,* July 3, 2000, p. 32: Joel Millman, "Services May Lead U.S. to Trade Surplus," *The Wall Street Journal,* December 4, 2000, p. A1: and John Motala, "Statistical Discrepancies in the World Current Account," *Finance & Development* 34(1), March 1997, pp. 24–25.

The Current Account and the Capital and Financial Account

The rule that total inflows and outflows need to be equal leads to an interesting bit of logic. If the current account balance is negative, then the capital and financial account balance must be positive. The reverse is also true. A country running a deficit on trade in goods and services must somehow "finance" this deficit by borrowing from foreigners. Remember that a deficit in trade in goods and services means that a country is consuming more than it is producing. In 1980, the U.S. was "paying" for the trade deficit with investment income. Looking at the capital and financial accounts for the same year, the U.S. was investing more overseas than foreigners were investing in the U.S.

The U.S. International Investment Position

A country's international investment position is related to the capital account in its balance of payments. The capital account in a balance of payments statement shows the flow of capital to or from a country during the year. A country's international investment position reflects these capital flows and all previous capital flows. This allows one to compare the size of the country's foreign assets with the size of its foreign liabilities. If the assets exceed the liabilities, the country is a net creditor (positive balance). If the liabilities exceed the assets, the country is a net debtor (negative balance).

The U.S. net international investment position over the period 1976–2006 is shown in Figure 12.4. The dramatic decline in the U.S. position since 1980 reflects the U.S. current account deficits. Since the current account deficits reflect greater spending than U.S. income, another way to view the decline in the U.S. international investment position is that foreigners have been financing (loaning) the excess spending through a capital inflow into the U.S. This makes the U.S. the world's largest debtor nation.

Figure 12.4 The Net International Investment Position of the U.S., 1976–2006

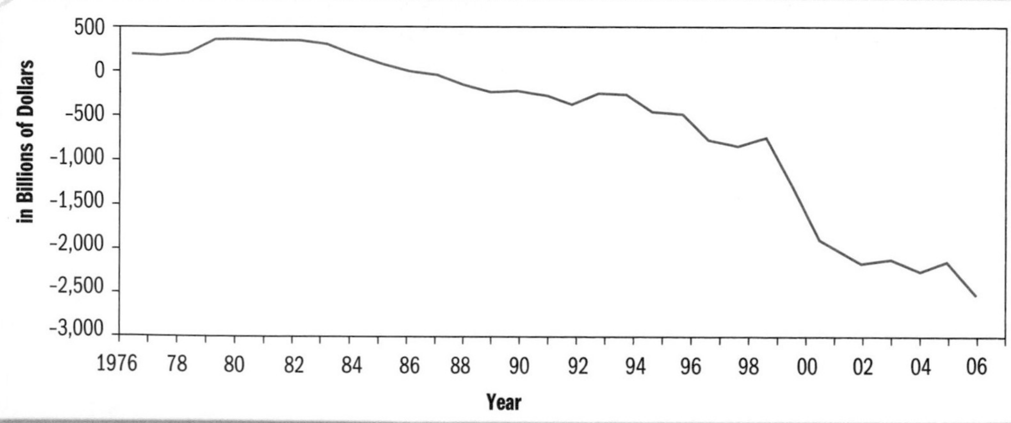

Source: http://www.bea.gov/newsreleases/international/intinv/

Until the late 1990s, it was fairly typical for U.S. investments overseas to be larger than foreign investment in the U.S. This discrepancy created rising positive investment income for the U.S. The income could then "finance" a deficit in merchandise trade. However, since 1983, the U.S. has invested less overseas than foreigners have invested in the U.S. The U.S. essentially has been financing its current account deficit by borrowing from the rest of the world and by selling U.S. assets. This situation is neither good nor bad. A deficit in goods and services has to be offset somewhere else in the balance of payments. This may take the form of investment income, inflows of capital, or, in the case of some developing countries, positive unilateral transfers.

Current account surpluses have to be balanced as well. A current account surplus means a capital and financial account deficit. Investors in a country will have to purchase foreign assets in excess of what foreigners are purchasing in that country. This may not necessarily be advantageous as the capital account surplus means that there will be less capital for investors to invest in their own country since capital will be moving to other countries. Because rates of economic growth are sensitive to capital investment, growth may slow at some point in the future. Also, exporting capital may lower the rate of growth of productivity and the growth of real wages.[9] However, exporting capital may lead to rising investment income, which would enable the country to consume more in the future.

Balance of Payments Stages

A popular misconception regarding a country's international trade position is that deficits are bad and surpluses are good. However, if we examine the different stages of the balance of payments, following a country's development from poor to rich, we come to a different conclusion.[10] A poor country usually has abundant labor and scarce capital. To raise its GDP per capita, the country must increase the amount of capital per worker, which is difficult to do. First, capital is scarce. Second, many poor countries are seeing their populations and labor forces rising rapidly, which makes it even more difficult to increase capital per worker. A solution is to import foreign capital in the form of foreign direct investment. This creates a capital and financial account surplus and a current account deficit. Over time, the foreign direct investment may lead to an increase in exports, which creates a trade surplus. However, investment income may be negative, as the return to the foreign investors must be paid. As the debt is paid, the country shifts to a current account surplus and a capital and financial account deficit. This financial account deficit may eventually lead to a surplus in investment income. If the investment income surplus becomes large enough, then the trade balance may shift into a deficit, which is offset by a positive investment income. Until the early 1980s, the U.S. fit this pattern almost perfectly. However, you should not infer from this discussion that current account deficits are never a problem. The point is that, in many cases, deficits are typical for economies at different stages of development.

---

[9]Not surprisingly, unions around the world have always been less than enthusiastic about FDI. They quite rationally realize that the export of capital to other countries is not in the long run interest of their members.

[10]For a more complete explanation, see "In Defense of Deficits," *The Economist*, December 16, 1995, pp. 68–69.

SUMMARY

1. A nation's Gross Domestic Product (GDP) is equal to the total output of final goods and services a nation produces in a year. It is a conservative estimate of total output as a number of activities are excluded from the calculation. Nominal GDP is adjusted for price changes to arrive at real GDP.
2. GDP can be divided into several different types of spending: consumption, investment, government purchases, and the trade balance, exports minus imports.
3. In an economy closed to international trade, GDP must be consumed, invested, or purchased by the government. In an open economy, GDP will equal the sum of consumption, investment, government purchases, and exports minus imports.
4. In an open economy, international trade does not have to balance. The amount exported does not have to equal the amount imported. The imbalances of international trade for an open economy are equal to the difference between the economy's output and its total domestic spending.
5. The trade imbalance equals the change in a country's borrowing or lending to foreigners.
6. The trade imbalance also equals the country's outflows of income—savings or taxes—and its injections of income—investment or government purchases.
7. The trade balance is a way for a country to balance its production and consumption over periods of time longer than a year.
8. The balance of payments is a record of a country's economic transactions with all other countries. Each transaction that causes an inflow of dollars (money) into the U.S. receives a positive sign, and each transaction that causes an outflow of dollars (money) from the U.S. to foreigners receives a negative sign.
9. The balance of payments statement identifies economic transactions as current account transactions, capital account transactions, or financial account transaction. Transactions involving goods, services, investment income, or unilateral transfers appear in the current account of the balance of payments. Transactions involving international sales or purchases of assets appear in the financial account.
10. Since total inflows and outflows of dollars will be equal, a current account deficit will be matched by an equal capital and financial account surplus or a current account surplus will be matched by a capital and financial account deficit.
11. In many cases deficits are typical for economies at different stages of development. In 2006 the U.S. had a trade balance of –$838.3 billion, a balance on goods and services of –$758.5 billion, a balance on goods, services, and investment income of –$721.9 billion, and a current account balance of –$811.5 billion. The current account deficit of the U.S. in 2006 was offset by a capital and financial account surplus of $800.5 billion.

KEY CONCEPTS AND TERMS

- national income accounting p. 274
- real GDP p. 275
- nominal GDP p. 275
- intertemporal trade p. 281
- leakages of income p. 281
- injections of income p. 281
- balance of payments p. 285
- balance on current account p. 285
- balance on financial account p. 286
- balance on capital account p. 286
- merchandise trade balance p. 287
- balance on services p. 288
- balance on goods and services p. 288
- balance on investment income p. 288
- balance on goods, services, and income p. 288
- unilateral transfers p. 289
- change in assets abroad p. 290
- official reserve assets p. 290
- Special Drawing Rights (SDRs) p. 290
- International Monetary Fund (IMF) p. 290
- change in foreign assets p. 291

PROBLEMS AND QUESTIONS FOR REVIEW

1. What items are excluded from the calculation of GDP?
2. Why is it necessary to adjust nominal GDP for price changes?
3. What are the different components of GDP in an open economy?
4. How are GDP and domestic spending related in a closed economy? In an open economy?
5. If GDP is equal to $10 trillion and the sum of C, I, and G is $9 trillion, then the country must have a trade surplus. Show why this is true.
6. What are the different leakages of income and injections of income in an open economy?
7. Explain the relationship between a country's trade balance and the other leakages of income and injections of income.
8. Assume that S, I, G, and T were equal to 10, 20, 30, and 40, respectively. What would be the value of $X - M$?
9. If $S + T$ is greater than $G + I$, then the country must have a trade surplus. Create a numerical example to show that this must be true.
10. China currently has consumption that is less than half of GDP. Explain how this statistic might be related to China's merchandise trade surplus.
11. A trade deficit is a way for a country to trade current consumption for future consumption. Explain why this statement is true.
12. What does the term balance of payments mean?
13. What economic transactions cause an inflow of dollars? An outflow of dollars?
14. What is the meaning of a deficit (surplus) in the: (a) merchandise trade balance, (b) balance on services, (c) balance on goods and services, (d) balance on investment income, (e) balance on goods, services and income, (f) balance on current account, and (g) balance on capital account?
15. Suppose that a country had a balance on current account equal to a positive $100 million. Further assume that the country had a merchandise trade deficit of $90 million. Explain how it is possible for this to happen.
16. Given the following information concerning a hypothetical economy calculate: (a) merchandise trade balance; (b) balance on services; (c) balance on goods and services; (d) balance on investment income; (e) balance on goods, services, and income; (f) unilateral transfers; (g) balance on current account; (h) balance on capital and financial account; and (i) the statistical discrepancy.

Exports of Merchandise	$500
Imports of Merchandise	400
Exports of Services	150
Imports of Services	100
Income Receipts on Assets Abroad	100
Income Payments of Foreign Assets	150
Unilateral Transfers, Net	–10
Change in Assets Abroad	500
Change in Foreign Assets	400

17. Describe the stages that a country's balance of payments may go through as the country moves from being poor to rich.

SUGGESTED READINGS AND WEB SITES

Bureau of Economic Analysis (www.bea.doc.gov)

A convenient web site for past and current balance of payments statistics for the U.S.

"Figures to Fret About," *The Economist,* July 11, 1998, p. 76.

A good article on the pitfalls of trying to read too much into current account statistics.

"In Defence of Deficits," *The Economist,* December 16, 1995, pp. 68–69.

A concise explanation of why current account deficits may be appropriate for different types of economies.

International Monetary Fund (www.imf.org)

The official web site of the IMF.

IMF, *Balance of Payments Yearbook,* Washington, D.C: IMF, 2003.

A good basic reference for balance of payments statistics for most of the world's countries.

IMF, *International Financial Statistics,* Washington, D.C.: IMF, selected issues.

A monthly publication of the IMF containing balance of payments and other economic data for most of the world's countries.

John Matola, "Statistical Discrepancies in the World Current Account," *Finance & Development* 34(1), March 1997, pp. 24–25.

In Chapter 1, it was mentioned that world imports and world exports don't match. This article will allow the students to see exactly why.

OECD (www.oecd.org)

The official web site of the OECD.

OECD, *Main Economic Indicators,* Paris: OECD, 2003.

A good source of information on the national income accounts for different groups of countries.

"Ownership-Based Trade," *International Economic Trends,* Federal Reserve Bank of St. Louis, August 2002, p. 1

A very nice one page article on the activities of U.S. MNCs abroad, foreign MNCs in the U.S., and the effect their activities have on reported trade flows.

Pakko, Michael R., "The U.S. Trade Deficit and the 'New Economy'," *Federal Reserve Bank of St. Louis Review* 81(5), September/October 1999, pp. 11–19.

An interesting analysis of how changes in the structure of the U.S. economy may be reflected in the current account using the tools developed in this chapter.

Peter Reuter and Edwin M. Truman, *Chasing Dirty Money: Progress on Anti-Money Laundering,* Washington, D.C.: Institute for International Economics, 2004.

A book that answers the questions about the movement of money associated with illegal activities in the world economy.

"Services May Lead U.S. to Trade Surplus," *Wall Street Journal,* December 4, 2000, p. A1.

A short but detailed article on the growing U.S. trade surplus in services.

"The Trade Gap May Be Inflated," *Business Week,* July 3, 2000, p. 32.

A short but interesting article on the difficulties in gathering the standard trade statistics and why this matters.

"What Drives Large Current Account Deficits?" *International Economic Trends,* Federal Reserve Bank of St. Louis, May 2001, p. 1.

A good place to start learning about analyzing macroeconomic imbalances and their effects on the current account.

Chapter 13

International Transactions and Financial Markets

"The world's capital markets are experiencing a revolution. . . . [the early 1980s had witnessed] the progressive demise of barriers and regulations which hinder the movement of capital around the world. This process, combined with some powerful new financing techniques, is creating an almost global capital market.

The lines of demarcation between domestic and international capital markets are increasingly blurred, as are those between the different instruments for raising capital: equity, bonds, and loans. The structure of the financial institutions serving the markets is also changing. And the pace of change, in the structure of the markets, the instruments and the institutions, is accelerating."

—EUROMONEY

INTRODUCTION

In the previous chapter, you learned that the total inflows and outflows of money in a country result from its economic interactions with the rest of the world. In most cases, these interactions require that one currency is exchanged for another currency. This exchange of currency raises two important questions. First, how do these exchanges occur and what institutions are involved in the process? Second, how much domestic currency would be needed to obtain the desired amount of foreign currency? This chapter will answer the first question, and Chapter 14 will address the second question.

The exchange of domestic currency for foreign currency occurs in the foreign exchange market. This market has developed as individuals, businesses, and governments need to obtain foreign currency to conduct the types of international transactions that we described in the previous chapter. We begin our analysis by examining the institutions that participate in this market. In the previous chapter, you learned that there were items in the balance of payments that occur in the current account and in the financial account. These financial account transactions included foreign direct investment and money flowing into and out of a country to purchase financial assets such as stocks and bonds. Since we discussed foreign direct investment in Chapter 6, our focus in this Chapter is on the flows of money used to acquire financial assets. We will address why these capital flows occur both in the short and the long run and how international flows of capital can be used to reduce risk. Once you understand what motivates these capital flows, we will look at the major participants in these international flows of capital. The final section of the chapter describes how the Eurocurrency markets work, as this market has become an important mechanism for financing international trade.

THE FOREIGN EXCHANGE MARKET

In the first half of the book, we were concerned with imports and exports of goods and services. Individuals and firms are constantly buying goods and services from other individuals and firms in other countries. This inherently gives rise to the need to change one currency into another currency. An example may help to illustrate this point. If a U.S. firm buys a Jaguar, then at some point U.S. dollars would have to be traded for British pounds. The British producer has to pay the workers, the rent, suppliers of the car's sub-components, repay the loan at the bank, and pay taxes to the British government. All of these claims on the British producer's gross revenue are paid in pounds because the pound is the U.K.'s national currency. Jaguar workers in the U.K. would have trouble buying groceries with dollars, just as we would have trouble buying groceries in the U.S. with pounds.[1] Generally, any transaction included in the current account we described in Chapter 12 would entail exchanging one country's currency for another country's currency. However, as you learned in Chapter 12, there are other reasons for money to move from one country to another that are not related to imports and exports of goods and services. For example, a company building a plant in another country would need to exchange its domestic currency for foreign currency in order to pay for the plant's construction. The same would be true of the purchase of financial assets such as stocks or bonds. The buyer would need to exchange his or her domestic currency for foreign currency in order to purchase the asset.

foreign exchange **currency or deposits in financial institutions of another country**

How would such transactions occur? Usually, they are facilitated by a commercial bank. The core of the foreign exchange market is a global network of commercial banks that purchase and sell foreign currency or foreign currency demand deposits or foreign exchange. **Foreign exchange** is a financial asset that represents a monetary claim that a resident of one country holds against the resident of another country. These financial assets may be currency, bank deposits, or other highly-liquid financial claims. Since the majority of the assets are bank deposits, foreign exchange generally refers to foreign currency bank deposits.

As Figure 13.1 illustrates, the foreign exchange market in the U.S. is comprised of three sub-markets: the retail foreign exchange market; the inter-bank (wholesale) foreign exchange market; and the market for foreign exchange derivatives such as futures.[2] In total, these three submarkets form an integrated foreign exchange market. Unlike the futures and options market, the foreign exchange retail and inter-bank markets do not have physical trading centers. Like the NASDAQ, they represent an over-the-counter market. Customers transact business with their local banks, and

[1]One may object that it is possible to use dollars outside the U.S. or that we can purchase foreign products without having to buy foreign currencies. This does not alter the discussion. At some point the dollars *would* be traded for pounds.

[2]The market for futures and options will be covered later in the chapter.

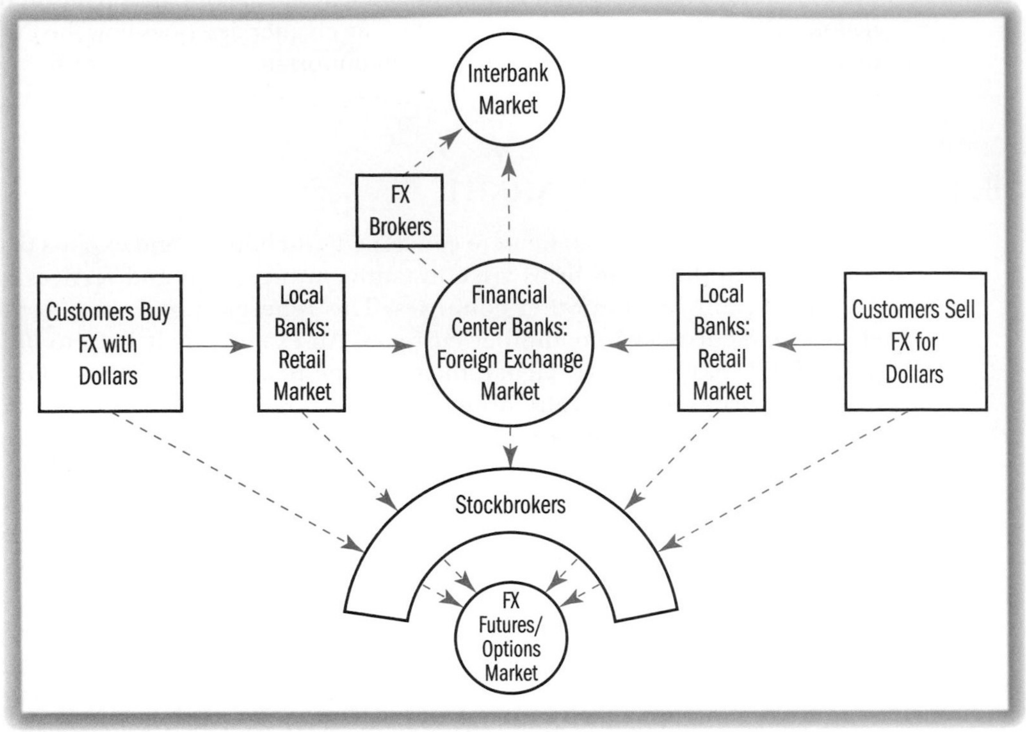

Figure 13.1 The Structure of the Foreign Exchange Market in the U.S.

financial center banks transact business directly with one another or through foreign exchange brokers.

Participants in the retail market are individuals, multinational firms, and nonbank financial institutions that purchase or sell foreign exchange to local banks. Participants in the interbank market are the international departments of large financial center banks mainly located in New York, London, Zurich, Frankfurt, Paris, Tokyo, and so forth. A participating bank generally has a trading room equipped with computer

Currency Trading

Figure 13.2 shows the world's largest foreign-exchange dealers. Citibank still holds the number one ranking in the latest *Euromoney* poll. It was also number one in last year's rankings. It is important to notice that the 25 largest currency traders account for approximately 75 percent of the total foreign exchange trading worldwide. With currency trading of approximately $2.0 trillion dollars per day, this translates into these 25 traders accounting for almost $1 trillion per day.

Figure 13.2 Major Foreign Exchange Dealers

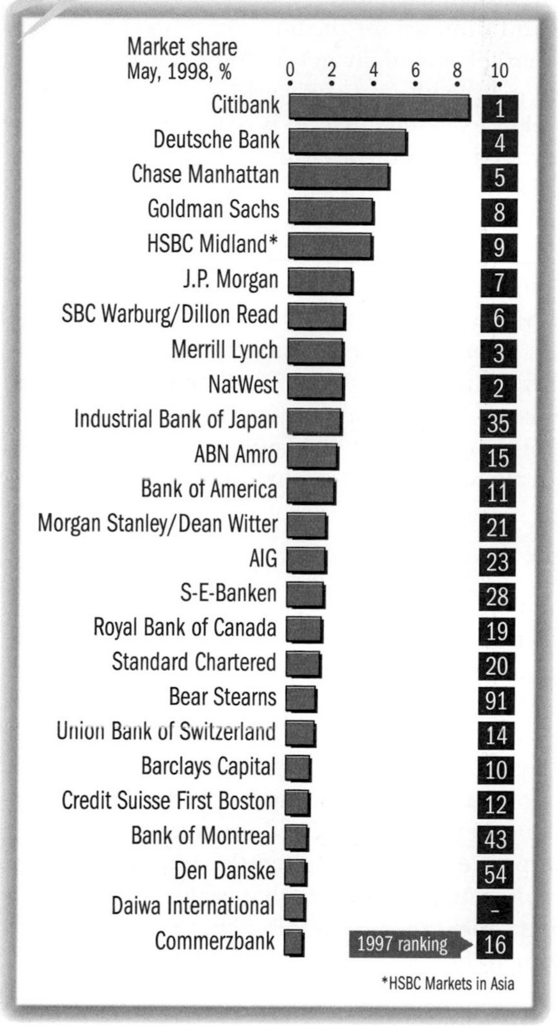

Source: *The Economist.* May 23, 1998, pp. 97.

terminals and telephones through which dealers make and receive price quotations and agree to transactions. Nonbank customers, local banks, and financial center banks all participate through stockbrokers in the exchanges that trade assets related to foreign exchange. Instant electronic communications have created a single integrated global market in foreign exchange.

The scope and dimensions of the foreign exchange market are truly extraordinary. First, the market essentially never closes. Virtually every minute of the day, every day of the week, people all over the world are exchanging one currency for another. Second, the foreign exchange market is reasonably free of obstructions for the industrialized and developing countries with open capital markets. The currencies in these countries are referred to as *freely convertible currencies.* With freely convertible currencies, money can move between countries without the impediments associated with trade in goods or services. For example, as it enters a country, money does not have to move through customs and no tariffs have to be paid. Given modern telecommunications technology, truly large sums of money can move freely from one country to another. Current estimates indicate that the daily volume of foreign exchange trading has reached $1.8 trillion. To put this into perspective, the output of the world economy is approximately $45 trillion per year. In a little less than one month, the value of trading in the foreign exchange market is in excess of the amount of goods and services produced in the world economy in a year.

Paying for Imports and Exports

The fundamental reason the foreign exchange market exists is that payments in international transactions are different from payments in a domestic economy. Most domestic payments are either cash payments or the customer pays when the merchandise is billed (open account). Cash payments are rare in international trade because of the burden it puts on the buyer (importer). Open-account payments are more common but are usually restricted to intrafirm payments within a multinational corporation.

Usually imports are paid for using a specific foreign exchange instrument. The problem is that in international trade, there may be a substantial period between when the exporter ships the goods and when the importer receives them. The problem is how to bridge this time gap in a way that is agreeable to both parties. The most common solution is a cable transfer. In this case, the importer instructs his or her bank to transfer the payment for the imports to the exporters account in another country. The worldwide network of banks makes this transfer relatively cheap. In most cases, the transfer would occur in two days.

The disadvantage of a cable transfer is that the importer essentially paid in advance for goods not yet received. Fortunately, there are instruments that allow the exporter to receive money quickly and for the importer to pay for the goods at about the same time they are received. A commercial bill of exchange or a bank draft is a written order by the exporter to the importer instructing the importer to pay on a certain date a specified amount of money either to the exporter or the exporters' bank. In many cases, these instruments are backed by a letter of credit. A letter of credit is a guaranty from the importer's bank that the commercial bill of exchange or bank draft will be paid by the bank. The beauty of these instruments is what happens when the exporter receives them. The exporter could hold the instruments to maturity. However, the exporter could also sell the instruments in the foreign exchange market for slightly less money than the face value. The holder of the instrument would receive a return for holding the instrument equivalent to this discount. Everyone is happy. The exporter has been paid. The importer does not have to pay for the goods before they are likely to arrive. The buyer of the instrument gets a rate of return on an investment that is presumably better than they could have gotten on an investment with equal risk.

Spot and Forward Exchange Rates

spot exchange rate the exchange rate that applies when the transaction is competed at the same time the price is agreed on

forward exchange rate the price of foreign exchange to be delivered at some point in the future

Most of the time when we refer to an exchange rate, we are talking about the **spot exchange rate**, or the exchange rate that is relevant to current foreign exchange transactions. However, there is a peculiarity with respect to international trade as opposed to domestic trade. Suppose that the Jaguar importer contracts to buy one hundred Jaguars. Given the distance from the U.K. to the U.S., the cars purchased today may not be delivered for three months or longer. How is this transaction handled? The manufacturer, of course, must assume the normal risks associated with producing and selling cars domestically. However, in the case of international sales, the company may be unwilling to assume the risk that the exchange rate will change over the next 90 days. Likewise, the importer does not want to deal with unanticipated exchange rate changes and is not willing to pay for the cars until they are delivered. A convenient way out of this timing problem for both parties is to use the **forward exchange rate**. The forward exchange rate is the price of foreign exchange to be delivered at some point in the future. In this case, the importer simply directs its bank to pay the producer in 90 days at a price and exchange rate agreeable to both parties today. The bank then sells a trade acceptance (an accepted commercial bill of exchange) in the local market to a speculator. Notice that the speculator has taken the risk in the hopes of making a profit. The importer, the manufacturer, and the bank have transferred the risk of exchange rate changes to the speculator.

The spot and forward exchange rates for major currencies are published daily in the *Wall Street Journal, The Financial Times,* and in most daily newspapers around the world. Currency quotations for a typical business day are shown in Table 13.1. This table also shows the forward rate of exchange for a few major currencies. Table 13.1 shows each currency expressed in either U.S. dollar equivalent (direct quote) or in foreign currency relative to the dollar (indirect quote). Also, one month, three month, six month and one year forward exchange rates are shown. Forward rates are quoted in the same manner as spot rates. Direct spot and forward exchange rates are expressed as domestic currency per unit of foreign currency and indirect exchange rates are expressed as foreign currency per unit of domestic currency. Direct and indirect quotes are always reciprocals of one another.

If the forward rate is less than the spot rate, the forward rate is said to be at a discount to the spot rate. If the forward rate is higher than the spot rate, the forward rate is said to be at a premium to the spot rate. To determine the percentage discount or premium for the forward rate relative to the spot rate when exchange rates are quoted on a direct basis, the following formula can be used:

$$[(\text{Forward Rate} - \text{Spot Rate})/\text{Spot Rate}] \times (360/N) \times 100$$

where N is the number of days to future delivery in the contract.

Table 13.1 Daily Quotations of Spot and Forward Exchange Rates

DOLLAR SPOT FORWARD AGAINST THE DOLLAR

Aug 22		Closing mid-point	Change on day	Bid/offer spread	Day's mid high	Day's mid low	One month Rate	One month %PA	Three months Rate	Three months %PA	One year Rate	One year %PA	J.P. Morgan Index
Europe													
Czech Rep.	(Koruna)	20.5006	−0.0173	868 - 143	20.5960	20.4250	20.4557	2.6	20.3806	2.3	20.2043	1.4	–
Denmark	(DKr)	5.5062	−0.0108	054 - 069	5.5317	5.4921	5.5009	1.1	5.4952	0.8	5.4864	0.4	110.30
Hungary	(Forint)	191.358	−2.4741	248 - 468	194.900	191.030	191.728	−2.3	192.448	−2.3	195.808	−2.3	–
Norway	(NKr)	5.9168	−0.0230	146 - 189	5.9610	5.9037	5.9139	0.6	5.9113	0.4	5.9431	−0.4	115.30
Poland	(Zloty)	2.8376	−0.0167	359 - 392	2.8684	2.8329	2.8356	0.8	2.8337	0.5	2.8456	−0.3	–
Russia	(Rouble)	25.7863	−0.0894	833 - 893	25.9107	25.7521	25.7968	−0.5	25.8028	−0.3	25.8883	−0.4	–
Slovakia	(Koruna)	24.9825	−0.1597	649 - 000	25.2430	24.9320	24.9528	1.4	24.8955	1.4	24.7630	0.9	–
Sweden	(SKr)	6.9452	−0.0093	433 - 471	6.9744	6.9281	6.9346	1.8	6.9175	1.6	6.8890	0.8	100.90
Switzerland	(SFr)	1.2075	0.0043	072 - 078	1.2111	1.2043	1.2046	2.9	1.1994	2.7	1.1820	2.1	107.10
Turkey	(Lira)	1.3336	−0.0305	325 - 346	1.3560	1.3325	1.3488	−13.7	1.3771	−13.0	1.5044	−12.8	–
UK (0.5022)[a]	(£)	1.9913	0.0079	910 - 915	1.9928	1.9804	1.9898	0.9	1.9863	1.0	1.9668	1.2	103.00
Euro (0.7399)[a]	(Euro)	1.3516	0.0026	514 - 517	1.3550	1.3452	1.3528	−1.1	1.3544	−0.8	1.3576	−0.4	129.10
SDR	–	0.6554	−0.0003	–	–	–	–	–	–	–	–	–	–
Americas													
Argentina	(Peso)	3.1638	0.0050	625 - 650	3.1650	3.1625	3.2190	−20.9	3.2644	−12.7	3.4281	−8.4	–
Brazil	(R$)	2.0143	−0.0216	133 - 153	2.0365	2.0050	2.0197	−3.2	2.0320	−3.5	2.0912	−3.8	–
Canada	(C$)	1.0619	0.0031	616 - 621	1.0665	1.0574	1.0613	0.6	1.0604	0.6	1.0578	0.4	134.60
Mexico	(New Peso)	11.0710	−0.0541	670 - 750	11.1493	11.0580	11.0895	−2.0	11.1294	−2.1	11.3580	−2.6	80.80
Peru	(New Sol)	3.1650	−0.0050	640 - 660	3.1710	3.1620	3.1628	0.9	3.1598	0.7	3.1626	0.1	–
USA	($)	–	–	–	–	–	–	–	–	–	–	–	85.90

Pacific/Middle East/Africa													
Australia	(A$)	1.2449	−0.0033	446 - 453	1.2544	1.2390	–	–	–	–	–	–	121.90
Hong Kong	(HK$)	7.8087	0.0032	084 - 090	7.8099	7.8052	7.8038	0.8	7.7929	0.8	7.7717	0.5	91.50
India	(Rs)	40.8950	−0.1900	900 - 000	41.0950	40.8000	40.9700	−2.2	41.0800	−1.8	41.5625	−1.6	–
Indonesia	(Rupiah)	9395.00	−45.0000	000 - 000	9455.00	9390.00	9399.50	−0.6	9415.00	−0.9	9565.00	−1.8	–
Iran	(Rial)	9259.00	−1.0000	400 - 400	–	–	–	–	–	–	–	–	–
Israel	(Shk)	4.1644	−0.0247	622 - 665	4.1825	4.1610	4.1598	1.3	4.1565	0.8	4.1704	−0.1	–
Japan	(Y)	115.035	0.7000	020 - 050	115.460	114.000	114.556	5.0	113.712	4.6	110.631	3.8	82.20
Kuwait	(Dinar)	0.2819	–	818 - 819	0.2820	0.2818	0.2820	−0.4	0.2822	−0.4	0.2828	−0.3	–
Malaysia[b]	(M$)	3.4825	−0.0150	800 - 850	3.5020	3.4800	3.4768	2.0	3.4656	1.9	3.4320	1.5	–
New Zealand	(NZ$)	1.4302	−0.0066	298 - 306	1.4514	1.4241	–	–	–	–	–	–	132.40
Philippines	(Peso)	46.5000	−0.3700	500 - 500	46.9400	46.4500	46.5455	−1.2	46.6365	−1.2	47.0600	−1.2	–
Saudi Arabia	(SR)	3.7510	0.0004	505 - 514	3.7514	3.7505	3.7489	0.7	3.7464	0.5	3.7415	0.3	–
Singapore	(S$)	1.5242	−0.0105	239 - 245	1.5332	1.5239	1.5207	2.7	1.5143	2.6	1.4907	2.2	103.60
South Africa	(R)	7.2521	−0.1480	471 - 571	7.3856	7.2465	7.2838	−5.2	7.3491	−5.4	7.6784	−5.9	–
South Korea	(Won)	944.100	−0.1500	900 - 300	946.900	943.100	942.100	2.5	938.100	2.5	929.600	1.5	110.40
Taiwan	(T$)	32.9560	0.0295	490 - 630	33.0200	32.9490	32.8610	3.5	32.7260	2.8	32.1810	2.4	86.20
Thailand	(Bt)	34.4800	−0.0750	600 - 000	34.6000	31.6000	34.4280	1.8	34.3350	1.7	34.0800	1.2	–
UAE	(Dirham)	3.6727	−0.0001	725 - 729	3.6729	3.6725	3.6719	0.3	3.6705	0.2	3.6653	0.2	–

[a]*The closing mid-point rates for the Euro and £ are shown in brackets. The other figures in both rows are in the reciprocal form in line with market convention.*
[b]*Official rate set by Malaysian government. The WM/Reuters rate for the valuation of capital assets is 3.80 MYR/USD. Bid/offer spreads in the Dollar Spot table show only the last three decimal places. J.P. Morgan nominal indices: Base average 2000 = 100. Bid, offer, mid spot rates and forward rates in both this and the pound table are derived from the WM/REUTERS 4pm (London time) CLOSING SPOT and FORWARD RATE services. Some values are rounded by the F.T.*

Futures, Options, and Swaps

futures contract a commitment to purchase or deliver a specified quantity of foreign currency on a designated future date

option a contract that gives the holder the option to buy or sell foreign exchange in the future

currency swap an agreement to exchange different currencies over a specified period of time

An alternative to using the forward exchange rate to make foreign currency transactions is a futures contract. A **futures contract** is a commitment to purchase or deliver a specified quantity of foreign currency on a designated date in the future. The price of the futures contract is determined competitively in an auction market when the contract is transacted. Futures contracts are less flexible than the forward exchange rate, as the former can only be obtained in standardized amounts and for specific points in time. Both the forward and the futures markets insulate buyers and sellers of foreign exchange from the risks of exchange rate changes. Foreign currency futures contracts are traded in organized markets like the International Monetary Market of the Chicago Mercantile Exchange.

A financial instrument related to futures contracts is an **option**. An option contract gives the holder the option to buy or sell foreign exchange at a future point in time. The main difference between an option and a futures contract is that the holder of an option is not obligated to actually buy or sell foreign exchange. They merely are acquiring the option to do so if they choose. Since options are cheaper than futures contracts, the potential for loss on an options contract is smaller.

A final future-oriented foreign exchange arrangement is the **currency swap**. In this arrangement, two parties agree to exchange different currencies over a specified period of time. In such a situation, a corporation might agree to deliver a large amount of one currency in the future for a comparable amount of another currency now. In addition, the holder usually agrees to make interest payments on the currency it receives while the other party makes interest payments on the currency it has received. At the end of the specified period, the two parties would then swap the currencies with one another and in essence the two parties would return to their original currency positions. Swaps are very popular in large part because they have lower transaction costs than those associated with futures or options markets.

The international markets in futures, options, and swaps have become very large. Futures and options volume is approximately $117 billion per day. However, most future-oriented financial products are traded directly among commercial banks. Total outstanding currency swaps at the end of 2004 were approximately $7.9 trillion. If one

The Role of the U.S. Dollar

In the world economy, the dominant currency is the U.S. dollar. It plays a unique role because it is so commonly used outside the U.S. To be used as money, an asset must perform three functions. First, it must serve as a medium of exchange. In this regard, the U.S. dollar is the world's most often used medium of exchange for international transactions. Second, it must be used as a unit of account. In this sense, the dollar is like the meter: everyone knows how long a meter is; likewise, virtually all the world's people know what a U.S. dollar is worth. Third, an asset must be used as a store of value. In a world where currencies may rapidly depreciate, many people use U.S. dollars as a way to save if the value of their domestic currency is uncertain. Indeed, there are more dollars outside the U.S. economy than there inside it. In a sense this is not surprising, as the U.S. economy is about one-third of the world economy. However, the use of the dollar in international transactions is much higher than this percentage.

Table 13.2 provides some data on the importance of the dollar. The table shows the use of the U.S. dollar, the Euro, the Japanese yen, the British pound, and the Swiss franc for several categories of transactions. The first column shows that the dollar is used for over 45 percent of foreign exchange trading. The percentages are even higher for the percentage of international bank loans and bond offerings. However, the Euro has become as important as the dollar for international bank loans and bond offerings. Given that the economy of the EU is roughly the same size as the U.S. economy, the percentages for this new currency are not surprising. However, one must remember the word *new*. The Euro is now as important as the U.S. dollar in international lending as a whole because a bond is simply a special type of long-term loan. As time passes, the dominance of the dollar may become less pronounced in the world economy.

Table 13.2 Relative International Importance of Major Currencies, 2001 (in percentages)

Currency	Foreign Exchange Trading	International Bank Loans	International Bond Offering
US Dollar	45.2%	50.3%	48.4%
Euro	18.8	51.0	44.3
Japanese Yen	11.4	–7.6	1.2
UK Pound	6.6	4.3	5.2
Swiss Franc	3.1	0.4	–0.2
Other Currencies	14.9	1.6	1.1

Source: Bank of International Settlements, *Triennial Central Bank Survey,* (Basel: Bank of International Settlements), March 2002.

adds the value of these products designed to deal with foreign exchange volatility to the value of direct foreign exchange trading, the sums are truly staggering. In the world economy, the trading of foreign exchange and financial products related to foreign exchange has become an extremely large business by any standard.

INTERNATIONAL FINANCIAL MARKETS

In Chapter 12, you learned that a large amount of the inflows and outflows listed in the balance of payments were not related to items listed in the current account. Money can also flow into a country for the purpose of buying domestic assets. Part of the motivation for these capital flows are related to FDI flows, which we discussed in Chapter 6. However, in many cases the motivation for the buying and selling of foreign exchange is linked to the desire to acquire financial assets. These international movements of portfolio capital are movements of money across borders for the purpose of purchasing financial assets. In this section, we examine the two major reasons for the movement of portfolio capital and the two different time frames over which they occur.

Financial Intermediation

The purpose of either a domestic or international financial market is to perform intermediation. What this means is putting two different market participants together to conduct an economic transaction. At any point in time in a domestic financial market there are individuals and/or firms who have more money than they currently wish to spend, as well as other individuals and firms who need more money than they currently have. The function of financial markets is to move money from the first group to the second. Without well-functioning markets, it would be difficult for these groups to find one another. Efficient financial markets improve the welfare of both savers and investors—and they also benefit the entire country. The benefit to the overall economy is a result of the positive correlation between investment as a percentage of GDP and the country's rate of economic growth. However, for these savings to have the maximum impact on economic growth, the country's financial markets need to efficiently move capital from savers to investors. International financial markets provide similar benefits to the world economy. The additional benefit of international financial markets is that the world economy's rate of growth would increase, as we showed in Chapter 6.[3] The argument for allowing the free flow of capital in the world economy is analogous to argument for allowing free trade in goods and services.

The major rationale for moving money from one country to another is a higher rate of return. The flow of capital between developed and developing countries is one example of capital flows seeking a higher rate of return. A distinguishing characteristic of international trade in goods is that developing countries tend to have a comparative advantage in labor-intensive products and a comparative disadvantage in capital-intensive products. What this implies is that capital is relatively scarce in developing countries. As a result, the rate of return on capital is relatively high. Fortunately for these countries there is an external source of capital in the developed countries. For the developed countries, the situation is reversed. Capital is relatively abundant and the returns to it are relatively low. Capital flows from the developed to developing countries could make both groups of countries better off in that investors from developed countries could earn a higher rate of return and the developing countries could obtain badly needed capital that could augment their rate of economic growth.

However, the majority of international portfolio capital flows are between one high-income country and another high-income country. At first this may seem strange, as most high-income countries are capital abundant relative to low- and middle-income countries. However, capital is not equally abundant among the high-income countries. As we discussed in Chapter 12, national savings rates are quite different among developed countries. As we will show in Chapter 15, different national savings rates lead to different national interest rates. This being the case, there is a substantial

[3]Increased rates of economic growth in the developing countries would typically mean more imports of goods and services from developed countries.

amount of capital which moves from one high-income country into other high-income countries. Further, financial markets in low- and middle-income countries are still relatively small. This means that a substantial portion of money to be invested by the high-income countries will of necessity, be invested in other high-income countries.

Risk Diversification

The movements of capital we have just described portray a one-way movement of capital in search of higher returns in foreign countries. However, consider a situation where the real rate of interest is 4 percent in the U.S. and 2 percent in Germany. Based on our earlier discussion, you would presume that capital would flow only one-way from Germany to the U.S. In general, this is not the case. Given these real interest rates, more capital probably would flow from Germany to the U.S., but there also would be some capital flowing from the U.S. to Germany. Either we have spotted some financial irrationality among U.S. investors or some other motive for the movement of portfolio capital is at work.

Modern portfolio theory illustrates that by diversifying a portfolio of financial assets, an investor can earn a higher rate of return for the same level of risk or the same rate of return with less risk. For example, suppose that there are two securities with an average yield of 10 percent. Further, suppose that the first security has a range of yields over time from 0 to 20 percent, and the second security has an analogous range of yields from 5 to 15 percent. The first security is clearly riskier than the second. Since the average yield is the same, an investor would clearly prefer the latter security (same yield, less risk). To explain the effect of diversification within a portfolio, we need to know how the returns of these two securities are related. For the moment, let's assume that the yields on the two securities are inversely related. This means that when the return on one security is high, the return on the other security is low. When this is the case, a portfolio containing both securities would be less risky than holding just one of the securities. This is the basic principle of **risk diversification**, which states that if the returns on various assets do not move together identically, holding a portfolio of assets will be less risky than holding a single asset.

risk diversification **the principle that holding financial assets with varying degrees of risk tends to be less risky than holding just one financial asset**

Risk diversification helps to explain two-way capital flows. In our example, if the return on German securities is inversely correlated with the return on U.S. securities, two-way capital flows will occur. The German investor could minimize risk by putting some capital in both the German and U.S. financial markets. The same reasoning would apply to U.S. investors. Given the large sums of portfolio capital available in both Germany and the U.S., large two-way capital flows between the two countries would not be surprising. Given the large number of countries with open capital markets and the range of financial assets available, there are many possibilities available to a mutual-fund portfolio manager to diversify risk.

Short-Run Movements of Portfolio Capital

In financial markets, the "short run" usually means a period of time less than one year. The large amount of portfolio capital moving from one country to another in the short run generally is simply a searching for a higher real rate of return. The rationale behind such movements is fairly clear. For example, consider a multinational firm with a cash balance in excess of what the firm will need over the next 30 days. Now assume that

LIBOR

One of the most important interest rates in the world financial markets is the London Interbank Offered Rate (LIBOR). LIBOR is set every day at 11:00 A.M. (London time) for seven major currencies. These currencies are the British pound, the Canadian dollar, the Euro, the U.S. dollar, the Australian dollar, the Japanese yen, and the Swiss franc. The rate is set by a panel of contributing banks that are chosen for their reputation, level of activity in the London market, and their perceived expertise in the relevant currency. LIBOR is set each day for the following maturities: overnight, 2 days, 1 week, 2 weeks, and 1–12 months. One can find daily LIBOR rates published in the *Wall Street Journal*. The LIBOR rate quoted in this publication is an average of rate quotes by the Bank of America, Barclays, Bank of Tokyo, Deutsche Bank, and Swiss Bank.

For the U.S. dollar, LIBOR represents the interest rate on Eurodollars traded between banks in London. This interest rate is one of the most important interest rates in world financial markets. This is because it is considered to be a virtually risk-free rate. As a result, it effectively becomes a benchmark for many other interest rates. A number of interest rates in the world are routinely quoted as LIBOR plus some amount such as LIBOR plus two percent.

In the U.S., LIBOR has huge impact on the U.S. housing market. Most U.S. mortgages pass through two entities. These are the Federal National Mortgage Association (FannieMae) and the Federal Home Loan Mortgage Corporation (Freddie Mac). LIBOR is used by these entities in determining the interest rate most Americans pay when they buy a house. In this case, globalization of the world's financial markets has truly come "home." An interest rate set in London on the U.S. currency by banks from a number of different countries becomes a major part of the interest rate that an American family pays on its mortgage in, say, a small town in the Midwest.

a higher real interest rate can be obtained by investing in Euros rather than Japanese yen for the next 30 days.[4] If the cost of moving capital from one currency to another is close to zero, it is difficult to criticize the multinational firm for moving short-run capital from one country to another in order to take advantage of this interest rate differential. Given that most multinational companies frequently experience this situation and have relatively low transaction costs for moving capital, it is not surprising that multinational firms (or purely domestic firms, for that matter) tend to move capital from country to country in order to maximize their short-run rate of return.

money market **a market for financial assets with maturities of a year or less**

In examining international financial markets, it is useful to begin with a discussion of domestic financial markets. This is because they are, in many respects, similar to one another. Domestic financial markets are segmented into the money market and the capital market. In a **money market**, financial assets that have a maturity of less than one year are traded. Money-market assets include short-term government debt, one-year notes, business commercial paper, and short-term certificates of deposit. These financial assets are a useful way for firms and individuals to earn a low-risk rate of return on money that will be needed in the immediate future. Thus, much of the capital flowing from one national financial market to another is primarily placed in money-market assets.

[4]You may recall that the real interest rate is the nominal or posted interest rate minus the expected rate of inflation.

Long-Run Movements of Portfolio Capital

In addition to short-term capital flows of portfolio capital, there are substantial amounts of capital flowing from one country to another for the purpose of purchasing financial instruments like stocks or bonds that have long maturities. For example, foreign nationals may invest in countries that have active secondary bond markets. Investors have different time horizons, and some investors are seeking a relatively high rate of return over a long period of time. If this is the case, investing in domestic and foreign bonds might be attractive to investors. In a **capital market**, financial assets that have a maturity of more than a year, are traded. Capital market assets include equities, corporate bonds, and government bonds. Many of us are familiar with the operations of the domestic capital markets. The prices of 30-year Treasury bonds and the value of the S&P 500 are commonplace pieces of financial information that describe two of the larger U.S. financial markets.

capital market **a market for financial assets with a maturity of more than 1 year**

For instance, suppose that a country has a relatively high national savings rate. Everything else being equal, real interest rates in this country will likely be below those of other countries that have lower national savings rates. If the investor has a low tolerance for risk and a long investment horizon, then investing in high-quality bonds in foreign countries may be an attractive option. For example, Japanese insurance companies and pension funds have invested large amounts of long-term capital in the U.S. bond market because real interest rates in the U.S. usually are higher than comparable rates in Japan. These Japanese institutions also have a long investment horizon in that insurance premiums and retirement savings today could be invested in long-term financial instruments, as the payments to individuals would not be made for decades. Japanese insurance companies and pension funds are not the only entities with long investment horizons. There are many individuals and firms in the world financial markets that are seeking investments with both an attractive rate of return and a long maturity.

Almost the same argument holds for international investment in equities. If an investor is seeking to maximize his or her long-run rate of return, there is a high probability that having a portion of one's investment portfolio in equities would be optimal. The only remaining issue is deciding what percentage of equities would be in domestic versus foreign markets. The rate of return on various equities in different countries would be an important issue. For example, there may be foreign equities with a higher potential rate of return than that available for domestic equities. In addition to rate of return, risk diversification also plays an important role. The rate of return in national equity markets around the world are not perfectly correlated with one another. In this case, having an internationally diversified portfolio of equities should yield better performance in the long run than would be the case with a purely domestic portfolio.

PARTICIPANTS IN THE INTERNATIONAL FINANCIAL MARKETS

Who is moving all this portfolio capital between countries? As we explained earlier, to a large extent the international financial markets are an extension of domestic financial markets. It should not be surprising, then, to learn that the institutions participating in international financial markets are mainly extensions of domestic financial institutions. Because we are discussing international markets, the movement of capital involves exchanging one currency for another in the foreign exchange market. The purpose of this section is to briefly describe the major participants in international financial markets and, by implication, participants in the foreign exchange market.

Commercial Banks

The commercial banks in a country are the center of the international financial markets. These institutions play a primary role for two reasons. First, commercial banks are at the heart of the domestic payments system in most countries, since both firms and individuals generally deposit large sums of currency in banks. In turn, banks lend these funds to other firms and individuals in need of money. Large commercial banks operating in the global economy perform the same functions by both accepting deposits and making loans to firms in many parts of the world. In such cases, banks move money from one part of their system to another and facilitate the international transmission of capital. A purely domestic bank in a large country conceptually does the same thing. For example, suppose that the California branch of a large U.S. bank temporarily accepts more deposits than it can prudently lend in California. What will the bank do with these excess deposits? It is quite possible that another branch of the bank in a different region of the country is loaning more money than it is taking in deposits. To maximize its profits, the bank would move money from the surplus branch to the deficit branch. This is not only good for the bank but this transfer of funds is also good for the U.S. economy. In moving the money from one branch to another, the bank has enabled the U.S. to move a resource such as capital from an area in which there is a capital surplus to an area in which there is a capital shortage. The capital would be more productively used in the latter area than in the former, resulting in a higher output of goods and services for the country as a whole. In attempting to maximize its own profits, the bank has created a positive externality for the U.S. economy by transferring capital from where it is less needed to where it can be more profitability put to use.

A second reason why large commercial banks operate globally and participate in the international capital markets is due to differences in national banking regulations. In some countries, commercial banks may be legally prohibited from engaging in activities that are permissible in other countries. This is known as regulatory asymmetry. When countries have different regulations, banks (or other financial institutions) may establish branches in other countries in order to engage in domestically prohibited activities. The classic example of this regulatory effect is in the area of investment banking.[5] Until very recently, U.S. law prohibited U.S. commercial banks from engaging in investment banking. Since the degree of bank regulation varies across countries, banks in many countries chose to participate in the international capital markets in order to evade these domestic banking regulations. It should be noted that there is nothing either illegal or unethical about this movement. If governments prohibit banks from engaging in certain activities that can be legally performed in other countries, it is not surprising that banks would choose to establish offshore branches to take advantage of these asymmetries.

[5]Investment banking refers to the underwriting (selling) of new issues of equities and bonds.

To engage in offshore or foreign banking, a domestic bank may choose one of three types of arrangements. The banking regulations imposed in the foreign country often dictate which one of the three arrangements is chosen by the domestic bank. The most limited type of offshore arrangement is an agency office located abroad. An agency office can arrange loans and transfer funds, but it cannot accept deposits. In the second offshore arrangement, a domestic bank can set up a subsidiary office abroad. In this case, the subsidiary can perform all of the functions typically associated with banking in that country. The only real difference between a foreign subsidiary bank and other banks within the foreign country is that the foreign subsidiary bank is owned and controlled by a bank in the home country. The advantage of having a subsidiary abroad is that the subsidiary may be able to engage in banking activities that would not be permissible in the home country due to regulations. The third arrangement is for the bank in the home country to set up a branch bank in a foreign country. The difference between this form of banking and a subsidiary bank is that a branch bank is usually subjected to both the home and the foreign country's bank regulatory requirements. The advantage of a branch bank is that the branch is a fully integrated part of the parent bank and not a legally separate entity.

Corporations

In addition to commercial banks, corporations increasingly participate in the international capital markets. Sometimes, corporations need additional capital to finance the expansion of their business. Usually, corporations raise additional capital by offering initial issues of equities or by issuing bonds of various maturities. In many cases, it may be advantageous for the company to issue these financial instruments in another country to take advantage of financial conditions in the foreign market. For example, suppose that a German firm needs to raise capital by issuing additional common stock. If the German firm believes or has forecasted the value of each Euro to be 1 Euro for a U.S. dollar, and the current exchange rate is 1.25 Euros to the dollar, the company might wish to issue new stock in the U.S equity market.[6] If the company's forecast of the long-run exchange rate were correct, it would be able to receive .25 additional Euros for every dollar by issuing the new stock in the U.S. However, if the company was incorrect in its exchange-rate forecast, issuing stock in a foreign currency could cost the firm part of the net proceeds received from the new stock issue.

Corporations may issue bonds in debt markets located outside their home country. Several reasons would motivate firms to issue foreign bonds. First, as with equities, the corporation may be trying to take advantage of a more favorable exchange rate. In the long run, it may take fewer units of domestic currency to pay back the debt than it would if the bond issue were denominated in the home country's currency. Second, in the long run there is the possibility that real interest rates may be lower in some countries than in others. If this is the case, then, everything else being equal, it may make sense for a company to raise funds in a foreign market. Third, the domestic capital market may be too small to support the issue of new bonds. For example, many of the smaller economies of Europe have capital markets that are too small to support major bond issues. Part of the excitement over the creation of the Euro is the creation of an

[6]There is a reason why the company may conclude this. See Chapter 16 on purchasing power parity for details.

EU-wide bond market. For companies in some of the smaller economies, an EU-wide bond market may offer better options for acquiring capital than was the case before the Euro. Fourth, the domestic capital market may be nonexistent, as many developing countries have no long-term bond market. For companies in these countries, the only alternative to bank loans is to issue bonds in foreign markets.

Nonbank Financial Institutions

Besides commercial banks and corporations, a number of nonbank financial institutions participate in international capital markets. The most important of these nonbank institutions are investment companies and insurance companies. Investment companies generally are organized into two operating divisions. One division is concerned primarily with offering services to individuals and investment organizations like pension funds. Since the firm's clients can benefit from the international diversification of their assets, in most cases large investment companies will allocate some of their assets outside the home country. Investment companies provide this service in several ways. First, they may help their clients purchase financial assets in other countries. Second, for the many investors who do not want to directly own foreign securities, investment companies may provide them with a mutual fund that invests in international equities and/or bonds. In this case, investors can invest some of their financial assets in foreign countries and leave the purchasing decisions in the hands of professional money managers. The second operating division of investment companies is concerned with underwriting new equity and bond issues. Since the amount of new issues in one capital market is inherently limited, investment companies frequently provide this service in a number of foreign markets.

The participation of insurance companies in international capital markets may be less noticeable than the participation of other financial entities such as banks. However, insurance companies usually have a large amount of long-term capital to manage. If an insurance company can invest the money only in the home market, its rate of return and/or level of risk may be inherently limited. As such, most insurance companies invest some of their assets outside the home country.

Speculators

A final group of participants in the foreign exchange market are speculators. Speculators are individual foreign exchange traders, financial institutions, or nonfinancial businesses that buy and sell foreign exchange in order to make a short-run trading profit. For example, say a U.S. currency trader buys British pounds early in the trading day at $1.4345 per pound and sells them later in the day at $1.4488 per pound. During the day, the dollar has depreciated slightly and the pound has appreciated slightly. If the trader had bought and sold one million pounds, the profit would be approximately $14,300 or a bit less than a one percent return. This profit may not sound like much until one considers this was accomplished in a *day*. The returns are high, but so are the risks. As with most markets for financial assets, the operation of large numbers of speculators is crucial in providing liquidity in this market. **Liquidity** is the property associated with being able to buy or sell something easily. It is always possible to buy or sell foreign exchange at the going price because there are always some market participants such as speculators willing to buy or sell in the hopes of making a profit. The activities of speculators also apply to the futures markets.

liquidity **the property associated with being able to buy or sell something easily**

EUROCURRENCY MARKETS

Eurodollar a dollar-denominated account that is located outside the U.S.

Eurocurrency an account denominated in a major currency that is located outside that country

Many of us have heard the term *Eurodollar*, but some of us have only a limited understanding of what the term means. A **Eurodollar** is a dollar-denominated account that exists outside the U.S. The Eurodollar market is part of a larger global market known as the Eurocurrency market. A **Eurocurrency** market is a money market in which accounts denominated in a particular country's currency are located outside that country. "Euro" is a holdover from the days when such accounts existed only in Europe. In reality, Eurocurrency accounts are now part of the global market and can be found in most of the world's major financial centers such as New York, London, or Tokyo. Most Eurocurrency accounts are denominated in U.S. dollars, Euros, Japanese Yen, or British pounds. In our explanation of these markets, we will focus on the Eurodollar market as an example because it is the largest portion of the overall Eurocurrency market. These markets are important because a large percentage of international trade is conducted in these few currencies.

For example, suppose that a Dutch oil firm buys crude oil from Saudi Arabia. The crude oil is priced and the transaction between the two countries occurs in U.S. dollars. The Dutch firm pays for the oil in U.S. dollars, and the Saudi oil company receives U.S. dollars in payment. Consider the position of the Dutch and Saudi firms in this transaction. The Dutch firm could buy the oil by converting Euros into dollars every time it needed to buy oil from Saudi Arabia and then use the dollars to buy the oil. However, since the Dutch firm pays a transaction fee for converting Euros into dollars, this would be inconvenient and costly. Now let us further assume that the Dutch firm is buying oil from Saudi Arabia regularly and, moreover, refining the crude oil into gasoline, some of which is sold to other countries. Some of the payments for this gasoline may be in Euros, but some will be in U.S. dollars. The Dutch firm does not mind having the dollars because it is going to need them to buy additional crude oil. If the firm has only a Dutch bank account denominated in Euros, this is inconvenient because some dollars would come in as receipts and would have to be converted into Euros. At some point, these Euros will need to be converted into dollars again to pay for crude oil. Unless the receipts and expenditures match perfectly, the firm is incurring conversion costs and inconvenience by constantly converting dollars into Euros and back again.

A solution to this problem is a Eurodollar account. For instance, the Dutch firm can set up a dollar-denominated account (a Eurodollar account) with a bank in London. In this case, notice that the firm is Dutch, the account is denominated in U.S. dollars, and the account exists in London. The Dutch firm can now deposit the U.S. dollars it earns from the sale of gasoline in this U.S. dollar-denominated account. Also, the firm can use this dollar-denominated account to pay for the crude oil when necessary. It is quite possible that the Saudi Arabian firm would have a Eurodollar account for the same sort of reasons.

As a customer service, commercial banks are willing to offer Eurocurrency accounts to potential customers. The banks participating in the Eurocurrency markets are taking deposits, but the question then becomes what to do with them. The solution is rather efficient. Much of world trade is conducted in U.S. dollars or the other currencies listed previously. Since much of world trade is financed in the short run, the banks have a demand for short-term loans. They can match maturities on these types of deposits with short-term loans for trade finance. The banks can offer services to both potential depositors and potential borrowers. This makes the Eurocurrency markets advantageous for all parties. Earners of foreign exchange need a place to deposit their currency, while some firms and individuals need to borrow major foreign currencies for short periods of time. The banks earn a rate of return on the difference between the interest rates for depositors and borrowers.

From their beginning in the late 1950s, the Eurocurrency markets have grown and are now valued at nearly $8 trillion. The Eurodollar market is about two-thirds of the total Eurocurrency market. This rapid growth can be attributed to several factors. First, the growth of world trade over the last several decades has been fairly rapid. As international trade in goods and services grows, and since trade among the major developed countries dominates world trade, the demand for accounts denominated in these currencies has grown. Also, much of world trade is conducted in U.S. dollars and a few other major currencies. Thus, as world trade has grown, there has been an even greater rise in the demand for a few major currencies.

SUMMARY

1. The core of the foreign exchange market in the U.S. is a network of commercial banks, located primarily in New York, London, Zurich, Frankfurt, Paris, and Tokyo that purchase and sell foreign-currency demand deposits or foreign exchange. The foreign exchange market is comprised of three submarkets: the retail foreign exchange market; the interbank (wholesale) foreign exchange market; and the foreign exchange futures and option markets at certain commodity and stock exchanges.
2. A large amount of capital flows from one country to another in the form of portfolio capital. The basic motives for portfolio capital flows are yield maximization and risk diversification. International movements of portfolio capital are associated with different national rates of return and the advantages of risk diversification.
3. The money market is a market where financial assets are traded that have a maturity of less than one year. A capital market is usually defined as a market where assets are traded with a maturity of more than a year. The purpose of any financial market is to perform intermediation by putting two different market participants together to move money from one group to the other.
4. Participants in the retail market are individuals, multinational firms, and nonbank financial institutions that purchase or sell foreign exchange to local banks. Participants in the interbank market are the international departments of large financial center banks. Nonbank customers, local banks, and financial center banks all participate through stockbrokers in the exchange that trades foreign exchange futures and options. The activities of speculators are critical in providing liquidity in the foreign exchange market.
5. Most international capital flows are handled by one of several types of financial institutions. Commercial banks are the center of the international capital markets. Corporations increasingly participate in the international capital markets by acquiring additional capital by issuing equities or bonds in another country. A number of different types of nonbank financial institutions also participate in the international capital markets. The most important of these institutions are investment companies and insurance companies.
6. The Eurocurrency markets are deposits of U.S. dollars and major currencies located outside the home country. These deposits occur because much of world trade is financed and paid for using one of the major currencies. As such, Eurocurrency markets are advantageous to all parties in reducing the transaction cost of international trade.

KEY CONCEPTS AND TERMS

- foreign exchange p. 299
- spot exchange rate p. 303
- forward exchange rate p. 303
- futures contract p. 306
- option p. 306
- currency swap p. 306
- risk diversification p. 309
- money market p. 310
- capital market p. 311
- liquidity p. 314
- Eurodollar p. 315
- Eurocurrency p. 315

PROBLEMS AND QUESTIONS FOR REVIEW

1. Why does the existence of international trade lead to the existence of a market for foreign exchange?
2. Describe the size of foreign exchange trading in relation to the world economy.
3. Explain why the forward exchange rate is useful in international trade.
4. If a company buys a product in a foreign country, what options does it potentially have for paying for the goods.
5. If the spot exchange rate of dollars for Euros is 1 dollar per Euro, and the forward exchange rate is 1.5 dollars per Euro, the forward rate is at a premium to the spot rate. Describe why this is true.
6. Look up the current spot and forward exchange rates for the U.S. dollar relative to the Euro, the British pound, and the Japanese yen. Is the dollar at a premium or a discount to each of these currencies?
7. Describe the difference between a futures contract and an option.
8. How does a currency swap work? Why have they become so popular?
9. What is the difference between a money market and a capital market?
10. How does capital mobility enhance individual welfare and a country's welfare? Does international capital mobility tend to enhance the welfare of the world economy?
11. What is the motivation for short-term flows of portfolio capital?
12. What are some of the reasons for long-term movements of portfolio capital?
13. "Don't put all of your eggs in one basket." Explain this saying in terms of risk diversification.
14. List and describe the different private-sector participants in the international capital markets.
15. What are the different organizational forms that banks can use to participate in global financial markets?
16. Speculators often have a bad reputation. Is this reputation warranted?
17. What is the Eurocurrency market? Who participates in this market?
18. What is the difference between the Eurodollar market and the Eurocurrency markets?
19. Why would a company such as Exxon maintain a Eurocurrency account?

SUGGESTED READINGS AND WEB SITES

"Capital Goes Global," *The Economist,* October 25, 1997, pp. 87–88.
A quick look at the increasing mobility of capital in the world economy.
Financial Times (www.ft.com)
The best source of information on European exchange rates.
Barbara Garson, Money Makes the World Go Around: One Investor Tracks Her Cash Through the Global Economy from Brooklyn to Bangkok and Back, New York: Viking Press, 2001.
An entertaining book on the details of capital flows in the world economy.
"Global Equity Markets," *The Economist,* May 5, 2001, pp. 1–33.
The fall in global equity markets in 2000 was a shock to the world economy. This survey explains the rise in equity prices and what led to the fall.

Maurice Obstfeld, "The Global Capital Market: Benefactor or Menace?" *Journal of Economic Perspectives* 12(4), Fall 1998, pp. 9–30.
A quick review of the basic facts of the international capital markets.
"Perils of the Hedge Highwire," *Business Week,* October 26, 1998, pp. 74–76.
A short but informative article on how firms decide to hedge their exposure to exchange rate changes.
Peter J. Quirk, "Money Laundering: Muddying the Macroeconomy," *Finance & Development* 34(1), March 1997, pp. 7–9.
An excellent short piece on the mechanics and effects of money laundering.
Jim Rogers, *Adventure Capitalist,* New York: Random House, 2003.
A sort of sequel to Investment Biker, this book is an entertaining look at the world economy through the eyes of an experienced international investor.
The Economist (www.economist.com)
An excellent source of information on exchange rates for major developed and developing countries on a weekly basis.
UNCTD, World Investment Report, Geneva: UNCTD, 2003.
Published annually, this report contains extensive information on global capital flows.
Wall Street Journal (www.wsj.com)
A good source of daily foreign exchange market information.

Chapter 14

Exchange Rates and Their Determination: A Basic Model

"The exchange rate is determined from day to day by supply and demand of home currency in terms of foreign currency. Each transaction is two-sided, and sales are equal to purchases. Any change in the conditions of demand or of supply reflects itself in a change in the exchange rate, and at the ruling rate the balance of payments balances from day to day, or from moment to moment."
—Joan Robinson

INTRODUCTION

The international value of a country's currency has become an inescapable part of the daily flow of economic information. Most individuals are aware that a country's exchange rate is important, but many of us do not have a clear idea of why the exchange rate matters or what causes it to change. As the chapter's opening quote indicates, the familiar tools of supply and demand analysis can be used to determine a country's exchange rate. In this chapter, you will learn why the supply and demand model works in analyzing exchange rates—in the same manner, in fact, that it works in analyzing the price of gasoline or pizza, for one dollar or one yen or one gallon of gasoline is indistinguishable from another. By the end of this chapter you should have a good grasp of why exchange rates are important and what factors cause them to change over the long run. Finally, it is obvious to even a casual observer that exchange rates change frequently. These frequent changes, or volatility, are a source of aggravation for individuals, businesses, and governments. The final part of the chapter explains what economists know about the effects of exchange-rate volatility on international trade.

EXCHANGE RATES

Let's return to our example in Chapter 13 in which a U.S. importer is purchasing British Jaguars. To purchase the Jaguars, the importer needs to obtain British pounds by exchanging dollars for pounds. The demand for foreign currency is derived from individuals demanding foreign goods and services. This relationship can also be applied in reverse. As individuals in the U.K. demand U.S. products, there is an increased demand for dollars. However, this raises the question of how many dollars must be exchanged to obtain the requisite number of pounds, or vice versa? In this example, the relevant exchange rate is the U.S. dollar–U.K. pound exchange rate. In general, the exchange rate is the price of one country's currency in terms of another. The demand for British pounds relative to the supply of pounds will determine the exchange rate, just as the demand for gasoline relative to the supply of gasoline determines the price of gasoline. Exchange rates fluctuate considerably over time. However, unlike the price of gasoline, changes in the exchange rate are expressed as changes in the value of the domestic country's currency. An increase in the value of a currency is referred to as **appreciation**. Analogously, a decline in the value of the currency is referred to as **depreciation**.

appreciation an increase in the value of a currency

depreciation a decrease in the value of a currency

For example, let's assume that the exchange rate is $2 per pound, which means that one pound costs $2. If the exchange rate increases to $3 per pound, we would say that the dollar has depreciated. Although the price has risen, each U.S. dollar is now worth less relative to British pounds. It now takes more dollars to buy a pound than it did before. If the exchange rate declines from $2 per pound to $1 per pound, we would say that the dollar has appreciated, as it now takes only $1 to buy one pound.

This example can be expressed in reverse, or by the number of pounds it takes to purchase a dollar. An exchange rate of $2 per pound is the same thing as an exchange rate of 1/2 pound per dollar. In this case, a depreciation of the dollar could be seen as a change in the exchange rate to 1/3 of a pound per $1. As before, note that each dollar is buying a smaller part of a pound. An appreciation of the dollar would be the change in the exchange rate to one pound per dollar. As we described in Chapter 13, when the exchange rate is quoted as a direct quote—domestic currency per unit of foreign currency—an increase in the exchange rate means that the dollar has depreciated. When the exchange rate is expressed as units of foreign currency per unit of domestic currency—an indirect quote—an increase in the exchange rate means that the dollar has appreciated.

The way that exchange rates are reported can create some confusion among nonspecialists. Exchange rates can be quoted either as domestic currency per unit of foreign currency (a direct quote) or as units of foreign currency per unit of domestic currency (an indirect quote). One can easily see both quotes in the same issue of a business publication such as the *The Financial Times*. Using the U.S. as an example, the exchange rate between the dollar and the British pound is almost always reported as dollars per pound (direct quote). However, the exchange rate between the dollar and the Japanese yen is usually reported as yen per dollar. The direct quote is based on one yen being worth approximately one U.S. penny. So the exchange rate of 110 yen to the dollar is somewhat easier to think about than .0090909 dollars per yen (indirect quote). Each country has its own conventions concerning how the exchange rate is reported for each foreign currency.

As we saw in the previous chapter, the spot market for foreign exchange is the market where transactions are concluded at the same time the price is agreed on. To measure the percentage appreciation or depreciation of the spot rate over time using direct quotes, the following equation is used:

$$\% \Delta \text{ in Spot Rate} = [(\text{beginning rate} - \text{ending rate})/\text{beginning rate}] \times 100$$

Since our purpose is to learn the basics of the foreign exchange market and exchange rate determination, we will view most transactions from the domestic country's point of view. Viewing the foreign exchange market from this perspective means that the exchange rate will be expressed as the number of units of domestic currency needed to obtain a unit of foreign currency. When showing movements in the exchange rate over time, a rise in the exchange rate means that the domestic currency has depreciated. If the exchange rate falls, the domestic currency has appreciated. For example, Figure 14.1 shows the movements in the value of the U.S. dollar with respect to the Canadian dollar, the U.K. pound, and the Japanese yen from 1980 through 2006, and for the Euro from 1999 through 2006. As the figure indicates, the U.S. dollar has both appreciated and depreciated against these four major currencies at different points in time.

THE DEMAND FOR FOREIGN EXCHANGE

demand for foreign exchange the demand for the currency of one country by residents of another country

You have learned that the **demand for foreign exchange** is a result of domestic residents demanding foreign goods and services, and that the exchange rate is simply the price of foreign exchange. Let's examine the demand for foreign exchange in more detail in order to learn what factors specifically affect this demand. Suppose that a U.S. importer wants to buy Jaguars, and suppose that a Jaguar costs 30,000 British pounds. The dollar price of the Jaguars depends on the exchange rate. If the exchange rate were $3 per pound, the Jaguar would cost the importer $90,000. While there might be some demand for Jaguars in the U.S. at this price, the quantity demanded would be fairly small. If the exchange rate fell to $2 per pound, the dollar price of the Jaguar would fall to $60,000 and the quantity demanded would be somewhat higher. If the exchange rate were $1 per pound, the car in question would cost only $30,000 and the quantity demanded in the U.S. would be even larger.

What we have just determined is a demand curve for foreign exchange as shown in Figure 14.2. As the exchange rate falls, the dollar appreciates and Jaguars become less expensive in dollar terms. As the car becomes less expensive, the quantity demanded increases. This is illustrated in Figure 14.2 as a movement from point A to point B to point C. When the only factor that changes is the price, in this case the exchange rate, one moves from one point to another point on the same demand curve. We call this movement a change in the quantity demanded. Note that the price of the car in terms of British pounds has not changed. The only thing that has changed is the exchange rate. As the exchange rate changes, the amount of goods the U.S. imports from Britain changes. The same principle applies to the demand for all British goods and services in general. At $3 per pound, a British vacation becomes fairly expensive for the average U.S. citizen. At $1 per pound, the same vacation would cost a lot fewer dollars. The same would be true of financial assets. British stocks and bonds would be relatively inexpensive at $1 per pound and fairly expensive at

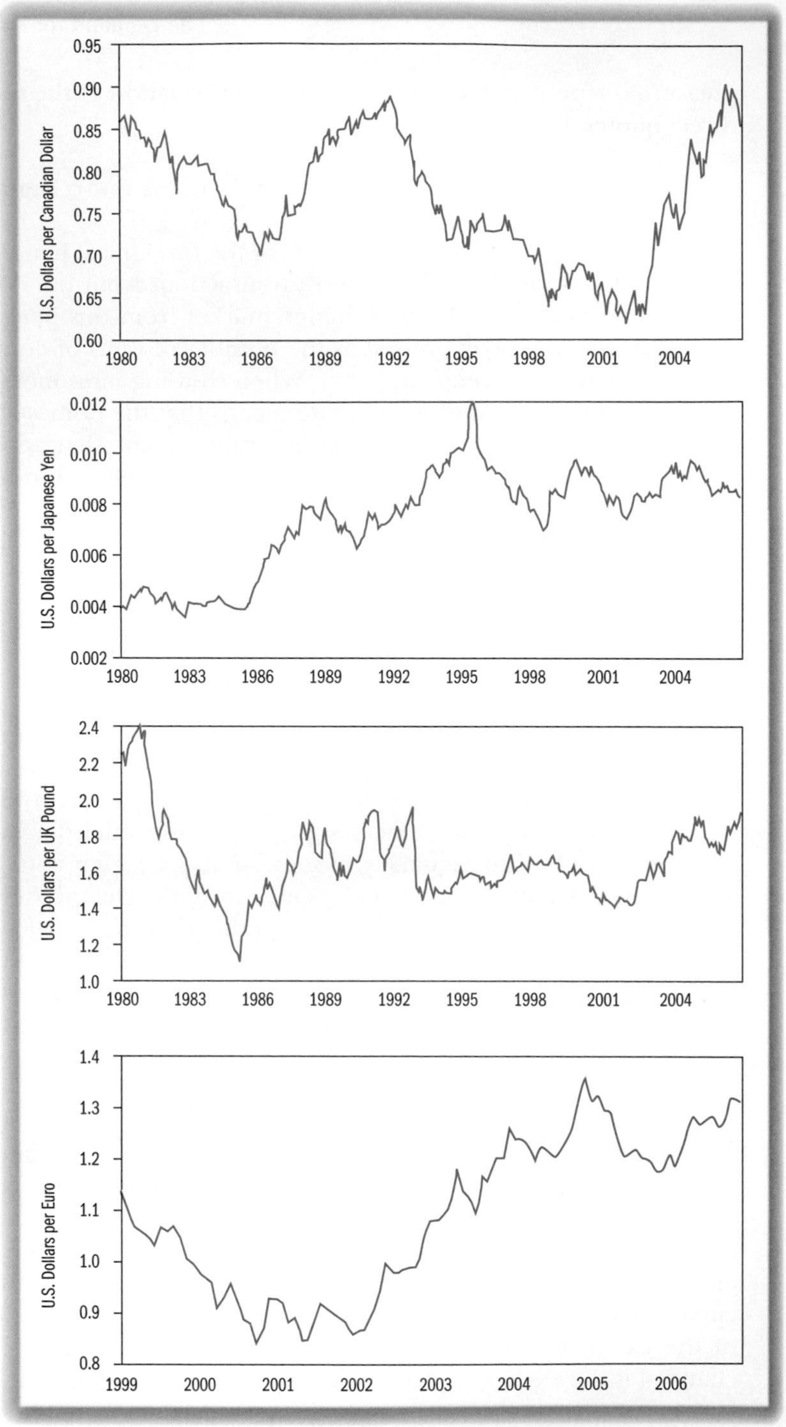

Figure 14.1 Foreign Exchange Rates of the U.S. Dollar

Source: IMF, *International Financial Statistics*, CD-ROM, Washington, D.C.: IMF, July 2007.

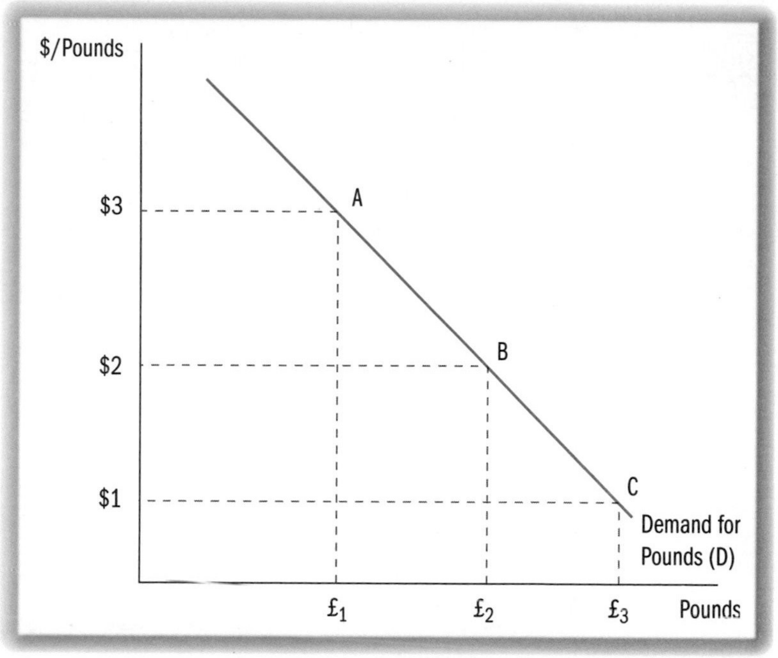

Figure 14.2 **The Demand for Foreign Exchange**

As the exchange rate changes, the quantity of pounds demanded changes. An appreciation of the dollar from $3 per pound would cause an increase in the quantity demanded.

$3 per pound.[1] As with any demand curve, one must distinguish between changes in the quantity demanded and changes in demand. For example, if any other factor that influences the demand for the good in question changes, the entire demand curve shifts.

Shifts in the Demand for Foreign Exchange

What would cause the demand curve for foreign exchange to change or shift? Conceptually, shifts in the demand for foreign exchange are not really any different from shifts in the demand for any other good or service. As with most goods and services, changes in the demand for foreign exchange are related to a country's income level, the relative price levels, and tastes and preferences. The two most important factors that shift the U.S. demand for British pounds are changes in U.S. income and prices in the U.S. relative to prices in the U.K. Keep in mind that we are only using the U.S. and the U.K. for illustrative purposes. The analysis can be generalized to other countries.

Changes in Domestic Income

If U.S. income changes, the demand for British goods will change along with the demand for most other products, both foreign and domestic. As U.S. income increases, the demand for all goods increases, including the demand for imported British goods.

[1]The impact of interest rates on the flow of capital between countries is considered in Chapter 15.

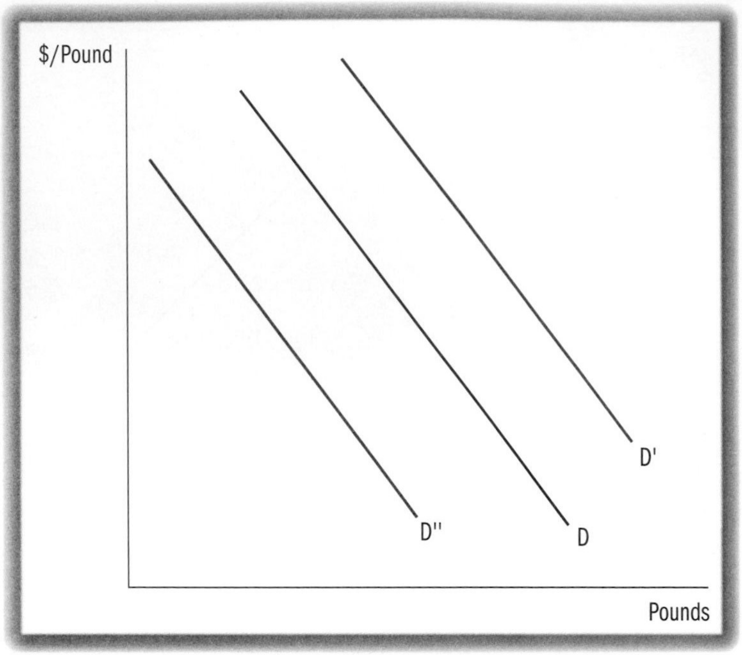

Figure 14.3 The Change in Demand for Foreign Exchange

An increase or decrease in U.S. income causes a rightward or leftward shift of the demand curve, respectively. This change in demand means that more or fewer pounds would be demanded at any given exchange rate. In a similar manner, a decrease or increase in British price, prices would shift the demand curve right or left, respectively.

This increase in U.S. income will cause an increase in the demand for British goods. The increase in the demand for British goods causes an increase in demand for British pounds in the foreign exchange market, and the demand curve shifts to the right. In Figure 14.3, we show the shift in the demand for foreign exchange from the original demand curve to the demand curve labeled D′. At any given exchange rate, notice that the amount of British pounds demanded in the foreign exchange market is now higher because U.S. income is higher. Analogously, a decline in U.S. income would cause a decline in the demand for British goods and a decline in the number of pounds demanded at any given exchange rate. In Figure 14.3, this is shown as a movement to the left in the demand for British pounds from the original demand curve to the demand curve labeled D″.

In general, when U.S. GDP rises rapidly, the income of U.S. citizens also rises, and the demand for Jaguars and other British goods increases. Importers will demand more cars to satisfy U.S. consumers and will demand more British pounds. On the other hand, when the U.S. has a recession, GDP declines and the income of U.S. consumers also declines. With lower consumer demand, the importer will demand fewer cars and fewer British pounds.

Changes in Relative Prices

The second factor that will change or shift the demand for foreign exchange is changes in relative prices between the two countries. Consider what would happen to

Income Changes and Trade

In the previous section, you learned that the rate of growth of domestic income tends to affect imports, while the rate of foreign economic growth tends to affect exports. We can illustrate the potential effects that income has on imports and exports using the U.S. as an example. GDP and income are highly correlated, and Figure 14.4 examines changes in U.S. GDP relative to foreign GDP. The bars in the figure measure the percentage difference between foreign GDP growth and U.S. GDP growth from 1992 to 2003. The difference is the trade-weighted average of GDP growth in Canada, Japan, Mexico, Germany, the U.K., China, Taiwan, Korea, France, Singapore, Italy, Hong Kong, Malaysia, the Netherlands, and Brazil—minus U.S. GDP growth. A positive percentage indicates that U.S. incomes were rising more slowly than incomes in the 15 largest trading partners, and vice versa. U.S. income growth was relatively slow, as the U.S. economy experienced a recession while foreign economies continued to grow. This led to a large positive growth differential. The growth differential narrowed during much of the 1990s to less than one percent. A large negative growth differential occurred in 1998 due to exceptionally fast growth in the U.S. economy relative to the 15 largest trading partners. As economic growth in the U.S. slowed in the late 1990s, the growth differential became positive. Everything else equal, a positive growth differential for the U.S. would tend to reduce imports and increase exports. A negative growth differential would tend to increase imports and reduce exports. As we will see, many factors affect imports and exports, but domestic income versus foreign income is an important one.

Figure 14.4 U.S. Trade Balance and GDP Growth Differentials

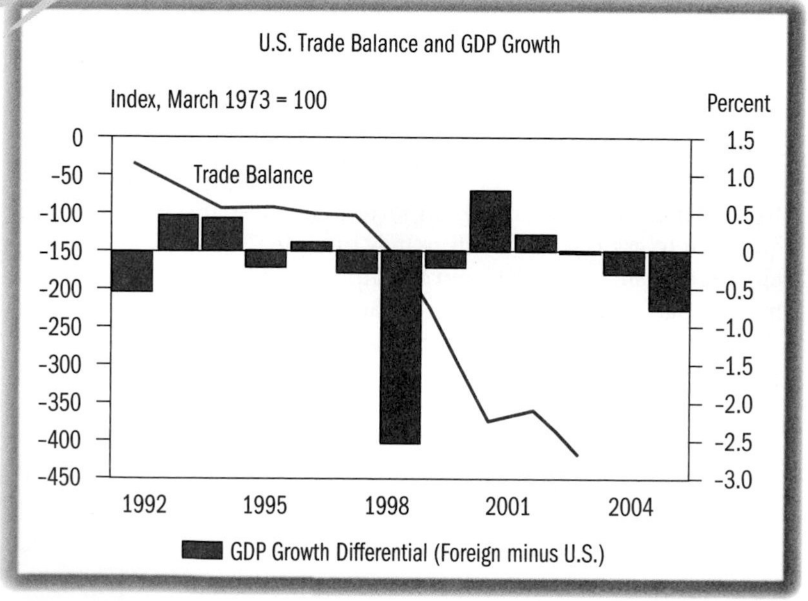

Source: International Transactions, Federal Reserve Bank of Cleveland, *Economic Trends,* October 2003. p. 8.

the demand for British pounds if prices for all goods and services rose in the U.K. If British prices increase (the pound price of Jaguars rises) with no change in the exchange rate, the dollar price of imported Jaguars and other British goods would rise in the U.S. As import prices of British goods increase, U.S. consumers would begin to substitute U.S.-produced goods and services for British-produced goods and services. As a result, the demand for British pounds would decline in the foreign exchange market. Everything else equal, the demand for pounds shifts to the left, as there are fewer pounds demanded at any given exchange rate.

The reverse phenomenon would occur if U.S. prices rose relative to prices in the U.K. For example, if the prices of U.S.-produced goods increase with no change in British prices, U.S. consumers would begin to purchase more of the relatively less expensive British goods. With the demand for British goods rising, the demand for pounds would rise along with it. In Figure 14.3, this movement is represented by an increase in the demand for British pounds in the foreign exchange market and at any given exchange rate there would be a larger number of pounds demanded.

In summary, if domestic prices rise relative to foreign prices, the demand for foreign exchange increases. If foreign prices rise relative to domestic prices, the demand for foreign exchange decreases. In practice, price level changes within a country are not so discrete. Most countries experience a continuous change in prices measured by the country's inflation rate. Our discussion concerning relative price changes and their impact on the demand for foreign exchange can be generalized to relative inflation rates between countries. Countries with high levels of inflation relative to their trading partners would tend to experience increases in the demand for foreign goods and foreign exchange. As we will see, this increase in demand will tend to cause a depreciation of the domestic currency over time.[2] In a simple model of exchange rate determination, three important factors tend to cause a change in the demand for foreign exchange: changes in domestic income; changes in foreign prices; and changes in domestic prices.

THE SUPPLY OF FOREIGN EXCHANGE

supply of foreign exchange **the amount of foreign exchange supplied in the foreign exchange market**

In our example, if it is U.S. importers who buy foreign exchange, then a reasonable question to ask is who will ultimately provide the **supply of foreign exchange** to the foreign exchange market? In our example, the supply of pounds in the foreign exchange market occurs as a result of the British demand for U.S. products. For example, consider a British importer who wishes to buy a U.S. computer network system priced at \$100,000. In order to purchase this product, the British importer needs to obtain the requisite dollars from a British bank by exchanging pounds for dollars at the current exchange rate. If the exchange rate were \$2 per pound, the importer would have to exchange (supply) £50,000 in order to obtain the computer network system. This British demand for dollars to buy U.S. goods effectively creates a supply of pounds in

[2]An extreme example of this would be *currency substitution*. This occurs where domestic residents face such high inflation that the domestic currency is not performing its store of value function. In this case, people start substituting foreign exchange for domestic currency. For a readable discussion of this, see Guillermo Calvo and Carlos A. Vegh, "Currency Substitution in High Inflation Countries," *Finance & Development* 30(1), March 1993, pp. 34–37.

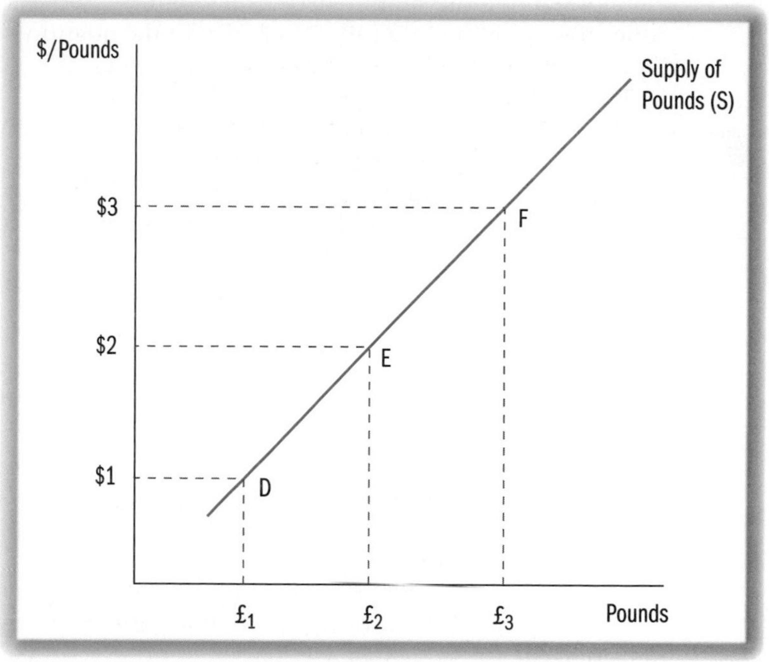

Figure 14.5 **The Supply of Foreign Exchange**

As the exchange rate changes, the quantity of pounds supplied changes. As the exchange rate increases, the dollar depreciates, and the quantity supplied of pounds to the foreign exchange market increases. This is because the British demand for imports increases.

the foreign exchange market. More generally, British demand for foreign goods would give rise to the same process of selling pounds in the foreign exchange market. What if the exchange rate were $1 per pound? The computer network system costing $100,000 in the U.S. would now cost the British importer £100,000. At that exchange rate ($1 per pound), there would be fewer computer network systems sold to the British. As a result, there would be fewer pounds supplied in the foreign exchange market. Finally, consider the same transaction at an exchange rate of $3 per pound. At this exchange rate, the computer network system would cost £33,333. At this price, the demand would be higher and the quantity of pounds supplied to the foreign exchange market also would be higher.

This relationship between the quantity of pounds supplied to the foreign exchange market and the exchange rate is shown in Figure 14.5. As the exchange rate moves from $1 per pound to $3 per pound, the quantity of pounds supplied to the foreign exchange market increases. Like any other supply curve, this supply of pounds slopes upward and to the right.[3] Everything else equal, as the exchange rate increases

[3]We have implicitly assumed that the British demand for U.S. products is elastic. This means that as the pound price of U.S. goods decline, the increase in the quantity of U.S. goods demanded is larger than the fall in price. Under these conditions, the total revenue of the exporting firm increases and the supply of pounds is positively sloped. Under conditions when the demand for U.S. products is inelastic, the supply of pounds will be negatively sloped.

one moves along the supply curve from point D to point E to point F. This movement along the supply curve is called a change in the quantity supplied. In our example, as the exchange rate increases, the dollar depreciates, U.S. goods become less expensive, the British buy more U.S. goods, and the quantity of pounds the British supply to the foreign exchange market increases. The supply of pounds to the foreign exchange market is dependent on the British demand for imports. The same would be true for any country. The amount of domestic currency supplied to the foreign exchange market depends on the foreign demand for imported goods.

Shifts in the Supply of Foreign Exchange

As we illustrated with the demand for foreign exchange, the supply of foreign exchange can change or shift in response to changes in the factors that influence it. The two most important factors that shift the supply of foreign exchange are changes in income and relative prices.

Changes in Foreign Income

Consider, for example, what would happen to the supply of pounds in the foreign exchange market if British income rises? With this increase in income, British demand for all goods and services increases, including the demand for U.S. exports (British imports). As British importers purchase more U.S. products, they need to sell more pounds in the foreign exchange market in order to obtain the necessary dollars. As a result, the supply of pounds to the foreign exchange market increases at any given exchange rate. This rightward shift in the supply of foreign exchange (pounds) is illustrated in Figure 14.6 as the shift of the original supply curve to the new supply curve labeled S′. The reverse would occur if income in the U.K. fell. Lower British incomes would lower the British demand for goods and services, including its demand for imports. This causes a decline in the amount of pounds sold in the foreign exchange market and produces a leftward shift in the supply of pounds. This effect is shown in Figure 14.6 as a shift in the original supply curve to the new supply curve labeled S″.

Changes in Relative Prices

A change in relative prices between the two countries similarly will shift the supply of foreign exchange. For instance, if prices in the U.K. rise relative to prices in the U.S., British demand for imports (U.S. exports) will rise. This increase in the supply of foreign exchange occurs as British consumers substitute relatively higher-priced domestic goods for relatively lower-priced U.S. goods. This effect is represented by a rightward shift of the supply curve in Figure 14.6. An opposite effect would occur if U.S. prices rose relative to British prices. As U.S. prices rise, British consumers substitute relatively lower-priced domestic goods for the higher-priced U.S. goods. As a result, British consumers purchase fewer U.S. goods and the supply of pounds in the foreign exchange market decreases. The supply curve in this case shifts to the left, as shown in Figure 14.6.

EQUILIBRIUM IN THE FOREIGN EXCHANGE MARKET

The concepts of the demand and supply of foreign exchange can now be combined to explain the equilibrium exchange rate. In our example, the demand for and supply of

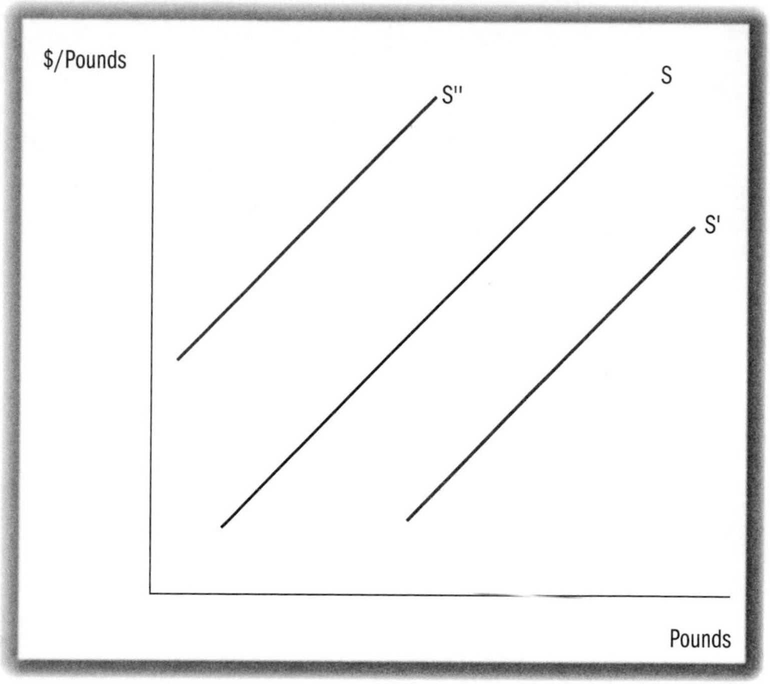

Figure 14.6 The Change in Supply for Foreign Exchange

An increase or decrease in British income would cause a rightward or leftward shift of the supply of pounds in the foreign exchange market. This change in supply means that at any given exchange rate, the quantity of pounds available changes. Changes in the relative price of British or U.S. goods can also shift the supply curve.

equilibrium exchange rate **the exchange rate where the quantity demanded of foreign exchange equals the quantity supplied**

pounds are shown in Figure 14.7. In this case, the **equilibrium exchange rate** occurs when the quantity of pounds demanded is equal to the quantity of pounds supplied. In our example, this equilibrium is shown in Figure 14.7 at $2 per pound, point E. At this exchange rate, the amount of pounds that U.S. consumers want to purchase exactly matches the number of pounds that Britons are willing to supply in order to obtain dollars. For many individuals, the term *exactly* may be troubling, because exchange rates fluctuate over the course of a trading day and considerably more than that over longer periods of time. The precise equilibrium shown in Figure 14.7 should be thought of as an equilibrium that the foreign exchange market would achieve if everything else remained constant. However, exchange rates move very quickly as economic conditions and expectations change. There are already several variables we have described that can influence exchange rates, and these variables are continually changing and thus the equilibrium exchange rate is constantly changing.[4]

[4]GDP statistics for most countries are published quarterly and price indexes are published monthly. However, the underlying income and relative prices are in constant flux.

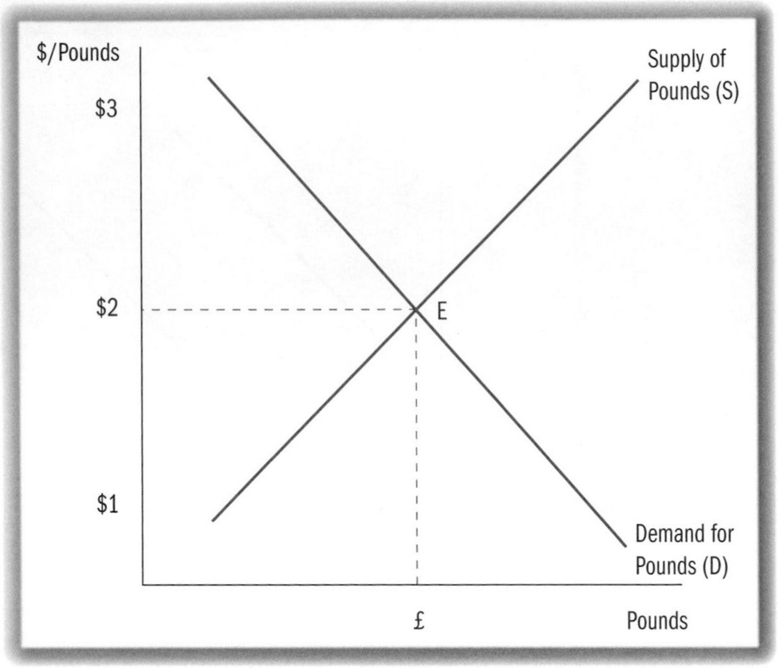

Figure 14.7 The Equilibrium Exchange Rate

Given income and relative prices in the U.K. and the U.S., equilibrium in the foreign exchange market occurs at point E, where the exchange rate is $2 per pound and the quantity of pounds exchange in the market is represented by £.

CHANGES IN THE EQUILIBRIUM EXCHANGE RATE

To illustrate the effect of changes in income and relative prices on the equilibrium exchange rate, we will describe several examples. As our first example, consider the case where the equilibrium in the foreign exchange market is $2 per pound, which is illustrated at point E in Figure 14.8. Now, assume that U.S. incomes increase, causing the demand for imports in the U.S. and the demand for British pounds to increase. The increase in the demand for pounds is illustrated as a shift the demand curve to D′. With the supply of pounds held constant, the equilibrium exchange rate has increased from $2 dollars per pound to $3 dollars per pound. This new equilibrium is shown as point F in the Figure. The demand for pounds has increased relative to the supply and the price of a pound in terms of dollars has risen.

A second situation showing how the exchange rate changes is illustrated in Figure 14.9. Suppose that the equilibrium in the foreign exchange market is currently at point E at the exchange rate of $2 per pound. Now, assume that the U.S. inflation rate is greater than the U.K. inflation rate (i.e., prices in the U.S. are rising faster than prices in the U.K). As a result of the rising relative U.S. prices, the demand for pounds increases as U.S. consumers buy more relatively inexpensive British goods. In addition, the supply of pounds decreases as U.S. exports fall because U.S. goods have become relatively more expensive in the U.K. The new equilibrium in the foreign

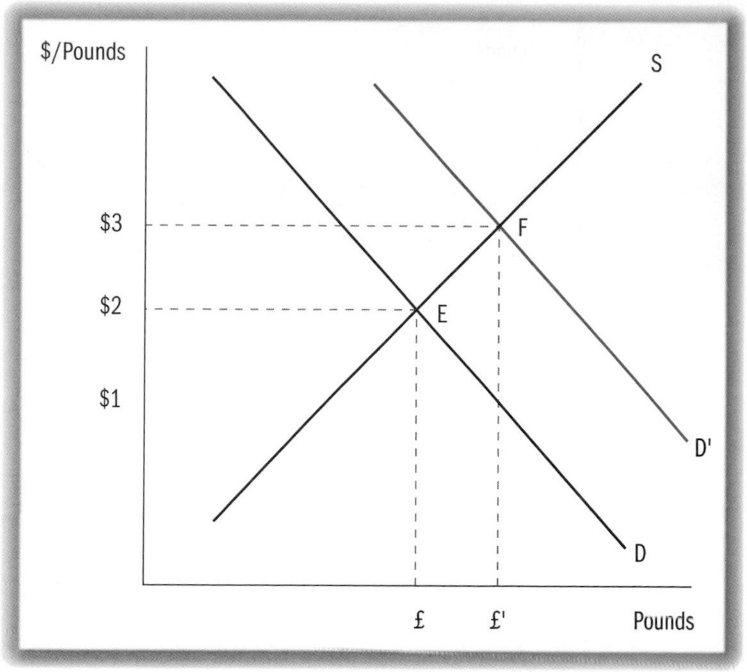

Figure 14.8 Change in the Equilibrium Exchange Rate

An increase in U.S. income causes a rightward shift in the demand for pounds. Everything else equal, the equilibrium exchange rate would increase and the dollar would depreciate.

exchange market is shown at point F, where the exchange rate is $3 per pound. Notice that the total volume of trade shown on the horizontal axis has not changed and trade is still balanced at the new exchange rate. The reason for this result will be discussed in Chapter 16. At this point, suffice it to say that the exchange rate is simply trying to correct for the change in relative prices between the U.S. and the U.K. The general principle is that countries with relatively high or low rates of inflation will tend to have currencies that depreciate or appreciate over time, respectively. The depreciation of the currency in the foreign exchange market is simply the market's way of compensating for differential rates of inflation.

Of course, there are many different combinations of events that could shift the demand and/or supply of foreign exchange and cause a change the exchange rate. Table 14.1 summarizes the effect of changes in the factors that can influence the equilibrium exchange rate. However, keep in mind that these are the effects of the various factors if all other factors remain constant. Many different combinations of these factors could occur, leading to a very large number of possible changes in the equilibrium exchange rate.

EXCHANGE RATE VOLATILITY AND INTERNATIONAL TRADE

As the examples presented in this chapter illustrate, changes in the exchange rate make international trade different from interregional trade within a large country

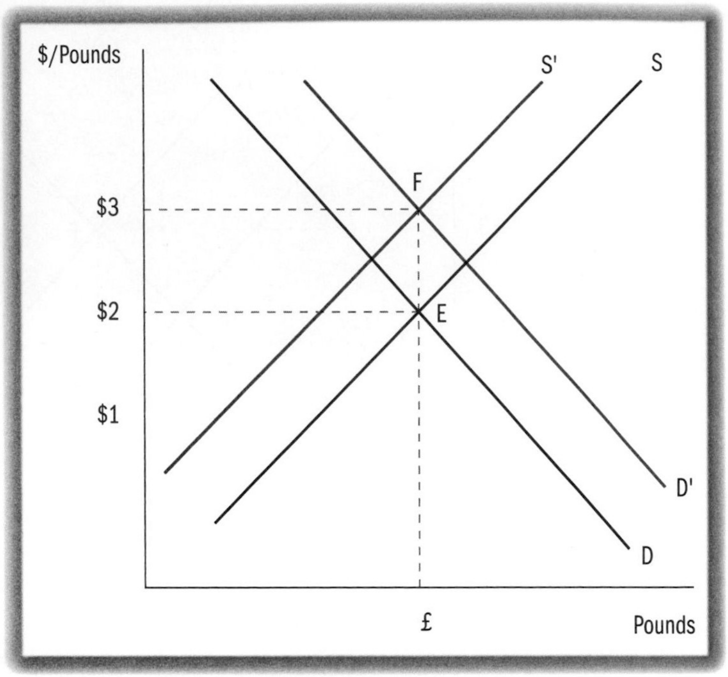

Figure 14.9 A Change in the Equilibrium Exchange Rate

An increase in U.S. prices would cause the exchange rate to increase and the dollar to depreciate. This occurs because U.S. demand for imports increases while the U.K. demand for U.S. exports decreases.

The Dollar as a Vehicle Currency

In this chapter, the dollar and the pound are treated as equivalent currencies. For example, if the U.S. wanted to buy British products, the U.S. importer would have to acquire pounds. In reality, many U.S. importers can purchase foreign goods with dollars. The dollar's role in international trade and finance goes even further. Exporters in many countries price their products in international markets in dollars, rather than in the local currency. A familiar example is crude oil, which is always quoted in dollar terms. This enables countries to trade with one another in dollar terms. For instance if a Mexican importer wanted to buy Brazilian products, the whole transaction might occur in dollars. It has been estimated that 90 percent of foreign exchange trades involve the dollar.[5] The point is that the dollar, and to a lesser extent the Euro and the Japanese yen, assumes a larger role in world trade than just the imports and exports of these countries. These currencies are truly international in the sense that they are freely acceptable as payment in many cases between unrelated countries.[6]

[5]See Craig S. Hakkio, "The Dollar's International Role," *Contemporary Policy Issues* 11(2), April 1993, pp. 62–75.

[6]It remains to be seen whether or not the Euro will at some point become a vehicle currency.

Table 14.1 Impact of Changes in the Demand and Supply of Foreign Exchange and the Equilibrium Exchange Rate

Change in Determinant	Change in the Dollar-Pound Exchange Rate	Change in the Value of the U.S. Dollar
Increase in U.K. demand for U.S. Exports	Decreases	Appreciation
Decrease in U.K. demand for U.S. Exports	Increases	Depreciation
Increase in U.S. demand for U.K. Exports	Increases	Depreciation
Decrease in U.S. demand for U.K. Exports	Decreases	Appreciation
Increase in U.S. Prices	Increases	Depreciation
Decrease in U.S. Prices	Decreases	Appreciation
Increase in U.K. Prices	Decreases	Appreciation
Decrease in U.K. Prices	Increases	Depreciation
Increase in U.S. Incomes	Increases	Depreciation
Decrease in U.S. Incomes	Decreases	Appreciation
Increase in U.K. Incomes	Decreases	Appreciation
Decrease in U.K. Incomes	Increases	Depreciation

such as the U.S. or Brazil. As our examples indicated, the price of Jaguars in the U.K. and/or the price of computer network systems in the U.S. can remain unchanged in the domestic currency but change considerably when denominated in foreign currencies. In the short run, exchange rate changes can be mitigated to a certain extent through the use of forward or futures markets for foreign exchange. However, using these markets is not free, and the reduction of risk can be purchased only at some additional cost. In addition, changes in exchange rates are difficult to forecast in the long run and impede the ability of individuals and businesses to make plans over any time horizon longer than six months. Taken together, both risk and uncertainty depress international trade and investment, but the degree to which they do so has been a matter of intense debate. In other words, the direction of the effect is no doubt negative but the exact magnitude of the effect is not known.[7] In any case, this type of risk and uncertainty do not exist in domestic trade. This creates a bias toward domestic as opposed to international transactions if exchange rates are allowed to fluctuate in response to changes in the factors that determine them.

Fluctuations in exchange rates also have led to a cottage industry in forecasting exchange rate changes. Even using our simplified demand and supply model, such

[7]For an excellent discussion of the issue of the effects of exchange rate volatility, see Michael D. McKenzie, "The Impact of Exchange Rate Volatility on International Trade Flows," *Journal of Economic Surveys* 13(1), February 1999, pp. 71–106.

Exchange Rate Pass Through

The model of the demand and supply of foreign exchange used in the chapter to determine the equilibrium exchange rate contained a very important assumption. This assumption embodied in our analysis was that when the exchange rate changes, the price of the imported product expressed in the domestic currency changes to reflect the new exchange rate. For example, suppose that the dollar appreciates by 10 percent against the British pound. In our analysis, we assumed that the dollar price of British imports would therefore fall by 10 percent. As we will see in Chapter 16, in the long run this price movement would generally occur. However, in the short run a change in the exchange rate may not perfectly "pass through" to the domestic price of imports.

We can employ a supply and demand model to show how this can occur. Consider Figure 14.10, where we illustrate U.S. imports from the U.K. The vertical axis shows the dollar price of imports sold in the U.S. market and the horizontal axis shows the quantity of imports demanded or supplied in the U.S. market. Given the exchange rate of $2 per pound, the demand and supply of imports are in equilibrium at point E. As the exchange rate changes, the demand for imports does not shift as the demand curve is dollar priced. However, as the exchange rate changes, the supply of imports will shift as the supply of imports is determined by the pound price of imports multiplied by the exchange rate (dollar per pound).

Figure 14.10 Exchange Rate Pass Through

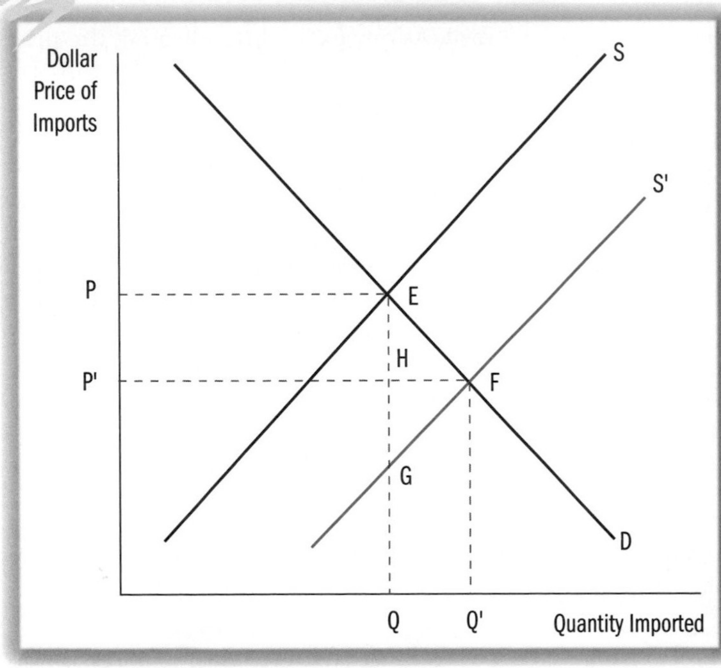

Now assume that the dollar appreciates from $2 per pound to $1.50 per pound. In this case, the supply of imports will shift downward or to the right. Thus, as the dollar appreciates, U.K. exporters are willing and able to supply more goods to the U.S. market. In the figure, this is shown as a rightward shift of the supply of exports from S to S′. The new equilibrium is would now be established at point F.

From the figure, it is clear that U.S. import prices have fallen from P to P′. However, U.S. import prices have not fallen by as much as the increase in supply. This would only occur if the supply curve were completely horizontal (perfectly elastic). Since the supply curve has a positive slope, the change in the U.S. price is less than the appreciation of the currency. A bit of arithmetic will show why this is the case. In the figure, the vertical distance from point E to point G shows the effect of the dollar appreciation on the supply of imports. The change in the dollar price of imports is shown by the vertical distance from point E to point H. The extent to which the appreciation of the currency is "passed through" to the domestic imported price is measured by the ratio of AH to AG. The closer that AH is to AG, the more that the appreciation of the dollar is passed through to the domestic imported price. The actual amount of the pass through depends on the slopes of the demand and supply curves. The more elastic (horizontal) the supply curve, the more that the exchange rate change will affect the domestic price. On the other hand, the more inelastic (vertical) the demand curve, the more that the exchange rate change will pass through to domestic prices.

Our discussions of exchange rate changes in the chapter assumed that the pass through was very high, virtually complete. This is a realistic assumption over medium- to long-run periods of time. However, in the short run, changes in the exchange rate may not be completely passed through to domestic import prices. Also, the degree of pass through may not be the same for all imported goods, because the pass through effect depends on the elasticities of the supply and demand curves in the short run. Estimating exchange rate pass through effects has been one of the more heavily researched issues in international economics. However, it has some practical significance, too, and we will refer to the concept of exchange rate pass through in later chapters.

an exercise is difficult. At minimum, a successful exchange rate forecast would need reasonably accurate forecasts of changes in the two countries' GDPs as well as similar forecasts of changes in their price levels. As we will see, these are not all the factors that affect the exchange rate. Even if the market were as simple as we have described in this chapter, such a forecast would frequently misforecast the actual exchange rate in the future. In many cases, one could misforecast the exchange rate by a considerable amount. The model that we describe does allow us to make some generalizations over the medium to long run. For example, if either country has a pronounced trend in its growth rate of GDP or its inflation rate, we might be able to make some general statements about the probability of the currency's depreciation or appreciation. However, it would be risky to use the model to make any sort of precise forecasts over shorter periods of time.

The basic supply and demand model described in this chapter is a useful representation of the world producers and consumers face in the long run. However, short-run changes in exchange rates are frequently caused by other factors that we have not yet included in the model. In the next chapter, we move from a long-run model of exchange rate determination to a model better suited to explaining both long- and short-run variations in exchange rates.

SUMMARY

1. The exchange rate is the price of one country's currency in terms of another country's currency. For example, in the U.S. the exchange rate refers to the number of dollars necessary to buy one unit of a foreign currency, such as a British pound.
2. Appreciation of the domestic currency is a decrease in the number of units of domestic currency necessary to buy a unit of foreign currency. Depreciation is an increase in the number of units of domestic currency necessary to buy a unit of foreign currency.
3. The demand for foreign exchange is related to changes in domestic income and changes in relative prices. If domestic income rises, the demand for imports and foreign exchange also will rise and vice versa. If domestic prices rise relative to foreign prices, the demand for imports and foreign exchange will tend to rise. A lowering of domestic prices relative to foreign prices generally reduces the demand for imports and foreign exchange.
4. The supply of foreign exchange is related to changes in foreign income and changes in relative prices. If foreign incomes rise, foreigners import more which translates into a need for foreign residents to sell their domestic currency. This creates a supply of foreign exchange. Likewise, an increase in foreign prices relative to domestic prices also induces foreigners to import more and sell their currency to purchase foreign exchange. A drop in foreign income or an increase in domestic prices relative to foreign prices tends to cause a reduction in the supply of foreign exchange.
5. The interaction of the supply and demand for foreign exchange determines the equilibrium exchange rate in a free market.
6. Everything else equal, a country that has faster economic growth than its trading partners will tend to find that its currency is depreciating in the foreign exchange market. A country that has slower economic growth than its trading partners will tend to find that its currency is appreciating in the foreign exchange market.
7. A country that has higher inflation than its trading partners will tend to find that the value of its currency is depreciating in the foreign exchange market. A country that has lower inflation than its trading partners will tend to find that the value of its currency is appreciating in the foreign exchange market.
8. Fluctuations in the exchange rate tend to depress the amount of international trade in goods and services relative to domestic trade in goods and services. This is because international transactions are inherently riskier than domestic transactions as the prices of foreign goods and services fluctuate more than the prices of domestic goods and services.

KEY CONCEPTS AND TERMS

- appreciation p. 320
- depreciation p. 320
- demand for foreign exchange p. 321
- supply of foreign exchange p. 326
- equilibrium exchange rate p. 329

PROBLEMS AND QUESTIONS FOR REVIEW

1. What does the term exchange rate mean?
2. What is meant by an appreciation of a currency such as the U.S. dollar? A depreciation?
3. Describe the difference between a direct quote of the exchange rate and an indirect quote.
4. Find the exchange rate quote for the U.S. dollar relative to the Euro, Japanese yen, British pound, Swiss Franc, Canadian dollar, and the Mexican peso. Which of these are usually quoted as direct quotes and which are indirect.

5. Suppose that the U.S. dollar/British pound exchange rate changed from 2 to 3. What is the percentage change in the exchange rate?
6. Describe how the demand for foreign exchange is related to domestic residents' demand for foreign goods and services.
7. If the number of units of domestic currency required to purchase a unit of foreign currency increases or decreases, what happens to the quantity demanded of the foreign currency?
8. What factors would cause the demand for foreign exchange in a country to increase or decrease?
9. Suppose that the U.S. economy enters a recession. Everything else equal, what would happen to the demand for foreign exchange and the exchange rate?
10. If the number of units of domestic currency per unit of foreign currency increases, the quantity supplied of foreign exchange increases. Explain why this statement is true.
11. What factors would cause the supply of foreign exchange to shift to the left or right?
12. Assume the inflation rate is 2 percent in the U.S. and 5 percent in Mexico. Everything else equal, what would happen to the exchange rate between the two currencies?
13. The equilibrium exchange rate is where the demand for foreign exchange equals the supply of foreign exchange. Once established, this equilibrium should never change. Explain why this statement is not likely to be true.
14. Using supply and demand curves for pounds, analyze the effect of each of the following on the dollar/pound exchange rate.
    a. The British economy slides into a recession.
    b. The U.S. economy grows unusually fast.
    c. The U.S. encounters severe inflation while prices are stable in the U.K.
    d. The U.S. economy slides into a recession.
15. Using the data provided in the text, describe the movements of the dollar relative to the Canadian dollar, the Japanese yen, and the British pound since 1980.
16. "Weak" currencies are usually associated the high inflation and "strong" currencies are usually associated with low inflation. Explain why these associations exist.
17. Why would domestic firms tend to have a bias towards buying and selling domestic goods and services as opposed to foreign goods and services?
18. Suppose that you were given the job of forecasting exchange rates. What is the minimum amount of information you would need to do your job?

SELECTED READINGS AND WEB SITES

R. Z. Aliber, *The International Money Game*, 5th edition, New York: Basic Books, 1987.

An excellent treatment of the operation of the foreign-exchange markets.

"Magnets for Money: A Special Report on Financial Centres," *The Economist*, September 15, 2007, pp. 1–20.

Much of the foreign exchange trading described in the chapter occurs in major financial centers. This article provides an extensive description of the world's major financial centers.

Olsen and Associates (www.oanda.com)

A comprehensive web site giving historical exchange rates and a currency calculator for 192 currencies.

Wall Street Journal (www.wsj.com)

A complete listing of exchange rates is given every Monday in a section entitled "World Value of the Dollar."

Chapter 15

Money, Interest Rates, and the Exchange Rate

"When U.S. interest rates have been significantly higher than foreign rates, capital has tended to flow to the United States, raising the value of the dollar; conversely, when U.S. interest rates have been significantly below foreign rates, capital has tended to flow abroad, depressing the dollar . . . the depreciation of the dollar in the late 1970s reflected, among other factors, our expansionary monetary policy. . . . The reversal of the dollar's decline in 1980 and its unprecedented appreciation through the middle of the decade reflected major change in U.S. macroeconomic policy . . . [T]he Federal Reserve initiated policies that led to a substantial rise in U.S. short-term interest rates."

—Economic Report of the President

INTRODUCTION

So far, we have examined the institutional details of the foreign exchange market and explained what determines the exchange rate. The model of exchange rate determination that we developed in the previous chapter explains some of the movement in exchange rates. Both the rate of inflation and the growth rate of GDP of a country usually do not change dramatically over short periods of time, such as one day to the next. Yet, exchange rates change almost every minute of every business day. As a result, we need to expand our model of exchange rate determination to include another factor that determines or influences exchange rate movements over short periods of time. This factor is short-term interest rates. Since interest rates have an important influence on the exchange rate, we need to describe what causes domestic interest rates to change. In the first part of the chapter, we will review and expand on what you learned in your Principles of Economics course concerning the supply and demand for money and the determination of the equilibrium interest rate within a domestic economy.

In the second part of the chapter, we will examine the relationship between interest rates and the exchange rate. As we will see, any change in interest rates will lead to changes in the inflows and outflows of (money) capital in a country's financial account and the changes in capital flows lead to changes in the exchange rate. By the end of the chapter, we will be able to examine how changes in interest rates, the exchange rate, the current account, and the financial account all interact with one another.

MONEY DEFINED: A REVIEW

When trying to determine how money affects the exchange rate, our first objective is to define the term *money*. Most individuals believe that they know what money is, but in fact, what constitutes money is not clear at all. The easiest way to describe money is to consider what it does. Money has to perform three separate but important functions. First, it must act as a medium of exchange. This is money's most important function. How would economic transactions be conducted in a world without money? Without money, every price of every good would be a relative price. For example, the price of a hamburger would be defined as what a hamburger is worth in terms of all other goods and services. In an advanced economy with a large number of goods and services, this relative pricing quickly becomes untenable. The price of one hamburger might be defined as four soft drinks or .04 tires. No one could possibly keep track of all the possible relative prices. The power of money is largely dependent on solving this relative-price problem. If there are 50,000 goods in any economy, there are only 50,000 prices. This is complicated but the alternative is far more complicated. Even if governments did not produce money, some item would emerge as a medium of exchange. In anything other than the simplest economy, something would emerge to serve as money.[1]

Money's second purpose is to function as a unit of account. This function is analogous to using standardized measures of length and weight. If no one could agree on how to measure length, how could one express how far it is from New York to Boston? Just having two common means of measurement in the U.S. creates enough problems. Thinking about moving from gallons to liters or from miles to kilometers is quite troublesome. Analogously, what if the U.S. had two commonly used currencies? In this case, an hour of labor, a magazine, or a CD would have two different prices. The efficiency of economic transactions is greatly enhanced if there is only one measure of money that is universally used as a unit of account. When this is the case, all economic transactions are easier to compare.

Money's final function is the store of value function. A simple way to explain this function is to consider the mismatch between your income and your consumption. For example, most of us are paid on a weekly, biweekly, or monthly basis. Our income does not come to us on a continuous basis. On the other hand, we spend some money practically every day. As a result, our streams of income and consumption do not perfectly match. In order to get around this mismatch of the timing of our income and the timing of our consumption, most of us store money in a convenient place such as a checking account. Since the money that is stored is not perishable, in the sense that food is, we can use money earned today to consume goods and services at some point in the future. Money thus provides a convenient way to smooth out any inconsistencies between money earned and money spent.

The store of value function of money can also help to solve the problem of storing money earned early in life for use later in life, such as saving for retirement. As long as money's value is sufficiently stable, money is useful in saving for the long run. One of the effects of inflation is that it damages peoples' ability to store money over long

[1]This concept can be linked to the problem of various national currencies. In the U.S., a soft drink is priced only in dollar terms.

money supply the total amount of money in an economy

periods of time. If inflation within a country is severe, individuals may begin storing their income and wealth in other forms such as commodities or foreign currencies that have a more stable value. Part of gold's allure has been that it retains its value over long periods of time independently of the value of money. In the modern world economy, individuals living in high-inflation countries may keep dollars or other "stable" foreign currencies as a way of storing value over long periods of time.

THE SUPPLY OF MONEY

M1 the sum of cash in the hands of the public and demand deposits in the U.S. economy

Now that we have defined what constitutes money, we can explain what comprises the total money supply in a modern economy. Coins and paper currency are money because they act as one of the primary mediums of exchange. Likewise, demand deposits held at commercial banks and other depository institutions are money because they provide the same function as currency. The sum of currency plus demand deposits is referred to as the **money supply**. In the U.S., the total quantity of currency plus demand deposits is called **M1**.[2] Internationally, this definition of the money supply is known as narrow money.

Other definitions of money are possible. There are a number of financial assets that are referred to as *near monies* that can be used as money in many circumstances.

What is the Supply of Money?

Even though the public can hold money for a variety of reasons, the supply of money that is relevant for the purposes of economic policy is a measure of money that will be used for economic transactions within a given period of time, such as a year. Unfortunately, in most countries such a perfect measure of the money supply does not exist. For example, in the U.S. neither M1 nor M2 is identical to the supply of money the public uses for short-run economic transactions. The primary reason why this is true is related to the existence of money market mutual funds. These funds can be used for transactions, as each account has limited check-writing capabilities. In addition, these accounts are also widely used as a parking place for funds between the purchase and sale of equities, bonds, and other long-term financial assets. As a result, M1 understates the amount of money that the public could use for short-run economic transactions, and M2 overstates this same amount. In this case, the central bank of the U.S. cannot know with certainty what the amount of money is that the public intends to use for short-run economic activities. To a greater or lesser extent, every country has this problem of defining what the relevant supply of money is. In the discussion that follows, we assume that there is a relevant supply of money under the central bank's control. However, one should keep in mind that the supply of money in an economy is not as clear-cut in most cases as central bankers or those following the state of the economy might like.

[2]In our discussion of the definitions of money, we have omitted several of the quantitatively less important components to reduce the maze of details. For example, travelers' checks are included in the M1 money supply. For an example of a more comprehensive definition of the money supply for the U.S., see any recent issue of the *Federal Reserve Bulletin*.

Near monies are highly liquid financial assets such as savings accounts, time deposits, and short-term government securities. In many cases, these assets cannot be spent as easily as can currency or a demand deposit at a local bank. An example of a near money is an account with a money market mutual fund. In the U.S., this is a common form of near money. In other countries, where this form of near money is less common, a large amount of near money is held in the form of time deposits. For the most part, near monies do not function as a medium of exchange but they can be readily converted into currency or demand deposits. For the U.S., M1 plus money market mutual funds and time deposits constitutes **M2**. In an international context, the term for M2 is called broad money.

M2 M1 plus near monies in the U.S. economy

Ultimately, the supply of money within a country is the result of a process that we need to describe. In order to do this we will need to look at an important part of the money supply known as the **monetary base (B)**. The monetary base (B) is composed of cash in the hands of the public (C) and the total quantity of bank reserves (R) on deposit at the central bank. In precise terms, the monetary base is:

monetary base (B) the sum of cash in the hands of the public and bank reserves

$$B = C + R$$

A country's money supply is equal to the monetary base multiplied by the banking **money multiplier**. The banking money multiplier is equal to 1 divided by the **reserve requirement**. In most countries, all depository institutions must keep a legal or required reserve on deposit at the central bank. This reserve requirement is an amount of funds equal to a specified percentage of its own deposits (r). For example, if the reserve requirement for banks is 10 percent, the money multiplier would be 10. Using these concepts, the money supply (MS) for a country becomes:

money multiplier the reciprocal of the reserve requirement

reserve requirement the percentage of deposits banks are legally required to keep on deposit with the central bank

$$MS = B \times 1/r$$

As a result, if the monetary base was $100 billion and r was .10, the money supply would be $1 trillion.[3] This relationship between the monetary base and the money supply is extremely important. When a central bank wants the money supply to change, it actually changes the monetary base or the money multiplier. The term "printing" money is literally equivalent to changing the amount of currency (C) contained in the monetary base. Printing money, however, is a relatively crude way to change the money supply within a country. In practice, governments or central banks can change the money supply by employing one of three tools.

The first tool that a central bank can use to change the money supply is the discount rate. The **discount rate** is the interest rate that the central bank charges commercial banks for borrowing reserves. When a commercial bank borrows reserves from the central bank, the monetary base rises by an equal amount. Given the money multiplier, as the total reserves of the banking system increase, the money supply increases by a multiple of that amount. When a central bank lowers the discount rate, commercial banks tend to borrow more from the central bank, bank reserves rise and the

discount rate the rate of interest charged by a central bank on loans to commercial banks

[3]For those interested in a more detailed treatment of these relationships when the economy has currency drains, see Appendix 15.1.

money supply rises. The reverse occurs if the discount rate is increased. However, using the discount rate to control the money supply is not very precise. For example, a change in the discount rate brings about a change in bank reserves. However, the amount by which reserves change is a function of how much banks wish to borrow. As a result, changing the discount rate will change bank reserves by an uncertain amount.

The second tool that a central bank can use to change the money supply is the reserve requirement. Two effects occur when the central bank changes the reserve requirement. First, changes in the reserve requirement change the amount of funds a bank must keep on deposit at the central bank. If the reserve requirement were lowered, banks would be able to hold a smaller fraction of their deposits as reserves and could make more loans, expanding the money supply. Second, changes in the reserve requirement change the size of the money multiplier. For instance, if the reserve requirement were lowered from 10 percent to 8 percent, the value of the money multiplier would rise from 10 to 12.5. In this case, each dollar in the monetary base is multiplied by a larger amount. As a result, a relatively small change in the reserve

International Differences in Reserve Requirements

In our previous example, we assumed that the reserve requirement was 10 percent, or .1. However, reserve requirements vary enormously even among developed countries. Since changes in the reserve requirement is an infrequently used tool to manage the money supply, countries have many options with regard to the level that they set the reserve requirement for their banks. The Table 15.1 shows some of these differences for a set of developed countries.

Table 15.1 Reserve Requirements for Selected Countries

Country	Reserve Requirement (1996)
Australia	.01
Austria	.05
France	.01
Germany	.02
Italy	.15
Japan	.012
Spain	.02
Switzerland	.025
U.S.	.10

Source: Adapted from Claudio E. V. Borio, "The Implementation of Monetary Policy in Industrial Countries," *BIS Economic Papers,* No. 47, July 1997, Basle: Bank for International Settlements, 1997.

requirement brings about relatively large changes in the money multiplier. These large changes in the money multiplier have substantial impacts on the money supply. For this reason, changes in the reserve requirement are infrequently used as a means of changing the money supply, as the effect on the money supply is potentially too powerful.

In countries with well-developed financial markets, the monetary base and the money supply are usually changed in a more precise fashion using open market operations. A central bank's **open market operations** refer to the buying and selling of bonds by the central bank in the open market. When the central bank buys or sells a bond, either the banking system's reserves change or the amount of currency in circulation changes. If the central bank buys a bond in the open market from a commercial bank, the central bank pays for the bond by increasing that bank's reserves by the amount of the purchase. If the central bank buys a bond in the open market from the public, the effect on commercial bank reserves is much the same. The individual who sold the bond receives payment by a check drawn on the central bank. When this check is deposited in a commercial bank, the banks reserves increase. In either of these two cases, this transaction increases the reserves of the banking system and the monetary base. As a result, the money supply will rise by a multiple of that amount.

open market operations the buying and selling of bonds by the central bank

The reverse would happen when the central bank sells a bond. In this case, the banking system's reserves fall, the monetary base falls, and the money supply declines. Given an estimate of the value of the money multiplier, a central bank using open market operations can precisely control the monetary base, and control the money supply with some degree of precision. The key institutional characteristic necessary for open market operations is the existence of an active secondary bond market.[4] The central bank needs to be able to easily buy and sell bonds in its attempts to control the money supply. If a secondary market for bonds does not exist, control of the money supply becomes much more difficult. Assuming such a market does exist; changing the money supply becomes relatively easy for the central bank. However, like any other asset, the money supply and changes in the money supply are only half the story. To determine the price of money, meaning the interest rate, one must also consider the demand for money.

THE DEMAND FOR MONEY

Having described how a country's money supply is determined, we can now turn our attention to the other side of the money market, the demand for money. In many respects, money is an asset much like any other asset. The main difference is that money is a very good substitute for practically all other goods and services. The decision to hold money balances is a portfolio decision, as firms and individuals have some desired level of money balances that they wish to keep on hand. As such, there are three major reasons for individuals and firms to hold money.

First, individuals and firms hold money because they may want to buy goods and services. In order to make these purchases, individuals and firms need money in the form of either cash or bank-account balances. This transactions demand for money

[4]A secondary market is where previously issued financial assets are bought and sold. This is distinct from a primary market, where newly issued financial assets are sold.

varies directly with the total amount of the purchases or nominal GDP. Second, individuals and firms hold money in case of an emergency that requires a financial purchase over and above their normal spending levels. Third, holding money yields no explicit rate of return.[5] Obviously, there is an opportunity cost to holding money, as interest income is forgone or sacrificed. When the opportunity cost of holding money (the interest rate) is high, individuals and firms will choose to hold a small amount of money as assets. As interest rates rise, individuals and firms would tend to move their assets out of money and into other financial assets that pay an explicit rate of return. The reverse is also true, the lower the interest rate, the greater the propensity of individuals and firms to hold a large amount of money as assets. The net result is that the demand for money by individuals and firms is inversely related to the interest rate.

demand for money the total demand for money by all firms and individuals in the economy

These three motivations for holding money combine to create the demand for money. The **demand for money** is the total demand for money by all firms and individuals in the economy. This demand for money is related to three factors. First, it is inversely related to the interest rate. As interest rates rise, the demand for money declines and vice versa. This relationship indicates that fluctuations in the interest rate will cause the demand for money to fluctuate. Second, the demand for money is directly related to the price level. As the price level rises, the average value of economic transactions (purchases or sales) rises. Thus, as the average price level increases, individuals and firms increase their holdings of money in order to maintain their real level of spending. Finally, the demand for money is directly related to the real level of economic activity or real income.[6] As the economy's real income rises, consumers buy more goods and services. In order to purchase these additional goods and services, consumers must increase their holdings of money.

In summary, the demand for money in an economy is inversely related to the interest rate and positively related to the price level and the level of real income. These relationships can be expressed in the following manner:

$$MD = f(-i, +P, +Y)$$

where i is the interest rate; P is the price level; and Y is real GDP. In the following section, we consider how the supply of money and the demand for money combine to determine interest rates within an economy.

THE EQUILIBRIUM INTEREST RATE: THE INTERACTION OF MONEY SUPPLY AND MONEY DEMAND

Having defined both the supply of money and the demand for money, we will now combine these two relationships in the money market to determine the equilibrium

---

[5]In the case of currency, this form of money earns no interest at all. In the case of an interest-bearing checking account, it does not earn as much interest income as one can earn on bonds or non-checkable deposits.

[6]In most cases, real GDP would be a useful proxy for the real level of economic activity.

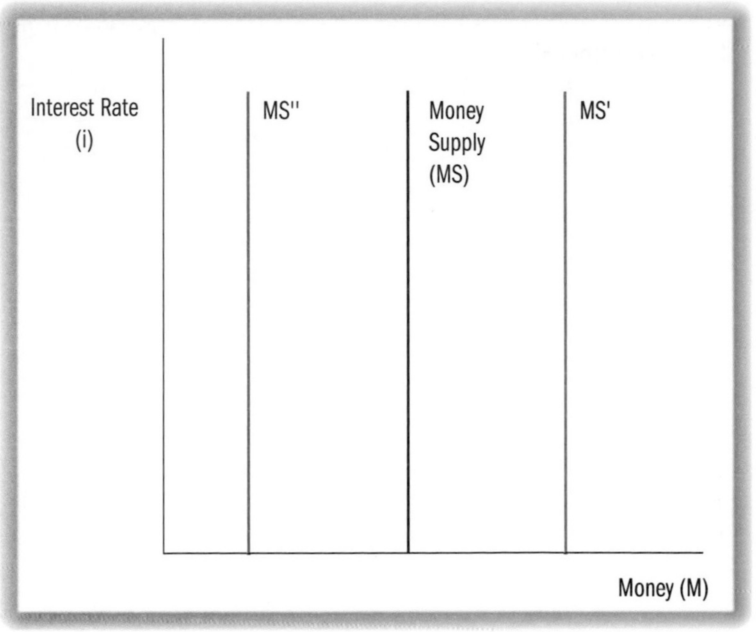

Figure 15.1 Changes in the Supply of Money

An increase in the money supply caused by an open market purchase by the central bank would shift the money supply curve to the right. A decrease in the money supply caused by an open market sale by the central bank would shift the money supply curve to the left.

price of money or the interest rate. Recall that the central bank determines the money supply through open market operations, the discount rate, and the reserve requirement. The supply of money is shown in Figure 15.1. We have graphed the money supply as a vertical line, meaning that the money supply is completely inelastic with respect to the interest rate. This means that as interest rates change, the money supply does not respond. By graphing the money supply in this manner, we have assumed that the central bank can determine the level of the money supply within the country at some arbitrary level.

Under these circumstances, the supply of money is affected only by the central bank's actions. If the central bank lowers the discount rate, lowers the reserve requirement, or purchases bonds, the supply of money increases. This increase in the money supply is represented by a rightward shift in the money supply in Figure 15.1. This is shown as MS′ in Figure 15.1. On the other hand, if the central bank raises the discount rate, raises the reserve requirement, or sells bonds, the supply of money declines. This is shown in Figure 15.1 as a shift in the money supply inwards or to the left and is represented by MS″.

The demand for money is illustrated in Figure 15.2. Like virtually all demand curves, the demand for money slopes downward, indicating that as interest rates fall, the amount of money that individuals and firms are willing and able to hold increases. This change in the amount of money demanded is illustrated in the figure by moving

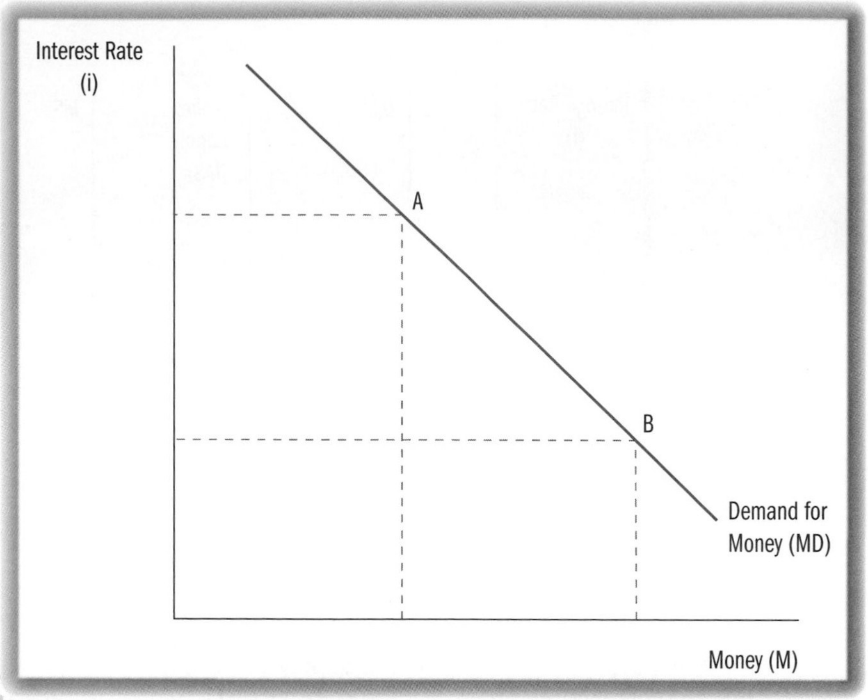

Figure 15.2 The Demand for Money

The demand for money depends on the interest rate. At higher interest rates, individuals will want to hold less money than at lower interest rates because the opportunity cost of holding money is higher.

from point A to point B. As interest rates change, individuals and firms adjust the quantity of money that they are willing and able to hold by moving along the demand curve. Like all demand curves, the relationship between the price and quantity demanded is based on the assumption that everything else has been held constant. In the case of the demand for money, the major determinants being held constant are real income and the price level. If either one of these determinants changes, the entire demand for money will shift.

Both increases and decreases in the demand for money (shifts) are shown in Figure 15.3. For example, if the level of real income and/or the price level increase, the demand for money will increase (shift) to the right as indicated by MD′. On the other hand, if real income and/or the price level decrease, the demand for money will decrease (shift) to the left as indicated by MD″.

By combining the supply and demand for money, we can determine the equilibrium interest rate in a country. The intersection of money demand and money supply determines the equilibrium interest rate. Given a particular level of income and prices (demand) and given the supply of money determined by the central bank, the equilibrium in the money market is at point E and the equilibrium interest rate would be equal to i as shown in Figure 15.4. This equilibrium in the money market occurs as

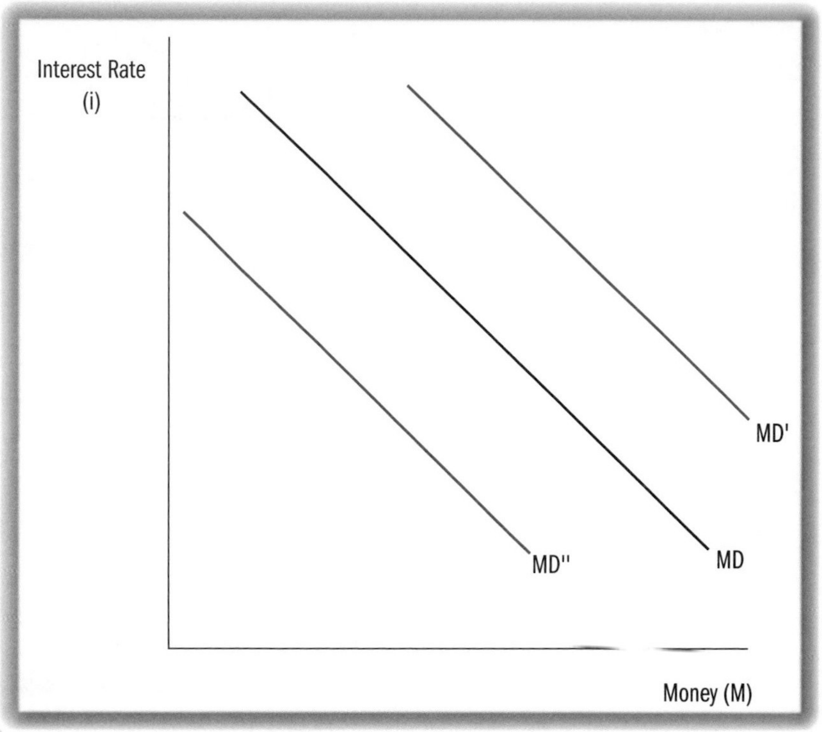

Figure 15.3 Changes in the Demand for Money

As prices increase and/or as real income increases, the demand for money shifts to the right (increases). As prices decline and/or as real income declines, the demand for money shifts to the left (decreases).

individuals and firms adjust their asset holdings. For example, at any interest rate higher than the equilibrium rate, the amount of money demanded by individuals and firms is less than the amount of money supplied. In this case, individuals and firms would buy financial assets that earn an explicit rate of return. By purchasing financial assets, the price of financial assets would rise causing a fall in interest rates until the money market achieves equilibrium. Conversely, if the interest rate is below the equilibrium rate of interest, the amount of money demanded by individuals and firms is greater than the amount supplied. As a result, individuals and firms would sell financial assets, causing the price of such assets to fall and interest rates to rise.

Now that we know how the equilibrium interest rate is determined, we can illustrate how the interest rate responds to changes in either the demand or supply of money. For example, assume that the money market is in equilibrium and the real income or the price level changes. A change in either one of these determinants shifts the demand for money and changes the equilibrium interest rate. Two examples of these changes in money demand are shown in Figure 15.5. First, assume that the money market is in equilibrium at point E, and the economy has an overall decline in real income. Such a decline in total real income is usually associated with a recession.

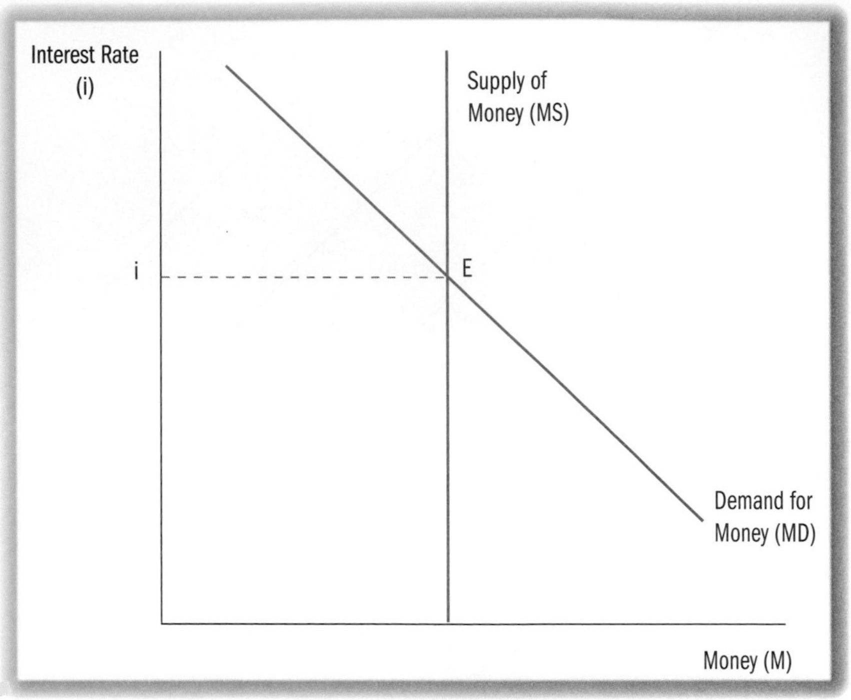

Figure 15.4 **The Equilibrium Interest Rate**

Equilibrium in the money market occurs at an interest rate, i, where the quantity of money demanded equals the quantity of money supplied.

As real income declines, the demand for money declines. This is represented by a shift in the demand for money from MD to MD′. As a result, the new equilibrium in the money market is at F, and the equilibrium rate of interest declines to i′.

Second, consider the effect that an increase in the price level would have on the equilibrium rate of interest. Again, assume that the money market currently is in equilibrium at point E and the price level increases. The rise in the price level brings about an increase in the demand for money, as more money is needed to purchase the same real volume of goods and services. In this case, the demand for money would shift outwards from MD to MD″. As a result, the new equilibrium in the money market is at G and the equilibrium interest rate rises to i″.

The standard analysis of the money market also considers the effect of changes in the money supply on the equilibrium rate of interest. As our analysis will indicate, in the absence of changes in the demand for money, the central bank can alter interest rates through changes in the money supply. The effect of changes in the money supply on the equilibrium rate of interest is illustrated in Figure 15.6. Let's assume that the money market has an initial equilibrium at point E, with an equilibrium interest rate of i. If the money supply increases from MS to MS′ with an unchanged demand for money, the new equilibrium in the money market is at F and the rate of interest declines to i′. On the other hand, if the central bank decreases the money supply from

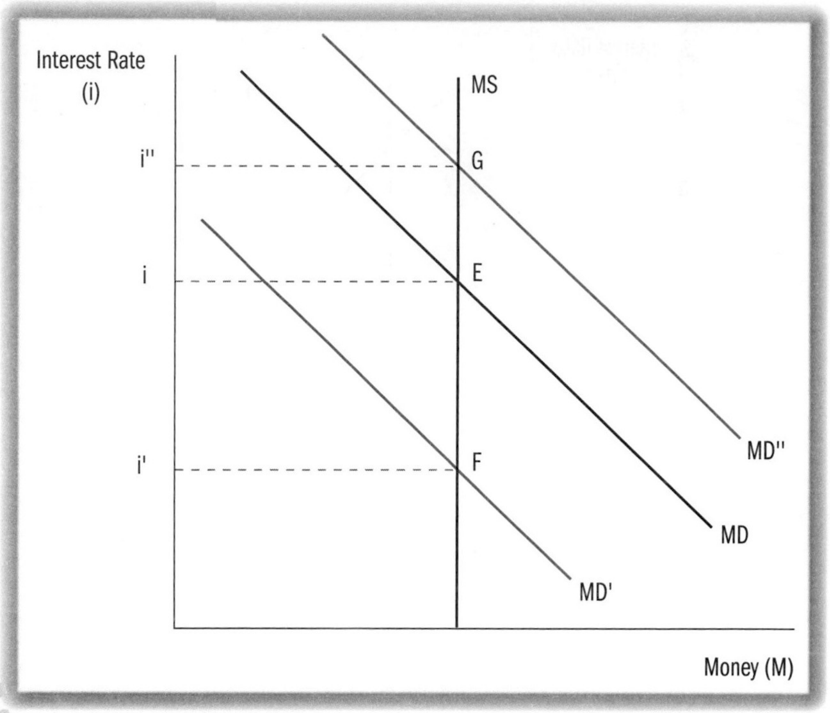

Figure 15.5 Shifts in the Demand for Money and the Equilibrium Interest Rate

When the money supply is held constant, the equilibrium interest rate changes whenever there is a change in the demand for money. If the demand for money decreases, the equilibrium interest rate will decline. If the demand for money increases, the equilibrium interest rate will rise.

MS to MS″, the new equilibrium in the money market would be at G and the rate of interest would rise to i″.[7]

As Figure 15.6 indicates, changes in the money supply have an obvious impact on an economy's interest rate. If the central bank changes the money supply for any reason, interest rates also will change. Given a stable money demand, a higher money supply implies lower interest rates. Analogously, a lower money supply usually will mean higher interest rates. As we indicated earlier, in developed countries changes in the money supply usually are accomplished using open market operations. The central bank buys bonds to increase the money supply and sells bonds to reduce it. In both cases, the central bank can alter the money supply and, therefore, interest rates.[8] As we will see in the next section, changes in the equilibrium interest rate usually translate into changes in the country's exchange rate.

---

[7]In more general terms, the central bank may adjust the rate of growth of the money supply that affects interest rates. It is rare for the money supply to actually decline for any extended period of time. A *decrease* in the money supply is in most cases really a slowdown in the rate of growth of the money supply relative to the rate of growth in the demand for money.

[8]We are consciously avoiding the issue of what the central banks target is. Whether or not the target is the interest rate or the money supply is not important in the current context. Changes in the money supply will affect interest rates and this in turn will have an effect on the exchange rate.

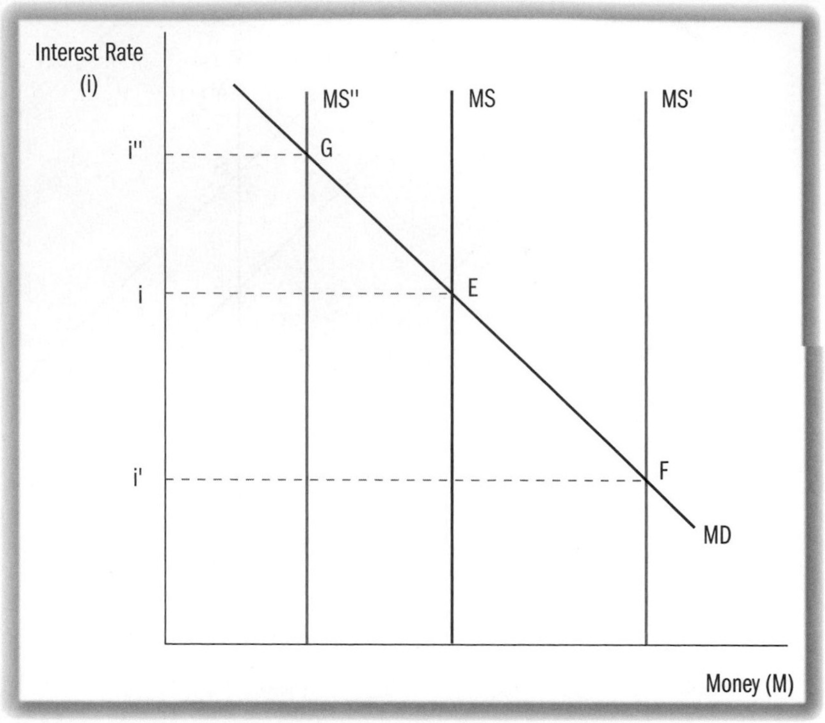

Figure 15.6 Shifts in the Supply of Money and the Equilibrium Interest Rate

When the demand for money is held constant, the equilibrium interest rate changes whenever there is a change in the supply of money. If the supply of money increases, the equilibrium interest rate will decline. If the supply of money decreases, the equilibrium interest rate will rise.

THE INTEREST RATE AND THE EXCHANGE RATE IN THE SHORT RUN

interest arbitrage the relationship between interest rates and the exchange rate in the short run

With our understanding of how interest rates are determined, we can now examine the relationship between interest rates and the exchange rate in the short run. This relationship is known as **interest arbitrage**. The relationship between these two rates hinges on the existence of international markets in which short-term capital can flow unimpeded between countries. To explain interest arbitrage, let's suppose that you are the chief financial officer (CFO) for a large U.S. multinational firm that maintains offices and/or production facilities in a number of countries. Further, let's assume that the firm has a positive cash flow and the CFO needs to maximize the short-run rate of return on this cash flow.[9] Essentially, this means finding the highest short-term return on the firm's idle cash balances. This highest short-term return might be in the U.S. or it might be in some foreign country.

[9]In simple terms, *cash flow* is total cash revenues minus total cash costs. In reality, the term is considerably more complex. For a more thorough treatment of cash flow, see Eugene F. Brigham and Louis C. Gapenski, *Intermediate Financial Management,* The Dryden Press, 1997.

However, with the presence of exchange risk, the comparison of interest rates between two countries is not a sufficient guide to allocate funds between the two countries. For example, assume that the interest rate in New York is 10 percent and that the interest rate in London is 12 percent.[10] In deciding where to invest $10,000, the CFO must compare the rate of return earned by the funds invested in New York with the rate of return earned by the funds invested in London, not the interest rates per se in New York or London. The CFO cannot conclude automatically that it is more profitable to invest in London just because London has a higher interest rate. In this case, the CFO who invests in London will not necessarily earn 12 percent. He or she will earn 12 percent only if the exchange rate (dollar/pound) remains constant. If the pound depreciates (the dollar appreciates), the CFO will earn less than 12 percent. If the pound appreciates (the dollar depreciates), the CFO will earn more than 12 percent.

For instance, assume that the current spot exchange rate is $2 per pound, and the CFO wants to invest the $10,000 in London. To do this, the CFO first must buy pounds (sell dollars) in the foreign exchange market. Once the 5,000 pounds have been purchased, the CFO can then invest in London. Assume that the CFO invests in London for three months at 12 percent. In three months, the London investment will be worth 5,150 pounds. Now, the CFO is interested in dollars, not pounds. To obtain dollars, the CFO must sell the 5,150 pounds in the foreign exchange market. In three months, if the spot exchange rate is still $2 per pound, the CFO will obtain $10,300, or 12 percent.

However, suppose that in 3 months the pound has depreciated (dollar appreciated) to $1.975 per pound. This movement in the exchange rate represents a depreciation of the pound of 5 percent. In this case, at the end of the three-month period, the CFO will receive only $10,171.25. He or she will have earned approximately 7 percent. This total return is actually the difference between the annual interest rate in London (12 percent) and the depreciation of the pound (5 percent). Of course, it is possible that in three months the pound might appreciate (dollar depreciate) to $2.025 per pound. In this case, the pound has appreciated by 5 percent. In three months the CFO will receive $10,428.75, or approximately 17 percent. This total return is actually the sum of the London interest rate (12 percent) and the appreciation of the pound (5 percent). In each of these cases, the CFO's total return on the funds that were invested in London is approximately equal to the rate of interest that prevails in London less any depreciation of the pound (or plus any appreciation of the pound).

This example illustrates that investing funds in a foreign country involves an exchange rate risk. To eliminate this risk, the CFO can buy pounds in the spot exchange market to make the investment and, at the same time, sell pounds in the forward foreign exchange market with a delivery date that coincides with the maturity of the investment. For the moment, assume that the change in the exchange rate over the investment period in the previous example is correctly reflected in the forward exchange rate. If the forward rate is equal to the current spot rate, it is more profitable for the CFO to invest funds in London. If the pound is selling at a forward premium, it is even more profitable to invest in London, because of the additional gain the investor receives by buying pounds in the less costly spot market and selling pounds in the expensive forward market.

[10] All interest rates and exchange rate changes are in per annum terms.

However, if the pound is selling at a forward discount, the gain due to the favorable interest rate differential in London must be compared to the loss suffered from buying pounds in the spot market, where pounds are expensive, and selling pounds in the forward market, where they are cheap. When the interest rate differential is greater than the forward discount, it is more profitable to invest in London. When the interest rate differential is less than the forward discount, moving funds to London is less profitable than investing in New York. In these examples, we have described the movement of funds between New York and London from a U.S. point of view. If it is profitable for a U.S. CFO or investor to move funds to London, it is profitable for a British investor to do so as well. The only difference is that the U.S. investor starts and ends with dollars, and the British investor starts and ends with pounds.

Under most circumstances, the movement of funds between countries continues until the forward premium or discount equals the interest rate differential. This implies that the interest rate differential is exactly balanced by the loss or gain of buying pounds in the spot market and selling pounds in the forward market. Under these circumstances, the rate of return on an investment in both countries is identical and there is no reason to move funds from one country to another. When this situation occurs, it is said that the forward rate is at interest parity, or, in other words, that interest parity prevails between the two countries.[11]

Now, consider what would happen if interest parity exists between the U.S. and the U.K., and suddenly the U.S. central bank decreases the money supply. As we illustrate in panel a of Figure 15.7, we show the money market in the U.S. with an initial equilibrium at E, and in panel b we show the foreign exchange market with an initial equilibrium at E′. As the U.S. central bank decreases the money supply from MS to MS′, equilibrium in the money market changes to point F and interest rates in the U.S. rise from i to i′. This rise in U.S. interest rates relative to interest rates in the U.K. gives both U.S. and U.K. investors an incentive to purchase short-term financial assets in the U.S. In order to purchase U.S. financial assets, the investors must first sell British pounds and buy U.S. dollars. The impact of the interest rate change on the exchange rate is shown in panel b. The selling of pounds to buy dollars in the foreign exchange market causes an increase in the supply of pounds from S to S′. With a larger supply of pounds, the equilibrium in the foreign exchange market changes to point F′ and the exchange rate declines from (\$/£) to (\$/£′). As a result, the dollar appreciates (pound depreciates) until interest parity is achieved. The rising interest rates in the U.S. have caused an appreciation of the dollar. Although not shown in the figure, it is also quite likely that U.S. investors' demand for pounds would decline as U.S. citizens invest more in the U.S. and less in the U.K.[12]

In Figure 15.8, we illustrate the opposite situation by considering what would happen if interest parity exists between the U.S. and the U.K. and suddenly the U.S. central bank increases the money supply. In panel a of Figure 15.8, we show the money market in the U.S. with an initial equilibrium at E, and in panel b we show the foreign exchange market with an initial equilibrium at E′. As the U.S. central bank increases the money supply from MS to MS′, equilibrium in the money market changes to point

[11]Appendix 15.2 presents a brief mathematical formulation of interest parity.

[12]We have assumed that the inflation rate or the price level in the U.S. remains constant. We allow for changes in the price level as a result of changes in the money supply in Chapter 16.

The Efficiency of the Foreign Exchange Market

In the preceding section, we considered the effects of interest rates on the exchange rate. More specifically, we showed that differences in interest rates should be systematically reflected in differences between the spot and forward (future) exchange rates. This interest parity condition contains an implicit assumption. This assumption was not mentioned explicitly because it can be controversial. We were assuming that the foreign exchange market is efficient. An efficient market is one where the price of an asset reflects all known information. As traders in the market acquire new information, the price of the asset changes. In our context, the "asset" happens to be foreign exchange. This is a standard assumption among economists when discussing the foreign exchange market. It was also an assumption that we made in our discussion of interest parity. But, it should be asked, are foreign exchange markets really efficient? It turns out that this is the subject of a furious debate among economists.

The standard way to test for efficiency in the foreign exchange market is to empirically examine the interest parity condition. The interest parity condition shows that the interest rate differential between counties is systematically related to the difference between the spot exchange rate and the forward exchange rate. This means that the interest rate differential is, in reality, a *forecast* of future changes in the exchange rate. As the interest rate differential changes, the difference between the spot and forward exchange rates will change. This implies a relatively simple test for market efficiency. If traders are making their decisions based on all current information, the interest rate differential should be a good predictor of future changes in the exchange rate.

The results of these tests have not been encouraging, as the interest rate differential has been found to be a poor predictor of the future movement of exchange rates. Empirical tests have shown two results. First, the interest rate differential does not do a good job of predicting the magnitude of changes in the exchange rate because it fails to adequately forecast large changes in the exchange rate. This result is discouraging, but like many other cases in economics, one may be able to predict the direction of change but not necessarily the magnitude of change. Secondly, in many cases, the interest parity condition does not predict the direction of change in the exchange rate. This means that the interest parity condition predicted an appreciation of a currency, when in fact the currency depreciated. It is this empirical result that calls into question the whole idea of market efficiency. Other, more sophisticated tests of market efficiency have yielded more mixed results. The debate among economists on this issue continues. This does not mean that the discussion in the chapter concerning interest rate parity is fundamentality incorrect. Like many issues in economics, analyzing the effects of changes in economic variables depends on the time frame used in the study. Most studies of market efficiency are considering a relatively short period of time, such as months. The effects that we describe, relating interest rate to exchange rate, may not be a perfect description of what happens in the very short run; these short-run dynamics of the relationship between interest rates and the exchange rate are still imperfectly understood. However, over longer periods of time, one can have more confidence in this relationship. Everything else equal, an increase in interest rates will usually lead to an appreciating exchange rate, and vice versa. The information in the text is helpful in understanding the general relationship between interest rates and the exchange rate, but it will not allow you to make a fortune trading foreign exchange in the short run.

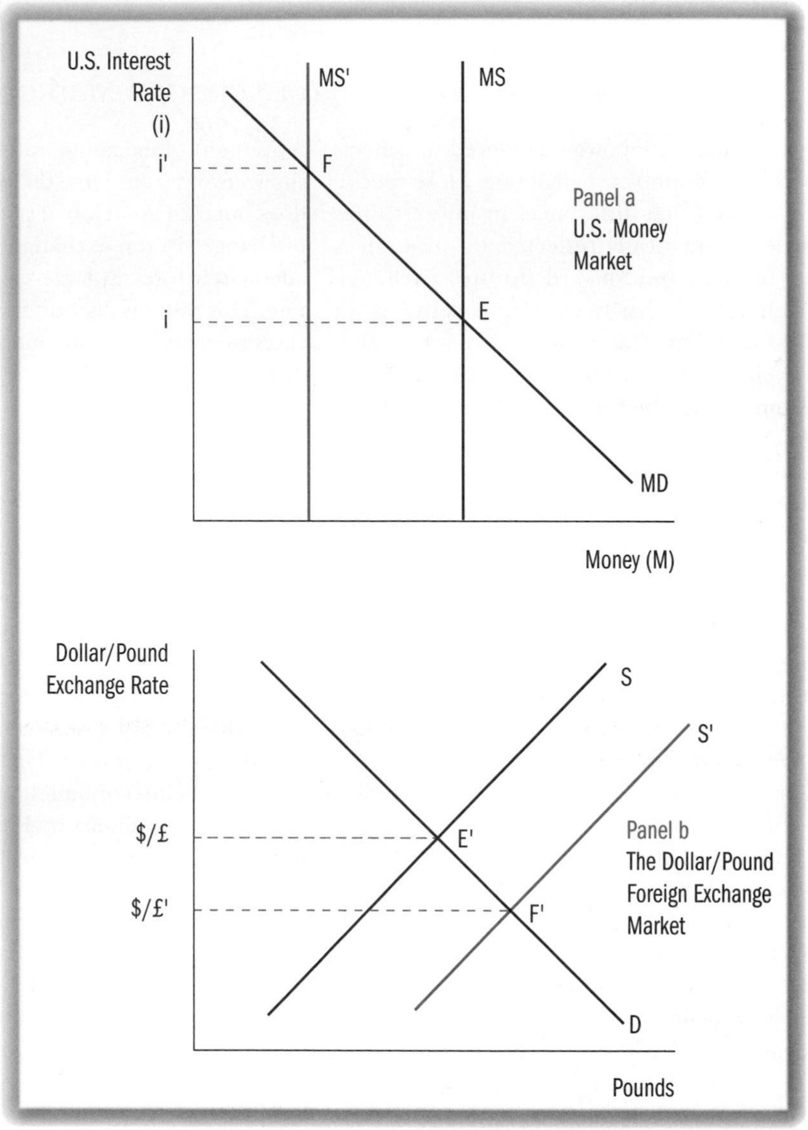

Figure 15.7 **Effect of a Decrease in the U.S. Money Supply on the Dollar–Pound Exchange Rate**

If the supply of money decreases, the equilibrium interest rate will rise. (Panel a). As the domestic interest rate rises, capital flows from the U.K. into the U.S. This capital inflow causes an increase in the supply of pounds, and the exchange rate declines. (Panel b).

G and interest rates in the U.S. fall from i to i′. This fall in U.S. interest rates relative to interest rates in the U.K. gives both U.S. and U.K. investors an incentive to purchase short-term financial assets in the U.K. In order to purchase U.K. financial assets, the investors must first buy British pounds and sell U.S. dollars. The impact of the interest rate change on the exchange rate is shown in panel b. The selling of dollars to buy

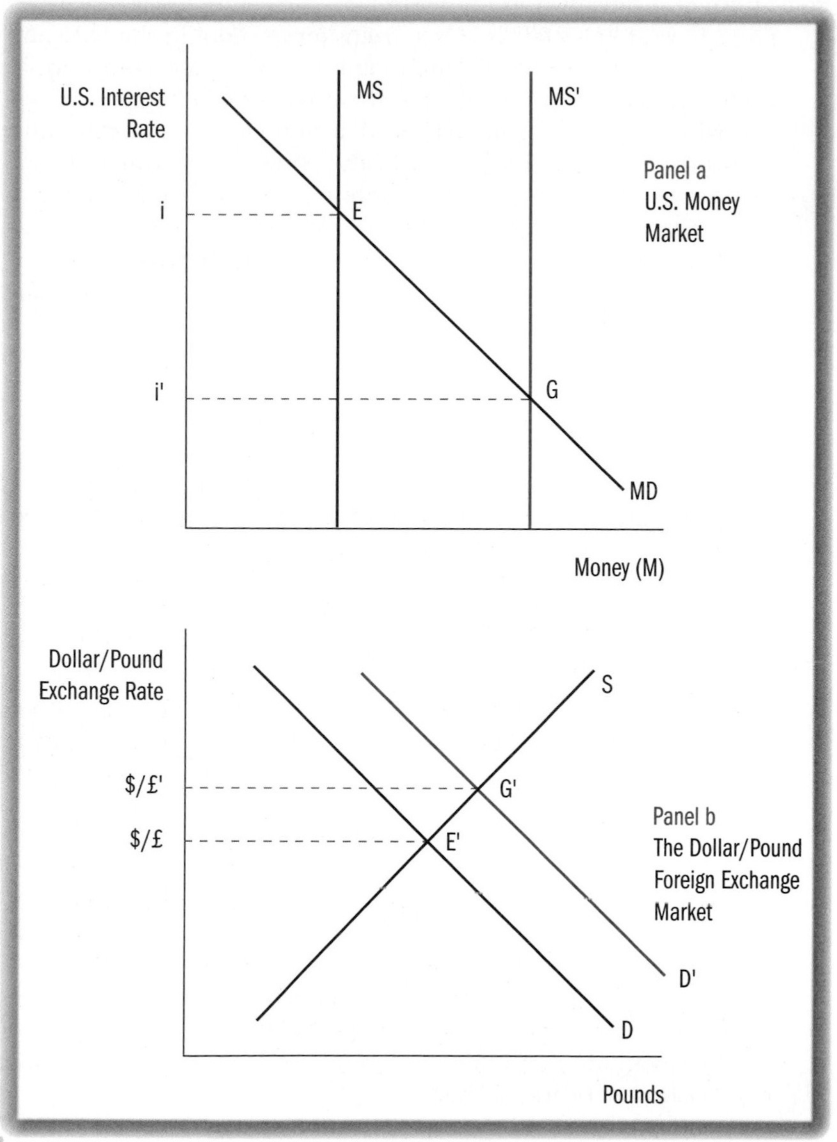

Figure 15.8 Effect of an Increase in the U.S. Money Supply on the Dollar–Pound Exchange Rate

If the supply of money increases, the equilibrium interest rate will decline. (Panel a). As the domestic interest rate falls, capital flows from the U.S. into the U.K. This capital outflow causes an increase in the demand for pounds, and the exchange rate rises. (Panel b).

pounds in the foreign exchange market causes an increase in the demand for pounds from D to D′. With a larger demand for pounds, the equilibrium in the foreign exchange market changes to point G′ and the exchange rate increases from ($/£) to ($/£′). As a result, the dollar depreciates (pound appreciates) until interest parity is achieved. The falling interest rates in the U.S. have caused a depreciation of the dollar.

Although not shown in the figure, it is also quite likely that U.K. investors' supply of pounds would also fall as U.K. citizens invest more in the U.K. and less in the U.S.

Although these two examples illustrate the effects of interest rate changes on the exchange rate for two countries, these results can be generalized to many countries. Everything else equal, an increase in a country's interest rate will tend to cause a capital inflow and an appreciation of the country's currency. The reverse would occur when interest rates decline. As interest rates fall, capital flows out of the country, and the country's currency would depreciate.

The mechanism that causes the exchange rate to change is the movement of capital between countries. The constant daily movement of exchange rates should now be more understandable. Changes in short-term interest rates and investors' expectations of changes in interest rates are constantly occurring. As interest rates change, both the volume and direction of worldwide capital flows change. As changes in capital flows occur, the supply and demand for foreign exchange changes, which in turn affects exchange rates. As such, one of the main contributors to exchange rate volatility is the volatility of interest rates. Since it is unlikely that interest rates will stop fluctuating any time in the near future, one should not be too optimistic about exchange rates becoming very stable any time soon.

INTEREST RATES, THE EXCHANGE RATE, AND THE BALANCE OF PAYMENTS

In the previous section, we showed what would tend to happen to the exchange rate if interest rates suddenly changed. The adjustment process that we illustrated was relatively smooth: as interest rates changed, the exchange rate changed in a predictable manner. In Chapter 12, we examined the various components of a country's balance of payments. A basic principle embodied within the balance of payments statement is that, over time, a country's inflows and outflows of money are balanced. The interaction of the current account and the capital/financial account jointly determined this balance. If the current account was negative, the balance of capital flows had to be positive. If the current account was positive, the balance of capital flows must be negative. We can further analyze this relationship between trade flows, capital flows, and the equilibrium exchange rate using the demand and supply of foreign exchange.

In describing the foreign exchange market and the determinants of the exchange rate in Chapter 14, we said that as the domestic price level and domestic income changed, trade flows between two countries would change. The result was that the equilibrium exchange rate would adjust to a new level. In a world where there are no capital flows between countries, price levels and income would primarily determine the exchange rate. Exchange rates and trade flows would respond to changes in incomes and price levels and a country's current account would continually balance. However, the world is not that simple. As the money supply and interest rates change, capital flows are affected. As capital flows change, the exchange rate changes. What we are able to do at this point is to analyze simultaneously the current account, capital flows, and the exchange rate.

To illustrate these relationships, let's examine Figure 15.9. In panel a, we have graphed the demand and supply of foreign exchange and the equilibrium in the foreign exchange market at E, where the equilibrium exchange rate is \$/£. Assume for the moment that capital flows between countries are zero, so that the demand and

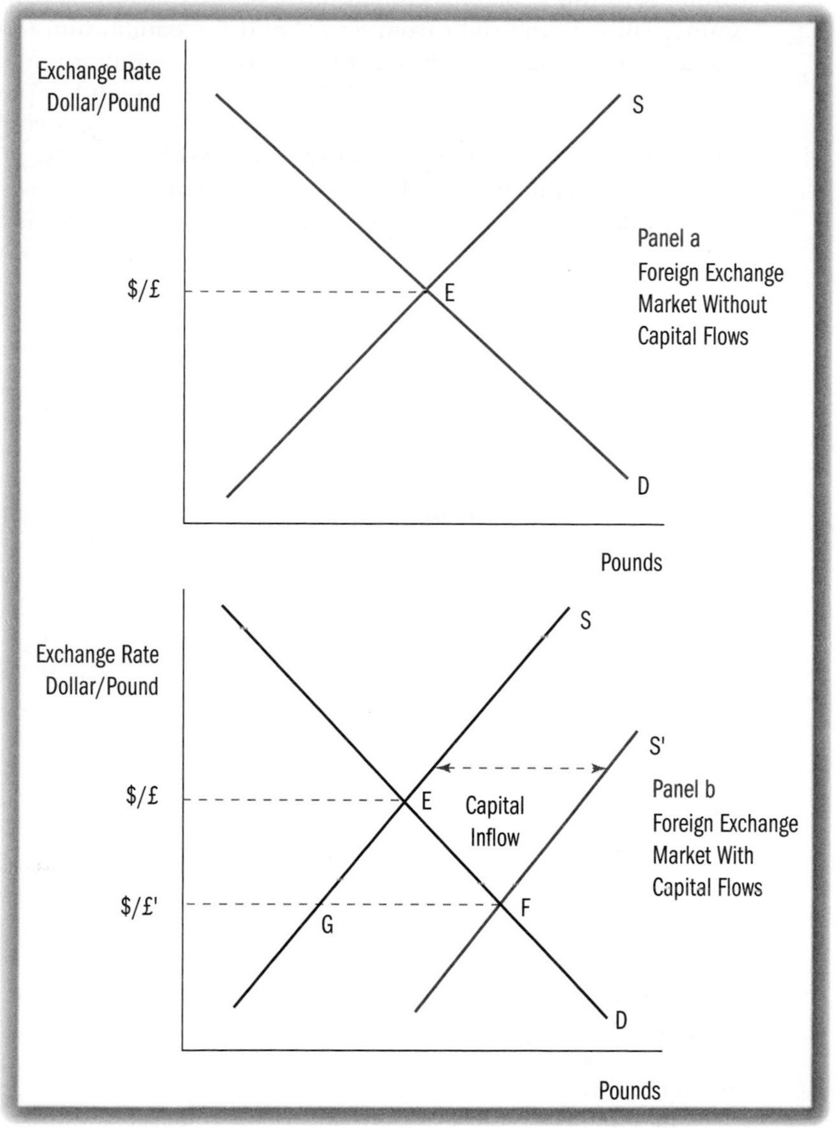

Figure 15.9 The Foreign Exchange Market With and Without Capital Flows

When there are no capital flows between countries, the demand and supply of foreign exchange will balance the current account (Panel a). When capital flows are introduced into the foreign exchange market (Panel b), the total inflows and outflows of foreign exchange balance. However, the new equilibrium balances both the current account and capital flows. In this case, an inflow of capital creates a current account deficit.

supply of foreign exchange represent a country's exports and imports of goods and services. In this case, the current account is balanced at the equilibrium exchange rate—meaning exports equal imports.

Now, let's introduce capital flows between countries. Assume that U.S. interest rates increase. In this case, investors will sell pounds and buy dollars in order to move capital into the U.S. This capital movement is shown in panel b, as the supply of pounds shifts to the right from S to S′ and the equilibrium in the foreign exchange market moves from point E to F. In this case, the equilibrium exchange rate changes from ($/£) to ($/£′) and the dollar appreciates (pound depreciates). What we can now demonstrate is the relationship between the current account and the capital/financial account in a country's balance of payments.

The original demand and supply curves (D and S) represent the demand and supply of British pounds considering current-account transactions only. The new equilibrium exchange rate occurs at the intersection of D and S′, where total inflows and outflows of pounds balance. However, this new equilibrium balances both the current account and capital flows. Even though total inflows and outflows of pounds balance, the current account may well be in deficit or surplus. In this situation, because of the capital inflows, the current account must be in deficit. This deficit is shown in panel b as the gap between points G and F at the new equilibrium exchange rate of ($/£′). At the new exchange rate, total imports of goods and services are shown where D and S′ intersect, point F. However, the inflow of capital causes the exchange rate to appreciate. This appreciation of the exchange rate causes the total export of goods and services to decline, point G. Total exports of goods and services are shown where the new equilibrium exchange rate crosses the original supply curve. At the new exchange rate, imports of goods and services are greater than exports of goods and services, indicating a current account deficit. While the overall balance of payments "balances," the current account is now in deficit, while capital flows are in surplus. This example generally describes the U.S. balance of payments position. Interest rates in real terms are relatively high in the U.S., and these high interest rates tend to attract foreign capital. This, in turn, creates a financial/capital account surplus. The result of this surplus is an appreciation of the dollar and a current account deficit. What we have shown is that as interest rates change, capital flows adjust, and the exchange rate moves to a new equilibrium. These movements in capital affect not only the exchange rate but also the size of the current account deficit.

In order to reinforce the fact that changes in capital flows affect the exchange rate, let's examine the impact of a decline in interest rates on a country's current account balance. For example, assume that interest rates in Japan decline. Figure 15.10 illustrates these relationships. Since we want to describe this situation from the Japanese viewpoint, we represent the exchange rate as the number of Japanese Yen per dollar, (Yen/$). As before, if the exchange rate rises, the yen is depreciating (dollar appreciating); and if the exchange rate falls, the yen is appreciating (dollar depreciating).

The equilibrium in the foreign exchange market shown in panel a at point E is based on the assumption that there are no capital flows between the two countries. As before, the equilibrium exchange rate equates imports of goods and services with exports of goods and services at the equilibrium exchange rate of (¥/$). In this case, Japan's current account is balanced.

Now, assume that capital can flow between the two countries and that Japanese interest rates fall. Investor reaction is predictable, as investors now have the incentive to move capital out of Japan and into the U.S. This action requires that investors buy dollars (sell yen) in the foreign exchange market, and the demand for foreign exchange, in this case dollars, increases from D to D′, as shown in panel b. The new equilibrium in the foreign exchange market is at point F and the exchange rate increases from (¥/$) to (¥/$′), and the yen depreciates (dollar appreciates). This change in the exchange rate affects trade flows. Exports of goods and services increase

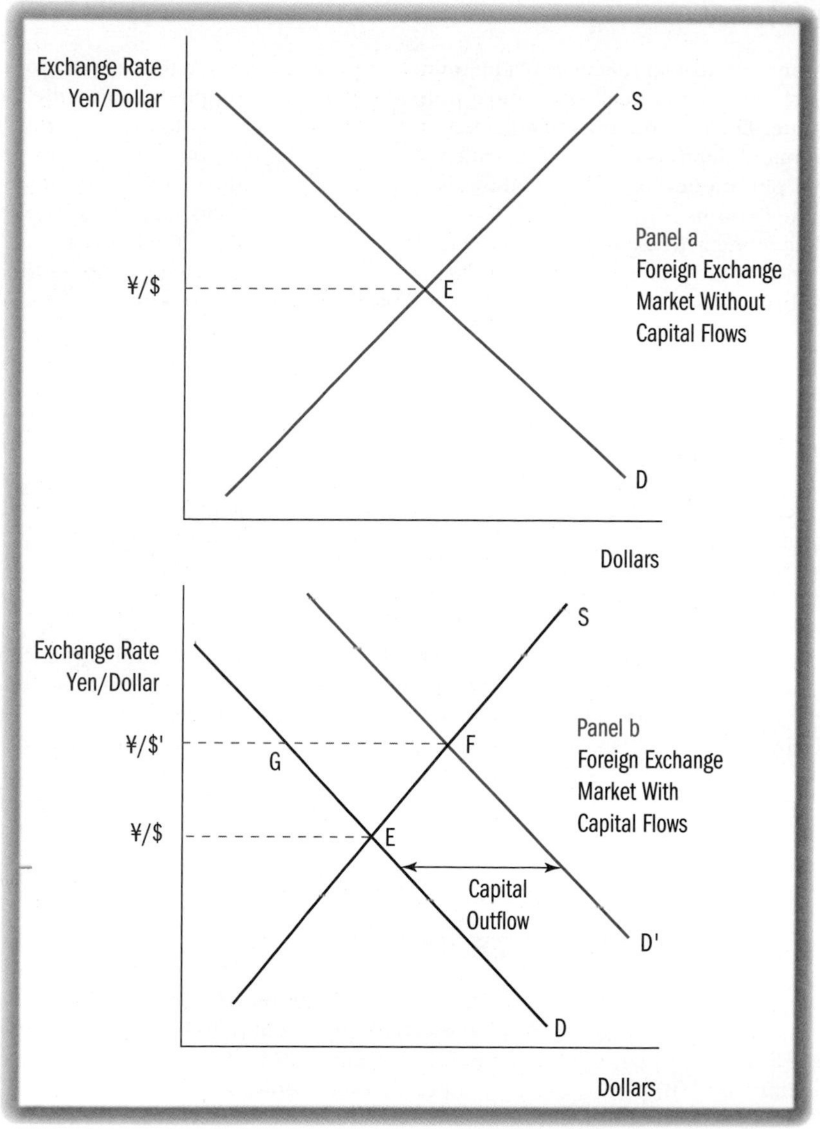

Figure 15.10 **The Foreign Exchange Market With and Without Capital Flows**

Again, when there are no capital flows between countries, the demand and supply of foreign exchange will balance the current account (Panel a). When capital flows are introduced into the foreign exchange market (Panel b), the total inflows and outflows of foreign exchange balance. However, the new equilibrium balances both the current account and capital flows. In this case, an outflow of capital creates a current account surplus.

as the yen depreciates because Japanese goods are now cheaper to foreign buyers. Imports of goods and services decrease as imports become more expensive for Japanese consumers. The result is that overall inflows and outflows of dollars still balance at point F in the foreign exchange market. However, the financial/capital account is now in deficit for Japan, represented by the gap from F to G, and the current account of Japan is in surplus.

SUMMARY

1. Money is an asset that acts as a medium of exchange, a unit of account and a store of value. The total quantity of currency and demand deposits in the U.S. is called M1. M1 plus money market mutual funds and time deposits constitute M2.
2. The monetary base is equal to cash in the hands of the public plus the total quantity of bank reserves. The monetary base is linked to the supply of money through the money multiplier. For policy purposes, the central bank changes the monetary base to change the money supply.
3. In practice, a country's central bank changes the money supply by changing the discount rate, changing the required reserve ratio, or by conducting open market operations. To increase the money supply, the central bank could lower the discount rate, reduce the required reserve ratio, or buy bonds. To reduce the money supply, the central bank could increase the discount rate, increase the required reserve ratio, or sell bonds.
4. Individuals' and businesses' demand for money is inversely related to the interest rate, positively related to the price level, and positively related to the level of real income.
5. When the demand for money is equal to the supply of money, the money market is in equilibrium. In the short run, an increase in the money supply lowers the interest rate, and a decrease in the money supply raises the interest rate. In the short run, an increase in the demand for money raises the interest rate, and a decrease in the demand for money lowers the interest rate.
6. Interest rates and exchange rates are interrelated through interest arbitrage. An increase in the money supply lowers the domestic interest rate and causes a capital outflow. The capital outflow increases the demand for foreign exchange and causes the domestic currency to depreciate. Similarly, a decrease in the money supply raises the domestic interest rate and causes a capital inflow. The capital inflow increases the supply of foreign exchange and causes the domestic currency to appreciate.
7. The foreign exchange market equates the total inflow of foreign exchange with the total outflow of foreign exchange. When a country has a capital inflow and the exchange rate appreciates, the current account moves to a deficit. When a country has a capital outflow and the exchange rate depreciates, the current account moves to a surplus.

KEY CONCEPTS AND TERMS

- money supply p. 340
- M1 p. 340
- M2 p. 341
- monetary base (B) p. 341
- money multiplier p. 341
- reserve requirement p. 341
- discount rate p. 341
- open market operations p. 343
- demand for money p. 344
- interest arbitrage p. 350

PROBLEMS AND QUESTIONS FOR REVIEW

1. List and explain the functions of money.
2. What are the components of the monetary base? What is the significance of the monetary base?
3. List and explain the different tools the central bank can use to control the monetary base.
4. The money supply is equal to the monetary base multiplied by the money multiplier. Explain why this statement is true.
5. What is the difference between the narrow and broad definitions of the money supply?
6. How is the reserve requirement related to the supply of money?
7. What is the discount rate? Explain how changes in the discount rate affect the supply of money.

8. If the U.S. suddenly adopted the reserve requirement that Germany uses, what would happen to the U.S. money supply?
9. A central bank can change the money supply by buying and selling bonds. Describe how this process affects the supply of money.
10. It is harder to control the money supply in a country that does not have an active secondary market for bonds. Explain why this statement is true.
11. Discuss how the demand for money is related to interest rates, real income, and the price level.
12. Suppose that the U.S. Federal Reserve decreases the money supply. Show the effects of this action on the interest rate and the exchange rate.
13. Describe the effects on the interest rate of changes in each of the following determinants of the demand for money:
    a. the domestic price level increases;
    b. domestic real incomes rise;
    c. the domestic price level declines;
    d. domestic real incomes fall.
14. Suppose that the Mexican central bank increases Mexico's money supply. Show the effects of this action on Mexican interest rates and the dollar–peso exchange rate.
15. Suppose that the demand for money in the U.S. declines. Explain and show the effects of this action on U.S. interest rates and the exchange rate.
16. Describe the relationship between interest rates in two countries and the spot and forward exchange rates.
17. Assume that the interest rate in New York is 12 percent and is 10 percent in London. What other information would an investor need to make a decision about where to invest?
18. Explain why capital flows cause imbalances in the current account.
19. Draw a graph illustrating that a current account deficit must be matched by a financial/capital account surplus.
20. Graphically show the situation where a country has:
    a. a current account deficit and a financial/capital account surplus;
    b. a current account surplus and a financial/capital account deficit.

SELECTED READINGS AND WEB SITES

IMF, *International Financial Statistics,* Washington, D.C: IMF, monthly.

The easiest source for information on the money supply (narrow or broad) and the monetary base for any country. In the same publication you can find information on the discount rate and/or other interest rates.

Imad A. Moosa, *Exchange Rate Forecasting: Techniques and Applications,* New York: St. Martin's Press, 2000.

An excellent survey of how exchange rate forecasting is done in practice. The book also includes some interesting case studies of exchange rate forecasting in action.

The Economist (www.economist.com)

A good source of information for the latest economic data the OECD countries and the larger developing countries.

The Financial Times (www.ft.com)

An excellent source of information on macroeconomic policies in Europe.

Wall Street Journal (www.wsj.com)

The best source for daily information on short-term U.S. interest rates.

APPENDIX 15.1

The Relationship Between the Monetary Base and the Money Supply

In the chapter, we assumed that individuals and/or businesses did not want to hold any currency. Since the financial system can create new money only on the basis of excess reserves, it is important to understand the logic and limits of the expansion process when individuals and/or businesses want to hold currency. We can accomplish this by employing the concept of the monetary base.

The monetary base includes all currency and coins in circulation plus the sum of the Federal Reserve accounts that depository institutions (total reserves of the depository institutions) own. The Federal Reserve directly controls the monetary base, or "high powered money," and is the ultimate source of the U.S. money supply. As you learned in this chapter, the money multiplier multiplied by the monetary base always, by definition, equals the money supply.

To see why this must be so, recall that the monetary base, B, consists of total depository reserves, R, plus cash in the public's hand, C. By definition, therefore:

$$B = R + C$$

In addition, a nation's money supply, MS, consists of total deposits, D, plus cash in the hands of the public, C. Again, by definition:

$$MS = C + D$$

Now, in equilibrium, all depository institution reserves are required reserves (R). This is:

$$R = [r]D$$

where r denotes the required reserve ratio imposed by the Federal Reserve.

To make the analysis as simple as possible, assume that the public wants to hold a constant fraction, k, of its money as cash and the rest as deposits. So that:

$$C = k(D)$$

Thus, the monetary base equals:

$$\begin{aligned} B &= [r]D + k(D) \\ &= [r + k]D \end{aligned}$$

or, total deposits of all financial institutions are:

$$D = B(1/[r + k])$$

To put this in terms of the money supply rather than deposits, remember that the total money supply (MS) includes not only deposits (D) but also currency (C).

$$\begin{aligned} MS &= D + C \\ &= D + k(D) \\ &= (1 + k)D \end{aligned}$$

Substituting for D, we can obtain:

$$\begin{aligned} MS &= (1 + k)D \\ &= [(1 + k)/(r + k)] \times B \end{aligned}$$

In the above equation, the money multiplier is equal to:

$$[(1 + k)/(r + k)].$$

APPENDIX 15.2

Interest Parity and Covered Interest Arbitrage

In the chapter, we described the interest-parity relationship without the use of equations. This appendix provides a brief mathematical formulation of this relationship. To make our analysis as simple as possible, let

A = the amount of dollars to be invested for three months

r_{US} = the three month interest rate in New York

r_{UK} = the three month interest rate in London

S = the spot exchange rate, dollars per pound

F = the three month forward exchange rate, dollars per pound

Consider a U.S. investor who has A dollars available for a three-month investment. The investor would invest in New York when:

$$A(1 + r_{US}) > A(1/S)(1 + r_{UK})F$$

The investor would invest in London when:

$$A(1 + r_{US}) < A(1/S)(1 + r_{UK})F$$

Interest parity prevails when the profitability of investing in London is equal to the profitability of investing in New York, which is when:

$$A(1 + r_{US}) = A(1/S)(1 + r_{UK})F$$

Now, define the forward difference (d) as follows:

$$\begin{aligned} d &= (F - S)/S \\ &= (F/S) - 1 \end{aligned}$$

The pound is at a forward premium when $d > 0$, and the pound is at a forward discount when $d < 0$.

Using the interest parity condition, and the definition of the forward difference, one obtains the following:

$$\begin{aligned} A(1 + r_{US}) &= A(1/S)(1 + r_{UK})F \\ (1 + r_{US}) &= (1/S)(1 + r_{UK})F \\ (1 + r_{US}) &= (F/S)(1 + r_{UK}) \\ r_{US} &= (F/S)(1 + r_{UK}) - 1 \\ r_{US} &= (d + 1)(1 + r_{UK}) - 1 \\ r_{US} &= d + r_{UK} + d(r_{UK}) \end{aligned}$$

The term $d(r_{UK})$ is assumed to be zero because it is the product of two small fractions. Thus,

$$r_{US} = d + r_{UK}$$

This shows that the currency of the low interest rate country is at a forward premium.

Chapter 16

Price Levels and the Exchange Rate in the Long Run

"In the long run we are all dead."
—John Maynard Keynes

INTRODUCTION

In the last two chapters, we described the factors that determine exchange rates and their movements. Among the factors we considered were changes in income, the price level, and interest rates. In the short run, all of these factors may change, leading to short-run volatility in exchange rates. We also described how changes in the money supply influence exchange rates in the short run. Changes in the money supply cause interest rates to fluctuate, which in turn influences exchange rates and the balance of payments.

In this chapter, we will discuss the determinants of the exchange rate over long periods of time. We extend our model of exchange rate determination by expanding the effects of changes in the money supply to include its impact on a country's price level (the inflation rate). Money supply changes affect not only interest rates in the short run but also the price level. Price changes lead to predictable changes in exchange rates, and this insight can help us determine what a particular bilateral exchange rate should be. In turn, this will enable us to define or describe a sort of benchmark exchange rate against which the current value of an exchange rate can be compared. As we will see, the current value of an exchange rate may differ significantly from this predicted (benchmark) value, and this difference can have important implications for international business.

THE LAW OF ONE PRICE

We begin our discussion of price levels and exchange rates with a simple but powerful statement known as the law of one price. Disregarding barriers to trade and transportation costs, the **law of one price** states that identical goods sold in competitive

law of one price the proposition that identical goods sold in competitive markets should cost the same everywhere when prices are expressed in terms of the same currency

arbitrage the process of moving goods from low-price markets to high-price markets

markets should cost the same everywhere when prices are expressed in terms of the same currency. For example, assume that the dollar–pound exchange rate is \$2 per pound. If a pair of shoes cost £200 in the U.K., the same pair of shoes should cost \$400 in the U.S. The price of the same pair of shoes in the U.S. and the U.K. expressed in a common currency should be identical. At the exchange rate of \$2 per pound, the price of £200 or \$400 is the same price.

What is even more interesting is why the law of one price should hold between countries. Suppose that the exchange rate is \$2 per pound and the identical pair of shoes cost £150 in the U.K. and \$400 in the U.S. Abstracting from transportation costs and barriers to trade, you could buy the shoes in the U.K. for £150 or \$300 and then ship the shoes to the U.S. and sell them for \$400. On this transaction, you could make a \$100 profit on each pair of shoes, or a 33 percent rate of return on the initial investment.[1] Given the profitability of moving shoes between the two countries, a couple of things would automatically occur. First, shoes would be exported from the U.K. en masse to the U.S. The export of shoes from the U.K. would reduce the local shoe supply in the U.K. market. As the local shoe supply fell in the U.K., the pound price of shoes would rise. Second, shoes would be imported into the U.S., and as the supply of shoes increased, the dollar price of shoes would decline. Over time, the price of shoes in the U.S. and the U.K. would tend to converge until shoe prices in the two countries became equal. This process is called **arbitrage**. Traders will tend to move goods from low-price markets to higher-priced markets and the process would continue until all excess profits disappear.

If this sounds to you like trade based on the law of comparative advantage, you are correct. The law of one price merely states comparative advantage in terms of currencies. However, everyone knows that prices for identical goods are not equal even within a large country such as the U.S.—and much less so in all international markets. Does this mean that the law of one price is useless? No, not at all. The appropriate way to think about the law of one price is that there is a tendency for prices of identical goods to equalize between countries. Because of transport costs, barriers to trade, and differences in tax rates and regulations, goods rarely sell for exactly the same price in international markets. When identical goods are selling at different prices in different international markets, over time the price differential should narrow.[2] Like the proverbial \$20 bill lying in the street, firms are unlikely to pass up a profitable opportunity.

The law of one price also provides us a convenient point of departure for several other concepts. Using our familiar example of the dollar–pound exchange rate, [R(\$/£)], the law of one price can be expressed more formally as a relationship between the exchange rate and the price of shoes in the U.S. and the U.K. This relationship between the two prices and the exchange rate can be expressed as follows:

$$P_{US} = [R(\$/£)] \times P_{UK}$$

where the exchange rate [R(\$/£)] is the number of dollars needed to buy a pound; P_{US} is the price of shoes in the U.S.; and P_{UK} is the price of shoes in the U.K. By

[1]Even by paying transport costs of, say, 10 percent, the trader would earn \$70, or a return of about 23 percent.
[2]This discussion should remind the reader of our earlier discussion concerning factor-price equalization in Chapter 4.

rearranging the terms slightly we can obtain the following relationship for the exchange rate:

$$[R(\$/£)] = P_{US}/P_{UK}$$

As the equations illustrate the exchange rate between the dollar and the pound is equal to the ratio of the price of shoes in the U.S. to the price of shoes in the U.K. Aside from the arithmetic, what does this really mean? Suppose that the price of shoes in the U.S. rose to $500 and the price of shoes in the U.K. remained constant at £200. What would businesses do if the exchange rate were still $2 per pound? They would begin to ship shoes from the U.K. to the U.S. In the foreign exchange market, the demand for pounds would increase, as U.S. consumers would need pounds to buy British shoes. As a result, the dollar/pound exchange rate would rise. This process would continue until shoes priced in both currencies once again cost the same. The increase in the exchange rate would continue until the exchange rate equaled $2.50 per pound. To extrapolate this simple example to many different goods, we need to broaden our analysis to a discussion of purchasing power parity.

Hamburgers and PPP

Is there an easier way to calculate PPP? Ten years ago, *The Economist* magazine published an article calculating PPP across countries based on the dollar price of Big Macs (yes, the hamburger). Initially the idea was something of a parody on PPP and the seriousness with which economists discuss it. However, what started as a joke has taken on a life of its own. The McPPP standard is now a staple of international economics because, over time, it has been found to work surprisingly well. Even though Big Macs are not tradable goods (unless the border is nearby) the annual calculations are not all that far from reality. In Figure 16.1, we have reproduced the estimates for 2007. The first column shows the price of a Big Mac in local currency. The next column shows the price in dollars at the current spot exchange rate. Dividing this dollar price by the U.S. price gives an implied PPP exchange rate in the third column. The fourth column is the actual spot exchange rate used in the calculation. The final column gives the amount by which the spot rate differs from the exchange rate that would be expected if all you did was compare the price of Big Macs.

The creators of the index did not take it too seriously at first. However, in the last 10 years economists have noticed that the McPPP works fairly well. The implied PPP is frequently not so different from estimates produced by much more sophisticated methods. Further, it has been found that, more often than not, currencies that McPPP finds to be overvalued or undervalued tend to move in the predicted direction over the next year. For example, the 1996 indexes correctly predicted the movement of exchange rates for 8 of the 12 major industrial countries. Of the seven currencies that moved by more than 10 percent, the index correctly predicted the direction of change six times.[3] It is rare in economics for something to be both amusing *and* perhaps even useful.

[3]See "Big MacCurrencies," *The Economist,* April 12, 1997, p. 71.

[4]See Li Lian Ong, "Burgernomics: The Economics of the Big Mac Standard," *Journal of International Money and Finance* 16(6), 1997, pp. 865–78. In this article, the author finds that Big Mac index performs just as well as most other indices used to test PPP.

Cash and carry

The hamburger standard, July 2007

	Big Mac prices: in local currency	Big Mac prices: in dollars	Implied PPP[a] of the	Actual Dollar Exchange Rate July 2nd	Under (−)/Over (+) Valuation Against the Dollar, %
United States[b]	$3.41	3.41			
Argentina	Peso 8.25	2.67	2.42	3.09	−22
Australia	A$3.45	2.95	1.01	1.17	−14
Brazil	Real 6.90	3.61	2.02	1.91	+6
Britain	£1.99	4.01	1.71[c]	2.01[c]	+18
Canada	C$3.88	3.68	1.14	1.05	+8
Chile	Peso 1,565	2.97	459	527	−13
China	Yuan 11.0	1.45	3.23	7.60	−58
Czech Republic	Koruna 52.9	2.51	15.5	21.1	−27
Denmark	Dkr 27.75	5.08	8.14	5.46	+49
Egypt	Pound 9.54	1.68	2.80	5.69	−51
Euro area[d]	€3.06	4.17	1.12[e]	1.36[e]	+22
Hong Kong	HK$12.0	1.54	3.52	7.82	−55
Hungary	Forint 600	3.33	176	180	−2
Indonesia	Rupiah 15,900	1.76	4,663	9,015	−48
Japan	¥280	2.29	82.1	122	−33
Malaysia	Ringgit 5.50	1.60	1.61	3.43	−53
Mexico	Peso 29.0	2.69	8.50	10.8	−21
New Zealand	NZ$4.60	3.59	1.35	1.28	+5
Peru	New Sol 9.50	3.00	2.79	3.17	−12
Philippines	Peso 85.0	1.85	24.9	45.9	−46
Poland	Zloty 6.90	2.51	2.02	2.75	−26
Russia	Rouble 52.0	2.03	15.2	25.6	−41
Singapore	S$3.95	2.59	1.16	1.52	−24
South Africa	Rand 15.5	2.22	4.55	6.97	−35
South Korea	Won 2,900	3.14	850	923	−8
Sweden	SKr33.0	4.86	9.68	6.79	+42
Switzerland	SFr6.30	5.20	1.85	1.21	+53
Taiwan	NT$75.0	2.29	22.0	32.8	−33
Thailand	Baht 62.0	1.80	18.2	34.5	−47
Turkey	Lire 4.75	3.66	1.39	1.30	+7
Venezuela	Bolivar 7,400	3.45	2,170	2,147	+1
Colombia	Peso 6,900	3.53	2,023	1,956	+3
Costa Rica	Colon 1,130	2.18	331	519	−36
Estonia	Kroon 30.0	2.61	8.80	11.5	−23
Iceland	Kronur 469	7.61	138	61.7	+123
Latvia	Lats 1.39	2.72	0.41	0.51	−20
Lithuania	Litas 6.60	2.61	1.94	2.53	−24
Norway	Kroner 40.0	6.88	11.7	5.81	−102
Pakistan	Rupee 140	2.32	41.1	60.4	−32
Paraguay	Guarani 10,500	2.04	3,079	5,145	−40
Saudi Arabia	Riyal 9.00	2.40	2.64	3.75	−30
Slovakia	Koruna 61.3	2.49	18.0	24.6	−27
Sri Lanka	Rupee 210	1.89	61.6	111	−45
UAE	Dirhams 10.0	2.72	2.93	3.67	−20
Ukraine	Hryvnia 9.25	1.84	2.71	5.03	−46
Uruguay	Peso 62.0	2.59	18.2	23.9	−24

[a]*Purchasing-power parity; local price divided by price in United States.* [b]*Average of New York, Chicago, Atlanta and San Francisco.* [c]*Dollars per pound.* [d]*Weighted average of prices in euro area.* [e]*Dollars per euro*

Sources: McDonald's; *The Economist.*

Figure 16.1 Purchasing Power Parity and the Big Mac

Source: *The Economist,* August 22, 2007.

PURCHASING POWER PARITY

Although interesting, the law of one price applies to only one good, like shoes. If the law of one price or a tendency toward the same price holds for shoes, it also should also hold for other goods. However, for the law of one price to hold, the goods in question must be tradable between countries. This means that traders (individuals or firms) must be able to move goods from the low-priced country to a high-priced country. In doing so, prices, after having been translated into a common currency in each country, would tend to be identical over time.

purchasing power parity (PPP) the theory that changes in exchange rates are related to price levels between countries

Purchasing power parity (PPP) is the theory that changes in exchange rates are related to changes in relative prices among countries. Where the law of one price states that the price of a good expressed in the same currency should cost the same everywhere, purchasing power parity simply extends this concept to the price of a representative market basket of goods. Purchasing power parity states that an exchange rate between two countries should equal the ratio of the price level in one country to the price level in the other country.

For example, if the price level in the U.S. doubled relative to the price level in the U.K., U.S. goods would now be twice as expensive as British goods. As a result, U.S. imports of British goods would increase and U.S. exports to the U.K. would decline, leading to an increase in the dollar/pound exchange rate and a depreciation of the dollar relative to the British pound. If the reverse occurred and the price level in the U.S. fell relative to the price level in the U.K., the dollar/pound exchange rate would decline and the dollar would appreciate relative to the pound. As with the law of one price, purchasing power parity should be thought of as a tendency or as a *long-run* concept.

For example, if a country has extremely high inflation relative to the rest of the world, its currency on average would depreciate relative to countries with low inflation. However, that said, it is clearly possible for a country's current exchange rate to deviate significantly from the value predicted by purchasing power parity as other determinants like interest rates change. This does not make purchasing power parity useless. Rather, large deviations from purchasing power parity become important. As exchange rates fluctuate over time, it is useful to have some type of benchmark that allows one to determine where the exchange rate should be based on a country's relative price level versus where the current exchange rate actually is. The best way to view purchasing power parity is as just that, a benchmark. In the long run, an exchange rate will tend to move toward this benchmark value.

Using the concept of purchasing power parity also helps to clear up some of confusion that the business press creates concerning exchange rates. Very often in the business press you will find statements like a currency is undervalued or overvalued, or that a currency is weak or strong. To make these statements, one has to have some benchmark exchange rate. Undervalued or overvalued implies that the currency has an underlying value that is different from the current exchange rate. Generally, that underlying value is based on purchasing power parity. Without this valuable concept, using these descriptors for currencies has no meaning.

Essentially, we use the concept of purchasing power parity in much the same way that we use the concept of perfect competition. In your Principles of Economics course, you discussed and analyzed a perfectly competitive market structure. Yet, perfectly competitive markets are, in practice, rarely observed. If these markets are so rare, why bother explaining them? Perfect competition is important as a benchmark to assess the degree of competitiveness (or lack thereof) in other market structures. Purchasing power parity is most useful for similar reasons. Actual exchange rates are rarely *exactly* at purchasing power parity. However, to assess whether or not the exchange rate is "high" or "low," one needs something to measure it against. It is precisely this use of purchasing power parity that makes it important.

Absolute Purchasing Power Parity

absolute purchasing power parity the theory that exchange rates are related to differences in the level of prices between countries

The first version of purchasing power parity we will describe is the version known as **absolute purchasing power parity**. Absolute purchasing power parity is the theory that the bilateral exchange rate between two countries is related to the ratio of the level of prices between two countries. We will continue using the same notation that we used for the law of one price in our discussion of absolute purchasing power parity. The only difference is that P_{US} represents the dollar price of a representative market basket of tradable goods in the U.S., and P_{UK} represents the pound price of the same market basket of tradable goods in the U.K. Using these relationships, the dollar/pound exchange rate predicted by absolute purchasing power parity is expressed as:

$$[R(\$/£)] = P_{US}/P_{UK}$$

In this case, if a particular basket of goods were to cost \$1,000 in the U.S. (P_{US}) and an identical basket of goods were to cost £500 in the U.K. (P_{UK}), the absolute version of purchasing power parity states that the exchange rate would be \$2 per pound.

Now, consider what would happen to the exchange rate if the price level doubled in the U.S.? For example, if P_{US} increased to \$2,000 and prices remain unchanged in the U.K. at £500, the purchasing power parity exchange rate would move to \$4 per pound. The purchasing power parity exchange rate has simply risen to offset the dollar's lower purchasing power. By rearranging the previous equation, we can obtain a slightly different version of this relationship:

$$P_{US} = [R(\$/£)] \times P_{UK}$$

When the relationship is expressed in this form, we see that when absolute purchasing power parity holds, prices in the U.S. (P_{US}) would be equal to the pound price of the market basket of tradable goods in the U.K. (P_{UK}) multiplied by the exchange rate, R(\$/£). For example, suppose that you take \$1,000, which would buy a representative market basket of goods in the U.S., and exchanged the dollars for pounds. This quantity of pounds should allow you to purchase exactly the same market basket of goods in the U.K. If the U.S. price level doubled to \$2,000, you should be able to do the same thing. You would just need to exchange \$2,000 for pounds rather than \$1,000 at the new exchange rate. Thus, if absolute purchasing power parity holds, the exchange rate may change in nominal terms, but in real terms the amount of goods you can buy has not changed. In the short run, if the exchange rate does not exactly match the ratio of the price levels between two countries, this difference will have an important implication for a country's trade flows.

Relative Purchasing Power Parity

We will now extend the concept of PPP one step further. The previous relationship describing PPP was based on the absolute prices of goods in the two countries. From the absolute version of purchasing power parity, it is possible to obtain another version of PPP known as relative purchasing power parity.

relative purchasing power parity the theory that a percentage change in the exchange rate is equal to the difference in the percentage change in price levels

Relative purchasing power parity between two countries states that the *percentage change* in the bilateral exchange rate is equal to the difference in the *percentage change* in the national price levels over any given period of time. Absolute purchasing power parity is a statement about absolute prices and exchange rate *levels*. On the other hand, relative purchasing power parity is a statement about price and exchange rate *changes* over time. Relative purchasing power parity is a very useful concept for one main reason. Normally, when discussing price changes we do not talk about the actual price level. When was the last time you heard of price changes in the U.S. or any other country described as "the price of the market basket went from this dollar amount to that dollar amount"? Although this is what has actually happened, price changes normally are reported as a percentage change in the price level (the rate of inflation) on an annual basis.

For example, suppose the rate of inflation in the U.S. was 10 percent in a given year and only 5 percent for the same year in the U.K. In this case, the relative version of purchasing power parity would predict that the dollar/pound exchange rate would increase by 5 percent or the dollar would depreciate by 5 percent relative to the British pound. This is shown in more formal terms as[5]

$$\%\Delta XR = \%\Delta P_{US} - \%\Delta P_{UK}$$

Aside from being more convenient, there is another reason that relative purchasing power parity is useful. When describing the absolute version of purchasing power parity, we assumed that the market baskets of tradable goods being compared in the two countries were identical. This requires that each country's market basket contain exactly the same goods and have exactly the same weights. Since national price indexes are weighted averages of many prices, it would be unlikely that two countries would have both the same identical goods in the basket and employ exactly the same weights in the basket. Because of these differences, each country's price index is slightly different from every other country's price index. These differences limit the usefulness of the absolute version of purchasing power parity, as the direct comparison of price levels between countries would be like comparing apples to oranges. However, a comparison of the changes in the price levels between countries may still be valid as long as the factors that cause price levels to change in each country are similar.

Purchasing Power Parity in the Short Run and the Long Run

> "Although the technical minutiae of PPP definitions may seem mundane, they in fact are central to many of the practical questions surrounding implementation of purchasing power parity."
>
> —KENNETH ROGOFF

[5]The equation for the relative version of PPP is only an approximation. The exact relationship is $\%\Delta XR = [(1 + \%\Delta P_{US})/(1 + \%\Delta P_{UK})] - 1$.

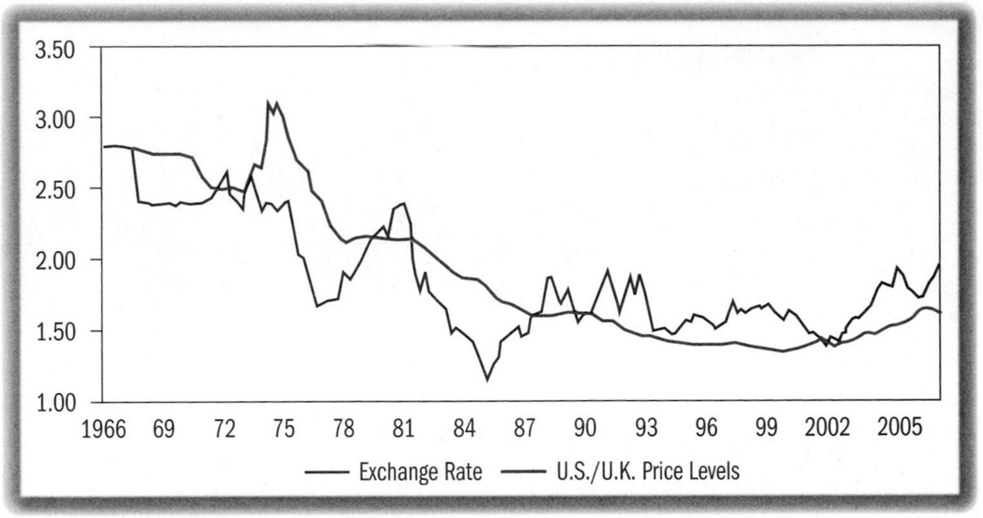

Figure 16.2 The Dollar/Pound Exchange Rate and Relative U.S./U.K. Price Levels, 1966–2006

Notice that the exchange rate and the relative price levels tend to move together in the long run. However, in the short run the deviation of the exchange rate from that predicted by PPP can be large.

Source: IMF, *International Financial Statistics*, CD-ROM, Washington, D.C.: July, 2007.

So far, we have emphasized that purchasing power parity should be viewed as a long-run concept. In this section, we present evidence that indicates that changes in relative prices and exchange rates do move together over long periods of time. However, in the short run, exchange rates can deviate significantly from purchasing power parity. We begin our discussion by examining the absolute version of purchasing power parity using the dollar per pound exchange rate. Figure 16.2 shows the dollar/pound exchange rate and the ratio of the U.S. and U.K. market baskets from 1966 to 2006.[6] Notice that the two series tend to move together over the long run. However, notice that in some time periods the deviation of the exchange rate from that predicted by this version of purchasing power parity is dramatic. This reinforces what we have described earlier. PPP is most useful as a long-run benchmark for what the exchange rate *should* be. However, PPP routinely fails as a short-run predictor of what the exchange rate actually *is*.

As we discussed earlier, the relative version of purchasing power parity may be better suited for examining changes in exchange rates. Recall that the relative version of PPP relates differences in national rates of inflation to changes in bilateral exchange rates. For example, we can again use the dollar–pound exchange rate. Figure 16.3 relates the percentage change in the dollar–pound exchange rate to the difference

[6]The market basket used for both countries is the Producer Price Index (PPI). The reason for using this basket instead of the more common Consumer Price Index (CPI) or the GDP deflator will be discussed below.

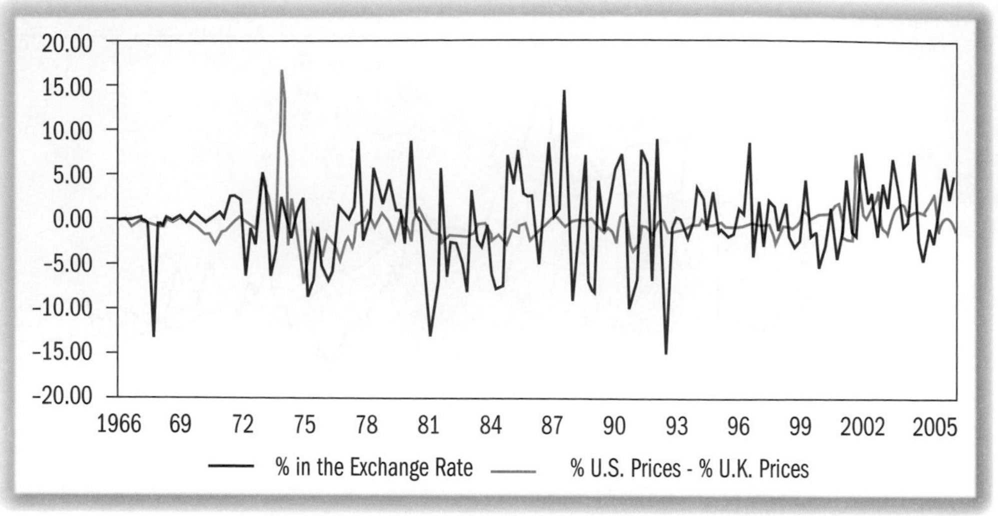

Figure 16.3 Percentage Change in the Exchange Rate and the Percentage Difference in Relative Prices, 1967–2006

Notice that the percentage change in the exchange rate and the percentage change in the relative price levels tend to move together in the long run. However, in the short run the actual exchange rate deviates substantially from that predicted by the relative version of PPP.
Source: IMF, *International Financial Statistics,* CD-ROM, Washington, D.C.: IMF, July 2007.

between the rates of inflation in the U.S. and the U.K. Notice that this figure is similar to Figure 16.2. Both the actual percentage change in the exchange rate and that predicted using PPP move in a similar direction over the long run. However, in the short run, the actual exchange rate deviates substantially from that predicted by the relative version of purchasing power parity. Relative PPP does seem to work "better" in the sense that the deviations are less severe than was the case for the absolute version of PPP shown in Figure 16.2.

With respect to our discussion of purchasing power parity, one has to decide if the cup is half full or half empty. Both versions of PPP fail as reliable predictors of short-run changes in the exchange rate. In this sense, the glass is half empty. Trying to use PPP to predict next month's bilateral exchange rate would be a fool's errand. However, over sufficiently long periods of time, the glass is half full as the two series tend to move together. In this sense, PPP is a useful benchmark. At some point, the market exchange rate tends to move toward the PPP exchange rate. Unfortunately, the exchange rate has a distressing tendency to "overshoot" the target in the other direction.

Our calculations are designed only to illustrate rough estimates of purchasing power parity for one bilateral exchange rate. However, empirical research conducted

[7]In the jargon of econometrics, the exchange rate seems to exhibit mean reversion behavior with respect to PPP. For more information on this point, see Jeffrey A. Frankel and Andrew K. Rose, "A Panel Project on Purchasing Power Parity: Mean Reversion Within and Between Countries," *Journal of International Economics* 40(1/2), February 1996, pp. 209–24.

over the last several decades tends to support the conclusion that PPP works much better in the long run than in the short run. Empirical tests concerning the validity of the absolute and relative versions of purchasing power parity have found that in the short run, the actual exchange rate may differ substantially from the predicted value.[8] Even the law of one price does not fare well in empirical tests.[9]

Over the years, economists have developed a number of explanations of why purchasing power parity fails many empirical tests. First, there is the question of which market basket to use in the calculating PPP. In practice, there are three price indexes that could be used in the calculation: the consumer price index (CPI), the GDP price deflator, and the Producer Price Index (PPI).[10] Economists have long debated which price index to use in calculating PPP. Since PPP is based on extrapolation of the law of one price to a group of tradable goods, the presence of nontradable goods in both the CPI and the GDP deflator make these indexes less desirable to use. The consensus is that calculating PPP based on the PPI is the best choice, as a higher proportion of the goods in this index for most countries are tradable goods.

Once the price index has been chosen, there is a secondary problem associated with how the price index is constructed in various countries. For example, the price of equipment to produce semiconductors might be included in the U.S. PPI but not in Bolivia's. Even when the products included in the price indexes are identical, the weights assigned to various products may differ. For example, rice would have a higher weight in the Japanese price index than it would in the U.S. price index, and the reverse would be true for beef. Since price indexes are weighted averages of the prices of various products, it is unlikely that any two country's price index would measure exactly the same products with identical weights.[11] As a result, comparing prices and price indexes across countries sounds conceptually simple but in fact it is fraught with difficulties. It is these difficulties associated with comparing two price indexes that may partially explain why purchasing power parity fails in empirical tests.

A second group of problems associated with testing PPP is concerned with barriers or market conditions that allow prices to diverge between two countries. First, transportation costs to move goods between countries are not zero. As a result, the higher the transportation costs to move a good between two countries, the more likely the prices of the same product in different countries will diverge. Businesses can more easily arbitrage diamond prices between countries than they can cement prices.[12] This means that even in a free market, some products could have widely different prices in various countries and these differences could persist indefinitely.

---

[8]For a review of the empirical tests concerning both the absolute and relative versions of PPP, see Kenneth Rogoff, "The Purchasing Power Parity Puzzle," *Journal of Economic Literature* 24(2), June 1996, pp. 647–68.

[9]For example, see Peter Isard, Kenneth A. Froot and Kenneth Rogoff, "Perspectives on PPP and Long-Run Exchange Rates," in Gene M. Grossman and Kenneth Rogoff, eds., *Handbook of International Economics,* Vol. 3, Amsterdam: North-Holland, 1995, pp. 1647–88.

[10]The PPI was formerly known as the Wholesale Price Index in the U.S. Many countries still use the latter term.

[11]Recently researchers have started constructing internationally comparable market baskets. While this research is promising, it is still too new to be empirically useful. See Robert Summers and Alan Heston, "The Penn World Table (Mark 5): An Expanded Set of International Comparisons, 1950–1988," *Quarterly Journal of Economics* 106(2), May 1991, pp. 327–68.

[12]A convenient way to think about this is that products with a high value-to-weight ratio, such as a diamond, are easily transported and these costs would form a negligible part of total cost. Cement would be just the reverse.

Second, differences in market structures between countries could cause the prices of the same product in two countries to vary. A product that is sold in a competitive market in one country will be less expensive than the same product sold in an imperfectly competitive market in another country. Thus, international differences in market structure could lead to international price differences for the same product. This phenomenon also occurs within a large country, such as the U.S. Identical products frequently sell at higher prices in smaller cities than in larger cities, as the increased competition in a larger city generally will keep prices lower than in less competitive markets.

Third, government policies also cause international differences in prices. For example, many products have tariffs in place in order to protect domestic industries. To the extent that tariffs on identical products differ between countries, the prices of identical goods may likewise differ. International price differences can also occur for goods that are subject to different nontariff barriers such as quotas. In addition, taxes also affect a product's price, and countries throughout the world use different methods of taxation. For example, countries in Western Europe extensively use the Value Added Tax (VAT) as a means of raising revenue, and this VAT tax impacts the final price of the product.[13] Comparing prices in Western Europe to prices in the U.S., which does not use the VAT, can lead to very different prices for the same product. Differences in other types of taxes and/or industrial policy can also contribute to different prices for the same product among countries. The net result is that prices for identical products between two countries may be substantially different due to market conditions, government policies, or barriers that inhibit the free flow of goods between countries.

A final problem associated with testing purchasing power parity is the existence of nontradable goods. The classic example of a nontradable good is a haircut. Haircuts may be cheaper in the U.S. than in Belgium. However, few Belgians would fly to New York just to get a haircut. Generally, nontradable goods are goods in which the transportation costs are so high relative to the value of the product that international trade does not occur. Typically, nontradable goods are associated with the housing industry and the service industry. Collectively, nontradable goods account for approximately 60 percent of GDP in the U.S. The problem associated with nontradeable goods is that their prices are determined wholly by *domestic* demand and supply. As such, prices of nontradable goods can differ greatly from country to country. For example, the supply and demand for housing in your local market determines the price of your home, not the price of homes in Tokyo. Since nontradable goods are not traded internationally, they should not be included in purchasing power parity calculations. However, virtually all price indexes calculated in every country contain a certain percentage of nontradable goods. Using the CPI, GDP price deflator, or to a lesser degree the PPI, to calculate PPP explicitly includes the price of nontradable goods. In addition, the prices of nontradable goods are implicitly included in many prices of goods that are traded. For example, marketing expenses and computer services are included in the

[3]The VAT is essentially a tax on the difference between total costs and total revenue for producers. Since it is usually levied on all firms, the amount of tax embodied on a complicated product, such as a car, can be quite substantial. This can lead to the seemingly strange phenomenon of European products selling at lower prices in the U.S. than they do in Europe.

prices of tradable goods. When comparing the price of a single product between countries, the prices may differ because the price of the goods is "contaminated," so to speak, by production costs that are nontradable. As a result, it becomes almost impossible to compare international prices for "purely" tradable goods. This means that it is very difficult to compare prices in Japan with those in the U.S. because nontradable goods are more expensive in Japan, making the calculation of purchasing power parity between the yen and the dollar less than ideal.

We began this section by illustrating that the actual exchange rate between the dollar and the British pound often does not match what purchasing power parity predicts. Many other empirical studies conducted over the last 30 years have come up with much the same result using different currencies, different versions of PPP, and different time periods. From these empirical failures of purchasing power parity, one might be tempted to dismiss the entire concept as useless.

However, *part* of the failure of PPP is one of measurement. The price indexes that we ideally would like to use to test the theory do not exist. As such, part of the reason PPP fails empirical tests is poor price data. However, even if perfect data did exist, it is likely that purchasing power parity would still fail some empirical tests. A good portion of the problem seems to be whether one is discussing the short run or the long run. If one uses this year's price differential between countries to predict movements in the exchange rate, then purchasing power parity will frequently misestimate the exchange rate. But suppose that the rate of inflation in the U.S. over the next five years averaged 10 percent and the average inflation rate of the U.K. was only 5 percent? What would happen to the dollar's value? Using purchasing power parity, one would state that, over time, the dollar would depreciate in value. Further, if you lengthened the time period, the probability of a wrong answer diminishes.

If purchasing power parity works fairly well in the long run, we might ask, then, just what is the long run? The empirical work on this issue yields a consistent consensus. It is rare for an exchange rate deviation from PPP to take fewer than three years to revert toward PPP. On the other hand, it is also rare for the process to take longer than five years.[14] Thus, the long run with regard to PPP is not substantially different from the long run in other applications in economics.

Nominal Exchange Rates in the Long Run

Given our discussion of purchasing power parity, we are now in a position to analyze changes in the nominal exchange rate over long periods of time. For example, many currencies have long-run trends in their nominal exchange rate. These long run trends are normally a result of some underlying factor within the economy. In addition, these long-run changes in the nominal exchange rate are important when making long-run business decisions concerning trade and investment.

To begin our analysis, first consider the implications associated with purchasing power parity. PPP indicates that changes in the nominal exchange rate are function of changes in relative prices between countries. To examine this relationship in more detail, we need to link a country's price level to its major determinant, the money supply.

---

[4]For an excellent summary of this literature, see Kenneth Rogoff, "The Purchasing Power Parity Puzzle," *Journal of Economic Literature* 34(2), June 1996, pp. 647–68.

Why Are Prices Lower in Poorer Countries?

When comparing price levels across countries, a striking empirical regularity stands out. The absolute price level among countries is positively correlated with the level of real GDP per capita. In other words, as real GDP per capita rises, so does the price level. This also means that the overall cost of living is lower in poor countries than it is in wealthier countries. For instance the cost of living in Mexico is lower than it is in the U.S.

There are two general explanations of this phenomenon. First, the economists Bela Balassa and Paul Samuelson both formulated an explanation along the following lines. Their explanation is that labor, on average, is less productive in poor countries than it is in wealthy countries. However, there is a productivity difference in poor countries between tradable goods and nontradable goods. Balassa and Samuelson posit that in tradable goods, workers in wealthy countries are much more productive than workers in poor countries. For nontradable goods, the differences in productivity between workers in wealthy or poor countries may be negligible. The key is that labor may shift between the two sectors in the long run. This means that wages in one sector influence wages in the other sector. In the tradable goods sector, workers in the wealthy countries earn high wages because their productivity is high. Since workers may shift from one sector to the other, high wages in the tradable goods sectors pushes up wages for workers in the nontradable sector. Across countries, there may not be very much difference in workers' productivity in the nontradable sector. The classic example is a haircut. A barber in either a wealthy or a poor country can give only so many haircuts. Nontradables are really cheaper in poor countries because workers are paid less per unit of output than they are in rich countries. This makes the prices of nontradables relatively more expensive in wealthy countries than in poor countries. As nontradables are a substantial component of almost any country's price index, prices overall will tend to be higher in wealthy countries than in poor countries.[15]

Jagdish Bhagwati, Irving Kravis, and Robert Lipsey developed the second explanation of the difference in national price levels. The central point of their argument is that wealthy countries have a higher endowment of capital. On average, tradable goods are probably more capital intensive than are nontradable goods. The greater endowment of capital in wealthy countries means that workers in tradable goods in these countries will be relatively more productive and earn higher wages. Nontradables usually are more labor intensive. Since poor countries tend to have an abundance of labor, their nontradables will be less expensive. The two explanations complement one another. In any case, there are sound economic reasons why the overall price level should be different between wealthy and poor countries. What does this have to do with PPP? If we assume that this phenomenon exists, it creates a problem in comparing price levels internationally. It is difficult to arbitrage the prices of nontradable goods. If nontradable goods are included in countries' price indexes, it becomes difficult to compare price indexes across countries. This would be particularly true when comparing price indexes between developed and developing countries. PPP applies to tradable goods, and the presence of nontradable goods in the price indexes makes applying PPP all the more difficult.[16]

---

[5]See Bela Balassa, "The Purchasing Power Parity Doctrine: A Reappraisal," *Journal of Political Economy,* December 1964, pp. 584–96 and Paul A. Samuelson, "Theoretical Notes on Trade Problems," *Review of Economics and Statistics,* May 1964, pp. 145–54.

[6]See Irving B. Kravis and Robert E, Lipsey, Toward and Explanation of National Price Levels, Princeton Studies in International Finance 52 (International Finance Section, Department of Economics, Princeton University), November 1983; and Jagdish N. Bhagwati, "Why Are Services Cheaper in the Poor Countries?" *Economic Journal* 94(374), June 1984, pp. 279–86.

As we illustrated in Chapter 15, equilibrium in a country's money market occurs when a country's money supply (MS) is equal to a country's demand for money (MD). A simple money demand function for a country can be defined as follows:

$$MD = k(P)(Y)$$

where k is amount of money people want to hold for every dollar of nominal income or GDP, (P)(Y). Using separate money demand functions for the U.S. and the U.K., this becomes:

$$MS_{US} = k_{US}(\text{Nominal GDP}_{US}) = k_{US}(P_{US}) \times (Y_{US})$$

$$MS_{UK} = k_{UK}(\text{Nominal GDP}_{UK}) = k_{UK}(P_{UK}) \times (Y_{UK})$$

Different factors determine the variables associated in both of these equilibrium relationships in the U.S. and the U.K. Recall that a country's central bank determines a country's money supply (MS). The ks represent the proportion of nominal GDP that the public wishes to hold in the form of money. As such, public preferences to hold money in each country determine this variable. In the long run, a combination of the growth rate of the labor force, the growth rate of the productivity of labor, and improvements in technology determine the real GDP (Y) of a country. If we take a ratio of these two equations for the U.S. and the U.K. and rearrange terms, we obtain:

$$(P_{US}/P_{UK}) = (MS_{US}/MS_{UK}) \times (k_{UK}/k_{US}) \times (Y_{UK}/Y_{US})$$

In this form, the price ratio between the U.S. and the U.K. is a function of the ratios of the money supplies (MS), the proportion of nominal GDP that the public wants to hold as money (k), and real GDP (Y). The left-hand side of the equation should look familiar. In our discussion of purchasing power parity, this term was the right-hand side of the equation determining the nominal exchange rate. Using that relationship, the nominal exchange rate becomes:

$$[R(\$/£)] = P_{US}/P_{UK} = (MS_{US}/MS_{UK}) \times (k_{UK}/k_{US}) \times (Y_{UK}/Y_{US})$$

When presented in this form, the nominal exchange rate is a function of relative prices between the U.S. and the U.K. The relative prices between the two countries are a function of the relative money supplies, the public's willingness to hold money, and real GDP in each country.

Now, consider the effect of a change in prices on the nominal exchange rate. For example, suppose that prices in the U.S. are rising faster than the prices in the U.K. This causes the price ratio (P_{US}/P_{UK}) to rise and the nominal exchange rate would adjust to this change by also rising. The rise in the nominal exchange rate indicates that the dollar has depreciated because of the relatively higher prices in the U.S.

The above relationship between prices and their underlying determinants allows us to ask the additional question: What caused U.S. prices to rise? As the relationship illustrates, if the ratio of prices between the U.S. and the U.K. is rising, then there must be a change in the ratio of money supplies, the public's willingness to hold money, or real GDP between the two countries. If prices in the U.S. (P_{US}) are rising faster than prices in the U.K. (P_{UK}), then one of underlying determinants must have changed—for example, if the U.S. money supply is rising faster than the U.K. money supply. Everything else equal, a rising ratio of money supplies (MS_{US}/MS_{UK}) implies a rising ratio of prices (P_{US}/P_{UK}). This change in the relative money supply in each country leads, in turn, to an increase in the dollar–pound exchange rate and a depreciation in the value of the dollar. Thus, we can explain differences in relative prices caused by differences in the money supply's growth rates.

In addition to changes in the money supplies, there are two other underlying determinants that could change and cause the price level to change. For example, the ks represent the proportion of income that the public wants to hold as money in the two countries. Consider what would happen if this proportion declined in the U.S. If the U.S. public chooses to hold less money, this means the public has chosen to buy more goods and services.[17] Everything else equal, this additional demand for goods and services would cause prices in the U.S. price to rise.[18] With a rising price level, the dollar/pound exchange rate rises and the dollar would depreciate.

The third factor that could cause a change in the ratio of prices between the two countries is a change in the ratio of real GDPs between the U.S. and the U.K. Suppose that real GDP in the U.S. declines, so that the ratio of GDPs between the two countries increases. Assuming that everything else remains constant, the ratio of prices between the U.S. and the U.K. would have to increase. The connection between a falling real GDP in the U.S. and a rise in prices in the U.S. is fairly clear, as the supply of goods and services decrease in the U.S. coupled with a constant money supply, prices in the U.S. rise.[19]

Putting all of this together, we can now make several general statements concerning the factors that change a nominal exchange rate in the long run. From purchasing power parity we know that a country's rising relative price level tends to cause the exchange rate to change in a predictable manner. As the price level in the U.S. rises relative to another country, the exchange rate (dollar/foreign currency) increases and the dollar depreciates. From this relationship we can examine the factors that cause the change in the price level. Most importantly, changes in the money supply can change the price ratio and thus cause the nominal exchange rate to change. Less obvious but still important are changes in the relative demands for money and changes in the relative rates of growth of real GDP. These three factors can lead to changes in the price ratio and changes in the nominal exchange rate in the long run.

THE REAL EXCHANGE RATE

Using PPP as a benchmark, we can define another important exchange rate. This additional exchange rate is called the *real exchange rate.*[20] The nominal price of a good is the price posted in the marketplace. Its real price is the nominal price adjusted for changes in the overall level of prices. For example, suppose that the price of a cheeseburger increases from $2.00 to $2.20 in one year. In nominal terms, the price of

[7]If k declines under the assumption that Y and M are constant, the only possible adjustment to make the Cambridge equation balance is to lower the price level.

[18]Remember that k_{uk} has not changed. Thus, P_{uk} does not change.

[19]This effect will be even clearer after our discussion of changes in aggregate demand in the next chapter.

[20]The real exchange rate also is sometimes referred to as the real effective exchange rate.

this good has risen by 10 percent. However, what has happened to the price of cheeseburgers in relation to the prices of all other goods? To answer this question, we need information on the general price level in the country. For our example, assume that the general level of prices in the U.S. over the same period increased by 3 percent. In this case, the real price of cheeseburgers increased by approximately 7 percent.[21]

If the price of cheeseburgers increased by 3 percent, and the general price level in the U.S. over the same period increased by 3 percent, then the real price of the cheeseburger would have remained constant. The real price of a cheeseburger can also decline. For example, assume that the price for a cheeseburger increases by 1 percent and the general price level in the U.S. over the same period increased by 3 percent. In this case, the real price of cheeseburgers would have declined by approximately 2 percent. Our point is that in a world where the overall level of prices is changing frequently, changes in the nominal price can be deceiving. An increase in the nominal price may or may not be an increase in price in real terms. Since the market participants react to changes in *real* prices, it is important to know what is happening to the real price of a good or service. In a similar vein, determining a country's real exchange rate is important, as trade flows respond to changes in the real exchange rate just like the demand and supply of cheeseburgers respond to the real price of cheeseburgers.

Before we define the real exchange rate more formally, consider the following example, which will give you an idea of what the real exchange rate means and why it is important. In the mid 1980s, the Mexican peso depreciated.[22] In a relatively short period of time, the peso–dollar exchange rate went from 50 pesos per dollar to nearly 1,000. The exchange rate continued to deteriorate and the peso depreciated from 923.5 pesos per dollar to 2,209.7 pesos per dollar. This movement in the exchange rate seems quite significant. However, we also need to consider what was occurring to the average level of prices in Mexico and the U.S. If prices were constant in both countries, the depreciation of the peso would have led to extremely large changes in trade flows. Mexican goods and services would have become so cheap that U.S. consumers would have purchased any Mexican products available in the open market. From the Mexican perspective, U.S. products would have become so expensive that selling any U.S. product in Mexico would have been exceptionally difficult.

However, the fact of the matter was that prices in both countries were not constant. During the mid 1980s, prices in Mexico rose by approximately 135 percent. On the other hand, prices in the U.S. rose by approximately 3.5 percent. As a result, the Mexican peso depreciated substantially just to offset the difference in the inflation rates in Mexico and the U.S. In *nominal* terms the Mexican peso had depreciated dramatically. However, in *real* terms the value of the Mexican peso was virtually unchanged.

For example, in 1986 you could convert a dollar into 923.5 pesos and then walk across the border and buy a couple of bottles of soda. What would this transaction look like a year later? You would change a dollar for 2,209.7 pesos and walk across the border and buy a couple of bottles of soda. Notice that on both trips your dollar bought you approximately the same amount of Mexican goods. The exchange rate had

[1]The equation to determine the percentage change in real value of the cheeseburger is $\%\Delta\text{Real Value} = [(1 + \%\Delta P_{\text{Cheeseburger}})/(1 + \%\Delta P_{\text{for the U.S.}})] - 1$.

[22]For the moment, we will ignore *why* the Mexican peso was devalued. The reasons why this type of situation occurs will be discussed in Chapter 18.

real exchange rate the relative price of two currencies after adjusting for change in domestic prices

changed dramatically in nominal terms. However, once adjusted for price differences between the two countries, the exchange rate had not changed in real terms. Mexican goods were no more or less expensive in terms of dollars. The change in the exchange rate basically offset the changes in the price levels between the two countries. However, as we will see this is not always the case.

The nominal or posted exchange rate is the relative price of two currencies. The **real exchange rate** is the relative price of two currencies after adjusting for changes in domestic prices within the two countries. For example, consider the dollar–pound exchange rate. The real exchange rate is defined as the dollar price of a British market basket of goods relative to a U.S. market basket of similar goods. Using our earlier notation, the real exchange rate (RXR) becomes:

$$[RXR(\$/£)] = [R(\$/£)][P_{UK}/P_{US}]$$

A numerical example may be helpful. Suppose that the nominal exchange rate [R($/£)] is $2 dollars per £, and the prices of a market basket in the U.K. and the U.S. are £50 and $100, respectively. This would make the dollar prices of the market baskets in the two countries equivalent. With a bit of arithmetic, the real dollar–pound exchange rate would be 1.

Now, consider what happens if the nominal exchange rate changes and the price levels in the U.K. and the U.S. do not. Suppose that the nominal exchange rate changes from $2 per pound to $3 per pound. The dollar has depreciated in nominal terms and it has also depreciated in real terms. The real exchange rate under these conditions would now be 1.5 instead of 1. There is a perfectly good reason for this change in the real exchange rate. Although prices of goods have not changed in the U.K., it now takes more dollars to purchase a market basket of goods in the U.K. In real terms the dollar is worth less in the U.K. The reverse is also true. Each pound will now buy more dollars. Since prices have not changed in the U.S., these additional dollars will buy more U.S. goods. The opposite situation could also occur. For example, if the nominal exchange rate changed from $2 per pound to $1 per pound and prices in both countries remained constant, then the dollar would have appreciated against the pound in both nominal and real terms. It would now take fewer dollars to buy a pound and each pound would be buying the same amount of goods and services in the U.K.

Consider another possibility. Suppose that prices in the U.S. increased from $100 to $200 and that the nominal exchange rate and prices in the U.K. remained constant. The nominal exchange rate has not changed but the real exchange rate has. In this case, the real exchange rate has changed from 1.0 to 0.5. This change in the real exchange rate indicates that the dollar has appreciated relative to the pound in real terms. Domestically, each dollar is worth less because there is inflation in the U.S. However, it takes the same number of dollars to buy a pound. These less valuable dollars are buying the same amount of pounds in the foreign exchange market and are buying the same amount of British goods. Relative to U.S. goods, British goods have become cheaper and it would not be surprising to see a large increase in imports from Britain.

We can now return to the example where the nominal value of the Mexican peso had changed dramatically over a short period of time. In our example, the nominal depreciation of the peso against the dollar was not a depreciation of the real exchange rate. Using the real exchange rate to analyze this situation, it now should be clear that the nominal exchange rate was simply moving in a manner to offset the changes in the ratio of U.S. prices to Mexican prices. Since this price ratio was falling dramatically, the nominal exchange rate was rising to offset it and the real exchange rate remained approximately constant.

Nominal exchange rates are observable in the foreign exchange market on a daily basis. Unfortunately, real exchange rates are not directly observable. As such, a change in the nominal exchange rate may or may not also mean a change in the real exchange rate. A change in the nominal exchange rate may just offset the inflation differentials, in which case the real exchange rate is unchanged. On the other hand, a nominal exchange rate change could easily be a change in the real exchange rate. As such, it can be difficult at times to know whether an exchange rate change is "real" or not. In Figure 16.4, we plot the nominal dollar–pound exchange rate and the real dollar–pound exchange rate from 1966 to 2006, using 1966 as the base year. As the figure illustrates, the nominal and real exchange rate often move together indicating both a real and nominal change in the exchange rate. However, the two exchange rates often do not move together, indicating that a nominal change in the exchange rate has not been offset by relative price changes or that relative price changes have not been offset by changes in the nominal exchange rate.

Without an understanding of the real exchange rate, one is likely to mistake every nominal exchange rate change for a real exchange rate change. This might lead one to

Figure 16.4 The Dollar/Pound Exchange Rate and The Real Dollar/Pound Exchange Rate, 1966–2006

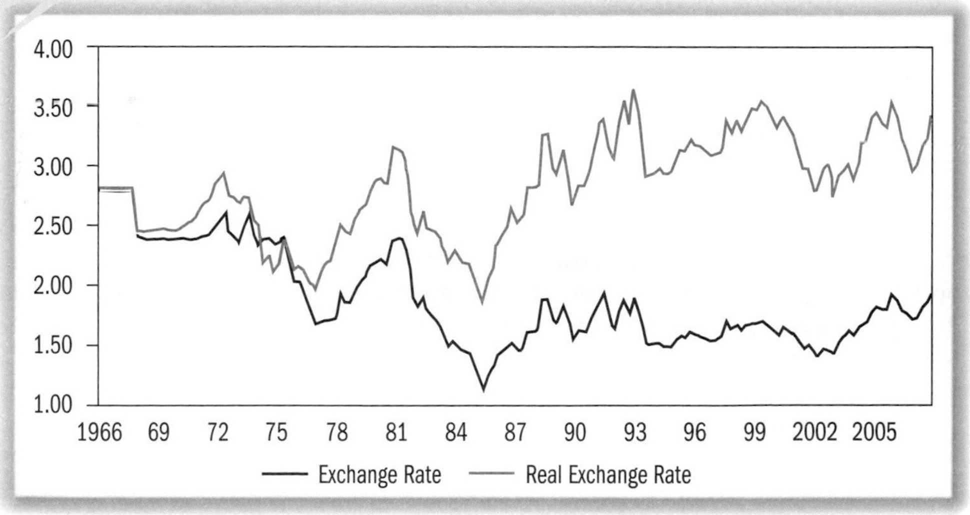

Notice that the nominal exchange rate and the real exchange rate often move together, indicating both a nominal and real change in the exchange rate. However, the two exchange rates often do not move together. This indicates that a change in the nominal exchange rate has not been offset by relative price changes or that relative price changes have not been offset by changes in the nominal exchange rate.

Source: IMF, *International Financial Statistics,* CD-ROM, Washington, D.C.: IMF, July 2007.

conclude incorrectly that every nominal depreciation of a currency would automatically result in foreign goods that are cheap in real terms. Making business decisions based on nominal exchange rate changes without regard for the difference in national rates of inflation could easily produce poor business decisions.

Changes in the Real Exchange Rate

In the last section, we described the real exchange rate between two countries and the importance of the real exchange rate. We are now in a position to describe why the real exchange rate may change in the long run. To examine changes in the value of the real exchange rate, recall that the real exchange rate is defined as:

$$[RXR(\$/£)] = [R(\$/£)][P_{UK}/P_{US}]$$

The Value of the Chinese Currency

Normally, an economic concept like purchasing power parity is something that only professional economists are interested in and captive student audiences are forced to learn. However, over the last decade the concept has become one of the most important policy issues in international economics. The issue has arisen in tandem with the rise of the overall U.S. current account deficit. As the overall U.S. trade deficit has increased to nearly 6 percent of GDP, the trade deficit with China has exploded. From 1999 to 2006, this bilateral deficit has risen from –\$68.7 billion to –\$233.1 billion. To many in Washington it is very convenient to blame China for being a major contributor to the overall U.S. trade deficit. In order to strengthen this argument, it would be even more convenient if China could be found to be doing something "wrong."

In this case, the Chinese are accused of "manipulating" the value of their currency (the renminbi). These suspicions are heightened because the renminbi is not a fully convertible currency. It is convertible for current account transactions but not for financial account transactions. This allows the Chinese government to limit exchange rate fluctuations and, more importantly, provide some insurance against an exchange rate shock. However, when this partial inconvertibility is coupled with large trade surpluses and large reserves of foreign exchange, the suspicions that the currency is being manipulated are harder to dismiss.

In the end, the debate about the value of the currency is about purchasing power parity. If one claims that the renminbi is "undervalued," one is essentially saying that it is below purchasing power parity. Fortunately, the International Monetary Fund routinely publishes the Real Effective Exchange Rate (REER) for a large number of countries. Since the REER essentially is a PPP calculation, one can simply chart the nominal and real exchange rates and check for "undervaluation." Figure 16.5 shows the two exchange rates since 1997. The Chinese currency does appear to be undervalued by about 8 to 10 percent. Critics of Chinese exchange rate policy do seem to have a point. The Chinese currency seems to be persistently "undervalued." However, making the case that this degree of undervaluation is causing the large trade deficit with China may be a bit less plausible. As we saw in Chapter 12, the cause of a country's trade deficit usually can be found in domestic macroeconomic imbalances. However, blaming foreigners for a domestic problem is neither new nor peculiar to American politicians.

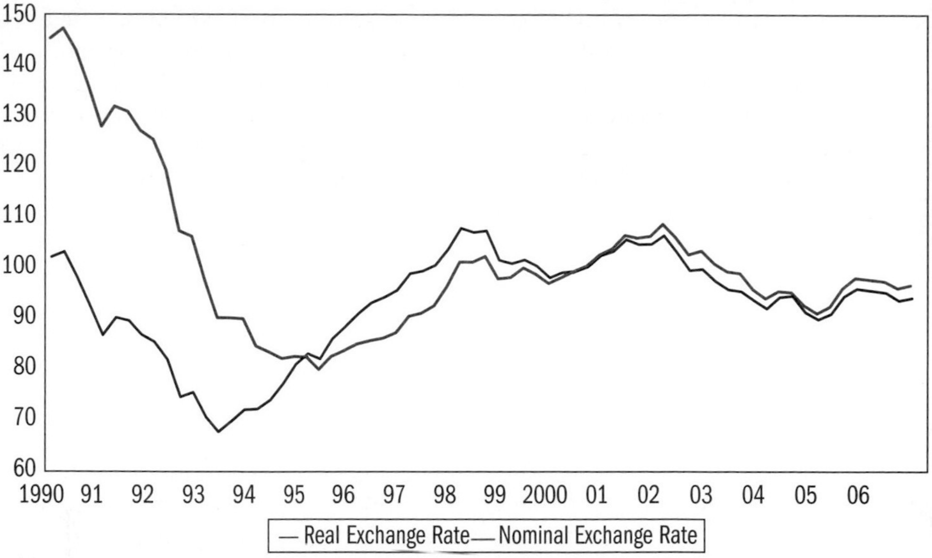

Figure 16.5 China's Nominal and Real Effective Exchange Rate, 1997–2006

Source: IMF, *International Financial Statistics,* CD-ROM, Washington, D.C.: IMF, July 2007.

In general, there are three major factors that would cause the real exchange rate to change in the long run. The first factor that can cause the real exchange rate to change is the foreign (world) demand for domestically produced products and domestic demand for foreign produced products. For example, assume that tastes or preferences by residents of the U.K. shift in favor of U.S. produced products. This change in demand for U.S. produced goods will tend to cause an excess demand at the prevailing nominal exchange rate and at prevailing prices. This excess demand for U.S. goods causes the real exchange rate to fall and a real appreciation of the dollar. Thus, a net real change in the demand for U.S. or U.K. produced goods will tend to cause the real exchange rate to change. A net real increase in the demand for U.S. produced goods causes a real appreciation of the dollar, and a net real increase in the demand for foreign produced goods by U.S. residents causes a real depreciation of the dollar.

The second factor that causes real exchange rate changes in the long run is changes in a country's overall productivity. Previously, we described how real changes in the demand for U.S. and foreign goods and services cause a change in the real exchange rate. As one might guess, real changes in the supply for goods and services must also be considered. Suppose that in the long run, both U.S. capital and labor become more productive, meaning that the amount of output produced for any given amount of capital and/or labor increases. If U.S. demand for this increased output remains constant, the increase in supply of U.S. produced goods will tend to cause an excess supply of U.S. goods at the prevailing nominal exchange rate and at prevailing prices. This excess supply of U.S. goods causes the real exchange rate to rise and a real depreciation of the dollar. Thus, a net real change in the supply of U.S. or foreign produced goods will tend to cause the real exchange rate to change. A net real increase in the supply of U.S. produced goods causes a real depreciation of the dollar, and a net real increase in the supply of foreign produced goods causes a real depreciation of the dollar. The effects of real supply changes might not be very noticeable from one year to the next, but the tendency for the real exchange rate to change would exist nonetheless.

real interest rate the nominal interest rate minus the expected rate of inflation

real interest parity the theory that changes in the real exchange rate are related to changes in the real interest rate

Changes in both the real demand and the real supply of goods are important in determining changes in the real exchange rate, but these changes are rather subtle and occur over long periods of time. One of the most salient characteristics of the floating exchange rate system is that real exchange rates can change substantially in the short run. Most of the short-run changes in the real exchange rate are related to interest rate changes. In Chapter 15, we described how changes in interest rates tend to change the value of the nominal exchange rate. What was neglected at that point in our discussion was that the changes in interest rates, in many cases, cause changes not only in the nominal exchange rate but also in the *real* exchange rate.

To examine how changes in interest rates influence the real exchange rate, first we need to define the **real interest rate**. The real interest rate is defined as the nominal interest rate minus the expected rate of inflation. In order to examine how real interest rate changes affect exchange rates, we need to examine, once again, the flow of portfolio capital between countries. To do this, we need to examine the **real interest-rate parity** condition. The real interest rate parity condition is the proposition that changes in the real exchange rate are related to changes in real interest rates. Since real interest rate parity is just a variation on our previous discussions of how interest rates affect capital flows, let's start by reviewing these effects. The nominal interest rate for both the U.S. and the U.K. is composed of both the real interest rate (r), and the rate of inflation (%Δ P), as follows:

$$i_{US} = r_{US} + \%\Delta P_{US}$$

$$i_{UK} = r_{UK} + \%\Delta P_{UK}$$

In Chapter 15, we described how international capital flows respond to national differences in nominal interest rates. Now, suppose that the real interest rate in the U.S. increases relative to the real interest rate in the U.K. In this case, capital would flow from the U.K. into the U.S. in search of the higher real rate of return. Unless the price ratios change in an offsetting way, this nominal decrease in the dollar–pound exchange rate will translate into a decrease in the real exchange rate. As such, the dollar appreciates both in nominal and real terms. The real interest parity condition simply gives us a convenient way of examining this relationship. The real interest parity condition results from the original interest parity condition that we developed in Chapter 15. This condition is given by:

$$r_{UK} - r_{US} = E[\%\Delta RXR(\$/£)]$$

Exchange-Rate Indexes

In virtually all of our examples of nominal and real exchange rates, we have been using a bilateral exchange rate such as the U.S. dollar and the British pound. However, one often hears that a country's currency did this or that. Frequently, no other country's currency is mentioned because in nearly all cases the commentator or writer is discussing some trade-weighted *exchange-rate index.* Since this term is commonly used, it would be useful to understand how it is constructed. An exchange-rate index is really an average of one currency's value against a number of other currencies. Creating such indices can be problematic. First, you have to decide how many countries to include. Conceptually, one would like to include all of them. As a practical matter, this is difficult to do on a daily basis.[23] In most cases, the index is constructed using a number of countries that constitute a large portion of a country's trade. Since the index will be some type of weighted average, the question becomes what weights to use. There are three choices. One could use weights based on the percentage of imports, the percentage of exports, or the percentage of the sum of imports and exports accounted for by each country. Most of the published indexes are also nominal exchange rate indexes. It would be preferable to use a real exchange rate index, which has the advantage of showing how much an exchange rate has changed once domestic price changes and price changes in other countries have been factored out. Nominal and real exchange rates tend to move together, but the movements do not always perfectly match. There are a number of different trade-weighted indexes for the U.S. dollar. One of the most common of these indexes is the J.P. Morgan index, which is displayed prominently each day in the *Wall Street Journal* or *The Financial Times.* (See Table 13.1 last column).

The J.P. Morgan index is a good example of the choices that must be made to create an exchange rate index. It is an average of the U.S. dollar versus nineteen currencies. This is not a comprehensive index, but the number of countries covered is fairly typical. Also, it is an import-weighted index. Finally it is a nominal exchange rate index and not a real exchange rate index. There is nothing inherently "wrong" with this particular exchange-rate index. However, one simply needs to think a little about how an exchange-rate index is constructed before using this information in a business environment. For example, the information could be misleading if you were a U.S. exporter to Latin America.

[3]The Federal Reserve Bank of Dallas produces an exchange rate index that does just that. However this index is only available on a quarterly basis.

In this equation, r refers to the real interest rate in either the U.S. or the U.K. and $E[\%\Delta RXR(\$/£)]$ refers to the expected percentage change in the real exchange rate.[24] Clearly, if a country's expected real interest rate changes, the real exchange rate must also change. For example, assume that the real interest rates in the U.S. and the U.K. are 10 percent and 5 percent, respectively. Thus, the real interest rate differential

[4]Appendix 15.2 provides a derivation of the interest parity condition. If one assumes that prices are constant, this condition is also the real interest rate parity condition. However, since real exchange rates and real interest rates are based on expected inflation rates, the real interest parity condition uses expected changes in interest rates and exchange rates.

is 5 percent and the real exchange rate would be expected to change by 5 percent. What would happen if the expected real interest rate in the U.S. increased from 10 percent to 15 percent? The expected real exchange rate would have to rise by 10 percent. Thus, if the expected real interest rate rises in a country, the expected real exchange rate would also rise. However, if real interest rates increase in the U.K., capital would flow into the U.K. from the U.S. Investors would buy pounds and sell dollars in the foreign exchange market. The investors' actions would cause the dollar to depreciate in nominal terms. If there were no changes in the price of goods and services in the two countries, the real exchange rate would also depreciate.

Empirically, real interest parity is analogous to purchasing power parity. Empirical tests usually confirm that much of the time real interest parity does not hold. However, as with purchasing power parity, real interest parity should be viewed as a tendency. If real interest rates increase, the real exchange rate has a tendency to appreciate. Perfect parity may not hold, but it would be odd for a real exchange rate to depreciate in the face of rising real interest rates. In most countries, the central bank can influence nominal interest rates through changes in the money supply. In many cases, this change in nominal interest rates also translates into changes in the real exchange rate. This course of events is extremely important in that it provides a mechanism by which changes in monetary policy affect the real exchange rate and the balance of payments.

SUMMARY

1. The law of one price states that, disregarding barriers to trade and transportation costs, identical goods sold in competitive markets should cost the same everywhere when prices are expressed in terms of the same currency. Although the law of one price does not hold for every good, there is a tendency for prices to equalize between countries.
2. Purchasing power parity (PPP) is an extrapolation of the law of one price to a group of tradable goods. PPP theory states that a bilateral exchange rate should equal the ratio of the price level in one country to the price level in the other country. As with the law of one price, PPP should be thought of as a tendency or as a long-run concept.
3. The absolute version of PPP is based on the absolute prices in two countries. The relative version of PPP is based on the difference in the percentage change in the national price levels over any given period of time. Absolute PPP is a statement about absolute price and exchange rate levels. Relative PPP is a statement about price and exchange rate changes over time expressed in percentage terms.
4. In the short run, the exchange rate observed in the market can and does deviate significantly from that predicted by either version of PPP. Both versions fail as reliable predictors of short-run changes in the exchange rate. However, PPP works fairly well in the long run.
5. Prices may not equalize perfectly between countries because of trade barriers, differences in competitive conditions, differences in taxes and regulations, and the presence of nontradable goods.
6. Long-run changes in the nominal exchange rate are a function of relative prices between the two countries. Changes in a country's price level also can be related to changes in the supply of money, money demand, and real GDP. Most importantly, the money supply growth rate would tend to change the price ratio and the nominal exchange rate.
7. The real exchange rate is the nominal exchange rate adjusted for changes in the price level of the two countries. The real exchange rate is important, as trade flows respond to changes in this exchange rate.

8. There are three major factors that would cause the real exchange rate to change in the long run. These are changes in the foreign demand for domestically produced products, changes in a country's productivity, and changes in the real interest rate between countries (the real interest rate parity condition).

KEY CONCEPTS AND TERMS

- law of one price p. 365
- arbitrage p. 365
- purchasing power parity (PPP) p. 368
- absolute purchasing power parity p. 369
- relative purchasing power parity p. 370
- real exchange rate p. 380
- real interest rate p. 384
- real interest parity p. 384

PROBLEMS AND QUESTIONS FOR REVIEW

1. What is the law of one price? Why is it useful?
2. If umbrellas are more expensive in the U.S. than in the U.K., describe the process of arbitrage that would tend to move the prices toward equality.
3. If a pair of shoes costs $100 in the U.S. and £500 in the U.K., what would the exchange rate have to be in order to satisfy the law of one price.
4. Describe the basic concept of PPP.
5. Compare and contrast the absolute and relative versions of PPP.
6. Assume a market basket of goods costs 500 pesos in Mexico and $2,000 in the U.S. What would be the exchange rate predicted by absolute PPP?
7. Explain why PPP works better in the long run than in the short run.
8. What would happen to the exchange rate if the ratio of domestic to foreign prices increased? Decreased?
9. Domestic prices should be equal to foreign prices multiplied by the relevant exchange rate. Carefully show why this is true.
10. Suppose that prices in the U.S. rise by 10 percent and prices in the U.K. rise by 2 percent. How much would the dollar tend to depreciate? Why?
11. Summarize the findings of empirical tests of PPP. From the theory and the empirical evidence, why is PPP still a useful concept?
12. How do changes in the supply and demand for money affect exchange rates?
13. If real GDP changes then the exchange rate may change. Explain why this is true.
14. What is the real exchange rate? Why is this exchange rate important?
15. Show how it is possible for the nominal exchange rate to depreciate and the real exchange rate to appreciate at the same time.
16. Suppose that a PPP calculation of the Japanese Yen/U.S. dollar exchange rate equaled 100. If the actual exchange rate was 200 yen to the dollar, what could one say about the "value" of the dollar relative to the yen?
17. List and explain the major determinants of the real exchange rate.
18. What is the real interest rate? Explain the relationship between the real interest rate and the real exchange rate?

SELECTED READINGS AND WEB SITES

Marcus Apslund and Richard Friberg, "The Law of One Price in Scandinavian Duty-Free Stores," *American Economic Review* 91(4), September 2001, pp. 1072–83.
An interesting test of the law of one price in a restricted geographic area.
Federal Reserve Banks (www.ny.frb.org; www.dallasfed.org; www.stls.frb.org)
Various Federal Reserve Banks in the U.S. produce different exchange rate indexes for the U.S.
Thomas M. Fullerton and Roberto Coronado, "Restaurant Prices and the Mexican Peso," *Southern Economic Journal* 68(1), July 2001, pp. 145–55.
A clever analysis of PPP by comparing fast food prices along the U.S.-Mexican border.
IMF, *International Financial Statistics,* Washington, D.C.: IMF, selected issues.
For selected countries, the IMF produces a real exchange rate index on a monthly basis.
OECD (www.oecd.org)
A source for purchasing power parity exchange rates for OECD countries.
Michael R. Pakko and Patricia S. Pollard, "Burgernomics: A Big Mac Guide to Purchasing Power Parity" *Federal Reserve Bank of St. Louis Review,* November/December 2003, pp. 9–27.
An interesting article exploring the details of the "Big Mac" index.
Alan M. Taylor and Mark P. Taylor, "The Puchasing Power Parity Debate," *Journal of Economic Perspectives* 18(4), Fall 2004, pp. 135–58.
The latest survey of research on PPP.

Chapter 17

Output and the Exchange Rate in the Short Run

"In some cases, by not putting policy issues in an international perspective, we provide students with the 'wrong' answers."
—Joseph E. Stiglitz

INTRODUCTION

In the previous chapter, we described the long-run relationship between the price level or rate of inflation and the exchange rate. As we have shown, many of the nominal fluctuations in the exchange rate are related to differences in national rates of inflation. When this is the case, changes in nominal exchange rates do not have a very important impact on an open economy in the short run. However, when a country's real exchange rate changes, this change has a noticeable impact on imports and exports. As we will see, when the currency depreciates in real terms, the current account balance tends to improve: exports tend to increase and imports tend to fall. If the currency appreciates in real terms, the current account balance tends to worsen. Exports tend to decline as they become more expensive to foreign consumers, and imports tend to rise as they become cheaper to domestic consumers.

In Chapter 12, you learned that imports and exports are becoming an increasingly large percentage of GDP for the U.S. As the U.S. economy becomes more open, changes in the level of imports and exports have a perceptible effect on GDP. Changes in the rate of growth of GDP in the U.S. are still most heavily influenced by changes in consumption, investment, and government spending. However, international trade has become a sufficiently large part of the U.S. economy that changes in foreign trade now have a nontrivial impact on the rate of growth of GDP. In many other countries, the effects of international trade on a country's growth rate are even larger due to the relative size of the international sector.

This brings us back to the importance of the real exchange rate in an open economy. Under these conditions, the real exchange rate becomes important because, in addition to affecting the level of international trade, it can also affect the rate of growth of GDP in the short run. These effects are the main point of this chapter. In order to examine how changes in the real exchange rate affect GDP, we present and describe a general model of output and price determination for an open economy.

Once this general model has been developed, we will be able to analyze how changes in the real exchange rate affect more important variables such as GDP. Finally, we consider the effect of real exchange rate changes on the composition of a country's output.

AGGREGATE DEMAND AND AGGREGATE SUPPLY: A REVIEW

aggregate demand **the relationship between the total quantity of goods and services demanded by all sectors of the economy and the price level**

In your Principles of Economics course(s), you developed and used a general framework for analyzing macroeconomic activity and events. This general framework was called the aggregate demand/aggregate supply model.

Aggregate Demand

Aggregate demand is the relationship between the total quantity of goods and services that all sectors of the economy demand and the price level, holding all other determinants of spending unchanged. The aggregate demand (AD) curve, shown in Figure 17.1, is a graphical representation of this relationship. The horizontal axis measures the total output of goods and services demanded (measured by real GDP). As one moves to the right, the value of real GDP increases, and vice versa. The vertical

Figure 17.1 The Aggregate Demand Curve

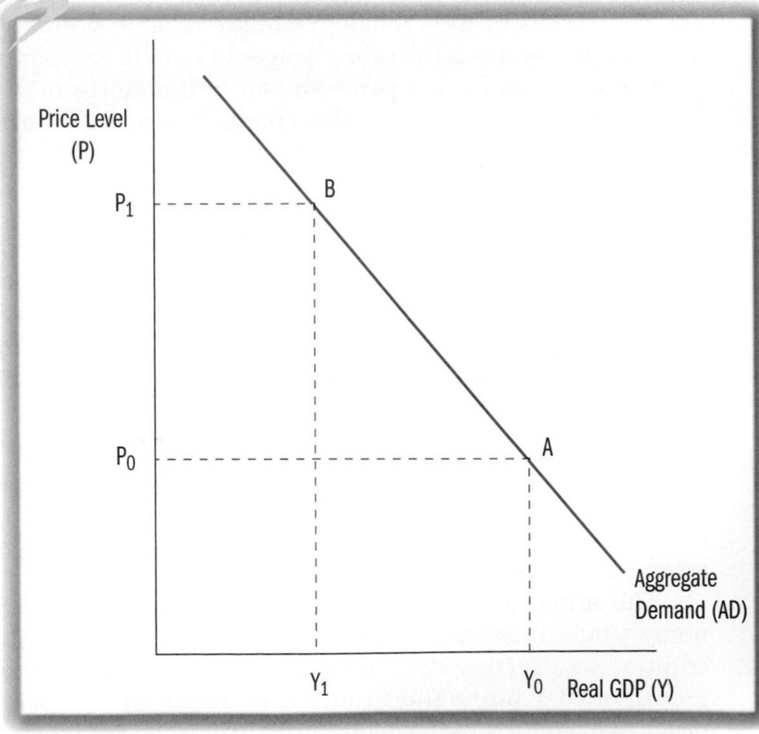

The aggregate demand curve slopes downward and to the right, indicating that as the price level changes, real GDP changes.

axis measures the price level of the economy (measured by the GDP price deflator). Notice that the AD curve slopes downward and to the right, indicating that as the price level declines, the quantity of goods and services demanded increases.

The negative slope of the aggregate demand curve suggests that it behaves in the same way as an ordinary demand curve—one describing, for example, the demand for cars. This is an easy but incorrect assumption to make concerning aggregate demand. In the case of an individual product, two effects occur as the price of that product falls. First, the consumer's real income rises. For a normal good, the increase in real income increases the amount consumed (the income effect).[1] Second, the lower price induces consumers to buy more of this product because it is now cheaper than other, similar products (the substitution effect). Neither of these effects are relevant to a change in the aggregate price level. First, if the aggregate price level falls, this means that the prices consumers pay are falling, and the prices that people receive (wages, rents, interest, and profits) are falling as well. As the entire price level falls, goods and services are cheaper, but incomes are lower as well. As a result, there is no additional demand as the price level declines. Second, the price level is a measure of prices in general, not of a particular price. As the price level falls, there is no substitution effect because prices in general are falling rather than the prices of a particular product.

wealth effect the effect of a change in wealth on consumption

interest rate effect the effect of a change in the interest rate on consumption

international substitution effect the effect of changes in the domestic price level on the consumption of domestically produced goods relative to foreign produced goods

This means that for the overall economy, the aggregate demand curve has a negative slope for different reasons.[2] First, when the price level changes, the value of people's real wealth changes—this is called the **wealth effect**. An increase in the price level reduces the value of accumulated financial assets and induces people to reduce their consumption of goods and services. As the price level changes, real wealth changes, and the aggregate quantity demanded changes.

Second, as the price level rises, interest rates increase—the **interest rate effect**.[3] The higher interest rates not only curtail the business community's investment but also curtail certain types of consumer spending, such as spending on housing and automobiles.[4] The net result is that as the price level increases, aggregate quantity demanded falls, and vice versa.

Finally, as the price level changes, it impacts a country's total exports and imports of goods and services—the **international substitution effect**. As the price level increases, the price of domestically produced goods rises relative to the price of foreign produced goods. As this occurs, foreign demand for domestically produced goods and services (exports) would decline, and domestic demand for foreign produced goods and services (imports) would increase. As a result, an increase in the price level increases a country's imports and reduces exports. Again, this means that as the price level increases, aggregate quantity demanded declines.

[1]A normal good is one where the percentage change in demand is equivalent to the percentage change in income.

[2]The following is a highly simplified explanation of the shape of the aggregate demand curve. It could also be derived from an aggregate expenditures-output model or even more formally using an IS-LM model. For details see Oliver Blanchard, *Macroeconomics,* 4th ed., Upper Saddle River, NJ: Prentice Hall, 2005.

[3]Aggregate demand assumes that everything else is constant. In this case, the money supply is assumed to be constant. What we have described is an increase in money demand, caused by an increase in the price level, with the money supply held constant. Under this circumstance, the interest rate has to increase.

[4]Actually, housing is included in total investment rather than consumption. This form of consumption is more technically known as residential investment. This is a somewhat annoying convention in some respects but it needs to be kept in mind when analyzing data on consumption and investment.

Putting these three effects together, as the price level increases from P_0 to P_1 in Figure 17.1, everything else equal, the aggregate quantity demanded (output of goods and services) declines from Y_0 to Y_1, and vice versa. This inverse relationship is shown as a movement along a given aggregate demand curve from point A to point B.

Changes in Aggregate Demand

change in aggregate demand **a shift of the aggregate demand curve**

Now, if one of the determinants of aggregate demand that has been held constant changes, the aggregate demand curve will shift. This is called a **change in aggregate demand**. An increase in aggregate demand is represented by a shift in the entire curve to the right from AD to AD′, as shown in Figure 17.2. The new aggregate demand curve indicates that at any given price level, society desires to buy more real goods and services. Whereas, a shift in the aggregate demand curve to the left from AD to AD″ indicates that aggregate demand has decreased. This shift indicates that at any given price level, society desires to buy fewer real goods and services.

To analyze the shifts in aggregate demand, it is useful to recall the expenditure approach to calculating GDP. In Chapter 12, we described this approach and indicated that there are four different sectors of an open economy that buy real goods and services. The first component is public consumption, C, or consumer spending on

Figure 17.2 Changes in Aggregate Demand

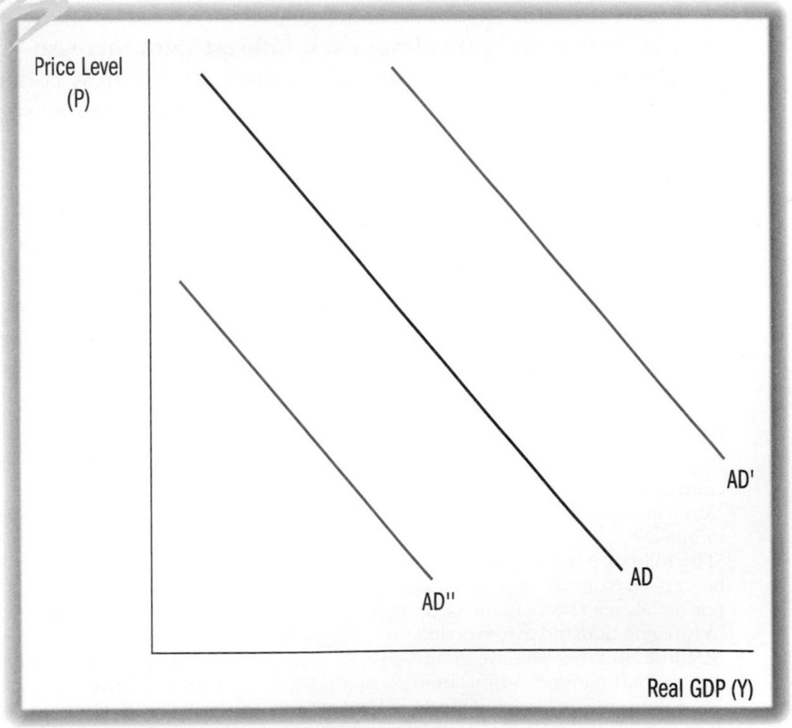

If any factor other than the price level changes, the aggregate demand curve will shift.

goods and services. The second spending component is business investment and public spending on new housing, I. The third component is spending by national, state, and local governments on goods and services, G, not including any government spending for transfer payments. Finally, there are two familiar foreign sector components, exports, X, and imports, M, of goods and services. Exports form an addition to total spending by adding foreign demand to domestic demand. Imports are subtracted from total spending, as they represent domestic spending on foreign goods and services. A country's aggregate demand is composed of consumption, investment, government spending, exports, and imports. If or when any of these components of aggregate demand change, the entire aggregate demand curve shifts in one direction or another.

A number of factors influence or determine each of the components of aggregate demand. For most countries, the largest component of aggregate demand is consumption spending, C.[5] Public consumption can change for a number of reasons that are not related to the price level. First, consumption is sensitive to changes in *consumer wealth.* Earlier in this chapter the discussion of wealth and consumption focused on how changes in the price level affected wealth. However, consumer wealth can change for reasons unrelated to the price level. As the level of consumer wealth increases or decreases, the level of consumption moves in the same direction. As consumption spending increases or decreases, the aggregate demand curve would shift to the right or left, respectively.

Second, *consumer expectations* about the future course of economic events can change current consumption and change the aggregate demand curve. The more confident consumers are about the future, the more likely they are to consume today and shift the aggregate demand curve to the right. The reverse is also true, and a decrease in consumer confidence would shift the aggregate demand curve to the left.

Third, the *degree of consumer indebtedness* also affects consumption and aggregate demand. When consumers have a very high level of indebtedness caused by past consumption financed by borrowing, they will have to pay off their existing debt and may have to reduce current consumption. In this situation, consumer spending falls and aggregate demand falls. Similarly, the reverse holds true.

Finally, the government can affect consumption and aggregate demand by adjusting the level of *taxes.* Higher taxes (or lower transfer payments) reduce society's after-tax income and result in lower consumption spending and a decrease in aggregate demand. Lower taxes (or higher transfer payments) increase consumption spending and increase aggregate demand. Given that the value of wealth, consumer expectations, consumer indebtedness, and tax levels frequently change, it is not surprising that consumption is not completely stable. Because consumption spending is a large component of aggregate demand, changes in consumer spending usually lead to shifts in the aggregate demand curve.

The investment spending component of aggregate demand, I, is even more unstable than consumption spending. We have already seen that investment spending is sensitive to interest rates. As shown in Chapter 15, interest rates can change even if the price level does not. If interest rates change, aggregate demand will change as investment

[5]Consumption spending in the U.S. comprises 70 percent of GDP. For the world economy, the weighted average is 61 percent. Data on the components of GDP are contained in the World Bank, *World Development Indicators,* 2007, Washington, D.C.: World Bank, 2007.

responds to the change in interest rates. The effect of interest rates on investment spending has two components. Investment spending includes business investment and investment by the public in housing. Higher interest rates tend to decrease both types of investment and shift the aggregate demand curve to the left. Lower interest rates tend to encourage both types of investment and shift the aggregate demand curve to the right. Just like the public, businesses have expectations of future economic conditions. As economic conditions improve or worsen, expectations of future economic conditions generally change in the same direction and cause a change in investment spending.[6] Finally, the government can influence the quantity of business investment by changing the level of *business taxation.* Increases or decreases in the level of business taxes tend to raise or lower investment spending and aggregate demand, respectively.

In addition, government spending can influence the level of aggregate demand. As government spending on goods and services increases, aggregate demand increases, and vice versa. Government spending can change due to changes in economic policy at the federal, state, or local level. Government spending in most countries is a sufficiently large component of total spending in the economy as to have a noticeable impact on aggregate demand even when spending changes are small.

Finally, aggregate demand may change due to a change in exports and imports. Changes in these two components are caused primarily by changes in incomes and changes in the exchange rate. Exports are very sensitive to changes in income in foreign countries. When foreigners have higher incomes, they can buy more goods and services both at home and abroad. As foreign incomes increase, exports of the U.S. or any other country tend to increase. In turn, this increase in exports increases aggregate demand. The reverse is true for a decline in foreign income. As income abroad declines, exports fall and aggregate demand declines. This is precisely why the U.S. is concerned about economic conditions outside the U.S. The more that fast economic growth happens in the rest of the world, the greater will be the change in U.S. aggregate demand. Conversely, slow economic growth overseas (or a recession in foreign countries) negatively impacts U.S. aggregate demand.

Further, movements in the *real exchange rate* can affect the level of exports and imports. As the dollar depreciates, a unit of foreign currency will buy more U.S. goods and services and a dollar will buy fewer foreign goods and services. This depreciation of the dollar causes foreign purchases of U.S. goods and services (exports) to increase and U.S. purchases of foreign goods and services (imports) to decline. These effects cause an increase in aggregate demand. In the opposite case, an appreciation of the dollar causes an increase in imports and a reduction in exports. This in turn causes a decrease in aggregate demand. Since exports are 10 percent of GDP and imports are 15 percent of GDP for the U.S., the effects of changes in income and the exchange rate have become more than trivial determinants of aggregate demand.[7] Table 17.1 provides a list of factors that can cause the aggregate demand curve to increase or decrease.

---

[6]In the case of investment, the accelerator magnifies this effect. Business investment responds to changes in the rate of growth of real GDP rather than change in the absolute level of GDP. A slowing of GDP growth would tend to lead to an absolute downturn in the amount of business investment. This is one of the reasons I is considerably more volatile than C. For more details on the determinants of investment spending see Oliver Blanchard, *Macroeconomics,* 4th ed., Upper Saddle River, NJ: Prentice Hall, 2005.
[7]For most other countries these effects are even larger. The weighted average of exports as a percentage of GDP in the world economy is 26 percent, or double that of the U.S.

Table 17.1 Determinants or Factors that Shift the Aggregate Demand Curve

Change in Consumption Spending
Change in Consumer Wealth
Change in Consumer Expectations
Change in Consumer Indebtedness
Change in Taxes
Change in Investment Spending
Change in Interest Rates
Change in Business Expectations
Change in Business Taxes
Change in Government Spending
Change in Federal, State, and Local Government Spending
Change in Exports and Imports
Change in Foreign Income
Change in Exchange Rates

Aggregate Supply

aggregate supply the relationship between the total quantity of goods and services that an economy produces and the price level

Aggregate demand, or total spending, is only one side of the output market. In order to determine the equilibrium price level and equilibrium level of total output (GDP) for an open economy, we need to describe total production (or supply) of goods and services. **Aggregate supply** is the relationship between the total quantity of goods and services an economy produces at various price levels, holding all other determinants of production unchanged. The aggregate supply (AS) curve is a graphical representation of aggregate supply as shown in Figure 17.3.

Notice that the aggregate supply curve slopes upward and to the right, indicating that as the price level rises, the quantity of goods and services produced by the economy increases. If this supply curve represented the supply of a particular good, the relationship between the price of the product and the quantity produced would be clear. At higher prices, producers would be willing to supply more goods and services. However, aggregate supply represents the economy's total production (supply) in the short run. In this case, a higher price level is necessary to induce a higher level of total production in the economy. In the case of the aggregate supply of a country, we assume that in the short run the economy's labor force, capital stock, stock of natural resources, and level of technology are all held constant. The upward slope of the aggregate supply curve is related both to a rising demand for the output of the economy and rising *unit costs* as the economy starts operating closer to full employment. Unit costs tend to rise because as output expands, the prices of some inputs used in the production of final goods will begin to rise even before the economy as a whole reaches full employment. This occurs as a result of different demand and supply conditions in the various input markets. Because the price level is a weighted average of different prices in the entire economy, if some prices are rising while the rest of the prices are constant, the price level on average may start rising even before the economy as a whole reaches full employment. One of the most important prices

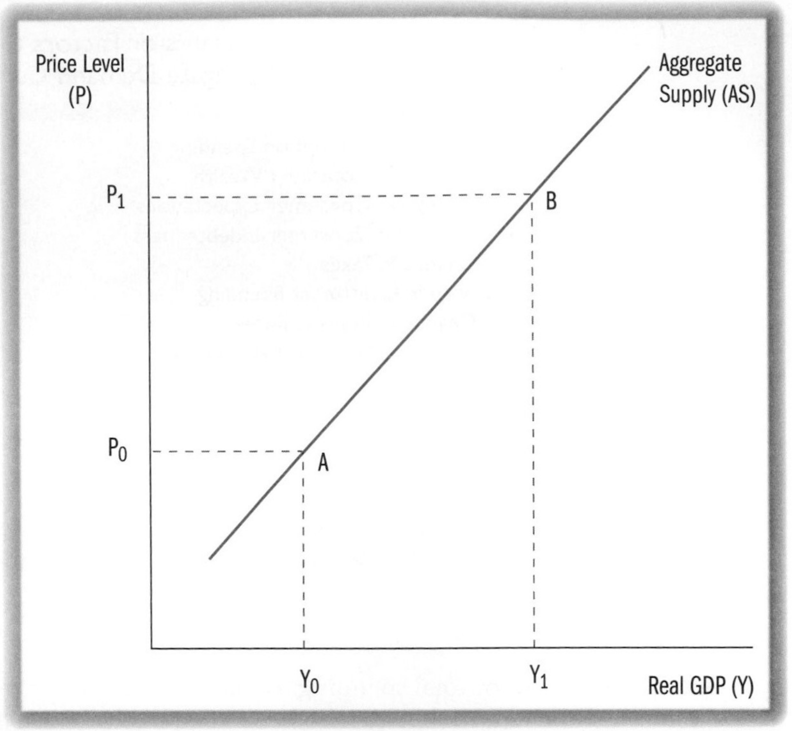

Figure 17.3 The Aggregate Supply Curve

The aggregate supply curve slopes upward to the right.

in the economy is the price of labor, or wages. As the economy expands output, hiring more labor causes the K/L ratio to fall in the short run. This results in a lower marginal output per unit of labor and in rising unit labor costs. This effect would contribute to rising production costs as output increases. The effect contributes to the positive slope of the aggregate supply curve. Thus, as the price level increases from P_0 to P_1 in Figure 17.3, everything else being constant, the aggregate quantity supplied (output of goods and services) increases from Y_0 to Y_1, and vice versa. This direct relationship is shown as a movement along a given aggregate supply curve from point A to point B.[8]

change in aggregate supply a shift of the aggregate supply curve

Changes in Aggregate Supply

Like the aggregate demand curve, the aggregate supply curve can shift if one of the determinants of aggregate supply that has been held constant changes. A **change in aggregate supply** means that per-unit production costs are rising (falling) for some reason unrelated to an increase in production (output). An increase in aggregate supply is

[8]For a more complete discussion, see Carl E. Case and Ray C. Fair, *Principles of Economics,* 8th ed., Upper Saddle River, NJ: Prentice Hall, 2006.

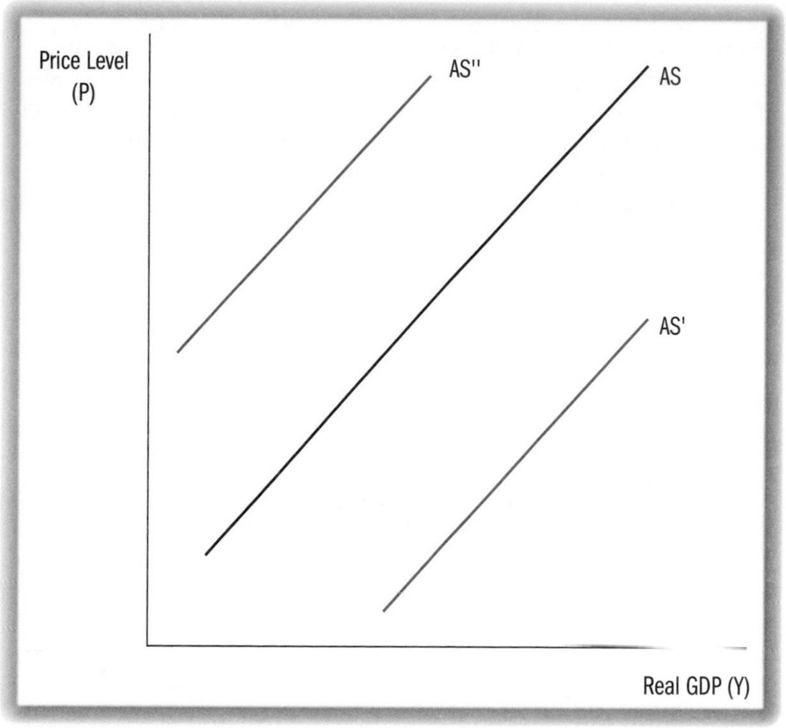

Figure 17.4 Changes in Aggregate Supply

If any factor other than the prices level changes, the aggregate supply curve will shift.

represented by a shift in the entire curve to the right, as shown in Figure 17.4, from AS to AS′. The new aggregate supply curve indicates that at any given price level, firms are willing and able to produce more real goods and services. Another way of stating this is that firms can produce the same level of output at lower unit costs, or unit costs for the firm have declined. A shift in the aggregate supply curve to the left from AS to AS″ indicates that aggregate supply has decreased or that unit costs of production have increased.

In the case of changes in the aggregate supply curve, we need to distinguish between two types of changes or shifts. For most countries, the aggregate supply curve will shift to the right on an annual basis as the level of potential real GDP for the economy increases.[9] For example, as the supply of an economy's *factors of production* (land, labor, and capital) increases over time, the aggregate supply curve will shift (drift) to the right.[10] In addition, increases in the *productivity* of a country's factors of production reduce a firm's unit costs and cause the aggregate supply curve to shift to the right. These movements in the aggregate supply curve are synonymous with a country's

[9]Potential real GDP is the amount of goods and services the economy could produce if it was operating at full employment.

[10]Here we are speaking of physical capital such as buildings and machinery rather than financial capital such as equities or bonds.

long-run economic growth. The faster the supplies of resources or productivity increase, the faster the economy can grow in the long run.

However, what we are interested in is a second type of shift in the aggregate supply curve. These changes or shifts in the aggregate supply occur over a relatively short period of time, such as a year. In describing these shifts, there are four major determinants of the aggregate supply curve that we need to consider. First, *input prices* used in the production of goods and services can change and cause a shift in the aggregate supply curve. For example, an increase in wages increases a firm's cost of production. As a result of the increased production costs, the aggregate supply curve declines (shifts to the left). A classic example of a change in input prices is an oil shock. An oil shock occurs when the price of crude oil increases dramatically in a relatively short period of time.[11] In most economies, oil (energy) is an important input in the production process of all goods. A large increase in the price of oil in a short period of time translates into an increase in production costs. This type of event causes a decrease in the aggregate supply curve (a leftward shift) as shown in Figure 17.4, and for any given level of output the price level is now higher. Fortunately, oil is a unique commodity, and it is difficult to find another raw material that is important enough to have the same effect on the aggregate supply curve. For example, increases in the price of coffee or orange juice are annoying, but they affect only that particular good. These price increases usually have little or no effect on production costs for the entire economy.

exchange rate shock a large change in the real value of a country's currency that occurs in a short period of time

A second factor that can cause the aggregate supply curve to shift is more common but less frequently noted. Over the last thirty years, many countries have experienced an exchange rate shock. An **exchange rate shock** occurs when there is a large change in the real value of a country's currency in a short period of time. For many countries, imports account for 20 to 30 percent of GDP, and many of these imports are crude materials or intermediate products that domestic producers use to produce final goods and services. A large exchange rate change can substantially change a firm's cost of production in a relatively short period of time. For example, a major depreciation of a country's currency will cause production costs to increase as the price of imported inputs rise. Such an exchange rate shock shifts the aggregate supply curve to the left. When a country's currency appreciates, the aggregate supply curve shifts to the right as production costs decrease as the price of imported inputs decline.

A third factor that can cause the aggregate supply curve to shift is changes in *business taxes,* such as sales taxes, excise taxes, and payroll taxes. An increase in overall business taxes increases production costs and causes the aggregate supply curve to decrease, whereas a reduction in overall business taxes causes the aggregate supply curve to increase.

A final factor that can shift the aggregate supply curve in the short run is a change in the public's *inflationary expectations.* For example, if the public perceives that inflation will increase rapidly in the future, it will begin to adjust its economic actions today. In many cases, this implies that producers will attempt to increase their prices today to stay ahead of the anticipated inflation. In addition, workers will attempt to receive larger salary increases today in order to protect their real wages and standards

[11]In the post World War II era there have been two oil shocks. The first occurred in 1973–74 and the second in 1979–80. Both led to increases in the price level coupled with lower output.

The Declining Importance of Oil

In the section above, we discussed the effects of an oil shock. An oil shock occurs when the price of oil rises dramatically in a short period of time. The world economy has been rocked by two oil shocks. The first occurred in 1973–1974. This first oil shock was caused by a major reduction in the supply of oil coming from the Middle East that resulted from a war between Israel and Egypt. The second oil shock occurred in 1979. This second shock again was triggered by political instability, this time in Iran. The loss of Iranian production for a number of months caused a large increase in the price of oil. Such events can be extremely disruptive for the world economy. World output can fall and the price level may rise in many, if not most, countries. The effects can be especially devastating for developing countries. A poor country with no oil resources may find paying for more expensive imports of oil difficult to do without reducing other necessary imports of food or important intermediate goods. This is especially true if a developing country is facing a loss of export revenue due to falling world demand for its exports. The consequences for developed countries are less serious. However, a drop in GDP coupled with an increase in the price level usually means a period of time when overall economic conditions are poor.

Fortunately, oil is not as important as it once was. As the real price of oil rises, the price of substitutes for oil will rise. Oil and other forms of energy become more expensive in real terms. Market forces work with respect to oil and other forms of energy in the same way as they do for virtually all other goods. As real prices increase, consumers and producers find ways to use less energy. This doesn't have to be decreed by anyone, it is necessary only for the government to allow the price of oil and oil related products to be priced by market forces. The results of this process can be seen in Figure 17.5. The figure

Figure 17.5 Energy Production and Consumption Per Dollar of Real GDP

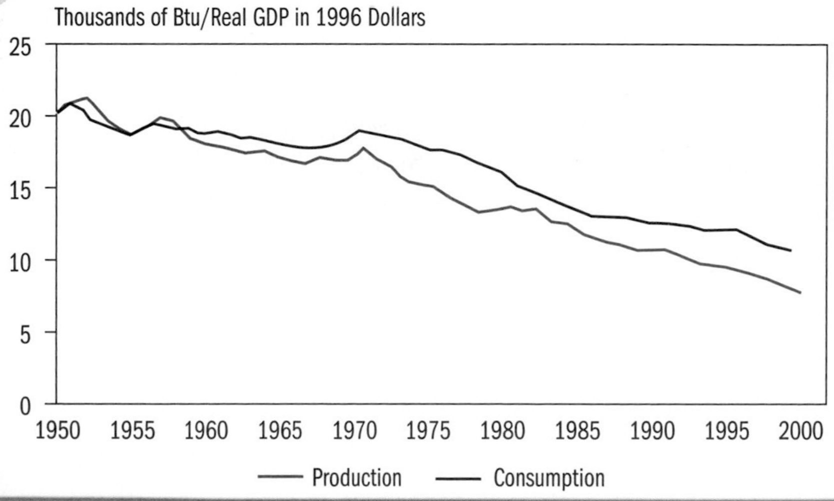

Source: Energy, Monetary Policy, and the Business Cycle, Federal Reserve Bank of Cleveland, *Economic Trends*, August 2002, p. 9.

(*continued*)

shows the ratio of energy consumption to GDP from 1950 to 2000 for the U.S. Fifty years ago, it took 20 cents of energy to produce a dollar of U.S. GDP. By 2000, the equivalent number was 10 cents. Relatively speaking, it takes half as much energy to produce a dollar of GDP now as it did in 1950. A rising price of oil would produce a smaller shift of the aggregate supply curve than was true only a few decades ago. Rising oil prices are still a problem, especially for developing countries. However, the macroeconomic effects are not as large as they once were.

of living. An increase in inflationary expectations tends to cause the aggregate supply curve to decline. Recaps of the factors that change the position of the aggregate supply curve are listed in Table 17.2.

Aggregate Equilibrium

With the discussion of aggregate demand and aggregate supply complete, we can now determine an open economy's equilibrium price level and real output. Figure 17.6 presents an open economy's aggregate demand and aggregate supply curves. The intersection of the two curves at point E determines an *open economy's equilibrium.* On the horizontal axis, the intersection indicates that the equilibrium level of real output (production and spending) for the economy occurs at Y_e. Analogously, the equilibrium price level achieved for the economy occurs at P_e. This equilibrium is determined as long as the aggregate demand and aggregate supply curves remain constant. If any of the underlying determinants or factors that can shift either the aggregate demand or aggregate supply curve change, the equilibrium level of output and the price level will change.

Table 17.2 Determinants or Factors that Shift the Aggregate Supply Curve

Change in Factor Supplies
Change in Labor Force
Change in Capital
Change in Land
Change in Entrepreneurial Ability
Change in Productivity
Change in Input Prices
Change in Raw Material Prices
Change in the Price of Labor, etc.
Change in Exchange Rate
Change in Business Taxes
Change in Inflationary Expectations

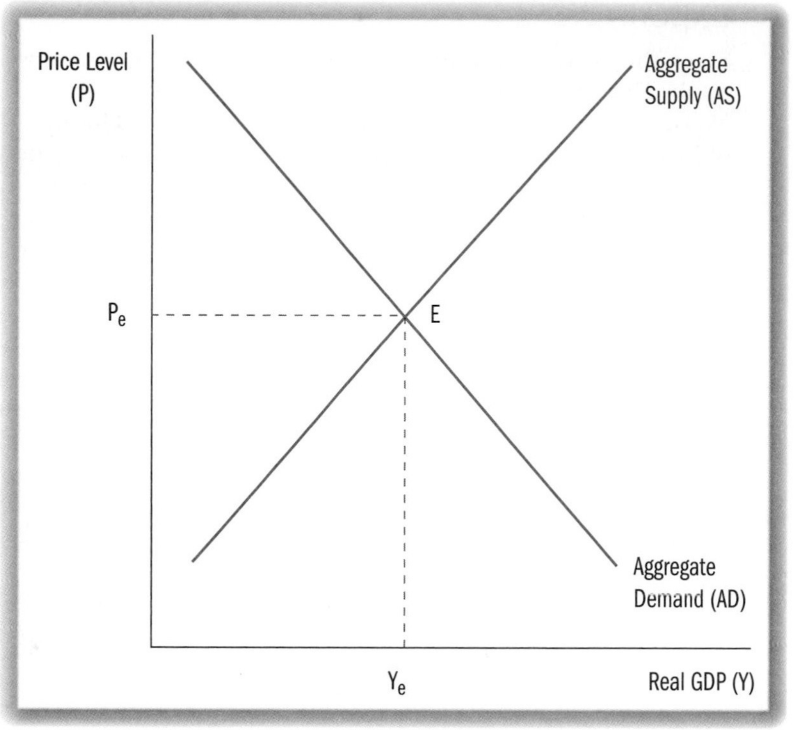

Figure 17.6 The Equilibrium Price Level and Equilibrium Real Output (GDP)

The intersection of aggregate demand and aggregate supply determines the equilibrium level of the real GDP and the price level.

Recall that in our separate discussion of aggregate demand and aggregate supply, changes in the exchange rate shift both the aggregate demand and the aggregate supply curves. As a result, changes in the exchange rate can affect an open economy's equilibrium level of output and the price level. We have discussed how changes in the exchange rate can affect a country's trade flows (exports and imports). However, what frequently goes unnoticed is that changes in the exchange rate can also have a noticeable impact on the entire economy.

DETERMINANTS OF THE CURRENT ACCOUNT

The intersection of aggregate demand and aggregate supply determines the equilibrium level of output and the price level for an open economy. Using this information, we can now describe how *changes* in aggregate demand and aggregate supply influence output. Unlike macroeconomics, the focus of our analysis is on one particular component of aggregate demand and aggregate supply—the current account. What we want to examine is how a change in the current account (defined, in this case, as exports minus imports) impacts the equilibrium level of output. As such, our analysis ignores changes in the other determinants of aggregate demand and aggregate supply.

Exports

Since the current account consists of exports and imports, we will analyze each separately. First, consider the level of a country's exports (X). In the short run, a country's exports are a function of two major determinants. The first determinant is the level of income in foreign countries, (Y_f). A country's exports depend on foreigners' ability to pay for the goods and services; as foreign incomes change, the level of a country's exports will also change. The size of this foreign-income effect depends on two factors. The first and most obvious factor is the size of the change in foreign income. If the change in foreign income is relatively small, the effect on a country's exports is likely to be small. The larger the change in foreign income, the larger the effect on exports. In addition, each country of the world has a unique country composition of its exports. For example, the dominant export markets for the U.S. are Canada (22.5 percent), Euro Area (15.0 percent), Mexico (13.1 percent), and Japan (5.6 percent). Because all countries' income levels change at different rates, changes in foreign income that affect a country's exports are weighted averages of changes in income among the country's trading partners.[12]

income elasticity of demand for exports the responsiveness of exports to changes in foreign income

The second factor that determines the size of the foreign-income effect on a country's exports is the income elasticity of demand for the country's exports. An income elasticity of demand measures the percentage change in a country's exports relative to the percentage change in foreign income. Using a simple formula this **income elasticity of demand for exports** becomes:

$$\eta_{(Y_f)} = [\%\Delta \text{ in X}]/[\%\Delta \text{ in } Y_f]$$

This income elasticity is normally a positive number indicating that as foreign incomes increase (decrease), a country's exports increase (decrease). A unitary foreign income elasticity occurs when foreign incomes change by 1 percent and a country's exports change by exactly 1 percent. For example, the elasticity of U.S. exports with respect to a change in foreign income is approximately one. The foreign income elasticity can be greater than one, which indicates that a 1 percent change in foreign income increases a country's exports by more than 1 percent. For instance, Germany and Japan have foreign income elasticities that are greater than one. For some countries such as Chile, Ecuador, and South Africa the foreign income elasticity is less than one, indicating that a 1 percent change in foreign income increases a country's exports by less than 1 percent. To a large extent, the size of a country's foreign income elasticity depends on the product mix of a country's exports. A country exporting a high percentage of products that have a high income elasticity of demand will tend to have a higher foreign income elasticity, and vice versa. Our main point is that changes in foreign income have a critical effect on a country's current account.

The second determinant of a country's exports is the real exchange rate (RXR). As we described in the previous chapter, when the real value of a country's currency appreciates (depreciates), the level of a country's exports declines (increases). The size of this exchange rate effect depends on two factors. The first and, again, most

[12]The composition of a country's exports can be found in *Directions of Trade* that is published annually by the IMF.

price elasticity of demand for exports the responsiveness of exports to changes in the real exchange rate

obvious factor is the size of the change in the real exchange rate. If the change in the real exchange rate is relatively small, the effect on a country's exports is likely to be small. The larger the change in the real exchange rate, the larger the effect on exports. Again, since bilateral exchange rates change by different magnitudes, changes in a country's real exchange rate are a weighted average of changes in bilateral exchange rates.

The second factor that determines the size of the exchange rate effect on a country's exports is the sensitivity of a country's exports to changes in the real exchange rate. This is referred to as the *price elasticity*. As such, a given percentage change in the real exchange rate will cause a certain percentage change in the level of a country's exports. This **price elasticity of demand for exports** is defined as:

$$\eta_{(RXR)} = [\%\Delta \text{ in X}]/[\%\Delta \text{ in RXR}]$$

The sensitivity of a country's exports is inversely related to changes in the real exchange rate. For example, a price elasticity of –1 (a unitary elasticity) indicates that a 1-percent appreciation in the real exchange rate causes a 1-percent decline in a country's exports. In addition, a price elasticity of –2 indicates that a 1-percent appreciation in the real exchange rate causes a 2-percent decline in a country's exports.

In summary, changes in foreign income, the income elasticity of demand for exports, changes in the real exchange rate, and the price elasticity of demand for exports determine a country's export sensitivity. As we will see, this export sensitivity in turn determines the sensitivity of a country's aggregate demand to changes in each of these determinants.

Imports

income elasticity of demand for imports the responsiveness of imports to a change in domestic income

As with exports, a country's imports are a function of two major determinants in the short-run. The first determinant is the level of domestic income (Y_d). As an economy's income rises, individuals tend to buy more goods and services. As such, some of society's extra spending will go to the purchase of foreign goods and services. As domestic income rises, the level of imports rises. As domestic income falls, the level of imports declines. Again the size of this effect depends on two factors, the first being the size of the change in domestic income. A large change in domestic income will have larger effects on imports than will a small change. The second factor that determines the size of the domestic income effect on a country's imports is related to the income elasticity of the demand for imports. This **income elasticity of the demand for imports** is defined as:

$$\eta_{(Y_d)} = [\%\Delta \text{ in M}]/[\%\Delta \text{ in } Y_d]$$

The income elasticity of the demand for imports can be unitary, less than one, or greater than one. If the income elasticity is unitary, this implies that a 1-percent change in domestic income causes a 1-percent change in imports. The domestic income elasticity could be greater (less) than one, which would indicate that a 1-percent change in domestic income yields a greater (less) than 1-percent change in a country's imports. The size of the change in domestic income, as well as the value of the income elasticity of the demand for imports, determines the total effect of a change in domestic income on the level of imports.

The second major determinant of a country's level of imports is the real exchange rate (RXR). As a country's currency appreciates in real terms, imports become cheaper and usually increase. If a country's currency depreciates in real terms, imports become more expensive and tend to decrease. Again the magnitude of the effect depends on two factors, the first being the size of the change in the real exchange rate.

The Price and Income Elasticities of Exports and Imports

Table 17.3 gives the absolute value of the price elasticity of demand for total imports and total exports, and the income elasticity of demand for total imports and total exports for the U.S., Japan, Germany, the U.K., Canada, other developed countries, and less developed countries. These elasticities were estimated using quarterly data from the first quarter of 1973 to the second quarter of 1985. The results show that the income elasticity of imports is between 0.35 for Japan and 2.51 for the U.K. For the U.S. the income elasticity of imports is 1.94. The absolute value of the price elasticity of demand for imports ranges from 0.47 for the U.K. to 1.02 for Canada, and this elasticity is 0.92 for the U.S.

In addition, the income and price elasticities for exports are also shown in the table. The estimated income elasticities for exports ranges from 1.54 for the U.S. to 2.26 for the LDCs. Finally, the absolute value of the price elasticity of demand for exports ranges from 0.44 for the U.K. to 0.99 for the U.S.

Table 17.3 Multilateral Trade Elasticities: Estimated Price and Income Elasticities

	Income Elasticity	Price Elasticity
Imports		
Canada	1.84	1.02
Germany	1.88	0.60
Japan	0.35	0.93
U.K.	2.51	0.47
U.S.	1.94	0.92
Rest of OECD	2.03	0.49
LDCs	0.40	0.81
Exports		
Canada	1.69	0.83
Germany	1.86	0.66
Japan	2.00	0.93
U.K.	2.07	0.44
U.S.	1.54	0.99
Rest of OECD	1.75	0.83
LDCs	2.26	0.63

Source: J. Marquez, "Bilateral Trade Elasticities," *Review of Economics and Statistics* 72(1), February 1990, pp. 70–77.

Table 17.4 Factors Determining the Current Account

Factor	Effect on	
Foreign Income Increases	Exports Increase	Current Account Increases
Foreign Income Decreases	Exports Decrease	Current Account Decreases
Real Exchange Rate Increases	Exports Increase Imports Decrease	Current Account Increases
Real Exchange Rate Decreases	Exports Decrease Imports Increase	Current Account Decreases
Domestic Income Increases	Imports Increase	Current Account Decreases
Domestic Income Decreases	Imports Decrease	Current Account Increases

Smaller changes in the real exchange rate would have a smaller effect on imports than would larger changes. The second factor that determines the magnitude of the effect is the price elasticity of demand for imports. The **price elasticity of the demand for imports** indicates the percentage change in imports relative to the percentage change in the real exchange rate. This price elasticity of the demand for imports is defined as:

price elasticity of demand for imports **the responsiveness of imports to changes in the real exchange rate**

$$\eta_{(RMR)} = [\%\Delta \text{ in M}]/[\%\Delta \text{ in RXR}]$$

Like the price elasticity of the demand for exports, this elasticity can equal 1 (a unitary elasticity), which indicates that a 1-percent appreciation in the real exchange rate causes a 1-percent increase in a country's imports. A price elasticity of 2 indicates that a 1-percent appreciation in the real exchange rate causes a 2-percent decline in a country's imports.

In summary, changes in domestic income, the income elasticity of demand for imports, changes in the real exchange rate, and the price elasticity of demand for imports determine changes in domestic income in the short run. In addition, import sensitivity determines the sensitivity of a country's aggregate demand to changes in each of these determinants. The effects of changes in the variables and the effects on exports, imports, and the current account are summarized in Table 17.4.

EXCHANGE RATE CHANGES AND EQUILIBRIUM OUTPUT IN AN OPEN ECONOMY

In the previous section, we considered the short-run factors that tend to influence a country's current account balance. We can now take our analysis one step further. In the short run, the aggregate demand curve is the link between the current account balance and the output of the entire economy. Because real exchange rate changes impact the current account, we can link real exchange rate changes to changes in the domestic economy's output.

Exchange Rate Appreciation

For example, suppose that the exchange rate is in equilibrium at point E as shown in panel a of Figure 17.7. The current nominal exchange rate equates inflows and outflows of foreign exchange at exchange rate (XR_e). In addition, let's assume that this initial exchange rate is associated with purchasing power parity. Since this equilibrium exchange rate determines a country's exports and imports, it also determines the

Figure 17.7 The Exchange Rate and Equilibrium Output

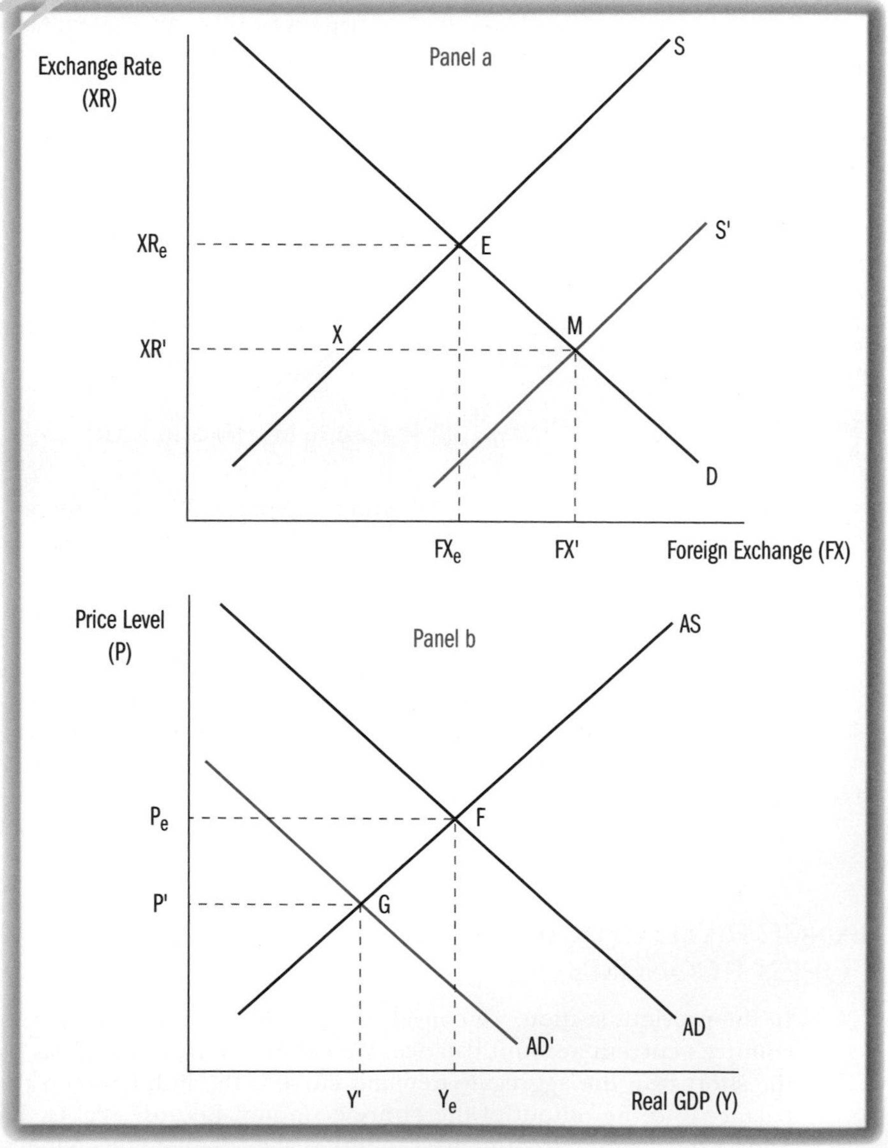

An appreciation of the currency will tend to cause a leftward shift of the aggregate demand curve.

The Dollar and U.S. Inflation in the 1980s

During the late 1970s and early 1980s, the U.S. economy experienced inflation that peaked at more than 10 percent. In response to this inflationary problem, the U.S. Federal Reserve adopted an extremely tight monetary policy that led to high real interest rates. Investors' response was predictable as U.S. investors reduced their purchases of foreign financial assets and foreign investors increased their purchases of U.S. financial assets. The result of these two responses was a large inflow of capital into the U.S. These flows had the effect of producing both large financial/capital account surpluses and current account deficits. The effect on the exchange value of the dollar is shown in Figure 17.8. The dollar appreciated by approximately 50 percent between 1980 and 1985.

The Federal Reserve's tight monetary policy had the desired effect on the inflation rate in the U.S. In Figure 17.9, you can see that inflation measured by the Consumer Price Index fell from nearly 15 percent in 1980 to just a bit over 1 percent in 1986. Given a very tight monetary policy, a decline in the inflation rate was not unexpected. However, the size of the decline in inflation was quite large. A part of this decline can be attributed to the large appreciation of the U.S. dollar. As the exchange rate appreciates, the prices of imported goods and services will tend to fall. The larger the appreciation is, the larger this effect will be. Further, falling prices for imported goods and services puts pressure on domestic producers who compete with imports. As import prices fall, it becomes more difficult for domestic producers to raise prices. The result is that an appreciating currency will tend to reduce inflationary pressures. The U.S. inflation rate would have fallen even without an appreciation of the dollar. However, the change in the exchange rate was a factor in the amount by which the rate of inflation eventually fell.

Figure 17.8 Nominal and Real Exchange Rates

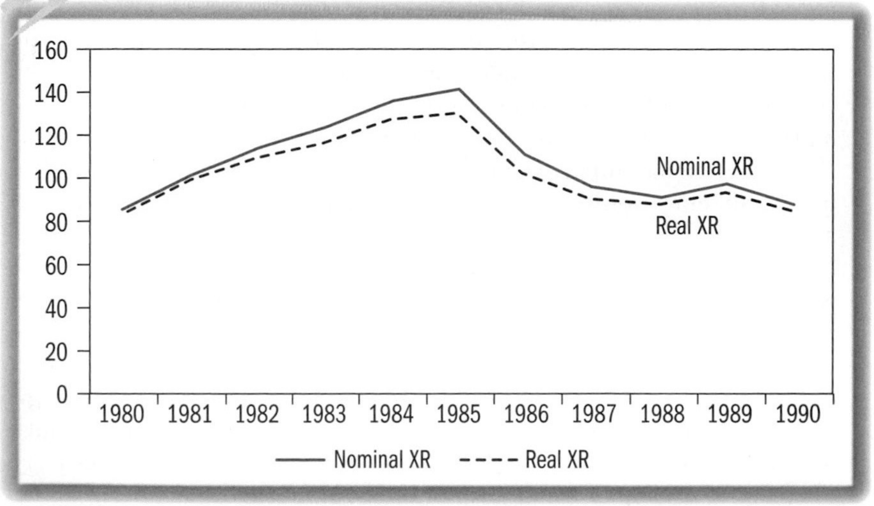

Source: Council of Economics Advisors, *Economic Report of the President,* Washington, D.C.: U.S. Government Printing Office, 1998.

(*continued*)

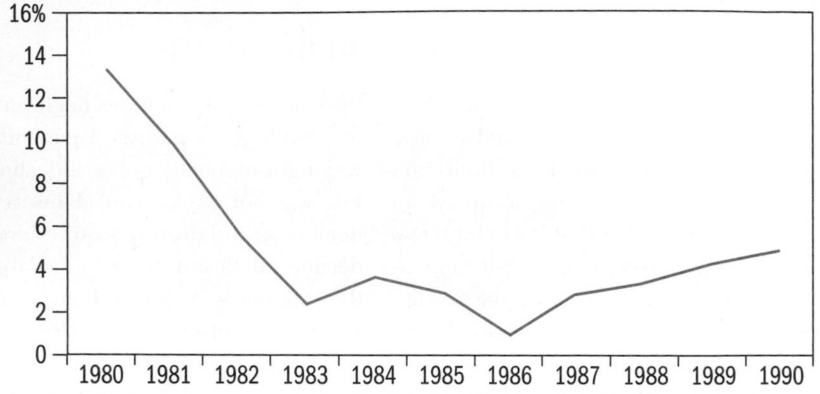

Figure 17.9 CPI Inflation

Source: Council of Economics Advisors, *Economic Report of the President,* Washington, D.C.: U.S. Government Printing Office, 1998.

initial level of aggregate demand shown in panel b of Figure 17.7. Assuming no capital flows between countries, foreign trade is balanced at FX_e and the overall economy will achieve an equilibrium at point F, with output of Y_e and price level P_e.

Now, assume that the real exchange rate changes. Suppose that the currency appreciates to XR′. This appreciation could be caused by a rightward shift of the supply of foreign exchange or by a leftward shift in the demand for foreign exchange. For the moment, let's assume that the real appreciation has been caused by an increase in the supply of foreign exchange from S to S′.

As the supply of foreign exchange increases, equilibrium in the foreign exchange market changes from point E to point M, and the real exchange rate appreciates from XR_e to XR′. What impact would this have on the domestic economy? This appreciation of the currency would cause exports to fall and imports to rise, resulting in a current account deficit.[13] This current account deficit would be equal to the difference between points M and X in panel a at the new equilibrium exchange rate. What effects would this current account deficit have on the real economy? As the current account moves into a deficit, the domestic economy's aggregate demand will decline as exports decline and imports increase. The aggregate demand curve would shift to the left from AD to AD′, as shown in Figure 17.7 (b). As a result of the shift in aggregate demand, the overall economy achieves an equilibrium at point G, with output of Y′ and price level P′. The effect of a real appreciation of the country's currency has been to cause a decrease in the equilibrium level of total output for the economy (real GDP).

[13]This current account deficit of course would be associated with a financial/capital account surplus.

Declining exports and rising imports cause this change in equilibrium output. While the effect on output is our primary concern, there is also an effect on the domestic price level. As the aggregate demand curve declines, the price level also falls. Aside from just observing the movements of the aggregate demand curve and the equilibrium level of output, the movement in the price level should make sense. For example, in the U.S. imports are approximately 15 percent of GDP. With an appreciating currency, two things occur that tend to put downward pressure on the price level. First, the price of imports declines as the currency appreciates. This occurs because it takes fewer dollars to buy any given amount of foreign exchange. In effect, imported goods and services become "cheaper." Second, many domestically produced goods and services compete with imports. With downward movements in the price of imports, the price of U.S. produced goods and services that compete with imports may fall or at least stay constant, as U.S. producers are unwilling to lose market share to imports. The net result of these two effects is that the domestic price level falls.

Exchange Rate Depreciation

As one can guess, the reverse occurs when a country's currency depreciates. For illustrative purposes, consider panel a Figure 17.10. In this case, the demand for foreign exchange has increased while the supply of foreign exchange has remained constant. The equilibrium in the foreign exchange market changes from point E to point X, and the equilibrium exchange rate changes from XR_e to XR'. If we assume that no capital flows between the two countries, the initial equilibrium indicates balanced trade. Also, we initially assume that this exchange rate, XR_e, is associated with purchasing power parity. As the exchange rate depreciates, a current account surplus would occur. Exports increase as the price of domestic goods and services falls in international markets and imports decline as the domestic price of imported goods and services increases. This current account surplus is indicated at the new equilibrium rate, XR', by the amount M to X.[14]

The effects of this depreciation of the currency on the country's domestic output and price level are shown in panel b of Figure 17.10. As the current account moves into a surplus, the economy's aggregate demand increases as more exports and fewer imports essentially means both a higher demand and output of domestic goods and services. With an increase in aggregate demand, the effects on domestic output are quite clear. As aggregate demand increases from AD to AD′, the equilibrium for the domestic economy changes from F to G, and domestic real GDP increases from Y_e to Y_2 as the total output of goods and services in the economy increases. Again, there is an effect on the country's price level. As aggregate demand increases from AD to AD′, the price level would also tend to rise from P_e to P'. The net result is that a depreciation of the currency leads to a higher level of output and a higher price level.

Exchange Rate Shocks

Our discussion of the effect of a country's currency depreciation implicitly assumed that the change in the exchange rate was not particularly large or dramatic. For example, consider the effects of a 75-percent depreciation of a country's currency

[14]Again, this current account surplus would be associated with a financial/capital account deficit.

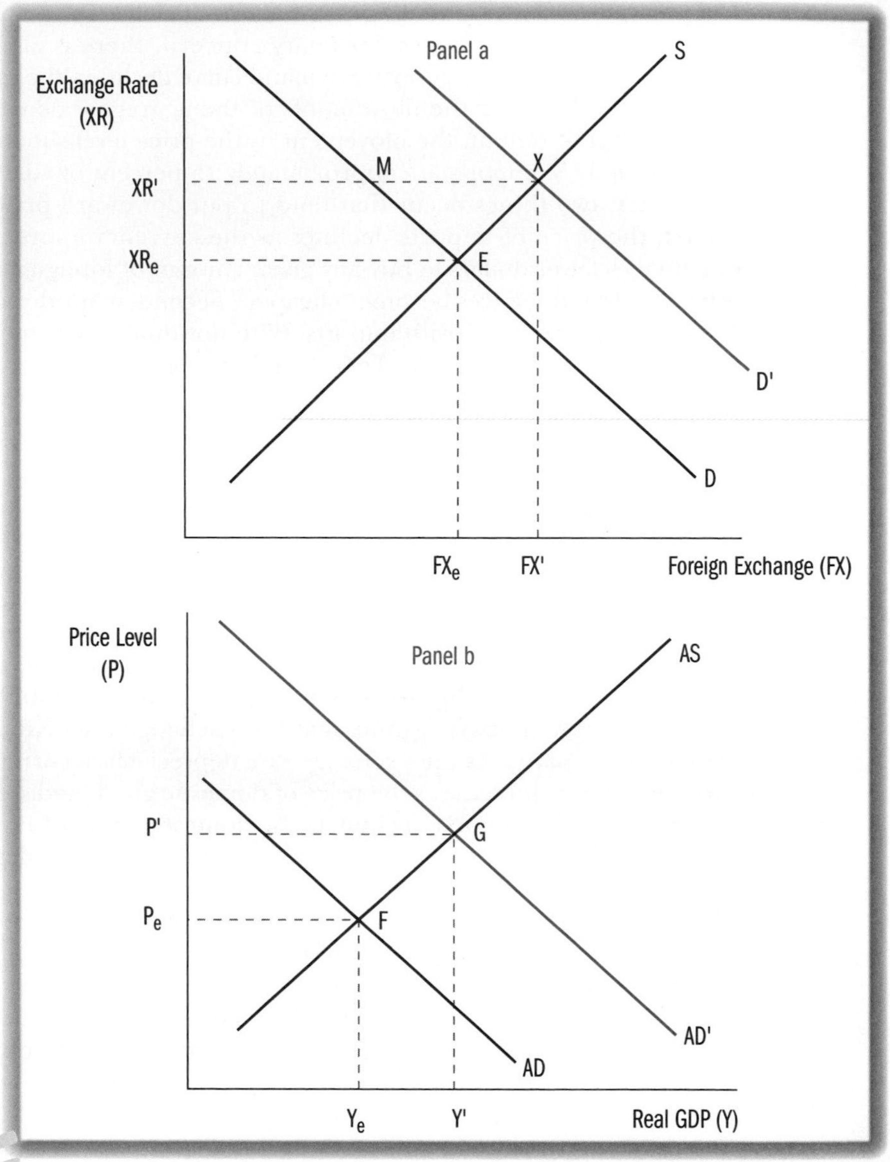

Figure 17.10 **The Effect of a Depreciation of the Currency**

A depreciation of the currency will tend to cause a rightward shift of the aggregate demand curve.

within one week. The effects of this dramatic depreciation are shown in panel a of Figure 17.11. In this case, the demand for foreign exchange has dramatically increased to D″ and the supply of foreign exchange has dramatically decreased to S″. The equilibrium in the foreign exchange market changes from point E to point F, and the equilibrium exchange rate changes from XR_e to XR″. This type of exchange rate change could occur if there were capital flight out of a country because of a domestic

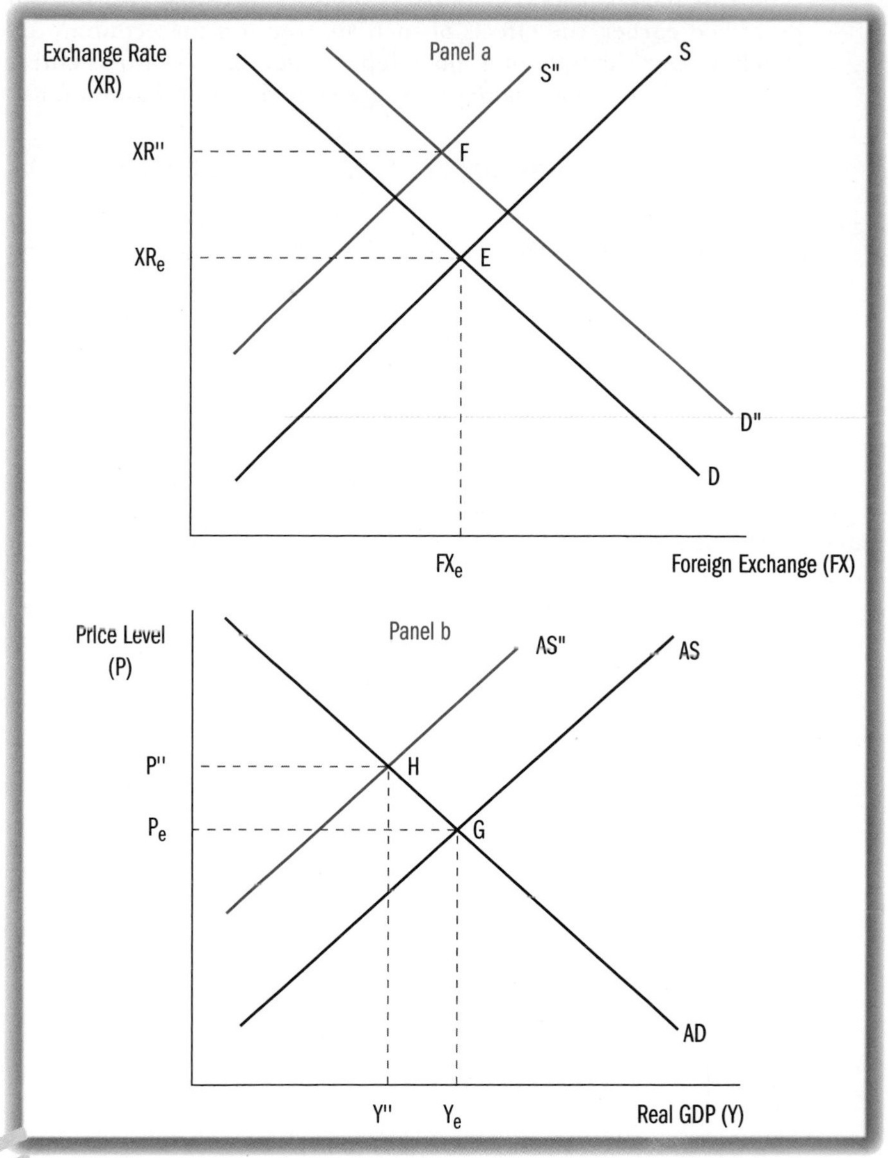

Figure 17.11 **The Effect of a Major Devaluation**

A major devaluation of the currency will tend to cause a leftward shift of the aggregate supply curve.

crisis or because the exchange rate had been "pegged or fixed" at an inappropriate level for a long period of time.[15]

The effects on the domestic economy in this type of crisis can be calamitous in the short run. In such a case, large changes in the exchange rate over a short period of

[15]For details on inappropriate "pegs," see Chapter 19.

time can have substantial impacts on a country's aggregate supply curve. As we described earlier, the effects of such an event on the economy are similar to an oil shock. In our example of a small depreciation of a country's currency, the exchange rate change caused an increase in aggregate demand. However, if the depreciation is

The Value of the Peso and the Performance of the Mexican Economy

Since the early 1980s, the value of the Mexican peso has had a drastic influence on the performance of the Mexican economy. In the early 1980s and between 1994 and 1997, Mexico experienced two textbook episodes of poor macroeconomic performance brought about by major devaluations of the Mexican peso. The value of the peso relative to the U.S. dollar is relevant, as over 75 percent of Mexico's trade is with the U.S. Figure 17.12 clearly depicts the two episodes of devaluation in the early 1980s and again in the mid 1990s.

The devaluations were so significant that the Mexican economy suffered from two exchange rate shocks. In Figure 17.13, one can see the damage that was done to Mexico's economic growth. In both cases, the economy deviated from its growth path and posted severe negative economic growth. While not shown, the effect on Mexico's inflation rate was also dramatic in both cases. Although exchange rate shocks are not unique to Mexico, the performance of the Mexican economy in response to a major devaluation of the currency is typical of the damage that such shocks can inflict on an otherwise healthy economy.

Figure 17.12 Pesos/Dollar

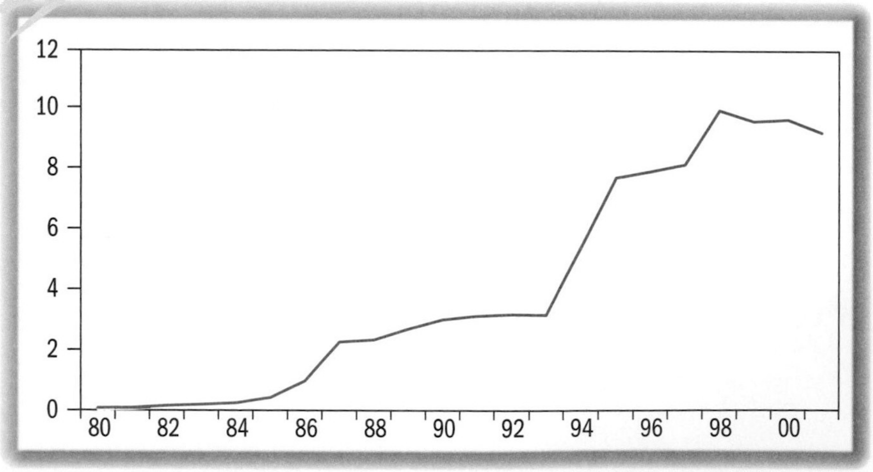

Source: International Monetary Fund, *International Financial Statistics,* Washington, D.C.: International Monetary Fund, June 2002.

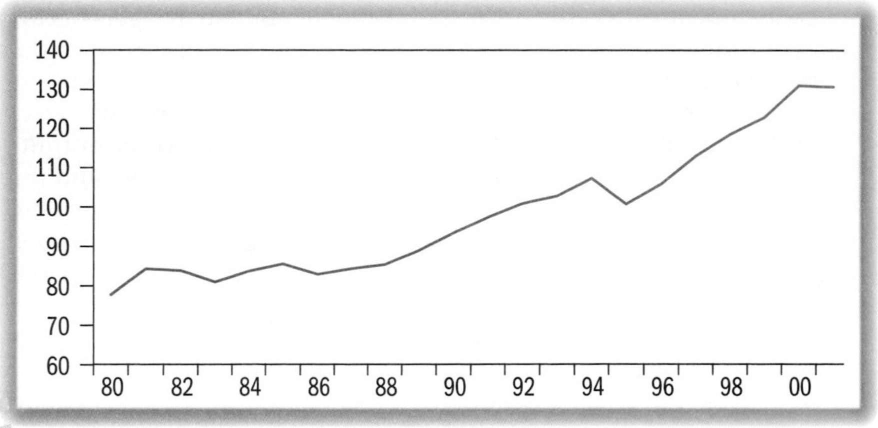

Figure 17.13 Mexico's Real GDP (1995=100)

Source: International Monetary Fund, *International Financial Statistics,* Washington, D.C.: International Monetary Fund, June 2002.

large, the effects on aggregate supply can be substantial. If the economy is open, the depreciation of the country's currency causes a large short-run increase in the costs of production for the entire economy.

Specifically, the depreciation could cause a leftward shift in aggregate supply, as shown in panel b of Figure 17.11. As aggregate supply decreases from AS to AS″, the equilibrium for the domestic economy changes from G to H. The economy's output moves from Y_e to Y″. This reduction in output may be enough to cause a major recession. In addition, the price level has increased from P_e to P″. The net result is that the economy is now faced with lower output and a higher price level. Such exchange rate shocks are uncommon among developed countries. However, they are unfortunately common for developing countries and avoiding these exchange rate shocks is a major task for policymakers in these countries.

CHANGES IN THE EXCHANGE RATE AND THE COMPOSITION OF OUTPUT

In this chapter, we have focused on the effects of changes in exchange rates on the economy's level of output. To a lesser extent, we have examined how changes in the exchange rate can affect a country's overall price level. At this point in our analysis, we want to examine the long-run effects of changes in exchange rates on the *composition of output* in an open economy. The critical distinction in this regard is the difference between tradable goods and nontradable goods. Recall that *tradable* goods are products like wheat or automobiles that are commonly sold in international markets. On the other hand, *nontradable* goods are products or services in which the costs of trying to arbitrage differences in prices across countries are too high. At first glance, it would seem that changes in exchange rates should affect the prices and output of tradable goods and not affect the prices and output of nontradable goods. However, what is frequently missed is that changes in the exchange rate in the long run also can change the price and output of nontradable goods.

Consider a case in which a country's currency appreciates in real terms. As the exchange rate changes, an open economy's equilibrium output and price level change. As indicated earlier, the equilibrium levels of output and prices both decline as exports decline and imports rise. As a result, the overall production of tradable goods in the economy falls. In addition, the price of tradable goods declines. This decline in the price of tradable goods makes nontradable goods relatively more expensive. In the long run, resources such as capital and labor will exit the tradable goods industries and flow into the nontradable goods industries, where the prices are relatively more attractive. In an economy operating at full employment, resources would move from the sector that is declining to the sector that is expanding. The net result is that an appreciation of the currency may have a positive effect on the economy's nontradable-goods sector. An example of this effect occurred in the U.S. economy during the early 1980s. With the dollar appreciating to historic highs, the tradable-goods sectors of the U.S. economy, such as manufacturing were quite depressed. At the time, there was gloomy talk of the "deindustrialization" of the U.S. economy. Overall, the U.S. economy in the 1980s experienced positive economic growth as the economy simply shifted production away from tradable goods to nontradable goods.

The opposite occurs when a country's currency depreciates. In this case, the production of tradable goods is stimulated. Prices in this sector rise and the output of tradable goods increases as exports increase and imports fall. In a relative sense the price of nontradables is falling. As a result, resources flow from the production of nontradable goods to the production of tradable goods. The point is that changes in the exchange rate have not only short-run effects on output and the price level in the entire economy, they have a long-run effect as well. As the real exchange rate changes, the relative price of tradable versus nontradable output changes. In turn, these price effects have a critical impact on the mix of production in the economy between tradable and nontradable goods. A depreciation of the currency may be good for the former and bad for the latter, and vice versa. Participants in the nontradable-goods sector of the economy may tend to feel that they are insulated from the effects of exchange rate changes. However, if the changes are large and persistent, that is not quite the case.

SUMMARY

1. The real exchange rate is important because it affects not only the level of international trade but also the rate of growth of GDP in the short run.
2. The general framework employed to analyze the effects of real exchange rate changes on domestic output and the price level is called the aggregate demand and aggregate supply model.
3. Aggregate demand is the relationship between the total quantity of goods and services that all sectors of society demand and the price level, holding all other determinants of spending unchanged. The aggregate demand curve slopes downward and to the right, indicating that as the price level declines, the quantity of goods and services demanded increases.
4. The negative slope of the aggregate demand curve occurs for several reasons. First, as the price level rises, the value of people's real wealth decreases and spending declines.

Second, as the price level rises, interest rates increase and spending declines. Finally, as the price level increases, the price of domestically produced goods rises relative to foreign goods, and exports decline and imports increase.

5. When one of the determinants of aggregate demand that has been held constant changes, the aggregate demand curve will shift. The consumption-spending component of aggregate demand changes as consumer wealth, consumer expectations, the degree of consumer indebtedness, and consumer taxes change. The investment-spending component of aggregate demand changes as the interest rate, business expectations, or business taxes change. As government spending on real goods and services changes, aggregate demand also changes. Finally, aggregate demand may change due to a change in exports and imports caused by changes in foreigners' incomes and changes in the exchange rate.
6. Aggregate supply is the relationship between the total quantity of goods and services an economy produces at various price levels, holding all other determinants of production constant. The aggregate supply curve slopes upwards and to the right indicating that as the price level rises, the quantity of goods and services the economy produces increases. The upward slope of the aggregate supply curve is related both to a rising demand for production and rising unit costs as the economy starts operating closer to full employment.
7. The aggregate supply curve will shift if one of the determinants of aggregate supply that has been held constant changes. In most years, the aggregate supply curve will shift right as the supply of an economy's factors of production over time increases, or as productivity increases. These movements in the aggregate supply curve are synonymous with the process of economic growth. In addition, a country's aggregate supply changes over a relatively short period of time if input prices used in the production of goods and services change, if exchange rates change dramatically, if business taxes change, or if inflationary expectations change.
8. The intersection of the aggregate demand and aggregate supply curves determines an open economy's equilibrium level of output and the price level. If any of the factors that can shift either the aggregate demand or aggregate supply curve change, the equilibrium level of output and price level will change.
9. Changes in the current account influence the equilibrium level of output. Changes in a country's level of exports occur if foreign incomes change or the real exchange rate changes. The size of the effect on exports depends on the magnitude of the change in income, the magnitude of the change in the real exchange rate, the size of the income elasticity of demand for exports, and the size of the price elasticity of demand for exports. Changes in a country's imports occur if domestic income changes or the real exchange rate changes. The size of the effect on imports depends on the magnitude of the change in income, the magnitude of the change in the real exchange rate, the size of the income elasticity of demand for imports, and the size of the price elasticity of demand for imports.
10. The link between the current account balance and the entire economy's output in the short run is through a country's aggregate demand. As the exchange rate appreciates (depreciates), the economy's current account becomes negative (positive) and the aggregate demand curve declines (increases). This change in aggregate demand causes the equilibrium level of the economy's total output to decline (increase) and the price level to fall (increase).
11. Dramatic changes in the real exchange rate can affect the domestic economy through changes in the aggregate supply curve. A large depreciation of a country's currency causes a large short-run increase in the cost of production for the entire economy and the aggregate supply curve decreases. This decrease in aggregate supply causes the equilibrium level of output to decline and the price level to rise.
12. Changes in exchange rates affect not only the level of short-run output in the economy but also the composition of that output in the long run. This may have a nontrivial impact on the mix of production in the economy between tradeable goods and nontradeable goods.

KEY CONCEPTS AND TERMS

- aggregate demand p. 390
- wealth effect p. 391
- interest rate effect p. 391
- international substitution effect p. 391
- change in aggregate demand p. 392
- aggregate supply p. 395
- change in aggregate supply p. 396
- exchange rate shock p. 398
- income elasticity of demand for exports p. 402
- price elasticity of demand for exports p. 403
- income elasticity of demand for imports p. 403
- price elasticity of demand for imports p. 405

PROBLEMS AND QUESTIONS FOR REVIEW

1. Why does the aggregate demand curve slope down and to the right?
2. List the different factors that shift the aggregate demand curve.
3. Show what would happen to the aggregate demand curve if:
   a. consumers decide to spend more.
   b. interest rates rise and business investment falls.
   c. government spending on goods and services falls.
   d. exports rise while imports remain constant.
4. The aggregate supply curve slopes upwards and to the right. Why is this true? Explain the different factors that shift the aggregate supply curve.
5. Show what would happen to the aggregate supply curve if:
   a. wages increased at a rapid rate.
   b. the price of oil increased dramatically in a short period of time.
   c. the exchange rate appreciated.
   d. the exchange rate depreciated.
6. Discuss how the following changes in aggregate demand or aggregate supply are likely to affect the level of output and the price level in the short run.
   a. An increase in aggregate demand
   b. A decrease in aggregate demand
   c. An increase in aggregate supply
   d. A decrease in aggregate supply
7. Assume that consumer expectations of future economic conditions improve. What effect would this tend to have on both output and the price level?
8. Show how a depreciating currency could lead to a higher price level.
9. If a country has a "strong" currency, this would make it easier to maintain stable prices. Show why this might be true.
10. What are the different factors that determine a country's level of exports?
11. Assume that the world economy expands by 5 percent this year. Further assume that country X has an income elasticity of demand for exports of 5 and country B has an income elasticity of demand for exports of 0.5. Show the differences that would occur in output and the price levels of the two countries over the course of a year.
12. Suppose that a low-income country exports mostly primary commodities with a low income elasticity of demand. Explain why world economic growth might benefit such a country to a lesser extent than a middle-income country that exports manufactured products with a higher income elasticity of demand.

13. List the different factors that determine a country's level of imports.
14. The U.S. has an unusually high income elasticity of demand for imports. If the U.S. economy had an exceptionally strong year of economic growth, what effects would this have on output and the price level?
15. What is the effect of changes in the real exchange rate on a country's current account?
16. Suppose that real interest rates in a country fell. What effect would this have on the real exchange rate and the current account? How would this affect equilibrium output and the price level?
17. How would a real appreciation of a country's currency affect its equilibrium output and the price level?
18. What are the effects of an exchange-rate shock on a country's equilibrium output and price level?
19. Explain the effects of real exchange rate changes on the composition of a country's output.
20. A persistent appreciation of a country's currency would tend to be good for the real estate market. Explain why this statement might be true.

SELECTED READINGS AND WEB SITES

"A Much Devalued Theory," *The Economist,* January 20, 1996, pp. 70–71.
An outstanding short article on devaluation as a means of curing a trade deficit and increasing economic growth.
Council of Economic Advisors, *Economic Report of the President,* Washington, D.C.: U.S. Government Printing Office, 2003.
An annual report providing a wealth of data and background information on the U.S. economy.
Federal Reserve Bank of St. Louis, *Foreign Economic Trends.*
A quarterly publication with an extremely good presentation of economic trends for the world's major economies.
Morris Goldstein and Mohsin S. Khan, "Income and Price Effects in Foreign Trade," in *Handbook of International Economics,* Vol. II, edited by R. W. Jones and P. B. Kenen, Amsterdam: North Holland, 1985, pp. 1041–1105.
An excellent source on the estimation of international trade elasticities.
A good source of information on the estimation of price and income elasticities in foreign trade.
OECD, *OECD Economic Outlook,* Paris: OECD, quarterly.
Data and analysis of current and future economic activity for the thirty OECD countries.
W. Charles Sawyer and Richard L. Sprinkle, *The Demand for Imports and Exports in the World Economy,* Brookfield, VT: Ashgate, 1999.
The most current source of price and income elasticities in world trade.
U.S. Department of Commerce, *Survey of Current Business,* Washington, D.C.: U.S. Department of Commerce, monthly.
A complete and up to date source of information on the U.S. economy.

Chapter 18

Macroeconomic Policy and Floating Exchange Rates

"Flexible exchange rates are a means of combining interdependence among countries through trade with a maximum of internal monetary independence; they are a means of permitting each country to seek for monetary stability according to its own lights, without either imposing mistakes on its neighbors or having their mistakes imposed on it."
—MILTON FRIEDMAN

INTRODUCTION

In Chapter 17, we investigated the effect of exchange rate changes on the equilibrium output level for the entire economy (GDP). To a lesser extent, we also examined the effect of exchange rate changes on a country's equilibrium price level. As we explained in Chapters 14 and 15, there are a number of reasons why a country's exchange rate is constantly changing over time.

In this chapter we describe fiscal policy and monetary policy, the two macroeconomic policies that governments employ to affect domestic output. Governments are generally committed to using fiscal and/or monetary policy to maintain full employment and price stability. In addition to these two effects, we will analyze the effects of both fiscal policy and monetary policy on the exchange rate, the current account balance, interest rates, and short-run capital flows within an environment of floating exchange rates.[1]

[1]The analysis in this chapter is frequently referred to as the Mundell-Fleming model. The model is named after the authors of two articles: Robert A. Mundell, "Capital Mobility and Stabilization Policy Under Fixed and Flexible Exchange Rates," *Canadian Journal of Economics* 29(4), November 1963, pp. 475–85; and J. Marcus Fleming, "Domestic Financial Policies Under Fixed and Under Floating Exchange Rates," *International Monetary Fund Staff Papers* 9(3), November 1962, pp. 369–79.

FISCAL AND MONETARY POLICY

fiscal policy a macroeconomic policy that uses government spending and/or taxation to affect a country's GDP

monetary policy a macroeconomic policy that uses changes in the money supply and/or changes in interest to affect a country's GDP

external balance the balance between inflows and outflows included in the current account

internal balance the preferred tradeoff between the rate of inflation and the rate of unemployment

Fiscal policy entails using changes in government taxation and/or government spending at the national level to affect the level of economic activity (GDP). **Monetary policy** is the use of changes in the money supply and/or interest rates to affect a country's GDP. Since the 1930s, most countries have been committed to using various combinations of fiscal and monetary policies in an attempt to maintain both full employment and price stability. What is less frequently discussed is that changes in both fiscal and monetary policies have predictable effects on the exchange rate, the current account balance, and short-run capital flows.

In this chapter we discuss the effects of fiscal and monetary policy in a floating exchange rate environment,[2] while assuming that the exchange rate and the current account balance are *not* explicit policy targets for a country. What this means is that the government does not employ fiscal and/or monetary policy in an attempt to generate a balanced current account but, rather, uses these policies to affect the output level and the price level.

Fiscal and monetary policy can be used to equilibrate the current account balance. In fact, this practice was fairly common several decades ago when governments adopted the sustainability of the nominal exchange rate and the current account balance as explicit policy targets. In the past, it was a common practice for governments to focus fiscal and/or monetary policy on obtaining what is known as an **external balance**. This involves the balancing of the inflows and outflows included in the current account. Using fiscal and/or monetary policy to obtain a specific external balance has become much less common since the demise of the fixed exchange rate system in the early 1970s.

Governments now tend to use monetary and fiscal policy to focus on a country's internal balance. **Internal balance** refers to the levels of unemployment and inflation that fit the preferences of the citizens of various economies or countries. For most countries, the focus of fiscal and/or monetary policy is on managing the growth rate of real GDP and the price level. In many cases, this focus on internal balance comes at the expense of external balance considerations. In effect, the exchange rate and the current account balance become secondary variables as countries attempt to manage the domestic economy and the exchange rate and current account balances adjust to these policies. For many countries this approach seems sensible, as the exchange rate and the current account are important. However, the state of the domestic economy is considered to be far more important. This focus on internal balance is not without a cost. Policies designed to achieve a desired internal balance may have large consequences for a country's external balance, and this is the point of this chapter. Governments may not like the results that specific fiscal and/or monetary policy changes have on the country's external balance. However, they are willing to accept these consequences as the price of maintaining a desired internal balance.

CHANGES IN FISCAL POLICY

In both developed and developing countries the government may use fiscal policy to influence the economy's short- to medium-term equilibrium. However, even if the

[2]The effects of changes in fiscal and monetary policy in a fixed exchange rate environment will be discussed in Chapter 19.

government is not actively using fiscal policy to influence the state of the economy in the short run, fiscal policy is still important. In most economies, government spending on goods and services is such a large part of GDP that any changes in this spending will have a critical impact on the economy. The weighted average of government spending on goods and services in the world economy is approximately 17 percent of GDP. Because most governments also spend a substantial amount on transfer payments, it is common for tax revenues and total government spending to comprise a substantially higher portion of GDP.[3] In addition, for many countries, a portion of total government spending is financed through borrowing. Consequently, changes in fiscal policy also impact a country's domestic financial markets and interest rates.

expansionary fiscal policy an increase in government spending and/or a decrease in taxes

demand for loanable funds the demand for loans by the private and public sectors of the economy

supply of loanable funds the amount of money available to be borrowed by the private and public sectors of the economy

Expansionary Fiscal Policy

Let's begin our analysis of the effects of fiscal policy on the domestic economy by assuming that the government initially has a balanced budget. That is, total government spending equals total government taxes collected.[4] Now, assume that this government adopts an **expansionary fiscal policy**. In this case, the government would choose to adopt some combination of lower tax revenues and/or higher government spending. Under these conditions, the expansionary fiscal policy leads to a government budget deficit. If the budget initially was in deficit or surplus, an expansionary fiscal policy would increase the former and decrease the latter. Under the above condition, the expansionary fiscal policy has to be financed. In this case, assume that the government borrows the shortfall of revenue rather than printing the money to finance the deficit.[5] As such, the government's extra borrowing has a predictable effect on interest rates, as shown in Figure 18.1.

The figure illustrates the **demand for loanable funds** in the economy, which is the total demand for loans in the economy. As the figure shows, this demand is indirectly related to the interest rate. This demand for loanable funds has two components. First, there is a private-sector demand for loanable funds. This demand comes from the public's consumption activities that may need to be financed (automobiles and consumer credit) and business's demand for loanable funds for investment in plant and equipment. Second, the government generates a public sector demand for loanable funds equal to the difference between total government spending and total government taxes collected.[6]

Along with this demand for loanable funds, there is an associated **supply of loanable funds**. This supply represents the total amount of money available to be borrowed. The supply of loanable funds, S, is illustrated in Figure 18.1 as perfectly inelastic (vertical). That is, the amount of loanable funds available in the domestic economy is not

[3]For details see World Bank, *World Development Indicators,* 2007, World Bank: Washington, D.C., 2007.
[4]In the post–World War II era, most governments do not have a balanced budget but rather have budget deficits. Although this is the case, it does not change our analysis.
[5]Printing money to finance a government budget deficit also requires the use of expansionary monetary policy. In our example, we want to examine the effects of fiscal policy in isolation by assuming that monetary policy is held constant.
[6]This is not quite true, as there may be other entities in the public sector that may also be borrowing. At a minimum, though, the federal government's demand for funds should be large relative to the needs of any other entities.

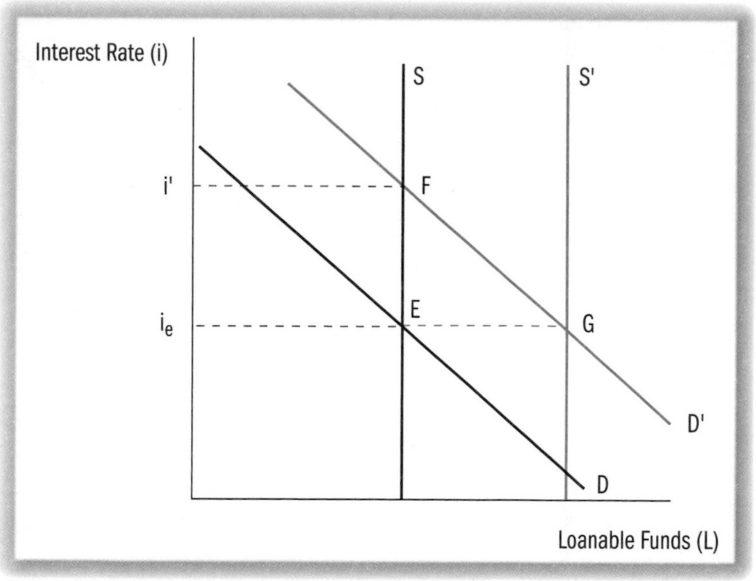

Figure 18.1 **Supply and Demand for Loanable Funds and Expansionary Fiscal Policy**

An expansionary fiscal policy causes an increase in the demand for loanable funds. In a closed economy, this would cause interest rates to rise. In an open economy, the rise in interest rates causes an inflow of capital and an increase in the supply of loanable funds. The net result is that an expansionary fiscal policy puts less upward pressure in interest rate when the economy is open.

related to the interest rate. In the short run, the amount of money held as savings by the public determines this supply of loanable funds.[7] Initially, assume that when the government budget is balanced, the demand for loanable funds is represented by D. Given this demand and supply for loanable funds, the equilibrium in the loanable funds market is at E at an equilibrium interest rate of i_e.

As the government adopts an expansionary fiscal policy, the government's added demand for loanable funds will cause the demand for loanable funds to increase from D to D′. With only domestic loanable funds available, the equilibrium would change from E to F and the interest rate rises from i_e to i′. In a closed economy, an expansionary fiscal policy causes interest rates to rise. However, in an open economy with freely flowing international capital, the rise in domestic interest rates causes an inflow of foreign capital as foreign investors see a higher rate of return. This effect occurred in the U.S. economy during the 1980s. U.S. interest rates rose as a result of an expansionary fiscal policy. As foreign capital moves into the domestic market, it augments the domestic supply of loanable funds. This additional supply of loanable funds from foreigners is illustrated in Figure 18.1 as a rightward shift of the supply of loanable funds from S to S′. As a result, the equilibrium in the loanable funds market changes from F to G, and the inflow of foreign capital lowers domestic interest rates from i′ back

[7]In practice, the supply curve probably has some small upward slope. However, savings in the short run is mostly a function of income rather than interest rates.

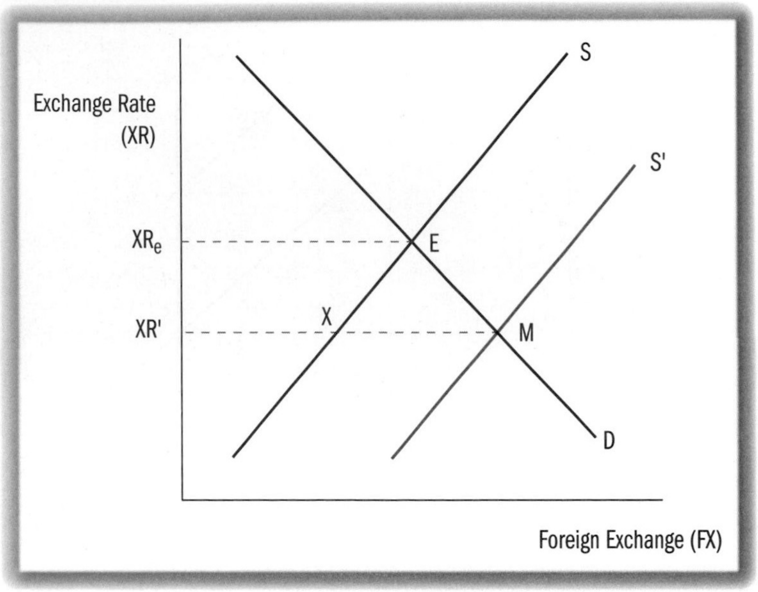

Figure 18.2 **Effects of Expansionary Fiscal Policy on the Exchange Rate**

An expansionary fiscal policy leads to an inflow of capital that causes the supply of foreign exchange to increase and the exchange rate to decline. The decline in the exchange rate or appreciation of the domestic currency causes exports to fall and imports to rise, resulting in a current account deficit.

toward i_e.[8] The net result of an expansionary fiscal policy in an open economy with freely flowing capital is that less upward pressure is put on domestic interest rates than would be the case in a closed economy.

Figure 18.1 indicates that a larger federal government budget deficit tends to increase domestic interest rates, and the higher domestic interest rates cause an inflow of foreign capital into the country. As we described in Chapter 15, the capital flows have an effect on the equilibrium exchange rate. This effect on the exchange rate is illustrated in Figure 18.2.

In Figure 18.2, we illustrate the demand and supply in the foreign exchange market before the government conducts an expansionary fiscal policy as D and S, respectively. The initial equilibrium in the foreign exchange market is illustrated at point E, with an equilibrium exchange rate of XR_e. Assume that at this initial equilibrium exchange rate there were no capital inflows into the domestic economy. This means that the current account was initially balanced (i.e., exports equal imports).[9] When the government adopts an expansionary fiscal policy and domestic interest rates rise, the inflow of foreign capital requires that foreign investors first sell foreign currency (buy

[8]Under the assumption of perfect capital mobility between countries, the supply curve will continue to shift to the right until the equilibrium interest rate falls to its original level, i_e. In addition, the more mobile capital is between countries, the closer the equilibrium interest rate will be to its original level. The less mobile capital is between countries, the closer the equilibrium interest rate will be to i_e.

[9]We could, of course, have started from a position of either a deficit or a surplus. The starting from a position of a current account balance simply is an expositional convenience.

domestic currency). The effect of the capital inflow is clear. The supply of foreign exchange increases from S to S′ and a new equilibrium is established at point M, with an equilibrium exchange rate of XR′. The decline in the exchange rate means that the domestic currency has appreciated in nominal terms.[10] The capital inflows encouraged by the higher interest rates result in a financial/capital account surplus in the country's balance of payments. The mirror image of this financial/capital account surplus is a current account deficit. If trade were initially balanced at the initial exchange rate, XR_e, the appreciation of the domestic currency causes a current account deficit. In Figure 18.2, this deficit in the current account is shown as the difference between the amount imported (M) and the amount exported (X) at the new equilibrium exchange rate, XR′. This indicates that an expansionary fiscal policy indirectly leads to a current account deficit as a result of the financial/capital account surplus.

In Figures 18.1 and 18.2, we have established two primary effects of expansionary fiscal policy. First, such a policy puts upward pressure on domestic interest rates. Second, this increase in domestic interest rates increases the flow of capital from abroad into the domestic financial markets. The associated increase in capital flows leads to an appreciating currency and a current account deficit (or a reduction in the surplus).

At this point in our analysis, we have not examined the effects of expansionary fiscal policy on the domestic economy. To examine these effects, we employ the aggregate demand/aggregate supply model that we described in Chapter 17. Figure 18.3 illustrates an economy's equilibrium before the government adopts an expansionary fiscal policy. Initially the economy's aggregate demand is represented by AD, and the economy is in equilibrium at point E, with real GDP at Y_e and the price level at P_e. As the government adopts an expansionary fiscal policy, the aggregate demand curve increases from AD to AD′ as spending in the domestic economy increases.[11] In a closed economy, this expansionary fiscal policy would lead to an increase in both domestic output, Y′, and the price level, P′, as the equilibrium changes from point E to point F.

However, in an open economy with capital mobility, the effects of expansionary fiscal policy are not quite so clear. The initial spending effects of an expansionary fiscal policy cause the aggregate demand curve to shift to the right from AD to AD′. However, this policy also causes the domestic currency to appreciate and worsens the current account balance as exports decline and imports increase. The deterioration of the current account balance shifts the aggregate demand curve to the left. In Figure 18.3, this would be shown as a movement of the aggregate demand curve from AD′ back toward AD and the economy's equilibrium moves from F back towards E. Clearly, in an open economy with capital mobility, expansionary fiscal policy has two conflicting effects. First, the expansionary fiscal policy *increases* aggregate demand as government reduces taxes and/or increases spending—the direct effect. Second, the expansionary fiscal policy *reduces* aggregate demand as the exchange rate appreciates and the current account balance deteriorates—the indirect effect. The net effect on aggregate demand, equilibrium output, and the price level depends on the magnitude of the two effects. As a result, expansionary fiscal policy in an open economy is less effective in changing equilibrium output than it is in a closed economy.

[10]If the rates of inflation have not changed in either country, the currency may have appreciated in real terms as well.

[11]There are some qualifications to this statement. For details, see the information on "crowding out" below.

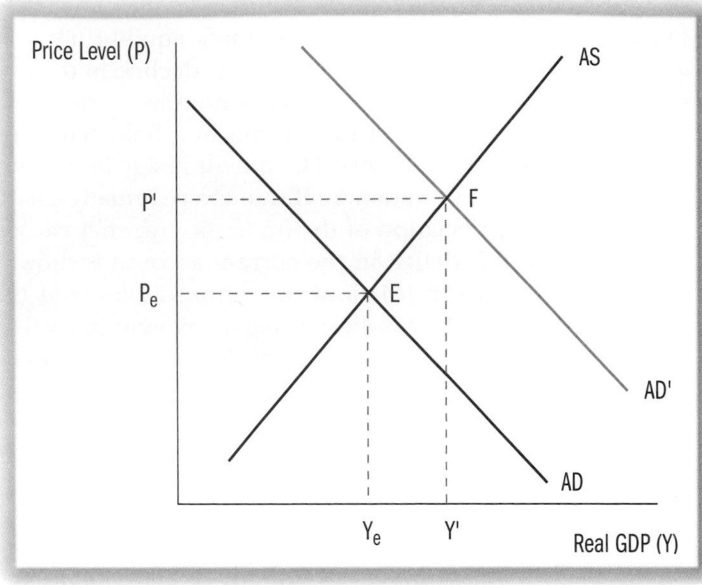

Figure 18.3 **Effects of Fiscal Policy on Equilibrium Output and Price Level**

An expansionary fiscal policy increases aggregate demand. In a closed economy, the increase in aggregate demand would cause an increase in both real output and the price level. In an open economy, the initial effect of expansionary fiscal policy is to increase aggregate demand. This policy also causes the domestic currency to appreciate and worsens the current account. As a result, the aggregate demand curve decreases, making fiscal policy less effective in changing equilibrium output.

Contractionary Fiscal Policy

contractionary fiscal policy a decrease in government spending and/or an increase in taxes

At this point, we need to consider the effects of a contractionary fiscal policy on an open economy. A **contractionary fiscal policy** would entail some combination of higher taxes and/or lower government spending. The adoption of a contractionary fiscal policy reduces a government budget deficit or increases the size of the government surplus. As with our previous example, we begin our analysis of the effects of a contractionary fiscal policy using the supply and demand for loanable funds, as illustrated in Figure 18.4. The economy's initial demand for loanable funds is represented by demand curve D, and the supply of loanable funds is represented by supply curve S, with an initial equilibrium at E and an equilibrium interest rate of i_e.

Everything else equal, if the government adopts a contractionary fiscal policy by increasing taxes and/or decreasing spending, the economy's overall demand for loanable funds shrinks from D to D′. As a result, a contractionary fiscal policy changes the equilibrium in the loanable funds market from E to F, and initially lowers the interest rate from i_e to i′. In an open economy with capital mobility, the lower domestic interest rate affects capital flows into the country. With the lower domestic interest rate, both domestic and foreign investors would tend to invest less capital in the domestic economy, and domestic investors would tend to invest more capital abroad. The net result is an outflow of capital from the domestic economy. This capital outflow affects the supply of loanable funds available domestically. This effect is illustrated as a leftward shift of the supply of loanable funds in Figure 18.4 from S to S′, and the equilibrium in the

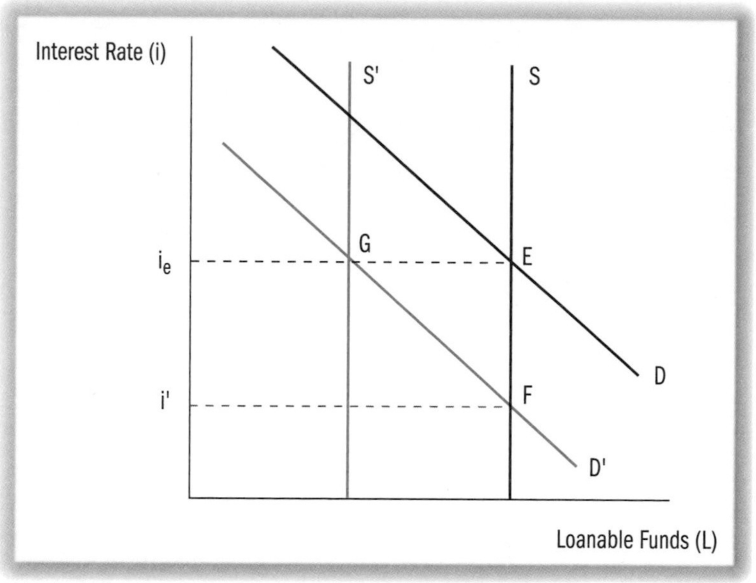

Figure 18.4 Supply and Demand for Loanable Funds and Contractionary Fiscal Policy

A contractionary fiscal causes a decrease in the demand for loanable funds. In a closed economy, this would cause interest rates to fall. In an open economy, the fall in interest rates causes an outflow of capital and a decrease in the supply of loanable funds. The net result is that contractionary fiscal policy puts less downward pressure on interest rates when the economy is open.

loanable funds market occurs at point G. The outflow of capital raises interest rates from i′ back toward i_e.[12] The net result is that in an open economy with freely flowing capital, a contractionary fiscal policy puts less downward pressure on domestic interest rates than would be the case in a closed economy.

A contractionary fiscal policy lowers the federal government budget deficit, which decreases domestic interest rates. In turn, the fall in domestic interest rates causes an outflow of capital. As investors move capital to foreign countries, the demand for foreign exchange in the foreign exchange market increases. This effect is illustrated in Figure 18.5, where the demand for foreign exchange has increased from D to D′. As a result of this change in the demand for foreign exchange, equilibrium in the foreign exchange market changes from E to X, and the exchange rate rises or the domestic currency depreciates from XR_e to XR′. Assuming that trade was initially balanced, the new equilibrium exchange rate affects the current account balance. The capital outflows cause the financial/capital account to become negative. The outflow of capital and the change in the exchange rate have a predictable effect on the current account. As the financial/capital account becomes negative, the current account would become positive. This current account imbalance is illustrated in Figure 18.5 as the

[12]Under the assumption of perfect capital mobility between countries, the supply curve will continue to shift to the left until the equilibrium interest rate rises to its original level, i_e. In addition, the more mobile capital is between countries, the closer the equilibrium interest rate will be to its original level. The less mobile capital is between countries, the closer the equilibrium interest rate will be to i′.

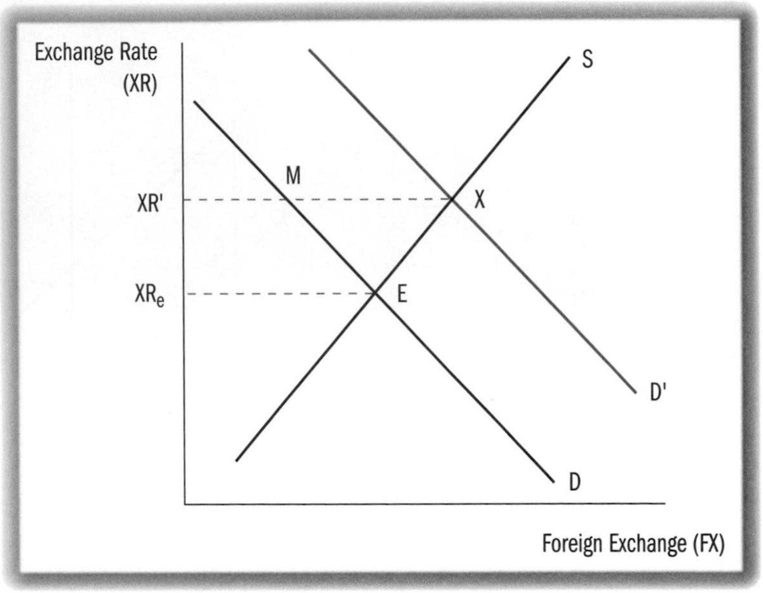

Figure 18.5 **Effects of Contractionary Fiscal Policy on the Exchange Rate**

A contractionary fiscal policy leads to an outflow of capital. This causes the demand for foreign exchange to increase and the exchange rate rises or the domestic currency depreciates. This depreciation of the domestic currency causes exports to rise and imports to fall, resulting in a current account deficit.

difference between the amount imported (M) and the amount exported (X) at the new exchange rate of XR′. The result is that a contractionary fiscal policy indirectly leads to a financial/capital account deficit and a current account surplus.[13]

In Figures 18.4 and 18.5, we have established two primary effects of a contractionary fiscal policy. First, a contractionary fiscal policy puts downward pressure on domestic interest rates. Second, this decrease in domestic interest rates increases the flow of capital from domestic to foreign financial markets. The associated increase in capital outflows leads to a rising exchange rate or depreciation of the domestic currency and results in a current account surplus (or a reduction in the current account deficit).

Now that we understand the impact of a contractionary fiscal policy on a country's exchange rate and its current account, we can analyze these effects on the economy. The effects of contractionary fiscal policy on the equilibrium level of output and the price level are shown using the aggregate demand/aggregate supply model in Figure 18.6. Before the contractionary fiscal policy is implemented, let's assume that the domestic economy is in equilibrium at point E, with an output level of Y_e and price level of P_e. As the government adopts a contractionary fiscal policy, the aggregate demand curve decreases from AD to AD′. In a closed economy, this contractionary fiscal policy would lead to a new equilibrium at F and cause a decrease in both domestic output, Y′, and the price level, P′.

[13]As before, if the current account was initially in surplus the surplus would simply get larger. If the initial starting position were a deficit, it would get smaller.

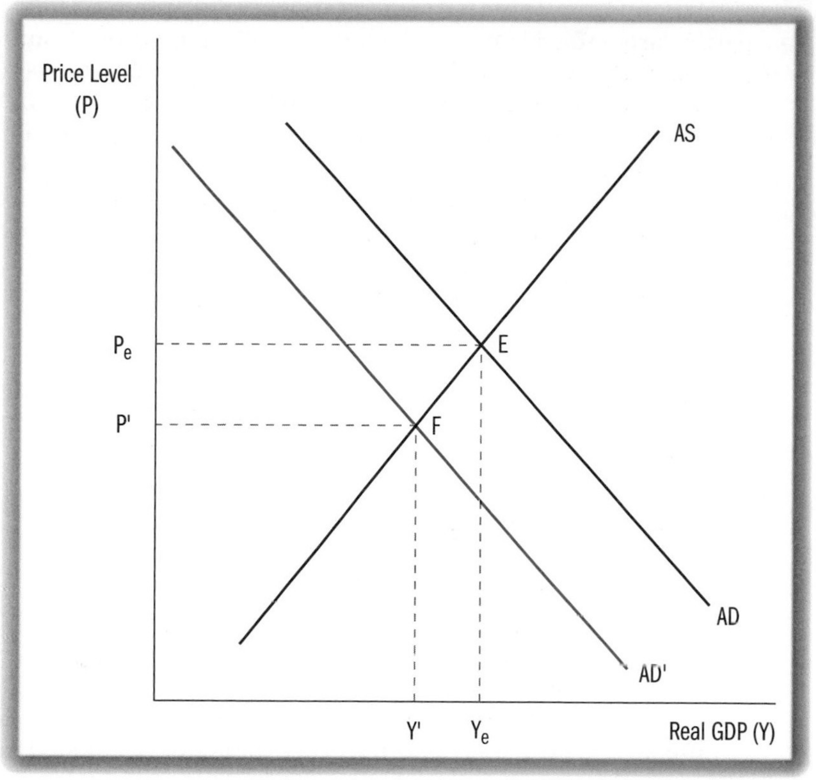

Figure 18.6 Effects of Fiscal Policy on Equilibrium Output and Price Level

A contractionary fiscal policy leads to a decrease in aggregate demand. In a closed economy, the decrease in aggregate demand would cause a decrease in both real output and the price level. In an open economy, the initial effect of contractionary fiscal policy is to decrease aggregate demand. This policy also causes the domestic currency to depreciate and improves the current account. This causes the aggregate demand curve to increase, making fiscal policy less effective in changing equilibrium output.

However, in an open economy with capital mobility, the effects of a contractionary fiscal policy are not quite so clear. Initially, a contractionary fiscal policy causes the aggregate demand curve to shift to the left from AD to AD′. However, a contractionary fiscal policy also causes the domestic currency to depreciate, and the current account balance improves as exports expand and imports decline. The improvement in the current account balance shifts the aggregate demand curve to the right. In Figure 18.6, this would be shown as a movement of the aggregate demand curve from AD′ back toward AD and the economy's equilibrium moves from F back towards E. Clearly, in an open economy with capital mobility, a contractionary fiscal policy has two conflicting effects. First, the contractionary fiscal policy *decreases* aggregate demand as government increases taxes and/or reduces spending—the direct effect. Second, the contractionary fiscal policy *increases* aggregate demand as the currency depreciates and the current account balance improves—the indirect effect. The net effect on aggregate demand and on equilibrium output and the price level depends on the magnitude of the two effects. As a result, contractionary fiscal policy in an open economy is less effective in changing equilibrium output than it is in a closed economy.

For open economies with international capital mobility, fiscal policy is not particularly effective in changing the equilibrium level of output or the price level. However, the main purpose of fiscal policy is to change the equilibrium output level and the price level from its current state to some more desirable level. In many cases, fiscal policy is designed to move the economy closer to full employment. In the current environment of floating exchange rates and relatively large short-run capital flows, fiscal policy has become a less effective tool for manipulating the level of output. There are a number of reasons why governments do not use fiscal policy to try to actively manage the economy's short-run state. One of the primary reasons is that with the demise of fixed exchange rates in the early 1970s, fiscal policy has become somewhat less powerful.[14]

Although changes in fiscal policy may not have the effects on output and the price level that they once did, their effects are not irrelevant. Changes in fiscal policy do affect variables such as the interest rate, the exchange rate, capital flows, and the current account balance. These effects are frequently noticeable in the economy and have an obvious effect on business decision making.

CHANGES IN MONETARY POLICY

discretionary monetary policy the use of monetary policy as a reaction to and/or to prevent unwanted changes in the economy's short-run performance

In the previous section, we described the effects of fiscal policy on the exchange rate, the balance of payments, and the overall economy. In this section, we change our focus to monetary policy, the other major tool governments use to manage a country's macroeconomic conditions. Recall that monetary policy is the central bank's attempt to influence the economy's performance in the short run by changing the growth rate of the money supply and/or interest rates. Most central banks in developed countries use what is known as discretionary monetary policy. **Discretionary monetary policy** entails using monetary policy in reaction to and/or to prevent unwanted changes in the economy's short-run performance. Recently, there has been increased interest in the substitution of some form of monetary rule for discretionary monetary policy. In this case, the central bank would focus on controlling a more limited variable, such as the price level, rather than trying to respond to or prevent short-run changes in economic activity.[15] For example, New Zealand and the EU are currently operating with a price stabilization rule. However, very few countries use a nondiscretionary (monetary rule) monetary policy.[16] In our discussion, we will describe the effects of both discretionary and nondiscretionary changes in the money supply and interest rates. In most cases, changes in monetary policy are the result of discretionary policy decisions. Even for countries operating with some type of monetary rule, there generally are periodic changes in the money supply and interest rates. As was the case with fiscal policy, what we are interested in are the effects that changes in monetary policy have on exchange rates and the current account balance, and by extension on a country's overall economy.

[14]We will see in Chapter 19 that fiscal policy is more effective in a fixed exchange rate regime.

[15]We will purposely avoid the acrimonious debate over rules versus discretion in monetary policy. For our purposes it does not make much difference.

[16]Countries that operate a currency board are in effect using a nondiscretionary monetary policy. For more on the operation of currency boards, see the relevant section in Chapter 19.

Expansionary Monetary Policy

expansionary monetary policy an increase in the money supply and/or a decrease in interest rates

We begin our analysis of monetary policy by describing the effects of an expansionary monetary policy. An **expansionary monetary policy** results when the central bank increases the money supply or increases the money supply's growth rate. While money supply growth figures are not usually front-page news, changes in interest rates normally are widely reported. The effect of an increase in the money supply is shown in Figure 18.7. The initial supply and demand for loanable funds in the domestic economy are shown as S and D, respectively. Given these market conditions, the equilibrium in the loanable funds market would occur at E with an equilibrium rate of interest of i_e. If the central bank increases the money supply, this affects the supply of loanable funds available in the domestic economy. As a result of the increase in the money supply, the supply of loanable funds increases from S to S′.[17] Assuming that the demand for loanable funds remains constant, this increase in supply would cause a change in the equilibrium from E to F, and the domestic interest rate declines to i′. Simply put, an increase in the money supply lowers the equilibrium interest rate.

Figure 18.7 Supply and Demand for Loanable Funds and Expansionary Monetary Policy

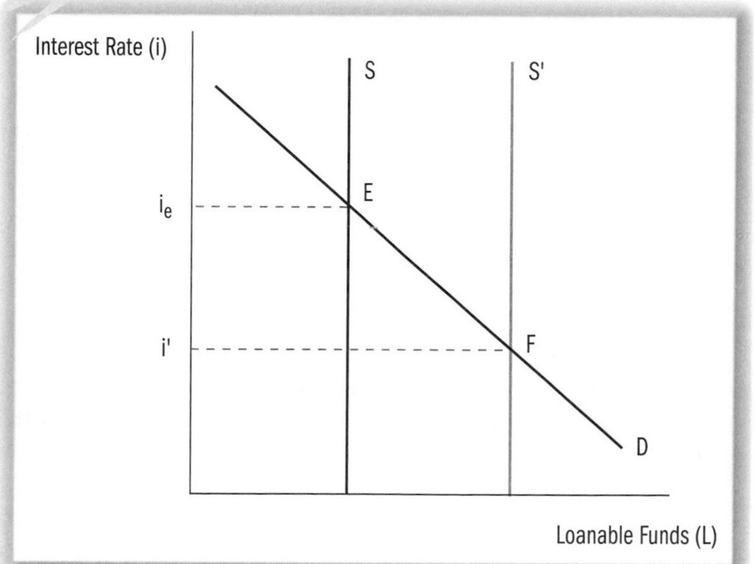

An expansionary monetary policy causes an increase in the supply of loanable funds. As a result, the equilibrium interest rate falls.

[17]Technically, a central bank in a developed country buys government bonds, which in turn increases banking-system reserves that bankers would prefer to loan to customers. The same effect on interest rates can be illustrated using the money market. See Chapter 14, for a description of the effects of an increase in the money supply.

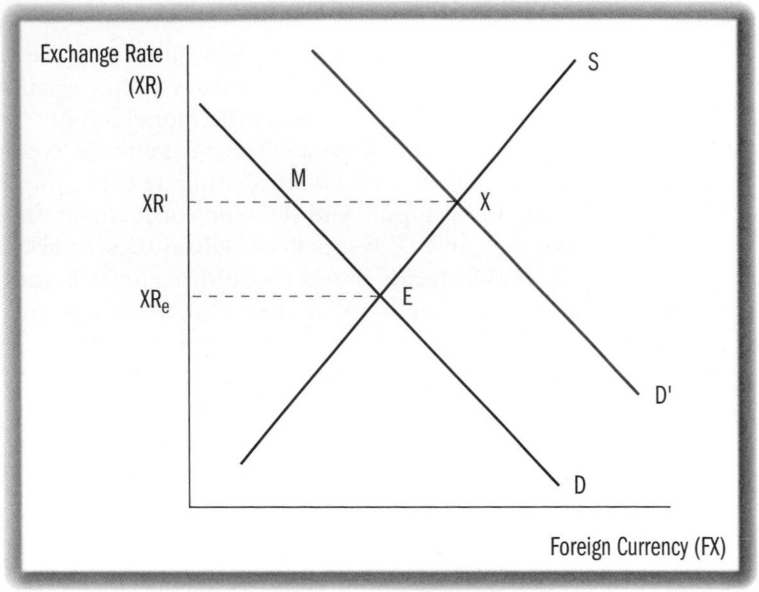

Figure 18.8 **Effects of Expansionary Monetary Policy on the Exchange Rate**

An expansionary monetary policy leads to a decrease in interest rates. This causes an outflow of capital that increases the demand for foreign exchange. As a result, the exchange rate rises and the domestic currency depreciates, which causes exports to rise and imports to fall, resulting in a current account surplus.

Now that we have established the effects of an increase in the money supply on interest rates, the remaining effects of monetary policy changes are similar to those we described for fiscal policy. The decrease in the domestic interest rate has a predictable effect on international capital flows. Foreign investors would be less likely to place their capital in the domestic capital markets, and domestic investors would be more likely to place their capital in foreign capital markets. The decrease in interest rates causes a capital outflow. This effect is shown in Figure 18.8. The demand for foreign exchange is increasing from D to D′. Everything else equal, this change in demand for foreign exchange causes the equilibrium in the foreign exchange market to change from E to X and the equilibrium exchange rate changes from XR_e to XR′. As capital flows out of the country, the capital/financial account worsens. If the current account initially was balanced, this effect causes a financial/capital account deficit.[18] As such, the depreciation of the domestic currency and the financial/capital account deficit translate into a current account surplus as exports expand and imports contract. This current account imbalance is illustrated in Figure 18.8 as the difference between the amount imported (M) and the amount exported (X) at the new exchange rate of XR′. An expansionary monetary policy indirectly leads to a current account surplus when capital is mobile between countries.[19]

[18]If the financial account were initially a deficit or a surplus, the former would worsen and the latter would be reduced.

[19]As before, if the current account was initially in surplus the surplus would simply get larger. If the initial starting position were a deficit, it would tend to get smaller.

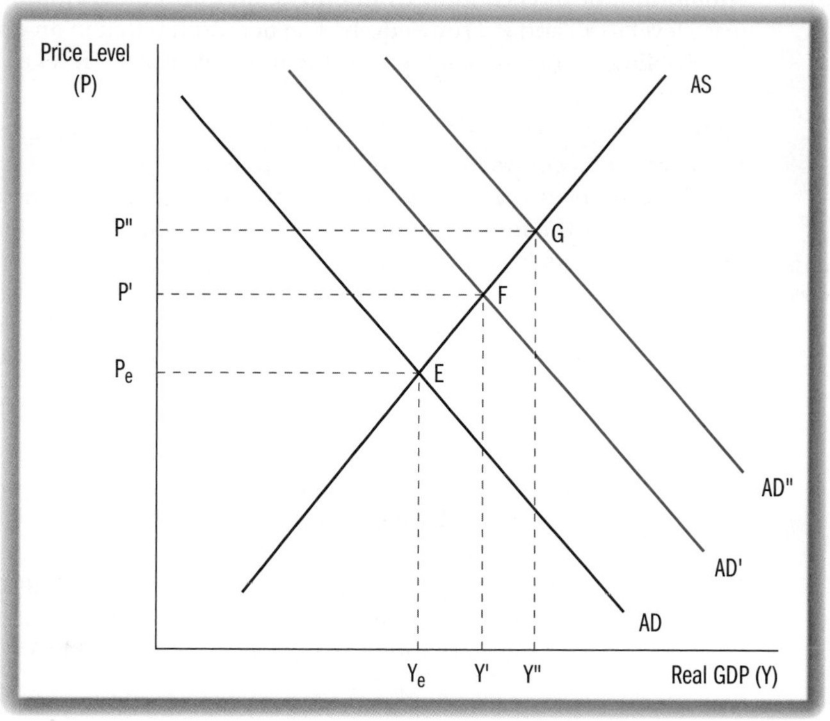

Figure 18.9 **Effects of Monetary Policy on Equilibrium Output and Price Level**

An expansionary monetary policy causes aggregate demand to increase as interest rates fall. In a closed economy, the increase in aggregate demand would cause an increase in both real output and the price level. In an open economy, the initial effect of expansionary monetary policy is to increase aggregate demand. This policy also causes the domestic currency to depreciate and improves the current account. Aggregate demand increases again, making monetary policy more effective in changing equilibrium output.

These movements in the exchange rate, the financial/capital account, and the current account tend to reinforce the initial effects of monetary policy on the domestic economy. In a closed economy, monetary policy is generally effective because lower interest rates increase both consumption and investment spending—the direct effect. This effect is illustrated using the aggregate demand/aggregate supply model shown in Figure 18.9. Assume that the economy initially is in equilibrium at E, with an output level of Y_e and a price level P_e. With an expansionary monetary policy, the increase in the money supply increases the aggregate demand curve from AD to AD′. This changes the equilibrium of the economy from E to F, and the equilibrium level of output increases from Y_e to Y′. Also, the equilibrium price level rises from P_e to P′. In an open economy with capital mobility, the fall in the interest rate induces a depreciation of the domestic currency as capital flows out of the country. The depreciation of the domestic currency, along with the capital outflow, induces an improvement in the current account as exports expand and imports contract—the indirect effect. The current account surplus, or at least an improving current account, shifts the AD curve even further to the right from AD′ to AD″. This additional increase in aggregate demand in turn changes the equilibrium of the economy from F to G, and the equilibrium level of output and the price level to Y″ and P″, respectively. The net result is that in an open economy with capital mobility, monetary policy is effective in increasing the level of economic activity.

Contractionary Monetary Policy

contractionary monetary policy a decrease in the money supply and/or an increase in interest rates

In the case of a **contractionary monetary policy**, the central bank decreases the money supply or reduces the money supply's growth rate. As the central bank decreases the growth rate of the money supply, the most noticeable effect is an increase in domestic interest rates. As before, we begin our analysis with the effects of a contractionary monetary policy on the supply and demand for loanable funds. In a developed country, a reduction in the growth rate of the money supply or a decrease in the money supply would occur when the central bank sells bonds. This action by the central bank reduces the amount of loanable funds available in the domestic economy. This effect is illustrated in Figure 18.10 as a decrease in the supply of loanable funds from S to S′. Assuming the demand for loanable funds is constant at D, the equilibrium in the loanable funds market changes from E to F, and the interest rate rises from i_e to i′.

This increase in the domestic interest rate will affect capital flows between countries as the increase in domestic interest rates attracts foreign capital. As foreign capital flows into the domestic economy, the equilibrium exchange rate will change. This effect is illustrated in Figure 18.11. The intersection of the original demand for foreign exchange, D, and supply of foreign exchange, S, determines the equilibrium at point E,

Figure 18.10 Supply and Demand for Loanable Funds and Contractionary Monetary Policy

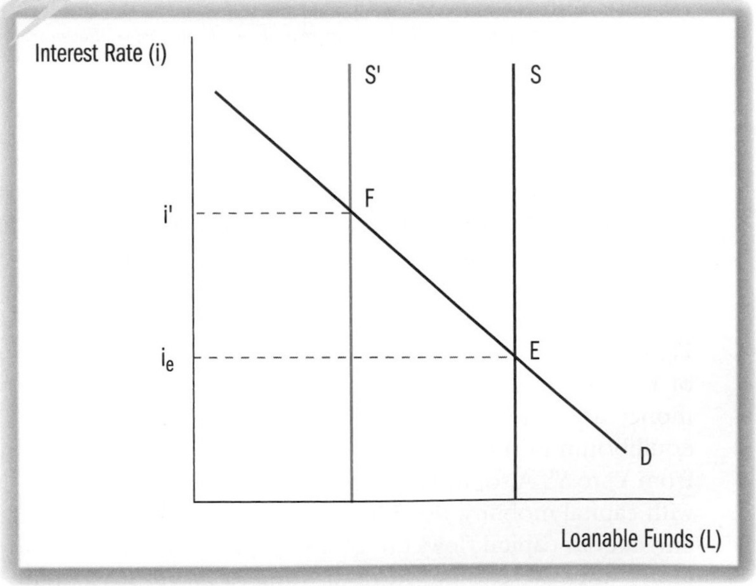

A contractionary monetary policy causes a decrease in the supply of loanable funds. As a result, the equilibrium interest rate rises.

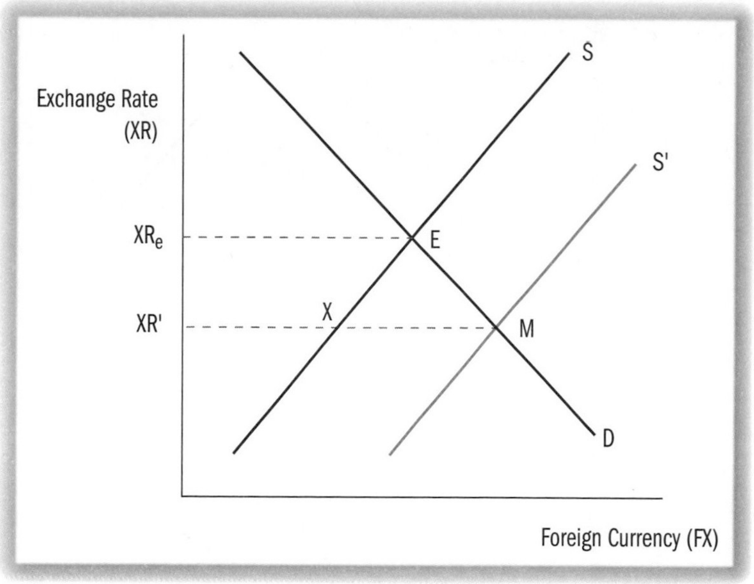

Figure 18.11 **Effects of Contractionary Monetary Policy on the Exchange Rate**

When the central bank adopts a contractionary monetary policy, the increase in interest rates causes an inflow of capital and increases the supply of foreign exchange. As a result, the exchange rate fall and the domestic currency appreciates, which causes exports to fall and imports to rise and a current account surplus.

with an exchange rate of XR_e. In order to buy domestic financial assets, foreign investors must sell foreign currency and buy domestic currency in the foreign exchange market. This capital inflow increases the supply of foreign exchange from S to S′. As a result, the equilibrium in the foreign exchange market changes from E to M, and the exchange rate falls from XR_e to XR′. The capital inflows into the country create a financial/capital account surplus. This financial/capital account surplus and the appreciation of the domestic currency leads to a current amount deficit, which is represented in Figure 18.11 as the difference between the amount imported (M), and the amount exported (X) at the new exchange rate of XR′.[20]

A contractionary monetary policy is effective in a closed economy because the increase in interest rates reduces the growth rate of consumption and/or investment. The effect of this reduction in total spending is illustrated in Figure 18.12 as a decrease in aggregate demand. The initial equilibrium is represented at point E by the intersection of aggregate demand, AD, and aggregate supply, AS, with an equilibrium level of output at Y_e and the price level at P_e. The direct effect of the contractionary monetary policy is illustrated by a leftward shift of the aggregate demand curve from

[20]As before, if the initial position was a current account deficit it would simply worsen. If the initial position were a surplus, it would tend to become smaller.

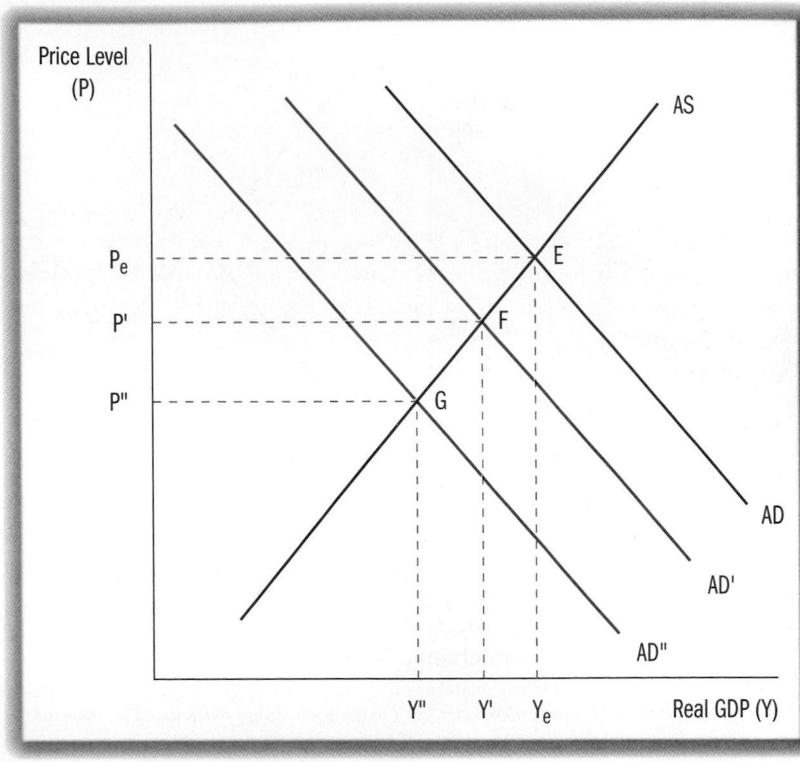

Figure 18.12 Effects of Monetary Policy on Equilibrium Output and Price Level

A contractionary monetary policy leads to a decrease in aggregate demand as interest rates rise. In a closed economy, this decrease would cause a decrease in both real output and the price level. In an open economy, the initial effect of a contractionary monetary policy is to decrease aggregate demand. This policy also causes the domestic currency to appreciate and worsens the current account. Aggregate demand decreases again, making monetary policy more effective in changing equilibrium output.

AD to AD′. At the new equilibrium illustrated at point F, the output level has fallen from Y_e to Y′, and the price level has declined from P_e to P′. In this case, the contractionary monetary policy has caused a decrease in output and the price level. If the economy is open and capital is mobile, the effects of a contractionary monetary policy are larger. In this situation, the increase in the interest rate induces an appreciation of the domestic currency as capital flows into the country. The appreciation of the currency along with the capital inflow induces a deterioration in the current account as exports contract and imports expand—the indirect effect. The current account deficit shifts the AD curve even further to the left from AD′ to AD″. This additional reduction in aggregate demand changes the economy's equilibrium from F to G, and the equilibrium level of output and the price level to Y″ and P″, respectively. In an open economy with freely flowing capital, both expansionary and contractionary monetary policy are highly effective in changing an economy's equilibrium level of output and the price level.

"Old" versus "New" Crowding Out

For many years, economists have discussed the issue of "crowding out" in the domestic economy. Crowding out refers to a government budget deficit's tendency to reduce the amount of money available to the private sector for borrowing. We can explain this concept using a couple of simple graphs. First, let's assume that the economy is closed to foreign trade. In Figure 18.13 we can show what might happen to private sector investment if the government budget deficit increases. Initially, we assume that the government budget is balanced and there is a supply of loanable funds (S) coupled with a private-sector demand for loanable funds (D). This would yield an equilibrium at point E with an interest rate of i_e. Next, assume that the government adopts an expansionary fiscal policy, which means that the budget goes from being balanced to a deficit. In this case, the demand for loanable funds rises to D′ and the equilibrium in the loanable funds market changes to point F. As such, the interest rate rises to i′. Since the supply of loanable funds is inelastic, government borrowing results in a reduction in private sector borrowing. Private-sector borrowing is still represented by the original demand curve (D). Total borrowing in the economy remains the same. However, a portion of private-sector borrowing has been "crowded out" by the new government demand for loanable funds. Total borrowing is still at L. Due to the higher interest rate, private-sector borrowing is now represented by L′ and point G on the original demand curve. To a greater or lesser extent, an increase in government borrowing reduces private-sector

Figure 18.13 Crowding Out in a Closed Economy

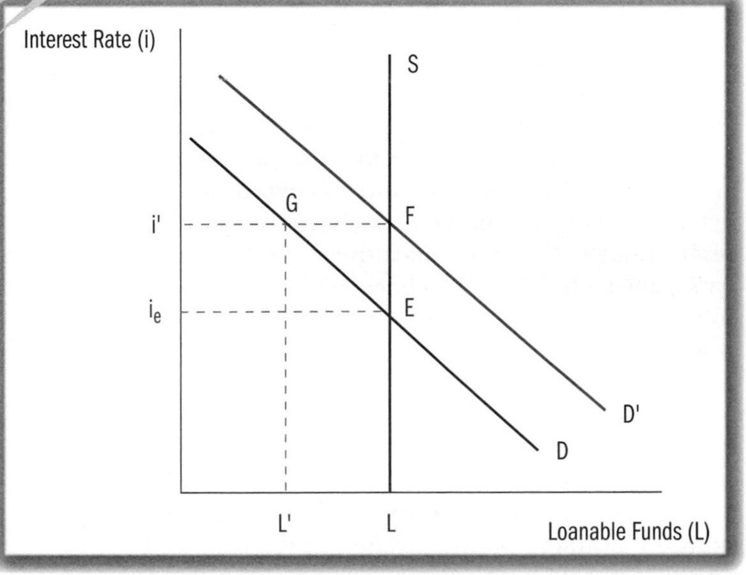

In a closed economy, an expansionary fiscal policy raises interest rates and crowd out private-sector borrowing.

(*continued*)

borrowing.[21] The government budget deficit has reduced the output of the interest-rate-sensitive sectors of the economy such as housing (i.e., residential investment), automobiles, and investment (nonresidential investment).

In an open economy with capital flows, the amount of crowding out will be reduced. As the increased government borrowing increases interest rates, inflows of foreign capital will mitigate this effect. This was shown previously in Figure 18.1. However, there are still casualties from the government budget deficit. The capital inflows tend to cause an appreciation of the currency shown in Figure 18.2. The interest rate-sensitive sectors of the economy are not affected as much as they are in a closed economy. However, there is still a cost. To a certain extent, the cost has been merely shifted to the exchange-rate-sensitive sectors of the economy. There is still a cost imposed on the domestic economy as a result of the expansionary fiscal policy. What has changed are the parts of the economy that are adversely affected by an increase in the government budget deficit.

[1]If the supply of loanable funds is not perfectly inelastic, the degree of crowding out will be less than complete. The reader will be spared the various details surrounding the degree of crowding out. It is probably less than complete, but is shown as such for convenience.

MONETARY AND FISCAL POLICY IN AN OPEN ECONOMY

We have just considered the effects of changes in fiscal and monetary policy on the exchange rate, the current account balance, and the state of the domestic economy. In this section, we extend our discussion of fiscal and monetary policy by considering the effects of simultaneous changes in both policies.

Before presenting the effects of different policy mixes on the domestic economy, we first want to consider how a country's government tends to use both policies to influence macroeconomic variables such as the growth rate of real GDP, the price level, the exchange rate, or the current account. Economists frequently describe the effects of government policies in terms of their effects on a country's external balance and internal balance. A country's current account balance represents a country's external balance, while a country's equilibrium level of output and the price level represent internal balance. Since there are two important variables included in a country's internal balance, the concept is more complicated. At any point in time, there is some optimal equilibrium for the economy with regard to its level of output and the price level. In the best of circumstances, such an equilibrium would imply a full-employment output level and a stable price level (no inflation or deflation). Since this optimal internal balance is rarely observed, governments frequently use fiscal and monetary policy together to achieve a more acceptable balance between the level of output and the price level. Governments can use fiscal and/or monetary policy to influence either their internal balance or their external balance. However, achieving both the optimal internal balance and a balanced current account simultaneously is another matter. In many cases, governments cannot simultaneously achieve both external and internal balance and have to choose which is more important.

Governments usually consider internal balance to be more important than external balance and frequently focus fiscal and/or monetary policy on achieving an optimal internal balance. As the quote at the beginning of the chapter indicates, a country's external balance usually is considered to be less important. Recall that although monetary and fiscal policy heavily influence the exchange rate and the current account balance, these variables are usually not the primary targets of these policies. Often, the public and the business press tend to think that the exchange rate and the current account balance are the primary targets of macroeconomic policies. In certain types of institutional arrangements, this may well be the case.[22] However, in an economy with floating exchange rates and open capital markets, macroeconomic policy is quite often focused on a country's internal balance.

policy mix **various combinations of fiscal and monetary policies used to influence external and internal balance**

Let's examine the potential effects of changes in fiscal and/or monetary policy on a country's external and internal balance. To make our analysis as simple as possible, we summarize the effects in Table 18.1. The rows in the table indicate the four types of government policies that we have already discussed. The columns indicate the effects of fiscal and monetary policy on the different macroeconomic variables of interest to the government. The table allows us to consider the **policy mix**, the effects of various combinations of fiscal and monetary policies.

Consistent Policy Mixes

Assume that a country's domestic economy is currently in a recession. In this case, the economy's real GDP is below the full employment output level. The government's

Table 18.1 Effects of Different Fiscal and Monetary Policies Under Flexible Exchange Rates and Capital Mobility

		Effect on			
		Equilibrium Output	**Equilibrium Price Level**	**Exchange Rate**	**Current Account**
Fiscal Policy					
Expansionary	-Direct	Increase	Increase	Appreciates	Deteriorates
	-Indirect	Decrease	Decrease		
	-Net	Little or no Effect		Appreciates	Deteriorates
Contractionary	-Direct	Decrease	Decrease	Depreciates	Improves
	-Indirect	Increase	Increase		
	-Net	Little or no Effect		Depreciates	Improves
Monetary Policy					
Expansionary	-Direct	Increase	Increase	Depreciates	Improves
	-Indirect	Increase	Increase		
	-Net	Large Increase		Depreciates	Improves
Contractionary	-Direct	Decrease	Decrease	Appreciates	Deteriorates
	-Indirect	Decrease	Decrease		
	-Net	Large Decrease		Appreciates	Deteriorates

[2]For some examples see Chapter 19.

most important objective would, therefore, be to increase the equilibrium level of output. The first column in Table 18.1 indicates the effects of monetary and fiscal policy on the country's equilibrium level of output. To increase output, the government would want to adopt an expansionary monetary policy and/or an expansionary fiscal policy. A combination of both would tend to increase the equilibrium level of output. In addition, there would be upward pressure on the price level as indicated in the table's second column. This additional pressure on the price level increases the risk of rising prices. However, when the economy is at less than full employment, that risk may be deemed to be acceptable at that point. Conducting both expansionary monetary and fiscal policies in combination has an unclear effect on the exchange rate. As the third column indicates, an expansionary fiscal policy would tend to cause the domestic currency to appreciate, while an expansionary monetary policy causes it to depreciate. The effect of these two policies in combination is unclear. The currency may appreciate or depreciate depending on the magnitude of the change in fiscal policy and monetary policy on the economy's domestic interest rates. Since the exchange rate effect is unclear, the effect of expansionary monetary and fiscal policy on the country's current account is also unclear. If the combination of expansionary monetary and fiscal policy causes lower interest rates for the domestic economy, the domestic currency would depreciate and the country's external balance would improve. If the policy mix causes domestic interest rates to rise, the domestic currency would tend to appreciate and the current account balance would deteriorate. From a policymaker's perspective, battling a recession and letting the country's external balance adjust to the change in interest rates is relatively safe. In this case, the domestic economy would improve as equilibrium output increases and the external balance is unlikely to change in either direction by a large amount.

A similar scenario emerges if a country's internal balance is such that the major domestic problem is inflation. When inflation is a problem, it is frequently the case that the economy is temporarily producing an output level greater than full employment. In this case, the government would employ a combination of contractionary monetary and fiscal policies. As indicated in Table 18.1, the effects of this combination of policies on a country's internal balance are clear. Both the equilibrium price level and equilibrium level of output (real GDP) would fall. Again, the effects of this combination of policies on a country's external balance are less clear. The contractionary fiscal policy would cause the domestic currency to depreciate while a contractionary monetary policy would cause the domestic currency rate to appreciate. The effects on a country's current account balance likewise are uncertain. As with the previous case, such a policy mix does not appear to be too problematic for the country in that its internal balance moves in the desired direction without dramatic changes in its external balance. In cases where governments adopt similar fiscal and monetary policies—that is, both expansionary and contractionary—a government can change the equilibrium level of output and the price level without making dramatic changes in its exchange rate or current account balance.

Inconsistent Policy Mixes

One would think that these cases where fiscal and monetary policies are consistent with one another should cover the feasible possibilities for mixtures of monetary and

The Japanese Economy in the 1990s

As most of you are aware, the Japanese economy is the world's second largest economy. It is roughly half the size of the U.S. economy and more than twice the size of the third largest economy, Germany. You may also be aware that all has not been well in the Japanese economy for quite some time. The economic boom in Japan during the 1980s suddenly ended in a recession in the early 1990s. In several ways, the Japanese economy has never really recovered. Economic growth in Japan has averaged less than 2 percent for the last decade. In many years, prices have actually *fallen*. Persistent deflation is a rare thing in any modern economy. In this environment, it is not surprising that unemployment has risen to over 5 percent, which for Japan is extremely high. The only bright spot in this bleak environment has been a persistent current account surplus. Even this needs to be viewed cautiously, as weak economic conditions tends to depress imports along with domestic consumption.

The response of the Japanese government has been the subject of much debate. Fiscal policy has been aggressively expansionary. The government budget deficit in recent years has been over 6 percent of GDP. For a developed country this is an astonishingly high number. The debate has focused on Japan's monetary policy. In one sense, the policy seems to be highly expansionary. Japanese interest rates have been less than 1 percent for a long time. However, monetary policy has not been as expansionary as it looks. With the collapse of the economy, the demand for loanable funds also collapsed. Much of the decline in interest rates was not the result of monetary policy but a decline in demand by business and the public. Broad money supply growth was anemic through most of the 1990s. To be fair, the monetary base and a measure of narrow money were rising a bit faster. However, in an economy with little economic growth and falling prices, money supply growth could safely have been more aggressive. The conclusion is that what superficially looks like a consistent policy mix in the face of a recession is not as consistent as it looks. A mix of expansionary fiscal and monetary policy should produce higher growth in GDP, a higher price level, and an uncertain effect on the current account. What actually occurred is stagnant growth in GDP, a falling price level, and a current account surplus. We cannot possibly cover all potential mixtures of fiscal and monetary policy in a short book. The mix of an aggressive fiscal policy and a neutral monetary policy is one such possibility. Fortunately, the Japanese central bank now appears to be pursuing a much more aggressive monetary policy, this gives one at least some reason to be cautiously optimistic about the future of the Japanese economy.

fiscal policies. However, this is not the case. Mixtures of fiscal and monetary policies that are consistent with one another (both expansionary or both contractionary) are consistent with internal balance objectives. Mixtures of fiscal and monetary policy that are inconsistent with one another (one expansionary and one contractionary) are inconsistent with internal balance objectives. For example, a mixture of a contractionary monetary policy and an expansionary fiscal policy produces an ambiguous outcome for the equilibrium level of output and the price level in the short run. Since the effect on a country's internal balance is unclear, the question becomes why would a government adopt such a policy mix?

In our previous discussion concerning policy mixes, we assumed that the same policymakers (government officials) were able to change both fiscal and monetary policy. In many countries this is not the case. On the one hand, a combination of the executive and legislative branches of government (e.g., a president or prime minister and Congress or the Parliament) controls fiscal policy. On the other hand, the central bank, acting independently of the elected government, determines monetary policy. When different policymakers are in control of fiscal and monetary policy, it becomes

The Twin Deficits

In the U.S. during the 1980s it became quite common to speak of the "twin deficits." The twin deficits referred to the simultaneous occurrence of a large government budget deficit and a large current account deficit. It is easy to see how these two deficits can be linked. In the early 1980s, the government budget deficit escalated rapidly, and at the same time, the current account deficit ballooned, as shown in Figure 18.14. The reasoning for this simultaneous occurrence is straightforward. An expansionary fiscal policy tends to increase domestic interest rates, which increases capital inflows and increases the current account deficit as indicated in Figures 18.1 and 18.2, respectively. In addition to the expansionary fiscal policy, something else was occurring. To battle inflation, the U.S. Federal Reserve reduced the growth rate of the money supply, which further pushed up real interest rates. This exacerbated the capital inflows resulting from an expansionary fiscal policy. Referring to Table 18.1, the results of this policy are fairly clear. A combination of an expansionary fiscal policy and a contractionary

Figure 18.14 Federal Budget Deficit and the Balance on Current Account for the U.S., 1980–1996

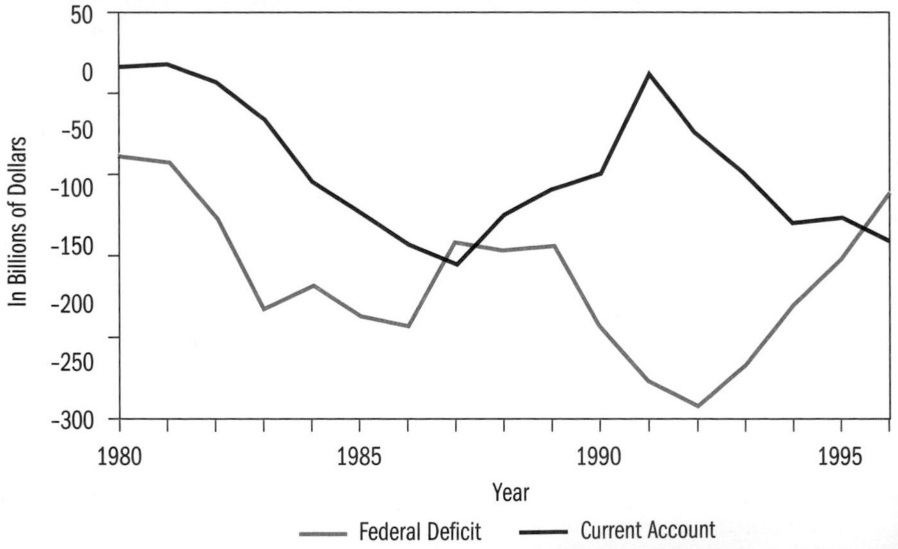

Source: Council of Economic Advisors, *Economic Report of the President,* Washington, D.C.: U.S. Government Printing Office, 1998.

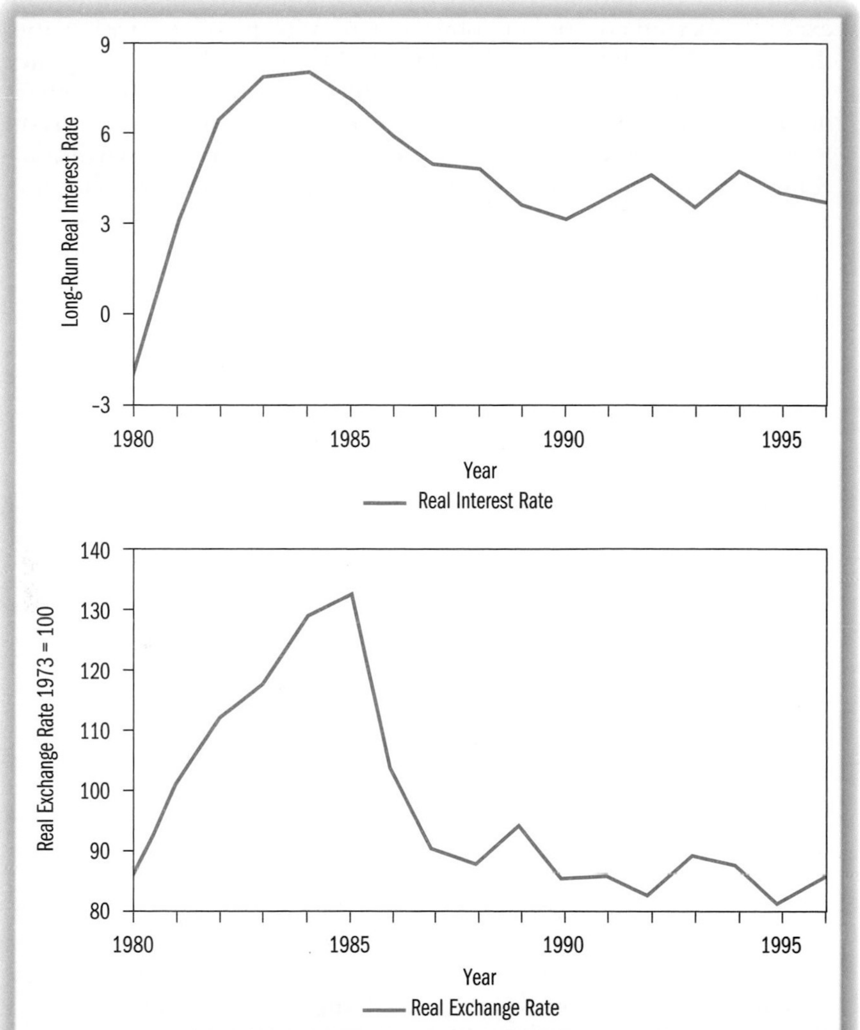

Figure 18.15 **U.S. Real Exchange Rate and Real Long-Run Interest Rate, 1980–1996**

Source: Council of Economic Advisors, *Economic Report of the President,* Washington, D.C.: U.S. Government Printing Office, 1998.

monetary policy would virtually guarantee an appreciation of the currency. This appreciation would in turn lead to an increase in the current account deficit. As the two policies were eventually "unwound," real interest rates fell and the dollar depreciated. These two effects are shown in Figure 18.15. Returning to Figure 18.14, notice that as the dollar depreciated, the current account deficit improved. The relationship between the government budget deficit and the current account is not always perfect. However, in certain circumstances, such as the U.S. during the 1980s, the government budget deficit and the current account may be inversely related.

possible for the two policies to be inconsistent with one another.[23] In the U.S., for example, elected government officials determine fiscal policy while the central bank—that is, the Federal Reserve—determines the course of monetary policy.

When policy mixes are inconsistent, they can have ambiguous effects on the domestic economy in the short run (i.e., internal balance). However, inconsistent policy mixes have explicit effects on a country's external balance. An expansionary fiscal policy coupled with a contractionary monetary policy causes the domestic currency to appreciate. This will cause a deterioration in the current account. In this case, both fiscal and monetary policies reinforce each other and the effect on a country's external balance can be quite significant. The same would be true of a contractionary fiscal policy coupled with an expansionary monetary policy. In this case, the domestic currency depreciates and the country's current account balance improves. The important point of our discussion is that these types of policy mixes can have extreme effects on a country's external balance.

For an individual firm operating in an economy that adopts inconsistent policy mixes, the effect of changes in the exchange rate change on the firm's competitiveness can be dramatic. For businesses competing with imports or attempting to export, such policy mixes have an exaggerated impact on the economy's tradable goods sector. An example of this type of situation is described in the box, The Twin Deficits.

TRADE FLOW ADJUSTMENT AND CURRENT ACCOUNT DYNAMICS

In our analysis concerning the effects of monetary and fiscal policy, we described how monetary and fiscal policies influence the current account balance via changes in interest rates, which in turn changes the exchange rate. However, implicit in our analysis was an assumption that there were virtually no time lags involved in producing these effects. In some cases, this may be a realistic assumption. First, changes in fiscal and/or monetary policy can be expected to influence interest rates fairly quickly if financial markets are efficient. Under conditions of high capital mobility between countries, capital can flow freely across national borders in response to changes in relative interest rates. This change in interest rates should cause a prompt change in the exchange rate. The result is that exchange rates can change fast in response to changes in interest rates caused by macroeconomic policy changes.

However, it is the response of trade flows (exports and imports) to changes in exchange rates that are a bit more problematic. In our analysis of the effects of macroeconomic policy changes, we assumed that as the exchange rate changes, trade flows (exports and imports) will respond (change) very quickly. This may not always be the case. If the exchange rate changes, the price of imports and exports may not change instantaneously. International trade in goods and services may move sluggishly in response to changes in prices when compared to the response of financial markets. The time it takes for an exchange rate change to influence the level of a country's exports and imports and, its current account balance may be as long as 6 months to 1 year.

---

[3]In many cases, the management of internal balance has been left to the central bank. It is becoming increasingly rare for governments in developed countries to actively use fiscal policy to influence the short-run state of the economy. This does not mean that fiscal policy has no effect on the economy. It is not being used as an active stabilization tool.

J-curve **the tendency for the current account balance to initially worsen when the currency depreciates**

In the long run, as a country's currency depreciates (appreciates), its exports expand (contract) and imports contract (expand). However, in the short run, as a country's exchange rate changes, the response of its exports and imports and its current account balance could very easily be in the opposite direction. In part, the problem with the adjustment of a country's current account to changes in the exchange rate is caused by the way in which international trade is conducted. In many cases, international trade in goods and services is conducted between the parties on a contract basis. For example, the importer may have contracted to purchase a certain amount of goods at a set price as specified in the contract. If the currency depreciates, the cost of the goods in domestic currency rises with the depreciation. In this case, the exchange rate change causes the value of imports to rise initially after the depreciation. In addition, the value of exports in domestic currency does not change as the exporters are being paid the prearranged price for their goods in domestic currency. The net effect is that the current account balance may initially worsen after a depreciation of a country's currency and only after a time lag will the current account begin to improve. This effect on a country's current account balance has been called **the J-curve**.[24]

The J-curve effect is shown in Figure 18.16. The horizontal axis is measured in units of time (months) and the vertical axis is the current account balance. Initially, at

Figure 18.16 The J Curve

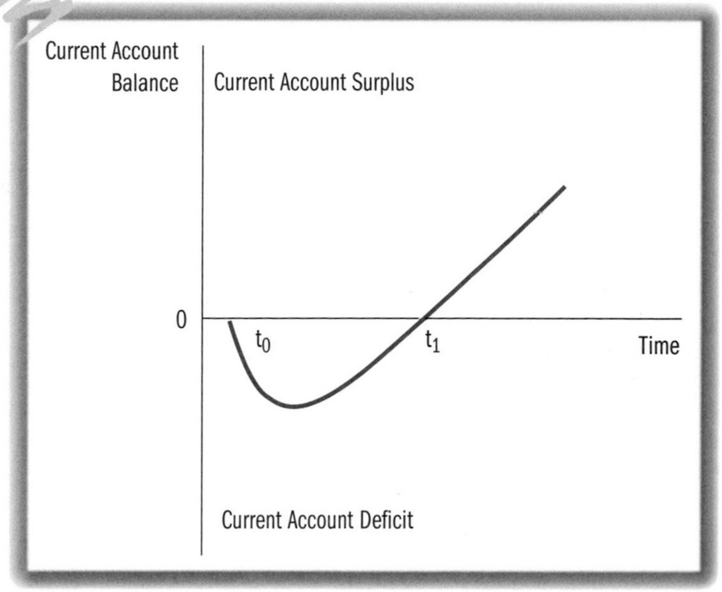

The J-curve illustrates the effect of a currency depreciation on the current account. A major depreciation of a currency initially causes a current account deficit. After a period of time, the current account moves in the direction of a surplus.

[4]The original work on the J-Curve is in Stephen Magee, "Currency Contracts, Pass Through and Devaluation," *Brooking Papers on Economic Activity,* 1973, 1, pp. 303–25.

time period t_0, the current account balance is zero. If the domestic currency depreciates, the current account balance does not immediately improve and, for a time, it may actually worsen. Only after international contracts are renewed to reflect the new exchange rate does the quantity of imports and exports begin to change. Imports will begin to decline and exports will begin to rise. Once this occurs, the country's current account balance will begin to improve. In the short run, the reaction of a country's current account balance can and many times will be the reverse of what was described in our previous analysis. For developed countries, this J-curve effect may last from 3 to 6 months to as long as a year. It does not fundamentally alter our previous analysis or conclusions. However, policymakers need to be prepared for this opposite effect. At a minimum a large depreciation of a country's currency is unlikely to immediately improve the current account balance, and it could easily make the current account balance worse in the short run.

SUMMARY

1. Governments use fiscal policy to change the level of taxation and/or government spending at the national level to affect the level of economic activity (GDP). Governments use monetary policy to change the money supply and/or interest rates to affect a country's level of economic activity. Both fiscal and monetary policies have predictable effects on the exchange rate, the current account, and short-run capital flows.
2. A country's exchange rate and its current account balance represent its external balance. A country's equilibrium price level and equilibrium level of output represent its internal balance. For most countries, the focus of fiscal and/or monetary policy is on managing their internal balances. In many cases, this focus on internal balance comes at the expense of external balance considerations.
3. Expansionary fiscal policy occurs when a government chooses to adopt some combination of lower tax revenue and/or higher government spending. In a closed economy, expansionary fiscal policy leads to a larger government budget deficit and causes domestic interest rates to rise. As a government adopts an expansionary fiscal policy, aggregate demand increases. In a closed economy, an expansionary fiscal policy would lead to an increase in both domestic output and the domestic price level.
4. In an open economy with international capital mobility, expansionary fiscal policy leads to a rise in interest rates, which causes an inflow of foreign capital. The inflow of foreign capital tends to lower domestic interest rates and causes the currency to appreciate. The capital inflows result in a financial/capital account surplus and a current account deficit. Expansionary fiscal policy causes the aggregate demand curve to increase, and also causes a deterioration of the current account balance, which causes aggregate demand to decrease. The net effect on aggregate demand, and thus, on equilibrium output and the price level depends on the magnitude of the two effects. As a result, expansionary fiscal policy in an open economy is less effective in changing equilibrium output than it is in a closed economy. However, changes in fiscal policy affect variables such as the interest rate, the exchange rate, capital flows, and the current account balance.
5. A contractionary fiscal policy in an open economy is not very effective in reducing the price level or real GDP. An increase in taxes or a cut in government spending would reduce aggregate demand. However, this policy would also lower interest rates and induce outflows of capital that would cause the exchange rate to depreciate. In turn, this depreciation would cause an improvement in the current account that would increase aggregate demand. This increase would partially offset the effects of a contractionary fiscal policy.
6. Expansionary monetary policy occurs when a government chooses to increase the money

supply or the money supply's growth rate. In a closed economy, expansionary monetary policy leads to a decline (increase) in domestic interest rates. As the government adopts an expansionary monetary policy aggregate demand increases. In a closed economy, an expansionary monetary policy would lead to an increase in both domestic output and the domestic price level.

7. In an open economy with international capital mobility, expansionary monetary policy leads to a fall in interest rates, which causes an outflow of foreign capital. The outflow of foreign capital tends to cause the exchange rate to depreciate. The capital outflows result in a financial/capital account deficit and a current account surplus. The effects of expansionary monetary policy cause aggregate demand to increase. It also causes an improvement of the current account balance, which causes aggregate demand to increase again. As a result, expansionary monetary policy in an open economy is more effective in changing equilibrium output than it is in a closed economy.
8. A contractionary monetary policy would lead to higher interest rates, lower output, and a lower price level. Capital mobility would tend to augment these effects. As the financial/capital account moves into surplus, the current account would tend to fall into a deficit. The current account deficit would tend to reduce aggregate demand even further.
9. Consistent policy mixes can be effective in solving internal balance problems. However, their effects on the exchange rate and the current account can be ambiguous.
10. Mixtures of fiscal and monetary policy that are inconsistent with one another are also inconsistent with internal balance objectives. Inconsistent policy mixes have unambiguous effects on a country's external balance.
11. In the long run, as a country's currency depreciates, its exports expand and imports contract. In the short run, as a country's exchange rate changes the response of its exports and imports, its current account balance could very easily move in the opposite direction. That is, the current account balance may initially worsen after a depreciation of a country's currency, and only after a time lag will the current account begin to improve. This effect on a country's current account balance has been called the J-curve.

KEY CONCEPTS AND TERMS

- fiscal policy p. 419
- monetary policy p. 419
- external balance p. 419
- internal balance p. 419
- expansionary fiscal policy p. 420
- demand for loanable funds p. 420
- supply of loanable funds p. 420
- contractionary fiscal policy p. 424
- discretionary monetary policy p. 428
- expansionary monetary policy p. 429
- contractionary monetary policy p. 432
- policy mix p. 437
- J-curve p. 443

PROBLEMS AND QUESTIONS FOR REVIEW

1. Define the terms fiscal policy and monetary policy.
2. Define the terms internal balance and external balance.
3. Graphically show what the demand and supply of loanable funds looks like.
4. Show the effects of an expansionary fiscal policy on GDP and the price level in a closed economy.
5. Contrast how an expansionary fiscal policy would affect interest rates in a closed economy and one with international capital mobility. Now show how this policy would affect the exchange rate and the current account.
6. What would be the effects of an expansionary fiscal policy on GDP and the price level in an open economy?
7. Capital mobility tends to make expansionary fiscal policy less effective. Show why this is true.

8. Show the effects of a contractionary fiscal policy on interest rates and the exchange rate in the absence of capital mobility. Now show what occurs if there is capital mobility.
9. Contrast the effects of a contractionary fiscal policy on real GDP and the price level assuming no capital mobility versus free capital mobility.
10. How would an expansionary monetary policy affect interest rates, real GDP, and the price level in a closed economy?
11. With capital mobility, an expansionary monetary policy would have a powerful effect on real GDP and the price level. Show why this is true.
12. Reducing inflation using monetary policy is easier if there is international capital mobility. Show why this is true.
13. Consistent policy mixes tend to produce the desired effects on the domestic economy but have uncertain effects on the exchange rate and the current account. Show why this is true.
14. Why is it possible to obtain inconsistent policy mixes?
15. Discuss the different effects of the following policy mixes:
    a. Expansionary fiscal policy and expansionary monetary policy.
    b. Expansionary fiscal policy and contractionary monetary policy.
    c. Contractionary fiscal policy and expansionary monetary policy.
    d. Contractionary fiscal policy and contractionary monetary policy.
16. A common policy mix in developing countries is a combination of an expansionary monetary policy and an expansionary fiscal policy. Show the effects of this policy mix on interest rates, the exchange rate, real GDP, and the price level.
17. Suppose that a government chose a policy mix of a contractionary monetary policy and an expansionary fiscal policy. Show the effects on the exchange rate and the current account.
18. Describe what the phrase twin deficits means.
19. Suppose that a domestic firm manufactures automobiles and is competing with foreign firms in the domestic market. Which policy mix would be clearly detrimental to this firm? Which policy mix would tend to assist them in competing with foreign firms?
20. Most developed countries tend to have government budget deficits most of the time. In effect this means that there are only two relevant policy mixes. Contrast the effects of these two relevant choices on the exchange rate and the current account.
21. Explain why a country's current account balance might deteriorate in the short run after the depreciation of the currency. Would this short-run effect be permanent?

SELECTED READINGS AND WEB SITES

Federal Reserve Bank of St. Louis (www.stlouisfed.org)
A good source of information on monetary and fiscal policy for major developed countries.

IMF, *Government Finance Statistics Yearbook,* Washington, D.C.: IMF, annual.
The most convenient source of information for information on fiscal policy around the world.

IMF, *World Economic Outlook,* Washington, D.C.: IMF, semiannual.
An important source of information, data, and forecasts of world economic activity.

IMF (www.imf.org)
A good general source of information on the world economy for both developed and developing countries.

Angus Maddison, *The World Economy: A Millenial Perspective,* Paris: OECD, 2001.
The single best source on historical changes in the world economy.

The Economist (www.economist.com)
The best source of information on economic conditions in the world economy.

Chapter 19

Fixed Exchange Rates and Currency Unions

"I have demonstrated that perfect capital mobility implies different concepts of stabilization policy from those to which we have become accustomed in the post-war period. Monetary policy has no impact on employment under fixed exchange rates while fiscal policy has no effect on employment under flexible exchange rates. On the other hand, fiscal policy has a strong effect on employment under fixed exchange rates while monetary policy has a strong effect on employment under flexible exchange rates."
—ROBERT MUNDELL

INTRODUCTION

Throughout most of our analysis concerning exchange rate changes and their effects, we have made several assumptions. First, we have assumed that exchange rates are completely free to adjust to their equilibrium level at all times. Second, we have assumed that all buying and selling of foreign exchange has occurred between individuals and/or companies located in the private sector. Third, we have assumed that national governments have not taken systematic actions to directly influence the value of their currency in the foreign exchange market. However, national governments frequently do buy and sell foreign exchange in the foreign exchange market.

So why would a government buy or sell foreign exchange? Like individuals and companies, governments frequently need foreign exchange to conduct economic transactions. For example, if a government purchases land to build a new consulate in a foreign country, it needs foreign exchange to make the acquisition. When the government buys or sells foreign exchange to conduct economic transactions, its participation in the foreign exchange market really is no different from that of a large corporation. We have not assumed that a national government never deals in foreign exchange. Rather, we have assumed that the government has allowed the value of the equilibrium exchange rate to be determined by market forces. This situation is reasonably descriptive of the involvement of many governments in the foreign exchange market since the early 1970s. However, letting market forces determine the value of the equilibrium exchange rate (i.e., freely floating exchange rates) is not typical of all national governments. No exchange rate system is perfect. For reasons we will outline in the next chapter, governments may choose to fix the exchange rate at some predetermined level, a fixed exchange rate. The purpose of this chapter is to study how the overall economy and economic policy change when the exchange rate is not allowed to float freely.

One of the reasons why we study fixed exchange rates is historical. Until the early 1970s, fixed exchange rates were the norm for all countries, as we describe in Chapter 20. For example, under a gold standard, each country's domestic currency was defined in terms of the amount of gold it could buy. In addition, each country's central bank was willing to buy or sell unlimited quantities of gold at the stated price. Since all currencies were defined in terms of gold, this maintained a fixed exchange rate between the various national currencies. In this case, fixed exchange rates were a natural part of a monetary policy based on gold. When the gold-standard monetary system broke up in the late 1920s, it was replaced by a system of fixed exchange rates known as the Bretton Woods system. Under Bretton Woods, most exchange rates were fixed from 1946 to the early 1970s. In order to understand the history of monetary systems, it is useful to have a basic understanding of how fixed exchange rate systems work.

inconvertible currency a currency that cannot be freely exchanged for another country's currency

The second reason we study fixed exchange rates is that a number of countries worldwide fix (peg) the value of their domestic currency to that of another country.[1] In addition, there are a number of countries in the EU that have taken a fixed exchange rate system one step further and have created a common currency—the Euro. A common currency in a large country such as the U.S. is just a fixed exchange rate system applied to all states within the U.S. By studying how fixed exchange rates work, we can learn a great deal about how the economies of many countries work and in the process learn something about how the various regions within a large economy such as the U.S. react to changes in the national economy.

INCONVERTIBLE CURRENCIES

The first method that a country can use to fix the value of its currency in the foreign exchange market involves making its currency inconvertible. An **inconvertible currency** is a currency that cannot be freely traded for another country's currency by domestic consumers and businesses. The common term used to describe this system is **exchange controls**. When a country adopts an inconvertible currency, the government, or more often the central bank, becomes a monopolist with respect to holding all foreign exchange. This implies that all residents and firms in the country are legally obligated to sell any foreign exchange to the government at a fixed price. Likewise, any resident or firm that needs foreign exchange must purchase it from the government at the same fixed price. Under a system of exchange controls, it becomes relatively easy for the government to "fix" the price of foreign exchange. While this system may sound odd, it is quite common among developing countries.

exchange controls a system where the government is the only legal buyer and seller of foreign exchange

Fixing the exchange rate using exchange controls is illustrated in Figure 19.1. The demand for foreign exchange is represented by D and has a negative slope. S represents

[1]According to International Monetary Fund data, there are 70 countries that have some type of fixed exchange rate system. See the *Annual Report on Exchange Arrangements and Restrictions,* published by the IMF.

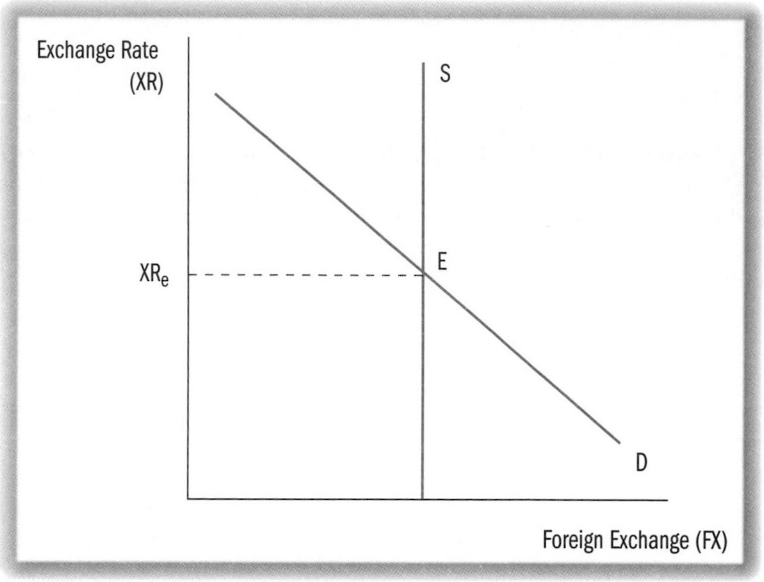

Figure 19.1 Demand and Supply of Foreign Exchange for an Inconvertible Currency

Initially, the demand and supply of foreign currency determines the fixed exchange rate posted by the government.

the supply of foreign exchange. Notice that the supply of foreign exchange is represented as perfectly inelastic—that is, it does not have a positive slope. The shape of the foreign exchange supply curve is different because there is only a single supplier of foreign exchange, the government. The intersection of the demand for foreign exchange and the supply of foreign exchange at point E, determines the fixed exchange rate that is posted by the government. Superficially, the illustrated equilibrium exchange rate looks to be the same as that under a flexible exchange rate system. The government has initially balanced the available supply of foreign exchange with the demand for foreign exchange at the equilibrium exchange rate of XR_e.

Now, for the exchange rate to remain fixed (constant) at the current exchange rate, XR_e, total outflows and inflows of foreign exchange must be equal at all times at the posted exchange rate, XR_e. In order to keep the exchange rate constant, the government must balance total inflows and outflows of foreign exchange at the fixed exchange rate. To accomplish this balance, most governments must seriously control the flow of capital into and out of the country. For example, domestic individuals' or companies' ability to purchase foreign financial assets and/or foreign direct investment is usually severely limited. Since exchange controls are more common in developing countries, government officials often argue that capital is usually scarce within their country and prohibiting capital from flowing abroad is in the best interest of the country's economic growth. In many cases the government may limit inflows of foreign capital, especially portfolio capital that can exit the country as easily as it entered. Very often, foreign direct investment flows into the country are relatively unrestricted or even encouraged, as an investment in facilities and equipment for a foreign firm

Currency Boards

A currency board system is an exchange rate system where the value of the domestic currency is irrevocably fixed to the value of another currency. In this sense, it is similar to the exchange control system just described. However, there is a major difference. In this system, the central bank holds no domestic currency, only foreign currency. As Hong Kong and Singapore have demonstrated, this type of exchange rate system can work quite well. On the other hand the recent collapse of the system in Argentina shows that it is not a panacea for all of a country's economic problems.

Before a country adopts a currency board system, it is prudent to examine the strengths and limitations of such a system. Essentially, a currency board helps to stabilize the exchange rate by ensuring that the money supply is fully backed by foreign exchange reserves. Like any fixed (pegged) exchange rate, a currency board makes a commitment to fix the value of the domestic currency relative to a foreign currency. With full backing, the currency board is able to make this commitment believable because it is able to redeem domestic currency for foreign currency at a fixed rate. However, the resulting stability carries a price. Most important is the fact that a country loses independent control of its monetary policy. In this case, the country is tying its economic fate to that of the foreign currency to which it is fixed (pegged). Without independence, the monetary authority also loses its ability to serve as a lender of last resort during a liquidity crisis.

All monetary authorities seek credibility, whether through reputation, explicit inflation targets, or exchange rate pegs. Currency boards help to establish credibility by ensuring full currency backing. Another characteristic of a currency board is that it is prohibited from buying or holding domestic treasury or commercial securities. Since a currency board is constrained to issue currency only in exchange for the reserve currency, it is powerless to create domestic money by extending credit as conventional central banks can do. Strict limits on a currency board's power to issue money constrain its operations in two important respects: the board cannot finance (i.e., monetize) the government's budgetary deficits, and it cannot regulate the nation's money supply by engaging in open market operations or discounting domestic bank held paper.

It is these two constraints that attract the most determined opposition to the currency board idea and, at the same time, inspire its greatest admiration. Currency boards are one particular monetary arrangement among many for establishing and maintaining confidence in a national currency, but they may not be the best choice in all situations.

cannot easily leave the country. The main principle embodied in limiting flows of capital into and out of the country is to make it easier to stabilize the demand for foreign exchange. In turn this makes it easier for the government to balance total inflows and outflows of foreign exchange at the fixed exchange rate.

Difficulties Associated with Exchange Controls

If one does not fully examine the implications of exchange controls, it initially seems to be a plausible method of fixing the exchange rate because the government has managed to initially balance the supply and demand for foreign exchange. Also, the government has eliminated the troublesome problem of wide swings in the nominal exchange rate. However, as a practical matter, exchange controls tend to cause a number of economic difficulties. First, there is the simple annoyance of dealing with a government bureaucracy every time one wants to exchange one currency for another. With an inconvertible currency, the government buys all foreign exchange earned by individuals and firms at the stated exchange rate and the government sells all foreign exchange requested by residents and firms within the country. As the government is the sole source of foreign exchange, the government bureaucracy is unlikely to provide the same quality service as a free market. In the case of a free market, if you do not like the foreign exchange service your bank provides, you can always switch banks. With exchange controls, one cannot legally switch providers. The efficiency losses of having only one provider of foreign exchange may be difficult to quantify, but they are there nonetheless.

A more serious difficulty arises with respect to the difference between the fixed nominal exchange rate and the real exchange rate. When a country fixes the exchange rate, the exchange rate is expressed in nominal terms. So long as the nominal exchange rate is close to its purchasing power parity value, then the nominal fixed exchange rate (peg) may be sustainable over time. However, as we described in Chapter 16, the real exchange rate may change even if the nominal exchange rate does not. A common problem in this regard is that a country's domestic inflation may not be equal to the rate of inflation in other foreign countries. As we described previously, controlling the money supply in developing countries is difficult due to the lack of open market operations. In this situation, changes in the government budget deficit easily can translate into large changes in the monetary base and the money supply. This, in turn, may lead to an increase in the domestic price level relative to the price level in foreign countries—in other words, a domestic inflation rate greater than the foreign inflation rate.[2] In such a case, the country's real exchange rate is changing even though its nominal value has remained constant. The result of this is that the real value of the domestic currency is appreciating and the nominal exchange rate is becoming overvalued.

We can demonstrate the effects of this situation in Figure 19.2, where the exchange rate is fixed at XR_e with an initial equilibrium at point E, where the demand (D) and supply (S) of foreign exchange intersect. Now, assume that the government adopts an expansionary monetary and fiscal policy and the domestic economy expands and the price level increases. As a result, of the nominal exchange rate being fixed, the real exchange rate increases and the domestic currency appreciates in real terms. The appreciation of the real value of the currency (imports are relatively cheaper) and the increase in domestic output (income) causes the demand for foreign exchange to increase from D to D′. However, since the nominal exchange rate is fixed, the government faces the an excess demand for foreign exchange at the current exchange rate. At the fixed exchange rate of XR_e, the demand for foreign exchange is now illustrated at point F instead of E and more citizens and firms are requesting foreign exchange from the government than the government can supply (in other words, there is a shortage of foreign exchange).

To balance the demand for foreign exchange with the supply of foreign exchange, the government can use one of three options. First, it could allow the exchange rate to

[2]One may wish to refer back to the section on the real exchange rate in Chapter 16 at this point.

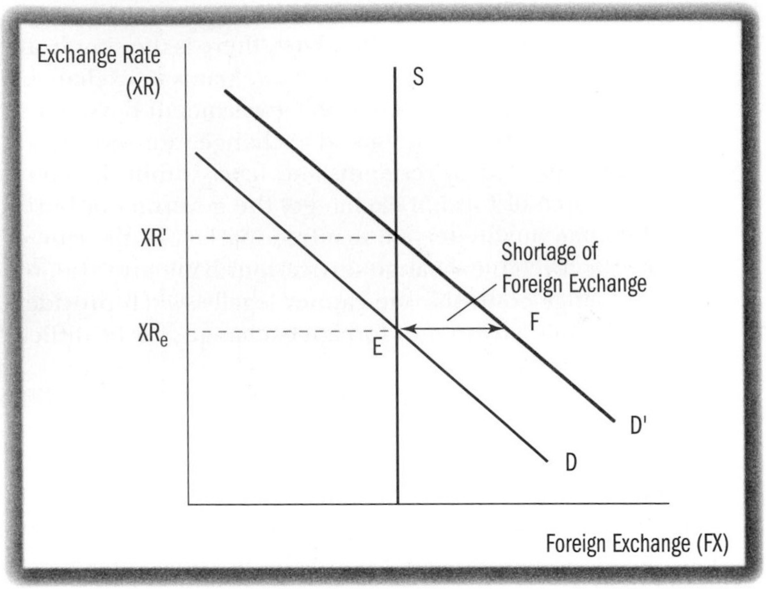

Figure 19.2 Demand and Supply of Foreign Exchange for an Inconvertible Currency—Policy Options

When the demand for foreign exchange increases, a shortage of foreign currency occurs. This shortage can be eliminated by depreciating the domestic currency, conducting contractionary fiscal and/or monetary policy, or by rationing the available supply of foreign exchange.

increase and the currency to depreciate from XR_e to XR′. However, if this depreciation of the exchange rate is relatively large, it might have serious macroeconomic consequences. Such a large depreciation tends to cause the difficult combination of higher inflation and a lower level of GDP. Second, the government could implement restrictive macroeconomic policies (contractionary fiscal and/or monetary policy) that would reduce the demand for foreign exchange. However, this type of policy amounts to sacrificing domestic economic growth to maintain the exchange rate.

The third and most common option available to the government is to ration the available supply of foreign exchange. Since the quantity demanded is greater than the quantity supplied, the government must decide who will get foreign exchange and who will not. Ideally, the government would provide foreign exchange for necessary imports and deny it for unnecessary imports. However, who is to say what is necessary and what is not? The government might easily determine requests for foreign exchange to import certain goods (food, energy, pharmaceuticals, spare parts, etc.). However, once the obvious choices are made, deciding who receives foreign exchange and who does not becomes quite arbitrary. For example, does one release foreign exchange for imported clothing if a domestic clothing industry exists? Even completely honest government officials are going to have a difficult time making decisions that are consistent with those that would have been made in a free market. There are imports that may not be absolutely "necessary" but that are very profitable to sell in the domestic market. In this type of situation, the demanders of foreign exchange may have a large incentive to share these profits with government officials who have the authority to release foreign exchange. As a result, the system contains large incentives for the corruption of government officials.[3]

The shortage of foreign exchange within a country, as illustrated in Figure 19.2, can become more severe over time. In Figure 19.2, imports became relatively cheaper as the real exchange rate appreciates and the demand for foreign exchange increases. However, what has been ignored is the effect of the real exchange rate's change on the country's exports. As the real exchange rate appreciates and the nominal exchange rate becomes overvalued, the country's exports become more expensive in foreign markets. This is especially true if the country exports primary commodities that are competitively priced in world markets. In this case, the supply of foreign exchange available to the country (derived from exports) decreases.

This combination of an increase in the demand for foreign exchange coupled with a decrease in the supply of foreign exchange is illustrated in Figure 19.3. As the real exchange rate appreciates, the supply of foreign exchange shifts from S to S′ and the demand for foreign exchange shifts from D to D′. The shortage of foreign exchange becomes even more acute and increases the gap from point G to F. The pressure placed on the government to deliver foreign exchange, at this point, increases. The rationing problem becomes more severe for the country as the amount

Figure 19.3 Demand and Supply of Foreign Exchange for an Inconvertible Currency—Policy Options

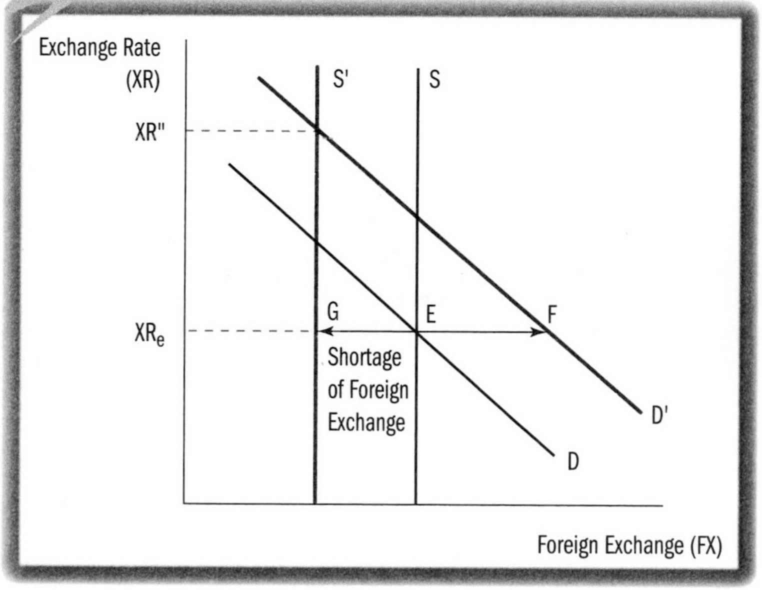

If the demand for foreign exchange increases and the supply of foreign exchange decreases, the shortage of foreign exchange becomes even more acute and increases the gap from G to F.

[3]The situation is somewhat like the periodic scandals involving government officials who have the authority to dispense contracts for goods and services to private-sector firms.

The Value of An Inconvertible Currency

If an inconvertible currency has become overvalued, the question becomes what the nominal exchange rate "should" be. Recall that domestic residents who possess foreign exchange are legally obliged to surrender it to the government. To a greater or lesser extent, there would be legal sanctions for failing to do this. Suppose that the penalties for illegally possessing foreign exchange are fairly small—say, a small monetary fine. If the currency becomes sufficiently overvalued, it may become logical (although illegal) to not surrender the foreign exchange to the government at the fixed price. Given that there is excess demand for foreign exchange, it is quite possible that you could find a buyer who would be willing to pay more than the fixed government rate. When the government attempts to fix any price, a *black market* will develop. If one observes that there is a black market for foreign exchange in a country, you don't even need to ask if there are exchange controls. The very existence of a black market means that the government's fixed price for foreign exchange is too low. In this case, there are only two remaining questions. First, how overvalued is the official exchange rate? The black market rate is a reliable guide to this. Empirical estimates have shown time and again that the black market rate will closely approximate purchasing power parity. This knowledge is both a blessing and a curse. It is good in the sense that one usually does not have to conduct tedious calculations of just how overvalued the exchange rate is. One can simply go out in the street and find out. However, the answer in some cases may be disheartening. If the black market rate is 50 percent above the official rate, there is likely to be a nasty combination of an austerity program and/or a large devaluation to bring the economy back into balance. Economists will likely be able to identify countries where there is a high probability of a major devaluation. When such a currency crisis will occur is another matter.

of imports declines and may well cause product and intermediate input shortages in the domestic markets.

An extremely overvalued exchange rate can make it very difficult for a government to regain external balance, as the options available to eliminate the shortage of foreign exchange become more difficult to adopt. First, the degree of macroeconomic austerity required to decrease the demand for foreign exchange by an amount necessary to correct this shortage increases and at some point may become truly draconian. Second, the size of the depreciation of the currency necessary to reestablish equilibrium likewise increases to XR″.

INTERVENTION IN THE FOREIGN EXCHANGE MARKET

intervention government buying and selling of foreign exchange

As the previous section illustrated, there are a number of problems associated with a country attempting to "fix" its exchange rate by making its currency inconvertible. As a result, many countries "fix" their currency to the currency of another country using a different method. For example, suppose that Mexico wants to fix (peg) the value of the peso to the U.S. dollar at some exchange rate and does not want to make the peso inconvertible. Mexico can accomplish this by using **intervention** in the foreign exchange market. Intervention simply refers to the government buying and selling

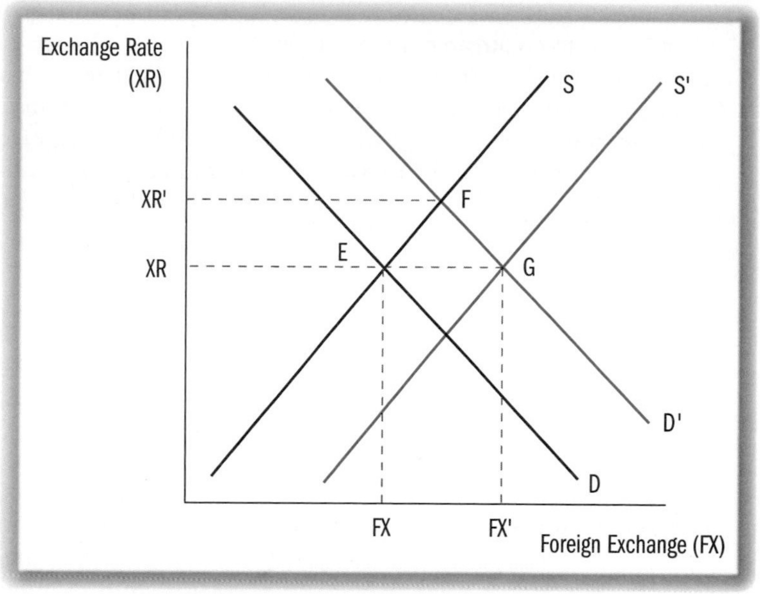

Figure 19.4 **Demand and Supply of Foreign Exchange and Government Intervention by Selling Foreign Exchange**

If the Mexican economy has a large increase in output, there will be an increase in imports and the demand for foreign exchange increases. In a floating exchange rate environment, the exchange rate would increase to XR′. In a fixed exchange rate environment, in order to maintain the current exchange rate the central bank would create an equilibrium in the foreign exchange market by supplying (selling) foreign exchange.

foreign exchange in the foreign exchange market to influence the value of the exchange rate. A country's central bank usually conducts intervention in the foreign exchange market, but this does not necessarily have to be the case. When the Mexican government sells foreign exchange, such as U.S. dollars, it increases the supply of foreign exchange in the market. This increase in the supply of dollars causes the exchange rate to change. On the other hand, if the Mexican government buys dollars in the foreign exchange market, this influences the demand for foreign exchange and causes the exchange rate to change. Likewise, any other shift in the demand or supply of foreign exchange also influences the exchange rate and would cause it to change. The "fixing" or "pegging" the value of a country's currency is illustrated in Figure 19.4. Suppose that the Mexican government wants to fix or peg the peso against the dollar at a level equal to XR. In addition, let's assume that at this exchange rate, the supply and demand for foreign exchange initially are in equilibrium at point E and the equilibrium quantity of foreign exchange exchanged in the market is denoted as FX.

Now, consider a situation where the Mexican economy is performing unusually well and economic growth is better than the historical average. As our previous analysis indicates, an increase in domestic output causes an increase in imports and the demand for foreign exchange shifts from D to D′. In a floating exchange rate environment, the equilibrium in the foreign exchange market would change from point E to F and the exchange rate would increase from XR_p to XR′. However, in the case of a fixed exchange rate, the government has made a commitment to keep the exchange rate constant at XR. In order to maintain this rate, the government (central bank) would need to create an equilibrium in the foreign exchange market at the current fixed exchange rate. This equilibrium is accomplished by the government supplying (selling) foreign exchange to the market. Of course, the government's sale of foreign exchange increases the supply from S to S′, and equilibrium in the foreign exchange market would occur at point G. In this fashion, the government maintains the exchange rate at XR and prevents a depreciation of the currency.[4] In this case, the supply and demand for foreign exchange are in equilibrium after the intervention and the equilibrium quantity of foreign exchange exchanged in the market increases from FX to FX′. In addition, Figure 19.4 could be used to illustrate the effects of an increase in U.S. interest rates relative to Mexico's interest rates. The only difference is that the change in interest rates causes a capital outflow from Mexico but the demand for foreign exchange still increases from D to D′, and the government must respond by supplying foreign exchange to the market from S to S′.

Government intervention also is used to stabilize the value of the currency in the reverse circumstances. For example, suppose that Mexico's interest rates increase relative to U.S. interest rates. In this case, capital would flow from the U.S. to Mexico, and the supply of foreign exchange increases in the foreign exchange market. We illustrate this effect in Figure 19.5, as the supply of foreign exchange shifts from S to S′. In a floating exchange rate environment, this movement in the supply of foreign exchange would translate into a change in equilibrium from point E to F, and a decrease in the exchange rate from XR to XR′. To maintain the exchange rate, the Mexican government would need to purchase foreign exchange. The government's purchase of foreign exchange would cause the demand for foreign exchange to increase from D to D′, and the equilibrium in the foreign exchange market would occur at point G. In this manner, the "fixed" or "pegged" exchange rate at XR could be maintained. In both cases, the government can maintain the exchange rate in the short run by either selling or buying foreign exchange.[5]

In the long run, the country can maintain the exchange rate so long as it can sell or buy foreign exchange. In theory, a country can buy foreign exchange (sell domestic currency) forever and keep its currency from appreciating.[6] However, a country can sell foreign exchange only for a limited period of time before it runs out. Mexico can sell dollars in the foreign exchange market only so long as it has the dollars to sell. As a result, in today's environment of mobile portfolio capital, these capital flows can be a blessing or a curse for a country with a fixed exchange rate. Inflows of portfolio capital create an additional supply of foreign exchange that allows the government to buy foreign currency with domestic currency. However, in the short run capital flows can be volatile and easily create problems when there is an outflow of portfolio capital from the country's domestic financial markets. If the exodus of capital is large

[4]In practice, the government usually would be committed to maintaining the exchange rate within some predetermined "band." The band might be a few percentage points either side of the target exchange rate. This allows the government to avoid continuously buying or selling foreign exchange in reaction to "small" changes in the exchange rate.

[5]One may have noticed that such intervention potentially is profitable. The government is buying foreign exchange when it is cheap and selling it when it is expensive.

[6]This statement ignores the long-run consequences of the intervention on the country's money supply and price level.

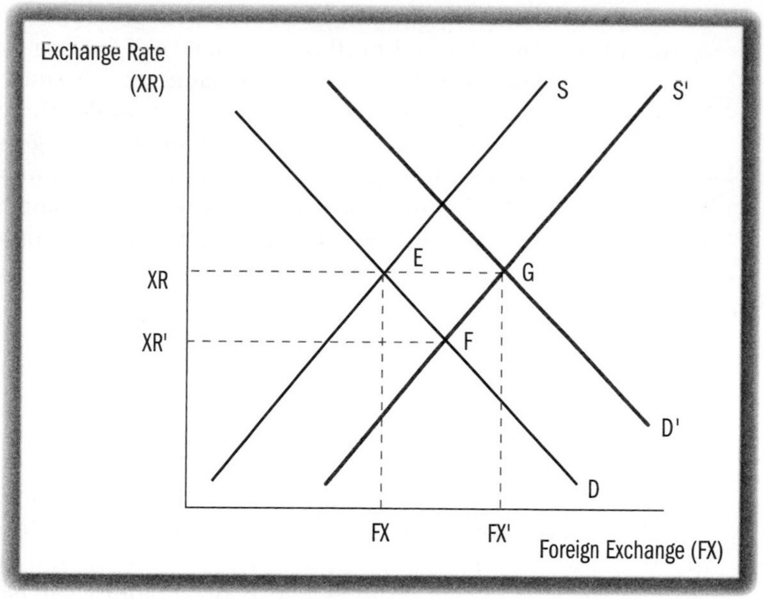

Figure 19.5 Demand and Supply of Foreign Exchange and Government—Intervention by Buying Foreign Exchange

If the Mexican economy has an increase in interest rates, an inflow of capital results and the supply of foreign exchange increases. In a floating exchange rate environment, the exchange rate would decrease to XR′. In a fixed exchange rate environment, in order to maintain the current exchange rate the central bank would create an equilibrium in the foreign exchange market by demanding (buying) foreign exchange.

enough, a "currency crisis" can emerge when the government cannot maintain the fixed exchange rate (peg) if foreign exchange reserves are insufficient in the short run. In this case the government might be forced into a major depreciation of its currency. This type of large and quick devaluation can have the serious consequences on the economy that we discussed in Chapter 17. While capital inflows can make it easier to maintain a pegged exchange rate, capital outflows can lead to a currency crisis. As a result of the effects of capital flows within a fixed exchange rate system, many countries have adopted restrictions or limits on inflows and outflows of portfolio capital.

Macroeconomic Adjustment under Fixed Exchange Rates: Part I

If a country can easily manage its exchange rate through intervention, then why don't more countries "fix" their exchange rates? This is a good question because businesses and individuals are subjected to the increased risk of adverse movements in exchange rates in a flexible exchange rate environment. As most of the industrialized countries of the world have adopted floating (flexible) exchange rates and have taken on the increase in risk associated with them, there must be some difficulties associated with a fixed exchange rate system. This is exactly the case. In our description of government intervention (Figure 19.4), the increase in the demand for foreign exchange by individuals and firms causes the government to intervene in the foreign exchange market by supplying foreign currency. At the fixed (pegged) exchange rate, the country's private sector is currently running a current account deficit. In Figure 19.4 the private sector inflows (supply) and outflows (demand) of foreign exchange are represented by points E and G, respectively. The government must finance this private sector deficit in the current account, i.e., intervention. For a while, the government can finance this deficit by selling its foreign exchange. However, the government cannot sell foreign exchange indefinitely. At some point, the government would run out of foreign exchange to sell. When this situation occurs, the government is forced to either depreciate its currency, make its currency inconvertible, or adopt a macroeconomic austerity program. Over time, in order for a country to maintain the "fixed" exchange rate, internal balance must be adjusted to be consistent with the fixed exchange rate. In this section we will study how this macroeconomic adjustment occurs.

In order to understand the adjustment of internal balance with fixed exchange rates, we will use the following example. Assume that a country's domestic economy is growing rapidly, and as a result, the demand for foreign exchange by the private sector increases. This increase in the demand for foreign exchange causes the private sector to have a current account deficit. This deficit at the current fixed exchange rate requires that the government sell foreign exchange in the foreign exchange market to maintain the exchange rate. As a result of these actions, there are several interesting consequences. To examine their effects on the domestic economy, we illustrate the initial position of the domestic economy in Figure 19.6. In this figure, aggregate demand and aggregate supply are represented by AD and AS, respectively. We assume

Figure 19.6 The Effect of Intervention on the Domestic Economy

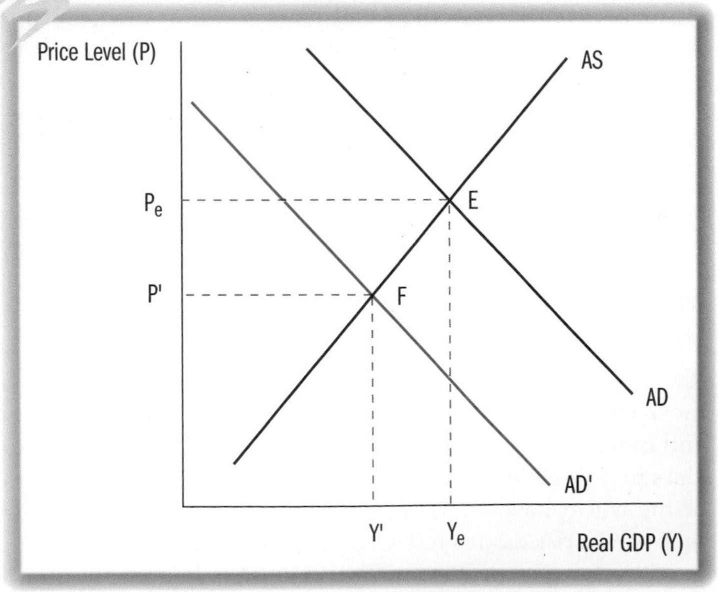

As the central bank intervenes in the foreign exchange market by selling foreign exchange to maintain the exchange rate, the domestic money supply falls. As the money supply falls, the economy's aggregate demand falls and both real output and the price level fall.

that the initial equilibrium of the domestic economy is at the full employment level of output Y_e, with the economy's price level P_e as represented by point E. If the country is fortunate, the current account deficit will provide enough of a drag on aggregate demand that the economy will not push past this full employment level. If the government has sufficient reserves of foreign exchange, it may be able to intervene simply until economic growth slows.

In fact, if the government does nothing but intervene in the foreign exchange market, the situation will quickly correct itself. This correction occurs because when a country intervenes in the foreign exchange market, the intervention changes the country's domestic money supply. While this effect on the domestic money supply is not very obvious, it is fairly straightforward. In this case, the government sells foreign exchange in the foreign exchange market to maintain the exchange rate. As it sells foreign exchange to individuals and firms, it is buying domestic currency from them. The government basically is swapping foreign currency for domestic currency. However, there is an important distinction. Foreign exchange is not part of the domestic money supply. In this process of intervention, the private sector gets more foreign exchange but has less domestic currency (money). By selling foreign exchange to the private sector, the government has reduced the economy's domestic money supply.[7] In particular, as the government sells foreign exchange, it reduces the country's monetary base by the amount of the intervention. As the monetary base contracts, the domestic supply of money also will contract by a multiple of the amount of the intervention.

In this case, the government intervention has two major effects. First, in the short run, the intervention stabilizes the exchange rate as we presented in Figure 19.4. Second, the intervention has set into motion an automatic adjustment process that virtually guarantees that the private-sector current account deficit will not persist in the long run. By examining Figure 19.6, we can see the automatic adjustment process of the domestic economy that occurs because of the intervention.

Because government intervention has caused the domestic money supply to fall, there is an impact on aggregate demand that must be considered. As the money supply falls, the aggregate demand of the economy falls from AD to AD′. The expanding domestic economy that was the genesis of the intervention would cease to be a problem as the equilibrium changes from E to F, and the level of output and the price level both decline. As this occurs the government's need to intervene in the foreign exchange market also would diminish, as falling output reduces the country's demand for imports (foreign exchange). In this case, the government has maintained the fixed exchange rate by reducing the equilibrium level of output or the rate of economic growth.

At first glance, this fixed exchange rate system may seem to be rather convenient. In fact, for some economists, the automatic adjustment process just described is preferred to the flexible exchange rate system. This fixed exchange rate arrangement has the advantage of not only "fixing" the exchange rate but also automatically adjusting the domestic economy to a sustainable external equilibrium. The level of economic growth that results in a private-sector current account deficit (surplus) automatically leads to a reduction (increase) in the domestic money supply. These changes in the money supply automatically change the domestic economy's aggregate demand and

---

[7]The effect of selling foreign exchange is almost exactly analogous to the central bank selling a government bond.

move the equilibrium level of output and the price level. The movements in the domestic equilibrium would continue until the external balance of a country balanced. Maintaining a fixed exchange rate through intervention means that a country cannot use discretionary monetary policy to influence the domestic economy. This loss of monetary policy occurs because in order for the country to maintain a fixed exchange rate, the domestic monetary base and, thus the money supply becomes a function of the country's external balance to the degree in which the government must intervene in the foreign exchange market.

Macroeconomic Adjustment under Fixed Exchange Rates: Part II

We just examined a situation in which the government fixed (pegged) the exchange rate via intervention in the foreign exchange market. With this fixed exchange rate system, intervention automatically adjusts the domestic economy to create a sustainable balanced *external* equilibrium. Total inflows and outflows of foreign exchange are balanced at the predetermined fixed exchange rate. As the old saying goes in economics, "there's no such thing as a free lunch." Such a conceptually consistent system comes with costs as well as benefits. Intervention in the foreign exchange market has the power to change the domestic supply of money. In a very real sense, a country's monetary policy becomes a captive of the external balance. If the external balance is in deficit (surplus), intervention reduces (increases) the supply of money and the economy adjusts to the lower (higher) money supply. The problem or the cost that this system imposes is that these automatic changes occur without regard to the state of the domestic economy.

For example, assume that a country's external balance is in deficit. Further, assume that the domestic economy is operating at an equilibrium level of output that is less than full employment. This situation implies that unemployment is higher than usual and reducing it is the primary domestic objective. Inflation is not much of a problem or it is of secondary importance. Because of the intervention in the foreign exchange market, the country's domestic money supply would still decline even though the domestic economy was below full employment. The country's external balance would be brought into equilibrium. However, the country's internal balance, that is, the balance between price stability and full employment, would be forced to adjust. In this case, the equilibrium level of output would contract and the economy's level of unemployment would become worse. To say the least, this adjustment is less than optimal for domestic policymakers. In some cases, the change in the money supply that the government's intervention causes will be consistent with the domestic economy's internal balance, while in other cases, there may be an inconsistency between a country's external and internal balance requirements.

This dilemma is summarized in Table 19.1. The first column indicates the state of internal balance or whether the domestic economy's most important problem is a lack of output (unemployment) or inflation. The second column indicates the position of the country's external balance (surplus or deficit). The third and fourth columns list the appropriate government policy response to solve internal and external balance problems, respectively. The last column indicates whether the monetary policy required to solve the country's internal and external balance problems are consistent.

Table 19.1 Combinations of Economic Conditions and Policy Response Requirements

Internal Conditions	External Conditions	Policy Response to Internal Balance	Policy Response to External Balance	Nature of Situation
Unemployment	Surplus	Expansionary	Expansionary	Consistent
Unemployment	Deficit	Expansionary	Contractionary	Inconsistent
Inflation	Surplus	Contractionary	Expansionary	Inconsistent
Inflation	Deficit	Contractionary	Contractionary	Consistent

Notice that there are two cases in the table where the monetary policy that solves the external balance problem is consistent with what is necessary to achieve or maintain internal balance. However, there are also two cases labeled inconsistent. In these two cases, a conflict emerges between what is necessary to maintain the exchange rate and the state of the domestic economy.

It is precisely these two cells that make a fixed (pegged) exchange-rate system a problem for some countries. Under a fixed exchange rate system, these two cases require the country to sacrifice the interests of internal balance in order to maintain the country's external balance. For example, if an external deficit occurs when the economy is at or less than full employment, the response of monetary policy (contraction of the money supply) that automatically occurs will move the economy further away from full employment. In this situation, the automatic adjustment requires the country to suffer a recession to maintain the fixed exchange rate. Also, if a country has an external surplus coupled with a period of inflation or a rapid period of economic growth, the response of monetary policy (expansion of the money supply) that automatically occurs will move the economy to even higher inflation and/or even more rapid economic growth. This would be the macroeconomic equivalent of pouring gasoline on a fire, as the country's external balance would be restored at the risk of additional domestic inflation.

Table 19.1 illustrates the dilemma of fixed exchange rates for governments. On the one hand, practically all participants in international trade prefer exchange rate stability over instability, and fixed exchange rates reduce or eliminate exchange-rate risk. On the other hand, a fixed exchange rate system virtually guarantees that from time to time there will be a mismatch between the monetary policy that is required and the country's external and/or internal balance. In the short run, a country has two ways out of this dilemma.

Fiscal Policy and Internal Balance

First, the government can assign monetary policy the role of achieving a country's external balance and can assign fiscal policy the role of achieving the country's internal balance objective. Under a fixed exchange rate system, fiscal policy can be highly effective in changing the equilibrium level of output and the price level. For simplicity, assume that the government initially has a balanced budget—that is, that government spending equals government taxes. Now, assume that the government adopts an

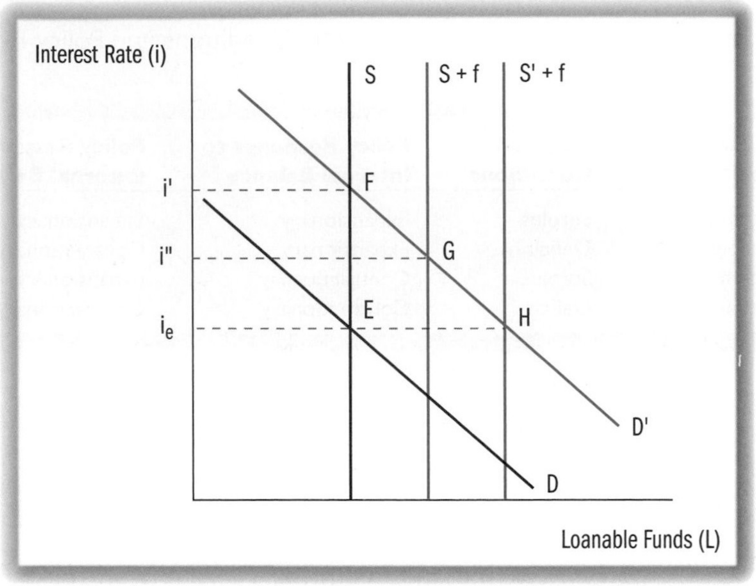

Figure 19.7 Supply and Demand for Loanable Funds and Expansionary Fiscal Policy

An expansionary fiscal policy causes an increase in the demand for loanable funds. In a closed economy this would cause interest rates to rise. In an open economy the rise in interest rates causes an inflow of capital and an increase in the supply of loanable funds (S + f). This policy also causes the central bank to intervene in the foreign exchange market and sell domestic currency causing an additional increase in the supply of loanable funds (S′ + f). The Net result is that expansionary fiscal policy put less upward pressure on interest rates.

expansionary fiscal policy. As such, the government chooses to adopt some combination of lower taxes and/or higher government spending.

Under these conditions, the expansionary fiscal policy leads to a government budget deficit that must be financed. In this case, we assume that the government borrows the shortfall of revenue. The government's extra borrowing has a predictable effect on the interest rate, as shown in Figure 19.7. Like our examples in Chapter 18, the figure illustrates the demand for loanable funds, D, and the economy's supply of loanable funds, S. In this situation, the equilibrium in the loanable funds market before the expansionary fiscal policy was at point E, with an equilibrium interest rate of i_e. As the government adopts an expansionary fiscal policy, the government's added demand for loanable funds will cause the demand to increase from D to D′. With only domestic loanable funds available, the equilibrium changes from E to F, and the interest rate rises from i_e to i′. In an open economy with freely flowing international capital, the rise in interest rates causes an inflow of foreign capital as foreign investors see a higher rate of return in another country. As foreign capital moves into the domestic market, the domestic supply of loanable funds is augmented by foreign capital. This additional supply of loanable funds from foreigners is illustrated in Figure 19.7 as a rightward shift of the supply of loanable funds from S to S + f. Thus, the inflow of foreign capital changes the equilibrium from F to G, and lowers domestic interest rates from i′ to i″.

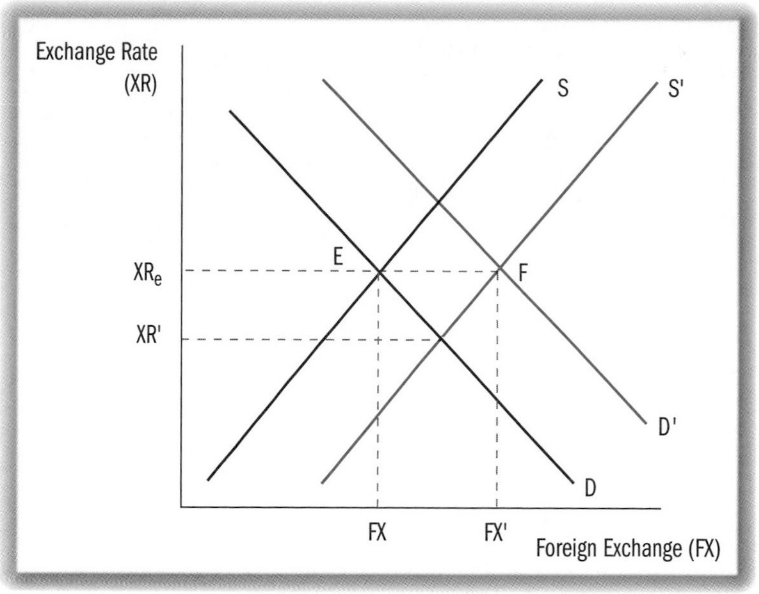

Figure 19.8 **Effects of Expansionary Fiscal Policy on the Foreign Exchange Market**

An expansionary fiscal policy leads to an inflow of capital. This, in turn, causes the supply of foreign exchange to increase and the domestic currency to appreciate. In order to maintain the exchange rate, the central bank would create an equilibrium in the foreign exchange market by demanding (buying) foreign exchange.

As shown in Figure 19.7, a larger federal government budget deficit tends to increase domestic interest rates, and the higher domestic interest rate causes an inflow of foreign capital into the country. The capital flow between countries has an effect on the foreign exchange market that is illustrated in Figure 19.8. The demand and supply of foreign exchange before the expansionary fiscal policy are shown as D and S, respectively. The initial equilibrium in the foreign exchange market is illustrated at point E and the country's fixed exchange rate is XR_e. When the government adopts an expansionary fiscal policy, the inflow of foreign capital requires that foreign investors first sell foreign exchange (i.e., buy domestic currency). The effect of the capital flow is clear. The supply of foreign exchange increases from S to S′ and the country's exchange rate would tend to fall from XR_e to XR′. Since this country has a fixed exchange rate, the fall in the exchange rate (appreciation of the currency) is not allowed to occur. In this case, the government must intervene in the foreign exchange market and buy foreign exchange. This intervention causes the demand for foreign exchange to increase from D to D′. In this manner the "fixed" or "pegged" exchange rate is maintained as equilibrium in the foreign exchange market changes from E to F.

The secondary effect of the government intervention is that the domestic money supply changes. In this case, when the government buys foreign exchange it also sells domestic currency, and the domestic money supply increases. The effect of the increase in the domestic money supply is to increase the amount of loanable funds available in the domestic economy. The supply of loanable funds in Figure 19.7

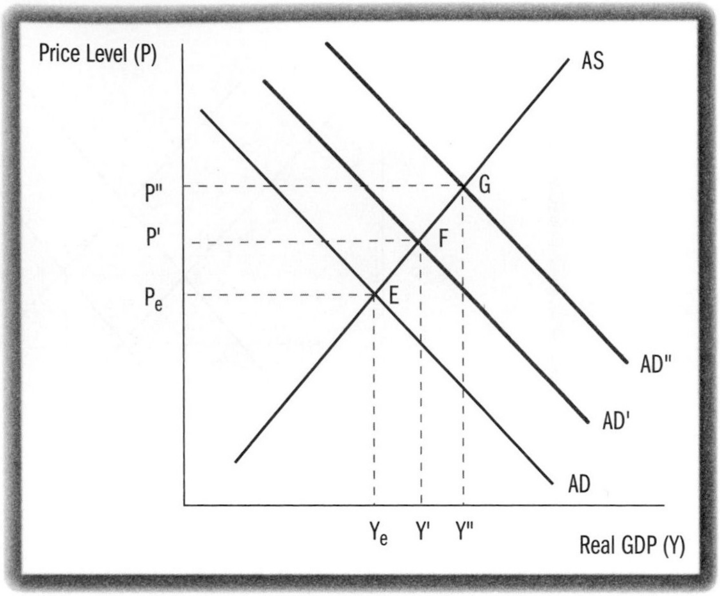

Figure 19.9 Effects of Expansionary Fiscal Policy on Equilibrium Output and Price Level

An expansionary fiscal policy causes the aggregate demand curve to increase. In a closed economy, the increase in aggregate demand would cause an increase in both real output and the price level. In an open economy, the initial effect of this policy is to increase aggregate demand. This policy also causes the central bank to intervene in the foreign exchange market by demanding (buying) foreign exchange. Aggregate demand increases again, making fiscal policy more effective in changing equilibrium output.

increases from S + f to S′ + f, the equilibrium in the loanable funds market changes from G to H, and domestic interest rates continue to decline from i″ toward i_e.

The Effects of Expanisonary and Contractionary Fiscal Policy

At this point in our analysis, we have not examined the effects of expansionary fiscal policy on the domestic economy. To examine these effects we employ the aggregate demand/aggregate supply model. Figure 19.9 illustrates the economy's equilibrium before the expansionary fiscal policy. Initially, the economy's aggregate demand is represented by AD and the economy is in equilibrium at point E, with real GDP at Y_e and the price level at P_e. As the government adopts an expansionary fiscal policy, the aggregate demand curve increases from AD to AD′. The initial effect of this expansionary fiscal policy is to move the economy's equilibrium from E to F and increase both domestic output to Y′ and the domestic price level to P′. In addition to this initial effect, the intervention in the foreign exchange market and the resulting increase in the money supply cause aggregate demand to shift even further to the right from AD′ to AD″. This additional increase in aggregate demand changes the economy's equilibrium from F to G, and the equilibrium output level and price level to Y″ and P″, respectively. The net result is that in an open economy with capital mobility and fixed exchange rates, the effects of expansionary fiscal policy are more pronounced.

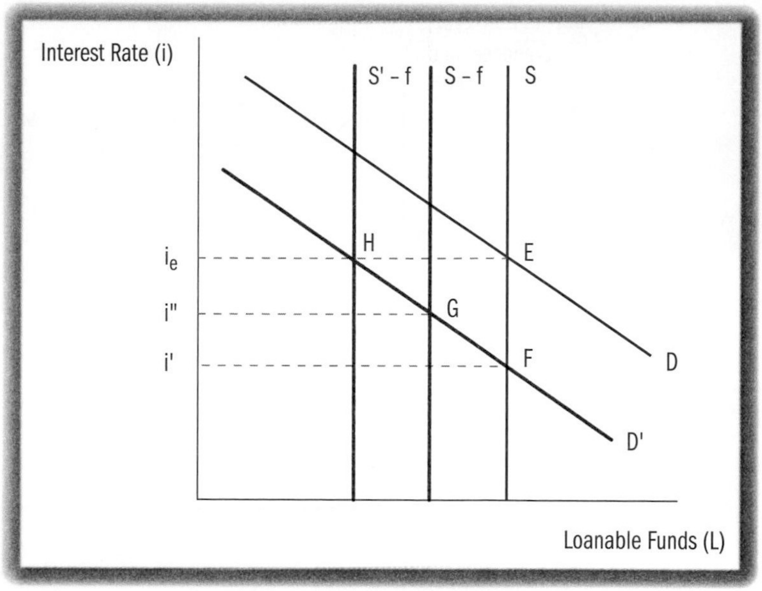

Figure 19.10 Supply and Demand for Loanable Funds and Contractionary Fiscal Policy

A contractionary fiscal policy causes a decrease in the demand for loanable funds. In a closed economy this would cause interest rates to fall. In an open economy, the fall in interest rates causes an outflow of capital and a decrease in the supply of loanable funds (S − f). This policy also causes the central bank to intervene and sell foreign exchange, causing an additional decrease in the supply of loanable funds (S′ − f). The net result is that a contractionary fiscal policy puts downward pressure on interest rates when the economy is open.

The effects of contractionary fiscal policy on the economy are similar but reversed. The case of contractionary fiscal policy entails some combination of higher taxes and/or lower government spending. As such, the policy reduces a government budget deficit or increases the size of the government's surplus. As in our previous example, we begin our analysis of the effects using the supply and demand for loanable funds as illustrated in Figure 19.10. In Figure 19.7, D and S represent the demand and supply curves for loanable funds, respectively. The initial equilibrium is at point E and an interest rate of i_e.

Everything else equal, if the government now adopts a contractionary fiscal policy, the economy's demand for loanable funds is reduced from D to D′. As a result, equilibrium in the loanable funds market changes from point E to F and the contractionary fiscal policy initially lowers the interest rate from i_e to i′. In an open economy with capital mobility, the lower domestic interest rate affects capital flows. Domestic and foreign investors have a tendency to invest less capital in the domestic economy and/or they will invest more capital abroad. This capital outflow affects the supply of loanable funds available domestically. This effect is illustrated as a leftward shift of the supply of loanable funds in Figure 19.10 from S to S − f. The outflow of capital changes the equilibrium in the loanable funds market from point F to G, and interest rates rise from i′ to i″.

A contractionary fiscal policy lowers the federal government budget deficit and decreases domestic interest rates. The lower domestic interest rates cause an outflow

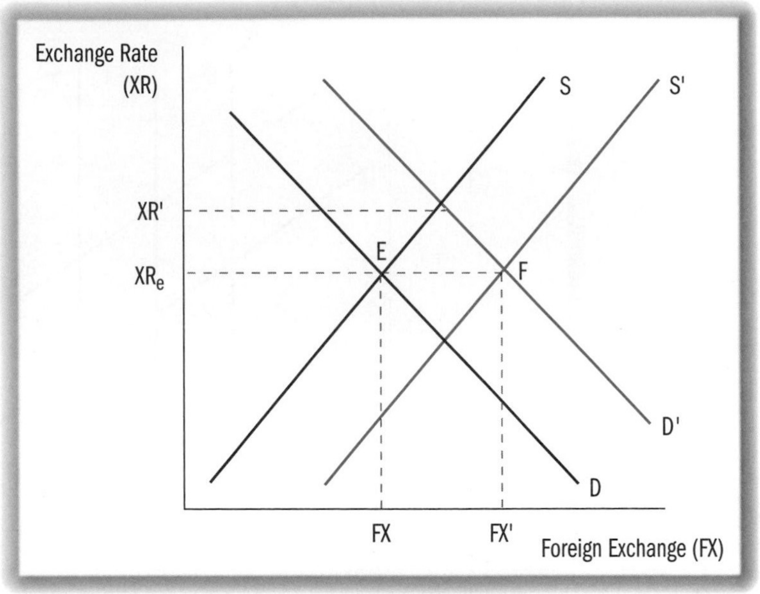

Figure 19.11 Effects of Contractionary Fiscal Policy on the Foreign Exchange Market

A contractionary fiscal policy causes an outflow of capital and the demand for foreign exchange increases. In order to maintain the exchange rate, the central bank would create and equilibrium in the foreign exchange market by supplying (selling) foreign exchange.

of capital. The effect of a contractionary fiscal policy on the foreign exchange market is fairly obvious. As domestic interest rates fall, outflows of capital occur. As investors move capital to foreign countries, the demand for foreign exchange in the foreign exchange market increases. This effect is illustrated in Figure 19.11, where the demand for foreign exchange has increased from D to D′. As a result of this change in the demand for foreign exchange, the exchange rate is under pressure to increase from XR_e to XR′. Since this country has a fixed exchange rate, the depreciation of the currency is not allowed to occur. In this case, the government must intervene in the foreign exchange market and sell foreign exchange. This intervention causes the supply of foreign exchange to increase from S to S′. In this way the "fixed" or "pegged" exchange rate is maintained as the equilibrium in the foreign exchange market changes from E to F.

The secondary effect of the government intervention is that the domestic money supply changes. In this case, when the government sells foreign exchange it also buys domestic currency, and the domestic money supply decreases. The effect of this decrease is to decrease the amount of loanable funds available in the domestic economy. In Figure 19.10, this is shown as a decrease in the supply of loanable funds from S − f to S′ − f. The equilibrium in the loanable funds market changes from point G to H and domestic interest rates continue to rise from i″ toward i_e.

Now that we know how contractionary fiscal policy impacts the loanable funds market and the foreign exchange market, we can analyze their effects on the macroeconomy. These effects are shown using the aggregate demand/aggregate supply

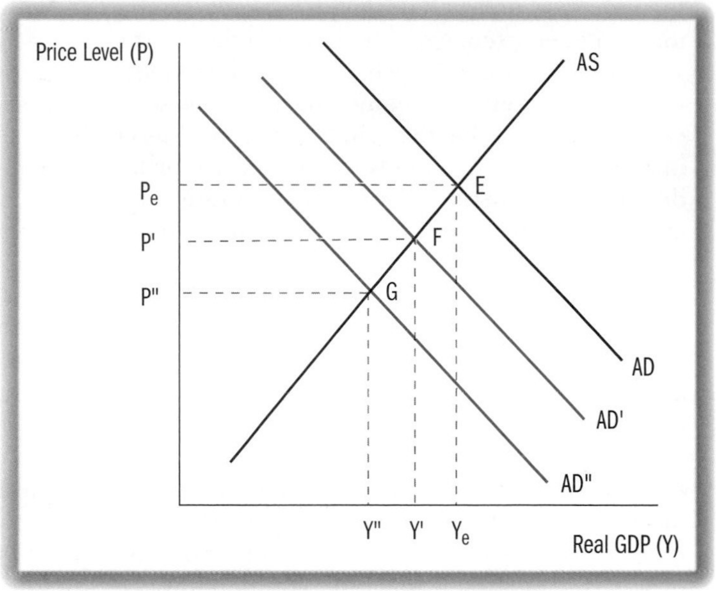

Figure 19.12 Effects of Contractionary Fiscal Policy on Equilibrium Output and Price Level

With a contractionary fiscal policy, aggregate demand decreases. In a closed economy, the decrease in aggregate demand would cause a decrease in both real output and the price level. In an open economy, the initial effect of this policy is to decrease aggregate demand. This policy also causes the central bank to intervene in the foreign exchange market by supplying (selling) foreign exchange, which causes aggregate demand to decrease again. This makes fiscal policy more effective in changing equilibrium output.

model in Figure 19.12. Before the contractionary fiscal policy is implemented, the domestic economy is in equilibrium at point E, with an equilibrium output level of Y_e and a price level of P_e. As the government adopts a contractionary fiscal policy, aggregate demand decreases from AD to AD′. The initial effect of this contractionary policy is to change the economy's equilibrium from point E to F, and decrease both domestic output to Y′ and the domestic price level to P′. In addition to this initial effect, the intervention in the foreign exchange market and the resulting decrease in the money supply cause aggregate demand to shift even further to the left, from AD′ to AD″. In turn, this additional decrease in aggregate demand changes the economy's equilibrium from point F to G, and the level of equilibrium output and price level to Y″ and P″, respectively. The net result is that in an open economy with capital mobility and fixed exchange rates, the effects of contractionary fiscal policy are more pronounced.

Sterilization

In the preceding discussion of impact of fiscal policy on the domestic economy, we assumed that monetary policy was assigned the task of achieving external balance. In order for the monetary policy to accomplish this, it was necessary to assume that intervention was allowed to affect the money supply of the country. In this section, we will examine the situation where intervention in the foreign exchange market is not allowed to change the money supply. This is one way of solving the mismatch between the monetary policy that is required and a country's external and/or internal balance under a fixed exchange-rate system in the short run.

sterilization the process of insulating the money supply from changes that would be caused by intervention

As we will see, it is technically possible to separate monetary policy from intervention in the foreign exchange market. This separation is known as **sterilization**. For example, assume that the private sector increases its demand for foreign exchange. This increase in demand causes the private sector to have a current account deficit. This deficit at the current fixed exchange rate requires the government to sell foreign exchange to maintain the exchange rate in the foreign exchange market. This sale of foreign exchange causes a decrease in the domestic monetary base and the money supply. A government (central bank) in a developed country that has an active bond market can easily offset this effect through open market operations. The government knows exactly how much the intervention has reduced the monetary base. This is because the government knows how much foreign exchange it sold and how much domestic currency it bought in the foreign exchange market.

In response to this intervention, the government could conduct open market operations in the domestic bond market by purchasing an equivalent amount of bonds. The intervention in the foreign exchange market reduces the monetary base. However, this reduction in the monetary base can be sterilized by purchasing the equivalent amount of bonds. The net effect of intervention and sterilization on the domestic supply of money is therefore zero. In principle, a government can keep the domestic money supply insulated from the intervention in the foreign exchange market.

Although sterilized intervention allows a government to separate its monetary policy from the effects of intervention in the foreign exchange market, there are several problems associated with its use. Sterilized intervention works best when the short-run deviations in the exchange rate from purchasing power parity are relatively small. In this case, intervention can be used to smooth out small deviations from purchasing power parity that might occur from time to time. If intervention in the foreign exchange market is sterilized, it is necessary that the exchange rate be kept fairly close to purchasing power parity. If not, there is a high probability that the policy will fail.

A common example of failure will illustrate the point. Let's assume the government is committed to a fixed exchange rate by selling foreign exchange. In order to do this in the long run, domestic inflation must be similar to foreign inflation. However, what often occurs in this situation is that domestic inflation is significantly greater than foreign inflation. In this case, the government will find itself in an unsustainable situation. It intervenes in the foreign exchange market to support the exchange rate and sterilizes the restrictive effects on the money supply. Over time, the exchange rate becomes increasingly overvalued. At some point the government's supply of foreign exchange becomes inadequate to maintain the exchange rate and the currency must be devalued. This can lead to a sharp devaluation with the attendant consequences that we discussed in Chapter 17.

Does this mean that sterilized intervention is a hopeless case? Not necessarily. There are two ways that sterilized intervention can work fairly well. The first involves a slight variation of what is meant by a fixed exchange rate. As we have just seen, it is difficult to fix (peg) a nominal exchange rate because the monetary policy necessary to maintain a nominal peg may at times conflict with an optimal monetary policy for the domestic economy. A useful variation in many cases is to fix (peg) the real exchange rate. In this case the nominal exchange rate would be allowed to change fairly

crawling peg the term used to describe the process of pegging (fixing) the real exchange rate

frequently. What is held constant is the real exchange rate. The common term for this system is a **crawling peg.** In order to explain how a crawling peg works, consider the equation below that we used to describe the real exchange rate.[8]

$$[RXR(\$/FC)] = [R(\$/FC)][P_{FC}/P_{US}]$$

Once again, notice that the real exchange rate (RXR), defined as dollars per unit of foreign currency, is equal to the nominal exchange rate, R, multiplied by the ratio of foreign prices, P_{FC}, to U.S. prices, P_{US}. The difficulty with maintaining a nominal exchange rate peg is that it requires the ratio of changes in domestic prices to changes in foreign prices to be constant. This means that the nominal exchange rate may be pegged but the real exchange rate is fluctuating. An alternative policy with respect to the exchange rate is to peg the exchange rate in real terms. Fortunately, it is not difficult for policy makers to maintain the real exchange rate. One simply has to calculate the differences in the two rates of inflation and allow the nominal exchange rate to change by that amount. In practice, the country may set a pre-announced rate of change in the nominal exchange rate based on these differences. Although participants in the foreign exchange market are facing an exchange rate that is changing, the amount of change is known in advance. Usually, the rate is changed on a pre-announced schedule such as daily or weekly. Even though the nominal exchange rate is changing, the real exchange rate is being held approximately constant. There is still a need for intervention to smooth out small changes in the actual exchange rate from the announced rate. However, since the real exchange rate is fixed, the exchange rate is more stable than it would be without intervention. Monetary policy in this case can now be used to focus on domestic economic conditions, *and* the exchange rate is in a real sense "stable."

Pegging the Exchange Rate with Monetary Policy

There is one last method of fixing the exchange rate that will require some intervention in the foreign exchange market from time to time. In some cases, a country may be willing to sacrifice discretionary domestic monetary policy in the interest of maintaining a fixed exchange rate. This choice may seem extreme, but for some countries it is quite sensible. Suppose that in an economic sense two countries are quite closely related. This relationship may have a couple of quantifiable aspects. First, the two countries may trade extensively with one another because of a combination of location, language, and similarity of business environments. Second, if the relationship is truly close, the correlation between changes in the GDPs of the two countries may be rather high. In many cases, this occurs because one country's GDP may be substantially larger than that of the other. In these circumstances, the smaller country might be fixing its exchange rate in nominal terms to the currency of the larger country. Citizens in both countries benefit from the security of a fixed exchange rate that makes trade and investment less risky, as a fixed exchange rate eliminates the exchange rate risk. As we indicated earlier in the chapter, there is frequently a cost imposed on the

[8]One might want to look back at the section describing the real exchange rate in Chapter 16 to review the concept of the real exchange rate.

country for adopting a fixed exchange rate. The smaller country's monetary policy may have to be sacrificed to keep the exchange rate fixed. However, in this circumstance can the smaller country really influence its domestic economy through monetary policy? If the larger country falls into a recession, there is a high probability that the smaller country will follow. In this case, would a change in monetary policy in the smaller country make much of a difference? If not, then the smaller country may feel that the most sensible long run policy run is to passively follow the monetary policy of the larger country. There may not be much of a loss in doing so, and the benefit is that exchange rate stability is maintained. This may require occasional intervention in the foreign exchange market to maintain the fixed exchange rate. However, in this case whether or not the intervention is sterilized or not is irrelevant. The smaller country will have a growth rate of the money supply and an inflation rate that is nearly identical to that of the larger country. Intervention is simply a way for the exchange rate to be made sufficiently stable in the short run.

CURRENCY UNIONS

currency union a situation in which two or more countries use the same currency

Considering all of the potential difficulties with maintaining a fixed exchange rate, one can take the analysis a step further. If maintaining a fixed exchange rate is such a headache for government policymakers, then why not simply do away with the problem of trying to fix the value of the currency against other currencies? If two countries are fairly committed to maintaining exchange rate stability between their two respective currencies, at some point a logical thing to do is to consider merging the two currencies and making a common currency. This is called a **currency union**. Whether or not countries take such a step depends on a number of factors. As with any economic policy decision, there are a number of benefits and costs associated with a currency union. In making this decision, the factors to consider are fairly straightforward. Unfortunately, the weighing of the costs and benefits is not exactly precise and the final decision on whether or not to form a currency union cannot be made with exact certainty.[9]

What, then, are the issues associated with adopting a currency union? Before the creation of the Euro, Austria had pegged its currency, the schilling, in nominal terms to the German Mark. Assume that the two countries were considering adopting a common currency. In this case, we will examine the costs and benefits from the Austrian perspective. Would it be a good idea for Austria to move from its current policy to a monetary union with Germany? What factors should be considered if Austria wanted to form a currency union with Germany?

monetary efficiency gain the gains that accrue to countries using a common currency

The first benefit is known as a **monetary efficiency gain**. Monetary efficiency gains are the gains that are derived from not having to change currencies in order to buy or sell goods or services across national borders. Since Germany and Austria trade heavily with one another, every time an Austrian or a German firm wishes to engage in a cross-border transaction there is an explicit loss in exchanging currency and an implicit loss of time and risk. To get some idea of this loss, assume that each of the fifty

[9] The original contribution on the analysis fixing an exchange rate is Robert A. Mundell, "The Theory of Optimum Currency Areas," *American Economic Review* 51, September 1961, pp. 717–25

states in the U.S. had a different currency. Conducting business among the various states would become much more complicated. Some of these monetary efficiency gains can accrue to both countries if they have a fixed exchange rate. However, even with a perfect nominal peg, both countries could gain further by adopting a common currency. A common currency between Austria and Germany would be easier for citizens of both countries to deal with than having two separate currencies. The largest cost for both countries is the loss of an autonomous monetary policy. If either country wished to pursue an independent monetary policy, it could not do so with a currency union. At some point in time, the joint monetary policy for the two countries would be less than optimal for each individual country. With a currency union, there would be an **economic stability loss** due to the currency union. Economic stability losses occur as a result of the inability of a country in a currency union to conduct an independent monetary policy. Whether or not a currency union is a good idea depends on the magnitude of the monetary efficiency gains versus the potential losses in terms of economic stability. What we now want to consider are the factors that tend to influence the size of the gains and losses for each country.

economic stability loss **the losses associated with the absence of an independent monetary policy for a country participating in a currency union**

A country's monetary efficiency gains are influenced by a number of factors. Although the gains on any one transaction are relatively small, the total gains can be quite large, and the gains increase as the volume of trade between the countries joining the monetary union increases. This establishes a general rule with regard to a currency union. The greater the amount of trade between the countries, the larger the monetary efficiency gains will be if the countries move to a common currency. Just how much trade is required between the countries to make the union profitable? Economists really cannot answer this question precisely. What we can say is that there would be more gains in a monetary union between Germany and Austria than there would be if the countries were Germany and, say, Portugal. This is because Germany and Austria trade more with one another than either one does with Portugal. The greater the trade, the greater the benefits is a useful generalization. However, there is not some type of precise cutoff point where a currency union is a good idea on one side and not a good idea on the other.

The gains of a monetary union can be extrapolated to the movement of factors of production between the countries joining the union. If capital is mobile between Germany and Austria, there will be additional gains for both currency traders and investors. Austrian banks might well have branches in Germany, and vice versa. For financial institutions, it is easier to set up branches across borders and conduct their business in a common currency. A common currency would have the benefits of making capital flows easier in the sense that it would now be unnecessary to exchange one currency for another, which increases the efficiency of the financial markets in both countries. The same type of argument would apply to flows of FDI between the countries. It would be easier to make direct investments across borders if you did not have to convert currencies. More importantly, not needing to convert currencies would eliminate some uncertainty with respect to the return on the investment. A direct investment could easily have a twenty- or thirty-year useful life. To calculate a possible return on this type of investment invariably would require "assuming" what the exchange rate would be over a long time horizon. The probability that this assumption might be wrong could easily wipe out expected profits in certain years. By forming a currency union, investors in both countries would be more likely to invest across borders.

Likewise, there are several factors that influence the losses in terms of economic stability of each of the countries joining the union. If labor can (and most importantly does) freely migrate between Germany and Austria, the losses associated with economic stability are reduced. For example, suppose that Austria suffers a recession and unemployment in Austria rises. If Austrian workers can and are willing to move to Germany to seek employment, the effects of the recession in Austria would be less severe. As a result of the labor force movement into Germany, it is not necessary for Austria to try to pursue expansionary monetary and fiscal policies in order to stimulate domestic demand. Second, the more similar the two countries' average rates of inflation, the smaller the economic stability losses in both countries. If the social preferences for inflation are similar in the two countries, there is less of a chance that the joint monetary policy would be undesirable for the two countries. Third, the economic stability losses are smaller if there is some form of common fiscal policy within the countries joining the union. In any country, fiscal policy tends to work to transfer income from faster growing regions to slower growing ones. If the taxation and spending systems of the two countries were somewhat integrated, the losses in economic stability would be diminished. The final factor is the most important in determining the size of the economic stability losses. The economic stability losses will be smaller the higher the correlation of GDP is between the two countries. For instance, if Germany were in a recession, there is a high probability that Austria would be in a recession. Thus, a joint monetary policy would most likely be appropriate for both countries. The lower the correlation is, the higher the probability that a joint monetary policy would be inappropriate for one of the countries. For the most part, it is exactly these arguments that lead countries within Europe to adopt the Euro, as the group of 12 countries determined that the benefits of a currency union outweighed the costs. At this point, the U.K. is considering joining the currency union and is weighing the benefits of joining against the costs.

THE INCOMPATIBLE TRINITY

In the previous two chapters, we covered two separate types of exchange rate systems. Most of the world's countries have opted for some form of floating exchange rate. This sort of system has the advantage of making it easier to manage the domestic economy or internal balance. In the following chapter, we covered the macroeconomics of a fixed exchange rate system. In that chapter, we showed that having fixed exchange rates makes monetary policy less effective. As one may have noticed, the existence of a fixed exchange rate as a policy goal may make internal balance more difficult to manage. In our discussion of the choice of an exchange rate system, this is a point that has been lingering in the background but not explicitly brought out. In part, the omission is present because, to economists, it has become deeply embedded in our thinking—so much sothat we typically say nothing about it. However, if one is not an economist, talking about the "incompatible trinity" (sometimes referred to as the "trilemma") has some value. In the 1950s, Robert Mundell pointed out that three policies were fundamentally incompatible. These policies are perfect capital mobility, fixed exchange rates, and an effective monetary policy. A country can accomplish two out of the three, but not all three together. In the previous two chapters, we have already shown this, to an extent. If the exchange rate is floating, monetary policy will be effective. If the exchange rate is fixed, monetary policy becomes less effective. However, in both chapters we assumed the existence of perfect capital mobility.

A floating exchange rate implies a conscious decision concerning the incompatible trinity. Countries using this system have chosen to let the exchange rate float and to allow capital mobility. This is not the only solution to the problem. As we will see in the next chapter, there have been other choices made at other times. In the past, countries chose to fix the exchange rate, allow capital mobility, and not be as concerned with monetary policy. Another type of international monetary system was designed for the policy choice of fixed exchange rates with a focus on internal balance. As we will see, this system eventually failed because it also allowed capital mobility. Since capital mobility was allowed, there was no explicit solution to the incompatible trinity. In any case, as we move through the modern history of international monetary systems, the incompatible trinity is a useful concept to keep in mind. The same will apply to much of our discussion in Chapter 20. The incompatible trinity may be an uncomfortable reality, but any exchange rate system that does not take this tradeoff into account may not be viable in the long run.

SUMMARY

1. Until the early 1970s, fixed exchange rates were the norm for all countries. We study fixed exchange rates because a number of countries still "peg" (fix) the value of their domestic currency to that of another country.
2. The most common method of fixing an exchange rate is for a country to have an inconvertible currency. Under this system, all residents and firms of the country are legally obliged to sell any foreign exchange to the government (central bank) at a fixed price. Likewise, any resident or firm that needs foreign exchange must purchase it from the government (central bank) at the same fixed price. In order to manage this exchange rate system, the country's government must always balance the demand for foreign exchange with the supply of foreign exchange.
3. Another method that a country can use to fix an exchange rate is by intervening in the foreign exchange market. Intervention consists of the government buying or selling foreign exchange to maintain the exchange rate.
4. Government intervention in the foreign exchange market to maintain the exchange rate affects the country's money supply as well. When a government buys foreign exchange to maintain the exchange rate, the country's money supply increases. This change in the money supply has an impact on the domestic economy's aggregate demand and automatically adjusts the domestic economy to a sustainable external equilibrium.
5. In some cases, the change in the money supply will be consistent with the domestic economy's internal balance. In other cases, there may be an inconsistency between a country's external and internal balance requirements.
6. The government can assign monetary policy the role of achieving a country's external balance, and fiscal policy the role of achieving a country's internal balance. Under a fixed exchange rate system, fiscal policy is highly effective in changing the equilibrium level of output and the price level. When the government adopts an expansionary fiscal policy, it leads to a higher government budget deficit and to an increase in domestic interest rates. In an open economy with mobile capital, the rise in interest rates causes an inflow of foreign capital. The inflow of foreign capital requires that the government intervene in the foreign exchange market and buy foreign exchange, which causes the domestic money supply to increase. The net result is that the effects of fiscal policy are more pronounced.
7. Sterilization is another method of solving the problem of finding an appropriate mix of

monetary and fiscal policy that is required to maintain both a country's external and internal balance under a fixed exchange rate system. Sterilization consists of offsetting the money supply effects of intervention by using open market operations. The net effect of intervention and sterilization on the domestic supply of money is zero. Using sterilization, a government can keep the domestic money supply insulated from the intervention in the foreign exchange market.

8. A variation on a fixed exchange rate system is for the government to fix the real exchange rate. In this case the nominal exchange rate is allowed to change while the real exchange rate is held constant. The term used to describe this system is called a crawling peg.
9. When two countries are committed to maintaining exchange rate stability between their two respective currencies, then at some point they may merge the two currencies into a common currency. The benefits of a currency union include the monetary efficiency gains, and the costs of a common currency include the loss of an autonomous monetary policy and the loss of economic stability. Whether or not a currency union is beneficial depends on the magnitude of the monetary efficiency gains versus the potential losses in terms of economic stability.
10. Unfortunately, it is impossible for a country to simultaneously have a fixed exchange rate, capital mobility, and an effective monetary policy.

KEY CONCEPTS AND TERMS

- inconvertible currency p. 448
- exchange controls p. 448
- intervention p. 454
- sterilization p. 468
- crawling peg p. 469
- currency union p. 470
- monetary efficiency gain p. 470
- economic stability loss p. 471

PROBLEMS AND QUESTIONS FOR REVIEW

1. What is an inconvertible currency?
2. Explain how a country can use exchange controls to maintain external balance.
3. List and describe the problems frequently encountered with the use of exchange controls.
4. Show how an exchange control system could lead to a "shortage" of foreign exchange.
5. Describe what intervention in the foreign exchange market is.
6. Show how a fixed exchange rate system using intervention would tend to lead to the automatic maintenance of external balance.
7. Show how a current account deficit and a fixed exchange rate could lead to a recession.
8. With fixed exchange rates, how could a current account surplus be related to inflation?
9. Under what cases is monetary policy consistent with both internal and external balance?
10. In what cases is monetary policy inconsistent with both internal and external balance?
11. Show the effects of expansionary fiscal policy for a country that has adopted a fixed exchange rate.
12. Describe why fiscal policy is effective in achieving internal balance when the exchange rate is fixed.
13. Describe how sterilization is the process of insulating the domestic money supply from intervention in the foreign exchange market.
14. Under what conditions does sterilization work best?
15. Describe how using sterilization to fix the exchange rate could lead to an exchange rate shock.
16. Carefully show how a crawling peg means a peg of the real exchange rate and a depreciation of the nominal exchange rate.

17. Why would a small open economy choose to adopt the monetary policy of a major trading partner?
18. Explain the benefits and costs to a country when it joins a monetary union.
19. Is the U.S. an optimum currency area? Why or why not?
20. Explain why a country cannot simultaneously have a fixed exchange rate, capital mobility, and an effective monetary policy.

SELECTED READINGS AND WEB SITES

Catherine Bosner-Neal, "Does Central Bank Intervention Stabilize Foreign Exchange Rates?" *Federal Reserve Bank of Kansas City Economic Review* 81(1), First Quarter 1996, pp. 43–57.

A good source on intervention in the foreign exchange market.

Charles Enoch and Anne-Marie Gulde, "Are Currency Boards a Cure for All Monetary Problems?" *Finance & Development* 35(4), December 1998, pp. 40–43.

A short readable guide to the current state of currency boards.

Farley Grubb, "Creating the U.S. Dollar Currency Union, 1748–1811: A Quest for Monetary Stability or a Usurpation of State Sovereignty for Personal Gain?" *American Economic Review* 93(5), December 2003, pp. 1778–98.

The creation of the U.S. monetary union was a long and messy process. This article is an excellent summary of how it occurred.

IMF, *Annual Report of Exchange Rate Arrangements and Restrictions,* Washington, D.C: IMF, annual.

The best summary of different exchange rate systems for most of the world's countries.

"Meddling in the Currency Market," *The Economist,* November 20, 1999, p. 96.

A quick introduction to intervention in the foreign exchange markets.

OECD, *EMU: Facts, Challenges & Policies,* Washington, D.C.: OECD, 1999.

A comprehensive guide to virtually all of the issues surrounding the implementation of the Euro.

"The ABC of A Currency Board," *The Economist,* November 1, 1997, p. 80.

A quick introduction to how currency boards work.

"The Etiquette of Merging Currencies," *The Economist,* December 9, 1995, p. 80.

A short article on the basics of optimum currency areas.

Chapter 20

International Monetary Arrangements

"So much of barbarism, however, still remains in the transactions of most civilized nations, that almost all independent countries choose to assert their nationality by having, to their own inconvenience and that of their neighbours, a peculiar currency of their own."
—John Stuart Mill

INTRODUCTION

During your lifetime, the world's dominant currency, the dollar, has to one extent or another been allowed to float to whatever level the foreign exchange market deems appropriate. The same is true for other major currencies such as the Euro, the Japanese yen, and the British pound. The current system, if it can be called a system at all, is a bewildering array of currencies that float, currencies that are fixed (pegged) to other currencies that float, and currencies that are inconvertible. Today, each country can determine how to manage the foreign exchange value of its currency. This has not always been the case. Until the early 1970s, most countries participated in an international monetary system that restricted their choices. Such systems had both costs and benefits. In this chapter, we will discuss the process of a country's adjustment to external imbalances as it actually occurred under the various international monetary systems that existed from the late 1800s to the present.

The purpose of this chapter is threefold. First, you will learn about the history of the two most widely used international monetary systems, the *gold standard* and the *Bretton Woods system.* Second, you will learn a method for analyzing the costs and benefits of the different types of international monetary systems. We have already completed much of this analysis earlier in the text. Our task in this chapter is to put this information into a more orderly form so you can examine alternatives to the current international arrangements. Finally, in the current environment, there is a lot of discussion concerning international monetary reform. There are good reasons for these discussions and you will learn why there has been no "reform" and why there may not be any grand reforms in the foreseeable future.

THE GOLD STANDARD

gold standard a former international monetary system where the value of each currency was fixed in terms of gold

official parity price the price of a currency in terms of gold in a gold standard system

Under the **gold standard**, which operated from about 1870 to 1914, each country defined the gold content of its currency. Under this system, one could exchange a piece of paper money for something of intrinsic value such as gold or silver. If you have ever examined an older dollar bill, you may have noticed the phrase "silver certificate" or "gold certificate" printed on it. In both cases, that particular U.S. currency literally could be redeemed for silver or gold. In the current environment, "Federal Reserve Note" has replaced that phrase. A dollar bill today can be exchanged for another brand new dollar bill. We no longer have a precious metal or anything tangible backing the currency.

Under the gold standard, the primary function of a country's central bank was to preserve the official parity between its currency and gold by buying and/or selling gold at the **official parity price**. The official parity price of a currency was the price of each country's currency in terms of gold. Since the gold content of each country's currency was known and fixed, exchange rates between countries also were fixed. When the U.S. was on the gold standard, there was little to no long-run inflation. Given the difficulties the U.S. and other countries have had with inflation, this alone would seem to make a gold standard desirable. In addition, the gold standard offered one huge advantage from an international business perspective: exchange rates were fixed for very long periods of time. As a result, businesses could trade and invest with little concern over changes in the exchange rate. To a businessperson of today, this would seem nearly a dream come true. In the current environment of volatile exchange rates, it is difficult to engage in any international transaction without worrying about the short- and long-term changes in exchange rates. A return to a gold standard would stabilize exchange rates. The fact that countries have not returned to it tells us that the gold standard does contain drawbacks that have been mostly forgotten. To understand the costs and benefits of the system, we need to describe how the international monetary system functioned during the period of the gold standard.

The Gold Standard and Monetary Policy

The gold standard was not only a means of fixing exchange rates between countries. More generally, it was a system that automatically managed a country's money supply. The fixed exchange rate was simply an offshoot of a broader method of economic stabilization. In Chapter 15 we discussed the money supply of a modern monetary system. In a gold-standard world, a country's monetary base consisted of gold or currency backed by gold. If a country had a balance of payments imbalance at the current fixed exchange rate, the gold standard system would automatically set into motion an adjustment process to correct the imbalance in the country's external balance.

For example, suppose that the U.S. had a balance of payments deficit at the current fixed exchange rate. In this circumstance, the rest of the world would be accumulating more dollars in the short run than they would want to spend. This excess supply of dollars in the foreign exchange market would cause the value of the dollar to depreciate if exchange rates were flexible. However, the price of a dollar *in terms of gold* was fixed, and the imbalance in the foreign exchange market would be corrected by gold outflows from the U.S. to the rest of the world. This exportation of gold from the U.S. occurred automatically. As dollars became cheaper in the foreign exchange market, it would make sense to purchase gold at the fixed price with the cheaper dollars. Traders could make a risk free, albeit small, profit on this transaction. Fixing the price of the currency in terms of gold would effectively keep the exchange rate stable in the short run.

However, this short-run fix might not hold in the long run—unless there was an additional adjustment process. The gold standard also provided this additional adjustment process. Recall from the previous example that if the U.S. had a balance of payments deficit, gold would flow out of the U.S. to the rest of the world. This outflow of gold has extremely important implications. When gold flowed out of the U.S., the monetary base would automatically decline or, at minimum, grow at a slower rate. As this occurred, the change in the money supply would set in motion forces (increases in interest rates, decreases in aggregate demand, etc.) that would tend to correct the balance of payments deficit. The converse occurred when a country had a balance of payments surplus. An external surplus resulted in an inflow of gold. This inflow of gold would automatically cause an increase in the money supply that would also quickly correct the balance of payments surplus.

In the modern context, we frequently use the terms *contractionary* or *expansionary* with respect to monetary policy. It is also common to hear the terms *increase* or *decrease* in connection with the money supply. In general, the use of these latter terms is not technically correct. A "contractionary" monetary policy generally is one under which there is a reduction in *the money supply's growth rate*. In a modern economy, it is rare for the money supply to actually decline for any extended period of time. Conversely, an "expansionary" monetary policy usually is one under which there is an increase in the money supply's growth rate. Under the gold standard, the terms *increase* or *decrease* had very precise meanings. It was not uncommon for the money supply to actually decrease for substantial periods of time whenever the country had an external deficit. This automatic adjustment to an external imbalance makes the domestic economy relatively unstable, as changes in the money supply affect real domestic economic activity. However, this automatic adjustment process did have the benefit of keeping the exchange rate fixed and the *long-run* level of prices relatively stable.

The Macroeconomics of the Gold Standard

Let's now examine the gold standard more carefully to show how the system operated. For example, suppose that real domestic economic activity was expanding. At some point, the economic expansion would put a strain on the country's overall balance of payments. This strain on the balance of payments is a result of two effects. First, the expansion results in higher incomes in the domestic economy, and the higher incomes result in an increase in the level of imports. Second, the expansion results in higher domestic prices, and higher domestic prices make imports relatively cheaper. Higher domestic prices would result in an increase in the level of imports. The net result is that the economic expansion causes a balance of payments deficit at the current fixed exchange rate. This situation is illustrated in Figure 20.1. The demand and supply of foreign exchange before the expansion of the economy are shown as D and S, respectively. The initial equilibrium in the foreign exchange market is illustrated at point E at the country's gold parity exchange rate, XR_p. As the economy expands, the

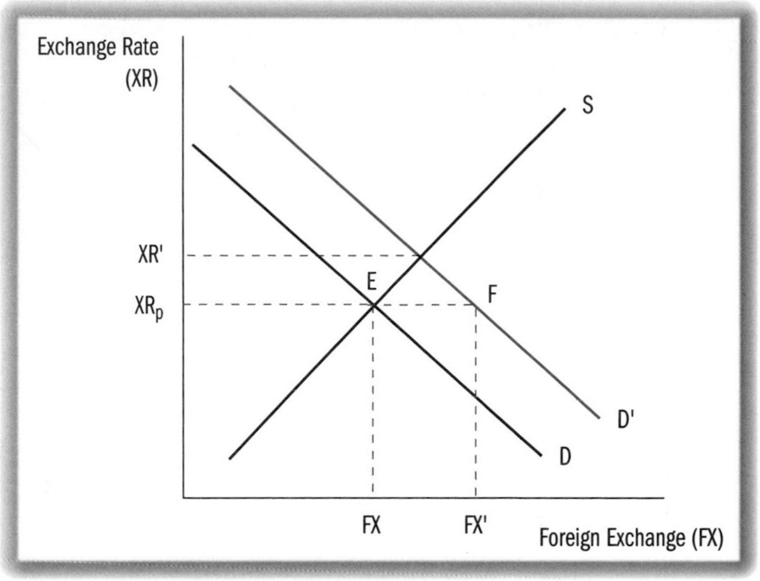

Figure 20.1 **Effect of Balance of Payments Deficit under the Gold Standard**
Under the gold standard, an increase in the demand for foreign exchange would cause an outflow of gold from the country and a contraction of the money supply.

increase in the level of imports causes the demand for foreign exchange to increase from D to D′. As a result, the balance of payments imbalance (deficit) at the gold parity exchange rate puts upward pressure on the exchange rate, and gold would flow out of the country. The gold outflow is represented by the amount from E to F.

In turn, the gold outflow would cause a decrease in the country's money supply. The actual contraction of the money supply could at times be extreme and have dire consequences for the state of the domestic economy. In Figure 20.2, we illustrate the effects of the monetary contraction. The initial equilibrium is illustrated at point E, with an equilibrium level of real GDP represented as Y_e with the price level at P_e. Since this macroeconomic equilibrium is associated with the balance of payments and exchange rate information given in Figure 20.1, we assume that this initial equilibrium occurs as a result of the economic expansion. However, as gold flows out of the country and the *contraction* of the money supply occurs, a change in the economy's aggregate demand results. As the money supply falls, both consumption and investment would decline as interest rates increased. As a result, the aggregate demand of the economy would decrease from AD to AD′ and the economy would move from E to F. The new equilibrium is illustrated with real GDP at Y′ and the domestic price level at P′. The effect of the gold outflow causes both real GDP and the price level to decline, and the domestic economy suffers a recession in order to bring the external balance back into balance at the fixed exchange rate.

This external adjustment automatically occurs as the changes in output and the price level induce an improvement in the country's balance of payments. As the equilibrium level of output declines, both consumption spending and the amount of

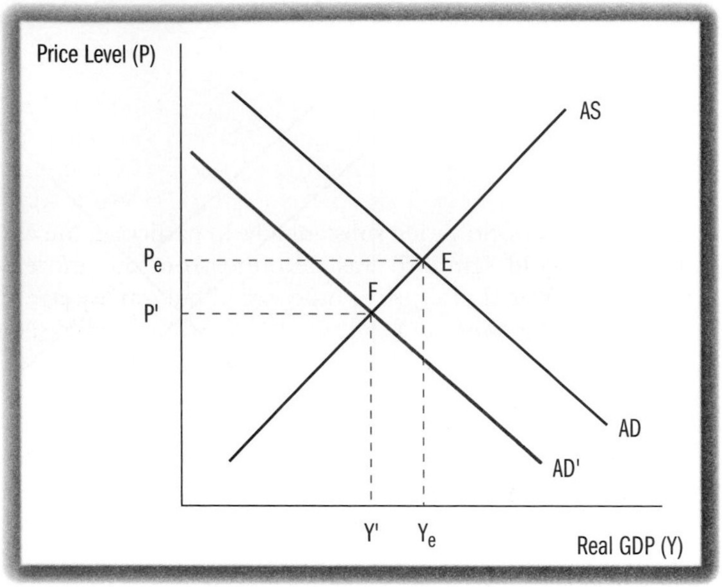

Figure 20.2 Effect of Balance of Payments Deficit on The Domestic Economy

Under the gold standard, an outflow of gold from a country would cause a contraction of the country's money supply and a decrease in aggregate demand. Both real output and the price level fall.

imported goods decline. In addition, the falling domestic price level also affects the level of imports, as domestically produced goods become relatively cheaper than foreign produced goods. This relative price effect further dampens the level of imports. Also, as domestic prices fall relative to foreign-produced goods, the level of exports increases as exports become cheaper. The net result of these adjustments is that the balance of payments tends to improve at the current fixed exchange rate. As this occurs, the outflows of gold from the country decline and at some point are eliminated. When the gold outflow ends, the country's money supply would stabilize (cease to fall) at a lower level. At this point, the domestic economy has completed its automatic adjustment to the external imbalance.

Costs and Benefits of the Gold Standard

One of the gold standard's major benefits is that the adjustment of the price level and output to an external imbalance is *completely* automatic. All that a country must do is fix its currency in relation to gold. Once a country has stated the gold content of its currency, all it needs to be willing to do is to buy or sell its currency (gold) at that stated price. The international monetary system then can be put on autopilot, so to speak. This is not much of an exaggeration. For most of the period that the U.S. adopted the gold standard, it had no central bank. The Second Bank of the United States was closed in 1837 and the modern Federal Reserve was created in 1913. Throughout this time period, there was virtually nothing that could be called a discretionary monetary policy in the U.S. In some senses, this automatic feature of the gold standard was very comforting because there was not any question about what would happen to a country if it had a balance of payments imbalance.

A second benefit of the gold standard was that it provided an anchor and, therefore, long-run price stability for a country. For example, the average rate of inflation for the U.S. under the gold standard was 0.1 percent per annum. In the case of the U.K. prices actually declined throughout the period (deflation). Compared to the current inflationary environment, this result is almost beyond belief. However, what proponents of the gold standard tend to forget is the short run. The gold standard most assuredly *does not guarantee short-run price stability*. From one year to the next, prices in a gold-standard world varied substantially. In particular, the character of the price changes under the gold standard was different from our more recent experience. In the post–World War II era, prices have varied but, on average, nearly always increase. The only remaining question is by how much? Under a gold standard, prices within a country may increase (inflation) some years and decrease (deflation) in others. The overall price level is relatively stable over a long period of time but it may vary substantially from one year to the next. In other words, deflation was just about as common as inflation. All of us are aware of the discomforts (costs) of inflation. However, the discomforts of a deflationary period are just as bad. When describing the benefit of the gold standard's ability to ensure price stability, one has to be careful. In the long run it does have that effect, but in the short run one must realize that prices can and will fluctuate.

In summary, the gold standard has two major benefits as an international monetary system. This system also has one extremely large cost for the countries that adopt it. Under this system, the overall balance of payments position heavily influences a country's money supply. A balance of payments deficit can mean a contracting money supply and a contracting economy. However, a balance of payments surplus can mean an overheated economy coupled with inflation. For example, under the gold standard the U.S. averaged a 1.4 percent increase in real per capita income per year. While GDP growth on average was healthy, the deviation from the average was relatively large. The gold standard guaranteed completely fixed exchange rates, but a large part of the system's cost was an extremely unstable GDP growth rate.

THE BRETTON WOODS SYSTEM AND THE INTERNATIONAL MONETARY FUND

gold-exchange standard an international monetary system where the price of one currency is tied to gold but all other currencies are tied to the value of that currency

The First World War essentially ended the international monetary system based on the gold standard. Between the end of that war and the Great Depression, governments periodically tried to revive the gold standard. These attempts invariably failed. In some sense, the period from 1914 to 1946 was similar to the current international monetary system, which is to say not much of a "system" at all. However, the governments' desire for some form of international monetary system was still strong. This desire led to a conference in Bretton Woods, New Hampshire, in July of 1944. At this conference, 44 countries essentially created a new international monetary system. This system usually is described as the "Bretton Woods" system. More precisely, this system is technically the **gold-exchange standard**. In this system, the U.S. dollar was tied to gold but all other currencies were tied to the dollar. In addition, the countries agreed to the creation of a new international monetary institution known as the *International Monetary Fund* (IMF). In this section, we consider how the Bretton Woods system functioned. Since this system and the IMF are inextricably bound together, we will also consider how the IMF played a key role in the operation of the international monetary system.

The Bretton Woods System

The purpose of the Bretton Woods system was twofold. First, countries had a strong desire to return to some form of international monetary system that featured fixed exchange rates. The period after the gold standard from 1914 up to World War II was characterized by exchange rates that were extremely unstable. Given that both business and governments had become used to stable exchange rates, this period of instability was very unsettling. Thus, the first objective of a new international monetary system was to develop some form of fixed exchange rates. The second purpose of the Bretton Woods system was to develop some method that would decouple the link between a balance of payments imbalance and the supply of money. In order to accomplish this objective, it was necessary to reduce the role that gold played in determining a country's money supply. It became necessary to link currencies to something other than gold. Both of these objectives were satisfied in a rather unique manner.

First, the price of gold was defined in terms of the U.S. dollar. The U.S. was to maintain the price of gold fixed at $35 per ounce. In addition, the U.S. would stand ready to exchange dollars for gold, or vice versa, at the stated price without restrictions or limitations. This requirement allowed the system to retain at least a small part of the old link to gold. Second, all other currencies were fixed in terms of the U.S. dollar. The Bretton Woods system was essentially a U.S. dollar standard, with the dollar linked to gold. Because all currencies were fixed to the dollar, they also were fixed in relation to one another. The international monetary system seemed ideal in that exchange rates were fixed and governments were now free to pursue a monetary policy consistent with internal balance—in other words, intervention coupled with sterilization. Thus, a country would no longer have to sacrifice internal balance considerations to maintain its external balance.

However, the Bretton Woods system was far from perfect. The inherent problem in what the system tried to accomplish is that it is logically impossible for all countries to have a balance of payments that balances in both the short and the long run. At best, one would hope that countries would have a balance of payments deficit over some period of time and surpluses over another, so that a country's balance of payments would "balance" in the long run. This long-run balancing was quite important for sustaining this type of international monetary system. In order to maintain fixed exchange rates in this system, it was necessary for governments to actively intervene in the foreign exchange market. In some cases, the governments would have to buy their own currency or sell foreign exchange (dollars) to prevent the domestic currency from depreciating. In other cases, they would have to buy foreign exchange (dollars) or sell their own currency in order to prevent the domestic currency from appreciating. In order to sell foreign exchange, it is necessary for the government to have a readily available supply. This selling of foreign exchange would occur when the country had a balance of payments deficit. Thus, the necessary reserves of foreign exchange to sell needed to be created in a previous period when the country had a balance of payments surplus and was accumulating foreign exchange. As such, it was important for countries to pursue internal policies that would ensure that the balance of payments "balanced" in the long run.

To more fully examine how the gold-exchange standard functioned, consider the following situation. Suppose that a country was currently in a recession and at the same time also had a current account deficit. In this case, the macroeconomic policies the government would need to pursue to obtain both an internal and external balance are inconsistent with one another. Internal balance considerations would suggest that the government should pursue expansionary monetary and/or fiscal policies. However, such policies would exacerbate the external deficit. In this case, the government might still prefer to fight the recession and keep the exchange rate fixed by selling previously accumulated foreign exchange. Once the domestic economy had recovered sufficiently, it might be possible to slow economic activity enough to reestablish external balance. If a country had sufficient international reserves in the short run, it might be able to deal with internal balance issues and temporarily ignore external balance considerations.

As outlined, the system could function over time if the balance of payments imbalances were short-run in nature. However, if the imbalances were persistent it would be difficult for the country to "finance" the balance of payments deficit using previously accumulated reserves. If the country kept pursuing policies that were inconsistent with internal and external balance, at some point the country might have no choice but to change the value of its currency and its relation to the U.S. dollar. If this situation occurred in enough countries, the devaluations would be so frequent that exchange rates would no longer be fixed. In other words, there needed to be some mechanism built into the international monetary system to encourage countries to maintain policies that would produce external balance and a stable exchange rate in the long run. In a gold-standard world, the enforcement mechanism was obvious. Balance of payments imbalances were by the nature of the system self-liquidating. In the Bretton Woods system, the mechanism was less obvious.

The International Monetary Fund

The embodiment of the Bretton Woods system was an institution known as the International Monetary Fund (IMF). In July 1944, 44 countries signed the Articles of Agreement of the International Monetary Fund. The IMF began operations in 1945, and its headquarters is in Washington, D.C. The IMF's initial function was to oversee the reconstruction of the world's international payments system. However, the Articles of Agreement also provided for the creation of a pool of international reserves that countries with temporary payments imbalances could draw on. Each country in the IMF was assigned a quota of money to contribute to the pool of funds. The size of this quota is related to a number of variables related to the country's importance in the world economy. One quarter of this quota was contributed in gold, and the country's own currency comprised the remaining three quarters of its quota. The size of the quota was also tied to a country's ability to borrow from the IMF. A country could borrow up to a fourth of its quota at any time without any conditions. As a country attempted to borrow more reserves from the IMF to finance an imbalance in its balance of payments, the institution would begin to impose "conditions" on this borrowing. Essentially the conditions the IMF imposed were that the borrowing government would have to pursue monetary and fiscal policies that were consistent with long-run external balance. Because most borrowing countries had external deficits, this invariably meant tighter monetary and/or fiscal policies. Thus, once a country had exhausted its own reserves, there was a limit to its ability to pursue inconsistent policies indefinitely. IMF loans are short-run loans that are designed to be repaid in 3 to 5 years.

In practice, these loans have proven to be troublesome because many of the countries borrowing from the IMF have serious imbalances in their balance of payments that may be difficult to correct in the short run. IMF-mandated conditions that will correct these problems in a short period of time might call for a combination of fiscal and/or monetary policy measures that can create a severe short-run economic contraction. The balance of payments problem may well be cured but the costs in terms of lost output may be high. Such lending also puts the IMF in the unenviable position of determining a sovereign country's macroeconomic policies. As one might imagine, this can make the IMF an unpopular institution. It is frequently forgotten that it was not the IMF that created the macroeconomic policies that led to the payments imbalance in the first place. However, the IMF is frequently involved in the solution to a macroeconomic problem at a time when the country's economy is not performing well. As a result, the IMF is a deeply unpopular institution in many developing countries.

The Demise of the Bretton Woods System

During the 1950s and 1960s, the Bretton Woods system functioned fairly well. However, there were a couple of problems that developed over time. The first problem with the system was that it was not symmetrical. The IMF would force a country with a chronic balance of payments deficit to pursue more restrictive monetary and fiscal policies that would eventually correct the problem. However, what would happen to a country with a chronic balance of payments surplus? As designed, the system allowed countries with a balance of payments surplus to accumulate reserves through intervention and then sterilize the effect of this intervention on the domestic economy. However, the result was that the Bretton Woods system had no real way to deal with chronic surpluses. Since the country would not be borrowing from the IMF, there was no way to force it to pursue policies that would correct this type of imbalance. In a gold-standard world, the system was symmetric in this regard. The system would correct both deficits *and* surpluses. In the Bretton Woods system, the deficits might get corrected but there was no effective way to deal with countries with persistent surpluses.

A second and more serious problem with the system developed over time. In the Bretton Woods system, all currencies were fixed to the dollar and the U.S. government was obligated to exchange dollars for gold at a fixed price. Thus, the system would function so long as the U.S. balance of payments was balanced in the long run. However, beginning in the mid 1960s, the U.S. developed a persistent balance of payments deficit. The U.S. dollar was the world's dominant reserve currency and was the heart of the system. All other countries wanted to hold dollars to use for intervention, and the U.S. was not obligated to correct this imbalance. Thus, the U.S. did not see the need to adjust domestic monetary and/or fiscal policy to reduce the external imbalance. Over time, this led to foreign central banks holding an increasing number of dollars. Surplus countries had to buy dollars and sell their domestic currencies to prevent their currencies from appreciating. By the end of the 1960s, an obvious problem had emerged. Foreign central banks were holding an amount of dollars that was larger than the U.S. stock of gold at the official price of $35 per ounce. Unless the U.S. was willing to change its economic policies, the situation increasingly was untenable.

In many respects, the end of the Bretton Woods system was fairly predictable. The U.S. was faced with a choice. It could:

1. change its macroeconomic policies to reduce or eliminate its external deficit,
2. have foreign central banks demand gold in exchange for the dollars that they were holding, or
3. devalue the dollar and let it float against gold and the other currencies.

The U.S. chose the latter option. The announcement by the U.S. in August of 1971 that it would no longer redeem dollars for gold effectively ended the Bretton Woods system. Over the next two years, there were periodic efforts by the member countries to reconstruct the system. However, since the U.S. was unwilling to change the policies that led to the problem in the first place, little was accomplished. The generalized global turbulence associated with the first oil shock in 1973 effectively ended any willingness by IMF members to reconstruct the system. For the last 30 years the world has been without a formal international monetary system. In the next section we will consider how the current system, or lack thereof, works.

THE POST–BRETTON WOODS ERA

clean float **an exchange rate system under which the government does not try to influence the exchange rate**

In the roughly thirty years since the breakup of the Bretton Woods system of fixed exchange rates, countries essentially have faced two options. The first has been to allow a relatively **clean float** of a country's exchange rate. Under the clean float option, the government has essentially left the exchange rate alone and allowed market forces to determine the value of the currency in the foreign exchange market. The second option for many countries has been to fix (peg) their exchange rate to the currency of another country or a group of countries. There are several variants of this second option. Thus, the world exchange rate system is often a confusing mix of various exchange rate arrangements. We use the word "system" here fairly loosely, as there is no system in the sense that the gold standard or Bretton Woods was a system. Currently, international monetary relations between countries are a rather loose collection of arrangements, and we present an explanation of each of the options available to a country in the next several sections.

Clean Floats

The first option, the clean float, is fairly straightforward. This option essentially is a policy of benign neglect that allows the exchange rate to constantly adjust to its equilibrium level. Adopting a clean float policy is the same as deciding that internal balance considerations are substantially more important than external balance considerations. In such a system, the government uses monetary and fiscal policy to achieve acceptable levels of economic growth and levels of inflation. The resulting mix of monetary and fiscal policies then determines the value of the exchange rate and also determines what the current and financial/capital account balances will be. These current and financial/capital account balances become almost purely residuals in response to macroeconomic policies set to achieve internal balance. As shown earlier, this is hardly an irrational response to the world in which we live. It can be argued that domestic economic conditions may be more important than the level of the exchange rate and the current account balance. However, as we have seen earlier, a clean float is not

The European Monetary Union

For more than 20 years, the European Union has been attempting to achieve the degree of exchange rate stability within Europe that the old Bretton Woods system had. As trade barriers fell in Europe and trade increased, the instability of exchange rates became increasingly important as a deterrent to both trade and investment. This led the EU to seek some form of an exchange rate regime that would promote more exchange rate stability. Over the past several years a new word—the Euro—has entered the jargon of international economics and business. The origins of the Euro can be traced back to the mid 1970s. With the breakdown of the Bretton Woods system, a number of members of the EU joined a system informally called "the snake." Essentially, this system was one in which a number of countries pegged their nominal exchange rates to the German mark. In 1979, this rather informal arrangement turned into the more formal European Monetary System (EMS). Countries could keep their nominal exchange rates fixed only by keeping their inflation rates and real interest rates close to those of Germany. This effectively meant that the German central bank (the Bundesbank) was setting monetary policy for all countries in the EMS. Discomfort among some EU members over this "German dominance of the EMS" was what led to negotiations for a single currency.

The initial negotiations for the single currency were held during 1987–1988. The EU issued the Delors report in June 1989 that recommended the creation of a new single currency. In the meantime, EU leaders abolished capital controls within the EU in July 1990. This was a necessary step in preparing European capital markets for a single currency and was considered the first step in a three-step process. The second step was the opening of the European Monetary Institute in Frankfurt, Germany, as a forerunner to a European central bank. In December 1995, EU leaders decided that the new currency, the Euro, would be launched in January 1999. It was further decided that the Euro would be valued in relation to the European Currency Unit (ECU), which was a synthetic currency tied to the value of a number of existing European currencies. All countries would not necessarily be part of the EMU. First, countries could "opt out" of the system, as did the U.K., Sweden, and Denmark. Second, countries were required to meet several "convergence criteria" in order to qualify for membership. Of the 12 remaining EU members, only Greece did not meet the convergence criteria.

The third step of the process started with the initial launch of the Euro on January 1, 1999. In the interim, the conversion rates between the Euro and the initial 11 national currencies (barring some emergency) were irrevocably fixed. Also, the European Monetary Institute became the European Central Bank.[1] The Euro could be used for financial transactions, and companies were allowed to keep their books in Euros. The Euro has been used for all transactions of the countries of the EMU since January 2002. Currently, 15 of the 27 countries of the EU use the Euro. In the previous chapter, we looked at a country's decision to join a currency union in terms of the monetary efficiency gains and the economic stability losses. The countries that are in the EMU have obviously decided that the gains are larger than the losses. The other twelve countries are free to join or retain their national currency indefinitely. One of the advantages of the EMU is that each country can make its own decision when the gains seem to be larger than the losses.

For the rest of the world, the effects of the Euro are small. Perhaps the only effect of note is the impact of the Euro on the U.S. dollar. First, the Euro has lead international investors to diversify more into Euro assets. Second, central banks are choosing to hold more of their reserves in Euros and less in dollars. Third, the dollar has been the currency of choice for invoicing trade and the pricing of some commodities. Any switch away from the dollar would be a switch toward the Euro and could reduce the demand for dollars. The bottom line is that the creation of the Euro may lead to a somewhat "weaker" dollar as the demand for dollars falls over time.

[1]For an excellent short history of the Euro, see "Eleven into One May Go," *The Economist,* October 17, 1998, pp. 81–82.

a costless choice. Under a clean float, a country's macroeconomic policies are such that monetary policy becomes very effective and fiscal policy is much less so. In the short run it is quite possible that the policy mixes can lead to an exchange rate that is far removed from a value consistent with purchasing power parity.

While a clean float policy may be optimal for the economy as a whole, it can be a serious problem for certain sectors of the economy. The macroeconomic policy mix could easily lead to a substantial real appreciation of the currency. This can lead to a situation where the economy as a whole has achieved its internal balance objective. For example, the economy might be growing at an acceptable rate and the rate of inflation might be rather subdued. However, the real appreciation of the country's currency will negatively impact the tradable goods portion of the economy. Providers of goods and services in international markets may find it increasingly difficult to compete with imports. On the other hand, exporters may find themselves losing business solely because of the appreciation of the country's currency. Although it is frequently less noticed, the reverse could be true. The policy mix could lead to an exchange rate that has depreciated substantially in real terms. In this case, the effects are more subtle but still exist nonetheless. The depreciation may lead to an expansion of the economy's tradable goods sector, as domestic production of these types of goods will increase. First, imports become more expensive and domestic production should rise to replace imports. Second, the country's goods become cheaper in international markets and exports also will rise. This is all well and good but there is a cost lurking here somewhere. If the macroeconomic policy mix has achieved its goal of something like full employment, then the resources needed to support production in the expanding tradable goods sector must come from somewhere. The rising prices and output in the tradable goods sector would tend to have a dampening effect on prices in the nontradable goods sector. As the relative price of nontradable goods falls, production of certain goods like haircuts and housing will grow at a slower rate. In the end, the policy of letting the exchange rate seek its own level may be optimal, but it is not costless. The point is that the periodic under- or over-valuations of the exchange rate can be quite uncomfortable for certain sectors of the economy. The tradeoff is one of overall internal balance versus potential negative impacts for certain sectors within the economy.

Fixing the Exchange Rate

For many countries, a policy of neglecting the exchange rate is not optimal. In many cases, international trade is a sufficiently large part of GDP that a country's external balance considerations cannot be safely ignored. In this case, a country may wish to fix (peg) its exchange rate. In some cases, this "peg" is fairly straightforward. A country may simply set the nominal value of its currency against that of another country's currency. In most cases, such a simple peg will invariably be to that of a larger country with which it does a substantial amount of trade and/or where cross border financial flows are large. If credible, this arrangement gives both traders and investors some insurance against sudden swings in the value of the exchange rate. However, one must keep in mind that the exchange rate has been fixed against one other currency and that the exchange rate is not fixed (pegged) against all currencies. If the currency that is being pegged against is itself floating, the value of a country's currency is still changing. For example, for a long time the value of the Austrian schilling was pegged to the value of the German mark. In the early 1990s, the German mark appreciated rapidly in real terms. Although the schilling was pegged to the mark, the result was that the schilling was appreciating along with the mark. While the nominal value of the exchange rate was not changing against the mark, its value against all other currencies was changing as the value of the mark changed.

One must keep in mind that such a nominal peg can be more apparent than real. The real value of the exchange rate can still change substantially. Of course, there is another cost to this type of arrangement. If Mexico wants to maintain a rigid nominal peg to the U.S. dollar, it is clear what it must do. In the long run, Mexico's inflation rate must almost exactly match the U.S. inflation rate. Otherwise it will be difficult for Mexico to maintain this fixed nominal exchange rate. Further, Mexico must be careful to keep domestic real interest rates in line with similar rates in the U.S., or else capital would start flowing between the two countries in such a way as to make it difficult to maintain the nominal peg in the short run. To do this, Mexico may have to pay a fairly high price for this policy. It will be necessary for Mexico to pursue monetary and fiscal policies that are similar to those that prevail in the U.S. To maintain such a rigid nominal peg means, for all practical purposes, that Mexico cannot use macroeconomic policy to maintain internal balance. So long as domestic economic conditions in Mexico are similar to those in the U.S., all is well. Mexico can maintain the fixed value of the peso and the price of doing so remains virtually zero. However, if domestic economic conditions in Mexico are or become substantially different from those in the U.S., Mexico faces an uncomfortable choice. It could either abandon the peg to the dollar, or it could pursue macroeconomic policies that are inappropriate given its state of internal balance. The price of this fixed exchange rate policy essentially would be the willingness to occasionally sacrifice internal balance to keep the exchange rate fixed. Again, this may be a sensible approach for some countries. But like any other policy choice, it comes with some costs.

As it turns out, there are a couple of ways that countries can *partially* avoid this dilemma. The first possibility is to fix the exchange rate in *real* rather than nominal terms. In the long run, international trade responds to changes in the real rather than the nominal exchange rate. It is a fairly simple matter for the government to determine what the purchasing power parity value of the exchange rate is at any particular time. Thus, in practice, the government could periodically change the nominal exchange rate to reflect differences in the rates of inflation between the two countries. This would allow the country to fix (peg) the real exchange rate and maintain monetary and fiscal policies that are somewhat different from those of the country to which its currency is fixed (pegged). Such a system has some of the advantages of a nominal fixed exchange rate. Traders and investors can be relatively sure of what the real value of the currency will be. However, there is still some uncertainty about what the nominal exchange rate might be in the future. To allay this uncertainty, governments pursuing such a policy may prefer to make the *rate* of devaluation somewhat constant. The official exchange rate may be allowed to change by a certain amount per day or per week. International trade frequently includes payment in the future for goods that will be received in the future. This feature allows traders to set up contracts for payment with some degree of certainty about what the nominal exchange rate will be in several weeks or months. There is still a problem, though, because the rate of change of the nominal exchange rate may have to be periodically adjusted. Domestic monetary and fiscal policy frequently may diverge from that of the other country. As this occurs, the rate of inflation in the two countries will diverge. This would require periodic adjustments in the rate of change of the nominal exchange rate. Thus, such a system has a bit more certainty than a free float. However, it is not nearly as stable as a credible fixed nominal exchange rate.

A second option is to fix the country's currency against a *basket* of currencies. This will almost inherently eliminate some of the problems of fixing the exchange rate against a single currency. If the domestic currency depreciates against one currency in the basket, it may appreciate against another currency. In the long run, such a system may yield a more stable exchange rate than would be the case if the currency were pegged to a single foreign currency. As sensible as this sounds conceptually, there are a couple of practical problems with such a system. First, construction of the basket is not all that clear. How many currencies should go into it? Which currencies are selected and which are excluded? Clearly, a country would want to include currencies that are important in the country's trade. However, *important* is a subjective term. How important is important? Should there be two currencies or five or ten? There are no clear-cut rules or parameters. Second, there is the issue of information. Should the government announce which currencies are being used in the basket? If it does, currency traders may notice when the local currency has depreciated or appreciated in the short run against the announced basket of currencies. This may make it more difficult for the country to maintain the peg. If a country attempts to keep the exact basket a secret, then some of the benefits of a fixed exchange rate are lost. Finally, such a system is more difficult for participants in private markets to handle. In this case, the government is simply committed to maintaining a fixed exchange rate against the basket and not any specific currency. As such traders operating mostly in one currency

Dollarization

Fixing a country's exchange rate may be technically difficult, and the choice of an exchange rate system has macroeconomic consequences. To avoid some of these difficulties, 26 countries do not use their own national currencies but instead use another country's currency as domestic legal tender. Historically, such a system is not new. However, the recent collapse of the currency board system in Argentina and the decision by Ecuador and El Salvador to start using the U.S. dollar has breathed new life into an old idea. Unfortunately, *dollarization* has become the current term for this system. However, the currency used does not have to be the dollar.

If the currency being used in place of the domestic currency is relatively stable in value, the country obtains the benefit of "inflation proofing" the domestic economy. The cost of the system is the loss of monetary policy. However, if inflation has been removed as a problem, then fiscal policy can be focused on managing domestic output. Dollarization is not a perfect solution to internal and external balance problems. However, for some countries it may be the least imperfect solution among the set of options they can choose from.

are really facing a floating exchange rate in the short run. The exchange rate is fixed on an overall basis, but not for a particular currency. This exposes traders to substantially more risk than would be the case if the bilateral exchange rate were fixed.

OPTIONS FOR INTERNATIONAL MONETARY REFORM

It is fairly safe to say that most participants in the world economy are not particularly satisfied with the current set of international monetary arrangements. Businesses genuinely dislike the current system of floating exchange rates, as exchange rate volatility greatly increases the risk of doing business in both the short run and the long run. In the short run, firms are forced to either take on the risk of exchange rate volatility or try to protect themselves from it by hedging in the foreign exchange market. If they do nothing, they stand to suffer periodic losses. Of course, sometimes they get lucky and make windfall gains. One strategy is to simply ignore the volatility and hope that the losses and the gains are roughly equal in the long run. However, this is cold comfort in the short run. A firm doing a substantial amount of business overseas can see its short-run profits whipsawed around because of exchange rate volatility. One may well ask why firms do not hedge their exchange rate exposure to insulate them from this type of risk. The answer is that hedging is not free. Hedging is simply one more form of insurance against a particular type of risk. As with any other form of insurance, it has costs. A firm has to consider whether or not purchasing this form of insurance is worth the cost in the long run. For many firms the answer is no, and those firms that do pay the cost would prefer more stable exchange rates that would allow them to avoid this expense. The current volatility of exchange rates also makes it difficult to plan more long-run types of business activity. Should a firm invest in expanding facilities and equipment in the home country or invest in new capacity overseas (FDI)? In making these judgments, the firm needs to consider the evolution of the relevant exchange rate over longer periods of time. If the current exchange rate is away from its long-run value and the firm does not perceive this, it can make a costly mistake. The bottom line is that the current exchange rate environment puts businesses in the position of having to *implicitly* forecast exchange rates, whether they want to or not. Even if the firm is not thinking much about exchange rates, doing so usually amounts to a forecast that the exchange rate will not change.

With respect to the current system, fluctuating exchange rates probably impose a significant externality on the world economy. Volatile exchange rates make international trade and investment more risky. Activities that entail more risk command a higher rate of return. In part, this is because risk is just another type of cost. To justify the higher costs, economic agents engaging in international trade need a higher rate of return to justify the higher costs. Since volatile exchange rates make international trade and investment more risky, fluctuating exchange rates also implicitly make international trade more costly. With higher risk and costs, you would expect to have less of any type of activity. The same is true of international trade. A big, though usually unrecognized cost, of volatile exchange rates is that they lower the total volume of international trade and investment. Economists have not been able to precisely estimate the size of this cost to the world economy. However, there is little doubt that there is some damage being done to the amount of world trade and investment.

Governments favor the current set of arrangements to about the same extent as the business community does. At a minimum, exchange rate volatility is an annoyance for countries like the U.S. It is at least a source of microeconomic concern, as an overvalued currency can seriously damage the economy's tradable goods sector. On the other hand, a temporarily undervalued currency can cause an unsustainable boom in the same sector, such as happened in Japan in the 1980s. At worst, a collapse in the currency's value can precipitate a macroeconomic crisis. Mexico has suffered through at least two crises in the last twenty years. The economic crisis in Asia in the late 1990s was at least partially attributed to serious short-run declines in the value of currencies. As much as governments may dislike the current exchange rate environment, there have been no serious multilateral moves toward a more stable system since the collapse of the Bretton Woods system in the early 1970s. With so much dissatisfaction with the current arrangements, there must be a compelling reason that no new system has emerged. There are good reasons for the current lack of motivation for a new system.

Figure 20.3 shows several of the central issues associated with any international monetary system.[2] On the horizontal axis, the degree of cooperation among countries in the international system is shown. Moving to the left in the figure, countries increasingly do not cooperate with one another and become more independent. At the limit, each country pursues whatever set of fiscal and monetary policies it deems appropriate given the country's state of internal balance. Moving to the right, countries would increasingly cooperate with one another. This cooperation may be necessary to smooth or enhance the international monetary system's operation. However, cooperation means that countries are willing to occasionally sacrifice internal balance considerations in order to achieve some level of exchange rate stability. The vertical axis plots the degree to which the international monetary system has some agreed-upon set of rules. At the top of the axis is an international system with rigid rules. At the bottom of the axis is a situation in which there are virtually no agreed-upon rules and countries exercise a great deal of discretion

Figure 20.3 is extremely useful in outlining some of the difficulties with past and potential international monetary systems. For example, in a historical context, the upper left-hand quadrant represents the gold standard. This system had two extreme characteristics. First, there were relatively rigid rules because each country had to define its currency in terms of gold at a fixed price. Thus, each currency's value was explicitly fixed against all other currencies. Except for fixing the currency in terms of gold, each country had great discretion. In modern terms, the system's rules took monetary policy out of the national government's hands. A country's external balance essentially determined the growth rate of the monetary base and the money supply. Second, with the exception of monetary policy, each country could do as it pleased with all other policies. There was no need to coordinate policies with other countries. Also, each country could autonomously set whatever commercial policy it wished. Tariffs and/or quotas could be set on international trade without obligation to any treaty such as GATT or an organization such as the WTO.[3] Despite the lingering

Figure 20.3 is adapted from "An Exchange-Rate Map, Part I," *The Economist*, May 21, 1988, p. 77.

[3]Of course, countries were not completely free in this regard. They had to be concerned with potential retaliation from other countries affected by adverse changes in commercial policy.

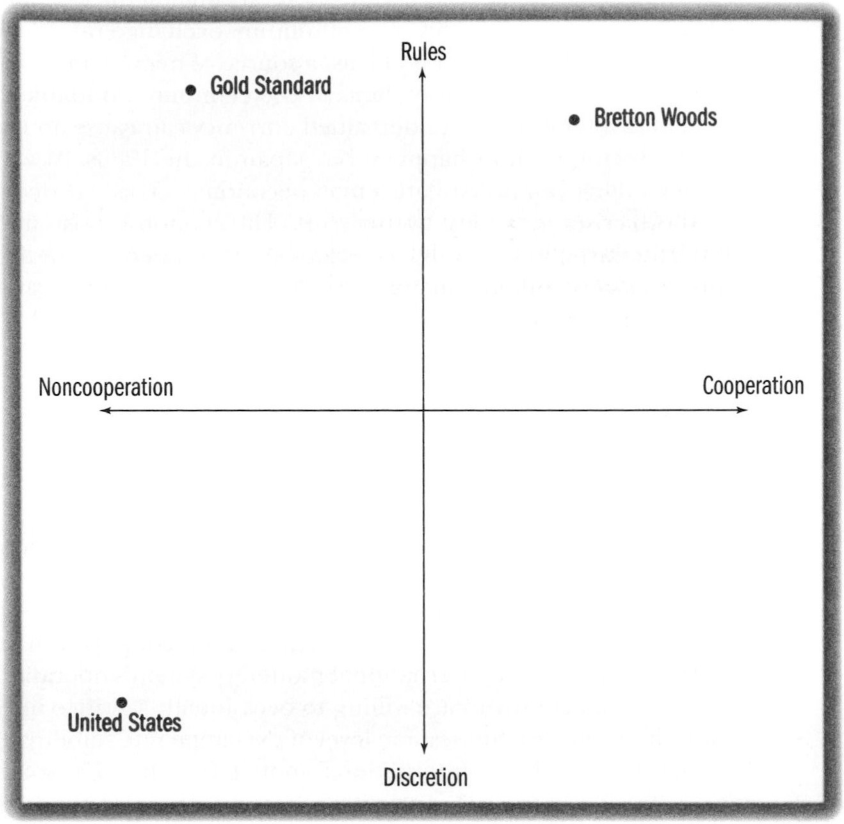

Figure 20.3 An Exchange Rate Map

Countries have the option of rules versus discretion and cooperation versus noncooperation in choosing an international monetary system.

nostalgia for the gold standard, it is unlikely to return. Countries would be loath to sacrifice monetary policy in the interests of exchange rate stability.[4]

The Bretton Woods system would be located in the upper right-hand quadrant of the figure. In this system there were rules that countries were obligated to follow in order to maintain a stable exchange rate. In addition, the country had obligations that went along with membership in the IMF. Although there were more rules than in the gold standard, they were somewhat less rigid. However, if a country's balance of payments were in chronic deficit, either the currency would have to depreciate or some form of discipline would be forthcoming from the IMF. Notice though that the two systems are similar in terms of rules. Where the two differ is in the degree of cooperation. Countries with fundamental imbalances would need to take steps to correct them. Otherwise, pressure would come to bear on other countries. For example, in the late 1960s the U.S. had chronic current account deficits that enhanced the

[4]This is not always the case. In some sense, the creation of the EMU is something like a return to a gold standard for the countries of the EU that are participating in it.

chronic current account surpluses in Germany and Japan, and vice versa. All three countries needed to cooperate in order to redress the problem. The U.S. needed to take steps to reduce the growth rate of GDP and imports; Germany and Japan needed to take steps to enhance domestic consumption and imports to reduce their current account surpluses. Since the countries involved were reluctant to take these cooperative steps, it became impossible for the system to continue.

The current system pursued in the U.S. can be found in the lower left-hand quadrant. In this case there are virtually no rules. Like the U.S., each country is free to pursue whatever policies it deems appropriate. This gives each country the maximum amount of discretion. Essentially, each country will be able to pursue the mix of fiscal and monetary policies that it considers best for internal balance. It can do this because, with no rules, the country can safely ignore or downplay exchange rate considerations.

This gives us the chance to demonstrate what would be necessary to come up with a new international monetary system. Such a system would presumably include a movement toward more stable exchange rates. The U.S. position is a useful starting point. Any movement toward more stable exchange rates would include at least one of two things: more rules and/or more cooperation. A move in a completely vertical direction back to the gold standard would probably prove to be unacceptable because of the loss of monetary policy. What would more likely emerge is a move from the U.S. position to the right and/or vertically. This is a move toward the lower right-hand quadrant. The G-7 countries made such moves in the late 1970s and the 1980s. Countries tried to achieve more exchange rate stability by increasing the level of cooperation. However, there were few, if any, rules. There was more cooperation, but since it basically was voluntary cooperation these agreements invariably failed. This is not too surprising in that countries tend to cooperate willingly when the policy mix needed to stabilize exchange rates matches the policy mix necessary for internal balance. If the two diverge, governments generally become uncooperative and again focus on their internal balance. In terms of a workable international monetary system, this quadrant does not seem to be very promising. At this juncture, the only realistic quadrant seems to be the lower left-hand quadrant. Countries do not seem inclined to go back to a system with a lot of relatively rigid rules, which makes a return to a rules-based system seem unlikely. Further, countries tend to focus on their internal balance first and consider external balance and the exchange rate only after the fact. This makes any move toward more cooperation unlikely. The current system, if it can be called that, is clearly messy and carries some costs for both the private and the public sector. However, given the preferences of most governments for autonomy in fiscal and monetary policy, it may be all that is feasible at this point.

SUMMARY

1. The current international monetary system is an array of currencies that float, currencies that are pegged to other currencies that float, and currencies that are inconvertible. In the current environment, each country can determine how to handle the exchange value of its currency.
2. The gold standard operated from approximately 1870 to 1914. Under this standard, each country defined the gold content of its

currency, and the primary function of a country's central bank was to preserve the official parity between its currency and gold by buying and/or selling any amount of gold at the official parity price. Because the gold content of each country's currency was known and fixed, exchange rates between countries were also fixed.

3. The gold standard was also a system that automatically managed a country's money supply. If a country had a balance of payments deficit at the current fixed exchange rate, gold would flow out of the country. This outflow of gold would cause the money supply to automatically decline, and the change in the money supply would set in motion forces that would tend to briskly correct the balance of payments deficit. The reverse would occur when a country had a balance of payments surplus.
4. In Bretton Woods, New Hampshire, in 1944, 44 countries created a new international monetary system called the gold-exchange standard. These countries agreed to the creation of a new international monetary institution known as the International Monetary Fund (IMF).
5. Under the gold-exchange standard, the price of gold was defined in terms of the U.S. dollar and the U.S. was to maintain the price of gold fixed at $35 per ounce. The U.S. would stand ready to exchange dollars for gold, or vise versa, at the stated price without restrictions or limitations. All other currencies were fixed in terms of the U.S. dollar. The Bretton Woods system was essentially a U.S.-dollar standard, with the dollar linked to gold.
6. In order to maintain fixed exchange rates in the gold-exchange standard, it was necessary for governments to actively intervene in the foreign exchange market. In some cases, the governments would have to buy their own currency or sell foreign exchange (dollars) to prevent the domestic currency from depreciating. In other cases, they would have to buy foreign exchange (dollars) or sell their own currency in order to prevent the domestic currency from appreciating. Thus, it was important for countries to pursue internal policies that would ensure that the balance of payments "balanced" in the long run.
7. The initial purpose of the IMF was to create a pool of international reserves upon which countries with temporary payments imbalances could draw. As a country attempted to borrow more reserves from the IMF to finance an imbalance in its balance of payments, the institution would begin to impose "conditions" on this borrowing.
8. The U.S. announcement in August 1971 that it would no longer redeem dollars for gold effectively ended the gold-exchange system.
9. In the roughly thirty years since the breakup of the gold-exchange system of fixed exchange rates, countries essentially have faced two options. The first option has been a relatively "clean" float of a country's exchange rate. In this case, the government has essentially left the exchange rate alone and let market forces determine the value of the currency in international markets. The second option for many countries has been to fix (peg) their exchange rate to a currency of another country or group of countries.
10. International monetary systems have two choices to make concerning rules versus discretion and noncooperation versus cooperation. The current system pursued in the U.S. can be described as a discretionary, noncooperating system in which the U.S. is free to pursue whatever policies it deems appropriate. The U.S. can do this because, with no rules, it can safely ignore or downplay exchange rate considerations.

KEY CONCEPTS AND TERMS

- gold standard p. 477
- official parity price p. 477
- gold exchange standard p. 481
- clean float p. 485

PROBLEMS AND QUESTIONS FOR REVIEW

1. Describe what the official parity price of a currency was under the gold standard. Why was it so important?
2. Suppose that under the gold standard, a country's currency was defined as 4 units for an ounce of gold. Describe what would happen if a country ran a balance of payments deficit and the exchange rate went to 5 units per dollar.
3. How would the price level and output adjust to a balance of payments deficit under the gold standard?
4. In a gold-standard world, what would be the problems associated with a country running a balance of payments surplus?
5. With a gold standard, aggregate demand was heavily influenced by the balance of payments. Show why this was true.
6. Consider the following statement. If a country is operating under a gold standard, it doesn't need a central bank.
7. Show why a gold standard produces long-run price stability but does not guarantee short-run price stability.
8. What is meant by the Bretton Woods system being a gold exchange standard?
9. Explain the operation of the Bretton Woods system.
10. What caused the Bretton Woods system to collapse?
11. In the Bretton Woods system, why was it necessary for the IMF to impose conditions when loaning foreign exchange to countries with balance of payments deficits?
12. A gold standard produced a symmetric response to balance of payments problems. The Bretton Woods system could only deal effectively with balance of payments deficits. Explain why this was true.
13. Briefly describe how the IMF works to deal with a country with a balance of payments deficit.
14. Graphically show what an IMF-mandated austerity program would look like.
15. Describe the demise of the Bretton Woods system. What was the role of the U.S. in this event?
16. Describe the costs and benefits of a clean float.
17. Suppose that a country wanted to peg its exchange rate. What are the issues involved in pegging to one currency versus pegging to a basket of currencies?
18. Describe how volatile exchange rates diminish the amount of international trade.
19. Plot the gold standard, the Bretton Woods system, a pegged exchange rate system, and a clean float on the graph used to show the tradeoffs involved in international monetary systems.
20. What are the major problems that countries face in developing a new international monetary system?

SELECTED READINGS AND WEB SITES

"An Awfully Big Adventure," *The Economist,* April 11, 1998. pp. S1–S22.
One in a series of articles on the Euro. The strength of this piece is the history of the Euro and a primer on the economics of a common currency.
Gaetano Antinolfi and Todd Keister, "Dollarization as a Monetary Arrangement for Emerging Market Economies," *Federal Reserve Bank of St. Louis Review* 83(6), November/December 2001, pp. 29–39.
A good review of the issues involved with small currencies converting to the use of the U.S. dollar.
Barry Eichengreen, *Globalizing Capital: A History of the International Monetary System,* Princeton, NJ: Princeton University Press, 1996.
A short readable history of the international monetary system.
"Getting out of a fix," *The Economist,* September 20, 1997, p. 89.
An excellent short list of the characteristics that help determine the optimal choice of an exchange rate system.

IMF (www.imf.org)

The official web site of the IMF. This Web site also contains reviews of exchange rate policy for all member countries.

Peter B. Kenen, *The International Financial Architecture: What's New? What's Missing?,* Washington, D.C.: Institute for International Economics, 2001.

A discussion of current attempts to improve the state of the international financial system and the International Monetary Fund.

R. I. McKinnon, *The Rules of the Game,* Cambridge: MIT Press, 1996.

This book contains an excellent discussion of the gold standard world.

Cait Murphy, "Dept. of Voodoo Economics," *Fortune,* November 26, 2001, p. 38.

A short essay on the costs and benefits of a "hard" currency peg.

Organization for Economic Cooperation and Development, *EMU: Facts, Challenges, & Policies,* Washington, D.C.: OECD, 1999.

A very thorough treatment of the Euro and the EMU.

"To fix or to float," *The Economist,* January 9, 1988, pp. 66–67.

It's old but still good. The description of how Texas adjusts to a payments imbalance within a fixed exchange-rate system (the U.S.) is an outstanding piece on how economies adjust in this sort of system.

Chapter 21

Capital Flows and the Developing Countries

"Countries don't go bust."
—WALTER WRISTON

"Yes, but their banker's do."
—IMF OFFICIAL

INTRODUCTION

In Chapter 11, we considered the effects of international trade on economic development. Despite the important effects of international trade on economic conditions in developing countries, our analysis was incomplete. As we saw in Chapter 12, there are a number of inflows and outflows of money in a country's balance of payments that are not included in the current account. Specifically, we have not completely considered how financial/capital account transactions affect economic development. In some previous chapters, we have touched on some of these issues. In Chapter 6, we briefly discussed the role of FDI in the world economy. In a few places in the second part of the book, we have looked at various aspects of financial/capital account transactions that affect the developing countries. The basic purpose of this chapter is to bring this material together in order to consider the role of capital flows in economic development.

In the first part of the chapter, we consider the reasons for the movement of capital from developed to developing countries. To more carefully consider the effects of this flow on economic development, we will define the different forms that these flows can take. These definitions should make it easier to understand some of the problems associated with capital flows into the developing countries. The most common problem associated with capital flows usually is the sudden depreciation of one or more developing country currencies. The second part of the chapter describes the various reasons why this can happen. Drawing on our earlier analysis of exchange rate changes in general, we will be able to apply the same tools in the context of the developing countries. This allows us to consider the macroeconomic consequences of these types of depreciations. The final part of the chapter considers the role of the IMF. For a number of reasons, the IMF is a controversial institution. The purpose of the section is to show why the controversy exists and to discuss the future of the IMF.

CAPITAL FLOWS TO DEVELOPING COUNTRIES

In the first half of the book, we touched on the reasons for capital flows to developing countries. The logic of these flows can be traced to the factor-proportions model covered in Chapter 4. On average, developing countries are capital scarce relative to the developed countries. Stated in reverse, developing countries typically are labor abundant relative to developed countries. Going one step further, the model implies that the scarce factor of production tends to be expensive and the abundant factor of production tends to be cheap. Frequently, these differences in factor intensities and factor prices are the basis for trade. Also, these differences in factor abundance can be the basis for the international movement of the factors of production. If possible, capital and labor will tend to migrate from countries where they earn a low rate of return to countries where the rate of return is higher. In this case, capital will move from capital-abundant countries to capital-scarce countries. In Chapter 6, we considered these movements and focused on the welfare effects in both the source and the host countries. Since most of these movements occur among developed countries, our focus in that chapter was on these movements. In this section, we will take a closer look at capital flows into the developing countries.

As we saw in Chapter 12, inflows of capital can be quantified as part of the overall balance of payments. Capital inflows in excess of outflows create a surplus in the financial/capital account. The other side of this surplus is an associated deficit in the current account. While not universally the case, financial/capital account surpluses coupled with current account deficits are common for developing countries. In this situation the current account deficit is being "financed" by a financial/capital account surplus. This financing should be simple, as capital should flow into countries where the rate of return is higher than it is in the source countries. However, these capital inflows mean that the country is borrowing from the rest of the world. In many cases, the result will be that a developing country is a net debtor. Conceptually, there is not a problem with this borrowing as long as the capital is used productively. If the borrowed capital is invested in profitable projects in the private sector, then the borrowing enhances the economic growth of the country. Assuming that the preconditions to growth we covered in Chapter 11 are met, private-sector capital flows to developing countries should be mutually beneficial. The same should be true for public-sector borrowing. It is common for governments in developing countries to borrow money for projects in the public sector. As long as this borrowing is channeled into public-sector investments that enhance economic development in a cost-effective way, such borrowing should not create any significant problems. Sadly, borrowing by governments in developing countries has a checkered history. As we will see in the next section, both for the public and private sectors, the form that this borrowing takes is important.

Debt versus Equity

debt borrowing by countries in the form of bonds or bank loans

When discussing borrowing, a critical distinction must be made between debt and equity. **Debt** is the situation where the borrower must repay all or part of the loan plus interest at certain points in time. In this case, the ability to pay off the loan over time is critical. In the international capital markets debt occurs in one of three forms. First, firms and/or governments in developing countries could issue bonds to raise capital. Usually, selling a bond involves a promise to make periodic interest payments to the bondholder with payment of the value of the bond due at the date of maturity. Usually, financing debt by issuing bonds occurs through government borrowing, as most private-sector firms in developing countries are not large enough to issue bonds in the global marketplace. Second, developing-country governments may be able to borrow money from commercial banks in the developed countries. This form of lending is referred to as *sovereign* lending. Loans by banks to governments go back hundreds of years. As indicated in the quotes at the start of the chapter, sovereign lending may not always work out well for the lender. Finally, developing-country governments may borrow money for projects from developed country governments or multilateral lending institutions such as the World Bank.

equity borrowing by countries in the form of FDI or investment in stocks

Capital also may flow into developing countries in the form of equity financing. **Equity** is a situation where the lender is also an owner in the company or project being financed. A common form of equity finance is foreign direct investment. The company providing all or part of the capital is to one extent or another involved in ownership and/or control of the project. A typical example would be an MNC building a production plant in a developing country. A second form of equity lending is the movement of portfolio capital between countries. As we saw in Chapter 1, portfolio capital is the movement of money from one country to another to purchase financial assets. In this case, capital is moving from primarily developed countries to developing countries to purchase stocks of companies located in developing countries. As such, the investor owns a part of the company through stock ownership but usually does not completely control the foreign firm. Equity finance is different from debt in one important respect. Debt payments have to be made no matter what the condition of the borrower is at the time the debt payment is due. Payments to the owners of equity are much more tied to current economic conditions. Owners of equity normally do not have a right to fixed payments in the form of a stream of income. Rather, they have a claim on all or part of the firm's assets.

The dimensions of debt and equity financing in developing countries are shown in Tables 21.1 and 21.2. With these tables, we can examine debt and equity in the developing countries in terms of the familiar stock and flow analysis. Table 21.1 shows how developing countries received capital inflows in 2005. In that year, total inflows of private-sector debt and equity to all developing countries were approximately $122 billion. Bonds and bank lending were $55.1 billion and 81.1 billion, respectively. Stocks and FDI in 2005 were nearly $66.7 billion and $280.8 billion, respectively. The table also shows the difference between these flows for low- and middle-income countries. As you can see, most of the flows of equity and debt in the table are relatively small. The importance of one number stands out. By far the largest flow of money into developing countries is FDI to middle-income countries. FDI accounts for approximately 70 percent of capital inflows into developing countries. In some of the discussions that follow, the

Table 21.1 Capital Flows to Developing Countries

Country Group	Net Private Capital Flows	Foreign Direct Investment	Portfolio Investment Flows		Bank & Trade Related Lending
			Bonds	Equity	
Developing Countries	$121,790	$280,795	$55,110	$66,680	$81,134
Low-Income Countries	10,327	20,522	−2,144	12,471	3,902
Middle-Income Countries	111,463	260,273	57,254	54,209	77,231

Source: World Bank, *World Development Indicators*, Washington, D.C.: World Bank, 2007.

focus will be on the problems caused by capital flows into developing countries. In this discussion, it is easy to forget that the majority of these flows are investments made by companies in land, plants, and equipment in middle-income countries. The nature of these investments is long term and represents the confidence investors have in the economic potential of these countries.

Table 21.2 shows the total stock of debt for the low- and middle-income countries. In 2005, the total amount of debt for all developing countries was approximately $2.7 trillion. Of this total, a bit more than $2 trillion was long-term in nature. The balance is short-term debt tied to trade financing and the like. Of this total, almost $1.4 trillion is held by developed country governments and multilateral lending agencies. The balance is held by the private sector or represents loans to countries by the IMF. Whether or not this is a large amount of debt depends on a number of factors. To start, consider the output of the developing countries. In 2005, the total output was $9.9 trillion. Once again, most of the outstanding debt is accounted for by the middle-income

Table 21.2 External Debt of Developing Countries

Country Group	Total External Debt	Long-term Debt	Public & Publicly Guaranteed Debt	Private External Debt	Use of IMF Credit
Developing Countries	$2,742,378	$2,147,179	$1,361,634	$785,545	$49,179
Low-Income Countries	379,239	338,595	298,209	40,385	8,322
Middle-Income Countries	2,363,139	1,808,585	1,063,425	745,160	40,857

Source: World Bank, *World Development Indicators*, Washington, D.C.: World Bank, 2007.

countries. However, in this case public-sector debt dominates the total. The middle-income countries alone owe governments and multilateral organizations approximately $1 trillion. If there is a difficulty here, it is the ability of developing countries to make timely payments on this debt. The next section covers some of the factors involved in their ability to do so.

Servicing Foreign Debt

Like all debt, money owed by citizens, firms, or the government of a developing country has to be repaid. In this case, there is one important difference. For most developing countries, foreign debt cannot be repaid in domestic currency. Repayment of foreign debt must be made in an acceptable foreign currency. When debt payments come due, foreign exchange must be available. In order to make timely payments on foreign debt, two factors become critical. We will discuss each of these factors in turn before looking at some other aspects of capital flows in developing countries. This is necessary because these two factors become important in some other contexts covered later in the chapter.

At any given time, inflows of foreign exchange may not exactly match outflows. In order to pay for imports and/or make payments on foreign debt, countries need to have an available fund of foreign exchange, called **foreign reserves**. Foreign reserves represent the stock of foreign exchange a country possesses at a point in time. In some time periods, inflows of foreign exchange will exceed outflows. In this circumstance, the stock of foreign reserves will rise. At other times, outflows may exceed inflows and the stock of international reserves will fall. International reserves are important in that they represent a cushion of foreign exchange. If inflows of foreign exchange temporarily decrease or outflows increase, the country can still pay for imports or debt repayments if the level of foreign reserves is sufficiently high. However, if this level is extremely low then a country may face the uncomfortable choice of imports versus debt repayments. There might not be enough foreign exchange for both. A related concept is the **debt/export ratio**. This ratio expresses the amount of debt repayment a country must make in relation to its earnings from exports. Since foreign debt must be paid in foreign exchange, the ability to make these payments is critical. The lower this ratio is, the easier it will be for a country to make debt repayments. However, if this ratio is high, the country may experience difficulties in repaying foreign debt. Putting these two concepts together, one can get a picture of a country that can afford to take on more debt. A country with a high level of international reserves coupled with a low debt/export ratio should be able to comfortably repay foreign borrowing. On the other hand, a country with a low level of reserves and a high debt/export ratio may have difficulty handling more borrowing. Neither factor is a perfect predictor of a country's ability to repay debt. However, the level of both factors influences the probability that a country will be able to handle different levels of foreign borrowing. The problem of debt is really a problem of a country not being able to make prompt payments on its foreign debt. If such payments cannot be made, there is the possibility of a **default**. A default occurs when a country cannot simultaneously pay all its debts. A default does not mean that a country is bankrupt; it simply means that it cannot currently pay *all* creditors. In this situation, a number of things can happen. One of these situations is that a default might trigger a major depreciation of the exchange rate.

foreign reserves the total stock of foreign exchange held by a country at any point in time

debt/export ratio the ratio of a country's debt payments to its exports

default the inability of a country to repay all of its foreign debt when it is due

EXCHANGE RATE SHOCKS

In Chapter 19, we briefly discussed exchange rate shocks. As you may recall, this situation occurs when there is a sudden depreciation in a country's currency. Technically, this is caused by a sudden shift in either the supply of and/or the demand for foreign exchange. This situation is illustrated in Figure 21.1. Suppose that the supply and demand for foreign exchange is in initial equilibrium at point A. Now assume that the supply of foreign exchange shifts to the left from S to S′. The new equilibrium would be at point B and the exchange rate would increase from XR to XR′, a depreciation of the domestic currency. A similar effect of the exchange rate would occur as a result of a sudden increase in the demand for foreign exchange. If the demand for foreign exchange shifted from D to D′, the new equilibrium would be at point C. Again the exchange rate would increase from XR to XR′. Any combination of these two shifts would cause the exchange rate to increase even further in the direction of point D. As we will see, it is also possible for the supply of foreign exchange to increase or the demand for foreign exchange to decrease. We can use the figure to illustrate this situation. Suppose that the initial equilibrium is at point D. Any combination of an increase in the supply of foreign exchange and/or a decrease in the demand for foreign exchange would cause the exchange rate to fall and the domestic currency to appreciate. This would mean movements of the equilibrium from point D in the direction of point A. We will be able to use this figure again to illustrate various situations where there are large movements in the exchange rate over relatively short periods of

Figure 21.1 The Effect of an Exchange Rate Shock on the Foreign Exchange Market

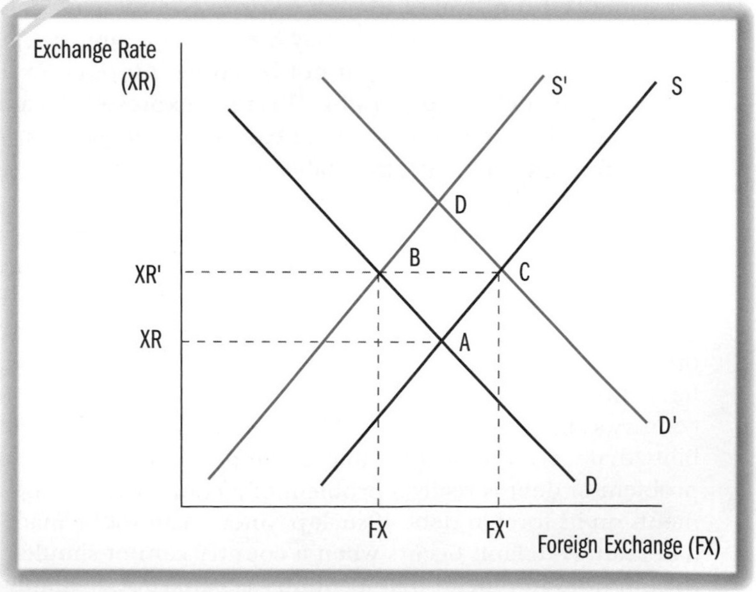

An increase in the demand for foreign exchange or a reduction in the supply of foreign exchange will increase the exchange rate.

time. In the following sections, we will cover some of the more common situations that can cause these sorts of short-run shifts.

Macroeconomic Consequences of Exchange Rate Shocks

Although an exchange rate shock could be due to either an appreciation or a depreciation of the currency, we will focus our attention on the latter. This is because, in most cases, a sudden depreciation is the most troublesome for the domestic economy. To analyze the macroeconomic consequences of an exchange rate shock, we need to review some of the material covered in Chapter 17. Like the previous analysis, we employ the aggregate demand/aggregate supply model to analyze these effects. Figure 21.2 shows the usual macroeconomic equilibrium. The price level (P) and real GDP (Y) are shown on the vertical and horizontal axis, respectively. As before, the aggregate demand curve (AD) slopes downwards and to the right and the aggregate supply curve (AS) slopes upwards and to the right. The intersection of these two curves occurs at point A. At this equilibrium, the price level is P and real GDP is Y.

Now assume that the exchange rate increases from XR to XR′, as was shown in Figure 21.1. The exchange rate shock has two effects. The main effect will be a decrease in aggregate supply. A large and sudden appreciation increases the cost of imports. As a result, the overall cost of production in the economy rises as well. This causes the AS curve to shift to the left to AS′. In Figure 21.2, this is shown as a movement in the equilibrium from point A to point B. This shift has two adverse effects on

Figure 21.2 The Effect of an Exchange Rate Shock on the Economy

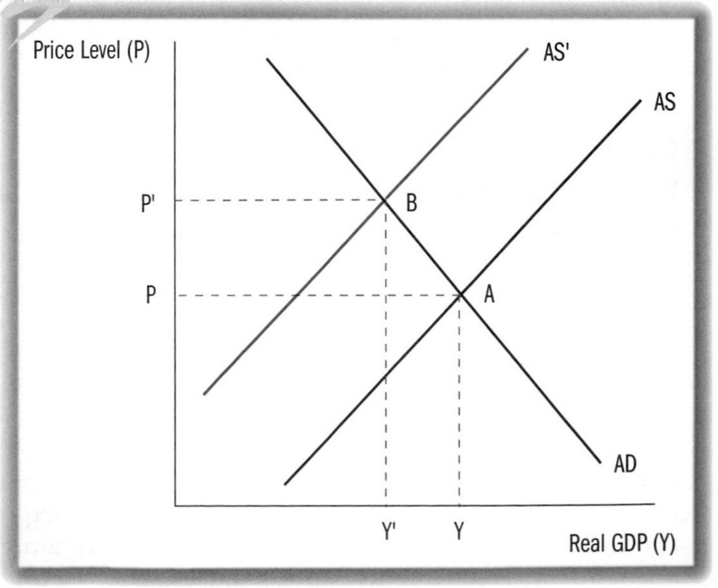

A major devaluation of the currency will tend to cause a leftward shift of the aggregate supply curve, causing equilibrium output to fall and the price level to rise.

the economy. First, the price level increases from P to P′. Second, real GDP declines from Y to Y′. Obviously, the larger the depreciation the larger the effects on the price level and real GDP will be. In the short run, an extremely large depreciation can have substantial effects on the domestic economy.

Such a shock would be an uncomfortable experience in a high-income country. An increase in the price level is virtually never a welcome occurrence. Likewise, the increase in the unemployment rate associated with a falling real GDP is not a good thing. However, for developing countries, this macroeconomic environment has more serious consequences. Inflation is especially hard on the poor. An inflation induced drop in real income of 10 percent is uncomfortable in a country with GDP per capita of $20,000. It is a much more serious problem in a country where GDP per capita is $2,000 or less. The same is true of the unemployment associated with a falling real GDP. In a developed country, there are social safety nets to help to cushion the economic blow of rising unemployment. In many developing countries, these social safety nets either are nonexistent or much less broad in their coverage. As we move through this material, keep in mind that the effects on the domestic economy caused by exchange rate shocks may have much more serious macroeconomic consequences than would be the case in high-income countries.

Sources of Exchange Rate Shocks

Unfortunately, exchange rate shocks are more prevalent in developing countries. Such shocks are rare in high-income countries. For high-income countries, exchange rates may be volatile. However the changes in the exchange rate usually are more muted and occur over longer periods of time. In this section, we will be able to see why this is the case. In developing countries, the sources of exchange rate shocks are a function of economic conditions that are common in low- and middle-income countries. In covering this material, keep in mind that the situations being described would be rare in a high-income country.

Commodity Price Shocks

In Chapter 11, we covered economic development in countries where the production of a primary commodity is an important part of overall economic activity. In that chapter, we indicated that the possession of natural resources can mean faster economic growth. However, it also was noted that an economic development strategy based on primary commodities sometimes creates costs for the economy overall. For these types of economies, there is an additional problem that could not be discussed earlier because we needed a model of exchange rate determination to explain this.

A commodity price shock can be illustrated using Figure 21.1. First, assume that the production of one or more primary commodities composes a substantial portion of a country's exports. This is not an unrealistic assumption because primary commodities account for approximately 40 percent of the exports of developing countries. Second, assume that exports and imports represent a nontrivial percentage of GDP. Again this is not unrealistic. Exports and imports account for 26.5 and 24.9 percent of the collective GDP of developing countries. Now assume that the price of a particular primary commodity falls dramatically in world markets. The immediate effect of this drop would be a large reduction of inflows of foreign exchange. This is shown in Figure 21.1 as a leftward shift in the supply of foreign exchange. The exchange rate would increase from XR to XR′ in a short period of time. The result of a major fall in the price of a primary commodity could be the depreciation of the domestic currency. However, is it not possible that the lower price of the commodity would be offset by an increase in the quantity demanded? As we showed in Chapter 11, this is rarely the case. The demand for primary commodities normally is inelastic. This means that as prices fall, the quantity demanded increases but not by very much. The result is that falling prices usually reduce the supply of foreign exchange. The effects of this depreciation are shown in Figure 21.2. The AS curve shifts to the left. As a result, the price level rises and real GDP falls. For some countries, falling commodity prices can lead to inflation, a lower real GDP, and higher unemployment.

For a country producing primary commodities, these effects can occur in reverse. Primary commodities also can increase substantially in price. If commodity prices increase, this can increase the supply of foreign exchange. Figure 21.1 depicts this as a rightward shift in the supply of foreign exchange. In this case, the exchange rate would decline from XR′ to XR. The macroeconomic effects of this can be seen in Figure 21.2. An appreciating domestic currency would lower the cost of imports. The effect of lower-cost imports would be to shift the aggregate supply curve to the right. This creates a very favorable macroeconomic environment as the price level falls from P′ to P and real GDP increases from Y′ to Y. If the appreciation is large and/or sustained, it could create rapid economic growth.

The two situations described above illustrate the advantages and disadvantages of a country being an exporter of primary commodities. If a primary commodity is important to an economy, the economy at times can grow rather fast. On the other hand, there may be times when these exports create a difficult macroeconomic environment. For these countries, the management of foreign reserves may be a critical issue. Suppose a country is subject to potential swings in the exchange rate caused by fluctuations in commodity prices. Usually, a country has little control over commodity prices. However, it may be able to mitigate wide swings in the exchange rate. If commodity prices are high, the government may want to limit the appreciation of the currency by buying foreign exchange. This can be done by selling the domestic currency and buying foreign exchange. This sort of intervention would decrease the boom associated with high commodity prices. In this situation, the government would be accumulating foreign exchange. A reasonable question is why would a country want to do this? The answer lies in the unfortunate reality that high commodity prices usually don't last forever. Periods of high commodity prices frequently are followed by low prices. If this happens too rapidly, the exchange rate could depreciate rather quickly. The previously accumulated foreign reserves then become useful. If the government has sufficient foreign reserves, foreign exchange can be sold to prevent the supply from falling too fast. This would help to offset the effects of an exchange rate shock. No country that is an exporter of primary commodities could hope to perfectly stabilize the exchange rate. However, for these countries the management of the level of foreign reserves is very important as a tool for stabilizing the economy in the face of wide swings in commodity prices.

Dutch Disease

The earlier development of a model of exchange rate determination allows us to illustrate one other problem associated with the exports of primary commodities. The textbook example of the problem is based on the real-world case of the Netherlands. In the early 1960s, the Netherlands began exporting relatively large amounts of natural gas. This increase in exports results in a rightward shift in the supply of foreign exchange. This effect is shown in Figure 21.3 as a movement of the supply curve from S to S′. As a result the exchange rate falls from XR to XR′. Since trade is balanced this means that exports increase from FX to FX′.

However, something else is happening that is not immediately obvious. The original supply curve (S) is the supply of exports excluding the new exports of natural gas. As the exchange rate falls, these exports become more expensive. Total exports increase, but what happens to exports of products that are not natural gas? At the new exchange rate, these exports are now FX″. Total exports have risen but these exports have fallen from FX to FX″. The appreciation of the domestic currency has reduced exports that are not natural gas. The country as a whole is better off but some exporters have been harmed. This is not a country specific example as the principle is general. Exports of primary commodities may make it more difficult to export other products. For a developed country such as the Netherlands, the effect may be an annoyance but it is not a critical factor in overall economic development. For a developing country, the problem may be more serious. In many cases, developing countries are just starting the process of industrialization. The start of this process may be developing labor-intensive industries exporting standardized products where an important consideration is production costs. In this case, the appreciation of the exchange rate caused by primary commodity exports may slow down the development of other export industries.

Figure 21.3 The Impact of Dutch Disease on Exports

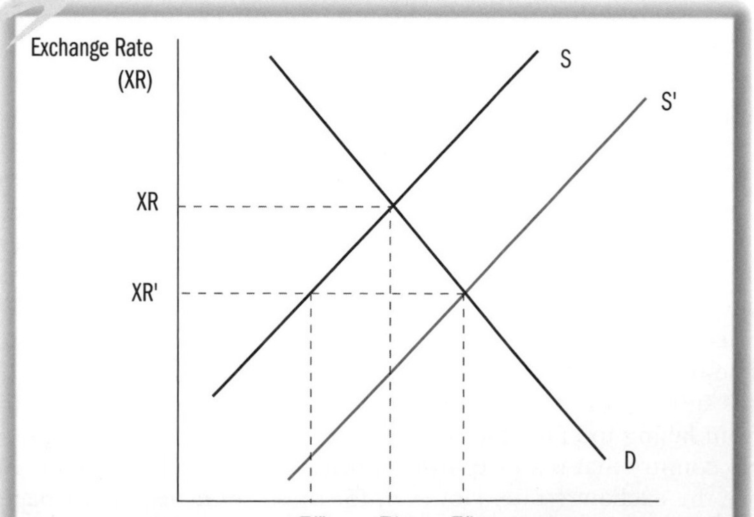

Exchange Controls

> "How many more fiascos will it take before responsible people are finally convinced that a system of pegged exchange rates is not a satisfactory financial arrangement?"
>
> —MILTON FRIEDMAN

In Chapter 19, we discussed fixed exchange rates. In that chapter, two different methods of fixing the exchange rate were covered: exchange controls and intervention. In this section we review the macroeconomic consequences of a large increase in the exchange rate when these forms of fixing the exchange rate become unsustainable. To begin our analyses, consider Figure 21.4. In this figure, equilibrium in the foreign exchange market is at point A where the demand and supply of foreign exchange intersect. The resulting equilibrium exchange rate is XR. However, the government desires an exchange rate that is below the equilibrium such as XR′. This exchange rate is inconsistent with balanced trade. At XR′ there is a current account deficit that is not completely offset by a financial/capital account surplus. The bottom line is that there is a shortage of foreign exchange equal to the difference between points B and C at the exchange rate desired by the government.

One way to deal with this situation is through exchange controls. In this case, the government becomes a monopolist with respect to foreign exchange. All foreign exchange legally must be surrendered to the government. The government then deals with the shortage of foreign exchange by rationing the available supply. However, let's

Figure 21.4 Effects of Exchange Controls

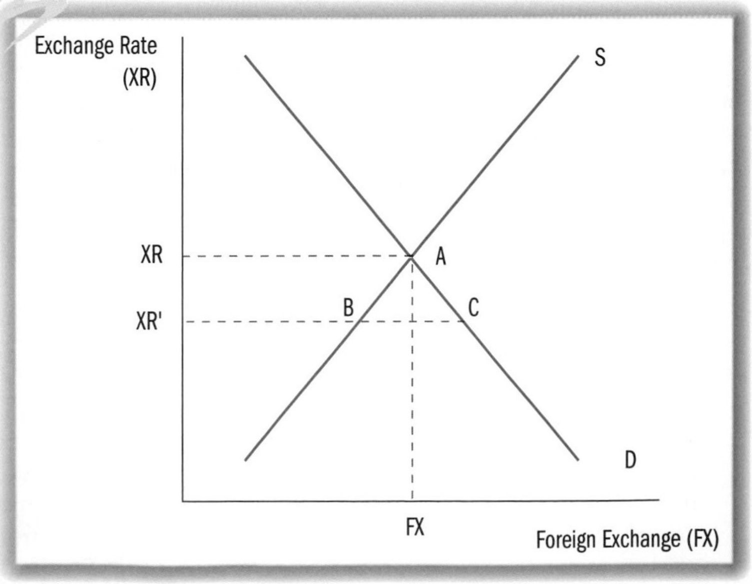

Equilibrium in the foreign exchange market is at point A where the demand and supply of foreign exchange intersect. However, if the government fixes the exchange rate at XR′, there would be a shortage of foreign exchange equal to the difference between points B and C.

Moral Hazard and the IMF

With increasing frequency, one often hears or reads about some sort of financial crisis in one or more developing countries. These situations are usually very similar to the examples we describe in the chapter. Generally, a country has borrowed heavily from both commercial banks in developed countries and international institutions, which make loans for economic development. At some point, the country finds itself in a position where it is unable to make all of the debt payments on their promised schedule. Very often this situation triggers a "crisis" that may spread from the original country to other countries. In many cases, this crisis leads to a series of negotiations involving the country, the country's creditors, and the IMF. The usual result of these negotiations is that the payments on the country's debt are "rescheduled." Rescheduled is a term used to imply the following process: The IMF agrees to loan the country more money to make current payments on the debt. In return, the country agrees to take steps to reduce the need to borrow more money or increase its ability to earn foreign exchange. The country's creditors agree to increase the maturity of the country's debt so that the country can more comfortably make scheduled payments. For the moment, the crisis has been resolved. However, notice what the lenders have done. They have agreed to loan more money to a country that has just experienced difficulties in paying the *existing* debt. In many similar situations, creditors/lenders would not do this.

The reason that creditors/lenders are willing to do this is related to the problem of *moral hazard.* Moral hazard refers to the tendency of market participants to engage in riskier behavior if they believe that they will not have to bear all of the costs of engaging in this behavior. If a moral hazard problem exists in a market, then one should look for some entity that is not governed by market forces. The suspect in this case is the IMF. Banks and other lending institutions may be willing to loan more to developing countries because the presence of the IMF reduces the probability of losses on these loans. Normally, if a country defaulted on its loans, the lenders would take an immediate loss. However, if the IMF provides money to prevent a default, then the creditors are protected from these losses. This encourages lenders to make loans that are riskier than they would make if the IMF didn't exist. In these situations, the IMF is not only "bailing out" the country, but it may also be protecting the earnings of commercial banks. Since both the countries and the lenders have been protected from the full costs of their behavior, their behavior may change. They may now engage in borrowing and lending that both parties know is risky because they have some confidence that the IMF will help them if the country experiences future problems servicing its debt. The stage is now set for yet another "crisis" at some point in the future.

suppose that the economy is growing. In this case, the demand for foreign exchange also is growing. In addition, suppose that the supply of foreign exchange is growing at a slower rate or in some cases actually declining. Why would this be the case? First, it may have to do with exports of primary commodities. Since the demand for these commodities may not be growing fast in the world economy, the supply of foreign exchange for the country may not be growing fast. Second, if the nominal exchange rate is pegged, the real exchange rate may be appreciating. In this case, labor in a developing country is getting more expensive. MNCs may choose to reduce production in this country and/or move production to other countries where the labor is now cheaper. The result is that, over time, the current account deficit may be growing.

This assumes that the domestic rate of inflation is still low. If this is not the case, then the problem becomes even worse. At some point, the fixed exchange rate may have to change. Using Figure 21.4, this would be shown as a movement of the exchange rate from XR′ back toward XR. Export earnings may become so low relative to the demand that the country cannot pay for essential imports such as food, fuel, and intermediate goods. Left unattended for too long, the exchange rate may have to increase by a large amount in a short period of time. The macroeconomic consequences should be familiar. In Figure 21.2, this would be shown as a leftward shift in the aggregate supply curve. As before, the price level would rise and real GDP would fall.

Intervention, Capital Flights, and Defaults

As was shown both in a previous chapter and earlier in this chapter, intervention in the foreign exchange market can be used to affect the exchange rate. There may be several reasons for this. In a developed country, intervention may be used to smooth out minor changes in the exchange rate in the short run. As was shown earlier in the chapter, intervention may be useful for a country that exports primary commodities. For other countries, intervention may be a way of avoiding the macroeconomic consequences of an overvalued exchange rate. This last situation is the focus of this section.

Consider a country in an inconsistent position with respect to internal and external balance. Suppose that the government wants to pursue rapid economic growth with relatively low inflation. In order to accomplish this, let's assume that the government pursues both expansionary fiscal and monetary policies. The effects are shown in Figure 21.5. The expansionary policies cause a rightward shift of aggregate demand

Figure 21.5 Effects of An Expansionary Macroeconomic Policy

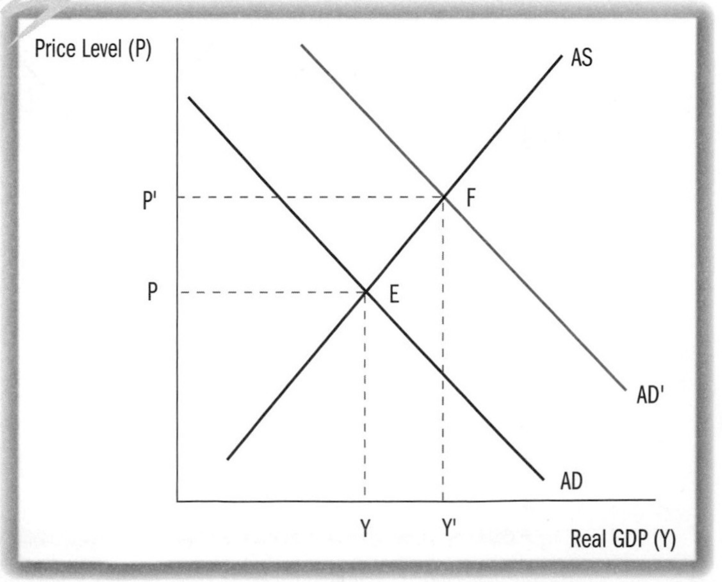

An expansionary fiscal policy causes the aggregate demand curve to increase and equilibrium output and the price level will rise.

from AD to AD′. Both real GDP and the price level (P) increase as the economy moves from equilibrium E to F. This situation may create a problem with respect to the country's external balance. To illustrate this, consider Figure 21.6. The initial equilibrium in the foreign exchange market is at point A with an exchange rate of XR. If the economy is growing rapidly, the demand for foreign exchange also may be increasing rapidly. The demand for foreign exchange may shift from D to D′. This would cause an increase in the exchange rate from XR to XR′. However, if imports are a large component of GDP, this may put further upward pressure on the price level. The economy may be growing rapidly but the price level may start reaching uncomfortably high levels.

Intervention in the form of selling foreign exchange makes this problem easier to deal with in the short run. Selling foreign exchange may stabilize the exchange rate as shown in Figure 21.6. The intervention shifts the supply of foreign exchange from S to S′. In turn, this reduces the tendency of the domestic currency to depreciate. A lower exchange rate helps reduce inflationary pressures by making imports cheaper. There is another effect. The other side of selling foreign exchange is buying domestic currency. To the extent that the government does not sterilize this effect, the growth rate of the money supply can be reduced. Again, this relieves some of the upward pressure on the price level.

The difficulty lies in the supply of foreign reserves. If the government has a large quantity of foreign reserves, intervention may be pursued as long as this supply is adequate. The question then becomes what happens if this source of foreign reserves is not enough to pursue intervention? One possibility was covered in the first section of

Figure 21.6 Effects of Intervention in the Foreign Exchange Market

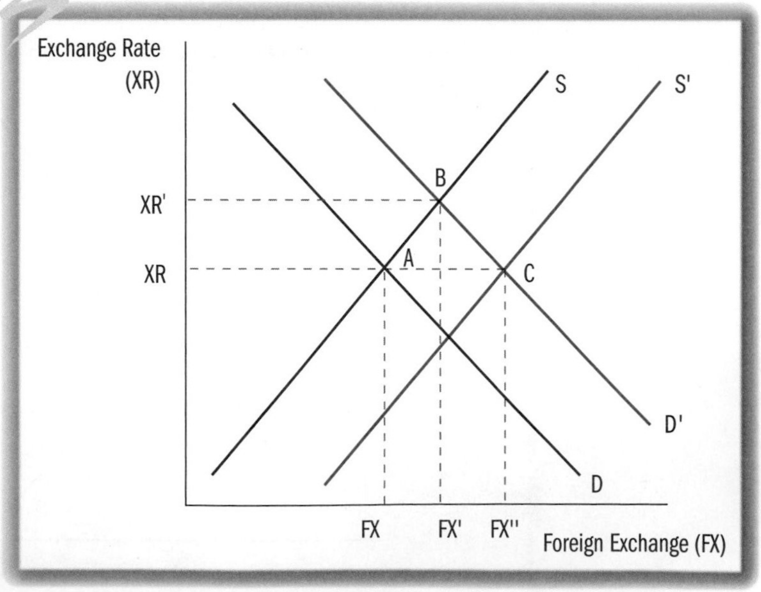

Intervention in the form of selling foreign exchange may stabilize the exchange rate at XR as the intervention shifts the supply of foreign exchange from S to S.'

the chapter. The government may be able to borrow foreign exchange from a commercial bank. This foreign exchange then is used to support intervention in the foreign exchange market. The good side of this strategy is that the economy may be able to continue to grow at a fast rate with relatively low inflation. The bad side is that the country is accumulating foreign debt. Further, the potential consequences of this policy are well known. What if a country loses access to borrowing foreign exchange for the purpose of intervention? The exhaustion of foreign reserves leads to a withdrawal of the government as a supplier of foreign exchange. The supply of foreign exchange in Figure 21.6 shifts rapidly to the left causing a large depreciation of the domestic currency. The macroeconomic consequences were described in previous sections. The aggregate supply curve shifts to the left. The price level rises and real GDP falls. A classic exchange rate shock has occurred.

In this situation, things can get even worse than described above. First, these events may be almost predictable. The data necessary to see this crisis unfolding is widely available. A sustained drop in a country's foreign reserves coupled with a current account deficit is an indication of potential problems. If the government's foreign debt also is rising, this is even more information indicative of potential problems. If the exchange rate is overvalued, exports may not be rising very fast. With a rising foreign debt, the debt/export ratio may be increasing. In this case, the possibility of an appreciation of the currency is slight. The probability of a depreciation becomes higher over time. The result is that capital starts leaving the country to avoid the losses associated with a depreciation. This creates an increase in the demand for foreign exchange that further increases the pressure for a depreciation. The lenders can see the same information. At some point, the country may be unable to secure further amounts of foreign exchange. An exchange rate shock is now unavoidable.

The aftermath of an exchange rate shock can lead to the following set of circumstances that are very common in developing countries. For a developing country that has just experienced an exchange rate shock, foreign reserves are now negligible and further borrowing of foreign exchange is not possible. The debt/export ratio for the country is very high. After making payments on the foreign debt, there is very little foreign exchange left for other imports. Because of the J-curve effect the devaluation has not improved the current account deficit. Imports have become much more expensive and exports have not yet risen. Real GDP has fallen and the price level has risen. Defaulting on the country's foreign debt now looks like a possible option. The creditors have become nervous that such a default at minimum will damage short-run earnings. What would normally occur is that the country and its lenders would work out an arrangement to reschedule payment of the debt in a mutually agreeable way. The short-run performance of the economy would be poor, but with better economic management, growth would eventually continue.

In the first section of the chapter, we showed that it is normal for a developing country to be a net borrower from the rest of the world. If the borrowed capital is invested in the public and private sectors and enhances long run economic growth, this borrowing should rarely cause serious economic problems. Borrowing for intervention in the foreign exchange market potentially is much more of a problem. The money borrowed for intervention was not invested for long run growth. This borrowing was used to support macroeconomic policies that were not sustainable. Such borrowing would not occur too many times before both countries and the international

The Asian Crisis and Financial Contagion

On July 2, 1997, the government of Thailand moved from a fixed exchange rate to a floating exchange rate, as the current account deficit had reached 8 percent of GDP. The depreciation was made worse by the flight of capital out of Thailand. One could have been excused for thinking that the implications of this event for the world economy would be slight. Unfortunately, this was not the case. Within months, capital started flowing out of Indonesia and Malaysia. From there the crisis spread to the Philippines, Hong Kong, South Korea, and Taiwan. A depreciation of the Thai bhat had triggered a flight of capital from an entire region. Instead of one exchange rate shock, the crisis was composed of a series of such shocks in countries with no obvious balance of payments problems. Further, this "Asian Crisis" led to the fear that the crisis might become global. Fortunately, those fears proved to be overblown. However, this sort of crisis was not a totally isolated event. Defaults on debt in some Latin American countries have occasionally led to capital flights from that region. These are examples of what is known as financial contagion. *Financial contagion* is the term used to describe the situation where an economic crisis in one country has repercussions in other countries.

For a number of reasons, these events are a source of intense study. Partially, this is because financial contagion can be observed in other contexts such as securities markets. Secondly, financial contagion doesn't always occur. A crisis in one country doesn't always spread to other countries. Third, financial contagion may have a number of causes that are not mutually exclusive. A crisis may spread more readily among countries that are linked together through trade and/or financial markets. A crisis in Mexico may spread more easily to Brazil than to South Korea. Also, in some cases investors may move in a "herd" that can cause a small crisis to become worse over time. Another factor may be whether or not the crisis was anticipated. Market participants may move more slowly in cases where the problem has been noticed beforehand. The reaction to an unanticipated event may be more severe. Whatever the explanation, financial contagion is not a new phenomenon and it is not likely to disappear. The task now is to understand these events to learn lessons about how to reduce their severity in the future.

capital market learned that such lending was risky for all parties. The fact that this situation still occurs has something to do with another institution in the world economy.

THE IMF AND DEVELOPING COUNTRIES

As we saw in the preceding chapter, the IMF was founded in the 1940s to be the centerpiece of the international monetary system. In the Bretton Woods system of fixed exchange rates, the IMF acted as a lender of foreign exchange to countries that needed to temporarily intervene in the foreign exchange market. The breakup of the Bretton Woods system in the early 1970s created something of a problem for the IMF. In effect, the institution had lost its central mission. Without a clearly defined new mandate the IMF has become more and more involved with the developing countries. In the next section, we will examine this new role for the IMF by looking at the various ways it now loans money to countries.

IMF Conditionality

The roots of the current antipathy toward the IMF can be traced back to its original mission. Traditionally, the IMF made short-run loans to countries with temporary balance of payments problems. In the world of the 1950s, the idea behind this lending was sound. The usual problem can be illustrated in panel a of Figure 21.7. Suppose that a country's exchange rate was initially in equilibrium at point A. Further assume that the domestic economy is in equilibrium at point A in panel b. Now suppose that the country pursues an expansionary fiscal policy. Remember that with fixed exchange rates fiscal policy is more effective than monetary policy. We will focus on the former to keep the analysis as simple as possible. In panel a the demand for foreign exchange will increase from D to D′. The new equilibrium is at point B. At the fixed exchange rate of XR, the country now has a current account deficit equivalent to the difference between A and B. The effects on the domestic economy of an expansionary fiscal policy are predictable. Aggregate demand moves from AD to AD′ and both the price level and real GDP increase. Now assume that the government is covering the deficit by using its own foreign reserves to shift the supply of foreign exchange from S to S′. The deficit is consistent with the fixed exchange rate only so long as the government has foreign reserves.

Now suppose that the government runs out of foreign reserves. The next stop is the IMF. Originally each country contributed 25 percent of a quota in dollars or gold and the balance of its quota in its own domestic currency. In total, the country could borrow up to 125 percent of its quota in five separate parts or tranches. Each tranche is now 37.5 percent of quota. The total quota is determined by a formula related to the relative size of the country's GDP in the world economy. The country can borrow its first tranche as a matter of right without any obligations. Once a country moves into the second or higher tranches the IMF begins to attach conditions to further borrowing. These conditions are the source of the term "conditionality." The higher the country goes, the stiffer these conditions. In a fixed exchange rate system, the conditions are clear. The government needs to take steps to reduce aggregate demand. In turn this will reduce the demand for foreign exchange and return the balance of payments to balance. This may be necessary in this system but it will not be popular. First, a decrease in aggregate demand will lower GDP and potentially increase unemployment. This is not a step any politician likes to take. There is a second and more philosophical problem. Higher levels of conditionality can put the IMF into the position of virtually dictating a country's macroeconomic policy. The effect of this can be that a country has handed overall economic policy to a group of advisors from a multilateral institution. In these circumstances, it is not surprising that the IMF is an unpopular institution in many countries. However, IMF conditionality was designed for the situation it faced in the 1950s and 1960s. Most borrowing was done by high-income countries that had temporary balance of payments problems that a bit of fiscal "austerity" could solve. In these circumstances, the IMF might not be popular but its lending did not lead to the controversial position it has today.

In many developing countries, the IMF and the austerity programs that come along with conditionality are more than unpopular. To understand why, it is necessary to put IMF conditionality into a developing country context. Understandably, the IMF has a difficult time enforcing conditionality. The result can be that the IMF has made

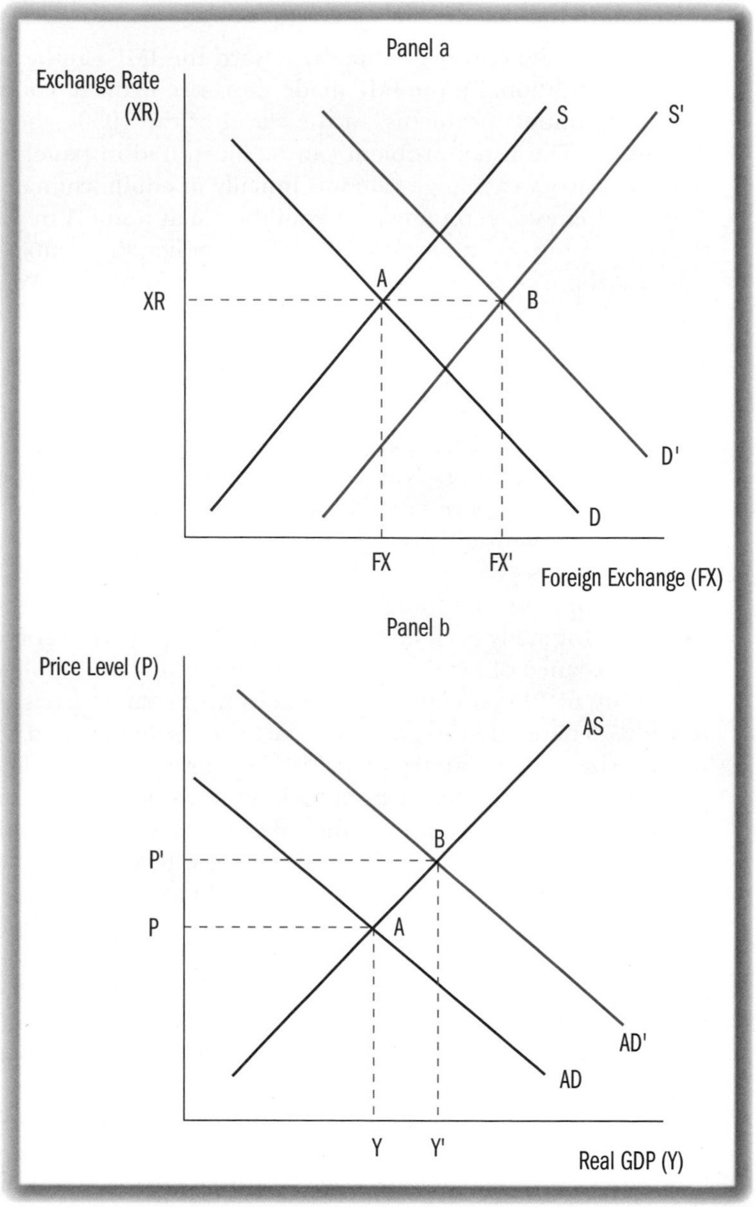

Figure 21.7 Macroeconomic Imbalances and the IMF

If a country pursues an expansionary fiscal policy, the demand for foreign exchange will increase from D to D′. At the fixed exchange rate of XR, the country now has a current account deficit equivalent to the difference between A and B. The effect on the domestic economy is an increase in aggregate demand moves from AD to AD′ and both the price level and real GDP increase. The current account deficit is consistent with the fixed exchange rate only so long as the government has foreign reserves.

conditional loans and the country has not made an adequate adjustment of its macroeconomic policy. The end of this process may be a highly indebted country that is forced to depreciate its currency due to a lack of foreign reserves for intervention. In certain circumstances, IMF conditionality can become even more difficult. Our previous discussions of exchange rate shocks showed that such shocks usually increase the price level and lower real GDP. As we indicated earlier, this combination is truly harsh in a developing country. If the IMF is involved in the countries macroeconomic policy, things can be even worse. This situation is shown in Figure 21.8. The exchange rate shock is shown as a leftward shift of aggregate supply from AS to AS′ and the price level increases and real GDP falls. Further assume that as a result of previous lending the IMF is attempting to impose tighter fiscal and/or monetary policies. The effect of these conditions would be to shift aggregate demand from AD to AD′. The effect of this shift would be to relieve some of the upward pressure on prices. Unfortunately, the combination of the shift of aggregate supply to the left and a fall in aggregate demand makes the drop in real GDP even worse. The dual effect of an exchange rate shock and IMF conditionality has the potential to create extreme economic hardship in a country that is by definition already poor.

Figure 21.8 Effects of a Major Devaluation and an IMF Austerity Program

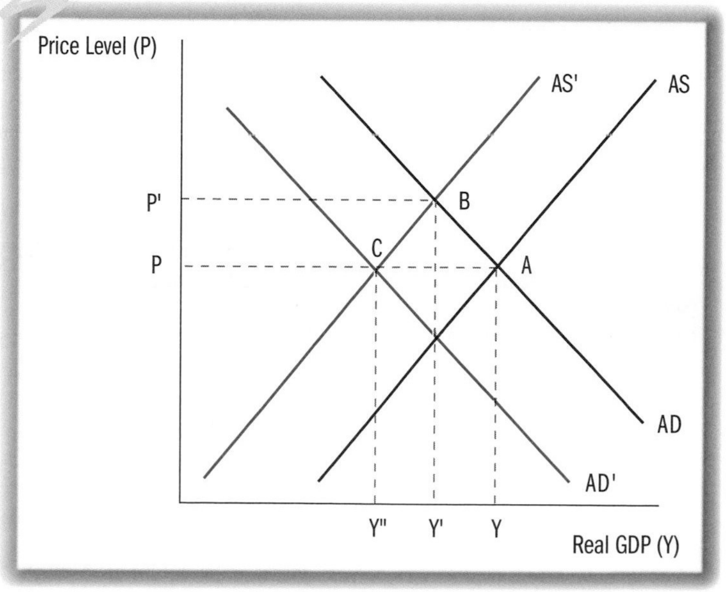

When a country has an exchange rate shock, the aggregate supply shifts from AS to AS′ and the price level increases and real GDP falls. If the IMF also imposes an austerity program on the country the aggregate demand shifts from AD to AD′. The combination of the shift of aggregate supply to the left and a fall in aggregate demand makes the drop in real GDP larger.

The Future of the IMF

The original purpose of IMF lending was to provide short-run loans of foreign exchange to countries with temporary balance of payments problems. IMF loans provided the necessary foreign exchange to support intervention activities until macroeconomic policies could be put into place that would correct the imbalance. Since the breakup of the Bretton Woods system, IMF lending has taken on a somewhat different character. These changes are reflected both in newer forms of lending by the IMF and the length of the loans.

Since the 1960s, IMF lending has taken on two characteristics that were not envisioned originally. Table 21.3 shows the newer forms of IMF lending. Notice that many of the newer programs are not related to traditional lending to support the value of the currency over a short period of time. This list represents a first shift in IMF lending. Loans are now made to explicitly cover exchange rate shocks caused by changes in commodity prices. In a similar vein, loans are now made to cover oil shocks. The newer lending programs are designed to enhance general economic development objectives. In reality, this is the meaning of structural adjustment and poverty reduction and

Table 21.3 Special Financing Facilities of the IMF

Year of Implementation	Name of Facility	Purpose
1963	Compensatory Financing	Assist countries experiencing either a sudden shortfall in export earnings or an increase in the cost of cereal imports caused by fluctuating world commodity prices.
1968	Compensatory & Contingency Financing	Assist countries experiencing either a sudden external shock.
1969	Buffer Stock Financing	To support international buffer stocks and to stabilize commodity prices.
1974	Oil Import	To finance an increase in oil import costs.
1975	Extended Fund	To create a longer time frame for countries experiencing adjustment lending.
1979	Supplementary Financing	To supplement funds by borrowing from some members and lending to other members.
1986	Structural Adjustment	Assist developing countries through concessional financing.
1987	Enhanced Structural Adjustment	Assist developing countries through concessional financing.
1993	Systematic Transformation	Assist and support countries as they change from a planned to a market economy.
1997	Supplementary Reserve	Assist countries in addressing balance of payments crises with large volume short-term, high interest rate loans.
1999	Poverty Reduction & Growth	Replaced the Enhanced Structural Adjustment and integrates poverty reduction with macroeconomic policies.

Source: www.imf.org

growth. A second trend is the length of the loans. Originally, loans from the IMF were to be repaid over a few years. Increasingly, IMF loans are more long run in nature. In both cases, the result is that IMF lending is now heavily oriented toward lending to developing countries. The institution has evolved from the center of the world's monetary system to an economic development institution.

If one looks closely at the newer programs initiated by the IMF, they look suspiciously like the loans and assistance provided by the World Bank. Increasingly the two institutions are becoming more similar. However, this movement is virtually all a movement of the IMF into lending for economic development. This is not to imply any criticism of the World Bank. It simply has stuck to its original mission. As we saw in Chapter 11, the World Bank primarily makes loans for individual projects in developing countries. The IMF has taken up the role of making loans to countries for less specific economic development programs. This lending takes on two general forms. First, as we saw in Chapter 11 many countries are now in the process of making the painful adjustment from failed import-substitution development policies to export promotion. One of the problems with this process is the balance of payments implications. In this transition, countries must open up highly protected domestic markets. Invariably this increases the level of imports. At the same time, they must increase exports. This may be difficult to do in the short run. Structural adjustment lending may ease this process and encourage more countries to make these sorts of policy changes. Second countries transitioning from planned economies to market economies face enormous balance of payments difficulties during this transition. Imports can expand rapidly, as domestic residents now have a much larger selection of goods to buy. On the other hand, firms in planned economies usually were not competitive in world markets. It may take time for these firms to restructure sufficiently for these countries to increase exports.

Theoretically, the IMF can contribute to the process of economic development. However, it faces several problems. The first is conditionality. Applying contractionary macroeconomic policies in a poor country can have devastating short-run effects on income in developing countries. Such austerity programs may be necessary, but implementing them is difficult in the context of high levels of absolute poverty. Second, the IMF is very involved in lending to large middle-income countries. Some of these countries have become heavily indebted to the IMF, commercial banks, and holders of sovereign debt in the form of bonds. At times, this puts the IMF into the position of mediating between the country and its creditors. This is a role far removed from anything envisioned in the IMF's original charter. Further, it can create the impression that the IMF now is just an extension of the private parts of the international capital markets.

All of these issues create problems for the institution. The nature of its lending has changed. This change is manifested in a blurring of the distinction between the IMF and the World Bank. Its image in developing countries is poor at best. Even in developed countries the perception is sometimes that the IMF has become too closely tied to major participants in the international capital markets. The problem is not new. Once the Bretton Woods system collapsed the role of the IMF became less clear. The two oil shocks of the 1970s temporarily gave the IMF a useful role in the world economy. Since then, its role is less clear. For any reform of the IMF to be meaningful, what the role of the IMF in world of mixed exchange rate systems needs to be made clearer.

SUMMARY

1. Capital tends to flow from the developed countries to the developing countries because of differences in factor abundance. Developing countries tend to run current account deficits that are offset by financial/capital account surpluses.
2. Borrowing by developing countries takes the form of either debt or equity. Debt is usually in the form of bonds or loans from banks in developed countries. Payments on debt have to made at certain points in time no matter what the economic condition of the borrower is. Equity borrowing is normally in the form of FDI or indirect investment in stocks.
3. In 2006, net borrowing by the developing countries was $402 billion. The bulk of this borrowing was equity in the form of FDI in the middle-income countries. In the same year, the total stock of borrowing by the developing countries was $2.7 trillion.
4. The foreign debt of the developing countries has to be repaid over time. Countries need an adequate supply of foreign reserves to make prompt debt payments. Further, foreign debt will be easier to service if the debt/export ratio is relatively low.
5. Exchange rate shocks occur if there is a sudden shift in either the demand for or the supply of foreign exchange. The most common type of exchange rate shock is a large reduction in the supply of foreign exchange. Such a shock causes a large depreciation of the currency.
6. A major depreciation of the currency typically causes a decrease in aggregate supply. The result of this change in aggregate supply is an increase in the price level coupled with a decrease in real GDP.
7. If a country is a major exporter of a primary commodity, then changes in commodity prices can cause exchange rate shocks. Also, exports of commodities may cause the currency to appreciate and make it more difficult for the country to export other products.
8. Some countries fix the exchange rate by making the government the only legal buyer and seller of foreign exchange. These exchange controls increase the probability that the currency becomes overvalued. In turn, this increases the likelihood of an exchange rate shock. Exchange control systems frequently lead to the creation of a black market in foreign exchange.
9. Countries can use intervention in the foreign exchange market to stabilize the exchange rate. If borrowing for intervention is too heavy, the country runs the risk of suddenly losing its ability to intervene. Concerns over this type of situation can lead to capital flight from a country. Financial contagion occurs when a shock in one country spreads to other countries, as in the Asian crisis of the late 1990s.
10. Since the early 1970s, the IMF has been heavily involved in lending to developing countries. This lending comes with conditions that influence the borrowing countries' macroeconomic policies. This "conditionality" has been controversial in the context of lending to developing countries.
11. Over time, IMF lending has broadened from pure balance of payments support to more general lending in support of economic development. This shift in focus has made IMF lending more similar to the activities of the World Bank.

KEY CONCEPTS AND TERMS

- debt p. 499
- equity p. 499
- foreign reserves p. 501
- debt/export ratio p. 501
- default p. 501

PROBLEMS AND QUESTIONS FOR REVIEW

1. Explain why capital tends to flow from developed to developing countries. Describe how these inflows into the developing countries show up in the balance of payments.

2. Define both debt and equity and explain the difference between the two.
3. Describe both the stock of debt owed by the developing countries and the flow of capital into these countries in a recent year.
4. Describe how the level of foreign reserves and the debt/export ratio affect the ability of a country to pay foreign debt.
5. Graph an exchange rate shock caused by a decrease in the supply of foreign exchange. Next, show how this shock affects a country's price level and real GDP.
6. How do commodity price shocks affect the exchange rate, the price level, and real GDP?
7. Show what happens to the exchange rate and the domestic economy when a country can no longer borrow to support intervention in the foreign exchange market.
8. Explain what the term IMF conditionality means.
9. Describe why the IMF is a controversial institution.
10. Over time, the IMF and the World Bank are becoming more similar. Discuss to what extent this statement is true.
11. Why would the government of a developing country need to borrow money in the international capital markets?
12. Borrowing in the form of debt is riskier than borrowing in the form of equity. Explain why this is true.
13. Describe the total external debt of the developing countries. How is this debt split between public and private sources? How much of the debt is incurred by low- versus middle-income countries?
14. Using the data in Chapter 1 or Chapter 11, calculate the debt/export ratios in total for low- and middle-income countries.
15. First, go to the Web site www.economist.com. On the left side, click on Weekly Indicators. Now click on Foreign Reserves. List the current amount of foreign reserves for China, India, Brazil, Mexico, and Turkey. Describe the differences in the level of foreign reserves for these countries.
16. First, go to the Web site www.economist.com. On the left side, click on Weekly Indicators. Next click on The Economist Commodity Price Index. Looking at the one month and one year changes in prices, describe the movements in prices for the various commodity indexes.
17. Economists sometimes use the phrase "the curse of oil" to describe the relatively poor economic performance of oil-exporting countries. Describe this phrase in terms of Dutch Disease.
18. Describe the concept of moral hazard. How does this relate to the IMF?
19. A country could experience an exchange rate shock even if its debt/export ratio is low if a country close to it experiences this sort of shock. Explain how this could happen.
20. How many different ways is it possible to qualify for a loan from the IMF?

SUGGESTED READINGS AND WEB SITES

Paul Blustein, *And The Money Kept Rolling In (And Out),* New York: Public Affairs, 2005.

A fascinating recounting of the role of the IMF in the recent economic turmoil in Argentina.

Guillermo A. Calvo and Frederic S. Mishkin, "The Mirage of Exchange Rate Regimes for Emerging Market Economies," *Journal of Economic Perspectives* 17(4), Fall 2003, pp. 98–118.

A good article on the choice of an exchange-rate system for developing countries.

Marcelle Chauvet and Fang Dong, "Leading Indicators of Country Risk and Currency Crisis: The Asian Experience," *Federal Reserve Bank of Atlanta Economic Review* 89(4), First Quarter 2004, pp. 25–37.

A look at whether or not the Asian crisis was predictable.

Barry Eichengreen, "Restructuring Foreign Debt," *Journal of Economic Perspectives* 17(4), Fall 2003, pp. 75–98.

The details on what happens after a default.

Finance & Development (www.imf.org)

An outstanding quarterly publication containing articles on economic development in general. This publication will give you a good feel for how the IMF views its role in economic development.

IMF (www.imf.org)

The main source of information on the IMF. The publication's section contains a wealth of information on capital flows and developing countries.

Graciela L. Kaminsky, Carmen M. Reinhart, and Carlos A. Vegh, "The Unholy Trinity of Financial Contagion," *Journal of Economic Perspectives* 17(4), Fall 2003, pp. 51–74.

A thorough look at financial contagion in the context of exchange-rate shocks.

"No Pain, No Gain," *The Economist,* December 13, 2003, p. 77.

Does a currency crisis reduce long-run economic growth? New research on the subject yields a surprising answer.

Norman Strong, "How to Default: A Primer." (www.leftbusinessobserver.com)

Defaults have become so common that there is now an "etiquette" to defaulting.

"The Dynamics of Debt," *The Economist,* October 6, 1988, p. 72.

Although this article is not new, some things never change. An excellent summary answer to the old question of how fast a country's debt can grow and still be "sustainable."

The Economist (www.economist.com)

See the "Emerging-Market Indicators" for a weekly summary of conditions in the major developing countries that includes exchange rates, current account balances, and the level of foreign reserves.

Michael Mussa, *Argentina and the Fund: From Triumph to Tragedy,* Washington, D.C.: Institute for International Economics, 2002.

A good case study on the relationship between the IMF and a large middle-income country.

www.jpmorgan.com

Look for the Event Risk Indicator (ERI) which reports on the likelihood of a major depreciation of a currency.

Carmen M. Reinhart and Kenneth S. Rogoff, "Serial Default and the 'Paradox' of Rich-to-Poor Capital Flows," *American Economic Review* 94(2), May 2004, pp. 53–58.

A surprisingly small amount of capital flows from rich to poor countries. This paper shows that the long history of defaults by poor countries may have something to do with this.

Appendix

GDP, Population, and Exports for Countries, 2005

GSP, Population, and Exports for U.S. Regions and States, 2005

Country Region State	Income Level	GDP (millions of $)	Population (millions)	GDP per Capita	Exports (millions of $)	Exports as a Percentage of GDP
United States	High	$12,416,505	296.410	$41,890	$904,383	7.3%
Euro Zone		$9,984,125	313.895	$31,807	$3,113,158	31.2%
Japan	High	$4,533,965	127.774	$35,484	$594,905	13.1%
Germany	High	$2,794,926	82.469	$33,891	$969,858	34.7%
SOUTHEAST		$2,781,655	74.946	$37,115	$174,590	6.3%
MIDEAST		$2,258,984	47.522	$47,535	$104,313	4.6%
China	Middle	$2,234,297	1,304.500	$1,713	$761,954	34.1%
FAR WEST		$2,233,889	51.005	$43,797	$175,704	7.9%
United Kingdom	High	$2,198,789	60.227	$36,508	$382,761	17.4%
France	High	$2,126,630	60.873	$34,936	$460,157	21.6%
GREAT LAKES		$1,823,333	46.276	$39,402	$144,653	7.9%
Italy	High	$1,762,519	58.607	$30,074	$367,200	20.8%
California		*$1,616,351*	*36.458*	*$44,335*	*$116,819*	*7.2%*
SOUTHWEST		$1,392,895	35.208	$39,562	$150,565	10.8%
Spain	High	$1,124,640	43.398	$25,915	$187,182	16.6%
Canada	High	$1,113,810	32.299	$34,484	$359,399	32.3%
Texas		*$989,333*	*23.508*	*$42,085*	*$128,761*	*13.0%*
New York		*$961,385*	*19.306*	*$49,797*	*$50,492*	*5.3%*
India	Low	$805,714	1,094.583	$736	$95,096	11.8%
PLAINS		$797,093	19.942	$39,970	$44,365	5.6%
Brazil	Middle	$796,055	186.405	$4,271	$118,308	14.9%
Korea	High	$787,624	48.294	$16,309	$284,419	36.1%
Mexico	Middle	$768,438	103.089	$7,454	$213,711	27.8%
Russian Federation	Middle	$763,720	143.114	$5,336	$243,569	31.9%
Australia	High	$732,499	20.329	$36,032	$105,825	14.4%
NEW ENGLAND		$679,249	14.270	$47,600	$42,096	6.2%
Florida		*$666,639*	*18.090*	*$36,851*	*$33,377*	*5.0%*
Netherlands	High	$624,202	16.320	$38,248	$402,407	64.5%
Illinois		*$555,599*	*12.832*	*$43,298*	*$35,868*	*6.5%*
Pennsylvania		*$486,139*	*12.441*	*$39,077*	*$22,271*	*4.6%*
Ohio		*$442,243*	*11.478*	*$38,530*	*$34,801*	*7.9%*
New Jersey		*$427,654*	*8.725*	*$49,017*	*$21,080*	*4.9%*
ROCKY MOUNTAIN		$405,753	10.230	$39,665	$17,480	4.3%
Michigan		*$372,148*	*10.096*	*$36,862*	*$37,584*	*10.1%*
Belgium	High	$370,824	10.479	$35,387	$334,298	90.2%

Country Region State	Income Level	GDP (millions of $)	Population (millions)	GDP per Capita	Exports (millions of $)	Exports as a Percentage of GDP
Switzerland	High	$367,029	7.437	$49,352	$130,898	35.7%
Turkey	Middle	$362,502	72.065	$5,030	$73,414	20.3%
Georgia		*$358,365*	*9.364*	*$38,271*	*$20,577*	*5.7%*
Sweden	High	$357,683	9.024	$39,637	$130,104	36.4%
North Carolina		*$350,700*	*8.857*	*$39,598*	*$19,463*	*5.5%*
Virginia		*$350,692*	*7.643*	*$45,885*	*$12,216*	*3.5%*
Massachusetts		*$320,050*	*6.437*	*$49,719*	*$22,043*	*6.9%*
Saudi Arabia	High	$309,778	23.119	$13,399	$181,440	58.6%
Austria	High	$306,073	8.233	$37,176	$123,987	40.5%
Poland	Middle	$303,229	38.165	$7,945	$89,288	29.4%
Norway	High	$295,513	4.623	$63,922	$103,780	35.1%
Indonesia	Middle	$287,217	220.558	$1,302	$86,226	30.0%
Washington		*$271,381*	*6.396*	*$42,431*	*$37,948*	*14.0%*
Denmark	High	$258,714	5.416	$47,769	$85,137	32.9%
Maryland		*$244,447*	*5.616*	*$43,529*	*$7,119*	*2.9%*
South Africa	Middle	$239,543	46.888	$5,109	$51,876	21.7%
Indiana		*$236,357*	*6.314*	*$37,437*	*$21,476*	*9.1%*
Minnesota		*$231,437*	*5.167*	*$44,790*	*$14,705*	*6.4%*
Greece	High	$225,206	11.104	$20,282	$17,044	7.6%
Tennessee		*$224,995*	*6.039*	*$37,258*	*$19,070*	*8.5%*
Wisconsin		*$216,985*	*5.557*	*$39,051*	*$14,924*	*6.9%*
Missouri		*$215,073*	*5.843*	*$36,810*	*$10,462*	*4.9%*
Colorado		*$214,337*	*4.753*	*$45,092*	*$6,784*	*3.2%*
Arizona		*$212,312*	*6.166*	*$34,431*	*$14,950*	*7.0%*
Ireland	High	$201,817	4.159	$48,525	$109,853	54.4%
Connecticut		*$193,496*	*3.505*	*$55,209*	*$9,687*	*5.0%*
Finland	High	$193,160	5.246	$36,820	$66,016	34.2%
Iran	Middle	$189,784	68.251	$2,781	$56,252	29.6%
Portugal	High	$183,305	10.549	$17,377	$38,133	20.8%
Argentina	Middle	$183,193	38.747	$4,728	$40,044	21.9%
Louisiana		*$180,336*	*4.288*	*$42,058*	*$19,232*	*10.7%*
Hong Kong, China	High	$177,703	6.944	$25,591	$292,119	164.4%
Thailand	Middle	$176,634	64.233	$2,750	$110,110	62.3%
Alabama		*$151,342*	*4.599*	*$32,907*	*$10,796*	*7.1%*
Oregon		*$141,831*	*3.701*	*$38,325*	*$12,381*	*8.7%*
Venezuela	Middle	$140,192	26.577	$5,275	$55,487	39.6%
South Carolina		*$140,088*	*4.321*	*$32,418*	*$13,944*	*10.0%*
Kentucky		*$138,616*	*4.206*	*$32,956*	*$14,899*	*10.7%*
Malaysia	Middle	$130,326	25.347	$5,142	$140,949	108.2%
United Arab Emirates	High	$129,702	4.533	$28,613	$115,453	89.0%
Czech Republic	Middle	$124,365	10.234	$12,152	$78,246	62.9%
Israel	High	$123,434	6.924	$17,827	$42,659	34.6%
Colombia	Middle	$122,309	45.600	$2,682	$21,146	17.3%
Oklahoma		*$121,558*	*3.579*	*$33,962*	*$4,314*	*3.5%*
Iowa		*$117,635*	*2.982*	*$39,447*	*$7,348*	*6.2%*
Singapore	High	$116,764	4.342	$26,892	$229,649	196.7%
Chile	Middle	$115,248	16.295	$7,073	$40,574	35.2%

Country Region State	Income Level	GDP (millions of $)	Population (millions)	GDP per Capita	Exports (millions of $)	Exports as a Percentage of GDP
Pakistan	Low	$110,732	155.772	$711	$15,917	14.4%
Nevada		*$110,158*	*2.496*	*$44,142*	*$3,937*	*3.6%*
New Zealand	High	$109,291	4.099	$26,663	$21,729	19.9%
Hungary	Middle	$109,239	10.087	$10,830	$62,109	56.9%
Kansas		*$105,228*	*2.764*	*$38,070*	*$6,720*	*6.4%*
Algeria	Middle	$102,256	32.854	$3,112	$46,001	45.0%
Philippines	Middle	$99,029	83.054	$1,192	$41,255	41.7%
Nigeria	Low	$98,951	131.530	$752	$42,277	42.7%
Romania	Middle	$98,565	21.634	$4,556	$27,730	28.1%
Egypt	Middle	$89,369	74.033	$1,207	$10,654	11.9%
Utah		*$88,364*	*2.550*	*$34,652*	*$6,056*	*6.9%*
Arkansas		*$87,004*	*2.811*	*$30,953*	*$3,862*	*4.4%*
Ukraine	Middle	$82,876	47.075	$1,761	$34,287	41.4%
District of Columbia		*$82,628*	*0.582*	*$142,087*	*$825*	*1.0%*
Kuwait	High	$80,781	2.535	$31,866	$45,011	55.7%
Mississippi		*$79,786*	*2.911*	*$27,413*	*$4,008*	*5.0%*
Peru	Middle	$79,379	27.968	$2,838	$17,206	21.7%
Nebraska		*$72,242*	*1.768*	*$40,853*	*$3,004*	*4.2%*
New Mexico		*$69,692*	*1.955*	*$35,655*	*$2,540*	*3.6%*
Bangladesh	Low	$60,034	141.822	$423	$9,294	15.5%
Kazakhstan	Middle	$57,124	15.146	$3,772	$27,849	48.8%
Delaware		*$56,731*	*0.853*	*$66,471*	*$2,525*	*4.5%*
Hawaii		*$54,773*	*1.285*	*$42,608*	*$1,028*	*1.9%*
New Hampshire		*$54,119*	*1.315*	*$41,158*	*$2,548*	*4.7%*
West Virginia		*$53,091*	*1.818*	*$29,195*	*$3,147*	*5.9%*
Vietnam	Low	$52,408	83.119	$631	$31,625	60.3%
Morocco	Middle	$51,621	30.168	$1,711	$10,641	20.6%
Slovak Republic	Middle	$46,412	5.387	$8,616	$31,956	68.9%
Idaho		*$45,891*	*1.466*	*$31,294*	*$3,260*	*7.1%*
Maine		*$44,906*	*1.322*	*$33,979*	*$2,310*	*5.1%*
Rhode Island		*$43,623*	*1.068*	*$40,860*	*$1,269*	*2.9%*
Qatar	High	$42,463	0.813	$52,230	$25,762	60.7%
Alaska		*$39,394*	*0.670*	*$58,792*	*$3,592*	*9.1%*
Libya	Middle	$38,756	5.853	$6,622	$30,110	77.7%
Croatia	Middle	$38,506	4.443	$8,667	$8,809	22.9%
Ecuador	Middle	$36,489	13.228	$2,758	$10,100	27.7%
Luxembourg	High	$36,469	0.457	$79,800	$18,390	50.4%
Slovenia	High	$34,354	2.001	$17,168	$18,633	54.2%
Angola	Middle	$32,811	15.941	$2,058	$23,400	71.3%
Guatemala	Middle	$31,717	12.599	$2,517	$5,381	17.0%
South Dakota		*$30,541*	*0.782*	*$39,059*	*$942*	*3.1%*
Montana		*$29,915*	*0.945*	*$31,668*	*$711*	*2.4%*
Belarus	Middle	$29,566	9.776	$3,024	$15,977	54.0%
Dominican Republic	Middle	$29,502	8.895	$3,317	$6,133	20.8%
Tunisia	Middle	$28,683	10.029	$2,860	$10,494	36.6%
Sudan	Low	$27,542	36.233	$760	$4,824	17.5%
Wyoming		*$27,246*	*0.515*	*$52,904*	*$669*	*2.5%*

Country Region State	Income Level	GDP (millions of $)	Population (millions)	GDP per Capita	Exports (millions of $)	Exports as a Percentage of GDP
Bulgaria	Middle	$26,648	7.740	$3,443	$11,725	44.0%
Syria	Middle	$26,320	19.043	$1,382	$5,760	21.9%
Serbia and Montenegro	Middle	$26,215	8.064	$3,251	$5,065	19.3%
Lithuania	Middle	$25,625	3.414	$7,506	$11,813	46.1%
North Dakota		*$24,935*	*0.636*	*$39,214*	*$1,185*	*4.8%*
Sri Lanka	Middle	$23,479	19.625	$1,196	$6,347	27.0%
Vermont		*$23,056*	*0.624*	*$36,954*	*$4,240*	*18.4%*
Lebanon	Middle	$21,944	3.577	$6,135	$2,337	10.6%
Costa Rica	Middle	$20,021	4.327	$4,627	$7,039	35.2%
Kenya	Low	$18,730	34.256	$547	$3,293	17.6%
El Salvador	Middle	$16,974	6.881	$2,467	$3,390	20.0%
Cameroon	Middle	$16,875	16.322	$1,034	$2,829	16.8%
Uruguay	Middle	$16,791	3.463	$4,849	$3,405	20.3%
Cote d'Ivoire	Low	$16,344	18.154	$900	$7,610	46.6%
Latvia	Middle	$15,826	2.301	$6,878	$5,161	32.6%
Iceland	High	$15,814	0.297	$53,245	$3,086	19.5%
Panama	Middle	$15,467	3.232	$4,785	$1,010	6.5%
Yemen	Low	$15,066	20.975	$718	$6,380	42.3%
Trinidad and Tobago	Middle	$14,358	1.305	$11,002	$9,035	62.9%
Uzbekistan	Low	$13,951	26.167	$533	$4,749	34.0%
Estonia	Middle	$13,101	1.346	$9,733	$7,667	58.5%
Bahrain	High	$12,914	0.727	$17,764	$9,866	76.4%
Jordan	Middle	$12,712	5.473	$2,323	$4,302	33.8%
Azerbaijan	Middle	$12,561	8.388	$1,498	$7,649	60.9%
Tanzania	Low	$12,111	38.329	$316	$1,481	12.2%
Ethiopia	Low	$11,174	71.256	$157	$883	7.9%
Ghana	Low	$10,720	22.113	$485	$2,490	23.2%
Botswana	Middle	$10,317	1.765	$5,846	$4,425	42.9%
Bosnia and Herzegovina	Middle	$9,949	3.907	$2,546	$2,402	24.1%
Jamaica	Middle	$9,574	2.655	$3,606	$1,500	15.7%
Bolivia	Middle	$9,334	9.182	$1,017	$2,671	28.6%
Uganda	Low	$8,724	28.816	$303	$853	9.8%
Albania	Middle	$8,380	3.130	$2,677	$658	7.9%
Honduras	Middle	$8,291	7.205	$1,151	$1,695	20.4%
Senegal	Low	$8,238	11.658	$707	$1,641	19.9%
Turkmenistan	Middle	$8,067	4.833	$1,669	$4,935	61.2%
Gabon	Middle	$8,055	1.384	$5,820	$4,920	61.1%
Nepal	Low	$7,391	27.133	$272	$850	11.5%
Paraguay	Middle	$7,328	5.899	$1,242	$1,688	23.0%
Zambia	Low	$7,270	11.668	$623	$1,720	23.7%
Congo, Dem. Rep.	Low	$7,103	57.549	$123	$2,050	28.9%
Mozambique	Low	$6,636	19.792	$335	$1,745	26.3%
Brunei Darussalam	High	$6,400	0.374	$17,112	$6,582	102.8%
Georgia	Middle	$6,395	4.474	$1,429	$867	13.6%
Mauritius	Middle	$6,290	1.243	$5,060	$2,144	34.1%

Country Region State	Income Level	GDP (millions of $)	Population (millions)	GDP per Capita	Exports (millions of $)	Exports as a Percentage of GDP
Cambodia	Low	$6,187	14.071	$440	$3,100	50.1%
Namibia	Middle	$6,126	2.031	$3,016	$2,070	33.8%
Macedonia	Middle	$5,766	2.034	$2,835	$2,041	35.4%
Malta	High	$5,570	0.404	$13,786	$2,276	40.9%
Chad	Low	$5,469	9.749	$561	$3,065	56.0%
Mali	Low	$5,305	13.518	$392	$1,109	20.9%
Burkina Faso	Low	$5,171	13.228	$391	$493	9.5%
Congo, Rep.	Middle	$5,091	3.999	$1,273	$5,000	98.2%
Madagascar	Low	$5,040	18.606	$271	$760	15.1%
Papua New Guinea	Low	$4,945	5.887	$840	$3,192	64.5%
Nicaragua	Middle	$4,911	5.149	$954	$858	17.5%
Armenia	Middle	$4,903	3.016	$1,626	$950	19.4%
Benin	Low	$4,287	8.439	$508	$561	13.1%
Haiti	Low	$4,268	8.528	$500	$470	11.0%
Niger	Low	$3,405	13.957	$244	$502	14.7%
Zimbabwe	Low	$3,372	13.010	$259	$1,820	54.0%
Guinea	Low	$3,289	9.402	$350	$890	27.1%
Equatorial Guinea	Middle	$3,231	0.504	$6,410	$7,177	222.2%
Barbados	Middle	$3,091	0.270	$11,446	$359	11.6%
Moldova	Middle	$2,917	4.206	$694	$1,091	37.4%
Lao	Low	$2,875	5.924	$485	$510	17.7%
Swaziland	Middle	$2,731	1.131	$2,414	$2,020	74.0%
Fiji	Middle	$2,729	0.848	$3,218	$702	25.7%
Kyrgyz Republic	Low	$2,441	5.144	$474	$672	27.5%
Tajikistan	Low	$2,312	6.507	$355	$909	39.3%
Togo	Low	$2,203	6.145	$358	$569	25.8%
Rwanda	Low	$2,153	9.038	$238	$125	5.8%
Malawi	Low	$2,072	12.884	$161	$520	25.1%
Mongolia	Low	$1,880	2.554	$736	$1,054	56.0%
Mauritania	Low	$1,850	3.069	$603	$565	30.5%
Lesotho	Middle	$1,450	1.795	$808	$649	44.7%
Central African Republic	Low	$1,369	4.038	$339	$128	9.3%
Suriname	Middle	$1,342	0.449	$2,988	$950	70.8%
Sierra Leone	Low	$1,193	5.525	$216	$158	13.3%
Belize	Middle	$1,105	0.292	$3,784	$215	19.5%
Cape Verde	Middle	$983	0.507	$1,939	$18	1.8%
Eritrea	Low	$970	4.401	$220	$10	1.0%
Antigua and Barbuda	High	$876	0.083	$10,551	$75	8.6%
Bhutan	Low	$844	0.637	$1,325	$250	29.6%
St. Lucia	Middle	$825	0.165	$5,001	$120	14.5%
Burundi	Low	$800	7.548	$106	$111	13.8%
Guyana	Middle	$787	0.751	$1,048	$551	70.0%
Maldives	Middle	$766	0.329	$2,327	$162	21.2%
Djibouti	Middle	$709	0.793	$894	$40	5.6%
Seychelles	Middle	$694	0.084	$8,258	$356	51.3%
Liberia	Low	$548	3.283	$167	$200	36.5%

Country Region State	Income Level	GDP (millions of $)	Population (millions)	GDP per Capita	Exports (millions of $)	Exports as a Percentage of GDP
Grenada	Middle	$474	0.107	$4,430	$40	8.4%
Gambia	Low	$461	1.517	$304	$8	1.7%
St. Kitts and Nevis	Middle	$453	0.048	$9,438	$50	11.0%
St. Vincent and the Grenadines	Middle	$430	0.119	$3,613	$38	8.8%
Samoa	Middle	$404	0.185	$2,183	$12	2.9%
Comoros	Low	$387	0.600	$645	$12	3.1%
Vanuatu	Middle	$341	0.211	$1,614	$38	11.2%
Guinea-Bissau	Low	$301	1.586	$190	$101	33.5%
Solomon Islands	Low	$298	0.478	$623	$102	34.2%
Dominica	Middle	$284	0.072	$3,938	$41	14.3%
Micronesia, Fed. Sts.	Middle	$232	0.110	$2,106	$20	8.6%
Tonga	Low	$214	0.102	$2,097	$10	4.7%
Marshall Islands	Middle	$144	0.063	$2,291	$9	6.2%
Kiribati	Middle	$76	0.099	$772	$1	1.3%
Sao Tome and Principe	Low	$71	0.157	$450	$5	7.1%

Note:

Euro Zone consists of Austria, Belgium, Finland, France, Germany, Greece, Ireland, Italy, Luxemburg, Netherlands, Portugal, Spain and Slovenia.

NEW ENGLAND region consists of Connecticut, Maine, Massachusetts, New Hampshire, Rhode Island, and Vermont.

MIDEAST region consists of Delaware, District of Columbia, Maryland, New Jersey, New York, and Pennsylvania.

GREAT LAKES region consists of Illinois, Indiana, Michigan, Ohio, Wisconsin.

PLAINS region consists of Iowa, Kansas, Minnesota, Missouri, Nebraska, North Dakota, and South Dakota.

SOUTHEAST region consists of Alabama, Arkansas, Florida, Georgia, Kentucky, Louisiana, Mississippi, North Carolina, South Carolina, Tennessee, Virginia, and West Virginia.

SOUTHWEST region consists of Arizona, New Mexico, Oklahoma, and Texas.

ROCKY MOUNTAIN region consists of Colorado, Idaho, Montana, Utah, and Wyoming.

FAR WEST region consists of Alaska, California, Hawaii, Nevada, Oregon, and Washington.

Source: World Bank, "Table 2.1 Population Dynamics," *World Development Indicators,* Washington, D.C.: World Bank, 2007

World Bank, "Table 4.2 Structure of Output," *World Development Indicators,* Washington, D.C.: World Bank, 2007

World Bank, "Table 4.5 Structure of Merchandise Exports," *World Development Indicators,* Washington, D.C.: World Bank, 2007

U.S. Department of Commerce, U.S. Census Bureau, Bureau of Economic Analysis, "Gross Domestic (State) Product" www.bea.doc/bea/regional/gsp

U.S. Department of Commerce, U.S. Census Bureau, Bureau of Economic Analysis, "Population SA1-3" www.bea.doc/bea/regional/spi

U.S. Department of Commerce, U.S. Census Bureau, Bureau of Economic Analysis, "Exports by State of Origin" www.census.gov/compendia/statab

Glossary

absolute advantage the ability of a country to produce a good using fewer resources than another country

absolute purchasing power parity the theory that exchange rates are related to differences in the level of prices between countries

ad valorem tariff a tariff that is measured as a percentage of the value of the imported good

administered protection increasing the tariff on a particular good by a country through the use of antidumping, countervailing duties, or escape clause regulations

aggregate demand the relationship between the total quantity of goods and services demanded by all sectors of the economy and the price level

aggregate supply the relationship between the total quantity of goods and services that an economy produces and the price level

antidumping law a law that does not allow an firm to sell its product in an foreign market for less than what it is sold for in its home market

appreciation an increase in the value of a currency

arbitrage the process of moving goods from low-price markets to high-price markets

auction quota the government auctions quotas in a free market in order to receive the quota rents

autarky a situation where a country does not engage in international trade

balance of payments a summary of all the international transactions of a country's residents with the rest of the world during a year

balance on capital account records that changes in the holding of nonfinancial assets including debt forgiveness and assets of immigrants

balance on current account an accounting of international transactions that includes goods, services, investment income, and unilateral transfers

balance on financial account records the difference between the holdings of foreign assets by domestic residents and domestic assets by foreign residents

balance on goods and services the difference between exports and imports of both goods and services

balance on goods, services, and income the summation of the merchandise trade balance, the balance on services, and the balance on investment income

balance on investment income the difference between income earned on foreign assets and payments to foreign residents on their assets

balance on services the difference between exports and imports of services

capital abundant the situation where a country has a high capital-to-labor ratio relative to another country

capital flows the flow of foreign assets into a country or the flow of a country's assets abroad

capital intensive the situation where the production of a good requires a high capital-to-labor ratio compared with that of another good

capital market a market for financial assets with a maturity of more than 1 year

capital-to-labor ratio (K/L) the amount of capital per unit of labor used to produce a good

change in aggregate demand a shift of the aggregate demand curve

change in aggregate supply a shift of the aggregate supply curve

change in assets abroad the change in the total amount of assets that domestic residents own

change in foreign assets the change in the amount of assets in a country that foreign residents own

clean float an exchange rate system under which the government does not try to influence the exchange rate

common agricultural policy (CAP) an agreement between the European countries to subsidize agricultural production uniformly. All EU member countries' farmers are paid subsidies by the EU rather than by each national government.

common external tariff an agreement between countries to eliminate their respective national tariff schedules and replace them with a common tariff schedule

common market an agreement between countries to maintain a free trade area, a common external tariff, and free mobility of capital and labor

comparative advantage the ability of a country to produce a good at a lower (opportunity) cost than another country

complete specialization the use of all of a country's resources to produce only one good

compound tariff a tariff that includes a specific tariff and an ad valorem tariff

constant costs the amount of a good (assumed to be unchanging) that a country must forego to produce each additional unit of another good

constant returns to scale a production condition in which proportionate changes in factors of production lead to proportionate changes in output

consumer surplus the difference between the price that a consumer would be willing to pay for a good and the actual market price

contractionary fiscal policy a decrease in government spending and/or an increase in taxes

contractionary monetary policy a decrease in the money supply and/or an increase in interest rates

cost, insurance, and freight a measurement of the value of imports that includes the cost of the good plus insurance and freight

countervailing duty a tariff imposed by a country that is designed to increase the price of the imported good by an amount equal to any export subsidies

crawling peg the term used to describe the process of pegging (fixing) the real exchange rate

currency swap an agreement to exchange different currencies over a specified period of time

currency union a situation in which two or more countries use the same currency

customs union an agreement between countries to maintain a free trade area and a common external tariff

dead-weight loss the loss of welfare by a country from the imposition of a tariff

debt borrowing by countries in the form of bonds or bank loans

debt/export ratio the ratio of a country's debt payments to its exports

decreasing costs the reduction in average costs that results from increases in a firm's output

default the inability of a country to repay all of its foreign debt when it is due

demand for foreign exchange the demand for the currency of one country by residents of another country

demand for loanable funds the demand for loans by the private and public sectors of the economy

demand for money the total demand for money by all firms and individuals in the economy

depreciation a decrease in the value of a currency

differentiated goods goods that compete in the same market or industry that appear different from one another on the basis of their features

discount rate the rate of interest charged by a central bank on loans to commercial banks

discretionary monetary policy the use of monetary policy as a reaction to and/or to prevent unwanted changes in the economy's short-run performance

dumping margin the difference between the domestic market price of a product and the foreign market value of the product

dynamic gains from trade the gains from trade that occur over time because trade causes an increase in a country's economic growth or induces greater efficiency in the use of existing resources

economic development the development of a standard of living in the developing countries equivalent to that of the developed countries

economic sanctions government interference with normal trade and capital flows to accomplish foreign policy goals

economic stability loss the losses associated with the absence of an independent monetary policy for a country participating in a currency union

economic union an agreement between countries to maintain a free trade area, a common external tariff, free mobility of capital and labor, and some degree of unification in monetary policy and other government policies

economies of scale the reduction in average costs that result from increases in the size (scale) of a firm's plant and equipment

effective rate of protection a measurement of the amount of protection provided to an industry by a country's tariff schedule

entrepot trade goods that are imported into a country and sometime later the same goods are exported to another country

environmental standards laws that apply environmental standards to manufactured products that may restrict imports

equilibrium exchange rate the exchange rate where the quantity demanded of foreign exchange equals the quantity supplied

equity borrowing by countries in the form of FDI or investment in stocks

escape clause a provision in U.S. law that allows temporary protection for U.S. industries that are under pressure from imports

Euro the new currency for the 15 countries of the European Monetary Union. This new currency has replaced the 15 national currencies.

Eurocurrency an account denominated in a major currency that is located outside that country

Eurodollar a dollar-denominated account that is located outside the U.S.

European Union an association of European countries that agrees to a free trade area and imposes a common external tariff

exchange controls a system where the government is the only legal buyer and seller of foreign exchange

exchange rate shock a large change in the real value of a country's currency that occurs in a short period of time

exchange rate the price of one currency in terms of another currency

expansionary fiscal policy an increase in government spending and/or a decrease in taxes

expansionary monetary policy an increase in the money supply and/or a decrease in interest rates

export promotion a development strategy based on developing industries in line with a country's comparative advantage

exports the part of domestic production that is sold to residents of other countries

external balance the balance between inflows and outflows included in the current account

factor-price equalization theorem the premise that international trade will reduce or equalize factor prices between countries

factor-proportions theory the theory that states that a country's comparative advantage is based on its endowment of the factors of production

factors of production resource inputs—e.g., labor and capital—used to produce goods

fiscal policy a macroeconomic policy that uses government spending and/or taxation to affect a country's GDP

foreign direct investment (FDI) a corporation's purchase of real assets, such as production facilities and equipment, in a foreign country

foreign exchange currency or deposits in financial institutions of another country

foreign exchange market the market where currencies are bought and sold

foreign reserves the total stock of foreign exchange held by a country at any point in time

forward exchange rate the price of foreign exchange to be delivered at some point in the future

free alongside a measurement of the value of imports that includes the price of the good shipped to the side of the ship but without loading costs

free on board a measurement of the value of imports that includes the price of the good loaded onto the ship but without the cost of international shipping or insurance

Free Trade Area of the Americas (FTAA) an agreement by 34 countries to pursue the implementation of an FTA for the Western hemisphere

free-trade area an agreement between countries to reduce or eliminate trade barriers between countries while maintaining separate national tariff schedules

futures contract a commitment to purchase or deliver a specified quantity of foreign currency on a designated future date

gains from trade the increase in world production and consumption resulting from specialization and trade

General Agreement on Tariffs and Trade (GATT) an agreement reached in 1947 that established principles to govern international trade. Until 1995 this organization administered multilateral trade agreements and settled trade disputes.

General Agreement on Trade in Services (GATS) commits WTO members to a set of agreed upon rules for trade in services

gold exchange standard an international monetary system where the price of one currency is tied to gold but all other currencies are tied to the value of that currency

gold standard a former international monetary system where the value of each currency was fixed in terms of gold

government procurement laws that direct a government to buy domestic-made products unless comparable foreign products are substantially cheaper

Gross Domestic Product (GDP) measures the market value of all final goods and services that a country produces during a given period of time

homogeneous goods one product is identical to every other product produced within an industry

horizontally differentiated goods similarly priced goods that are perceived to be different in some slight way

host country the country that receives the factor of production from another country

human capital the education, training, and job skills embodied in labor which increases its productivity

immigration the movement of labor from one country to another

imperfect competition a market structure in which firms have some degree of monopoly power, including monopolistic competition, oligopoly, and monopoly markets

import substitution a development strategy based on developing industries that will reduce imports

imports the part of domestic consumption and/or investment that a country purchases from foreign producers

income elasticity of demand for exports the responsiveness of exports to changes in foreign income

income elasticity of demand for imports the responsiveness of imports to a change in domestic income

inconvertible currency a currency that cannot be freely exchanged for another country's currency

increasing costs the increasing amount of a good that a country must forego to release enough resources to produce each additional unit of another good

indifference curve shows the consumption preferences of consumers which give the same level of satisfaction or utility

industrial policy a government policy designed to stimulate the development and growth of an industry

industrial structure the percentage of output that is accounted for by each industry within a country

infant-industry protection the argument that an industry's costs of production will be high when it is beginning, and as a result it will need protection from imports

injections of income additions to the circular flow of income that are not derived from current income (e.g., investment, government spending, and exports)

interest arbitrage the relationship between interest rates and the exchange rate in the short run

interest rate effect the effect of a change in the interest rate on consumption

interindustry trade international trade that occurs when a country either exports or imports goods in different industries

internal balance the preferred tradeoff between the rate of inflation and the rate of unemployment

international economics the study of the production, distribution, and consumption of goods, services, and capital on a worldwide basis

International Monetary Fund (IMF) a multilateral agency created in 1946 to promote international monetary stability and cooperation

international substitution effect the effect of changes in the domestic price level on the consumption of domestically produced goods relative to foreign produced goods

International Trade Organization (ITO) an organization conceived by the Bretton Woods conference to develop the international trading system. The actual implementation of the ITO did not occur because the U.S. Congress did not ratify the agreement.

intertemporal trade countries trading production for consumption at different points in time

intervention government buying and selling of foreign exchange

intraindustry trade index indicates the amount of intraindustry trade embodied in a country's international trade. The index is expressed as 1 minus the ratio of the absolute value of exports minus imports divided by exports plus imports.

intraindustry trade international trade that occurs when a country exports and imports goods within the same industry or product group

J-curve the tendency for the current account balance to initially worsen when the currency depreciates

labor abundant the situation where a country has a low capital-to-labor ratio relative to that of another country

labor intensive the situation where the production of a good requires a low capital-to-labor ratio

labor standards laws that apply labor standards to manufactured products that may restrict imports

labor theory of value the theory that the cost of a good is determined solely by the amount of labor used to produce it

law of one price the proposition that identical goods sold in competitive markets should cost the same everywhere when prices are expressed in terms of the same currency

leakages of income forms of income that are withdrawn from the circular flow of income (e.g., savings, taxes, and imports)

Leontief paradox the empirical finding that U.S. industries with trade surpluses were more labor intensive than U.S. industries with a trade deficit. This is contrary to the factor-proportions theory

licensing agreement a domestic firm licenses the right to produce and market a good or to use a technology to a firm in a foreign country

liquidity the property associated with being able to buy or sell something easily

M1 the sum of cash in the hands of the public and demand deposits in the U.S. economy

M2 M1 plus near monies in the U.S. economy

Maastricht Treaty an agreement between the European countries to establish an economic union and common currency, the Euro

macroeconomics the study of an entire economy's operation by examining the factors that determine the economy's total output

marginal rate of substitution the rate at which consumers are willing to substitute one good for another

marginal rate of transformation (MRT) the amount of one good that a country must forego to produce each additional unit of another good. This is another name for opportunity cost

merchandise trade balance the difference between exports and imports of goods

microeconomics the study of the production and consumption of various goods and services and how particular industries and markets work

mobile factor a factor of production that can move between industries or is mobile between industries

monetary base (B) the sum of cash in the hands of the public and bank reserves

monetary efficiency gain the gains that accrue to countries using a common currency

monetary policy a macroeconomic policy that uses changes in the money supply and/or changes in interest to affect a country's GDP

money market a market for financial assets with maturities of a year or less

money multiplier the reciprocal of the reserve requirement

money supply the total amount of money in an economy

monopolistic competition a market structure in which many firms produce slightly differentiated goods but each firm maintains some control over its own price

monopoly a market structure in which one firm supplies the entire industry for a particular good and maintains considerable control over its own price

most favored nation (MFN) when one country promises to offer another country having most-favored nation status the lowest tariff which it offers to any other country

Multifibre Arrangement a system of bilateral quotas for imports and exports of textiles and apparel in which each country is allowed to send or receive a specific quantity of textiles and/or apparel items

multilateral trade negotiations a process of reducing tariff and nontariff barriers to trade among member countries of GATT or the WTO

multinational corporations (MNCs) companies that own, control, or manage production and distribution facilities in several countries

national income accounting the process used by governments to keep track of GDP and its components

national treatment a multinational corporation as if it were a domestic firm, thus eliminating legal and/or regulatory restrictions that otherwise might apply to it as a foreign firm

nominal GDP the value of GDP in current dollars

nontariff trade barriers government policies other than tariffs that distort trade

nontradable goods goods whose transportation charges are so large that they become unprofitable to trade

North American Free Trade Agreement (NAFTA) an agreement to establish a free trade area consisting of the U.S., Canada, and Mexico

official development assistance (ODA) the transfer of resources from developed countries to developing countries to assist in the process of economic development

official parity price the price of a currency in terms of gold in a gold standard system

official reserve assets government holdings of gold or foreign currency used to acquire foreign assets

offshore assembly provisions the section of the tariff schedule that allows U.S. firms to export materials and parts of a good to foreign countries for final assembly; when the assembled goods are returned to the U.S., duties are assessed only on the value added in the foreign country

OLI approach a framework that explains why multinational corporations use foreign direct investment

oligopoly a market structure in which a few firms produce all of the output for an industry, and each firm has some control over its own price

open market operations the buying and selling of bonds by the central bank

opportunity costs the cost of a good is the amount of another good that must be given up to release enough resources to produce the first good

option a contract that gives the holder the option to buy or sell foreign exchange in the future

overlapping demands trade in manufactured goods is likely to be greatest among countries with similar tastes and income levels

perfect competition a market structure in which firms produce a homogeneous good and each firm has no control over its own price

perfect competition the market condition where there are many buyers and sellers of a good or factor of production and each buyer and seller has no control over the price of the good or factor

persistent dumping the sale of a product by a firm in a foreign market at a price below that sold in its domestic market over an extended period of time

policy mix various combinations of fiscal and monetary policies used to influence external and internal balance

portfolio capital the purchase of financial assets, such as stock and bonds, in a foreign country

predatory dumping the sale of a product by a firm in a foreign market at a price below that sold in its domestic market in order to drive competing firms out of business

price elasticity of demand for exports the responsiveness of exports to changes in the real exchange rate

price elasticity of demand for imports the responsiveness of imports to changes in the real exchange rate

primary products natural resources or the ability to produce certain agricultural products

producer surplus the difference between the price at which a good is sold and the minimum price that the seller would be willing to accept for it

product cycle the process where goods are produced and introduced in a developed country requiring heavy R&D expenses and refinement in production, followed by product stabilization in design and production, and finally complete standardization and production in a developing country

production function a graph showing the relationship between GDP and the factors of production

production possibilities frontier (PPF) a curve showing the various combinations of two goods that a country can produce when all of a country's resources are fully employed and used in their most efficient manner

protective tariff a tariff that is imposed by a government on a good to protect a domestic industry from foreign competition

public choice the economic analysis of the political process and government decision making

purchasing power parity (PPP) the theory that changes in exchange rates are related to price levels between countries

quota a government policy that limits imports of a product to a certain number of units

real exchange rate the relative price of two currencies after adjusting for change in domestic prices

real GDP a measure of GDP adjusted for changes in prices

real interest parity the theory that changes in the real exchange rate are related to changes in the real interest rate

real interest rate the nominal interest rate minus the expected rate of inflation

reciprocal demand the interaction of the demand by two countries for the other country's export good in determining the international exchange ratio

Reciprocal Trade Agreements Act passed in 1934, the general principles of this law remain the basis for all subsequent trade legislations in the U.S.

re-export trade goods are imported into a country and sometime later the same goods are subjected to a small transformation and exported to another country

regional trade agreements a trade agreement between two or more countries that provides tariff reductions for only those countries that are members of the agreement

relative purchasing power parity the theory that a percentage change in the exchange rate is equal to the difference in the percentage change in price levels

rent-seeking occurs when the government approves a program that benefits only a small group within society but the society as a whole pays the cost

reserve requirement the percentage of deposits banks are legally required to keep on deposit with the central bank

revenue tariff a tariff imposed by government on a good that is not domestically produced

risk diversification the principle that holding financial assets with varying degrees of risk tends to be less risky than holding just one financial asset

rules of origin laws that determine which country actually produced a good

Smoot-Hawley Tariff a high level of tariffs adopted by the U.S. in 1930 which caused a large decline in world trade

source country the country that sends the factor of production to another country

special drawing rights (SDRs) a form of international money created by the International Monetary Fund

special interest groups groups within a country that lobby for changes in laws and regulations that will benefit them

specific factor a factor of production is specific to an industry or is immobile between industries

specific tariff a tariff that is measured as a fixed amount of money per unit imported –$1 per ton

sporadic dumping the occasional sale of a product by a firm in a foreign market at a price below that sold in the home market

spot exchange rate the exchange rate that applies when the transaction is competed at the same time the price is agreed on

static gains from trade the increase in world production and consumption resulting from specialization and trade

sterilization the process of insulating the money supply from changes that would be caused by intervention

Stolper-Samuelson theorem the premise that international trade will reduce the income of the scarce factor of production and increase the income of the abundant factor of production within a country

structure of protection an analysis of the variation in tariffs by product for a country

supply of foreign exchange the amount of foreign exchange supplied in the foreign exchange market

supply of loanable funds the amount of money available to be borrowed by the private and public sectors of the economy

tariff a tax on imports imposed by a government

tariff equivalent the replacement of a quota with a tariff which restricts imports to the same level

Tariff of Abominations a very high level of tariffs adopted by the U.S. in 1828

technical barriers laws that apply technical standards to goods or services that may distort trade

terms of trade the relative price at which two counties trade goods

total factor productivity an increase in GDP not accounted for by changes in the labor force or the stock of capital

trade creation an efficiency gain that results from a free trade area because more efficient member countries displace less efficient member countries

trade deflection the diversion of exports to a country within a free trade area that has lower tariffs on a good

trade diversion an efficiency loss that results from a free trade area because less efficient member countries displace more efficient nonmember countries

Trade Related Intellectual Property (TRIPs) trade in intellectual property, such as music, software, writing, and pharmaceuticals, all of which are protected in the form of patents or copyrights

Trade Related Investment Measures (TRIMs) government policies in which foreign direct investment in a country is allowed only if the investing firm meets certain trade performance goals

trading possibilities curve a curve showing the various combinations of two goods that a country can consume through international trade

transfer pricing the over-pricing or under-pricing of goods in intrafirm trade of multinational corporations that is designed to shift income and profits from high-tax to low-tax countries

Treaty of Rome an agreement between six European countries to reduce tariffs and nontariff barriers to trade. It marked the beginning of the European Union

unilateral transfers grants or gifts extended to or received from other countries

vertically differentiated goods features that make one good appear different from competing goods in the same market based on very different product characteristics and very different prices

voluntary export restraint an agreement by a country to limit its exports to another country to a certain number of units

wealth effect the effect of a change in wealth on consumption

wholly-owned subsidiary a foreign operation incorporated in the host country and owned by a parent corporation in the source country

World Bank a multilateral institution that makes loans to developing countries to enhance economic development

World Trade Organization (WTO) a successor organization to GATT established in 1995. This organization administers multilateral trade agreements and settles trade disputes

Index

A

B

E

N

O